FIFTY CONTEMPORARY CHOREOGRAPHERS

'For those who think modern or contemporary dance is dead, this book opens a window of wonder, by revealing the intriguing and novel creations happening around the world. This book is the first of its kind to explore widespread contemporary dance diversity and its resulting rich global innovations. It is a must read for all those interested in contemporary dance.'

Constance Kreemer, *President of the Mel Wong Dance Foundation, Inc*

Praise for the first edition:

'Bound to become a well-thumbed resource tool.'
Dance Now

A unique and authoritative guide to the lives and work of prominent living contemporary choreographers, this fully updated new edition includes many new names in the field of choreography, alongside those considered masters of the modern age. Representing a wide range of dance genres, each entry locates the individual in the context of modern dance theatre and explores their impact. Those studied include:

- Jérôme Bel
- Richard Alston
- Doug Varone
- William Forsythe
- Phillippe Decouflé
- Jawole Willa Jo Zollar
- Ohad Naharin
- Itzik Galili
- Twyla Tharp
- Wim Vandekeybus.

With a new, updated introduction by Deborah Jowitt and further reading and references throughout, this text is an invaluable resource for all students and critics of dance and all those interested in the fascinating world of choreography.

Martha Bremser is an editor, writer and teacher. She edited the award-winning *International Dictionary of Ballet* (St James Press, 1993) and currently teaches English Literature and Critical Thinking at Channing School, London.

Lorna Sanders lectures within higher education both in the United Kingdom and in Europe. She is also course leader for 'Ballet Education Practice', a teacher's training course run by the Royal Ballet School/Royal Opera House Education departments.

ALSO AVAILABLE FROM ROUTLEDGE

FIFTY CONTEMPORARY CHOREOGRAPHERS

Second edition

Edited by
Martha Bremser and Lorna Sanders
With an introduction by Deborah Jowitt

Routledge
Taylor & Francis Group

LONDON AND NEW YORK

This second edition published 2011 by Routledge.
First edition published 1999 by Routledge.
2 Park Square, Milton Park, Abingdon, Oxon OX14 4RN

Simultaneously published in the USA and Canada
by Routledge
711 Third Avenue, New York, NY 10017

Routledge is an imprint of the Taylor & Francis Group, an informa business

Typeset in Times New Roman by
Book Now Ltd, London
Printed and bound in Great Britain by
CPI Antony Rowe, Chippenham, Wiltshire

British Library Cataloguing in Publication Data
A catalogue record for this book is available from the British Library

Library of Congress Cataloging in Publication Data
Fifty contemporary choreographers/edited by Martha Bremser and
Lorna Sanders—2nd ed.
p. cm.
1. Choreographers—Biography. 2. Choreography. 3. Modern dance. I. Bremser,
Martha. II. Sanders, Lorna.
GV1785.A1F54 2011
792.820922—dc22
[B]
2010035653

ISBN: 978–0–415–38081–2 (hbk)
ISBN: 978–0–415–38082–9 (pbk)
ISBN: 978–0–203–83129–8 (ebk)

CONTENTS

ALPHABETICAL LIST OF CONTENTS

CONTRIBUTORS

Joan Acocella is the dance critic for *The New Yorker*. She is the author of numerous publications, including *Twenty-Eight Artists and Two Saints* (2007) and *Mark Morris* (1993), and she has also edited *André Levinson on Dance: Writings from Paris in the Twenties* (with Lynn Garafola, 1991) and *The Diary of Vaslav Nijinsky* (1999).

Ann Cooper Albright is Professor of Dance and Theater at Oberlin College. She is the author of *Modern Gestures: Abraham Walkowitz Draws Isadora Duncan Dancing* (2010), *Traces of Light: Absence and Presence in the Work of Loie Fuller* (2007) and *Choreographing Difference: The Body and Identity in Contemporary Dance* (1997). She is also co-editor of *Moving History/Dancing Cultures* (2001) and *Taken by Surprise: Improvisation in Dance and Mind* (2003).

Alan Brissenden is a dance critic and historian who writes for *The Australian*, *The Adelaide Review* and *Dance Australia* as well as broadcasts for Radio Adelaide. His publications include *Australia Dances: Creating Australian Dance 1945–1965* (co-author, 2010), the Oxford Shakespeare edition of *As You Like It* (1993), *Shakespeare and the Dance* (1981) and numerous contributions to reference works and journals. An Honorary Visiting Research Fellow in English at the University of Adelaide, he was appointed a Member in the Order of Australia (AM) for services to the arts in 1996.

Judy Burns is a writer and critic based in New York. She was a contributing author to *Moving Words: Re-Writing Dance* (ed. Gay Morris, 1996) and has written for *Dance Research Journal*, *DCA News* and *Women in Performance* (for which she has also been an editor).

Ramsay Burt is Professor of Dance History at De Montfort University. His publications include *Writing Dancing Together* (with Valerie Briginshaw, 2009), *Judson Dance Theater* (2006), *Alien Bodies* (1997) and *The Male Dancer* (1995, revised 2007). With Susan Foster, he is founder editor of *Discourses in Dance*.

Debra Cash is a writer, teacher, lecturer and broadcaster specializing in the performing arts, design, and cultural policy. She was dance critic for *The Boston Globe* for 17 years and was also dance critic for the National Public Radio WBUR Online Arts website. She has contributed articles to numerous publications including *The Oxford Encyclopedia of World History* (2008) and *The Boston Phoenix, Wall Street Journal Online, Opera News, The Village Voice* and *Dance Magazine*.

Anita Donaldson is Dean of Dance at the Hong Kong Academy for Performing Arts. Previously held posts include Head of Research and Graduate Studies at the Laban Centre in London, and Dean of Performing Arts at the University of Adelaide in Australia. She was awarded the Medal of the Order of Australia in 2003 for services to dance and the performing arts.

George Dorris founded *Dance Chronicle* with Jack Anderson, co-editing the magazine from 1997 until 2007. He contributes regularly to *Ballet Review* and was an Associate Editor of *The International Encyclopedia of Dance* (1998) and a senior researcher on the Popular Balanchine Project of The Balanchine Foundation.

Rachel Duerden lectures in Dance at Manchester Metropolitan University. Her book on Antony Tudor was published in 2003. She is currently working on a co-authored study of the choreography of Mark Morris, with Bonnie Rowell.

Jennifer Dunning has been a dance critic and reporter for *The New York Times* since 1977. Her publications include *Geoffrey Holder: A Life in Theater, Dance and Art* (2001), *Alvin Ailey: A Life in Dance* (1996) and *But First a School: The First Fifty Years of the School of American Ballet* (1985).

Ben Felsenburg is a freelance writer and researcher living in London. His writing has appeared in *The Jewish Quarterly* and *Metro.co.uk*, among other journals.

Ellen Gaintner is a freelance researcher and writer on dance. She danced with Nashville Ballet II for two years and is now the assistant to the artistic director, Paul Vasterling.

Sandra Genter is Professor Emerita of Dance at Barnard College, Columbia University. Her work has appeared in *Dance Chronicle, Dance Research Journal* and regularly in *Ballet Review*. She covers dance festivals including at Montpellier in France, New York City's Lincoln Center Festival and Brooklyn Academy's Next Wave Festival.

Marianne Goldberg is an artist, writer and choreographer. She has written a number of articles in *Artforum, Dance Research Journal, Dance Theatre Journal, The Drama Review* and notably *Women & Performance*.

Nancy Goldner is a dance writer living in New York. She has been the dance critic for *The Nation, The Christian Science Monitor* and *Dance News*, among other publications. Her books include *Balanchine Variations* (2008), *Choreography by George Balanchine: A Catalogue of Works* (edited, 1983), *Coppélia: New York City Ballet* (with Lincoln Kirstein, 1974) and *The Stravinsky Festival of the New York City Ballet* (1972).

Robert Greskovic is a dance critic, lecturer and teacher living in New York. He is the author of *Ballet 101* (1998) and served as editorial advisor to *Danshnikov. In Black and White* (2002) and consulting editor of *The Best Ever Book of Ballet* (1996). He covers dance for *The Wall Street Journal*, and his writing has also appeared in *The Village Voice, The Los Angeles Times, The New York Times* and other publications in the United States and abroad.

Helena Hammond is Lecturer in Dance at the University of Surrey. She has written for *Dancing Times* and *Dance Gazette*, is a contributor to *The Ballets Russes: The Art of Costume* (2010) and is completing a book project on the politics of historical representation in dance.

Dale Harris was, until his death in 1996, a distinguished New York writer on music and dance and Professor of Arts and Humanities at Sarah Lawrence College, Bronxville, New York, and lastly at Cooper Union in New York City. He was dance critic for *The Wall Street Journal* and a music critic for *The Washington Post*. His other writings include contributions to *Ballet News, Ballet Review, Dancing Times, Opera, Opera Canada* and a number of newspapers.

Donald Hutera writes and lectures about dance, theatre and live performance for *The Times* of London, *Dance Europe*, *Animated*, *Dance Umbrella*, *The Dance Consortium* and many other publications and websites. He co-authored (with Allen Robertson) *The Dance Handbook* (1988) and received commissions to research and create the works *Scary Grant*, *Choreographus Interruptus* and *Finger Dances*.

Stephanie Jordan is a Research Professor in Dance and Director of the Centre for Dance Research, Roehampton University, London. She is author of *Stravinsky Dances: Re-Visions across a Century* (2007), *Moving Music: Dialogues with Music in Twentieth-Century Ballet* (2000) and *Striding Out: Aspects of Contemporary and New Dance in Britain* (1992). She has also written for a number of dance journals.

Deborah Jowitt teaches at New York University and has been principal dance critic for New York's *Village Voice* since 1967. Her books include *Jerome Robbins: His Life, His Theater, His Dance* (2004), *Time and the Dancing Image* (1988), *The Dance in Mind: Profiles and Reviews 1976–1983* (1985), *Dance Beat: Selected Views and Reviews 1967–1976* (1977) and the anthology *Meredith Monk* (1997), which she edited. She has also contributed to a number of newspapers, magazines and journals.

Angela Kane is Professor and Chair of Dance at the School of Music, Theatre and Dance at the University of Michigan. She has worked as Company Historian for the Paul Taylor Dance Company since 2003 and has published widely in *Dance Research*, *Dance Theatre Journal*, and *Dancing Times*, as well as contributed to the *International Encyclopedia of Dance* (1998). She was one of four writers commissioned to prepare the anniversary publication, *Paul Taylor Dance Company: The First Fifty Years* (2004).

Kathryn Kerby-Fulton is the Notre Dame Professor of English at University of Notre Dame, Indiana. She publishes on medieval literary culture and also on dance history.

Josephine Leask is London Correspondent for *The Dance Insider* and has contributed to a wide range of dance magazines and books. She also lectures on Cultural Studies and Dance Criticism at The London Studio Centre and recently worked as a dramaturg on Aletta Collins's piece for The Place's 40th anniversary, 'This Is The Place'.

Giannandrea Poesio is Principal Lecturer and Media and Performance Coordinator at London Metropolitan University, and dance critic for the weekly *Spectator*. His publications include *To and by Enrico Cecchetti* (2010) and *L'Italia e la danza* (with Alessandro Pontremoli, 2008). He has also contributed to *Dancing Times, Danza e Danza, Chorégraphie, Dance Research*, and a number of books, including *Rethinking the Sylph* (edited by Lynn Garafola, 1997).

Jennifer Predock-Linnell is Professor of Dance at the University of New Mexico. She has published work on the choreographic process, dance and psychology, contemporary choreographers, and dance and technology. She co-edited *Teaching Dance Studies* (with Larry Lavender, 2005), to which she also contributed two chapters.

Stacey Prickett is a Principal Lecturer in Dance Studies at Roehampton University, London. In addition to numerous conference presentations, she has contributed to *Dance and Politics* (ed. Alexandra Kolb, forthcoming), *Dance in the City* (1997) and articles in journals ranging from *Dance Research* and *Dance Chronicle* to *Pulse* and *South Asia Research*.

Jane Pritchard is Curator of Dance for the Victoria and Albert Museum, London.

Henia Rottenberg is Lecturer at Kibbutzim College and co-editor of *Dance Today: The Dance Magazine of Israel*. She has published articles in a number of journals and is one of the contributors to *Dencentring Dancing Texts* (ed. Janet Lansdale, 2008).

Bonnie Rowell is a Principal Lecturer in Dance Studies at Roehampton University, London, with a particular interest in dance analysis and contemporary choreography. Publications include *Dance Umbrella: The First 21 Years* (2000) and chapter contributions to various anthologies including *Contemporary Choreography: A Critical Reader* (2009).

Lesley-Anne Sayers was, until her untimely death in 2010, a Research Fellow in Dance at Roehampton University, London, with a special interest in set design and the visual arts. She also taught twentieth-century dance for the Open University and contributed to a number of journals including *Dance Now* and *Dance Theatre Journal*. She co-edited *The Dynamic Body in Space: Developing Rudolf Laban's Ideas for the 21st Century* (2010) and contributed to *The Continuum Companion to Twentieth-Century Theatre* (2002). She lived in Cheltenham, England.

Elizabeth Schwyzer is a dance and arts writer based in Santa Barbara, California. She holds degrees in Art History and Dance from the University of California, Berkeley.

Karen Vedel is a member of the research group 'Dance in Nordic Spaces' at Tampere University, Finland and has written extensively on the history of dance in Denmark in the twentieth century. Her publications include *Religion, Ritual, Theatre* (co-editor and contributing writer, 2008) and *Dance and the Formation of Norden: Emergences and Struggles* (forthcoming). She is a Member of the Board of Directors of the Congress on Research in Dance (CORD).

Sarah Whatley is Professor of Dance at Coventry University. She specializes in dance analysis and was project leader for the Siobhan Davies digital archive project (www.siobhandaviesreplay.com).

Liesbeth Wildschut is lecturer at Utrecht University in The Netherlands, where she teaches dance history, dance theory and dance dramaturgy. She is Chair of the Dutch Society for Dance Research, co-editor of the series *Danswetenschap in Nederland* and co-editor (with Jo Butterworth) of *Contemporary Choreography: A Critical Reader* (2009).

Yu-Ling Chao is Associate Professor at the Graduate School of Performing Arts, National Taiwan University of Arts. She is a freelance dance writer and the founding editor of *Taiwan Dance Magazine* (Taipei). Her publications include *Sociology of Dance: An Introduction to the Theories and Practices* (2008, in Chinese).

EDITORS' NOTE

This book was commissioned as a contribution to the 'Fifty Contemporary . . .' series intended to provide, in handbook form, introductory guides to fifty practitioners or thinkers in various fields.

In setting out to determine the scope of a book on choreographers, we decided that the notoriously fluid description 'contemporary' would, in this case, mean living choreographers whose work, spanning the decades from the late 1940s to the present, has often exemplified postwar trends in choreography. We therefore did not limit ourselves to a specific definition of the genre known as 'contemporary dance'. As Deborah Jowitt's Introduction suggests, the world of dance nowadays is witness to the blurring of boundaries, as choreographers once considered on the fringe of the dance world now undertake major commissions for established ballet companies, whereas the traditional balletic concentration on technique and music has increasingly worked its way into the practices of independent choreographers working with their own companies. As Deborah Jowitt summarizes it, 'the "contemporary" scene is as diverse as individual notions of contemporaneity.'

In terms of numbers, we have bent the rules slightly, in that one of our fifty entrants is a collective – Pilobolus. But the choreographers included here are not intended to form a canonical or exclusive group. What we have tried to do in our selection – so far as is possible in a book about people and not dance forms – is to suggest the range (geographical and stylistic) of dance phenomena in these decades: the explosion of variegated activity in New York since the 1950s, the emergence of British New Dance since the 1970s, the French *nouvelle danse*, the ballet experimentalists in Europe, and those areas where dance merges into other art forms, such as opera, drama, performance art and the installation. The careers discussed here also highlight the internationalism of the life of the professional choreographer today.

A note on the entries

Each entry consists of four sections:

1   An essay on the choreographer's career by a commissioned contributor.
2   A biographical sketch, with essential details of birth, education and training, career, dance company affiliations and awards/honours.
3   A list of choreographic works, as comprehensive as possible, by year of premiere. Any significant later version of a work is usually noted alongside the original version: there are some exceptions here, usually involving a change of the work's title.
4   A list of Further Reading, subdivided into interviews, articles and books. Items are listed in chronological order. We have generally not included the normal review columns from newspapers and dance periodicals, though where a review has been substantial enough to become a feature article, or when little other available written material exists, then we have retained it. For the most part, we have confined ourselves to English-language material, except in a few cases, where the most substantial writing exists in other widely spoken European languages. Where journals – usually quarterlies – designate issues by season (e.g. Winter 1988), we have preferred to list them thus; sometimes periodical series are inconsistent in this respect, and so some citations here include volume and issue numbers instead.

ACKNOWLEDGEMENTS

Many thanks are owed to all the contributors whose critical essays form the backbone of this book. As for the factual sections of the collection, it is impossible to list individually all those who helped with the task of compiling the material, particularly the works lists. However, general thanks must be made to all those contributors, companies and choreographers who gave valuable help in providing information and answering factual queries at various stages of the project.

Special mention must be made of Ian Bramley (and the Laban Library where he worked), who worked on this edition at a crucial stage in its development, Carol Maxwell, who helped with final keying and editing under an extremely tight deadline and Mark Hawkins-Dady, who provided essential editorial assistance and advice throughout. I would also like to thank my editors at Routledge, particularly Rosie Waters, who originally commissioned this edition and who was a patient and supportive colleague during her time overseeing the project.

Finally, I would like to extend my warmest thanks to Lorna Sanders, my co-editor on the second edition, without whose careful research, dogged determination and cheerful perseverance this edition would never have come to fruition. Her contribution has been vital and I am indebted to her.

MB

INTRODUCTION

In 1975, the erudite and cantankerous Lincoln Kirstein delivered the following broadside against the 'soi-disant "modern"-dance': 'Essentially, the modern dance tradition is a meager school and is without audience, repertory, or issue; it never gained a mass public, a central system, nor a common repertory...' [1] It was, in other words, no threat to opera house ballet and, more particularly, no threat to the New York City Ballet, the company that Kirstein and George Balanchine founded in 1933.

Those critics judging modern dance (or 'contemporary dance', 'new dance', 'postmodern dance', etc.) by the rules and standards of the danse d'école inevitably find it wanting. In 1968, the London critic A.V. Coton referred to Paul Taylor's already highly developed and idiosyncratic aesthetic as 'this free-style mode of non-ballet dance'.[2] Modern dance choreographers have always had to defend themselves against charges that they lack identifiable 'technique' and indulge in careless public improvisation. This last, along with notions of 'self-expression', was (mistakenly) believed to be the legacy of Isadora Duncan, whose reputation was tainted by the flocks of young girls experiencing 'freedom' in Grecian tunics. In the early days of Twyla Tharp's choreographic career, it was often assumed that because of the vernacular sputter of her movement style, her dancers were improvising. To counteract this, she created structures rigorous enough to attest to planning and hours of studio sweat. After all, if the three performers in her 1970 The Fugue, dancing only to the sound of their own boots on an amplified floor, end in perfect unison, not only is predetermined choreography a given, but also a new kind of virtuosity is clearly abloom.

It is true, however, that modern dance has never scorned the amateur. Before the Second World War in Germany, Rudolf Laban and his disciples pieced together immense 'movement choirs' out of

1

cadres of workers in various cities, creating idealistic proletarian spectacles unfortunately apt for being absorbed into the National Socialists' propaganda machine. In Britain, where Laban emigrated in 1938, children with no thought of becoming professionals learned to express themselves through dance. Mary Wigman's Dresden studio offered both a professional training programme and *Tanzgymnastik* classes for the general public. Through organizations such as the New Dance Group in New York, fervently left-wing American dancers of the 1930s organized after-school and after-work classes to proclaim art as the birthright of the masses. In New York in the 1960s, members of Judson Dance Theater and their followers used non-dancers in their works as a way of querying the primacy of the studio dancer.

Kirstein was right about several things but not about the spin he put on them. Like contemporary concert-hall music, serious modern and post-modern dance rarely build huge audiences, perhaps because of choreographers' willingness – indeed, their frequent mission – to challenge the expectations and sensibilities of the public or to present unsettling images of contemporary life. To scholars and admirers of modern dance, its glory lies in its diversity. Although, as in modern painting, 'schools' may arise and imitators abound, at the core of each style is the single artist's way of moving and feeling, fuelled by his or her vision of what dance means in the world and how the world reveals itself in dance.

At this point, it must be stressed that one of the ironies of dance history is that the cross-pollination of ballet and modern dance has not only produced hybrids, but it has also occasionally created ballet-makers trained in the classical lexicon, such as William Forsythe, who are more 'contemporary' in outlook than some choreographers who have come up through modern dance. And only in its early years could modern dance be considered to have anything at all in common with modernism as a movement in the arts. In 1959, as one of the New York City Ballet's occasional 'novelties' George Balanchine and Martha Graham each choreographed the two separate halves of *Episodes*, using for music the entire small *œuvre* of Anton Webern; Balanchine's ballet was cool, mysterious and astringently contemporary, whereas Graham chose to set a historical biography (of Mary, Queen of Scots) in her by-then-traditional dramatic style.

★★★

It is instructive to look at J.E. Crawford Flitch's 1912 *Modern Dancing and Dancers* (by modern, Flitch meant not 'antique').[3] There, along with Russian ballerinas and Loïe Fuller, Isadora Duncan and Ruth St Denis, the acknowledged foremothers of what came to be called 'modern dance', are the skirt dancers of the music halls and West End shows. Flitch's inclusion of these performers, who flourished in the late nineteenth and early twentieth centuries, was astute. Each woman was adept at creating a personal image on stage. By manipulating a skirt while performing movements drawn from ballet, step-dance and social dance, the performer could tease an audience with glimpses of stockinged thighs, adopting the persona of a shy maiden, a hussy, a dreamy romantic. She could also, however, enthral the *ton* by designing more abstract images out of the swirling shapes of skirt, arms and arching back, as did British music hall star Alice Lethbridge. George Bernard Shaw did not care for Lethbridge and could be savage about amateurish skirt dancers, but he waxed rhapsodic over Letty Lind in *Morocco Bound* in 1892.[4]

Fuller, Duncan and St Denis got their start as small-part actresses, musical comedy chorus girls and variety-show skirt dancers. But they took their theatrical savvy into new directions, dignifying dance by associating it with great art or music or philosophical ideas. Plying her yards of shimmering silk under innovative lighting that she designed herself, Fuller expanded skirt dancing into dazzling transformations — becoming fire, budding flowers, butterflies, water. No wonder the symbolist poets fêted her. No wonder her Art Nouveau jewel-box theatre was a much-frequented site at the 1900 World's Fair in Paris.

At a time when dancing was 'show business' and dancers morally suspect, Duncan and St Denis insisted on the ability of choreography to deal with lofty ideas and emotions. This, along with the freedom of the body to be expressive in ways not prescribed by the academy, was their bequest to contemporary dance. Both were widely read; both nurtured themselves on the ideas of the French theoretician François Delsarte (1811–71), as systematized by such American disciples as Steele McKaye and Genevieve Stebbins. Delsarte's enthusiastically reasoned linking of the body's postures and gestures, the heart's emotions and the mind's thoughts helped these dance soloists to dignify the body and make it a vehicle for complex expression. They transformed themselves from show dancers to 'salon artists', performing in the homes of the wealthy, and finally into 'interpretative' dancers who could fill a concert hall and excite debate.

Duncan's plastic evocations of an idyllic Greece went beyond fashionable statue-posing. Dancing to Chopin, Bach, Wagner and Gluck, she translated current ideas about nature, freedom, individual will, evolution and even electrical energy onto her womanly body. To a charmed European public, she stood, too, for the American vigour hymned by Walt Whitman, whose poetry she adored and on which she modelled some of her own public utterances. St Denis's goddesses, dancing girls and harem women went beyond the popular orientalist fantasies to show the metamorphoses from the physical to the spiritual: the deity who dances out the temptations of the senses, only to renounce them all (*Radha*, 1906); the worshipper whose rippling arms become one with the smoke of her offering (*The Incense*, 1906); the geisha who casts off her robes, dance by alluring dance, to reveal herself as a goddess (*O-Mika*, 1912).

These vivid women, and others like Maud Allan (whose lascivious 1906 *Vision of Salomé* thrilled Edward VII), set a fashion for artful solo recitals. The first works of those American dancers – Martha Graham, Doris Humphrey and Charles Weidman – who linked dance with modernism as a force in art and architecture, came out of Denishawn, the school and company founded in 1914 by St Denis and her husband Ted Shawn, a great proselytizer for virile male dancing. Humphrey's first solos were the hoop and scarf dances that could succeed either on the concert stage or, given their scanty costuming, on a vaudeville bill. Even as Humphrey and Weidman were presenting their first bravely modern works, Weidman also offered such titles as *Rhythmic Patterns of Java* (1929), and many of Graham's first solos presented her as the same Chinese maidens and Arabic temptresses that she had played at Denishawn.

Contemporary dance, *pace* Kirstein, has not been without systems. These have usually arisen, however, out of the needs and ideals of individual creators, most of whom were also the stars and directors of their companies. In the early twentieth century, various systems of movement to promote an expressive and efficient body developed in the wake of Delsartism. In Switzerland, Emile Jaques-Dalcroze's exercises, aimed primarily at musicians, correlated motion with the rhythms, pitches and phrase shapes of music. In Russia in the 1920s, the theatre director Vsevolod Meyerhold developed his biomechanical exercises, in part to train actors to negotiate the constructivist sets that were a vital part of his enterprise. Nikolai Foregger's physical training system, *Tafiatrenage* (taffy-pulling), fed directly into the machine dances that he considered a vital expression of twentieth-century life. Laban built 'Eukinetics', analyzing the expressiveness of the body's motion in relation to space and time. It became the custom for modern dance choreographers to design training systems based on their views of dance and the particular demands of their themes.

★★★

From the first compositions (around 1913) of Mary Wigman, the great pupil of Dalcroze and Laban, German *Ausdruckstanz* was allied not just with 'expression' (the name translates as 'Expression Dance') but with Expressionism. Wigman spoke of her creative process as a mystical communion with unknown forces:

> I shut myself in my golden room, leaned my head against the softly singing Siamese gong, and listened to myself deep within. I did so until a pose emerged out of the musing and resolved itself into the stylistically corresponding gesture.[5]

In her desire to find and project the gestural essence of an inner state, Wigman can be seen in relation to the Expressionist painters, several of whom were her friends. National Socialism, the Second World War and the post-war politics of a divided Germany rubbed the radical sheen off Wigman's career and robbed *Ausdruckstanz* of much of its impetus. But, in the first two decades of her career, she trained and/or inspired a host of followers and gave modern dance two of its great early subjects: the human body and psyche as sites for conflicting forces and the tension between the individual and the group.

Beginning in the late 1920s, American choreographers, too, were driven to express atavistic forces and committed to what Doris Humphrey termed 'moving from the inside out'.[6] By the 1930s and the socially conscious Depression years, they also felt a responsibility to articulate the spirit of the times and of their nation. Like many writers and painters, they gravitated towards native themes and images (breaking the habit of looking to Europe for inspiration became something of a moral imperative).

Graham in the 1930s turned her back on the exoticism of her Denishawn years and on the impressionistic studies of much 'interpretive dancing'. ('Why should an arm try to be corn; why should a hand try to be rain?' she wanted to know.[7]) Whether the choreographer was Graham, Humphrey, her colleague Weidman, the Wigman-trained Hanya Holm,

Helen Tamiris or their followers, the work tended to be as stripped down and powerful, as reduced to its essence as modern architecture and design. Given that their medium was the human body and spirit, the choreographers could not achieve total abstraction, but they worked at distilling feeling into action. Believing that dance form and style sprang from emotional responses to life, Graham and Humphrey each created training techniques expressing potent dualities: Graham's based on contraction and release, Humphrey's on fall and recovery; both translated human struggle and aspiration into physical principals.

★★★

At least twice in the brief history of contemporary dance, renegade choreographers have rebelled against everything they have been taught and pared dance back to a state of ardent simplicity. From this point, they gradually reintroduced, albeit in altered form, elements they had dispensed with. In the United States, critics like John Martin or Edwin Denby noted how the 'moderns' began to modulate their attack, broaden their vocabularies and subject matter, and entertain the notion of role-playing. By the 1940s, Graham had entered the period of her great dance-dramas: *Letter to the World* (1940), *Deaths and Entrances* (1943) and *Night Journey* (1947). Cinematic in their play with time and space, mixing myth and psychology via Jungian insight, these dances generated immense theatrical power. A one-time member of the Humphrey-Weidman Company, José Limón, who had been inspired to dance by a performance of the great German dancer-choreographer Harald Kreutzberg, created his brooding images of a tormented hero in such masterworks as *The Moor's Pavane* (1949).

Inevitably, as upstarts mature into established artists, they attract disciples and imitators; and ultimately others react against the prevailing styles. Among the next generation of choreographers were some mavericks, who turned away from the increasingly dramatic and literary nature of modern dance, much as George Balanchine reacted against the story ballets he had been raised on. Coming to prominence early in the 1950s, Alwin Nikolais, a pupil of Wigman-trained Hanya Holm, embedded nimble dancers in landscapes of light, altering their forms through ingenious costuming and movement, even as Loïe Fuller and the Bauhaus artist Oskar Schlemmer had done before him. Erick Hawkins, Martha Graham's partner from 1938 until 1950, created poetic images of simplicity in gentle and harmonious nature rituals. And it was in the 1950s that Merce Cunningham, another former

Graham dancer, began his controversial and thoroughly eye-opening reinvestigations of time, space and compositional procedures.

***

Redefining 'nature' has been a crucial mission in the development of contemporary dance. Cunningham's vision of nature was neither the evocation of ancient and pastoral harmony that Isadora mounted in defiance of the Industrial Revolution nor was it the urban landscape of grappling social forces that the early moderns explored. As Cunningham's colleague, the radical composer and theorist John Cage, wrote, 'Art changes because changes in science give the artist a different understanding of nature.'[8] Ideas from eastern philosophy and particle physics (some of them remarkably similar) shaped the aesthetic that Cunningham began to develop in the early 1950s. The apparent negation of causality in quantum mechanics, the fact that even our choices may be the result of chance or random selection – such theories found parallels in Cunningham's methods and in his vivid, disquieting stage pictures. His was a 'nature' so up-to-date that many could not recognize it as such.

Viewing space as an open field, Cunningham upset the convention of central focus, long a dominant feature of proscenium stage presentations. His compositional strategies included such chance procedures as tossing coins on charts to determine path, sequence, personnel and even movement. (Ever the vanguardist, he began, when just past 70, to adapt these methods to a new way of inventing movement through the computer program Life Forms.) His beautifully trained dancers never played roles onstage or appeared to influence one another enduringly. In keeping with the Zen Buddhist principles he and Cage subscribed to, he allowed each element of a dance to reveal its own nature with a minimum of manipulation, with music, décor, lighting, costumes and choreography existing as separate strands that come together only at the final rehearsal. The contemporary world mirrored in the process and formal practice of his dances was one of complexity and unpredictability. It still makes many people uncomfortable, but even considering the international spread of Graham technique or the explosion of *Tanztheater* in response to Pina Bausch's work in Wuppertal, Cunningham has possibly had more indirect impact on contemporary dance-making in the latter half of the twentieth century than anyone else.

Certainly his ideas, and more particularly Cage's, sparked the influential revolution of the 1960s in New York, most of which occurred under the auspices of Judson Dance Theater, a group of smart and irreverent choreographers as iconoclastic and, in a way, as idealistic as the radicals of the 1920s and 1930s. They, too, wanted to understand the essence of dance, but coming of age as artists in a vastly altered political and social climate, their questions and methods were different.

It is still debated whether the group, whose most prominent members included Yvonne Rainer, Trisha Brown, Steve Paxton, David Gordon, Lucinda Childs, Elaine Summers, Robert Rauschenberg, Robert Morris, Alex Hay and Deborah Hay, ought to be considered (along with Simone Forti) the first wave of 'postmodernists' in dance, as Sally Banes proposed in her important book *Terpsichore in Sneakers*. Yvonne Rainer originally used 'post-modern' to mean coming after modern dance, and certainly the Judson artists not only came after modern dance but also felt it had had its shining hour, and were not about to repeat its effects or subscribe to its philosophies. In the preface to the second edition of her book, Banes distinguished several strands, spanning three decades, of post-modernism in dance.[9] The term applies perhaps most neatly to choreographers of the 1980s and 1990s, whose artistic strategies and interests were more in tune with post-modernism in art and architecture than were those of the Judson group and the independents, who began to sprout around them (such as Meredith Monk, Kenneth King and Twyla Tharp).

The radical dancers, composers and painters of the 1960s have been compared to the Dadaists operating in Switzerland, Germany and Paris around the time of the First World War. True, some Judson performances echoed the witty and obstreperous playfulness of Dada performances, where poets and painters read simultaneously, where nonsense syllables were gravely recited, where musicians banged on instruments and where, according to Tristan Tzara, the act of demanding 'the right to piss in different colours', and following it up with demonstrations, counted as a performance activity.[10] However, neither the Judson dancers nor John Cage in his seminal composition courses at the New School for Social Research in New York were this nihilistic in their rowdiness. At a time when young people worldwide were questioning the political and social establishment, these artists were querying the separation of the arts, the hierarchical arrangement of compositional elements, the elitism and potential eradication of individuality inherent in much academic training. Further, if, according to Cage, any noise could be part of a musical composition, why could not any movement be considered dance?

Exploration of everyday movement, the use of untrained performers, dances structured like tasks or ingenious games, objects used literally, process as a possible element of performance, absence of narrative or emotion, avoidance of virtuosity and glamour to seduce an audience – these gave many dances of the 1960s a resolute purity similar in intent, if not in style, to the dances of the 1930s. And the iconoclasm of the 1960s, like that of the 1930s, initiated another cycle of invention, development, imitation and potential stagnation.

***

American contemporary dance emerged from the 1960s with a new look. The various individual styles developed by such choreographers as Brown, Gordon, Tharp, Paxton and Childs were seeded in part from ordinary behaviour, rough-and-tumble athletics, Asian martial art forms and the casual dislocations of rock and roll; they little resembled the dominant 'modern' dance. The loose, fumbly duets of Paxton's contact improvisation, Gordon's complicated word play, Childs's exacting rhythmic patterns of travelling steps, the liquid-bodies dancing and brainy structures Brown built, Tharp's equally rigorous experiments with a style that, increasingly, drew on black vernacular dancing for its casual wit and complexity – however difficult these styles were to execute, they bred dancers more focused on the business of doing than of showing, dancers who aimed to look more spontaneous and more relaxed than, say, the Graham-trained dancer. Analyzing her processes in 1976, Brown remarked, 'If I am beginning to sound like a bricklayer with a sense of humor, you are beginning to understand my work.'[11]

Following Cunningham's example, and perhaps Balanchine's too, many American choreographers of the 1970s tended to focus on movement and form, believing that these were in themselves expressive. However, radical choreographers elsewhere were not fighting to free dance of literary-dramatic trappings; they had other vital agendas. Butoh – a style and an artistic movement – developed in Japan during the 1960s as part of a reaction in all the arts against the rapid Westernization of the post-war years. The impulse of the two men acknowledged as founders of butoh, Tatsumi Hijikata and Kazuo Ohno (the latter performing into his eighties) was, like that of the Americans in Judson Dance Theater, transgressive and anti-conventional in expertise, but it took a different and darkly dramatic form. Like the work of radical contemporary Japanese writers, painters and theatre directors, butoh emphasized poverty of means, bad taste and extreme physical and spiritual states. It moved with excruciating slowness. Although the style might refer to traditional Japanese theatre and folk forms as well as to firmly transplanted German *Ausdruckstanz*, it shattered all conventions, presenting the body with its imperfections magnified: toed in, club footed, twitching, grimacing, knotted with tension, the dancer creeps into the skin of the foetus, the cripple, the spastic. Images of violence, eroticism and androgyny continue to permeate the work, offset by irony and absurdity. A main goal of the many butoh artists continues to be getting in touch with the inner self; for Hijikata (who died in 1986), it was also a search for the Japanese body in relation to the landscape and customs that spawned it. These goals link him with the expressionism of early modern dance, with Wigman's sense of the German soul and the Americans' quest for 'American' forms and spirit:

> The body is fundamentally chaotic; the Japanese body particularly, which in comparison with the coherent body of the Occidental (both religiously and culturally), is unsure in its stance. Occidentals have their feet planted firmly on the ground, forming a pyramid, whereas the Japanese seem to be performing acrobatic feats on oil paper. Therefore, they have to find their balance on twisted legs.[12]

The influence of butoh has extended not only to such Japanese artists as Eiko and Koma (based in New York) but also to the non-Asian choreographers in Canada, the United States and Europe.

The term *Tanztheater* is applied to the work of choreographers besides Pina Bausch, but it is she who made it world-famous. This renascence of bold contemporary dance in the Germany of the 1970s shared with *Ausdruckstanz* its essentially dark nature and view of life as a struggle of adversarial forces. In the work of Baush, who died in 2008, these forces were no longer located within the body as much as they were outside it; in her hours-long theatrical spectacles, performers persisted in impossible or humiliating tasks, or battled one another. Involving singing, speech and motion (and, beginning in the 1990s, more 'dance'), her pieces were collages of small intense scenes, which acquired a ritualistic fervour through the use of almost numbing repetition. With immense theatricality, they often presented life as a no-win battle of the sexes in an inertly bourgeois world. Compared to the abstract images of society in struggle, which the early modern dancers created, Bausch's society was without visible ideals or heroes.

★★★

Looking back over the last decades of the twentieth century, one may note the remarkably accelerated growth of innovative contemporary forms in countries such as Great Britain, France, Spain, Belgium, the Netherlands and Canada, which either had scant history of modern dance performance or came late to it. Martha Graham's formidable technique was already over 30 years old when Robin Howard fell in love with it and founded the London School of Contemporary Dance (1966) and London Contemporary Dance Theatre (1967). Less than five years later, a choreographer like Richard Alston, groomed in the Graham tradition, was already attracted to a less emotion-laden aesthetic inspired by Cunningham. Mary Fulkerson and her fostering of release work and contact improvisation soon after its 'invention' by Steve Paxton also influenced Alston's company Strider, and the historian Stephanie Jordan sees the explosion of British 'fringe' dance beginning in the late 1970s as being triggered in part by the arrival on the scene of the first graduating class trained by Fulkerson at Dartington College of Arts in Devon.[13] In effect, England was getting its first look at new trends abroad at the same time that choreographers like those associated with the X6 Collective (Fergus Early, Maedé Duprès, Jacky Lansley, Emilyn Claid and Mary Prestidge) and those who presented work under X6's auspices (Rosemary Butcher and others) were creating Britain's 'New Dance'.

An intriguing aspect of the post-modern scene has been the ways in which contemporary choreographers built on the radical experimental work of the 1960s, gradually reintroducing in new guises much of what was discarded. Virtuosity, once told to stay in the ballet world where it belonged, now often works in ironic companionship with the unassuming, everyday look cultivated by dancers during the 1960s. Someone slouches or saunters onto the stage, perhaps wearing street clothes, then off-handedly flings a leg towards the roof. The French choreographer Jérôme Bel includes 'ordinary people' in his dances, but, unlike choreographers of the 1960s, presents them in frankly entertaining ways. Some choreographers, such as Belgium's Wim Vandekeybus, Britain's Lloyd Newson or the United States' Elizabeth Streb (three highly dissimilar artists), began by reconstruing virtuosity as ordeal or as risk. Putting dancers in what looks like danger or working them to a point of visible exhaustion induces in spectators sensitized by the fitness craze a kinaesthetic response, different in quality but similar in effect to that caused by a ballet dancer's phenomenal leap. Although two of those mentioned have moved into narrative, Streb has continued to develop daring athletic work on increasingly complicated equipment; her danc-ers may rebound from trampolines, swing in harnesses or walk within and on the rim of a gigantic revolving wheel set on edge.

Improvisation, for some time unfashionable in modern dance because of its aforementioned connotations of 'free expression', gained credibility in the 1960s in connection with task or game structures that depended on individual interpretation of rules in performance. During the early 1970s, the Grand Union – which included former Judson Dance Theater mavericks like David Gordon, Trisha Brown and Steve Paxton – charmed (or alarmed) adventurous audiences with their wholly unplanned pre-sentations. When spectators know that a performance is improvised, they are drawn into the process, aware that they are experiencing a heady kind of mind-body virtuosity involving on-the-spot decisions and instant responses. Nigel Charnock is proud to let theatre-goers know that no two performances of his *Stupid Men* (2007) are alike. Berlin choreogra-pher Felix Ruckert has built on the notion of task or game structures developed in the 1960s; for instance, to create his 2005 *Messiah Game* he devised 'a syllabus of rules that allow for improvisation, spontaneity, and chance'[14] (others of Ruckert's structures incorporate audience members into the performance, further heightening their perception of the unex-pected). Some choreographers use improvisation more subtly – perhaps giving the performers a degree of freedom to choose in performance from among various composed phrases and movements or, like Susan Marshall, making it a vital part of the creative process. During the 1980s, Dana Reitz, who once likened her composition-improvisation strategies to those of jazz musicians' ringing changes on a known melody,[15] created solos so elegant and formally coherent that people were often unaware of the role that spontaneity played.

Contact improvisation, as Steve Paxton formulated it in the 1970s, was an 'art sport', a totally improvised duet form that featured exchanges of weight, with partners clambering over each other or levering one another off the floor. Because they so rarely use their hands to initiate moves, the action, although it can look erotic or competitive, never seems manipulative. Contact improvisation is still practised worldwide in its 'pure' form, but it also opened up new possibilities for a genera-tion of choreographers.

In the 1980s, a rekindled interest in emotion and narrative surfaced among choreographers who had been nurtured on the Cunningham aesthetic. Economic pressures, feelings of political helplessness and the spread of AIDS may have had some influence in spawning themes of dependency, helplessness and anger. In response, a gritty physicality derived in part from contact improvisation has become, in the works of choreographers from countries as diverse as Canada, Croatia and Venezuela, a metaphor for flawed human relationships and oppressive societies. With the fall of communism and the Berlin Wall, Eastern European countries once part of the Soviet bloc have hastened to nurture contemporary forms that had been disapproved of and suppressed by former regimes, and provocative works from South America challenge repressive ideologies. The lifts and supports in many current pieces are neither effortless nor attractive; they may be about a person who can hardly stand up trying to help another, about the terrible weight of a human body, about embraces that never quite work, about diving through the air and daring someone to catch you.

These contacts are not always tender. Post-modern dance and dance theatre alike often feature a violence that is more unabashed and far less glamorous than its equivalent in classic modern dance. Thinking over the contemporary scene of the last decades, one not only garners images of fierce, unstopping energy (as in the work of Stephen Petronio) but also more obviously dramatic ones of boots stomping, of people hauling one another around in painful or humiliating ways, of ordeals as punishment. In Jean-Claude Gallotta's *Docteur Labus* (1988), created for his Grenoble-based Groupe Emile Dubois, a man raised a woman by sticking his fingers in her ears; another pulled his partner around by a hand jammed into her mouth.

Radical artists of the 1960s occasionally presented the nude body as a statement against both censorship and prudery. In the 1970s, a climate that fostered free love and a return to nature engendered poetic presentations of nakedness that could be equated with innocence. In the twenty-first century, stripping someone of clothes can suggest not only erotic possibilities, as in the male duet in John Jasperse's *Fort Blossom* (2000), but also a stripping away of identity.

A sentence by Jasperse about *Fort Blossom* resonates with various inquiries into the body that have permeated scholarly discourse over the last two decades: 'In *Fort Blossom*, through a very personal look at the body (alternately medical, eroticized and/or aestheticized), the audience is invited to examine contemporary notions of how we experience the body as both owners and spectators.'[16] Although innovators of the 1960s and into the 1970s vaunted a natural human body over a trained and polished one, it is difficult to imagine any of them designing the movements for a quite spectacular dance on the effects of a muscular disease on the human body, as Wayne McGregor did in 2004 with *AtaXia*.

Many of the elements that characterize post-modernism in art and architecture also figure in contemporary dance forms. The emphasis is less on discovering personal vocabularies and training others in idiosyncratic techniques than it once was. Eclecticism is no longer a pejorative term. Just as interior decorators mate Queen Anne with the Bauhaus, choreographers feel free to borrow from, say, ballet and street dancing in the same work. Choreographers such as Karole Armitage and Michael Clark have mixed ballet-born vocabularies with pop imagery. Twyla Tharp built her phenomenal style by mingling the slouchy complexity and casual manners of jazz with ballet's linear precision.

Critics of post-modernism have deplored its addiction to making references to the past as purposeless nostalgia and pastiche. I would contest that, in dance, such references often do point out ironic structural parallels or disassemble the traditional so that new meanings may be squeezed out. One example is Pina Bausch's disconcertingly desolate and poignant update of Bluebeard (*Blaubart*, 1977). William Forsythe's *Impressing the Czar* (1988) deconstructed *fin-de-siècle* Russian art and social politics. In *Last Supper at Uncle Tom's Cabin / The Promised Land* (1990), Bill T. Jones used fragments of text and action drawn from Harriet Beecher Stowe's anti-slavery novel (with a performer representing Stowe as reader and commentator), poses from Leonardo da Vinci's masterpiece and a number of other 'texts' to inquire into religious faith and the often subtle nature of prejudice against blacks, women and homosexuals. Equally political, Matthew Bourne's all-male *Swan Lake* (1995) not only wreaked gender havoc on a nineteenth-century classic but also aimed darts at monarchy's power plays in general and Britain's royal family in particular. David Gordon's *Dancing Henry V* (2004) interwove Shakespeare's words with movements and additional text to create an eloquent – though subtle and unfailingly witty – denunciation of leaders who take their nations into war claiming that God is on 'our' side.

The fascination with history takes many different forms and includes revamping classics or the music associated with them. Bourne has made a career out of revisiting famous ballets, operas and films. Using Prokofiev's music for the ballet *Romeo and Juliet*, Angelin Preljocaj recast Shakespeare's plot as a battle between the military of an unspecified communist state and a crew of homeless rebels in *Roméo et Juliette*

(2005). He has set his *Noces* (1989) and *Rite* (2001) to two of Igor Stravinsky's most magisterial ballet scores. Javier De Frutos has choreographed four works in *Le Sacre du Printemps*, Molissa Fenley danced the entire score as a solo ordeal in her 1988 *State of Darkness* and Finnish choreographer Tero Saarinen used it to create a powerful private drama, *Hunt* (2002).

Explorations of history also extend to personal, racial and cultural heritages. Meredith Monk's great music-theatre-dance work *Quarry* (1976) could be said to pre-figure this trend and exemplify a form of non-linear narrative akin to mosaic. In recent years, a number of contemporary choreographers worldwide have been exploring their roots or expanding upon an inherited tradition. While Alvin Ailey built two of his most famous early pieces, *Revelations* (1960) and *Blues Suite* (1958), on African American religious fervour and urban jazz, later generations of dance-makers investigating the black experience, such as Jawole Willa Jo Zollar and David Rousseve, have employed speaking and singing, as well as dance, to render more specific dramatic insights into cultural phenomena. In very different ways and to different degrees, Akram Khan and Shobana Jeyasingh in Britain and the late Chandralekha in India have built contemporary works on reinterpreted classical Indian techniques: Kathak, Bharatanatyam and Kalaripayat, respectively. In the United States, Ronald K. Brown moulded a juicy style that owes much to his ancestors' African roots, even though his choreography tends to focus on more contemporary themes, and Rennie Harris used his expertise as a hip-hop artist to re-envision Shakespeare's *Romeo and Juliet* (as *Rome & Jewels*, 2000). In France, Vincent Mantsoe kneads and stretches his ingrained African way of moving to create new ritual journeys.

Post-modernist eclecticism fosters the incorporation or plundering of other forms – club dancing, hip hop, burlesque, cinema, literature, closed-circuit television, digital manipulation – whether to enhance a work's visual texture as Philippe Decouflé has done with film – or to ignite ideas and visions by rubbing disparate 'texts' together. Choreographers such as Wim Vandekeybus and Lloyd Newson have become absorbed in the possibilities of cinema – not just to accompany dance but as film–dance creations. On the other hand, Matthew Bourne's *Play Without Words* (2002) turned a film (Joseph Losey's *The Servant*) into a chilling piece of live theatre, with each principal character allocated to three performers (an intriguing contemporary vision that could be related to Martha Graham's practice in works like *Seraphic Dialogue*,

1955, and *Clytemnestra*, 1958). Designers for Merce Cunningham and Trisha Brown have used a process known as motion capture to create décor, and choreographers everywhere have begun to experiment with computer-generated imagery and techniques that juxtapose live dancers with virtual ones.

Post-modernism even embraces an artist like Mark Morris, who in some ways might be considered a throwback to Balanchine because of his emphasis on music and musicality, and to Paul Taylor's modern-dance world of sunny innocence and midnight depravity. Such practices as blending exalted feeling with down-to-earth manners, embracing culture via its music and social conventions, and downplaying or reversing traditional gender roles define Morris as undeniably contemporary. So do his references to past styles. But the evocations of Balkan dance, early German modern dance, Greek friezes, scarf dancers or down-and-dirty dancing are not simply quotations but transformations. As a contemporary classicist and something of a utopian, Morris can be considered in relation to such Arcadian painters as Milet Andrejevic, Thomas Cornell and Lennart Anderson, whose works show people in contemporary clothing, posed in fields or city parks like mild Dionysian revellers, nymphs or gods on the brink of mythic encounter.

Because of dance's ephemerality, styles of the past are continually being recycled in a more literal way too. Ballet choreographers recreate late nineteenth-century Russia; Asian choreographers pay homage to Martha Graham. Great choreographers, such as Taylor, who had developed his style by the early 1960s, flourish untouched by current fashions in choreography. In a larger sense, the 'contemporary' scene is as diverse as individual notions of contemporaneity and as subject to individual adventurousness. For Jiří Kylián, known for his lush movement style, to make a piece like *Last Touch* (2003), which suggests 'a silent Strindberg play performed at a butoh dancer's pace,'[17] is as daring in its way as John Jasperse's *Prone* (2005), in which half of the audience view the performance while lying on a gleaming installation of air mattresses.

Much of the presumed cutting-edge dance of the past two decades can be characterized by its frequent social, political and historical concerns, its voracious strain of eclecticism, its interest in text and narrative. These interests may broaden and deepen dancing itself or, as some fear, weaken movement invention. When choreographers turn to writing plays, does this mean that dance no longer serves their expressive needs? To what extent will digital wizardry serve live dancing as more than a gimmick? Which artists who consider themselves 'contemporary' are responding directly to contemporary life and which are simply shaping their ideas in accord with current trends is a question that can probably not be answered until the passage of time gives us perspective. We should, however, be grateful that modern dance did not become a powerful monolithic entity like ballet and that choreographers can remain utterly susceptible to the world around them, able to design the present, even sometimes the future, on moving bodies.

Deborah Jowitt

Notes

1 Klosty, James (ed.), *Merce Cunningham* (1975), 2nd edition with a new foreword, New York: Limelight Editions, 1986, p. 89.
2 Coton, A.V., *Writings on Dance, 1938–68*, London: Dance Books, 1975, p. 152.
3 Flitch, J.E. Crawford, *Modern Dancing and Dancers*, London: Grant Richards and Philadelphia: J.B. Lippincott Co., 1912.
4 Shaw, George Bernard (22 November 1892), collected in *Music in London, 1890–4*, London: Constable, 1931, p. 102.
5 Wigman, Mary, *The Language of Dance*, trans. Walter Sorell, Middletown, CT: Wesleyan University Press, 1966, p. 33.
6 Humphrey, Doris, letter to her parents, 8 August 1927, Doris Humphrey Letters (New York Public Library).
7 Armhage, Merle (ed.), *Martha Graham: The Early Years* (1937), New York: Da Capo Press, 1978, p. 67.
8 Cage, John, *Silence: Lectures and Writings*, Middletown, CT: Wesleyan University Press, 1973, p. 194.
9 Banes, Sally, *Terpsichore in Sneakers* (1980), 2nd edition with a new preface, Middlebury, CT: Wesleyan University Press, 1987.
10 Goldberg, RoseLee, *Performance: Live Art 1909 to the Present*, New York: Harry N. Abrams, 1979, p. 41.
11 Livet, Ann (ed.), *Contemporary Dance*, New York: Abbeville Press (in association with the Fort Worth Art Museum, Texas), 1978, p. 51.
12 Viala, Jean and Nourit Masson-Sekine, *Butoh: Shades of Darkness*, Tokyo: Shufunotomo, 1988, p. 188.
13 Jordan, Stephanie, *Striding Out: Aspects of Contemporary and New Dance in Britain*, London: Dance Books, 1992, p. 61.
14 Guzzo Vacarino, Elisa (ed.), *Body and Eros*, catalogue of the Festival Internationale di Danza Contemporanea, La Biennale di Venezia 2007. Venice: Marsilio Editori, 2007, p. 109.
15 Jowitt, Deborah, 'Dana Reitz', *The Drama Review*, 24(4) (T88), December 1980, p. 36.
16 Jasperse, John. www.johnjasperse.org/index.php?name=rep4
17 Jowitt, Deborah, *The Village Voice*, March 17–23, 2004, p. 75.

FIFTY CONTEMPORARY
CHOREOGRAPHERS

RICHARD ALSTON

Richard Alston has a sophisticated awareness of the arts, finding the stimulus for his work from a wide range of subjects, and he creates dances that benefit from repeated viewing. Although he has choreographed dances with no sound accompaniment, music has become the starting point for the majority of his creations. He immerses himself in the sound and the structure of the score before moving into the studio. He creates all the movement himself; he does not ask his dancers to improvise, but he chooses his dancers for the qualities they will bring to the dance. Their input is, therefore, crucial to the production and consequently all his dance works have a humanity, which enriches their appeal for the audience. The range of music he uses brings variety to an evening of Alston's well-crafted choreography that was described in *The New York Times* as evoking 'the gentle lyricism of Frederick Ashton, the rhythmic intensity of Merce Cunningham and the keen musicality of Mark Morris'.[1]

Alston combines the innovative and temporal expectations we have of a 'contemporary' choreographer. His career epitomizes the changing aesthetics and politics that have shaped British dance since the 1960s. If, in the twenty-first century, Alston has been accused of being 'old school', it is because he has retained a passion for steps and a joy in harmonious movement rather than a straining after effects. As a student at the London School of Contemporary Dance (LSCD) (1967–70), he was one of the first in Britain to benefit from a systematic training in modern dance. The school aimed to develop essentially Graham-style performers, but its syllabus also included regular classes in classical ballet, historical dance and choreography. Significantly, it was the breadth of training that appealed most to Alston. Among the teachers at The Place Theatre who influenced him were Viola Farber, Belinda Quirey and Pytt Geddes. Farber introduced Alston to Cunningham's movement with which he felt more comfortable than with Graham's technique. Quirey's historical dance course gave him an appreciation of how the quality, shape and space of movement could be intrinsically expressive, while the T'ai Chi that Geddes taught the Eastern style of movement in which the weight is low and the body and arms move freely. Alston experimented with a range of techniques and structures – in the 1970s he added Release techniques that he studied under the guidance of Mary Fulkerson – so much so that, even before modern dance became established as a mainstream form in Britain, Alston was regarded as its first rebel.

Initially, his decision to eschew the current 'contemporary dance' form was most marked in theme rather than content. Whereas the evolving Graham-influenced genre sought out expressionistic subject matter, Alston chose to create works about dancing itself. In 1971, his choice of title for *END, which is never more than this instant, than you on this instant, figuring it out and acting so. If there is any absolute, it is never more than this one, you, this instant, in action, which ought to get us on* was an intended criticism of the narrative works that increasingly typified the repertories of London Contemporary Dance Theatre (LCDT) and Ballet Rambert.

Alston, however, was no *enfant terrible*. His emphasis on movement – on motion, not emotion – links his choreography to the work of George Balanchine, Merce Cunningham and Frederick Ashton, who balanced the need to present narrative with a passion for actual movement. All the four choreographers find expression in formal elements. There is a close correlation between subject and structure, and as Alston became more experienced in developing the dance elements themselves as themes, his structures became more complex. In *Nowhere Slowly* (1970), *Windhover* (1972) and *Blue Schubert Fragments* (1974), for example, the main choreography was organized as solos and duets. These occurred predominantly *sur place*, with simple walking and running sequences moving the dancers from one place to the next. A decade later, his organization of movement around 'nuclei' (Alston's own term) had evolved into large-scale, multi-layered structures in which transitional phrases were as complex as the nuclei themselves. Among works that illustrate this are *Dangerous Liaisons* (1985), *Strong Language* (1987) and *Okho* (1996). The subject is the realization of their sound accompaniments in dance terms. In *Dangerous Liaisons*, Alston analyzed the ticks, clangs and chimes of Simon Waters' electronic tape to find its rhythmic progression. In *Okho*, the source was the weighty sound of the Djembe (African drum), whereas the challenge for Alston in *Strong Language* was to make 'dance sense' of the myriad rhythms in John-Marc Gowans' collage tape.

In *Strong Language*, the contrasts between and within the various sound sections can be detected in Alston's naming of four of them: 'String of sounds', 'Strumming', 'Swing and sway' and 'Funk'. Rhythmic phrases are juxtaposed with one another to highlight differences in sound quality and cadence, whereas the larger and linear structure of

Dangerous Liaisons was Alston's *raison d'être*, his organizing principle in *Strong Language* derives from the shorter, overlapping rhythms of Gowans' multi-track tape. Thus, the progression in *Strong Language* is episodic, and Alston uses repetition as his main structuring device. It is most evident in 'Strumming', a complicated five-minute dance of continually repeated material. Through a succession of entrances and exits, dancers join in this undulating adagio section, either singly or in pairs. Sometimes, they create larger unison groups; elsewhere, their accumulations occur as overlapping, canonic layers of movement. The fact that the same choreography is common to all is not always obvious, but, in seeing it repeated and re-echoed by different dancers, from different areas of the stage, the full shape and patterning of the material is revealed.

Repetition is a recurring structural device in Alston's work. As his choreography has become more complex, he has attempted to aid perception and continuity by repeating key material. This gives strength to his works; repetitions are presented in variations, in the use of canon and in the increasing numbers of dancers. The title of one of his dances, *Doublework* (1978), alludes to repetition: although the principal aim was to create a dance essentially about duets, a secondary goal was the re-stating of material at various points in the dance. Repetition also reinforces certain movement preferences: the high, bent elbow in the lunges of *Connecting Passages* (1977) and *Soda Lake* (1981), and in the parallel *retirés* and leaps of *Rainbow Bandit* (1974) and *Rainbow Ripples* (1980); the springing, turning *sissonnes* in *Soda Lake*, *Dutiful Ducks* (1982) and *Pulcinella* (1987); and the sudden shifts of weight onto and out of *fondu-retire*, which propel the dancers in many works. These choices express much about Alston's particular movement concerns.

His most favoured motifs illuminate two very telling prerequisites of the Alston style: coordination and the ability to move easily, either at great speed or extremely slowly. Impulse and ongoing momentum originate from deep within the torso, with small shifts in the hip or back providing the impetus for larger movement. Emanating from the spine is a sense of centre line – a lateral extension of the torso – which often produces *épaulement* and *éffacé* positions.

What characterizes Alston's style most is its openness, physically and philosophically. Much of this stems from the many types of dance training and performance that he encountered during his formative years. With his first company, Strider (1972–75), he attempted to fuse the tilts and twists of the Cunningham technique with the fluid, tension free concepts of release work. Then, while studying in New York with Cunningham and the former Ballets Russes de Monte Carlo teacher, Alfredo Corvino, he spent much of his free time seeing a wide spectrum of work – from the virtuosities of Balanchine's choreography (New York City Ballet) to the pedestrian non-performances of the American post-modernists. After Alston's return from New York in 1977, other Cunningham traits were observed in his choreography, particularly the clarity of *contrapposto* torso positions and precision at speed.

Influences on Alston as a choreographer were consolidated during his 12-year association with Rambert, first as resident choreographer (1980–86) and, to a lesser degree, when he was artistic director (1986–92), a period in which his choreographic maturity was evident. In an interview, he revealed that one of the reasons why he decided to join the company was his interest in seeing how a work evolves with repeated performance, a luxury not available with occasional pick-up companies. As a repertory company, Rambert provided him with opportunities to revise his choreography, either during the early performances of a work or when re-casting it, sometimes years later, as could be seen in the revivals of *Rainbow Ripples* in 1985, *Wildlife* in 1992 and *Roughcut* in 1999 for his own company. He has also significantly reworked productions, so there were two versions of *Mythologies* (1985 and 1989) and he revisited *Bell High* (1980) as *Hymnos* (1988).

Ballet Rambert also facilitated Alston's first three-way collaboration. Previously, for Strider, he had commissioned scores from contemporary composers (such as Anna Lockwood and Stephen Montague). His interest in the visual arts had begun even earlier. (Before attending the LSCD, Alston had studied theatre design at Croydon Art College.) However, the opportunity to work in larger theatres, with greater technical (and financial) resources, only arose once Alston joined Rambert. The most immediate effect of this was his incorporation of commissioned designs from the photographer David Buckland (*Rainbow Ripples*), painter Howard Hodgkin (*Night Music* (1981) and later, *Pulcinella*) and from lighting supremo Peter Mumford. (Mumford designed the lighting for almost all Alston's work for Rambert and he created the sets for several works too.) But it was in *Wildlife* (1984) that Alston realized his long-time ambition for a dance–music–design collaboration.

Wildlife was a landmark for Alston, not least because it confirmed his ability to work as part of a collaborative team. Importantly, this ability relates also to the reciprocal relationship that he developed with his dancers during the rehearsal process – one which became crucial when, two years later, he assumed the role of artistic director. Though the concept of *Wildlife* developed out of lengthy discussions with the composer Nigel Osborne and designer Richard Smith, Alston created the choreography at breakneck speed. Not only did the six dancers learn quickly but they were also instrumental in forging *Wildlife*'s taut and angular style. The zig-zag contours of Smith's kites and the explosive bursts of energy in Osborne's music meant that, in *Wildlife*, Alston addressed extremes of movement – both physically and dynamically – for the first time. (It was also for the first time that he worked with a commissioned score in a truly *musical* way.) Such extreme possibilities of movement demanded that the dancers be receptive to the rapid changes of body position and flow in *Wildlife*'s faster sections and also to the contrasting *adagio* control (especially in the central male–female duet).

The qualities introduced in *Wildlife* were developed further in *Dangerous Liaisons* the following year and in *Zansa* (1986), the latter of which Alston described as '*Wildlife* Mark II'. Though *Zansa* features the same angularities and urgent rhythms (and a second commissioned score by Osborne), it was more sophisticated, spatially, than any previous Alston work. This is particularly evident in his manipulation of groups. The multiple crossings of the blue-clad ensemble and the double duets for two couples dressed in yellow, both connected at crucial points – sequentially and thematically – by the interweavings of the female protagonist, together resulted in Alston's finest and most densely textured choreography.

Zansa was created in the same year that Alston became artistic director. However, though the years of Alston's directorship were important for introducing a range of modern and post-modern choreographers including Trisha Brown, Lucinda Childs, Merce Cunningham and David Gordon to Rambert's repertoire, they were the least distinguished for his own choreography. Sadly, they were also the years during which recession-hit dance companies were being forced to compromise artistic vision for the sake of box-office sales. As director, Alston resisted such pressures, even though audiences – and Rambert's own board – believed the repertory he built to be too austere in its focus on formalist works. In the autumn of 1992, Alston decided to take a short sabbatical to work with the French dance company Régine Chopinot/Ballet Atlantique. The outcome of this sortie was the creation of *Le Marteau sans maître* (1992; and a revival of *Rainbow Bandit*).

It was the most exciting statement by Alston in over six years and, at the time of *Le Marteau sans maître*'s premiere in December 1992, there was talk of the work being restaged for Rambert the following year. Ironically, on Alston's return to London, only days after the premiere, he was dismissed by the Rambert board. Dance politics thus proved to be more powerful than the pursuit of an individual aesthetic.

What followed for Alston was a two-year period of enforced free-lance activity before embarking on another full-time commitment. From September 1994, he began to direct his own company. Changes of policy and personnel at The Place (the home of LCDT and LSCD since 1969) led to considerable reorganization, and, as artistic director of the Contemporary Dance Trust, Alston assumed responsibility for spearheading developments both at The Place Theatre and LSCD. He also established the Richard Alston Dance Company of ten dancers. This has focused on Alston's own choreography (on average he has created two new productions a year for it since its establishment in 1994) but allows for dancers with the company to make occasional contributions. With this venture, Alston has presented his own choreographic credo, and without aiming to be at the cutting edge of dance, he is constantly taking risks.

The repertoire of the Richard Alston Dance Company ranges from crowd-pleasers, most recently *Red Run* (1998), *The Devil in the Detail* (2006) and *Shuffle it Right* (2008), to music by Heiner Goebbels, Scott Joplin and Hoagy Carmichael, respectively, to more intimate works. One strand of Alston's choreography draws on his fascination for music from the past that is often domestic in scale, which enables him to dwell on intimate relationships with gentle movement. These could be seen in productions from *Night Music* to *Light Flooding into Darkened Rooms* (1997). Alston's duets, like his movement, are not gender-specific and he delights in the changing qualities the change of gender can give to a movement or work. Nevertheless, male dancers have provided considerable inspiration, so that to celebrate his 60th birthday in 2008, he put together a compendium of choreography entitled *The Men in My Life* (2008).

Alston's productions now are rarely elaborately decorated, but they are well-lit to enhance the sculptural qualities that are so importantly combined with his plenitude of rhythm. Productions may look simple, but what Alston is presenting is clarity of structure which, as he has pointed out, parallels the English taste in unembellished architecture and a fascination for mathematics. Alston's choreography is all about looking at moving bodies within the performance space. As Alastair Macaulay noted, 'No choreographer surpasses Alston in making the maximum 3-D detail from a dancer's body'.[2]

Angela Kane
(updated by Jane Pritchard)

Notes

1 Christopher Reardon, 'Richard Alston's Second Chance', *New York Times*, 9 May 2004.
2 Alistair Macaulay, 'Move to the Rhythm and Dance', *Financial Times*, 4/5 January 1997.

Biographical details

Born in Stoughton, Sussex, England, 30 October 1948. **Studied** at Croydon College of Art, 1965–67; London School of Contemporary Dance, from 1967; with Merce Cunningham in New York, 1975–77; also with Alfred Corvino and Valda Setterfield. **Career:** Worked as a choreographer for London Contemporary Dance Theatre, 1970–72 and for own company Strider (founded with Gulbenkian Award), 1972–75; also choreographed while studying with Cunningham, presenting programme at the Cunningham Studio, New York, 1976; resident choreographer, Ballet Rambert (London), 1980–86; guest choreographer, Second Stride, 1982–83; artistic director, Ballet Rambert (Rambert Dance Company from 1987), 1986–92; founder, Richard Alston Dance Company, in residence at The Place Theatre, London, 1994. Has also choreographed for Royal Danish Ballet, Scottish Ballet, Extemporary Dance Theatre, Royal Ballet, English National Opera, Compagnie Chopinot, Ballet Black, Balletheater Munich and Shobana Jeyasingh Company. **Awards and honours:** Chevalier dans l'Ordre des Arts et des Lettres, 1995; CBE, 2001; Critics Circle Award, 2008; Chair of Youth Dance England, 2010.

Works

Transit (1968); *Matrix* (1968); *Something to Do* (1969); *Still Moving Still* (1969); *Cycladic Figure* (1969); *Winter Music* (1970); *Fall* (revised version of *Cycladic Figure*, 1970); *Departing in Yellow* (1970); *Pace* (1970); *Broadwhite* (revised version of *Departing in Yellow*, 1970); *Nowhere Slowly* (1970); *Goldrush* (1970); *END, which is never more than this instant, than you on this instant, figuring it out and acting so. If there is any absolute, it is never more than this one, you, this instant in action, which ought to get us on* (1971); *Shiftwork* (1971); *Cold* (1971); *Strider* (1971, reworked as duet *After Follows Before*, 1972); *Who is Twyla Tharp?* (1971, retitled *Traffic* 1972); *Combines* (1972); *Balkan Sobranie* (1972); *Routine Couple* (1972); *Thunder* (1972); *Tiger Balm* (1972); *Windhover* (1972); *Headlong* (originally *Trailer, a work-in-progress*, 1973); *Interior* (with others, 1973); *The Average Leap Forward* (1973); *Lay-Out* (1973); *Rainbow Bandit* (1974); *Blue Schubert Fragments* (1974); *Soft Verges/Hard Shoulder* (later known as *Soft Verges*, 1974); *Split* (with D. Greenwood, 1974); *Slow Field* (1974); *Souvenir* (1975); *Zero Through Nine* (1975); *Two Saints in Three Acts* (1975);

Standard Steps (1975); *Compass* (1975); *Slight Adventure* (film, 1975); *Solo Soft Verges* (1976); *Edge* (1976); *UnAmerican Activities* (1976); *Connecting Passages* (1977); *Rainbow Bandit* (new version, 1977); *Blueprint* (1977–78); *Home Ground* (1978); *Breaking Ground* (1978); *Doublework* (1978; revised version, 1982); *The Seven Deadly Sins* (1978); *Distant Rebound* (1978); *Unknown Banker Buys Atlantic* (1978); *Behind the Piano* (1979); *Elegiac Blues* (1979); *Dumka* (1979); *Bell High* (1980); *Schubert Dances* (1980); *The Field of Mustard* (1980); *Landscape* (1980); *Rainbow Ripples* (1980); *Sugar* (1981); *The Rite of Spring* (1981); *Soda Lake* (1981); *Swedish Dances* (1981); *Berceuse* (1981); *Night Music* (1981); *Bellezza Flash* (1982); *The Kingdom of the Pagodas* (1982); *Dutiful Ducks* (1982; revised version, 1986); *Crown Diamonds* (1982); *Apollo Distraught* (1982); *Fantasie* (1982); *Chicago Brass* (1983); *Facing Out* (1983); *Java* (1983; revised version, 1985); *The Brilliant and the Dark* (1983); *Midsummer* (1983); *Voices and Light Footsteps* (1984); *Wildlife* (1984); *Coursing* (1984); *Mythologies* (1985; new version 1989); *Dangerous Liaisons* (1985); *Cutter* (1985); *Zansa* (1986); *Pulcinella* (1987); *Strong Language* (incorporating material from *Cutter* 1987; video version, 1988); *Rhapsody in Blue* (1988); *Hymnos* (1988); *Cinema* (1989); *Pulau Dewata* (1989); *Dealing with Shadows* (1990); *Roughcut* (1990); *Cat's Eye* (1992); *Le Marteau sans maître* (1992); *The Perilous Night* (1993); *The Best* (1993); *Delicious Arbour* (1993); *Rumours, Visions* (originally *Les Illuminations*, 1993); *Romance, with Footnotes* (1993); *Shadow Realm* (1994); *Sad Eyes* (includes *Lachrymae*, 1994); *Something in the City* (1994); *Movements from Petrushka* (1994, new production, 2010); *Weep No More* (1994); *Stardust* (originally *Sometimes I Wonder*, 1995); *Secret Theatre* (1996); *Orpheus Singing and Dreaming* (1996); *Bach Measures* (1996; revised version *Beyond Measure*, 1996); *Okho* (1996); *Brisk Singing* (1997); *Light Flooding into Darkened Rooms* (1997); *Red Run* (1998); *Early English* (1998); *Dance of the Wayward Ancients* (1998); *Waltzes in Disorder* (1998); *Slow Airs Almost All* (1999); *Short Bursts of Brisk Singing* (1999); *A Sudden Exit* (1999); *The Signal of a Shake* (2000); *Tremor* (2000); *Fever* (2001); *Unrest* (2001); *Strange Company* (2001); *Water Music* (2001); *Touch and Go* (2002); *Stampede* (2002); *Overdrive* (2003); *Never Told* (2003); *Shimmer* (2004); *Gipsy Mixture* (2004); *Such Longing* (2005); *Volumina* (2005); *The Devil in the Detail* (2006); *Proverb* (2006); *Sheer Bravado* (2006); *Fingerprint* (2007); *Nigredo* (2007); *Walk Through a Storm* (2008); *Lazy River* (2008); *Shuffle it Right* (2008); *The Men in My Life* (2008); *Blow Over* (2008); *Carmen* (2009); *Serene Beneath* (2009); *Alert* (2009); *Even More* (2010).

Further reading

Interviews with Sarah Rubidge in 'The Rambert Reaches Sixty', *Dance Theatre Journal*, Summer 1986; with Barbara Newman in 'Richard Alston', *Dancing Times*, January 1987; with Sophie Constanti in 'Richard Alston: The Humanistic Approach', *Dance Theatre Journal*, Autumn 1989; with Angela Kane, in 'Shared Enthusiasms', *Dance and Dancers*, October 1991; with Stephanie Jordan, in 'Interviews with Richard Alston and Nigel Osborne', *Choreography and Dance*, 1(4), 1995; with Allen Robertson, in 'Full Circle', *Dance Now*, Spring 1995; with Siobhan Davies, 'Artistic directions: Siobhan Davies and Richard Alston in Conversation', *Dance Theatre Journal*, 15(1), 1999; with Lyndsey Winship, in 'Clarity and Grace', *Dance Now*, 13(2), 2004; with Lydia Polzer, in 'Dance about Dance', *Dancing Times*, April 2004; with Debra Craine, in 'Man of the Moment', *Dance Now*, Summer 2005; with Barbara Newman, in 'Outstanding Achiever', *Dancing Times*, May 2009.

Articles: Sophie Constanti, 'Passion in Parts', *Dance Theatre Journal*, Spring 1985; Alastair Macaulay, 'The Rambertians', *Dancing Times*, May 1985; Alastair Macaulay, 'Second Striders Past and Present', *Dance Theatre Journal*, Summer 1986; Barbara Newman, 'Richard Alston', *Dancing Times*, January 1987; Special Issue of *Dance Theatre Journal*, Summer 1987, includes: Judith Mackrell's 'Rambert 1987', Stephanie Jordan's 'Alston's Rambert', Alastair Macaulay's 'Rambert's Alston', and 'Choreography by Richard Alston'; John Percival, 'Rambert under Alston', *Dance and Dancers*, June 1989; Angela Kane, 'Twenty-one Years of Choreography', *Dance Research*, Autumn 1989; Sophie Constanti, 'The Humanistic Approach', *Dance Theatre Journal*, Autumn 1989; Stephanie Jordan, 'British Modern Dance. Early Radicalism', *Dance Research*, Autumn 1989; Angela Kane, 'Cunningham – Alston: Rambert's Double Indemnity', *Dancing Times*, April 1990; Peter Brinson, 'To Be Ahead', *Dance and Dancers*, June 1990; Judith Mackrell, 'Post-modern Dance in Britain', *Dance Research*, Spring 1991; Alastair Macaulay, 'Back at The Place', *Dancing Times*, January 1995; Richard Alston, 'Passing Through Time, *Dance Theatre Journal*, Summer 1996; Judith Mackrell, 'Secret Theatres', *Dance Now*, Summer 1996; Alastair Macaulay, 'Real Dancing, and/or Richard Alston', *Dancing Times*, January 1998; Jane Pritchard, 'Study Aid, parts 1 and 2', *Dancing Times*, April and May 2002; Zoë Anderson, Richard Alston Dance Company, *Dancing Times*, April 2005; Zoë Anderson, 'Richard Alston Dance Company', *Dancing Times*, May 2006; Mary Clarke, 'Richard Alston Dance Company at Sadler's Wells', *Dancing Times*, May 2007; Richard Alston, 'Talking Point', *Dancing Times*, October 2008.

Books: Joan W. White (ed.), *Twentieth-Century Dance in Britain: A History of Major Dance Companies in Britain*, London, 1985; Stephanie Jordan, *Striding Out: Aspects of Contemporary* and *New Dance in Britain*, London, 1992; Jane Pritchard, *Rambert: A Celebration*, London, 1996; Judith Mackrell, *Out of Line*, London, 1992; Sarah Rubidge, *Essential Alston*, London, 1998; Ross McKim, *The Essential Inheritance of the London Contemporary Dance Theatre*, London, 2001.

LEA ANDERSON

One of the brightest discoveries of contemporary British dance in the mid-1980s was The Cholmondeleys (pronounced 'chumleez'), a hilariously, startlingly original trio named after an Elizabethan painting hanging in the Tate Gallery. Choreographer/dancer Lea Anderson, like her company co-founders Teresa Barker and Gaynor Coward, was a graduate of London's Laban Centre for Movement and Dance. A drop-out from St Martin's School of Art, she fronted rock bands prior to emerging from the Laban chrysalis. This background may help to explain her visual flair and her early habit of constructing dances with the impact of a pop single; even some of her later full-length work possesses the deliberate consecutiveness of an album or a music gig.

Another reason for the brevity, and scaled-down detail, of the first Cholmondeleys pieces was the size and nature of the venues they played: cramped clubs, rough pubs, even a space in a tunnel beneath the Thames or on board a small riverboat-cum-art-gallery. This was fringe/ chamber/cabaret dance. Perhaps Anderson, with her eye for offbeat, code-like gestures and telling physical quirks, was simply a born miniaturist.

In any case, she and her collaborators shared a unique view of human behaviour expressed in movement. The dances had a certain 'pop' quality but were refreshingly free of predictability or cliché. Anderson's kinetic vocabulary sprouted from her observations of everyday body language mixed in with images, or moments, seized from cinema, magazine graphics and the plastic arts. Her inventive use of Celtic jigs, Spanish dance, sports moves and the like is a further demonstration of her satirical magpie mentality. Her rhythmic sense, evident in her unison work and tight patterning, was either acute or, as some critics have said, obsessively tidy, even rigid.

The dancers themselves flouted convention. None had the body of classical ballet's fairy-tale princesses, or the showgirl willowiness common in mainstream contemporary dance. These young women were supple but sturdy, with a hidden reserve of hip, working-class character. When they eventually courted the glamorous, donning designer Sandy Powell's black rubber ball gowns or candy-coloured, feather-trimmed party frocks, it was with an ironic awareness that these were costumes, whether funny, beautiful or both. (Powell is a regular collaborator, along with Steve Blake, composer of peculiarly perky, brassy, powerfully percussive music, and Drostan Madden, a master of mix-and-match pre-recorded sound manipulation. That Anderson's creative cohorts, onstage and off, are her friends lends her work a trusting, generous tone that usually avoids insularity.)

In early pieces, The Cholmondeleys were dry-humoured comedi-ennes, eager to scratch the itch out of formal dance rules; yet they also had no qualms about tickling the funny bone before delivering, with a flourish, a fast fist to the chest. Got up like white-faced, full-frocked ballerinas in their titular début dance *The Cholmondeley Sisters* in 1984, Anderson and Barker thumbed their noses at classical stereotypes by concentrating on distractions (sweets, lipstick and hairpins) rather than proper poses. The ritualistic *Dragon* (1985) started as a driven solo and ended as a trio, each new dancer repeating the same fierce, weighted moves executed by the first. *Baby, Baby, Baby* (1986), one of The Cholmondeleys' most popular dances, was perfectly timed to a Nina

Simone recording and marked by the knowing, low-key, flutter-fingered idiosyncrasy of which Anderson is so fond. There was more gravity in *Marina* (1987), where vaguely aquatic moves were emotionally highlighted with shards of Bizet, Verdi and Rossini and *No Joy* (1987), in which sign language and facial manipulation were used to make distressing suggestions about levels of power and limits of communication.

As The Cholmondeleys expanded to include new members like the late Rossana Sen, Emma Gladstone (an erstwhile member of Matthew Bourne's Adventures in Motion Pictures), and Alexandra Reynolds (formerly half of the Sisters Bon Bon), so did Anderson's interest in choreographing for men as well as women. Men had made a token appearance in *Baby, Baby, Baby*, but in 1988, officially, the all-male The Featherstonehaughs (pronounced 'fan-shaws') were born. In *Clump* (1987), one of their first dances and a tense, cunning, examination of masculine group mechanisms, Anderson had six men stomping, slouching and strutting their way in and out of Tweedledum-Tweedledee conformity.

Working with both sexes has enabled Anderson to test herself on a more ambitious scale. Since the unexpectedly epic *Flag* (1988), in which the two companies explored together the clichés and patterns of nationalism, she has taken risks with full-length, collage-like shows often built around a theme. In these, she combines or separates The Cholmondeleys and The Featherstonehaughs as she sees fit. Both troupes participated in the funny, wistful and anarchic *Birthday* (1992), and in 1993's *Precious*, a piece predicated on aspects of alchemy and featuring free-flowing choreography.

Flesh and Blood (1989, revised version 1997) sent The Cholmondeleys alone into a more introspective state, in a piece that dwelt on obsession and fanaticism à la Joan of Arc. (It has the distinction of being the first post-modern dance to be set for A-level students.) The springboard for *Cold Sweat* (1990) was a diversity of climates and the way in which that affected movement and mood. *Walky Talky* (1992), set in and around a huge bed, employed spoken text and a gentle sensuality to help to bring The Cholmondeleys' sisterly intimacy to the foreground. Anderson turned to road movies as inspiration for *Metalcholica* (1994), as seven biker women teamed up in search of escape. In *Car* (1995), the company freed itself from the confinement of theatres and took to the road, touring to public spaces throughout Britain with three 15-minute shows set in, on, and around one sleek Saab 9000. Examining the role of the automobile as icon, the Cholmondeleys appeared as cool chicks in catsuits, identically dressed Jackie Kennedys *c.* 22 November 1963, and Dadaists in back-to-front period clothes.

The Featherstonehaughs developed a collective identity distinct from their distaff siblings. *The Show* (1989), *Big Feature* (1991) and *The Featherstonehaughs Go Las Vegas* (1995) consisted of short, sharp pieces strung together for an engaging gang of guys free of narcissistic macho attitude. Perhaps even more than The Cholmondeleys, The Featherstonehaughs have come in all shapes and sizes, with backgrounds in such occupations as medicine, hairdressing and tree surgery (further proof that Anderson rates a performer's personality above technical training). They mine something substantial out of a frisky, witty and deceptively casual style. Their performances are a seemingly loosely packaged collection of sophisticated, dance-based games whose starting-points range from cowboy and gangster movies and religious tableaux to boxing, show-biz superficiality and Sinatra. They also hit emotive notes of anxiety, anger, passion and tenderness without being ponderous. Working with men has elicited some of what is best in Anderson's dance making: her ability to twist and subvert pop culture and kitsch to her own ends, her application of cinematic editing techniques to dance and her penchant for cocking a snook at social role models.

With flair and imagination, Anderson has shown herself capable of breaking The Featherstonehaughs out of the formulas she created for them. Inspired in part by the films *Das Boot* and *Performance*, *The Bends* (1994–95) was originally staged as part of an all-night extravaganza in a London club. *Immaculate Conception* (1992) took place out of doors, as Anderson tried to fuse the effects of *film noir* and Renaissance frescoes. For 1997's *The Featherstonehaughs Draw on the Sketch Books of Egon Schiele*, she hooked her fastidious and beguiling aesthetic to that of the mannered, morbid Viennese painter Schiele, with striking results.

Anderson has choreographed for theatre and film, and television has afforded her the space to deploy her skills as a filmmaker. Apart from creating pieces for the small screen, she has written and presented two seasons of *Tights, Camera, Action!*, a television series based on her pick of short dance films from the archives of the British Channel 4 station. She has also received commissions from dance and theatre companies, and taken up innovative, large-scale projects. In 1989, the French government invited her to Paris to choreograph the British section of a parade commemorating the bicentennial celebrations of the French

Revolution: two years later she staged *Opéra sportif*, an open-air athletics theatre event involving more than 100 performers in Leicester. Other work of this kind includes *Stargazer* (1998), an observance of a solar eclipse in Cornwall commissioned by Tate St Ives, and *Sportorama* (1999), a performance involving 140 sports people, musicians and dancers.

Anderson underwhelms some British critics, especially those who adhere to a more traditional credo. They say that she has not developed much beyond the small, jokey talent she had when she started out, that she can do little more than concoct absurdist vignettes, getting stuck in choreographic grooves and surrounding herself with dancers as incapable of virtuosity as she is. It is true that at times some of her work has seemed habitually clever rather than inspired, and she has occasionally lapsed into the choreographic doldrums bred by over-familiarity.

By the end of the 1990s, it appeared as if some of Anderson's creative steam had run out. Because of funding shortfalls, her output of shows had become more sporadic. She also began to recycle material, sometimes with diminishing returns. *Smithereens* (1999) was an intriguing coupling of a deliberate cookie-cutter uniformity of movement with seductively dark undertones of decadence. The tri-part *3* (2001) seemed, however, to mine similar subject matter too closely. Anderson's two companies performed both of these productions together, whereas in the full-length *Double Take* (2004) they only shared the bill. Made to mark the 20th anniversary of The Cholmondeleys, this retrospective evening's major interest was in gender swapping: *Flesh and Blood* was revisited by The Featherstonehaughs, whereas highlights from their past repertoire were executed by their female counterparts. In 2006, Anderson revived *Flag* for two new groups of dancers. Ranging in age from 12 to 19, and recruited from two schools in Kent, they were dubbed The Colquhouns and The Marjoribanks. The piece was restaged the following year for the re-opening of the Royal Festival Hall on London's Southbank. These latter-day re-inventions of some of her best work were well received. Not so *Yippeee!!!* (2006), a live 'anti-musical' that sampled at some length seven of the more surreal dance numbers choreographed for Hollywood by Busby Berkeley. This was a comeback of sorts, for which Anderson was lambasted with some of the most damning reviews of her career.

Anderson has hardly lacked kudos or invitations. In 2002, she received an MBE. Throughout 2003, she was an artist-in-residence at the University of California, Davis, and at The Circus Space, London. Nor has she been idle. Besides writing, mentoring, conducting workshops and even devising dance for radio, she has on average produced two to three films or live projects per year for colleges and lower-profile companies.

Some of Anderson's recent work has been on smaller-scale, cabaret-style entertainments designed for easy touring and to appeal to non-dance audiences. *Russian Roulette* (2008) was a deliberate gamble. Using the dark, feverish tone of Dostoevsky's writing as inspiration, could she concoct six new performances in ten weeks featuring eight company members plus a string of special guests? The answer was yes. Each show was presented in south London's Royal Vauxhall Tavern, whereas *Dancing on Your Grave* (2008) toured extensively. Here, Anderson's brief was simple but macabre: what happens when a music hall act bases its performance entirely on death? Three dancers and two musicians – Anderson's long-time collaborator Steve Blake and The Flea Pit Orchestra's Nigel Burch – were billed, with tongue-in-cheek, as the 'corpse de ballet'. The dancing, while adroit, seemed supplementary to the music. Blake, on banjo, and Burch, on ukulele, each wrote their own tunes, yet in terms of style they dovetailed perfectly. The result was inventive and diverting, even if all the morose, gruesome charm ulti-mately had nowhere much to go.

Anderson's goal for 2010 was to give The Featherstonehaughs their due by reviving the *Egon Schiele* show and crafting a new work for them. Entitled *Edits*, it was fashioned in collaboration with her long-time pals Simon Corder doing the lights, the Oscar-winning costume designer Sandy Powell and Blake. Anderson has remarked that she hopes to be making dances for her two groups well into her and their middle age, meaning she is likely to remain a force in British dance for some time to come.

Donald Hutera

Biographical details

Born in London, 13 June 1959. **Studied** at Middlesex College, 1977; art at St Martin's School of Art, London, 1978–79; dance at the Laban Centre, London, 1981–84. **Career**: Co-founder and choreographer of the female dancing trio, *The Cholmondeley Sisters* (renamed The Cholmondeleys), 1984; company became a quartet in 1988; also co-founder and choreographer of a male sextet, The Feath-erstonehaughs, in 1988. Presented two series, *Tights, Camera, Action!* for British television, 1992, 1994; also provided choreography for Todd Haynes's film *Velvet Goldmine* (1998). **Awards and honours** include Bonnie Bird Award, 1988; Dig-ital Dance Awards, 1989, 1990; *Time Out* Awards, 1990, 1991, 1992; Venice Film Festival Award, 1994; London Dance and Performance Award, 1990; Rencontres

Chorégraphiques Internationales de Bagnolet, 1991; Laban Centre Honorary Fellow, 1997; MBE for services to dance, 2002.

Works

The Cholmondeley Sisters (1984); Pole Dance (1984); Health and Efficiency (1984); Dragon (1985); Signals (1985); Kolo (1985); Cutty Sark (1985); The Clichés and the Holidays (1986); Baby, Baby, Baby (1986); La Paloma (1986); The Fly and the Crow (1986); Heel in the Earth (1986); Renoir, mon triot (1986); Marina (1987); Down by the Greenwood Side (opera, 1987); Bow Down (opera, 1987); But We Don't Know What . . . (1987); No Joy (1987); Fishwreck (1987); Carriage of Arms (1987); Clump (1987); Wear 2 Next (1988); The Big Dance Number (1988); Pastorale (1988); Venus in the Mourning (1988); Parfum de la nuit (1988); The Futurists (1988); Flag (1988; reworked 2006, restaged 2007); Slump (1988); Flesh and Blood (1989; film version 1990; revised version 1997); The Show (1989); Just So (musical, 1989); The Earl O' Murray (1989); Factor 6 (1990); Marseillaise (1990); Cold Sweat (1990); Le Jeu interior de tennis (1990); Sardinas (film, 1990); On (theatre production, 1991); Big Feature (1991); Opéra sportif (1991); Cross Channel (film, 1991); Birthday (1992); Walky Talky (1992); Immaculate Conception (1992); Perfect Moment (1992, TV version of Birthday); Jesus Baby Heater (film, 1992); Khovanschina (opera, 1992); Precious (1993); Dirt (1993); Metalcholica (1994); Waiting (film, 1994); Spectre de la rose (film, 1994); Joan (solo for television, 1994); Cabaret (musical, 1994); 24-Hour Featherstonehaughs (1994; touring as The Bends); The Featherstonehaughs Go Las Vegas (1995); Car (1995; film version 1996); Mask of Orpheus (1996); An Audience with the Victims of Death (1996); Offal Dance for Scott Walkers Meltdown (1996); The Featherstonehaughs Draw on the Sketchbooks of Egon Schiele (1997; film version, Lost Dances of Egon Schiele, 2001; revived 2010); Velvet Goldmine (feature film, dir. T. Haynes, 1998); Out on the Windy Beach (1998); Stargazer (1998); Smithereens (1999); Sportorama (1999); Absolute Joy (film, 1999); 3 (2001); 1½ (2002); Performance Perfect (2002); Double Take (2003; full length version, 2004; film version, 2005); Yippeee!!! (2006; revised version 2007); Toothpaste Kisses (2007); Russian Roulette (2008); Dancing on Your Grave (2008); Edits (2010).

Further reading

Interviews with Barbara Newman, in 'Lea Anderson of the Cholmondeleys', Dancing Times, November 1987; with Valerie Briginshaw, Dance Matters, Summer 1995; with Ian Bramley, '3-way Conversation', Dance Theatre Journal, 17(3), 2001; with Barbara Newman, 'Lea Anderson. 103 pieces later', Dancing Times, December 2004; with Martin Hargreaves, in 'Happy Returns', Dance Theatre Journal, 20(1), 2004; with Donald Hutera, in 'Boys will be Girls', The Times, April 2004; with David Jays, 'The Stupidest Name in Dance', Dancing Times, February 2009.

Articles: Judith Mackrell, 'Cholmondeleyism', Dance Theatre Journal, Summer 1986; Sophie Constanti, 'Easing the Load', Dance Theatre Journal, Summer 1987; Sarah Rubidge, 'Political Dance', Dance Theatre Journal, Autumn 1989; Sophie Constanti, 'First and Last', Dancing Times, January 1990; David Hughes, 'Cholmondeleys', Dance Theatre Journal, Summer 1990; Jann Parry, 'Opéra sportif', Dance Theatre Journal, Summer 1991; Klaus Witzeling, 'Lea Anderson at Kampnagel', Ballett

International, July 1994; Sherril Dodds, 'Lea Anderson and the Age of Spectacle', *Dance Theatre Journal*, Winter 1995/96; Valerie Briginshaw, 'Getting the Glamour on Our Own Terms', *Dance Theatre Journal*, Winter 1995/96; Josephine Leask, 'Separate Stages', *Ballett International*, August 1998; Sherril Dodds, 'Breaking the Boundaries of High Art', *Dancing Times*, February 2001; Martin Hargreaves 'Profile: Lea Anderson', *Dance Theatre Journal*, 18(3), 2002; David Jays, 'The Chums and The Fans 20th Anniversary Tour', *Dancing Times*, July 2004; 'Russian Roulette: Images and Memories of the Cholmondeleys and the Featherstonehaughs', *Dance Theatre Journal*, Summer 2010.

Books: Allen Robertson and Donald Hutera, *The Dance Handbook*, Harlow, Essex, 1988; Judith Mackrell, *Out of Line: The Story of British New Dance*, London, 1992; Sherill Dodds, 'A Streetwise Urban Chic', in Janet Adshead-Lansdale (ed.), *Dancing Texts: Intertextuality and Interpretation*, London, 1999; Stephanie Jordan, *Preservation Politics: Dance Revived, Reconstructed, Remade*, London, 2000; Valerie Briginshaw, *Dance Space and Subjectivity*, London, 2001; Janet Lansdale (ed.), *Decentring Dancing Texts*, Basingstoke, 2008; Susan Leigh Foster, 'Throwing Like a Girl'?', in Jo Butterworth and Liesbeth Wildschut (eds), *Contemporary Choreography*, London, 2009.

KAROLE ARMITAGE

If, during her professional beginnings with the ballet company of the Grand Théâtre de Genève, the young American Karole Armitage made any kind of splash dancing *corps de ballet* roles, our dance literature does not prominently record it. By 1977, however, after a year in the Merce Cunningham Dance Company, the wiry young woman from Kansas had come to some notice. The newcomer was paired with the choreographer himself in a duet from his new *Squaregame*. Furthermore, Armitage's rangy reach and delicate control of Cunninghamian complexity told of personal distinction quite apart from that of being chosen to work directly alongside the maestro himself. With her almost pixie-like face, enigmatically impassive and framed by a precisely fringed haircut, Armitage gently drew her viewers into her expert way with Cunningham's art. In Arlene Croce's essay on the Cunningham season that offered the premiere of *Squaregame* and the local début of Armitage, the critic singled out the 'duet in which [Cunningham] supports the most talented of his new dancers, Karole Armitage'.

More roles and more notice followed at an increasing pace. Soon, the notable dancer put on her own show. Her choreographic début work, *Ne* (1978), took place in a high school gymnasium. It featured Armitage and two other dancers, some neon light tubes, and a rock band called

The The. Croce found the event impressive. She called Armitage's vision 'new' and 'right', suggesting that *Ne* would be remembered because of 'its audacity for bringing concert dance together with punk-rock music'.

By 1981, Armitage had left Cunningham. In the process, she had punked her smooth hairdo into feathery spikes and she gained further notice the same year with perhaps her most ambitious work to date: a hurricane-wild and thunderously loud creation for six dancers, including Armitage, as well as five musicians, including Rhys Chatham, the composer. Called *Drastic Classicism*, the two-part work had chic costuming by Charles Atlas (e.g. stiff tutus over skinny trousers). The high-decibel sound level of the score prompted the management of the small-space theatre, New York City's Dance Theater Workshop, to provide earplugs for the faint of eardrum. In impact, Armitage's dance inventions had the air of Cunninghamian and ballet-schooled moves put in a blender and set at higher and higher speed.

Following in the footsteps of Loie Fuller and Isadora Duncan, Armitage decided to pursue her choreographic career in Europe, partly in England, but primarily in France and Italy. Ironically, Britain's Michael Clark, the ballet dancer turned new-wave choreographer whom Armitage profoundly inspired and influenced, first worked with her in New York, during one of her returns to home turf. What might be called the Atlas phase of Armitage's career was played out during the first half of the 1980s. Atlas not only provided Armitage with original and eye-catching design elements for her works but also collaborated with her on film and video projects of his own direction.

This period culminated in 1985 with a suite of dances, $-p = dH/dq$, later re-titled *The Watteau Duets*. In this series of unconventional *pas de deux*, Armitage, partnered by the former Cunningham dancer Joseph Lennon, sometimes put herself on pointe. The space-age-ballerina look to these moments no doubt recalled the pointework choreography Armitage explored in *GV-10*, a 1984 commission from the Paris Opéra Ballet's director Rudolf Nureyev for his troupe's experimental wing.

The latter half of the 1980s marks the Salle period of Armitage's work, identifying her collaboration with the American post-modernist/neo-expressionist painter David Salle. This phase began with a grand concoction for American Ballet Theatre called *The Mollino Room* (1985), starring Mikhail Baryshnikov. First unveiled on the opera house stage of Washington, D.C.'s Kennedy Center and subsequently given on the even vaster stage of New York's Metropolitan Opera House,

Armitage's work for male dancer, solo couple and subsidiary ensemble couples tickled the fancy of some in the know and aroused the ire of other critics. (*The New York Post*'s Clive Barnes characterized the affair with phrases like 'pretentious monstrosity' and 'a cultural con job'.) Set to astringent music by Paul Hindemith and an acidly funny routine by the comedy team Nichols and May, *The Mollino Room* was withdrawn from repertory before it could hit its stride. Salle's décor and costumes were wilfully disconnected and uncommonly handsome; Armitage's casting and choreography were largely witty and confidently discursive.

Some of Armitage's most lavish creations occurred during this time. In 1986, when the choreographer founded her own company, Armitage Ballet, she choreographed *The Elizabethan Phrasing of the Late Albert Ayler*, a three-act work that built on the scheme of *The Mollino Room*. Sometimes Armitage would dance, on and off pointe, in the pieces of this period. Other times, she presented work made on the talented, unknown ballet dancers she hired. Salle's high-profile art world colleagues also worked with Armitage, notably the controversial and fun-loving Jeff Koons. Throughout these and later creations, Armitage was an inspired director. Though her design elements came from a range of hands – Salle, Koons and Christian Lacroix – her stage pictures regularly achieved final results of indelible and spectacular dance theatre that can only be called Armitagean.

With some exceptions, Armitage's artistic collaboration with Salle ended, as did their personal relationship, about 1990. Around this time, the choreographer, who had become an art world favourite, lost some momentum in her US career as choreographer. Instead, she flourished in Europe, choreographing for companies from Monte Carlo to Berlin. But while she earned her living abroad, she was broadening her range at home. The American Film Institute invited her to study filmmaking, which she did from 1992 to 1995 in Los Angeles. She also freelanced as a choreographer for music videos and touring rock shows, including work with the Dyvinals, Milli Vanilli, Madonna and Michael Jackson.

Without her own troupe, Armitage created primarily for European ballet companies. These works have consistently intermingled her interests in *danse d'école* methods with bold costuming and stage decoration. The 'company' credit for *The Dog is Us* (1994) lists Deutsche Oper Ballett, Berlin and six poodles. The last named 'performers' are also part of Salle's set, which showed six clear-coloured niches framing as many standard French poodles, each seemingly dressed in human-scale evening gowns and gesticulating evening-gloved arms.

After writing and directing her own 1992 film, *Hall of Mirrors*, Armitage appeared in Salle's first film project, *Search and Destroy* (1994). The title, derived from a military manoeuvre inspiring the name of the play that gave the film its script, resonates with Armitagean philosophy. In promotional work and artistic deed, Armitage has zeroed in on the state of her dance culture and, with relish, the postmodern ballerina-turned-dance-maker looks for the nearest sitting duck and zaps it.

After freelancing with a variety of German, Swiss, French and Italian companies, Armitage was appointed in 1995 as Artistic Director of MaggioDanza, the resident ballet company at the Florence Opera House. Here she continued her ambitious theatrical mixtures of music, dance and spectacle – and her fondness for working with noted designers – until 1998. In 1997, she choreographed Handel's *Apollo e Dafne*, transforming the allegorical symbols of the original into modern-day imagery, the choreography underpinned by a full orchestra of contemporary instruments and with set and costume designs by the period-film director/designer James Ivory.

Two more collaborations with Ivory followed: Armitage provided the choreography for the Merchant Ivory films *The Golden Bowl* (2000) and *The White Countess* (2005). Other notable collaborations in Florence include *Pinocchio* (1998), with sets by Andrea Branzi and costumes by Jean Paul Gaultier, and *Scheherazade* (1995), with sets by painter Philip Taaffe. Next, Armitage became an associate choreographer at the Ballet de Lorraine in Nancy, France in 1999, a position she held until 2002. Although there she created the ballet *Rave* (2001), which was made into a television programme for the European TV channel Arte, and directed her first opera, Bartók's *Bluebeard's Castle* (2002), at the Opéra de Nancy, she later performed at Amsterdam's National Theater. Invitations to direct opera, including productions of Gluck's *Orfeo ed Euridice* at Teatro San Carlo in Naples and Rameau's *Pygmalion* at the Théâtre du Châtelet in Paris, followed.

Her return to the States was gradual. In 2004, The Joyce Theater in New York asked her to create a new work, resulting in the critical success *Time is the Echo of an Axe Within a Wood*, which Jennifer Dunning described in *The New York Times* as 'one of the most beautiful dances to be seen in New York in a very long time'. That same year, she returned to Italy to direct the Venice Biennale International Festival of Contemporary Dance. One year later, she again made New York her artistic home when she founded her company, Armitage Gone! Dance.

The company's seven dancers represented her ideal – 'masters of ballet technique, not ruled by it', as she told *The New York Times*. She created another big success with her ballet *In This Dream that Dogs Me* (2005). Three days before its premiere, Armitage told Kirstin Hohenadel that her 'greatest ambition is to innovate constantly'. She has continued to do so: in 2009, productions ranged from *Three Theories* (2010), a work based on theoretical physics, to *Itutu*, a collaboration with African pop band Burkina Electric, as well as a project with French novelist Muriel Barbery. She has even conquered Broadway, choreographing first the innovative production *Passing Strange* (2006), then the 2009 revival of *Hair*, for which she received a Tony Award nomination. Fluent in ballet and modern, popular and Eastern dance forms, Armitage is a kind of choreographer-of-all-trades, adapting herself to the project at hand with the ease of a native speaker. In 2010, her company continued to thrive in New York.

Robert Greskovic
(*updated by Ellen Gaintner*)

Biographical details

Born in Madison, Wisconsin, United States, 3 March 1954. **Studied** at the North Carolina School of the Arts, and with Bill Evans, University of Utah, 1971–72; also a scholarship student at the School of American Ballet and the Harkness School of Dance, New York; studied in London at London Dance Centre and The Place, 1972–73. **Career**: Danced with Geneva Ballet, Switzerland, 1973–75 and with the Merce Cunningham Dance Company, 1976–81; began choreographing for own group from 1978, becoming artistic director of the Armitage Dance Company, based in New York, sometimes appearing as Armitage Gone! Dance (from *c.* 1983), and becoming the Armitage Ballet from 1986; artistic director of MaggioDanza, Florence, 1995–98; associate choreographer for Ballet de Lorraine, Nancy, 1999–2002; and artistic director of the Venice Biennale International Festival of Contemporary Dance, 2004; returned as artistic director of Armitage Gone! Dance, New York, from 2005. Has also choreographed for American Ballet Theatre, Ballet de Monte Carlo, Bavarian State Opera Ballet (Munich), Charleroi Danse, Extemporary Dance Theatre, Deutsch Oper Ballett (Berlin), Lyons Opéra Ballet, Les Nomades (Lausanne), Oregon Ballet Theater, Paris Opera Ballet, Tasmanian Dance Company, Alvin Ailey American Dance Theater, The Washington Ballet, Bern Ballet, Kansas City Ballet, Ririe Woodbury Dance Company, White Oak Dance Project, Wendy Whelan and Albert Evans of New York City Ballet, Rambert Dance Company, Ballet National de Cuba, Greek National Ballet, ABCDance Company, Introdans, for the singers Madonna and Michael Jackson, and for various feature films. **Awards and honours** include Guggenheim Fellowship, 1986; Chevalier dans l'Ordre des Arts et des Lettres, 1992; Officer dans l'Ordre des Arts et des Lettres, 2002; Grand Prix Roscigno Danza, 2005.

Works

Ne (1978); *De We Could* (1979); *Objectstacle* (1979); *Vertige* (1980); *Drastic-Classicism* (1981); *It Happened at Club Bombay Cinema* (1981); *The Last Gone Dance* (1983); *Paradise* (1983); *A Real Gone Dance* (1983); *The Nutcracker* (with Rosella Hightower, 1983); *Parafango* (for television, 1983); *Slaughter on MacDougal Street* (1983); *Contact* (1984); *Tasmanian Devil* (also known as *G-Vehicle*, 1984); *GV-10* (1984); *Ex-Romance* (1984); *The Watteau Duets* (original title −*p* =*dH*/*dq*, 1985); *The Mollino Room* (1985); *The Elizabethan Phrasing of the Late Albert Ayler* (1986); *Les Anges ternis* (The Tarnished Angels, 1987); *Les Stances à Sophie* (1987); *Duck Dances* (1988); *Kammerdisco* (1988); *GoGo Ballerina* (1988); *Contempt* (1989); *Without You I'm Nothing* (film, dir. Boskovitch, 1989); *Forty Guns* (1990); *Dancing Zappa* (1990); *Jack and Betty* (1990); *The Marmot Quickstep* (1991); *Renegade Dance Wars* (1991); *Overboard* (1991); *Vogue* (video clip for Madonna, 1991); *Chain of Desire* (film, dir. Lopez, 1991); *Segunda Piel* (1992), *Happy Birthday Rossini* (1992); *In the Closet* (video clip for Michael Jackson, 1992), *Hall of Mirrors* (film, dir. Armitage, 1992); *Hucksters of the Soul* (1993); *I Had a Dream* (1993); *Hovering at the Edge of Chaos* (1994); *Tattoo and Tutu* (1994); *The Dog is Us* (1994); *Search and Destroy* (film, dir. Salle, 1994); *Scheherazade* (1995); *The Predators' Ball* (expanded version of *Hucksters of the Soul*, 1996); *Weather of Reality* (1997); *Tersicore* (1997); *Apollo e Dafne* (1997); *Pinocchio* (1998); *Nadaswaram* (1998); *Mirror's Edge* (1998); *The Last Lap* (1999); *Life Story* (1999); *Up at the Villa* (film, dir. Haas, 1999); *Schrodingers Cat* (2000); *Concerto Conciso* (2000); *Tango Mortale* (2000); *Yo, Giacomo Casanova* (2000); *The Birds* (2000); *The Golden Bowl* (film, dir. James Ivory, 2000); *Rave* (2001); *Power Surge* (2001); *Drastic Remix* (2001); *Rave 1* (2001); *Broken Glass* (2002); *Bluebeard's Castle* (2002); *SZ110* (2002); *Pinokkio* (2002); *Sonata da Caccia* (2002); *Melodien* (2002); *Living Toys* (2003); *Orfeo ed Euridice* (2003); *Pigmalion* (2004); *10 Poems* (2004); *The Double Life of Zefirino* (2004); *Time is the Echo of an Axe Within a Wood* (2004); *In This Dream that Dogs Me* (2005); *Ligeti Essays (Songs)* (2005; expanded 2007); *The White Countess* (film, dir. James Ivory, 2005); *Gamelan Gardens* (2006); *Visual Brainstorming* (2006); *Scenes from a Country Bunny* (2006); *Cantus Articus* (2006); *Passing Strange* (2006; production opened on Broadway 2008); *Hair* (musical, 40th anniversary concert performance, 2007); *Gathering His Thoughts* (2007); *Gran Partita* (2007); *Connoisseurs of Chaos* (2008); *Ariadne Unhinged* (2008); *Between the Clock and the Bed* (2008); *Summer of Love* (open air preview 2008); *Hair* (2009); *The Watteau Duets* (1985; revised 2009); *Drastic-Classicism* (1985; revised 2009); *Mashup* (2009); *Arctic Song* (2009); *Made in Naples* (2009); *It's Gonna Get Loud* (2009); *The Blue Rider* (2009); *Itutu* (2009); *Rite of Spring/Summer of Love* (2009); *Three Theories* (2010).

Further reading

Interviews with Otis Stewart in 'Madonna of the Rock', *Ballett International*, January 1985; with John Mueller, in 'Making Musical Dance', *Ballet Review*, Winter 1986.

Articles: Marcelle Michel *et al.*, 'Danser au soleil', *Pour la Danse*, October 1980; Jochen Schmidt, 'What Moves Them and How', *Ballett International*, June/July 1982; Jann Parry, 'Of a Feather, Flock', *Dance and Dancers*, November 1982;

Alastair Macaulay, 'Not Actually Extemporising', *Dance Theatre Journal*, May 1983; Odon-Jérôme Lemaître, 'Paradise de Karole Armitage', *Pour la Danse*, January 1984; Otis Stewart, 'Karole Armitage', *Pour la Danse*, February 1985; Robert Greskovic, 'Armitagean Physics, or the Shoes of a Ballerina', *Ballet Review*, Summer 1985; Jean Claude Diénis, 'Karole Armitage, danseuse de haut volt', *Danser*, September 1985; Elizabeth Zimmer, 'Out There with Karole Armitage', *Dance Magazine*, May 1986; Roger Copeland, 'The Objective Temperament', *Dance Theatre Journal*, Autumn 1986; Judith Mackrell, 'Kitsch and Courtship at the Umbrella', *Dance Theatre Journal*, Spring 1986; J. Johnston, 'The Punk Princess and the Postmodern Prince', *Art in America* (Marion, OH), October 1986; Anita Finkel, 'New York: Thème de Karole', *Ballett International*, April 1987; Stuart Otis, 'The Neoclassical Phrasing of the Now; Karole Armitage', *Ballet Review*, Winter 1988; special Armitage issue of *Les Saisons de la Danse*, October 1993; Francesca Pedroni, 'Armitage in Florence', *Ballett International*, December 1995; Nancy Dalva, 'Reviews: New York City', *Dance Magazine*, February 1997; Christopher Reardon. 'Return of the Punk Ballerina', *Dance Magazine*, January 2001; Joan Acocella, 'Drastic Classic', *The New Yorker*, 22 March 2004; Elizabeth Zimmer, 'Taming the Gypsy in Her Soul', *Dance Magazine*, February, 2007, Deborah Jowitt, 'Worlds of Change', *The Village Voice*, 30 January 2008; Deborah Jowitt, 'All Punked Up', *The Village Voice*, 11 March 2009; Joan Acocella, 'Twos and Threes', *The New Yorker*, 4 May 2009.

Books: Arlene Croce, *Going to the Dance*, New York, 1982; Deborah Jowitt, *The Dance in Mind*, Boston, 1985; Arlene Croce, *Sight Lines*, New York, 1987; Allen Robertson and Donald Hutera, *The Dance Handbook*, Harlow, Essex, 1988; Peter Schjeldahl, *Karole Armitage and David Salle: Three Years of the Ballet Stage*, Kyoto, Japan, 1989; Sally Banes, *Writing Dancing in the Age of Postmodernism*, Hanover, NH, and London, 1994; Karole Armitage and Kyoichi Tsuzuki, *Art Random: David Salle and Karole Armitage 19*, Kyoto, Japan, 1995.

JÉRÔME BEL

The problem of trying to write about the French dance artist Jérôme Bel here is that his ideas and performance work directly attack so many of the assumptions underlying much choreographical practice. Does Jérôme Bel even belong in a book about contemporary choreography? He uses the term 'realizer' rather than 'choreographer' to describe himself. While choreography, he says, concerns setting steps and movements into sequences, what he himself does is more concerned with ideas and concepts. The pieces his company has performed in his name in some ways amount to a series of provocations that undermine the assumption that the artist's name is a sign and guarantee of authorship, authenticity and originality. His international reputation, however, necessitates his inclusion in this book. One of the things that can come as a shock, when one sees a piece by Bel, is the realization that he does not subscribe to the notion that contemporary dance is an open field whose practitioners embrace the freedom to invent a new and previously inconceivable aesthetic. What can make this uncomfortable for a spectator is the accompanying realization of how much one may have believed in this romanticized view of contemporary dance without knowing it.

In his twenties, Bel danced for Angelin Preljocaj, Joëlle Bouvier and Regis Obadier, who were key figures in the rapid expansion of French contemporary dance during the 1980s. By 1992, he was feeling dissatisfied with the sort of work in which he had been performing. Finding himself with a healthy bank balance after helping Philippe Decouflé create the opening ceremony for the Winter Olympics in Albertville, Bel decided to spend two years living frugally in Paris and used this time to find a direction for himself as an artist. He read books about dance history and by French philosophers whose ideas had been affected by the events in Paris in May 1968, in particular Roland Barthes and Michel Foucault.

This was a time when other dancers of his generation – including Boris Charmatz, Emmanuelle Huynh, Benoît Lechambre, Xavier Le Roy, Loïc Touzé and Christophe Wavelet – were forming groups to discuss dance, philosophy and politics. These groups collectively wrote essays and manifestos (which were not always finished or published) and criticized current dance practice, often from a libertarian, anticapitalist point of view.[1] Two key areas of concern were the institutional context of dance and the importance of dance history. Companies in France were benefiting from supportive arts policies and funding, but a side effect of the way these systems worked was the creation of a format which, as Xavier Le Roy has observed, 'influenced and sometimes to a large degree also determined how a dance piece should be. Most of the time, producers and programmers have to significantly follow the rules of global economy'.[2] Bel, Le Roy and others began making works that challenged the largely tacit assumptions about what dance might be, thus engaging in a kind of institutional critique. In their view, the dance market also depended on a particular view of the relationship between contemporary dance and its history. As Bel himself put it, the older generation of French choreographers 'lost themselves to the illusion that they were totally without forefathers and would always have to invent things from scratch'.[3] Bel and his contemporaries therefore began deliberately to investigate past works. He was close to those involved in projects by the Quatuor Albrecht Knust company, remembering in particular their presentation in 1996 of Yvonne Rainer's 1970 piece *Continuous Project Altered Daily*.

In 1994, Bel created *Nom donné par l'auteur* (*Name Given by the Author* – that is, a dictionary definition of 'title') for himself and Frédéric Seguette. This was initially performed for close associates. It involved entirely logical but increasingly irrational combinations of a small group of everyday objects that might be found in any bourgeois interior, including a hair dryer, vacuum cleaner, dictionary, ball and a tin of table salt. The piece was entirely worked out in advance of rehearsals and destabilized conventions about dancers' self-presentation and use of space. English-speaking writers sometimes use the word 'deconstruction' to describe this approach. In France, however, Laurent Goumarre's definition of 'deceptive' art has gained currency that combines perception (of the material body rather than its imagined potential to evoke metaphysical ideals), conceptual art and deception.

Bel's second piece, *Jérôme Bel* (1995), which launched him on the international dance scene, pushed his 'deceptual' approach in a challenging and provocative direction. Where Roland Barthes had written about 'writing degree zero', Bel explored what dancing degree zero might be.[4] Four naked dancers performed on a bare stage lit by a single light bulb held by a woman who wrote 'Thomas Edison' in chalk on a blackboard at the back. Two dancers wrote, in chalk, their names, measurements, telephone numbers and bank balances. A fourth wrote 'Stravinsky, Igor' and then sang the entire score of *The Rite of Spring*. The piece comprised a series of ironic statements about the bare minimum of what being human means while foregrounding the materiality of bodies, their functions and social construction. They wrote on their bodies in lipstick, the woman inscribing 'Christian Dior' down her leg. At one point, she pressed her hair between a male dancer's closed legs and then pulled it back out. Later, they urinated and then used this to wash off some of the chalk letters, leaving the sentence 'Eric chante Sting' (Eric sings Sting), after which a man named Eric appeared and sang a song by the English pop star. In 2004, *Jérôme Bel* was the subject of an unsuccessful civil prosecution in Dublin, when a member of the audience took the International Dance Festival of Ireland to court for, in his view, wrongly describing the piece as dance.[5]

In *Le Dernier Spectacle* (*The Last Performance*, 1998), Bel wanted to make a piece for himself and three other dancers entirely out of existing choreography created by others. Of the choreographers he approached, only Susanne Linke gave permission, so an extract from her 1978 piece *Wandlungen* was one of four units of material whose repetitions made up the piece. A man said he was Jérôme Bel, though he was not, set an alarm on his digital watch and then stood blankly waiting for it to go off before exiting. Another, dressed for tennis, said he was André Agassi and played tennis against the back wall for a couple of minutes. Another, dressed in a black Renaissance costume, said he was Hamlet and recited the soliloquy 'To be or not to be'. A woman in a white silk dress said she was Susanne Linke and danced an extract from *Wandlungen*. Then one after another the three men, also in dresses, danced it. These four repetitions lasted nearly 30 minutes, their gradual familiarity increasingly making spectators aware of the endurance of watching. Later, performers returned to say they were not Bel, Agassi, Linke or Hamlet, and performed the related material in logically developed ways. The piece ended with an empty stage as a recorded voice read out the names of all the people who had reserved tickets for that evening's performance. Whether performers are or are not who they say they are (it was, e.g., Jérôme Bel who said he was not Jérôme Bel) depends on the way representations circulate within society. This, according to Foucault, is the meaning of the surrealist artist Magritte's painting of a pipe with the inscription underneath, 'this is not a pipe'.[6] Just as *Jérôme Bel* made audiences aware of the constructedness of bodies, *Le Dernier Spectacle* drew attention to the constructedness of performative signs.

Gerald Siegmund suggests that, by calling his fourth piece 'the last performance', Bel was announcing his premature retirement. When commissioned to make a new piece in 2000, he therefore asked Xavier Le Roy to make it for him, although Bel is named as the author of *Xavier Le Roy* and collects the royalties when it is performed. (Should this piece therefore be discussed in an article on Bel's work?) Le Roy says he made a piece as much like Bel's work as he could. Two dancers, wearing long blonde wigs that obscured their faces, appeared as Charlie Chaplin, Hitler, Christ on the cross, Michael Jackson and Marilyn Monroe. These were examples of movement clichés whose over-familiarity meant that their performance created a disturbing blankness.

The title of his next work, *The Show Must Go On* (2001), announced Bel's return to dance making. It was constructed around 18 pop songs, played one after the other. These records were so well-known that, on the one hand, listeners almost did not hear them while, on the other, they were triggers for the layers of public and private association they had accumulated. In typical Bel fashion, each song inspired an absolutely literal interpretation of a single element in its lyrics. Thus, while the stage remained empty for 'Tonight' and 'Let the Sunshine In', the performers only made their entrance when The Beatles actually sang the words 'Come Together' and did not move again until David Bowie sang the chorus of 'Let's Dance'. Commissioned by Paris's Théâtre de la Ville, it was Bel's first opportunity to explore the resources of a large conventional stage; thus during 'Yellow Submarine' the cast climbed through a trapdoor to sing along to 'beneath the waves' from beneath the stage. A large part of the Parisian audience demonstrated their disapproval by walking out, invading the stage or persisting with slow hand claps.

The Paris Opéra commissioned *Véronique Doisneau* (2004) for and about a retiring 'sujet' – someone who dances in the *corps de ballet* and sometimes performs minor roles. During this, Doisneau talked to the audience about her life and career, said how much she earned, and demonstrated extracts from her repertoire. Pointing out that what audiences often find most magical about the ballet can be excruciatingly boring and odious to perform, she showed what she dances during the second-act adagio of *Swan Lake*. This mostly consists of holding a pose for a long, boring wait until the musical cue to change to another position. Bel adopted a similar format for *Made in Thailand* (2004), a duo for himself and Pichet Klunchun, master of the Thai classical masked dance style 'khon'. They talked about their careers and demonstrated their work to one another and for the audience. The piece refused to fall into the trap of finding in movement a supposedly universal language that transcends cultural differences. History shows that the road to such universalization brings with it appropriation and exoticization.

By the early 2000s, Bel had become one of the best known exponents of conceptual, or deceptual, dance. Since 2002, he has programmed the biennial Belgian arts festival at Klapstuk. There are now agencies promoting indigenous conceptual choreography in former communist European countries, and notable conceptual choreographers are working in Africa and Brazil, but not, significantly, in New York.[7] What had begun as an anti-capitalist critique of the institutionalized dance world had inevitably been re-appropriated within the mainstream. Bel was in his thirties before he showed his work in public, and since then has slowly made a comparatively small number of beautifully constructed, highly economical and extremely smart works. These generate moments of sometimes witty, but sometimes uncanny and uncomfortable, absence which challenge the expectation that good art projects a powerful, reassuring presence. At their best, their blankness becomes a screen that reflects back to spectators their own desires and expectations with a directness that reminds them of their own potential for innovation and change. As Bel himself wryly observes, 'Sometimes I think people are getting more and more clever watching us be more and more stupid'.[8]

Ramsay Burt

Notes

1 For example, Groupe 20 Août – see Isabelle Launay, 'Les Signataires du 20 Août, état du grève à Kerguéhennec: corps en suspens' *Mouvement*, January–March (1999) and the 2001 Manifesto for a European Performance Policy – see André Lepecki, 'Concept and Presence: The Contemporary European Dance Scene' in Carter, Alexandra (ed.), *Rethinking Dance History*, London and New York, (2004).

2 Quoted in Helmut Ploebst, *No Wind No Word: New Choreography in the Society of the Spectacle*, Munich, 2001.

3 Quoted in Gerald Siegmund, 'Dialogue with the Body (II): In the Realm of Signs: Jérôme Bel', *Ballett International/Tanz Aktuell*, April, 1998.

4 Roland Barthes, *Writing Degree Zero*, London, 1967.

5 See André Lepecki, *Exhausting Dance: Performance and the Politics of Movement*, London and New York, 2006.

6 Michel Foucault, *This is Not A Pipe*, Los Angeles, 1982.

7 See Gia Kourlas, 'How New York Lost its Modern Dance Reign', *The New York Times*, 6 September 2005.

8 Quoted in Tim Etchells, 'More and more clever watching more and more stupid: Some thoughts around rules, games and *The Show Must Go On*', *Dance Theatre Journal*, 20(2), 2004.

Biographical details

Born in France, 1964. **Studied** for 1 year at the Centre Nationale de Danse Contemporaine at Angers, 1984–85. **Career**: Danced in the 1980s for Angelin Preljocaj, Joëlle Bouvière, Regis Obadia, Daniel Larrieu, Caterina Sagna among others; assistant director to Philippe Decouflé for the ceremonies of the XVIth Winter Olympic Games, Albertville and Savoie, 1992; began creating work in 1994 with *Nom donné par l'auteu*; has also created work for the Paris Opera Ballet; curated with Alain Platel, the Klapstuk Festival, Leuven, 2003; also participated in 'Parallel Voices', the first series of conversations between artists curated by Jonathan Burrows, hosted at the Siobhan Davies Dance Studio, London, 2007. **Awards** include New York Dance and Performance Award ('Bessie'), 2005; Routes Princess Margriet Award, 2008.

Works

Nom donné par l'auteur (1994); *Jérôme Bel* (1995); *Shirtology* (1997); *Le Dernier Spectacle* (1998); *Xavier Le Roy* (2000); *The Show Must Go On* (2001); *The Last Performance* (une conférence) (2004); *Véronique Doisneau* (2004); *Made in Thailand* (with Pichet Klunchun, 2004); *The Show Must Go On 2* (2004); *Pichet Klunchun and Myself* (2005); *Isabel Torres*, (version of *Véronique Doisneau* for Teatro Municipal of Rio de Janeiro, 2005); *Lutz Förster* (2009); *Cédric Andrieux* (2009); *A Spectator* (2009); *3 Abschied* (with Anna Teresa De Keersmaeker, 2010).

Further reading

Interview with Una Bauer, in 'Jerome Bel: An Interview', *Performance Research* 13(1), 2010.

Articles: Arnd Wesemann, 'At Point Zero of the Dancer's Body', *Ballett International/Tanz Aktuell*, March 1998; Gerald Siegmund, 'Dialogue with the Body (II): In the Realm of Signs: Jérôme Bel', *Ballett International/Tanz Aktuell*, April 1998; Laurent Goumarre, 'Deceptive art', *Art Press*, September 1998; Gerald Siegmund, 'The Endgame of Dance', *Ballett International/Tanz Aktuell*, January 1999; Isabelle Launay, 'Les Signataires du 20 Août, état du grève à Kerguéhennec: corps en suspens' *Mouvement*, January–March 1999; Christophe Wavelet, 'L'Après-spectacle', *Mouvement*, June–September 2000; Arnd Wesemann, 'The Fun Generation finally gets a theatre', *Ballett International/Tanz Aktuell*, November 2000; Andrew Brown, 'Intimacy with Strangers', *Dance Theatre Journal*, 17(2), 2001; Tim Etchells, 'More and more clever watching more and more stupid: Some thoughts around Rules, Games and *The Show Must Go On*', *Dance Theatre Journal*, 20(2), 2004; Michael Seaver, 'Naked in the Presence of his Enemies', *Dance Magazine*, November 2004; Kristin Hohenadel, 'Nondances That Spur Critics to Brawl and Audiences to Sue', *New York Times*, 20 March 2005; Rose Lee Goldberg, 'Jerome Bel: Dance Theater Workshop', *ArtForum*, Summer 2005; Roslyn Sulcas, 'Unless You Have Another World, Dance Will Do', *The New York Times* (Sunday feature), 24 February 2008; Una Bauer, 'The Movement of Embodied Thought', *Performance Research*, 13(1), 2010.

Books: Helmut Ploebst, *No Wind No Word: New Choreography in the Society of the Spectacle*, Munich, 2001; RoseLee Goldberg, *Performance Art: From Futurism to the Present*, New York, 2001; Alexandra Carter (ed.), *Rethinking Dance History*, London, 2004; André Lepecki, *Exhausting Dance: Performance and the Politics of Movement*, London, 2006; Ramsay Burt, *Judson Dance Theater: Performative Traces*, London, 2006; Gerald Siegmund, *Abwesenheit. Eine performative ästhetik des Tanzes: William Forsythe, Jérôme Bel, Xavier Le Roy, Meg Stuart*, Bielefeld, 2006; Janet Lansdale (ed.), *Decentring Dancing Texts*, Basingstoke, 2008.

MATTHEW BOURNE

Considered in relation to the various trends that characterize British modern and post-modern dance, Matthew Bourne's is a unique and isolated case. Bourne is not interested in abstract compositions or experimenting with new means of expression. His principal aim is to create dances in which the theatrical element is particularly evident, for he believes strongly in what can be called pure 'theatre magic' – whether it be the refined scenario of a ballet classic or the spectacular panache of a Busby Berkeley musical. In every work, from *Overlap Lovers* (1987), the first he created for his group Adventures in Motion Pictures, Bourne's personal adaptation of theatre magic is instantly recognizable.

Without seeking the assistance of the latest technology, Bourne can create impressive imagery and situations, merely by drawing from the language of dance. An example is his version of the familiar ballet *The Nutcracker* (1992). The first act of Bourne's version ends with a skating tableau: female dancers stand on one leg and hold their skirts as if they are floating in a winter breeze. By nothing more than a simple visual trick, an effective stage illusion is immediately created.

The inspiration for these images comes mainly from Bourne's own multi-faceted cultural background. Prior to embracing dance as a profession, Bourne was an enthusiastic fan of almost every form of performing art. As he has confirmed in interviews, he used to attend the theatre more than twice a week on a regular basis. Old films of musicals held a particular fascination for him. It is not merely incidental, therefore, that many of the images absorbed during those years provide the backbone to his works. *The Percys of Fitzrovia* (1992) is derived from the works of Noël Coward; *Deadly Serious* (1992) draws on the films of Alfred Hitchcock; and both the skating scene and the Kingdom of the Sweets scenario in his *Nutcracker* refer, respectively, to the choreographies of Frederick Ashton and Busby Berkeley.

The fact that theatre is fundamental to Bourne's choreography also dictates that narrative is a constant in his creations. Although some of his early works do not have a defined plot as such, narrative elements are always present in his works. This undoubtedly contributes to the accessibility and, therefore, the popularity of Bourne's choreography. Another important factor is the choreographer's innate sense of comedy, which can find expression in sharp satire, subtle irony or dark humour.

Bourne's movement vocabulary is characterized by the constant adaptation of the dance idiom to a dramatic context. Although one can speak of the 'Bourne style', it is difficult to define its technical elements. As a student at the Laban Centre in London, Bourne received a heterogeneous training that included some of the major dance techniques, ranging from Graham technique to ballet. His own vocabulary originally grew from this combination of styles and techniques, but it developed through the years, taking in other forms of movement and expression and eventually acquiring its own individuality. A significant trait is his use of music. This is especially evident in such creations as *Highland Fling* (1994) and *Swan Lake* (1995), where the dance action is set to familiar, pre-existing scores rather than to scores composed for the occasion. Bourne manages to capture the essence of the original music, giving a personal and distinctive choreographic reading of it. A notable example of his willingness to reinterpret a score is the disco sequence in *Highland Fling*, set to the Scottish dance of Løvenskjold's 1836 score *La Sylphide*.

In 1992, the director of Britain's Opera North commissioned a new version of *The Nutcracker* from Bourne, as part of the celebrations to mark the centenary of Tchaikovsky's death. Although Bourne and his company were already a familiar presence on the British dance scene, this was the work through which the young choreographer acquired his first taste of wider popularity. Bourne's *Nutcracker* retains part of the original scenario, although the context and action differ considerably from their nineteenth-century antecedent. A gloomy Victorian workhouse, within which orphans try to enjoy themselves, is humorously juxtaposed with the plush surroundings of the traditional *Nutcracker* Christmas party. The Kingdom of the Sweets, too, is subjected to some radical alterations: it becomes a caricature of contemporary society wherein people, being apparently literally 'sweet', lick one another. Several tongue-in-cheek references to illustrious choreographic examples from the past – such as Ashton's *Les Patineurs* – punctuate the work. The dance vocabulary is an amalgam of techniques and styles, ranging from ballet (although pointe shoes are never used) to disco dancing. Although the work was revised in 2002 and re-titled *Nutcracker!*, most of its original dramaturgic features were carefully retained.

Highland Fling is structured according to a similar formula. As with *The Nutcracker*, *Highland Fling* – subtitled *A Romantic 'Wee' Ballet* – is a contemporary adaptation of a familiar nineteenth-century ballet, this time August Bournonville's *La Sylphide*. The original storyline is retained almost in its entirety, while the time and the context of the action are updated to today. The Sylph becomes the product of James's drug-induced hallucinations, and the second act, focusing on James's vain struggle to join the sylphs, becomes an allegory of man's struggle and realization of his limitations. Cultural references to other nineteenth-century ballets occur throughout, mainly in the form of choreographic parody. Once again, the dance vocabulary is a combination of different styles, although ballet is the predominant one.

In Bourne's *Swan Lake*, these techniques of parody and cultural reference are again used to equal effect. With *Swan Lake*, the choreographer took perhaps his greatest risk by reinterpreting one of the most familiar and best-loved of nineteenth-century ballet scores, Tchaikovsky's 1877 masterpiece. Bourne's prince is a tortured soul who longs for freedom within the constrictive world of court society and identifies this freedom with a male swan who has haunted his dreams since childhood. In an effective reinterpretation of the famous 'white act' of the ballet, the unhappy prince finds himself in a moonlit park where he encounters the swan and his group of swan companions — but rather than ballerinas in tutus, these are male, bare chested and barefooted. As in the original libretto, the lead swan has a doppelgänger: Bourne's equivalent of the evil Black Swan is a leather-clad youth who crashes the royal ball and seduces the queen, driving the prince mad with despair. Isolated and rejected by society, the prince is finally rounded on by the corps of swans, who peck both him and the intervening chief swan to death. Once again the cultural references are strong, from the butterfly ballet-within-a-ballet that recalls Jerome Robbins's *The Concert* (1956) to the ballroom dancing sequences that bring to mind the imagery of Hollywood musicals. But the strongest scenes are undoubtedly the 'white' or swan scenes, which reveal Bourne's true choreographic genius.

Some critics regard the reinterpreted classics as significant landmarks in Bourne's career, as if the revising and updating of ballets from the past indicated an artistic change of direction for him. Others consider such works as an alarming signal of the choreographer's lack of inventiveness — and indeed, his 1997 version of *Cinderella* did not explore to the full the many symbolic and metaphorical possibilities offered by the story or the music. Still, it is difficult to give credit to either point of view. When analyzed in detail, these works do not reveal a drastic departure from Bourne's artistic canon. Rather, they provide evidence of a cultural and artistic quest for new materials; as such, they represent but a facet of Bourne's interests that spread across all the performing arts.

Since the creation of *Cinderella* Bourne has not tackled any other title of the ballet repertoire, focusing instead on choreographic readings and adaptations of cinema works. In *The Car Man* (2000), subtitled 'an auto erotic thriller', the narrative of the 1946 Hollywood classic *The Postman Always Rings Twice* is cleverly interwoven with that of George Bizet's opera *Carmen*. The result is a thought-provoking hybrid that is rich in inter-textual references of every kind, including direct visual quotations from recent blockbusters such as *Titanic* (1997). An inter-textual approach to cinema narratives is also what underpins *Play without Words* (2002), an Olivier Award-winning creation for the National Theatre in London, which crosses the boundaries between dance, pantomime and drama. Its storyline is inspired by that of Joseph Losey's 1963 film *The Servant*, and, as explained by the title, is 'acted' only through movement. *Edward Scissorhands* (2005), based on Tim Burton's popular film with the same title, can be seen as yet another tribute to Bourne's fondness for the big screen. In this production too, inter-textual references to ballet classics and Hollywood musicals abound, although, according to many, less effectively than in any of the works mentioned above. Still, *Edward Scissorhands* should not be numbered amongst Bourne's other dance creations, for it is, in the words of its own creator, a 'dansical' – namely a work that combines the traits of a dance works with those of a musical comedy.

Indeed, musical comedy is another area of interest for Bourne, within which his creative skills have found a fertile ground and often with prize-winning results. This is the case with *Oliver!* (1994), *My Fair Lady* (2002), *South Pacific* (2002) and, most notably, the West End hit *Mary Poppins* (2004) which he co-choreographed (with Stephen Mear) and co-directed (with Richard Eyre). Such ability to move successfully amidst a variety of theatre genres is certainly synonymous with Bourne's unique cultural and artistic openness, a quality that remains a guiding principle of both his work and that of his company, New Adventures, which he created after resigning in 2002 from the post of Artistic Director of his first company, Adventures in Motion Pictures.

Giannandrea Poesio

Biographical details

Born in London, 13 January 1960. **Studied** at the Laban Centre, London, 1982–85, received a BA in Dance and Theatre. **Career**: Danced with Laban Centre's Transitions Dance Company, 1985–86, Adventures in Motion Pictures (founder member), London, from 1987, and Lea Anderson's The Featherstone-haughs (founder member), London, 1988; began choreographing for Adventures in Motion Pictures, 1987, becoming its artistic director in 1987; resigned as artistic director of Adventures in Motion Pictures and created the company New Adventures, 2002; appointed Sadler's Wells Associate Artist, from 2005. Has also staged works for the Royal Shakespeare Company, Aix-en-Provence Festival, Malmö Stadsteater (Sweden) and National Youth Theatre (London). **Awards and honours** include The Place Portfolio, 1989; Bonnie Bird Choreography Award, 1989; Barclays New Stages Award, 1991; *Time Out* Award, 1995; Olivier Award for Best New Dance Production (*Swan Lake*), 1996; Laban Centre Honorary Fellowship, 1997; Astaire Award 1999; Tony Award for Best Direction of a Musical, 1999; Tony Award for Best Choreography, 1999; *Evening Standard* Award, 2000; OBE for Services to Dance, 2001; Olivier Award, 2002 and 2005; Hamburg Shakespeare for the Arts, 2003; Theatre Managers Special Award (TMA), 2007.

Works

Overlap Lovers (1987); *Spitfire* (1988); *Buck and Wing* (1988); *The Infernal Galop* (1989); *As You Like It* (play by Shakespeare, 1989); *Singer* (play by Peter Barnes, 1989); *Children of Eden* (musical by Stephen Schwanz, 1990); *Leonce and Lena* (play by Lyndsay Posner, 1990); *The Terra Firma* (opera by Steve Martland, 1990); *Town and Country* (1991); *A Midsummer Night's Dream* (opera by Britten, 1991); *Showboat* (musical by Oscar Hammerstein, 1991); *The Nutcracker* (1992); *Deadly Serious* (1992); *The Percys of Fitzrovia* (1992); *The Tempest* (play by Shakespeare, 1993); *Late-Flowering Lust* (for television, 1993); *Drip – A Love Story* (for television, 1993); *Highland Fling: A Romantic 'Wee' Ballet* (1994); *Oliver!* (musical by Lionel Bart, 1994); *Peer Gynt* (play by Ibsen, 1994); *Swan Lake* (1995; also televised); *Little Red Riding Hood* (for television, based on Roald Dahl story, 1995); *Watch Your Step!* (gala; music by Irving Berlin, 1995); *Cinderella* (1997); *The Car Man* (2000); *Play Without Words* (2002); *Nutcracker!* (2002); *My Fair Lady* (musical by Alan Jay Lerner and Frederick Loewe, 2002); *South Pacific* (musical by Rodgers and Hammerstein 2002); *Mary Poppins* (musical by Richard M. Sherman and Robert B. Sherman, 2004); *Edward Scissorhands* (2005); *Dorian Gray* (2008).

Further reading

Interview with Allen Robertson in 'High Voltage', *Dance Now*, Autumn 1995; with Mark Wilder in *Gay Times*, November 1995; with Christopher Bowen in *The Scotsman*, 2 April 1996; with Debra Craine, 'Man of the Moment', *Dance Now*, Summer 2005; with Alison Kirkman, 'Matthew Bourne's New Adventures in *The Car Man*', *Dancing Times*, August 2007; with Louise Bennett, in 'Portrait of Matthew Bourne', *Dancing Times*, August 2008.

Articles: Sophie Constanti, 'Dance Umbrella 1988', *Dancing Times*, December 1988; Jann Parry, 'Adventures in Motion Pictures: Company at a Crossroads', *Dance Theatre Journal*, Summer 1990; James Belsey, 'Dance Scene: Adventures in Motion Pictures', *Dancing Times*, May 1991; Judith Mackrell, 'Gingering up the Dolly Mixture', *The Independent*, 14 August 1992; Fiona Burnside, 'Matthew Bourne and Kim Brandstrup: Telling Other Men's Tales', *Dance Theatre Journal*, Spring/Summer 1994; Giannandrea Poesio, 'Spotlight on Matthew Bourne', *Dancing Times*, January 1994; Jann Parry, 'AMP's *Swan Lake*', *Dance Now*, Winter 1995; Christopher Benson, 'Matthew Bourne: Giving the Classics a Shot of Irony, *Dance Magazine*, May 1997; Louise Levene, 'Cinderella Makes Progress', *Dance Theatre Journal*, 14(1), 1998; Ian Bramley, 'The Return of the Narrative: Ian Bramley finds Matthew

Bourne and Mark Murphy Telling Tales', *Dance Theatre Journal*, 14(4), 1999; Elisabeth Marshall, 'Matthew Bourne's *Nutcracker!* Study Aid', *Dancing Times*, June and July 2006; Katie Gregory, '*Nutcracker!*', *Dancing Times*, February 2008; Zoë Anderson, '*Dorian Gray*', *Dancing Times*, October 2008.

Books: Judith Mackrell, *Out of Line: The Story of British New Dance*, London, 1992; Alastair Macaulay, *Matthew Bourne and His Adventures in Motion Pictures*, London, 2000; Alastair Macaulay, 'Matthew Bourne, Dance History and *Swan Lake*' in Alexandra Carter (ed.), *Rethinking Dance History*, London, 2004; Vida Midgelow, *Reworking the Ballet: Counter-Narratives and Alternative Bodies*, London, 2007.

RONALD K. BROWN

Ronald K. Brown made a name for himself, in the first decade of his career, as a choreographer who seamlessly fused styles or influences as various as West African traditional movement, urban club dancing and mainstream modern dance. His work was both spiritual and confidently gay-themed, filled with propulsive eruptions and fluid travel, the universally familiar product of a specific black sensibility. He set his dancers on abstract yet fervent journeys across the stage and by implication through life. Brown likes to say that he and his performers bear 'evidence' – the name of his company – of the truths of their lives and of the communities to which they belonged. 'Who will tell your grandmother's stories?' a friend once asked him. He never forgot that.

Brown was already considered a major and distinctive voice in New York modern dance when, in 1999, the Alvin Ailey American Dance Theater commissioned a piece called *Grace* that almost instantly became a classic and brought him a new, larger and more international audience than ever he might have dreamed of. An intensely emotional but fluid journey to some promised land, led by a woman who may be a manifestation of divinity, *Grace* is set to Duke Ellington's wistful, prayer-like 'Come Sunday', black dance music by Roy Davis, Jr., and Afro-Pop by Fela Kuti, and is typical of Brown's work in its inextricable blending of the sacred and mundane, the public and the private and theme and physicality. 'Few today can match the depth of his ability to marry message and medium,' Anna Kisselgoff, *The New York Times* dance critic, once wrote.

But *Grace* was also more than sophisticated and glossy enough to fill the stages the Ailey company performed on, so much bigger and more formal than the intimate dance theatres where Evidence/A Dance Company had appeared. The dance's paths and patterns looked newly expansive and the choreography blossomed in an atmosphere of gleaming deluxe costumes and set designs that Brown could never have afforded. The Ailey commission, the first of three, brought new validation to Brown and his work and placed him within a specific historical context. He was now definitively a black choreographer, his work performed by a black-identified company that also happened to be one of the most popular and successful dance troupes in the world.

Alvin Ailey's death in 1989 had marked the end of one kind of black dance, or dance created and largely performed by black artists, and the solidification of another kind. A new generation of black modern-dance choreographers like Brown, Jawole Willa Jo Zollar and Reggie Wilson could draw inspiration from the African and Caribbean forms that nourished black dance pioneers like Pearl Primus from the 1940s on. But now readily identifiable 'black' themes, among them the effects of slavery and racism on black Americans, were replaced for many black choreographers by a focus on men and women who had moved on with the times, their lives far more solidly and unremarkably a part of the texture of American life. At the same time, it is difficult to conceive of a white choreographer having made *Grace*, with its implicit allusions to black spirituality and its sense of a specific community.

What makes Brown and his work most distinctive, however, is his emphasis on inclusiveness and his success in making dances that succeed in drawing all viewers in. Everyone, after all, wants in some way to give testimony or bear witness to their lives and experiences, and there is much common ground to be shared. Working on a piece to be called *Redemption* at the American Dance Festival in 2004, he wrestled with the traditional idea of God as the cleanser of sins. 'Then when I looked up "redeem" it meant to turn over, to turn in, to cash in — the idea that it was something that a human could do,' Brown told the dance writer Byron Woods. 'So I started playing with the idea — oh, we can redeem each other.' Man did not have to wait for God to act, Brown reasoned. 'It's something we do with each other that leads to redemption as well. That became the journey of the piece. How do we take each other to this stage of redemption, this sacred space, this clean space and this space where we feel free?'

Nothing human is unknowable, no matter how unfamiliar it may seem. Brown's 1998 *Better Days* was inspired in part by the oddly spiritual quality he felt in the slow heavy house music to which gay men danced and by clubs like the now-defunct Better Days, where the men 'could find love and sex and dance their hearts out'. In rehearsal for one section of the dance, set in an imaginary club, all but one of Brown's male dancers convincingly suggested the promise of heat – and sadness – as each paired off with another. One hung back, dancing the sequence as steps rather than an experience. 'Straight boys do this, too,' Brown called out gently to the dancer.

A major inspiration for Better Days was writing by Brown's favourite gay black poets. An avid reader, Brown often does considerable research into themes. He has also frequently collaborated with black writers in his dances, unsurprisingly enough, given that he nearly chose journalism over a career in dance.

Born in the late 1960s, Brown grew up in Bedford-Stuyvesant in Brooklyn, not a place then known for its middle-class amenities. Encouraged by his mother in his artistic endeavours, he knew by the age of nine that he wanted to be a dancer, dressing in black tights and a white T-shirt as Arthur Mitchell, the black New York City Ballet star and a founder of the Dance Theatre of Harlem, for a Black History Month assignment in second grade. He studied dance in summer classes at the Police Athletic League, taught by a cast member of the Broadway musical The Wiz, and in high school took ballet at a neighbourhood dance school. His mother and three younger siblings served as audience for shows he presented that once included his own version of Ailey's Revelations, seen on a class trip to a performance by the Ailey company.

But before embarking on college training in journalism after his graduation from the Edward R. Murrow High School of Communications in 1983, Brown spent the summer on a scholarship at the Mary Anthony Dance Studio, where he studied modern dance, ballet, composition and teaching. He also performed with Anthony's troupe and presented his own dances in choreography workshops at the studio every three months. He had in effect made his choice of dance as a career.

A no-nonsense teacher who quietly influenced generations of modern-dance choreographers, Anthony drilled into her students the importance of such old-fashioned virtues as craft and an appreciation of clear form and content. It could be a frustrating experience for young choreographers finding their own style, and Brown left after two years with Anthony to study and perform with Jennifer Muller, whose style he identified with. He continued to work on his own dances, and after four years was ready to go out on his own, though he continued to perform with other choreographers. Around the same time, he joined a group of gay black writers, part of a larger national group, and was impressed by their notion that gay black men must create their own history because they had no movement of their own. Comparable choreographic influences have been the work of Bebe Miller, David Rousseve, Bill T. Jones and Ann Carlson.

A significant early piece was *Evidence*, a solo that he created in 1984. Inspired by the death of a beloved uncle, the dance addressed black ethnicity and family life. Brown was interested to learn from a Jewish woman in the audience of how much she identified with the subject matter. The following year, at the ripe age of 19, Brown founded Evidence.

His work in those years dealt head-on and idealistically with political and social issues including AIDS, to which a former lover had succumbed. His 1994 *Dirt Road*, performed to his own writing, poems by Donald K. Woods and Essex Hemphill, and songs by Aretha Franklin, Billie Holiday, Sylvester and others, was a non-linear narrative about cultural assimilation and loss. He began increasingly to incorporate spoken text into his choreography, which also grew more energetic as he explored the high-energy physicality of his performers and his own extraordinary gifts as a dancer.

By 1993, however, he was also moving towards the blend of vernacular or club dance and West African traditional forms for which he became known. At the American Dance Festival in Durham, North Carolina, the following year, Brown met and began to work with the Ivory Coast choreographer Rokya Kone. In 1995, he was a resident choreographer with Kone's Jeune Ballet d'Afrique Noire and Souleymane Koly's Ensemble Koteba D'Abidjan. Black modern-dance choreographers were travelling to Africa in the 1990s to immerse themselves in intensive, almost academic study of West African dance forms, much as Primus had decades before. But the experience had a profound effect on Brown's philosophy of dance and work, giving his characteristic ground-hugging movement a new curved fluency, as Kisselgoff observed, for a resilience that feels like the physical embodiment of the spirituality that attracts him.

Brown, who performs with his company, moves with a passion, urgency and easy whole-bodied abandon that other dancers are not quite able to match. That juiciness flows like a current through all his choreography, as does his gift for the deft expression of momentary shifts of characters and emotional and dynamic extremes.

Over the years, Brown has developed a work process that began with insistent visions or images, sometimes from his reading, which he then recorded in notebooks that might cover nearly a year of observations and work. Some percolated images eventually end up inspiring a piece or suite of dances. Brown has tended to teach performers new choreography by dancing it out in the performers' midst. As much an expression of the inclusiveness that identifies his treatment of his themes, he draws his performers into dancing with him as he repeats the material, rather than presenting it as a series of steps to be learned. Climb into the piece, he once told a group of students in rehearsal at the Juilliard Dance Division, don't put it on.

Jennifer Dunning

Biographical details

Born in Brooklyn, New York, 18 July 1966. **Studied** and performed with Mary Anthony from 1983 and Jennifer Muller from 1985. **Career:** Founded Evidence/A Dance Company, 1985; resident choreographer, Jeune Ballet d'Afrique Noire and Ensemble Koteba D'Abidjan, 1995; Alvin Ailey American Dance Theater Premiers *Grace*, 1999; has also created work for the African American Dance Ensemble, Philadanco, Cleo Parker Robinson Dance Ensemble, Dayton Contemporary Dance Company, Ailey 2, Cirque Folkloric Dance Theater, and Jennifer Muller/ The Works. **Awards and honours** include New York Dance and Performance Award ('Bessie'), 1998; John Simon Guggenheim Memorial Foundation Fellowship in Choreography, 2000; Black Theater Alliance Award for Choreography, 2000; AUDELCO (Black Theater Award), 2003; National Endowment for the Arts Choreographers' Fellowship, 2008; United States Artists Rose Fellowship Award, 2006.

Works

Evidence (1984); *Dirt Road* (1994); *Combat Review/Witches in Response* (1995); *Lessons* (1995); *Ebony Magazine* (1996); *Better Days* (1998); *Upside Down* (1998); *Grace* (Alvin Ailey American Dance Theater, 1999); *High Life* (2000); *Walking Out the Dark* (2001); *Serving Nia* (Alvin Ailey American Dance Theater, 2001); *Come Ye* (2003); *Redemption* (2004); *Blueprint of a Lady* (2005); *Ife/My Heart* (Alvin Ailey American Dance Theater, 2005); *Order My Steps* (2005); *Truth Don Die* (2006); *One Shot: Rhapsody in Black and White* (2007); *Two-Year Old Gentlemen* (2008).

Further reading

Interview with Melanie White Dixon, in 'Telling Stories, Keepin' it Real: A Conversation with Ronald K. Brown', *Attitude*, Spring 2000.

Articles: Bert Wechsler, 'Tendrils Entwine', *Attitude*, Spring, 1990; Tobi Tobias, 'Battle Cries', *The Village Voice*, 11 February 1992; Nicole Dekle, 'Ronald

K. Brown – Upcoming Choreographer', *Dance Magazine*, July 1995; Cynthia West, '*Combat Review/Witches in Response*', *Attitude*, Fall 1994/Winter 1995; Bernadine Jennings, 'Ron K. Brown/Evidence', *Attitude*, Spring/Summer 1998; Kevin Giordano, 'Reviews, New York City: Ronald K. Brown/Evidence', *Dance Magazine*, December 1998; Tobi Tobias, 'Saving Grace', *New York* magazine, 10 January 2000; Rose Eichenbaum, 'Leap of Faith', *Dance Magazine*, January 2000; Doris Hering, 'Passing the Flame', *Dance Magazine*, February 2001; Joan Acocella, 'The Spirit Moves', *The New Yorker*, 17 December 2001; Tobi Tobias, 'Disserving Nia', *New York* magazine, 24–31 December 2001; Jennifer Dunning, 'The Complexities of Love', *The New York Times*, 3 July 2002; Deborah Jowitt, 'Hidden Stories', *The Village Voice*, 7 February 2006; Deborah Jowitt, 'Keeping Truth Alive', *The Village Voice*, 30 January 2007; Deborah Jowitt, 'Ronald K. Brown's Spirit Moves', *The Village Voice*, 19 February 2008; Gus Solomons, Jr., 'Ronald K. Brown/Evidence', *Dance Magazine*, May 2009.

Books: Rose Eichenbaum (photographs and text) and Clive Barnes (foreword), *Masters of Movement: Portraits of America's Great Choreographers*, Washington, DC, 2004.

TRISHA BROWN

Trisha Brown's dances are shaped by dreams of levitation, by geometry, enigma, physics, by memory, mathematics and geography, by language. Her gestural imagery challenges perception of the moving body, making the impossible appear possible. Imagining that dancers can fall not only down but also up or sideways, Brown makes the rules of life seem arbitrary, offering an exhilarating transcendence of physical limits. Since 1962, her choreography has explored the interplay of intellect and instinct, paradoxes of logic and non sequitur, interpenetrations of present and past, coincidences of abstract form and mythic action and the edges between visibility and invisibility.

Brown was born in rural Aberdeen, Washington, where she immersed herself in her wilderness environment, in dance and in athletics. While attending Mills College in California she studied modern dance technique and composition derived from the teachings of Martha Graham and Louis Horst. At a workshop with the dance innovator Anna Halprin, she explored experiential anatomy, task-based improvisation, breath and vocalization and sensory awareness of the environment. This led to further investigations of experimental structures in the early 1960s in New York City – improvisational 'rulegames' with Simone Forti, indeterminate dances and spoken text with Yvonne Rainer, 'happenings' with Robert Whitman, Fluxus events with poets and composers and performance pieces with Robert Rauschenberg.

At the Merce Cunningham Studio, Brown was introduced to chance organization of movement and stage space. The aesthetic philosophy of the composer John Cage also became a source of ideas through his performed lectures and through Robert Dunn's Cage-sponsored composition course. Dunn emphasized conceptual strategies for composing dances, influenced by chance scores, Bauhaus approaches to materials and structure, Eastern philosophy and existentialism. Brown presented her earliest works with Judson Church Dance Theater, the home of a revolutionary movement in dance composition that evolved from Dunn's classes. *Trillium* (1962), *Lightfall* (1963) and *Rulegame 5* (1964) were highly physical responses to improvisational scores. In *Trillium* she took simple instructions to sit, stand or lie down to illogical conclusions and ended up 'lying' flat out in the air, suspended.

During the late 1960s, Brown initiated a series of autobiographical pieces exploring self-transformation and gesture: *Homemade* (1965), *Inside* (1966), *Skunk Cabbage, Salt Grass and Waders* (1967), *Ballet* (1968) and *Dance with a Duck's Head* (1968). Full of physical and emotional risk, these were personally created rituals in which Brown posed the self as a dilemma, making identity vulnerable to disassembly. More performance-art pieces than dances, their predecessors were 'happenings'. Brown conflated private and public spaces by using a barely converted industrial loft as both home and studio, putting domestic gestures into her dances like found objects. She overlaid personal history with live improvisation, exorcizing, for example, the violence of hunting experiences as a teenager with her father. She pursued sudden disorientations in off-balance moves, hurling herself, plummeting and rebounding. With filmic projections she took metaphoric flight from the constraints of femininity, using props like tutus and tightropes to fulfil fantastical images.

From 1968 to 1975 Brown created a series of suspension works, constructing specialized surfaces and devising equipment that enabled dancers to traverse them. In *Planes* (1968), *Man Walking Down the Side of a Building* (1970), *The Floor of the Forest* (1970), *Leaning Duets* (1970), *Walking on the Wall* (1971), *Roof Piece* (1971) and *Spiral* (1974), she suspended dancers in unusual relationships to gravity. She celebrated downtown Manhattan's architecture, its raw interior lofts and expansive outside spaces. She estranged pedestrian activities by shifting around the ways that floors, walls or ceilings frame them: three women navigated a huge peg-board wall, using holes as hand and footholds; a man keeled forwards atop a seven-storey building and ambulated downwards perpendicular to it; performers climbed in and out of clothing strung horizontally across a huge pipe grid rigged at eye level in an empty room. Dancers walked on the walls of the Whitney Museum, viewed by spectators as if from a tall building looking down, or they cantilevered out from pillars in a loft space, spiralling their way around horizontally until they reached the ground. Elevated above the city, performers stationed on rooftops relayed gestures across a mile-long span of skyline.

Overlapping these works, from 1971 to 1975, Brown invented eight dances in a new 'accumulation' genre, including *Accumulation* (1971), *Group Primary Accumulation* (1973), *Accumulation with Talking* (1973) and *Group Primary Accumulation: Raft Version* (1974). She pared movement down to sparse gestures played out serially, following mathematical dictates. Standing or prone, in solo or unison group forms, in museums, parks or floating on rafts on a lagoon, in silence or while talking, she and her dancers articulated one move, then another, then returned to the first, moved on to the second, added a third, and so on until they had accumulated a list of basic flexions and rotations of the joints, negating any rationale for moving other than being attentively present.

Structured Pieces (1973–76) – including *Sticks, Discs, Mistitled (5 Clacker), Spanish Dance, Solo Olos* and *Figure 8* – and *Pamplona Stones* (1974) were composed of activities with objects and were formal considerations of geometric line or metric time. Presented in lofts, galleries and museums, these works reflected a sensitivity to architecture and space similar to sculptural installations in the visual arts. Dancers performed tongue-in-cheek tricks with long white poles, 'sat' in chairs turned on their sides or ran as cardboard discs were thrown under their feet. The objects as non-human partners gave the pieces a material, external quality and facilitated communication about balance, weight state or line. There was both risk and absurdity in these tasks, and the possibility of success or error was approached in a matter-of-fact way.

Indoors or outdoors, spectators of the *Accumulations* or *Structured Pieces* moved from site to site to encounter the dancer-objects, who became part of architectural features or the ambient motion of the surroundings (e.g. that of bicyclists, pedestrians, rainstorms) evoking a palpable connection between person and place. In *Locus* (1975), Brown created a virtual room for the human body: an imaginary cube, its faces subdivided into 26 points that corresponded to letters of the alphabet. Gesturing to each point with mechanical motions of the joints such as hinging, rotating or leaning, Brown intended no emotional or narrative content. As anatomical structure fulfilled line and volume, the body became an insistently formal entity, the skeletal system articulating angles of 45, 90 and 180 degrees. The dance, freed from connotation, became animated by a structural language of grids, angles and semaphore-like moves.

Although in the early 1970s Brown was interested in the sheer presence of the performer in the moment of performing, from 1976 to 1983 she memorized spontaneous moments. *Locus* gave her tools to graph complex movement three dimensionally. In *Line Up* (1976), she asked dancers to remember improvised phrases on the basis of permutations of lines. In her 1978 breakthrough solo, *Watermotor*, Brown tapped memory by choreographing moments from her personal history, placing them amidst fluid, multidirectional moves. In *Accumulation with Talking Plus Watermotor* (1979), she developed this approach by splicing gestures from *Watermotor* into a standing *Accumulation*, and layering this with extemporaneous speaking. She cut between two stories and two dances at once, pushing order-making capacity to the limit, overcoming possible disintegration or memory loss.

Brown set improvised forms with her company in the proscenium works *Glacial Decoy* (1979), *Opal Loop* (1980), *Son of Gone Fishin'* (1981) and *Set and Reset* (1983). These pieces range from the interior and the cryptic to the outgoing and geometrical. In high-flying ensemble moves from improvisation and recall, responding to instructions like 'act on instinct', dancers met, interlocked for an instant and passed on, guided by intricate cueing systems. Timing was malleable, gauged to the effects of gravity on the off-kilter moving body. The space between bodies was charged with comings and goings, near or actual collisions and split-second unisons. Anatomical functions became choreographic principles as the group extended, folded or rotated. Any part of the body was free to combine with any other in an overall democratic vision of the relation between limbs and torso, center stage and periphery and individual and group.

From *Trillium* to *Set and Reset*, Brown honed the fit between formal structure, or the dance score, and raw material, or the movement. Engaging the score kinaesthetically, dancers physically manifested its idea. Linked to mathematical and geometric progression in minimal art, Brown's structures have subverted subjective compositional choice, so central to expressionist modern dance. Hewn from principles greater than the choreographer's personal imagination, Brown uses what she calls 'dance machines' – objective mechanisms that collaborate with the choreographer to determine the where, when and how of the dance.

Over time, *Set and Reset* has become a landmark of contemporary repertory, part of the formal curriculum for state arts education in France and regularly studied and restaged by university students in Britain and the United States.

In *Accumulation* and *Locus*, Brown built structures in front of the audience, so that the excitement of discerning them became a pleasure of viewing. In later multi-layered works, the formal structure became a nearly invisible under-girding, subliminally suggesting priority of thought as a foil to the instinctive dancing. The 'machine' in *Primary Accumulation* was mathematical serial progression; in *Man Walking Down the Side of a Building* spatial progression from top to bottom; in *Locus* numerical–linguistic–spatial coordination of gestures; in *Line-up* the forming and dissolution of lines and in *Set and Reset* a rectangular progression that traced the stage edges.

Each of Brown's formal structures elicited from the dancers an integral clarity in terms of anatomical and spatial intention. Feeding into this developing physical knowledge were Brown's studies, from the early 1970s onwards, of alternative approaches to dance training – Kinetic Awareness with Elaine Summers, the Alexander Technique and, since 1985, Susan Klein Technique. Brown relearned how to articulate each body part separately or in coordination, expanding range and diversity of motion. Her signature sequential style evolved from fluid joints, responsive without obstruction. Release techniques encourage ergonomic efficiency and Brown began to divest her designs of ornament, using limbs as levers or shifting weight like a hydraulic press. Physical dynamism found an analogy in technological power. Her 'dance machine' works intertwined America's dual love of technology and wilderness, the raw material of unrestricted movement civilized by the mechanized score.

By 1985, as the kinaesthetic sources of her dancing became integrated with her formal concerns, Brown no longer used 'dance machines' as organizing principles and, instead, focused more on movement ideas that evolved from the physical state of the body. In *Lateral Pass* (1985), *Newark* (1987) and *Astral Convertible* (1989), dancers loped by with large-bodied, muscled momentum, shifting from floor-bound to upright, airborne positions. Rather than use partnering for presentational display, they assisted one another to realize movement more fully. The entire group became a mechanism to heave individuals airborne, so that partnering became a sort of acrobatic cantilevering as bodies hurled, thrust, swung and rebounded, building and dispersing architectural forms, constantly changing plane, direction and dimension.

A high degree of virtuosity gives these works a striking theatricality. Contributing to this, beginning in 1979, Brown collaborated with composers and visual artists on large-scale productions for the proscenium theatre. She commissioned musical stores by Robert Ashley, Laurie Anderson, Peter Zummo, Richard Landry, John Cage and Alvin Curran. Visual presentations by Robert Rauschenberg, Fujiko Nakaja, Donald Judd, Nancy Graves, Elizabeth Murray, Kenjiro Okazaki and Roland Aeschlimann established environments inside the theatre, obscuring dancers in fog or dissecting space into quadrants with richly coloured drops that spanned the proscenium horizon. Neon-coloured sculptures flew in and out as dancers careened around them. Larger than life-size photographs travelled silently across the back wall, or car-light-studded towers blinked like an airport terminal at night. Enmeshing gesture and visual effect in *It's a Draw* (2002), Brown performed a 20-minute solo while drawing on a 8½′ × 10′ surface that dominated the stage.

Brown designed many of her formal structures to challenge the traditional relationship of dance to the theatrical frame and she carried her sensitivity to environmental space into the proscenium theatre. She composed movement explicitly for the stage edge, so that entrances and exits, visible through sheer wings, questioned conventional boundaries of vision. For example, she arranged a quartet to slide in and out of view, laterally: as one dancer slipped offstage, another replaced her way across on the other side, creating an illusion that the one just out of view continued on invisibly, the proscenium unable to frame or contain her.

In 1990, following her large-scale geometric works, Brown turned to softer chamber forms that explored processes of perception, whether in the performer's or the spectator's mind. In *Foray Forêt* (1990), *For MG: The Movie* (1991) and *Another Story as in Falling* (1993), she began to build character out of abstract form. In 1986, Brown's choreography for Lina Wertmuller's opera production of *Carmen* had pressed abstraction into confrontation with high drama and character; in *For MG*, with an object-like performing presence that still carried Judson influences, dancers fulfilled purely physical acts that suggested isolated moments of a story. Mythic, archetypal figures emerged: a woman running, a man standing still. When they did so long enough their exertions became metaphorical acts of endurance.

The operatic, seemingly at odds with Brown's protean language, has increasingly engaged her interest. Directing her first full-scale opera, Monteverdi's *L'Orfeo* at the Théâtre de la Monnaie in Brussels (1998, with the dance elements presented as *Canto/Pianto* in the previous year), she made a commitment to buoy the singers with gestural energy so that, as critic Melanie Eskenazi remarked, when Orfeo is confronted with his loss 'you are made to see the grief falling through every part of him'. Her near hallucinatory, bare-bones staging of Schubert's *Winterreise* (2002) matched three company dancers with baritone Simon Keenlyside, alternating landscapes of human vulnerability and the relentless facts of nature. *L'Amour au théâtre* (2009) is an elegant abstract rendering of portions from Jean-Philippe Rameau's Baroque opera, *Hippolyte et Aricie*, and in Summer 2010, it was paired with her direction of Rameau's one-act opera, *Pigmalion*.

Having collaborated with some of the most important abstract visual artists of her day, Brown has been recognized as an accomplished printmaker and visual artist. In 2008, the Walker Art Center in Minneapolis presented 'So That the Audience Does Not Know Whether I Have Stopped Dancing' as part of 'The Year of Trisha', exhibiting her drawings of the previous three decades and incorporating Brown 'performing' a new drawing especially for inclusion in the show. Brown's first solo gallery exhibition, in 2009, showed drawings distinguished by a sense of mark making, implied gesture and an exploration of shifting patterns in sequence.

Brown has also stayed on the cutting edge of digital art. In *How Long Does the Subject Linger on the Edge of the Volume . . .* (2005), a collaboration with computer scientists Marc Downie, Paul Kaiser and Shelley Eshkar, the patterns made by dancers wearing reflective markers were captured by 18 infrared cameras and fed into artificial intelligence software that generated spontaneous scenic effects, which echoed the transience of shifting relationships.

In these works, movements, placed like objects in time and space, suddenly become loaded with story or metaphor, but feeling dissolves back into geometrics. The dancers stand for nothing other than what they are, yet in their play with front, back, nearness or distance, emotional meanings emerge as unexpected insights. The works are studded with empty spaces that evoke contemplation. Sometimes in the breaks between moves, the body gestures reflexively, turbulently, inscrutably or incoherently or abruptly enters into prolonged stillness. Movement ideas become so clear that the thinker disappears and only the articulation of form in visible.

Marianne Goldberg
(updated by Debra Cash)

Biographical details

Born Patricia Brown in Aberdeen, Washington, United States, 25 November 1936. **Studied** at Mills College in Oakland, California, obtaining a BA degree in dance, 1958; studied with Anna Halprin in Marin County, California, 1959, with José Limón, Merce Cunningham and Louis Horst at Connecticut College, summers 1955, 1959 and 1960 and with Robert Dunn, New York, 1960. **Career:** Taught dance at Reed College, Portland, Oregon, 1958–59; moved to New York, after having met Yvonne Rainer and Simone Forti, 1960; becoming one of the founder members of Judson Dance Theater, 1968 and Grand Union, 1970–76; founded Trisha Brown Company, 1970, remaining choreographer and director ever since. Served on US National Council on the Arts 1994–97; has also developed career as visual artist, with first solo exhibition in 2009. **Awards and honours** include Fellowships in Choreography from Guggenheim Foundation, 1975, 1984 and National Endowment for the Arts, 1977, 1981, 1982, 1983, 1984; Creative Arts Medal in Dance from Brandeis University, 1982; Honorary Doctorate in Fine Arts from Oberlin College, 1983; New York Dance and Performance Award ('Bessie'), 1984, 1986; *Dance Magazine* Award, 1987; Laurence Olivier Award, 1987; Chevalier dans l'Ordre des Arts et des Lettres (France), 1988 – elevated to Officier in 2000 and to Commandeur in 2004; MacArthur Foundation Fellowship Award, 1991; Samuel H. Scripps American Dance Festival Award, 1994; New York State Governor's Arts Award, 1999; Doris Duke Award, 2000; National Medal of Arts, 2003; Benois de la Danse Prize for Lifetime Achievement, 2005; Nijinsky Award, 2006; Mills College Distinguished Achievement Award, 2008.

Works

Trillium (1962); *Lightfall* (1963); *2 Improvisations on the Nuclei for Simone by Jackson Maclow* (1963); *Improvisation on a Chicken Coop Roof* (1963); *Falling Solo with Singing* (1963); *Chanteuse Eccentrique Américaine* (1963); *Rulegame 5* (1964), *Target* (1964); *Motor* (1965); *Homemade* (1965); *A String* (consisting of *Motor, Homemade, and Inside,* 1966); *Skunk Cabbage, Salt Grass and Waders* (1967); *Medicine Dance* (1967); *Planes* (1968); *Snapshots* (1968); *Falling Duet* (1968); *Ballet* (1968); *Dance with a Duck's Head* (1968); *Yellow Belly* (1969); *Skymap* (1969); *Man Walking Down the Side of a Building* (1970); *Clothes Pipe, The Floor of the Forest, and Other Miracles, etc.* (1970); *Leaning Duets* (1970); *The Stream* (1970); *Walking on the Wall* (1971); *Leaning Duets II* (1971); *Falling Duet II* (1971); *Accumulation* (1971); *Rummage Sale and the Floor of the Forest* (1971); *Roof Piece* (1971); *Accumulation 55'* (1972); *Primary Accumulation* (1972); *Theme and Variations* (1972); *Woman Walking Down a Ladder* (1973); *Accumulating Pieces* (1973); *Accumulation with Talking* (1973); *Group Accumulation I* (1973); *Group Primary Accumulation* (1973); *Structured Pieces I* (1973); *Sticks* (1973); *Spanish Dance* (1973); *Group Primary Accumulation: Raft Version* (1974); *Figure 8* (1974); *Split Solo* (1974); *Drift* (1974); *Spiral* (1974); *Pamplona Stones* (1974); *Structured Pieces II* (1974); *Locus* (1975); *Pyramid* (1975); *Structured Pieces III* (1975); *Solo Olos* (1976); *Duetude* (1976); *Line Up* (1976); *Structured Pieces IV* (1976); *Watermotor* (solo; 1978); *Splang* (1978); *Accumulation with Talking Plus Watermotor* (versions of the three earlier pieces, 1979); *Glacial Decoy* (1979); *Opal Loop* (1980); *Son of Gone Fishin'* (1981); *Set and Reset* (includes *Decoy* and *Opal Loop,* 1983); *Lateral Pass* (1985); *Carmen* (opera by Bizet, 1986); *Newark* (1987); *Astral Convertible* (1989); *Foray Forêt* (1990);

Astral Converted (SO") (1991); *For MG: The Movie* (1991); *One Story as in Falling* (1992); *Another Story as in Falling* (1993); *Yet Another Story as in Falling* (1994); *If You Couldn't See Me* (solo, 1994; duet version with Mikhail Baryshnikov, *You Can See Us*, 1995); *Long and Dream* (with Steve Paxton, 1994); *M.O.* (1995); *Twelve Ton Rose* (1996); *Accumulation with Talking Plus Repertory* (1997); *For Merce* (1997); *Orfeo* (opera by Claudio Monteverdi, 1998); *Canto/Pianto* (1997*); *Five Part Weather Invention* (1999); *Groove and Countermove* (2000); *Rapture to Leon James* (2000); *El Trilogy* (2000); *Luci mie traditrici* (opera by Salvatore Sciarrino, 2001); *Geometry of Quiet* (2002); *It's a Draw* (2002); *Winterreise* (song cycle by Franz Schubert, 2002); *Present Tense* (2003); *O Ziozony/O Composite* (2004); *How Long Does the Subject Linger on the Edge of the Volume . . .* (2005); *Da gelo a gelo* (chamber opera by Salvatore Sciarrino, 2006); *Floor of the Forest* (2007); *I Love My Robots* (2007); *L'Amour au théâtre* (2009).

*Tricia Brown Company website cites *Canto/Pianto* as 2008. This work premiered in 1997, at the American Dance Festival, Duke University. See Jack Anderson, 'The Tension and Serenity, Not the Plot, of 'L'Orfeo'', *New York Times*, 27 June 1997, p. 111.

Further reading

Interviews with Sally Sommer, in 'Trisha Brown Making Dances', *Dance Scope*, Spring 1977; in 'Dialog on Dance', in *The Vision of Modern Dance*, Jean Morrison Brown (ed.), Princeton, NJ, 1979; in *Contemporary Dance*, Anne Livet (ed.), New York, 1978; with David Sears, in 'Forever New', *Dance News*, October 1981; with Marianne Goldberg, in 'Trisha Brown', *Drama Review*, Spring 1986; with Christy Adair, in 'Trisha Brown Dance Company at Sadler's Wells', *New Dance*, January 1988; with Marianne Goldberg, in 'Trisha Brown's Accumulations', *Dance Theatre Journal*, Autumn 1991; with Yvonne Rainer, in 'Trisha Brown', *Bomb Magazine*, October 1993; with Carol Pratl, in 'Trisha Brown', *Dance Europe*, June/July 1997; with Mike Dixon, in 'The Language of Structure', *Dance Theatre Journal*, 18(4), 2002.

Articles: Sally Sommer, 'Equipment Dances: Trisha Brown', *Drama Review*, September 1972; Sally Sommer, 'Trisha Brown Making Dances', *Dance Scope*, Spring/Summer 1977; Sally Banes, 'Gravity and Levity: Up and Down with Trisha Brown', *Dance Magazine*, March 1978; Mona Sulzman, 'Choice/Form in Trisha Brown's Locus: A View from Inside the Cube', *Dance Chronicle*, 2(2), 1978; David Sears, 'A Trisha Brown/Robert Rauschenberg Collage', *Ballet Review*, Fall 1982; Camille Hardy, 'Trisha Brown: Pushing Postmodern Art into Orbit', *Dance Magazine*, March 1985; Michael Huxley, 'Lines of Least Resistance: Trisha Brown Company', *New Dance*, Spring 1986; Allen Robertson, 'Gravity's Rainbow', *Ballet News*, September 1985; Marianne Goldberg, 'Trisha Brown: All of the Person's Person Arriving', *Drama Review*, Spring 1986; K. Kertsee, 'Dancing with Carmen', *Art in America*, April 1987; Deborah Jowitt, 'Trisha and France: A Love Story', *Dance Magazine*, September 1990; Elizabeth Kendall, 'Trisha Brown Comes Down to Earth', *Dance Ink*, April 1991; Sally Sommer, 'The Sound of Movement', *Dance Ink*, Spring 1993; Roslyn Sulcas, 'Trisha Brown: Choreography That Spans Continents and Oceans', *Dance Magazine*, April 1995; Trisha Brown and Bill T. Jones, 'Body Politics, Postmodernism and Political Correctness', in *Ballett International*, August 1995; Rita Felciano, 'Trisha Brown', *Dance Now*, Spring 1996; Wendy Perron,

'Trisha Brown on Tour', *Dancing Times*, May 1996; Jack Anderson, 'Trisha Brown', *Dancing Times*, March 2003; Marcia B. Siegel 'Making Chaos Visible,' *Hudson Review*, Spring 2003; Danielle Goldman, 'Steve Paxton and Trisha Brown: Falling in the Dynamite', *Dance Research*, Summer 2004; Lisa Kraus, 'Flying in a New Galaxy', *Dance Magazine*, April 2005; Ramsay Burt, 'Against Expectations: Trisha Brown and the Avant-garde', *Dance Research Journal*, Summer 2005; Claudia la Rocco, 'Toughest Moves in Dance: The Last Ones', *The New York Times*, 3 February 2008; Deborah Jowitt, 'Trisha Brown Rounds up Four Decades of Choreography', *The Village Voice*, 6 May 2009; Joan Acocella, 'Think Pieces: Return of the Judsonites', *The New Yorker*, 24 May 2010.

Books: Don McDonagh, *The Complete Guide to Modern Dance*, New York, 1976; Anne Livet (ed.), *Contemporary Dance*, New York, 1978; Peter Wynne (ed.), *Judson Dance: An Annotated Bibliography of the Judson Dance Theater and of Five Major Choreographers*, Englewood Cliffs, NJ, 1978; Sally Banes, *Terpsichore in Sneakers: Post-modern Dance*, Boston, 1980; Sally Banes, *Democracy's Body: Judson Dance Theater, 1962–1964*, Ann Arbor, Michigan, 1983 (reprinted, Durham, North Carolina, 1993); Deborah Jowitt, *The Dance in Mind*, Boston, 1985; Lise Brunel, *Trisha Brown* (in French and English), Paris, 1987; 'Trisha Brown: An Informal Performance,' in *Breakthroughs: Avant-garde Artists in Europe and America, 1950–1990*, New York, 1991; Hendel Teicher, *Trisha Brown: Dance and Art in Dialogue, 1961–2001*, Cambridge, MA, 2002; Michael Huxley and Noel Witts (eds), *The Twentieth Century Performance Reader*, 2nd edition, London, 2002; Sally Banes and Andrea Harris (eds), *Reinventing Dance in the 1960s*, Madison, 2003; Joyce Morgenroth (ed.), *Speaking of Dance: Twelve Contemporary Choreographers on their Craft*, New York, 2004; André Lepecki, *Exhausting Dance: Performance and the Politics of Movement*, London, 2005; Ramsay Burt, *Judson Dance Theater: Performative Traces*, London, 2006; Peter Eleey (ed.), *Trisha Brown: So That The Audience Does Not Know Whether I Have Stopped Dancing*, Minneapolis, 2008.

CHRISTOPHER BRUCE

Christopher Bruce maintains that his ballets are not essentially about movement but about ideas. They may not have an obvious storyline and may be episodic in structure, but they generally include dramatic or emotive elements that make an immediate impact on the audience. Although the works portray recognizable experiences, they are also open to a variety of interpretations, and Bruce prefers his audience to watch them unencumbered by pre-conceived notions. For this reason he usually avoids programme notes, and many of the titles of his works (such as *Land* (1985), *Waiting* (1993), *Crossing* (1994) and *Meeting Point* (1995)) leave their subject without narrative boundaries. Although the ideas are central to the productions, Bruce's concern is to create a dance, not a statement.

CHRISTOPHER BRUCE

Bruce was encouraged to dance by his father, and his training from the age of 11 was in ballet, tap and acrobatics. After two years he was accepted into the Rambert School. The 1960s were Bruce's formative years. Working with Walter Gore's London Ballet and Ballet Rambert, while that company still focused on classical ballet, exposed him to narrative works and to the use of *demi-caractère* dancing, as well as to the understated yet universal drama of Antony Tudor. He learned to appreciate the importance of theatrical presentation and recognized the high standards Marie Rambert instilled into all her choreographers. The 1960s were a period of change in British dance, and after Ballet Rambert's 1966 reconstitution, which turned the company once again into a more creative ensemble, Graham technique, as transplanted into Britain, became part of his experience.

At this time Bruce attracted attention as a dancer for his superb interpretation of the title role in Glen Tetley's *Pierrot Lunaire*. For two decades he was recognized as 'one of the most potent and sharply focused dancers in Britain', and he was compared with the great French dancer Jean Babilée, with whom he shared a remarkable stage presence and the ability to act through dance. Appearing in a wide repertory of ballets, from the title roles in Nijinsky's *L'Après-midi d'un faune* in 1967 and Fokine's *Petrouchka* in 1988, to created roles such as Prospero in Tetley's *The Tempest* (1979), provided Bruce with a rich background for his own choreography. In his own productions the creation of the central role of the Poet in *Cruel Garden* (1977), happily recorded for posterity, remains a particularly potent memory.

Tetley's impact on Rambert was considerable, particularly given his ability to marry classical and contemporary choreography. Like Bruce, Tetley's background included working with classical, contemporary and popular dance forms. Tetley encouraged Bruce in his first choreographic experiments, and Bruce's starting point for his third creation, *Wings* (1970), was movement developed from a section of Tetley's *Ziggurat*. Bruce was also encouraged by Rambert's associate director, Norman Morrice. (Morrice had enabled him to create his first dance role in *Realms of Choice* and then gave him opportunities to choreograph.) Morrice's own ballets at this period moved away from specific dramas to more universal themes, and he invited a variety of American contemporary choreographers to work with Rambert. Among them was Anna Sokolow, whose works ranged from pop ballets (*Opus 65*) to socially aware dramas (*Deserts*).

If the work of these choreographers provided the context for Bruce's own choreography, it must be stressed that he did not imitate them but found encouragement from their creative range. Bruce's first ballet, *George Frideric* (1969), to music by Handel, reflected a trend for setting light, lyric dance to baroque music (as seen in Paul Taylor's *Aureole*). It was a competent first work and did not reveal to the audience the agony of its slow creation. It remains one of Bruce's few dances that simply reflect its music. Indeed, with many of his early works Bruce tried to avoid expressing, or responding to, music, claiming in an interview that he did not want his dances to be reliant on another art form. For some productions, including *Duets* (1973), *Weekend* (1974) and *There Was a Time* (1973, inspired by the Trojan Wars), the electronic scores were added after the choreography was more or less complete. From the mid-1970s Bruce began to feel more confident in choosing scores, responding particularly to the compositions of George Crumb and also commissioning material from Philip Chambon, whom he met in 1984, for *Swansong* (1987), *Nature Dances* (1992) and *Stream* (1996). With some scores, such as the folk songs used for *Ghost Dances* (1981), Janácek's *Intimate Pages* quartet (1984) and Stravinsky's *Symphony in Three Movements* (1989), Bruce waited a number of years to find the right opportunity to create dances. Since the 1980s, he has responded to pop songs (mostly from the 1960s) by Billie Holliday, Joan Baez, Bob Dylan, John Lennon, The Rolling Stones and Jimi Hendrix.

Bruce's second work, *Living Space* (1969), was more dramatic. Danced to poems by Robert Cockburn, Bruce's choreography sometimes took its literal cue from the spoken words; and this trend continues to be seen in his productions to song cycles, such as *Sergeant Early's Dream* (1984) and *Rooster* (1991), which use select phrases mimetically. Bruce has also been stimulated in his work by literature – fact and fiction, poetry, prose and journalism. He never puts an epic work on stage, preferring to select themes that can be successfully conveyed in dance. *Swansong* was, in part, inspired by a description of a political prisoner's torture in Oriana Fallaci's novel *A Man*. Although *Sergeant Early's Dream* was primarily an excuse for some lively dances to Irish and American folk songs, it also drew on John Prebble's description of Highland clearance and migration in the nineteenth century. *Dancing Day* (1981), *Cantata* (1981) and *Ceremonies* (1986) derived from a fascination with the mixing of the sacred and secular in medieval and Renaissance society, as conveyed in the life of alchemist Dr John Dee and in such novels as Umberto Eco's *The Name of the Rose*.

Although Bruce has achieved some of the most striking translations of literature into dance, knowledge of a source work is never essential for the appreciation of the choreography. This is as true of the use of the poems of Federico García Lorca as it is of the use of sections of novels. A work such as his stunning *Cruel Garden* draws on Lorca's musical compositions and sketches as well as his poems, plays and film scripts, to create from his life and experience a multi-layered collage. It was a collaborative creation with Lindsay Kemp, who shared Bruce's fascination with Lorca. Undoubtedly, some of the richness of the ideas came from Kemp, who claimed, 'I think of myself as Cocteau to Christopher's Massine' – but the humanity of the work, with its expression of Lorca's concern for oppressed minorities, derives from Bruce's personal convictions. The subject matter of Bruce's work has attracted attention because it reflects his sensitive awareness of the larger social, political and ecological issues of our time. Bruce has said, 'I don't do my ballets to get social messages across; these things just come naturally out of me'. Nevertheless, on occasions the choice of subject matter is intentional. *Ghost Dances*, which draws on pre-Hispanic death culture, is dedicated to 'the innocent people of South America who . . . have been continuously devastated by political oppression'. *Waiting*, set to music celebrating Nelson Mandela's release from prison, was based on images of life in a South African township. *Berlin Requiem* (1982), developing themes from Kurt Weill music and Bertolt Brecht's words, portrayed the decadence and fall of the Weimar Republic. *Berlin Requiem* was choreographed to a planned scenario, but the shape of many of Bruce's ballets emerges when working with his dancers in the studio.

Observations on the brutality and futility of war have recurred in such works as *Land* and *for these who die as cattle* (1972) (created under the working title of *The Warriors* until Bruce read Wilfred Owen's war poem, which conveyed precisely the situation he had already choreographed). Taking their cue from the title of Arne Nordheim's music, *Warsaw*, critics initially discussed *Land* as referring back to the rape of Poland, but later revivals have made them aware of its more immediate relevance to contemporary situations in, for example, Bosnia. In both *Cattle* and *Land*, as well as other less harrowing but nevertheless intense works such as *Intimate Pages*, the women – or one central strong woman – provide the work's emotional focus.

Bruce's knowledge of the international dance repertory also colours his work. *Meeting Point*, created for the UNited We Dance Festival (to mark the fiftieth anniversary of the signing of the United Nations

Charter) deliberately evoked the opening and closing sections of Kurt Jooss's *The Green Table*; and *Land*, with its sense of loss, has choreographic resonances of Tudor's *Dark Elegies*.

Bruce's creative stimulus is, on occasion, strongly autobiographical. *Weekend* reflected the stress of touring on his family, *Swansong* the struggle to come to terms with the end of his performing career. His love of children was seen clearly in *Ancient Voices of Children* (1975), *Preludes and Songs* (1980), *Four Scenes* (1998) and *Hush* (2006), created when his own children and grandchildren were growing up. In other works the autobiographical element is retrospective. Discussing *The Dream is Over* (1986) in the television programme on John Lennon in which it was first shown, he said, 'I thought it would be nice to do something about my contemporaries, and the times we went through, and Lennon's lyrics seemed to speak for us and what we felt about life.'

Settings for Bruce's productions are uncluttered but apt, allowing space for movement. Initially, he regularly turned to Nadine Baylis and John B. Read, whose combined talents gave the reformed Rambert its visual signature. For more elaborate productions he has worked with Pamela Marre and Ralph Koltai. Marre provided the neon-lit bar that disappeared to become a barren landscape for *Berlin Requiem* and Koltai the blood-spattered bull ring of *Cruel Garden* (originally presented at The Roundhouse in London). Walter Nobbe, responsible for painterly and evocative landscapes enhanced by lighting, was a regular collaborator and for the past two decades Bruce has worked effectively with his wife, the artist Marian Bruce. He has also designed some of his own productions, contributing the costumes for *Swansong* and the Andean landscape for *Ghost Dances* (Belinda Scarlett designed the half-tattered costumes symbolizing the characters' transition from life to death).

As a creator of dances Bruce cannot be pigeonholed. His choreography combines elements of the varied styles he has worked with, usually based on classical and contemporary dance. His range is further extended by incorporating popular and folk dance. He finds this useful, as popular and folk dance, like pop songs and folk music, give his work both universality and a sense of particular community. His dancers thus appear as real people with recognizable emotions. His own 'esperanto folk dance', incorporating circles and lines, often with arms linked as in a Greek syrtaki dance or 'Zorba chain', has become a signature motif. The folk element has been present from his first work: *George Frideric* included heel-toe steps. The feet are often parallel, without concern for turnout, and Bruce's works often feature small, quick steps which contrast with bold circular gestures – full-skirted swirls and scooping movements, twisting the torso. Bruce exploits a low centre of gravity seen in lunges and deep *pliés* characteristic of contemporary dance.

Bruce has choreographed more than 70 productions, not only ballets but also musicals, plays, operas and works for television. Much of his working life has been based at Rambert – as student, dancer and choreographer – although for a decade from the mid-1980s he worked as a freelance choreographer. Even then, he held long-term contracts, first with English National Ballet and then with the Houston Ballet. Since resigning from directing Rambert in 2002, Bruce has adopted a slower pace of creation, although he stages his popular successes internationally, thus getting to know new dancers. Bruce has always preferred to create works on groups of dancers he is familiar with, supervising new productions of his own works and new casts in revivals. In this way he has regularly returned to specific companies, most notably Nederlands Dans Theater, Cullberg Ballet in Sweden, the now defunct Gulbenkian Ballet of Lisbon, Ballet du Grand Théâtre Genève and Houston Ballet. As an artistic director of Rambert Dance Company, he benefited from having worked internationally and having built up relationships with a range of like-minded choreographers whom he invited to work with his dancers. He was also able to draw on his experience of seeing his own ballets programmed in different situations. As a director, just as when he choreographs, his concern was to make lively contact with his audience. Productions may have a serious message or be comic, but Bruce never loses his awareness of the fact that he is working in the theatre.

Jane Pritchard

Biographical details

Born in Leicester, England, 3 October 1945. **Studied** at Benson Stage Academy, Scarborough and Ballet Rambert School, London. **Career**: Performed with Walter Gore's London Ballet, 1963; joined Ballet Rambert in 1963, becoming leading dancer in modern roles, from 1966; choreographer for Ballet Rambert (becoming Rambert Dance Company in 1987), from 1969, becoming associate choreographer, 1975–87, and associate director, 1975–79; associate choreographer for London Festival Ballet (becoming English National Ballet in 1989), 1986–91; resident choreographer, becoming associate choreographer, Houston Ballet, from 1989; artistic director, Rambert Dance Company, 1994–2002. Has also staged works for Royal Ballet, Scottish Ballet, Batsheva Dance Company, Munich Opera Ballet, Gulbenkian Ballet Company, Australian Dance Theatre, Royal Danish Ballet, Royal Swedish Ballet, Tanz-Forum (Cologne), Nederlands Dans Theater, Geneva Ballet, Cincinnati Ballet, Dutch National Ballet, San Francisco Ballet, Zurich Ballet, Basle Ballet, Ballett Krefeld-Mönchengladbach, Ballett Mainz, Deutsche Ballett

Berlin, Dusseldorf Ballet; has worked as choreographer/producer of operas, musicals, and television programmes. **Awards and honours** include *Evening Standard* Award, 1974 and 1997; Prix Italia, 1982; International Theatre Institute Award, 1993; CBE, 1998; De Valois Award for Outstanding Contribution to Dance at National Dance Awards, 2003; Rheinische Post Theater Oscar, at Theater Krefeld-Mönchengladbach 2004; Honorary Life Membership of Amnesty International, 2002.

Works

George Frideric (1969); *Living Space* (1969); *Wings* (1970); *for these who die as cattle* (1972); *Joseph and the Amazing Technicolour Dreamcoat* (musical, 1972); *There Was a Time* (1973); *Duets* (1973); *Weekend* (1974); *Unfamiliar Playground* (1974); *Jeeves* (musical, 1975); *Ancient Voices of Children* (1975); *Voices* (1976); *Black Angels* (1976); *Girl with Straw Hat* (1976); *Promenade* (1976); *Echoes of a Night Sky* (1976); *Cruel Garden* (with Lindsey Kemp, 1977); *Responses* (1977); *Labyrinth* (1979); *Night with Waning Moon* (1979); *Sidewalk* (1979); *Interactions* (1980); *Il ballo del ingrate* (opera, 1980); *Venus and Adonis* (1980); *Preludes and Songs* (1980); *Dancing Day* (1981); *Cantata* (1981); *Combattimento di Tancredi e Clorinda* (opera, 1981); *Ghost Dances* (1981); *Holiday Sketches* (1981); *Village Songs* (1981); *Agrippina* (opera, 1982); *Berlin Requiem* (1982); *In Alium* (1982); *Concertino* (1983); *Curses and Blessings* (with Jirí Kylián, 1983); *Silence is the End of Our Song* (1983); *Intimate Pages* (1984); *Sergeant Early's Dream* (1984); *Remembered Dances* (1985); *Mutiny* (musical, 1985); *Land* (1985); *Ceremonies* (1986); *The World Again* (1986); *The Dream is Over* (1986); *The Winter's Tale* (play, 1987); *Swansong* (1987); *The Changeling* (play, 1988); *Song* (1988); *Gautama Buddha* (1989); *Les Noces* (1989); *Symphony in Three Movements* (1989); *Journey* (1990); *Rooster* (1991); *Nature Dances* (1992); *Kingdom* (1993); *Moonshine* (1993); *Waiting* (1993); *Crossing* (1994); *Meeting Point* (1995); *Quicksilver* (1996); *Stream* (1996); *Four Scenes* (1998); *God's Plenty* (1999); *Hurricane* (2000); *Grinning in Your Face* (2001); *Cyrano de Bergerac* (play, 2004); *Three Songs, Two Voices* (2005); *A Steel Garden* (2005); *Hush* (2006); *Shift* (2007); *Dance at the Crossroads* (2007).

Further reading

Interviews in 'Curtain Up', *Dance and Dancers*, June 1986; with Ann Nugent, in 'Waiting with Certainty', *Dance Now*, Autumn 1993; with Sheron Wray, in 'Confronting the Boss', *Dance Theatre Journal*, 13(2), 1997; in Jo Butterworth and Gill Clarke (eds), *Dancemakers' Portfolio: Conversations with Choreographers*, Bretton Hall, 1998.

Articles: Charles Gow, 'Christopher Bruce', *Dancing Times*, March 1973; Noël Goodwin, 'Elegiac Images', *Dance and Dancers*, September 1975; David Dougill, 'Where Bruce Gets His Ideas From', *Classical Music*, 2 October 1976; Noël Goodwin, 'Shadows and Substances', *Dance and Dancers*, September 1981; Nadine Meisner, 'A Dream by the Ocean', *Dance and Dancers*, December 1984; Sophie Constanti, 'Ballet Rambert', *Dance Theatre Journal*, Summer 1985; Sophie Constanti, 'London Festival Ballet and Christopher Bruce', *Dancing Times*, July 1988; Kathrine Sorley Walker, 'Violence and Poetry', *Dance and Dancers*, August 1988;

Angela Kane, 'Christopher Bruce's Choreography: Inroads or Re-Tracing Old Steps?', *Dancing Times*, October 1991; Christopher Bruce, 'There's Always an Idea', *Dance and Dancers*, January 1993; Ann Nugent, 'Waiting with Certainty', *Dance Now*, Autumn 1993; Christopher Bruce, 'The Christopher Bruce Manifesto', *Dancing Times*, November 1994; Judith Mackrell, 'Mission – Impossible?', *Dance Now*, Autumn 1995; Kathrine Sorley Walker, 'Christopher Bruce and Rambert Dance Company', *Dancing Times*, July 1996; Josephine Leask, 'Diversity in Unity, *Ballett International*, 7, 1996; Josephine Leask, ' Love and War', *Dance Theatre Journal*, 15(3), 1999; Jan Murray, 'A Man of Many Passions', *Dance Australia*, June/July 1999; Mike Dixon, 'His Last Piece ever for 5 Busy Women?', *Ballettanz*, January 2002; Norman Morrice, 'A Tribute to Christopher Bruce', *Dancing Times*, February 2003.

Books: Richard Austin, *The Birth of a Ballet*, London, 1976; Clement Crisp, Anya Sainsbury and Peter Williams, *Ballet Rambert: 50 Years and On*, London, 1981; John Percival, *Modern Ballet*, London, 1981; Peter Brinson and Clement Crisp, *The Pan Book of Ballet and Dance*, London, 1981; Allen Robertson and Donald Hutera, *The Dance Handbook*, Harlow, Essex, 1988; Jane Pritchard, *Rambert: A Celebration*, London, 1996; Jane Pritchard, *Swansong Study Notes*, Rambert Dance Company, London, 1998; Ross McKim, *The Essential Inheritance of London Contemporary Dance Theatre*, London, 2001.

JONATHAN BURROWS

Jonathan Burrows, in his early career, developed a movement language with little emphasis given to theatrical components, its focus being directed instead towards the detail of movement itself. In more recent work, Burrows has explored the potential of working with untrained dancers, combining what Deborah Jowitt has referred to as 'everyday behavior and ingenious lunacy'. His works from the early days have been characterized by a range of movement material that is apparently very far from the classical ballet training of the choreographer and, therefore, also very different from the work of his contemporary at the Royal Ballet School, Michael Clark. Hallmarks include energy and attack, even – perhaps especially – in the context of small details, dramatic variations in rhythms and speed, and the use of stillness, as evident in, for example, *The Stop Quartet* (1996).

A fascination with detail – of movement, of different performers' ways of moving, of different means of communication – is a continuing theme in Burrows' work. This last, in particular, has continued to develop over the years, as Burrows has explored the range of possibilities offered by the individual qualities of his collaborators, both trained and untrained dancers. It is interesting that his fruitful collaboration with composer Matteo Fargion, for example, has led from dancer–musician collaborations to works involving them both as 'dancers', such as *Both Sitting Duet* (2002) and the works that followed, *The Quiet Dance* (2005) and the *Speaking Dance* (2006), making a triology of Burrow–Fargion investigations of the nature of dance and music and of the expressiveness of the 'ordinary' human body. His fascination with human movement itself has led Burrows to examine his own performative qualities, to question his relation to 'technique' and to relish working with other, untrained dancing bodies, all of which offer different insights into the work of choreography. Focus is one of his central concerns: the focus of one dancer on another, in particular, is key in many works, especially duets (*Singing*, 2003; *Weak Dance, Strong Questions*, 2001 and *Both Sitting Duet*), which show how the issue of communication between people – or lack of it – can be a powerful theme for dance.

Burrows' background is in classical ballet, and, at the Junior School of the Royal Ballet School, where he was trained, Morris Dancing was also taught. This latter form is one occasionally referred to by critics – especially in the early years of Burrows' career – and indeed by Burrows himself, as a possible influence on his style, although it is less apparent in more recent works. As a choreographer, he made some early works for Sadler's Wells Royal Ballet and the Royal Ballet Choreographic Group before striking out on his own; a few dancers to form the Jonathan Burrows Group. As a young dancer, he danced for a while with Rosemary Butcher, and has returned to dance with her again in between projects of his own; she has spoken of Burrows' inherent ability to attend to detail and precision – to work, as it were, in a small way. The influence of Butcher is evident occasionally in *The Stop Quartet*, with its relaxed quality of 'flung' gestures and low centre of gravity.

While making experimental work at the Riverside Studios, Hammersmith, early in his career, Burrows was exposed to various manifestations of New Dance, and he has since acknowledged the influence of Steve Paxton, among others. He has also expressed admiration for Bronislava Nijinska, specifically *Les Noces*; more recently Burrows has said, 'I don't think there is a single performance that I have made that hasn't quoted [*Les Noces*] directly in some way.'[1] Other acknowledged influences are David Gordon and Lucinda Childs. It is interesting to consider possible reflections of these practitioners' styles in Burrows' choreography: the pared-down, minimal approach of

Childs, for example, might find parallel in Burrows' abstraction of movement ideas or in the importance he gives to clear rhythmic manipulation, albeit in a very different way. In both, we see the potential of tiny detail to become germane to the development of a dance idea. David Gordon's quirky sense of humour and interest in the foibles of the individual human being find echoes in the strange, evocative, sometimes very witty gestures, poses and movements that are sprinkled throughout Burrows' work. The influences of Steve Paxton and contact improvisation – the partner work, taking weight, taking risks, trusting and having to trust people – are also apparent as contributing features. At the same time, however, it is also clear that Burrows possesses a distinctive choreographic 'voice': in his assimilation and transformation of such influences and ideas, he is able to manipulate those ideas in an original way for each different work.

The critic Judith Mackrell once described aspects of Burrows' style as emanating from the influences of folk dance, classicism and more weighted, 'post-modern' movement. Burrows himself, in speaking about the process of choreography, mentions the use of so-called 'images' in dance making, relating the process and effectiveness to homeopathy and thereby illustrating his commitment to a concept of abstraction:

> You start with a 100 per cent solution which would be say 100 per cent image . . . Then, as in homeopathy, you dilute it by one hundred times – the actual solution gets weaker but the potency gets stronger. So once the images were found, the idea was to dilute it by concentrating more and more on the physical sense of it and letting go more and more of the emotional sense of it. Thereby producing something which was less confrontational, less demanding and therefore more powerful.[2]

Various points that Burrows makes, and the ideas he seems to be dealing with, suggest the need for a different approach to each work, according to its demands, and point to his notion of refining and paring down images and movements so that the emotional impulse can be totally removed and the movement freed to speak for itself. What is interesting is Burrows' absorption in the materials of dance itself and his belief in dance's ability to be relevant to and expressive of the human condition without the trappings of theatre, lighting (although this aspect has sometimes been important in his work), costume, thematic development or 'issues'. Instead, he puts all those elements on one side to focus on what might be described as the unique distinguishing features of dance *per se*; and, importantly, dance in relation to music. It is clear that the idea outlined above in 1994 has been pursued consistently and through different means, including different approaches to collaboration, and the involvement of untrained dancers, but through all this, the notion of communication through movement. Burrows has said that he wishes to avoid imposing meaning or over-directing the audience. Too much information makes it 'difficult for [audiences] to see what they're seeing'.[3]

Burrows' classical background is evident in the versatility, strength and physical understanding of movement for its own sake that underpins so much of his earlier work, perhaps even when it is least 'classical' – as in *Very* (1992), for example, which is non-balletic and often pedestrian in appearance. Evident also is the tight structural clarity of Burrows' work, which could be seen as a 'classical' attribute in some sense.

Edward Thorpe, however, once wrote:

> Burrows's wide-ranging choreographic conceptions have nothing in them that is recognisably classical, except that the dancers' balletic training has given them the agility, suppleness, balance, control and stamina that his works demand. He uses many everyday, naturalistic movements, poses and gestures that are recognisable as common body-language, supercharged with a strange assortment of sudden stampings, falls, twists, flurries and angled limbs together with deliberately awkward lifts – humping sacks comes to mind – and moments of stasis, very often in a prone position, to create an elaborate dance structure that is continually fascinating to watch even without trying to impose narrative ideas upon it.[4]

Thorpe was writing in 1991, but it is interesting to compare Burrows' own more recent comments on the relationship of technique to choreography in his work. In interview with Lydia Polzer (2004), he reflects on his work with untrained dancers which, he said, 'refreshed my eye and ... freed me from my own over-concern with technique. That doesn't mean I'm against technique ... [b]ut I needed to come back at it from a different perspective.'[5] Again, in interview with Sarah Frater, Burrows revealed more about his attitude to the dancing body and its expressive potential when he remarked that:

[o]ne of the revolutions in contemporary dance is allowing different body types on stage, which is a huge relief to audiences. Instead of seeing a super-being, which reduces them to a lesser being, they see themselves. It's a quality that Matteo and I bring to our performances. An acceptance of failure. The more we fail, the funnier it gets.

(Burrows, in Frater, 2009)

In Burrows' work, it is possible to perceive invention and skill in the construction of original dance movements and phrases into a coherent dance work, one that has a dynamic excitement and imaginative delineation of movement and a richness that can sustain the interest without the need for the spectator to read specific or even hinted-at 'meanings'. This links in turn with Burrows' own comments on the homeopathic parallel and the idea that something may be most effective when most abstracted. See, for example, the use of stillness in *The Stop Quartet*, and Burrows' reference to 'holes' in the music through which the dance can be seen and *vice versa*,[6] and also the deliberately restricted perspective of the film work, for example, *blue yellow* (1995) made for Sylvie Guillem and the film version of *Very* (1993). The audience must create the imaginative space for the dance to exist within. But also, and more extremely, in his later work, Burrows has used untrained dancers alongside himself as performer, allowing the highlighted differences in movement style and articulation to become the focus of interest and value.

John Percival wrote of *Hymns* (originally a duet, then extended to include a trio for three other men) that the duet shows two men who 'undertake proudly minimal, pious parades' and that the three other men 'engage in schoolboy . . . gestures where attitudes are hinted through tiny confrontations'.[7] Those 'tiny confrontations' in this early (1988) work indicate a very economical approach to movement; such containment and understatement can be very telling about a choreographer's approach and Burrows has continued to explore them through his later work. In 2004 he said, 'I could say that I'm committed to the idea of using movement even at a time when many other choreographers are finding many other ways to be choreographers.'[8]

Stoics (1991) is a work that, unlike *Hymns*, could be seen as violent, dangerous and even nasty at times, as Burrows himself has suggested. Highlighted in this work is the potential of the movement itself, rather than any facial expression, to be expressive of emotion or passion. The choice of some of Mendelssohn's *Songs Without Words* for solo piano is especially interesting, particularly in view of the fact that the dance seems to be dealing with an inability to communicate, with people speaking different languages or not understanding each other. *Stoics*, as Burrows has explained, is so called because of the idea of the 'stiff upper lip' that characterizes a certain type of social behaviour, maintained none the less at the same time as a sense of humour throughout life's difficult events.

Audiences have perceived *Stoics* as funny rather than menacing, however, and it is easy to see why, because the dynamic shaping of the movement, whether it be aggressive, violent or threatening, is somehow channelled differently, so that it is never focused one person on the other – though dancers may stop to watch or contemplate each other from time to time. There is the sense of being an outsider, of looking at foreign customs, social interaction, war-dances (and this is equally true of *Very*) – but not quite, because the fact of each dancer stopping to watch the other 'breaks the frame' and highlights instead the human capacity for mutual misunderstanding. The hint of potential violence is made much more explicit, however, in small moments in *Very*; but these are not developed thematically and so again the sense of possible danger is dispelled.

Burrows' movement style in the 1990s was frequently characterized by a powerful impetus from the exact centre – not from the centre of the body, but rather from deep at the point of attachment; for example, in the shoulder or hip joint – which very quickly dissipates, with a 'flung' quality, so that directions do not seem to be important, or focused (although it should be said that in some works the focus is very clearly articulated, as in *Very* and several sections of *The Stop Quartet*). It is the constant awareness of a centre from which movements emanate, however violently, that contributes much to the clear focus of the structure or the way in which the movements are structured. There is a contrasting moment of repose in *Stoics*, for example, during some close partner work when Burrows crouches down and allows his partner to climb on to his back and then to be carried around by him. Her carriage is characteristically upright, and hands are joined again, but this time one hand is placed gently on top of the other. This relaxing of the tension in the moment diffuses the tension of the whole for a brief span, albeit to a limited extent, because of her ramrod posture and direct gaze; it is not weakening but softening.

Clement Crisp wrote (in the *Financial Times* in 1994) of the early works that 'Burrows saw lives that were a stifled cry of pain and his movement, wild, autistic, sometimes very funny, provided an exact parallel without descending into mimicry'. He also noted that *Very* was 'too cussed and uncommunicative' (suggesting the misfiring of communication in *Stoics* taken to extremes), but that in *Our* (1994), 'movement is fluid, structure more relaxed in outline and broader in dynamic range'. Both *Our* and *Very* recall *Stoics* in different ways. In *Our*, it is the intensity of focus one dancer directs towards another at various times, although with perhaps less sense of the ridiculous and more of the hopeless. In *Very*, there is a similar sense of struggling to achieve something or find something, for example, in the forced *attitude* with arched back, and the purposeful, clearly articulated gestural movements of hands brushing across the body, front and back.

In the programme note for *Our*, Burrows included a quotation by Baudelaire: 'To express at once the attitude and the gesture of living beings whether solemn or grotesque, and their luminous explosion in space'. He explained that the reason for using this text was 'to gently give those people [whose intuitive response might be blocked by working too hard] a framework in which to see [*Our*]'. This suggests a perceptive view of audiences as well as the conviction that dance can communicate something of life. Perhaps, it indicates an awareness of the need for work to be 'accessible' – that is, that dance should make some attempt to reach its audience, while challenging them at the same time.

Sophie Constanti, writing in *The Guardian* of *Our*, felt that 'here, Burrows seems as concerned with stillness as with action and has discarded many of the more homespun eccentricities of his works in favour of a more noble exploration of the soul of contemporary human kind'. Constanti seems to suggest that 'homespun eccentricities' are an aberration. It might be argued, however, that they represent, or manifest in some way, an existentialist approach to dance and art and that the detail of human eccentricity, the mundane, the everyday are the stuff of life rather more than 'a more noble exploration of the soul of contemporary human kind'. Exploration, however, is a running theme in Burrows's work, as his later collaboration with theatre director Jan Ritsema, *Weak Dance, Strong Questions*, demonstrates. Again a duet, which is evidently Burrows's favoured format, this 50-minute piece involves the performers – Burrows and Ritsema – in 'a state of perpetual questioning', answering these questions 'by movement'.[9]

Chris de Marigny likened Burrows's work to Trisha Brown's in its 'rhythmic complexity'. This comparison, taken in conjunction with the choreographer's acknowledged debt to Childs, Nijinska and Morris Dancing points to the importance of rhythm, which is given a privileged place in Burrows' structuring of both movement phrases and whole works, exemplified brilliantly in *Both Sitting Duet*. Although the rhythmic structures that Burrows uses are sometimes less obviously highlighted than in these other choreographers and styles, surely in certain works (such as *Both Sitting Duet*) they are key to the dynamic clarity and effectiveness of the pieces. There is nothing arbitrary about the play of speed, stillness and rhythm, and this is further underlined when looking at works with music.

Sometimes, the music has its own clear rhythmic shaping and Burrows counterpoints that with movement phrases of sometimes quite complex rhythmic change, as in, for example, both *Hymns* and *Stoics*. At other times, the relationship is more fluid and more to do with atmospheric layering and the possibility of glimpsing each component through 'holes' in the others, as the audience glimpses Sylvie Guillem through the doorway in *blue yellow*: a spatial exploration of the same idea, which encourages imaginative engagement on the part of the audience to create a space – literal, aural or conceptual – for the dance to inhabit. Or, again, it is a conceptual space, as in *Weak Dance, Strong Questions* or *Both Sitting Duet*, that invites the audience to join in the process of exploring the nature of dance itself.

The trilogy comprising *Both Sitting Duet*, *The Quiet Dance* and the *Speaking Dance* is not only concerned with an exploration of the nature of dance but also of dance–music relationships and our perception of these: how they operate, how they bear meaning for us, how we engage with either or both and with each other with reference to either or both. By juxtaposing sound that is not like 'music' with movement that is not like 'dance', performed by people who do not look like 'dancers' (as in, not young, thin, highly-trained – though Burrows himself is, of course, highly trained), the choreographer invites us again and again to contemplate the wonderful expressiveness of human movement, of the human voice, of a human interaction. Like John Cage's *4'33"*, but arguably more entertaining, these works not only encourage us to look and listen more carefully to see and hear what is there, but also give us deliciously witty and poignant illustrations of what there, might be, could be, in this endlessly rich and fascinating world of sound and vision and life. 'Questioning and exploration should be about opening every door, even those that may seem on the surface too recognisable to open.'[10]

Rachel Duerden

Notes

1 In Polzer, Lydia, 'Two Men, Two Chairs', *Dancing Times*, November 2004.
2 Chris de Marigny, 'Burrows: Our Thoughts', *Dance Theatre Journal*, 11(2), 1994.
3 Jonathan Burrows, 'Playing the Game Harder: Jonathan Burrows in Conversation', *Dance Theatre Journal* 18(4), 2002.
4 Edward Thorpe, 'Talking to an Engima', *Dance and Dancers*, June/July 1991.
5 Polzer, op.cit.
6 See Burrows' comments in Nadine Meisner's 'Closing in on Ballet', *Dance Theatre Journal*, 13(2), 1996.
7 John Percival, 'Home Reviews: Victoria Marks, Jonathan Burrows', *Dance and Dancers*, November/December 1988.
8 Polzer, op. cit.
9 Andrew Brown, 'Asking Questions: Andrew Brown at NOTT Dance 2002', *Dance Theatre Journal*, 18(2), 2002.
10 Burrows, op.cit.

Biographical details

Born in Bishop Auckland, County Durham, England, 1960. **Studied** at the Royal Ballet School, London, 1970–79, under Richard Glastone: winner of an Ursula Morton award for student piece of choreography, *3 Solos*. **Career**: Danced with the Royal Ballet, London, 1979-91, and with the Rosemary Butcher Dance Company; early pieces choreographed for Extemporary Dance Theatre, Spiral Dance Company, Sadler's Wells Royal Ballet and the Royal Ballet Choreographic Group; founded Jonathan Burrows Group in 1988, which became a resident company at The Place Theatre, London, 1992–94, and entered into several co-productions with theatres in Ghent (Belgium), Angers (France) and Utrecht (Netherlands), 1995-96; choreographer-in-residence, South Bank Centre, London, 1998-89; associate artist at Kunstencentrum Vooruit, Ghent, Belgium 1992–2002; has also choreographed for Frankfurt Ballet. **Awards and honours** include Frederick Ashton Choreographic Award, 1990; Digital Dance Award, 1992; *Time Out* Award, 1994; Prudential Award, 1995; Dance Artist Fellowship (Arts Council England), 2000; award from Foundation for Contemporary Performance Arts, New York, 2002; New York Dance and Performance Award ('Bessie'), 2004.

Works

Catch (1980); *Listen* (1980); *Cloister* (1982); *The Winter Play* (1983); *Hymns, Parts 1–3* (1985); *Squash* (1985); *Hymns* (1986); *A Tremulous Heart Requires* (1986); *Hymns: Complete Version* (1988); *dull morning cloudy mild* (1989); *Stoics* (1991); *Very* (1992; film version, dir. Adam Roberts, 1993); *Our* (1994; film version, dir. Adam Roberts, 1994); *Hands* (film; dir. Adam Roberts, 1995); *blue yellow* (film solo; dir. Adam Roberts, 1995); *The Stop Quartet* (1996; film version, dir. Adam Roberts, 1996); *Walking/music* (1997); *Quintet* (1997); *Weak Dance, Strong Questions* (2001); *Both Sitting Duet* (2002); *Singing* (2003); *The Quiet Dance* (2005); *Speaking Dance* (2006); *Cheap Lecture* (2009); *The Cow Piece* (2009).

Further reading

Interviews with Edward Thorpe, in 'Talking to an Enigma', *Dance and Dancers*, June/July, 1991; Chris de Marigny, in 'Burrows: Our Thoughts', *Dance Theatre Journal*, Spring/Summer 1994; with Myriam Van Imschoot, in 'Lost in the Singing of Oneself', in *De Morgan* (Belgium), 3 May 1996; with Ismene Brown, in 'One Step Beyond', *Daily Telegraph*, 22 October 1996; with Kevin Volans, in dance issue of *The Full Score*, Autumn/Winter 1996; with Edith Boxberger, in 'Liberating the Imagination', *Ballett International*, December 1996; in Jo Butterworth and Gill Clarke (eds), *Dancemakers' Portfolio: Conversations with Choreographers*, Bretton Hall, 1998; in 'Playing the Game Harder: Jonathan Burrows in Conversation', *Dance Theatre Journal*, 18(4), 2002.

Articles: 'Young Classical Choreographers', Dance Study Supplement 4, *Dancing Times*, January 1990; Angela Kane, 'Dance Scene: The Jonathan Burrows Group', *Dancing Times*, June 1991; Carol Brown, Eleanor Brickhill, Ann Nugent, 'Three by Three', *Dance Now*, Spring 1993; Marilyn Hunt, 'Jonathan Burrows: The Laughter of Recognition', *Dance Magazine*, October 1993; 'Leading Lights', *Dance Now*, Spring 1994; Ann Nugent, 'Dream Ticket', *Dance Now*, Summer 1994; Sophie Constanti, 'Jonathan Burrows' New Work for Sylvie Guillem', *Dance Theatre Journal*, Winter 1995/96; Sophie Constanti, 'Jonathan Burrows Group', *Dancing Times*, July 1996; Nadine Meisner, 'Closing in on Ballet?', *Dance Theatre Journal*, 13(2), 1996; Rachel Duerden, 'Jonathan Burrows: Exploring the Frontiers', *Dancing Times*, March 2001; Ian Bramley, 'Select Coverage: Ian Bramley at Dance Umbrella 2001', *Dance Theatre Journal*, 17(4) 2001; Sanjoy Roy, 'Dance Now: Flying High: Dance Umbrella 2001: Jonathan Burrows/Jan Ritsema', *Dance Now*, Winter 2001–02; Andrew Brown, 'Asking Questions. Andrew Brown at NOTT Dance 2002', *Dance Theatre Journal*, 18(2), 2002; Jonathan Burrows, 'Weak Dance Strong Questions' *Performance Research – A Journal of Performing Arts*, June 2003; John Percival, 'Silver Jubilee: Dance Umbrella at 25: Johnathan Burrows; Matthew Hawkins', *Dance Now*, Winter 2003–04; Lydia Polzer, 'Two Men, Two Chairs', *Dancing Times*, November 2004; Efrosini Protopapa, 'Choreographic Practice and the State of Questioning', *Dance Theatre Journal*, 20(3), 2004; Lydia Polzer, 'Two Men, Two Chairs,' *Dancing Times*, November 2004; Daniela Perazzo, 'The Sitting Duo Now Walks, Or the Piece That Lies Quietly Underneath', *Dance Theatre Journal*, 21(2), 2005; Jenny Gilbert, 'Dance Umbrella 2005: Jonathan Burrows & Matteo Fargion', *Dance Now*, Winter 2005–06; Zoë Anderson, 'Dance Umbrella 2006: Jonathan Burrows and Matteo Fargion in "Speaking Dance"', *Dancing Times*, December 2006; Jane Simpson, 'Jonathan Burrows and Matteo Fargion', *Dance Now*, Winter 2006–07; Daniela Perazzo, '"Speaking Dance": The Storm After the Calm', *Dance Theatre Journal*, 22(2), 2007; Amita Nijhawan, 'Movers and Shakers: De-ciphering Practice', *Pulse – South Asian Dance in the UK*, September 2008; Sanjoy Roy, 'A Couple of Blokes, a Couple of Chairs', *Dance Now*, Spring 2008; Joseph Houseal, 'London', *Ballet Review*, Winter 2008–09.

Book: Janet Lansdale (ed.), *Decentring Dancing Texts*, Basingstoke, 2008.

ROSEMARY BUTCHER

Rosemary Butcher trained at Dartington College during the mid- to late 1960s, taking extra classes in Graham technique at the then new London School of Contemporary Dance alongside Richard Alston and Siobhan Davies. She went on to further studies in North America, studying the techniques of Doris Humphrey and Merce Cunningham. The artists to have the greatest influence on her, however, were those at the vanguard of American post-modern dance, such as Yvonne Rainer, Trisha Brown, Steve Paxton, Anna Halprin, Elaine Summers and Lucinda Childs. Butcher returned to England at a significant time in the development of British dance, and although she is renowned for her idiosyncrasy, she became, through both her teaching and her choreography, an influence on a new generation of British artists who were making radical departures from established norms under the umbrella title of New Dance.

Looking retrospectively at Butcher's work is particularly rewarding; the phases of her artistic development become clear with an underlying continuity of theme and concern. An early work, *Landings* (1976), met with some acclaim, as did *Anchor Relay* (1978). The originality of the work, in terms of its cool and relaxed contrast to the dramatic style of Graham technique, in itself commanded attention. The use of pedestrian movement, repetition and improvisation was at this time still dynamically varied and physical. The influence of Doris Humphrey could be seen in Butcher's emphasis on fall and recovery, and athleticism contrasted with soft, sensual communication between dancers.

The increasing minimalism of Butcher's work in the late 1970s and early 1980s, was centred upon the pull of gravity and the transfer of weight within the body and between dancers, and involved a deliberate banality of performance. These were approaches Butcher shared with many visual artists at the time, as her work engaged with conceptualism. Butcher did not think like a theatrical choreographer; her concern was to explore process as part of the work, and her compositions in this period were characterized by a very limited dynamic range and performed most often in silence.

Butcher's work is appreciative of simple 'natural' forms rather than speculative with a highly developed language. It draws on aspects of release work and contact improvisation, and draws the spectator into the physical sensuality of the simplest movement. In even her most minimalist works there was a sense of poetic space, of resonant silence and the qualities of stillness. In her later works, Butcher was to allow these aspects a more expressive presence.

Although Butcher's works concentrate the eye and mind on movement stripped of virtuosity and display, her style often suggests a sense of isolation and perhaps an existential malaise. In *Spaces 4* (1981), for example, dancers hold and support one another with Butcher's usual contemplative sensuality, but their actions can easily suggest consolation rather than nurturing or enabling. There is a sense of resignation, and of inertia, which can sometimes threaten the spirit of human vitality and creative resistance that is so central to the notion of dance. During the 1980s, however, the calmly meditative qualities of Butcher's work and her tendency to explore only within a limited dynamic were gradually taking on new expressive potential; and this in itself gave rise to a more energizing sense of artistic control. The sense of the choreographer having loosely structured what was essentially an exploration for the dancers was fading. But, far from detracting from the qualities that her minimalism had enabled audiences to rediscover in simple movement, Butcher's more expressive collaborations now helped audiences to appreciate her concerns more fully.

By *The Site* in 1983, for example, Butcher was allowing her dancers to work with imagery rather than the abstract instructions of earlier works. This work was one of Butcher's many successful collaborations with the sculptor Heinz-Dieter Pietsch and with the use of soundscapes, created in this instance by Malcolm Clark. Although the movement was limited in range and dynamic, the work achieved a powerfully dramatic sense of threat, of community and isolation, and of urban wasteland. In *The Site*, and *Imprints* (also 1983), the formal qualities that had hitherto been of a primarily abstract interest now took on a more powerfully expressive resonance.

With *Flying Lines* (1985), Butcher's preoccupation with weight and gravity allowed also their opposites in light, soaring movements. The mesmeric qualities of her use of repetition were particularly successful in this work – partly, perhaps, because Michael Nyman's accessible use of musical repetition helped audiences to understand better what Butcher was doing and gave them a means of allowing it to affect and involve them. Rather than experiencing repetition as monotonous, the audience experienced an overpowering sense of liberation and heightened awareness of the smallest development.

In 1987, again in collaboration with Michael Nyman and Heinz-Dieter Pietsch, Butcher produced one of her most successful works,

Touch the Earth (1987), in which many of her developing interests and concerns appeared to come to fruition. Originally performed at the Whitechapel Art Gallery, it went on to be performed in a very different space at the Queen Elizabeth Hall, also in London, and was later televised. The broad theme, as in many of her works, was territory. Sources included ideas about the loss of the Native American's way of life described in T.C. McLuhan's book *Touch the Earth*. Although the work, as always with Butcher, was suggestive rather than narrative or overtly didactic, the programme note invited the audience to draw parallels with the (then) very recent Chernobyl nuclear disaster. Nyman's music looked to the rhythms and tempo of processions and to the singing gondoliers of Venice, while Pietsch's set was inspired by the materials used by ancient farmers.

Throughout her career, Butcher has sited her dancers in a wide range of performance environments; her work relates closely and sensitively to its particular environment, be it studio stage space, a gallery, a church or a warehouse. But there is a deeper sense in which Butcher's work is concerned with the environment of the human being; it is as if dance can be a way of claiming back lost spatial relations, as if the aim of the movement is to reclaim physical memories and to put us back in touch with the earth and its sensual rhythms. Butcher has always been thought of as the apolitical exception to the rule within the politicized arena of New Dance. She has never concerned herself with sexual politics in the overt way that many of her contemporaries have done, but her basic affiliation with ecological and environmentalist attitudes is an important aspect of her work, whether or not this has been her conscious intention.

Even in her period of greatest minimalism, Butcher's casual movement could look dreamy, its deliberation indolent, its simple physicality sensual and its use of space impressionistic. It is perhaps easier to be abstract in dance when the dancers are doing more rather than less; when the convoluted complexities of a highly technical movement vocabulary distance the audience from the dancers. In retrospect, the quality of their neutrality has always made Butcher's dancers to some extent politically and dramatically resonant – one looks for a context beyond the physicality of the dance.

Despite fluctuating financial support, Butcher has shown herself capable of constant renewal, and her work has steadily developed in a number of interesting and sometimes surprising directions. In the late 1980s and early 1990s, she produced a number of particularly grand conceptions, such as collaboration with architects Zaha Hadid and John Lyall on a three-part work, *d1*, *d2* and *3D* (1989–90) for a variety of different sites. She has also shown a strong interest in the adaptation of her work for film; in *Of Shadows and Walls* (1991), she worked with filmmaker Nicola Baldwin on an installation, which involved the use of 12 video monitors. Moving into the twenty-first century, Butcher's work remains true to her austere and idiosyncratic language and has entered into new and rewarding dialogues with a range of different sites, themes and media. In 2003, her work *White* (2003) engaged with projected pre-recorded video images mixed live by Martin Otter in collaboration with the dancers, contrasting live and pre-recorded movement. This trend has continued: in 2008, *Episodes of Flight* used images (created by Matthew Butcher and Melissa Appleton) of digital architectural landscapes. Her conceptualism and use of deliberate monotony have been developed and explored over a long and distinctive career and she continues to find new enthusiastic audiences.

Siting her work as part of an installation in gallery spaces such as Tate Modern, and embracing new technology, point both to Butcher's consistency of interest and to her openness to new possibilities. Her work invites comparisons and parallels, particularly with artists working in the visual arts, and Butcher remains a unique presence in British dance. She has also been an important influence on a wide range of British artists including Sue Maclennan, Miranda Tuffnel, Gaby Agis, Ashley Page and Jonathan Burrows. However, given that her work has contributed more generally to the expansion of our ways of seeing and siting dance, Rosemary Butcher's influence goes much further.

Lesley-Anne Sayers

Biographical details

Born in Bristol, England, 4 February 1947. **Studied** at Dartington College of Arts, Devon, 1965–68, under Ruth Foster and Flora Cushman; studied in the United States, 1967–68, including with Dorothy Madden at University of Maryland and at the Martha Graham School, New York; studied with Merce Cunningham, Trisha Brown, Yvonne Rainer, Lucinda Childs and Meredith Monk, 1970–71; also attended workshops by Anna Halprin and Doris Humphrey. **Career**: Danced with Elaine Summers' Intermedia Dance Foundation while in the United States, 1970–71; first choreography, for Scottish Ballet's Moveable Workshop, 1974; founded Rosemary Butcher Dance Company in 1976; appeared regularly at Dance Umbrella and at Dartington festivals, 1978–86, subsequently staging works independently; teaching posts and choreographic residencies include Dunfermline College, 1973–74, Dartington College, 1980–81, and the Laban Centre 1997–2002; presented 'In Retrospect' retrospective at Royal College of Art, 1997; also holder of postdoctoral fellowship in the Performing Arts, University of Surrey/ Middlesex University, 2003–06, and senior research fellow, 2006–07. **Awards and honours include** Royal Society of Arts Scholarship, 1977; Greater London Arts Award, 1986; *Time Out* Dance and Performance Award, 1987; Wingate Scholarship, 1999; Fellowship, Arts Council England, 2000–02; Jerwood Award, 2002.

Works*

Uneven Time (1974); *Multiple Event* (1974 for Dance Theatre Commune; 1976 for Rosemary Butcher Dance Company); *Ground Line* (1976); *Pause and Loss* (1976); *Landings* (1976); *Passage North East* (1976); *Space Between* (1977); *White Field* (1977); *Empty Signals* (1977); *Theme* (1978); *Anchor Relay* (1978); *Suggestion and Action* (1978); *Catch Five – Catch Six* (1978); *Touch and Go* (1978); *Uneven Time* (1978); *Suggestion and Action* (1978); *Dances for Different Spaces* (1979); *Landscape* (1979); *Solo Duo* (1979); *Five Sided Figure* (1980); *Six Tracks* (1980); *Solo from Instruction* (1980); *Spaces 4* (1981; TV version, 1984); *Shell: Force Fields and Spaces* (1981); *Field Beyond Maps* (1982); *Traces* (1982); *Imprints* (1983); *The Site* (1983); *Night Mooring Stones* (1984); *Flying Lines* (1985); *Touch the Earth* (1987; TV version, 1988); *Silent Spring* (1989); *After the Crying and the Shouting* (1989); *d1* (1989); *d2* (1990); *3D* (1990); *Of Shadows and Walls* (1991); *Body as Site* (1992–93); *After the Last Sky* (1995); *Unbroken View* (1996); *Fractured Landscapes, Fragmented Narratives* (1995–97); *SCAN* (2000–01); *Undercurrent* (film, 2001); *Still-Slow-Divided* (2002); *White* (2003); *Images Every Three Seconds* (2003); *Vanishing Point* (film, 2004); *Hidden Voices* (2004); *The Return* (film, 2005); *Six Frames – Memories of Two Women* (2005); *The Hour* (2005); *Aftermath* (film, 2006); *Episodes of Flight* (2008).

*Published sources vary; dates cited here are in accordance with Rosemary Butcher's website, which is the most up-to-date source.

Further reading

Interview with Ros Anderson, 'Transforming over Time', *Dance Theatre Journal*, 21(3), 2006.

Articles: Timothy Lamford, 'Rosemary Butcher Dance Company at the Hammersmith Studios, *New Dance*, Spring 1997; Dee Conway, 'Rosemary Butcher', *New Dance*, Winter 1983; Alastair Macaulay, 'One at a Time', *Dance Theatre Journal*, Spring 1983; Peri Mackintosh, 'Rosemary Butcher Dance Company, Riverside Studios', *Dance Theatre Journal*, 1(1), 1983; Sarah Rubidge, 'Traces', *Dance and Dancers*, February 1983; Sally Watts, 'New British Dance', *Dancing Times*, May 1984; Lesley-Anne Davis, 'Collaborations', *Dance Theatre Journal*, Spring 1985; Stephanie Jordan, 'Rosemary Butcher', *Dance Theatre Journal*, 4(2), Summer 1986; Christopher Crickmay, 'Dialogues with Rosemary Butcher: A Decade of Her Work', *New Dance*, Spring 1986; Judith Mackrell, 'Kitsch and Courtship at the Umbrella', *Dance Theatre Journal*, Spring 1986; Nadine Meisner, 'An English Pioneer', *Dance and Dancers*, February 1987; John Percival, 'What's New?', *Dance and Dancers*, July 1987; Stephanie Jordan, 'London', *Ballet Review*, Winter 1988; Judith Mackrell, 'Post-modern Dance in Britain', *Dance Research*, Spring 1991; Rosemary Butcher, 'What is Dance?', *Dance Now*, Summer 1992; Nadine Meisner, 'Body as

Site – Image as Event', *Dance and Dancers*, May 1993; Andrea Phillips, 'The Body as Site', *Dance Theatre Journal*, Spring/Summer 1993; Sherril Dodds, 'The Momentum Continues', *Dance Theatre Journal*, 13(3), 1997; Sophie Constanti, 'Rosemary Butcher in Retrospect', *Dancing Times*, April 1997; Nadine Meisner, 'Rosemary Butcher', *Dance Now*, Summer 1997; Sophie Constanti, 'Rosemary Butcher in Retrospect', *Dancing Times*, April 1997; Rosemary Butcher, 'What's Past is Prologue: New York Revisited', *Dance Theatre Journal*, 14(4), 1999; Niki Gladstone, 'A Vast, Slow Rushing', *Dance Theatre Journal*, 16(2), 2000; Andrew Brown, 'Asking Questions,' *Dance Theatre Journal*, 18(2), 2002; David Jays, 'Rosemary Butcher and Cathy Marston', *Dancing Times*, April, 2004; Sanjoy Roy, 'Rosemary Butcher', *The Guardian*, 6 November 2008.

Books: Janet Adshead (ed.), *Choreography: Principles and Practice, Report of the 4th Study of Dance Conference*, University of Surrey, 4–7 April, 1986; Allen Robertson and Donald Hutera, *The Dance Handbook*, Harlow, Essex, 1988; Stephanie Jordan, *Striding Out: Aspects of Contemporary and New Dance in Britain*, London, 1992; Judith Mackrell, *Out of Line: The Story of British New Dance*, London, 1992; Thea Barnes *et al.*, *Practice as Research and Research in Practice: Papers from the Research Day*, Laban Centre, London, 30 June, 1998; Janet Adshead-Lansdale (ed.), *Dancing Texts: Intertextuality in Interpretation*, London, 1999; Sally Totenbier *et al.*, *Dance, Culture and Politics: Papers from the Laban Centre London Research Conference*, 22 June 2000; Rosemary Butcher and Susan Melrose (eds), *Rosemary Butcher: Choreography, Collisions and Collaborations*, Middlesex University, Enfield, 2005.

LUCINDA CHILDS

The name Lucinda Childs conjures up an upright, elegantly severe presence. Her work is the epitome of choreographic minimalism, with a stripped-down vocabulary performed along geometric floor plans in rigorous structures that repeat or mutate minutely and precisely over time. Her style, derived from ballet and Cunningham technique, is aligned to maximum function and clarity even though the arms are used in a relaxed manner. Her demeanour, and that of her dancers, is not just neutral, but deeply cool and impersonal, or as Susan Sontag said, 'transpersonal'.[1]

A member of the Judson generation of post-modernists, Childs initially worked with a radically simplified vocabulary: walking, turning, small skips and later, leaps. In certain ways, Childs's work seems the perfect embodiment of the analytic post-modernism that Sally Banes has identified as an outgrowth of the Judson Church dance experiments.[2] Rejecting the overt, intentional expression of classic modern dance, with its carefully honed technique, measured phrasing and its significant lighting and music (let alone the codified, virtuosic vocabulary and spectacular presentation of ballet),[3] this new approach tended to objectify movement, both in the sense of doing away with subjective, emotive rationales for dance and in the sense of making movement itself a detached object of scrutiny.[4]

Unlike the game or chance structures used by many of her Judson-era contemporaries early in their careers, Childs's work did not tend to incorporate improvisation or the pedestrian, rather, it was disciplined and controlled to an extreme. This has been most apparent in her precise, deceptively simple choreographic structures. In one of her early Judson pieces, *Museum Piece* (1965), Childs placed coloured circles from an enlargement of a section of Seurat's painting *Le Cirque* on the floor, and then stepped backwards from dot to dot, looking through a mirror, enacting what was to become her ongoing concern with point of view.[5] Her evocation of Seurat seems like a particularly appropriate way to begin considering dance as energy visually conceived in space and time,[6] since in pointillism precisely spaced dots of colour interact with one another to bring a flat canvas to a pulsating three dimensionality. Throughout her works, Childs has explored the importance and the great difficulty of seeing movement clearly.[7] Some of her early dances seemed to push the limits of how 'simple' a dance could be and still elude the viewer's complete perception. Many of the dances suggested the shimmering visual ambiguity of Op Art.

Over the years, Childs's choreographic vocabulary gradually expanded to include ballet-derived steps while retaining her geometric structure and visual clarity. What has grown and developed since the early 1970s has been the way in which the steps are assembled, accumulated, varied through re-viewing from different points of view and intensified through repetition or doubling. Her choreography for unison ensembles or contrapuntal units is rarely about the evocation of community; rather it focuses on the power of choreography within a structure that is larger than individuals or pairs. Even when her dances suggest dramatic subtexts through partnering, these interactions support or elaborate spatial patterns rather than advance a story or mood.

Childs's work with Robert Wilson in *Einstein on the Beach* (1976) opened up new structural principles for her, spatially, in the expanded architecture and precisely focused geometries of a proscenium stage. Childs has noted that 'Wilson is able to transform that space because of the way he plays into the classical lines and, in some surrealistic way, also plays against those existing architectural values.'[8] Like Wilson,

Childs both exploits and transforms the proscenium in her use of ensemble; spare, angular vocabulary; rigorous attention to spatial placement and scale; repetition and shifts in point of view; and, most importantly, her emphasis on the diagonal.[9] All point to the pure geometry of the stage space on a scale that is larger than individual human beings. Sensitively designed sets have played their part in this effort as well, such as Sol LeWitt's oversize projections of the dancers in *Dance* (1979) and Frank Gehry's two-layer set for *Available Light* (1983).

Childs's involvement in *Einstein* also suggested a new form of temporal structure in the form of music. Her dances of the early 1970s were performed in silence and organized by elaborate counts.[10] Inspired by Wilson's collaboration with Philip Glass, Childs tended during the later 1970s and 1980s to structure her dances around and against the duration, tempi and rhythms of minimalist compositions whose precise, repetitive, gradually shifting structures paralleled her own choreographic concerns. That interest in repetitions has expanded to encompass the canons, themes and variations and other techniques of classical and contemporary composers, including in contemporary works with romantic or baroque overtones by composers such as Gavin Bryars, György Ligeti, Iannis Xenakis and Henryk Górecki. In keeping with Childs's tight control of the choreographic process, music, design and dance all evolve in a completely unified project.[11] Beginning in the late 1980s, Childs choreographed for a number of ballet companies and also choreographed and directed both classical and contemporary opera. She has found regular audiences – and regular funding – in Europe, which recognized her with honours that have included appointment to the rank of Commandeur dans l'Ordre des Arts et des Lettres by the French government in 2004. Childs's work has become less explicitly analytic and closer to traditional concepts of choreography, although it continues to build, for aesthetic ends, on the insights of the earlier analysis. Formalism has become less a polemic and more an aesthetic.

In *Four Elements* (1990), which Childs choreographed for Rambert Dance Company, the diagonal was enacted not only as a pathway, as in so many Childs dances, but also from numerous vertical perspectives. It appeared in versions of arabesques and lifts; it was also subtly distorted into an arc by a tilted head in an off-centre turn, or the angle of an over-the-back lift, or was momentarily brought into focus in the stress of two dancers pulling against one another. In *Largo* (2001), danced by perhaps the most poised human on the planet, Mikhail

Baryshnikov, the soloist kept returning to a balanced fourth position, one foot ahead, the other behind, and transferred his weight between them. Each step was light on the toes, with an occasional soft turn-on-a-dime spin and an arm that lifted and hung over his head like a fruit-laden branch. Minimalist in form, the piece carried an undertow of resignation and remembrance. In *Ten Part Suite* (2005) for Boston Ballet, Childs replaced austere geometries with rococo curlicue as the dancers performed to violin sonatas by Corelli in contained, private lanes that would not have been out of place at Versailles.

Childs has sustained her connection with her minimalist colleagues even as their works have grown similarly elaborate and her own involvement in opera, particularly in European houses, has continued. She created dances for the première of John Adams's opera *Doctor Atomic* (2005), directed by Peter Sellars at the San Francisco Opera, and revived her *Dance with Music* to Philip Glass for the Ballet de l'Opéra National du Rhin, where she has regularly worked as a choreographer and stage director. And as a performer, she returned to working with Robert Wilson, appearing in his production of Bach's Passion of St John at the Théâtre du Châtelet in Paris in 2007. A documentary by Patrick Bensard of La Cinémathèque de la Danse, broadcast by the French and German Arts television programme ARTE in 2009 and distributed through film festivals and on DVD, contextualized her career; and the thirtieth anniversary revival of *Dance* with original films by Sol LeWitt have reintroduced this important figure to new audiences. Ecstatic and disciplined, Childs's work remains at the intersection of post-modern dance and classicism.

Judy Burns
(revised and updated by Debra Cash)

Notes

1 Susan Sontag, 'For "Available Light": A Brief Lexicon', *Art in America*, December 1983. Sontag uses this word to make a distinction between Yvonne Rainer's 'neutral doer' and a more elevated impersonality in which grace is without inwardness, which Sontag located in Kleist's essay on puppetry and in George Balanchine's choreography.

2 Sally Banes, *Terpsichore in Sneakers*, Middletown, Connecticut, 1987.

3 See Yvonne Rainer, 'A Quasi Survey of Some "Minimalist" Tendencies in the Quantitatively Minimal Dance Activity Midst the Plethora; or an Analysis of *Trio A*', *Work 1961–73*, Nova Scotia, 1974.

4 Banes, op. cit.

5 Banes, op. cit.

6 A number of writers, notably Sally Banes, have accurately identified and discussed Childs's visual emphasis, but that visualness can be further defined. Much of the power of Childs's choreography – the 'shimmering' quality of these early dances, for example – lies in the structurally focused tension between kinetic energies and precise spatial placements or pathways; this effect was enhanced in the late 1970s and the 1980s when Childs incorporated airborne movements and musical pulse. See also Susan Sontag's discussion of repetition (1983).

7 Childs, quoted in Banes, op. cit.

8 Sophi Constanti, 'Swimming Against the Tide', *Dance Theatre Journal*, Spring 1991.

9 Ann Daly's observations concerning Robert Wilson's use of the diagonal to offset the horizontal and vertical in the proscenium as well as her paraphrase of Wilson's comment, 'counterpoint clarifies', are suggestive in regard to Childs's own practices. See Ann Daly, 'The Closet Classicist', *Danceview*, Winter 1993–94.

10 Sontag (1983), op. cit. Sontag implies a connection between Seurat's belief that beauty has an 'objective, measurable basis' and Childs's own aesthetic, and asserts that time and space come together through counting.

11 For some descriptions of the connection between specific music and Childs's dances in the early 1980s, see Nancy Goldner, 'The Festival May Be New Wave, But the Dancing Celebrated the Tried and True', *Christian Science Monitor*, 8 November 1983, and Allen Robertson, 'Be Am Is Are Was Were Been', *Soho News*, 25 March 1981.

Biographical details

Born in NewYork, 26 June 1940. **Studied** at Sarah Lawrence College, Bronxville, New York (earning BA degree in Dance, 1962), the American Ballet Center, New York, and with Merce Cunningham. **Career:** Danced with Judson Dance Theater, from 1963, working as choreographer (mostly of own solos), *c.* 1962–66; founding dancer, choreographer and director, Lucinda Childs Dance Company, New York, from 1973. Has staged works for Bavarian State Opera Ballet, Rambert Dance Company, Lyon Opera Ballet, Ohio Ballet, Paris Opera Ballet, Boston Ballet, Los Angeles Opera, San Francisco Opera, White Oak Dance, the Martha Graham Company, Ballet de l'Opéra National du Rhin, Pacific Northwest Ballet, Les Ballets Monte Carlo and MaggioDanza, Florence; has also worked extensively in opera. **Awards and honours** include Obie Award, 1976; Guggenheim Fellowship, 1979; New York Dance and Performance Award ('Bessie'), 2001; Commandeur dans l'Ordre des Arts et des Lettres, 2004.

Works

Pastime (1963); *Three Pieces* (1963); *Minus Auditorium Equipment and Furnishings* (1963); *Egg Deal* (1963); *Cancellation Sample* (1964); *Carnation* (1964); *Street Dance* (1964); *Model* (1964); *Geranium* (1965); *Scarf* (1965); *Museum Piece* (1965); *Screen* (1965); *Agriculture* (1965); *Vehicle* (in *Nine Evenings of Theater and Engineering*, 1966); *Untitled Trio* (1968; revised version, 1973); *Particular Reel* (1973); *Checkered Drift*

(1973); *Calico Mingling* (1973); *Duplicate Suite* (1975); *Reclining Rondo* (1975); *Congeries on Edges for 20 Obliques* (1975); *Radial Courses* (1976); *Mix Detail* (1976); *Transverse Exchanges* (1976); *Solo: Character on Three Diagonals* (from opera *Einstein on the Beach* by Philip Glass, 1976); *Cross Words* (1976); *Figure Eights* (1976); *Plaza* (1977); *Melody Excerpt* (1977); *Interior Drama* (1977); *Katema* (1978); *Dance* (1979); *Mad Rush* (1981); *Relative Calm* (1981); *Formal Abandon, Part I* (solo, 1982); *Formal Abandon, Part II* (quartet, 1982); *Available Light* (1983, revised later the same year); *Formal Abandon, Part III* (1983); *Cascade* (1984); *Outline* (1984); *Première Orage* (1984); *Field Dances* (dances in opera *Einstein on the Beach* by Philip Glass, 1984); *Portraits in Reflection* (1986); *Clarion* (1986); *Hungarian Rock* (1986); *Calyx* (1987); *Lichtknall* (opera by Erhard Grosskopf, 1987); *Mayday* (in collaboration with Sol LeWitt, 1989); *Perfect Stranger* (1990); *Four Elements* (1990); *Rhythm Plus* (1991); *Oophaa Naama* (1992); *Concerto* (1993); *One and One* (1993); *Impromptu* (1993); *Chamber Symphony* (1994); *Trilogies* (1994); *Commencement* (1995); *Solstice* (1995); *Kengir* (1995); *From the White Edge of Phrygia* (1995); *Hammerklavier* (1996); *Don Carlo* (opera by Guiseppe Verdi, 1997); *On the Balance of Things* (1998); *Sunrise of the Planetary Dream Collector* (1998); *Moto Perpetuo* (1998); *Histoire* (1999); *Macbeth* (opera by Guiseppe Verdi, 1999); *Variete de Variete* (2000); *Description of a Description* (2000); *The Chairman Dances* (2000); *Handel/Corelli* (2001); *Largo* (2001); *White Raven* (opera by Philip Glass, 2001); *Lohengrin* (opera by Richard Wagner, 2001); *Underwater* (2002); *Chacony* (2002); *Daphnis et Chloe* (2003); *Opus One* (2003); *Orfeo ed Euridice* (opera by Gluck, 2003); *Mandarin Merveilleux* (2004); *Parsifal* (opera by Wagner, 2004); *Firebird* (2005); *Ten Part Suite* (2005); *Doctor Atomic* (opera by John Adams, 2005); *Rossignol and Oedipus Rex* (opera by Stravinsky, 2007); *Symphony of Psalms* (2007); *Tempo Vicino* (2009); *Songs From Before* (2009).

Further reading

Interviews with Daryl Chin, in 'Talking with Lucinda Childs', *Dance Scope*, Winter/Spring 1979–80; with Connie Kreemer, in *Further Steps: Fifteen Choreographers on Modern Dance*, New York, 1987; with Bernadette Bonis, in 'Lucinda Childs. La danse post-moderne a cassé l'idée d'objet d'art', *Danser*, September 1990; with Sophie Constanti, in 'Swimming Against the Tide', *Dance Theatre Journal*, Spring 1991; with Jörn Rohwer, in 'Timeless Everyday', *Ballett International*, October 1995.

Articles: Jill Johnston, 'Judson 1964: End of an Era', *Ballet Review*, 1(6), 1967; Lucinda Childs, 'Notes: '64–'74', *Drama Review*, March 1975; John Percival, 'Robert Wilson, Lucinda Childs at the Royal Court Theatre', *Dance and Dancers*, October 1978; John Percival, 'Paris International Dance Festival: American Emphasis', *Dance and Dancers*, December 1979; Barry Laine, 'Dance Forecast, 1980–81', *Ballet News*, September 1980; Barry Laine, 'In Search of Judson, *Dance Magazine*, September 1982; Deborah Rawson, 'Child's Play', *Ballet News*, December 1984; Camille Hardy, 'Lucinda Childs Dance Company', *Dance Magazine*, July 1986; Iris Fanger, 'The New Lucinda Childs', *Dance Magazine*, October 1989; Lyn Garafola, Reviews: New York City', *Dance Magazine*, January 1990; Ann Daly, 'The Closet Classicist', *Danceview*, Winter 1993–94; Joseph Mazo, 'Lucinda Childs Returns', *Dance Magazine*, February 1994; Ann Nugent, 'Newly Minted, *Dance Now*, Winter 1994; Roslyn Sulcas, 'Reviews: International', *Dance Magazine*, March 1996; Maria Shevstova, 'La Maladie de la mort', *Dance Theatre Journal*, 14(1), 1998; Thomas

Hahn, 'On Stage: Backstage with Lucinda', *Ballett International*, June 2000; Iris Fanger, 'Lucinda Childs and Parcours: Celebrating a Quarter Century of the Road Less Taken . . .', *Dance Magazine*, October 2000; Emma Manning, 'More is Less', *Dance Europe*, December 2002; Deborah Jowitt, 'Lucinda Childs, Philip Glass and Sol LeWitt "Dance" at Bard's Summerscape', *The Village Voice*, 15 July 2009; Joan Acocella, 'Think Pieces: Return of the Judsonites', *The New Yorker*, 24 May 2010.

Books: Don McDonagh, *The Complete Guide to Modern Dance*, New York, 1976; Peter Wynne (ed.), *Judson Dance: An Annotated Bibliography of the Judson Dance Theater and of Five Major Choreographers*, Englewood Cliffs, NJ, 1978; Anne Livet, *Contemporary Dance*, New York, 1978; Sally Banes, *Terpsichore in Sneakers*, Boston, 1980; Arlene Croce, *Going to the Dance*, New York, 1982; Sally Banes, *Democracy's Body: Judson Dance Theater 1962–1964*, Ann Arbor, MI, 1983 (reprinted, Durham, NC, 1993); Lucinda Childs Dance Foundation, *25th Anniversary of Lucinda Childs Dance Company*, New York, 2000; Sally Banes and Andrea Harris (eds), *Reinventing Dance in the 1960s*, Madison, WI, 2003; Joyce, Morgenroth (ed.), *Speaking of Dance: Twelve Contemporary Choreographers on Their Craft*, New York, 2004.

MICHAEL CLARK

Michael Clark has attracted considerable attention since the early 1980s for a number of reasons. Most obviously, his anarchic blend of technically proficient dance performance based on classical *danse d'école* with incongruous, often subversive use of costumes, props, music and thematic material has provoked responses of delight and disapproval in varying measure. His popularity (and notoriety) over a period of years has given him a status in the dance world and beyond that has allowed him to pursue, develop and refine his interests in a number of contexts. Catherine Wood writes, 'Over the course of three decades, [Clark] has repeatedly used the concrete and delimited space of the stage to perform a world of his own making, creating self-portraits that are also allegories of community'.[1] Through his work, Clark arguably raises important issues about ballet – and, by extension, 'high art' in general – and its place and value in contemporary society. How does ballet embody contemporary life, attitudes, visions or hopes? How does it reflect contemporary anxieties, challenges and shifting landscapes?

As well as inspiring a widely diverse critical response, Clark's work has attracted a new audience for dance. Characteristic features of his style include clear references to, and manipulation of, classical ballet technique (and ballet's tradition) juxtaposed with rock music, exaggerated and often deliberately shocking costumes, the use of non-dancers, such as personal friends and family, and post-modern references to contemporary issues – frequently made in a childlike or playful way. His interest in classicism is apparent throughout his work, although the extent to which Clark may be seen to be redefining classicism, or developing a new strand within it, critics have sometimes found hard to assess. In reference to ballet, he has spoken of Balanchine's *Apollo* as:

> . . . an amazing piece of work, but I hate the idea that you can't create anything new, that everything is just a pastiche of what has gone before. If ballet is going to survive then it will be because dancers and choreographers challenge it. You have to re-define classicism – I couldn't do a piece that was just made up of classical vocabulary. You have to add new words to the language or it dies out.[2]

After early studies in Scottish dancing, Clark trained in ballet at the Royal Ballet School, where one of his contemporaries was the dancer and choreographer Jonathan Burrows. Scottish dancing itself makes an appearance in some of Clark's works, such as *Morag's Wedding* (1984) and the third part of the Stravinsky Project, *I Do* (2007). The classical foundation of his training, however, extends throughout his work, underpinning all his choreography and embodied in his chosen themes.

Clark's own performance style demonstrated considerable accomplishment: his fluid, clear line, highly arched feet, strong extensions, speed and precision are facets of classical technique to which dancers aspire. These qualities drew attention when he was a very young dancer, and the choreographer Richard Alston exploited some of the potential of Clark's ability in, for example, *Soda Lake* (1981). It is easy enough to trace links back to this in Clark's own choreographies – for example, in the use of precision in rhythm and weight changes, and in the clarity of shape, movement and phrasing, evident in his work, *Swamp*, made for Rambert in 1986 and revived in 2004 for the same company. Also apparent is the influence of Merce Cunningham (as in Alston's work) in the manipulation of fast, technical, clear work of limbs and torso placement, for example, in Clark's solo in *No Fire Escape in Hell* (1986).

Clark frequently foregrounds the more obvious facets of classical ballet – the outward rotation of the legs from the hip socket, the opening of the whole body in confident, outward-focused movement (evidence of a strong Cecchetti influence), the strong extension of legs and feet, the use of strength and control both in sustained movement and in fast footwork and jumps. Like Cunningham, and like Twyla Tharp in her very different way, Clark combines apparently 'straight' ballet with incongruous tilts and twists of the body, and off-balance shifts of weight and changes of direction. Unlike them, though, he sometimes makes ballet movements look distorted or dream-like because of the odd, unexpected juxtaposition of direct quotations (such as *cabrioles*, *pirouettes* and so on being couched in peculiar phrases), but also, of course – and this aspect is driven home sometimes before all the rest – because of the very idiosyncratic, imaginative and sometimes perverse (or subversive) choice of collaborators and their contributions in terms of costume, set, props and music.

In *Because We Must* (1987), there is extensive use of classical vocabulary – both specifically and in inflection – and many references to ballet, such as barre work as well as more obvious 'steps' and align-ment of the body, control and attack. The appearance of the nude guitarists, and of Clark standing in a barefoot fifth position, suggests the possibility that the parallel, or turned-in, or otherwise different aspects of movement vocabulary simply act in a 'chromatic' way. To push the musical parallel further, the chromaticism may escalate but tonality never completely dissolves.

Although Clark's own dance style was classically beautiful in its clar-ity, balance, harmony and supreme control, he sometimes uses his danc-ers somewhat differently – that is, by exploiting their own technical accomplishments and their individuality. Dancers do not need to become 'Clark clones' necessarily (except occasionally – as seemed to be the intention at times in *O* (1994, revised 2005)), and the use of non-dancers – his friends and his mother – shows further diversification.

Richard Glasstone, Clark's teacher at the Royal Ballet School, has written of the important influence of ballet and specifically the Cecchetti *ports de bras* and directions of the body in Clark's work, not only in his own performance style, but also quite specifically in his choice of movement ideas from which to develop choreography.[3] Glasstone likens Clark to Frederick Ashton in this respect. As early as 1984, Clark told Alastair Macaulay of his perception of the central importance of ballet in his work, the physical understanding it provides, as well as the speed, total control of weight, sense of movement and line and so on.[4]

Certainly, one can see this in much of Clark's work, sandwiched, with more or less prominence, among the punk post-modern. Glasstone asks whether, in fact, the distortions introduced by Clark might not eventually be refined and made more safe, as pointe work was. Jann Parry also comments on the 'pelvic shift' evident in *Mmm...* (1992, revised 2006) and *O* in these terms, suggesting links to Balanchine's manipulation and extension of the canon of classical ballet. However, Clark's idiosyncratic approach has frequently divided critics and posed a serious challenge in terms of what constitutes an appropriate response to his work.

Fiona Burnside, considering the problems of characterizing and responding to Clark's work, writes:

> ...he may ransack the past for ideas or images but only to illustrate some aspect of the present ...The dislocated values of the fragmented twentieth century society are present in all his works and not less so in this one [*O*] merely because the more extravagant trappings of his anarchism are less evident.[5]

Burnside suggests that Clark has an ability as a creator and manipulator of movement that has sometimes been obscured by fashionable trappings. Certainly, the theatrical and shocking aspects of his work may distract the audience's attention too much from a paucity of invention or, when invention is there, from the value of it. This does beg some questions about the nature and intention of post-modern dance, and of audiences' response to, and critical engagement with, the work. Is it appropriate, for example, to attempt to separate out the movement material from the overall context of fragmented and subversive images and structures? Critics have clearly been hard pressed at times to find the right approach to writing about the work (see David Hughes below), partly because the theatrical colour and diversity and the gleefully subversive imagery present a compelling spectacle that demands its own response regardless of the extent to which the material itself may be inventive and skilfully structured.

Mmm... and *O* both link themselves to the Diaghilev period and, beyond that, to classicism and notions of the binary opposites Apollo and Dionysos. Clark himself said in 1994:

> Stravinsky was more or less disowning *The Rite* when he came to write *Apollo*, and though the music is more purified and less violent, the works are two sides of the same coin. It's that thing of opposites confirming one another. *The Rite* is the music of Dionysos, of drunkenness and ecstasy and abandon and submission to inevitable change.

After all, the ritual in *The Rite* was the one that changed winter into spring. I wanted a quality there of the phrase doing a dancer, rather than the dancer doing a phrase. In contrast, Apollo is the Sun God. He's in control, he divides day from night, a god of clarity. Apollo moves to make the only possible choice from one reason to the next, and you could say that my difficulty with all this is that we work in a society that doesn't consider dance as something we *need*, and it is so hard to relay these matters to audiences nowadays.[6]

In much, or even all, of Clark's work, there is evidence of post-modern references to (and reframing of) the past, specifically through the medium of ballet, and this provides an underlying current throughout.

Clark could be seen, perhaps, as working more in the tradition of Balanchine in terms of the expansion of the classical vocabulary into realms often perceived as ugly or distorted, going counter to the prevailing ethos. Ballet's deep-rooted tradition and discipline, and its proven ability to develop and change through changing cultural climates, have shown its resilience and provided a rich resource for future choreographers. As Clark noted in relation to *O*:

I realise now that I'm looking for rigour ... I've begun to understand more recently about the precision and definition of ballet dancing, and how I require that in my work ... I like the fearlessness that goes with youth, but I love what experience brings. I used to be drawn to the individuality of performers – like Leigh Bowery or old lovers – who were untrained, but now I'm more interested in stretching other people, but they've got to be better than me to start with.[7]

Nadine Meisner, writing in 1984, maintained that Clark

... knows his sources intimately. He respects the music's narrative sub-text. He evokes Balanchine, occasionally even quoting him directly, as in touching of fingers between Apollo and Terpsichore, which Balanchine took from Michelangelo's image of God giving life to Adam.[8]

This may well be true, and be convincingly argued. However, this view could reflect, rather, Meisner's own intimate knowledge of sources, and her reading of their use in *O*. Perhaps Clark plays games with his critics by hinting in this way, making references and knowing or anticipating that they will respond with just such erudite speculation. There is no doubt, though, of Clark's deep respect for and valuing of the classical tradition, because his work is so very clearly rooted in it, despite all the trappings of post-punk anarchy in some works. This respect surely extends to the repertoire of ballet, too, and the possibility offered for cross-referencing almost to vanishing point.

Jann Parry (1992) also remarks on the visual links to *Apollo*, and the link between *Rite* and *Apollo* in ballet's history, through the Sun King – Louis XIV, who gave ballet its 'academic foundation' – and the sacrifice to the god of the sun in *Rite* to ensure the return of spring. As she says, 'Clark's Apollonian fifth positions were a recall to order in the midst of his irreverent experiments with movement and music'.[9] This could be seen in earlier work, too. In *Because We Must*, for example, Clark could be seen as 'professing his faith' (reminiscent of Nureyev's 'sign of the cross' every day) through the demonstration of the fifth position. In this instance, as noted above, it was a barefoot rendition, which itself carried a number of resonances – vulnerability, technique as a skill acquired or superimposed on the body.

David Hughes, in a review of *Mmm...*, demonstrates how dance critics have felt the need to find different ways of responding to Clark's work and articulating the significance of that response. Hughes chose to locate Clark's work firmly in the post-structural world of 'Masochism, minors, mother, Michael, myths: *posting the modern*':

> Clark is a product of a moment of history, the punk aesthetic, the post-modern, the parodic, pop art, performance art, dance itself. A product not of a moment of history, but of histories, then, conflated in a moment. This is the condition of the work itself, a compacting of references and a series of images which run into each other through their connecting elements.[10]

Perhaps it is the case that Clark has drawn together some central or recurrent premises of post-modernism. The question remains whether Clark has contributed something beyond superficial originality, or successfully controlled the disparate elements of his work, and, indeed, whether these are appropriate criteria of excellence in relation to his work at all.

Shortly after the appearance of *O*, Michael Clark's career seemed to flounder: a commission from the Royal Ballet was ultimately dropped, and the dancer/choreographer sustained a serious knee injury, which necessitated the cancellation of a ten-year retrospective in 1995. In early 1997, however, Clark was able to return to the studio, and was awarded a Wingate Scholarship to take a film course in New York. His long-term interest and involvement in video and filmmaking (evidenced in his collaboration with Charles Atlas) made this a logical next step for his further development as a creative artist.

His return to choreography after battling with not only injury but also drug addiction was, in some critics' view, a little tentative, and a number of writers suggested that Clark should focus more firmly on where his skills lie, and let go of 'juvenile detritus', as Luke Jennings describes the combination of 'unremitting rock and punk' music and costumes that are 'well past their shock-by date' in *OH MY GODDESS* (2003).[11] Jennings also, however, exhorts Clark to 'trust his choreographic instincts, which are fine and true', and this is a sentiment echoed by several other critics since his return to the stage in the late 1990s. However, although Clark's attachment to certain music, design and themes (which seem destined to irritate at least half of the critical community) remained strong in some instances, it is also the case that the very disjunctive combination that he has favoured continues to challenge pre-conceptions about dance and our response to it. As Jenny Gilbert remarked in relation to *Before and After: The Fall* (2001), 'Juxtaposing beauty with ugliness – a string of serenely perfect attitudes next to hideous plastic fried-egg props – makes you see each with different eyes'.[12]

The return to two Stravinsky works (*O* and *Mmm...*), and the choreographing of a third (*I Do*, 2007, based on *Les Noces*) to complete Clark's Stravinsky Project, presented an opportunity to reconsider Clark's achievement overall and his position in relation to the ballet tradition that nurtured him. Through Clark's deep mining of the potential of ballet combined with his own lived context, he offers new insights not only into familiar masterworks, into the genre of ballet itself, but also into the role of the artist in contemporary society. This trilogy may be seen as the culmination of years of work, revisiting and re-working ballets, and bringing them together in a way that announces the project of his career as a whole – the fundamental influence and significance of ballet, the inextricable connectedness to the world he lives in, his position and responsibility as a creative artist in this context. Clark's work can be seen to reflect the artistic, political and social landscape of the past 30 years, but his engagement with that landscape at the same time offers both critique and celebration, and – of course – is itself instrumental in the forming of that landscape as it shifts and changes.

Rachel Duerden

Notes

1 Catherine Wood, 'Because We Must', *ArtForum International*, 47, 1, 2008, p. 396.
2 See Clark's comments in Keith Watson, 'Time for the Tutus to Come Off', *Guardian* (Arts section), 3 May 1994.
3 Richard Glasstone, 'Michael Clark's Use of Ballet Technique', *Dance Now*, Winter 1994.
4 Alastair Macaulay, 'Michael Clark Talks!', *Dance Theatre Journal*, Autumn 1984.
5 Fiona Burnside, 'Michael Clark's O', *Dance Theatre Journal*, Autumn 1994.
6 Clark quoted by D. Watts, 'An Impure Queer in a Dickhead World', *City Life*, April 1994.
7 Ibid.
8 Jann Parry, 'Mmm... Michael Clark', *Dance Now*, Summer 1992.
9 Nadine Meisner, 'Michael Clark and Company', *Dance and Dancers*, September 1984.
10 David Hughes, 'Michael Clark's *Mmm...*', *Dance Theatre Journal*, Spring 1992.
11 Luke Jennings, 'Silver Jubilee: Dance Umbrella at 25: Michael Clark', *Dance Now*, Winter 2003/04.
12 Jenny Gilbert, 'The Michael Clark Company', *Dance Now*, Winter 2001/02.

Biographical details

Born in Aberdeen, Scotland, 2 July 1962. **Studied** Scottish dance as a child; studied with Richard Glasstone at The Royal Ballet School, London, 1975–79; also attended a Merce Cunningham summer school. **Career:** Dancer with Ballet Rambert, London, 1979–81; dancer and choreographer with Karole Armitage Company, from 1981; choreographer-in-residence, Riverside Studios, London, 1983; founder, Michael Clark and Dancers, 1984, beginning long-standing collaboration in costume design with Leigh Bowery and BodyMap; career interrupted by injury, 1995, resuming in 1998 with *current/SEE*; Artistic Associate of the Barbican, from 2005. Has choreographed for numerous companies, including Paris Opera Ballet, Groupe de Recherche Chorégraphique de l'Opéra de Paris (GRCOP), Extemporary Dance Theatre, Scottish Ballet, London Festival Ballet 2, Rambert, Phoenix Dance Theatre, English Dance Theatre, Mantis Dance Company, and Staatsballett Berlin; has also collaborated on several projects with filmmaker Charles Atlas. **Awards and honours** include Wingate Scholarship, 1997; Olivier Award, 2005.

Works

Belongings (c. 1975–79); *Surface Values* (1980); *Of a Feather, Flock* (1981, revised version, 1982); *A Wish Sandwich* (1982); *Rush* (1982); *Parts I–IV* (1983); *Sexist Crabs* (1983), *12XU* (1983), *1st Orange Segment* (1983), *Morag's Wedding* (1984);

Flippin' Eck/O Thweet Myth-tery of Life (1984); *New Puritans* (1984); *Do You Me?*
I Did (1984); *Le French Revolting* (1984); *HAIL the Classical* (1985; film version by
Charles Atlas, *Hail the New Puritans*, 1986); *Angel Food* (1985); *Not H.air* (1985);
Our Caca Phoney H Our Caca Phoney H (1985); *Drop Your Pearls and Hog it, Girl*
(1986); *Swamp* (revised version of *Do You Me?* *I Did*, 1986; film version by Charles
Atlas); *No Fire Escape in Hell* (1986; video version, 1986); *Pure Pre-Scenes* (1987);
New Gods (1987); *Because We Must* (1987, film version by Charles Atlas, 1989); *I am
Curious Orange* (1988; film version by Charles Atlas); *Rights* (1989); *Heterospective*
(1989); *Wrong* (1989); *Wrong Wrong* (1991); *Bog 3.0* (1992); *Mmm . . .* (1992); *O*
(1994); *Yet* (1998); ~ (1998); *Current/SEE* (1998); *Before and After: The Fall* (2001);
Should, Would, Can, Did (2003); *Satie Stud* (2003); *Rattle Your Jewellery* (2003);
OH MY GODDESS (2003); *Nevertheless, caviar* (2003); *Swamp* (revival, 2004); *O*
(revival, 2005); *Mmm . . .* (revival, 2006); *I Do* (2007); *Stravinsky Project* (culmination of *O*, *Mmm...*, *I Do*, 2007).

Further reading

Interviews with Alastair Macaulay, in 'Michael Clark Talks!', *Dance Theatre Journal*,
Autumn 1984; with Chris de Marigny (also interviewing Charles Atlas), in 'Hail,
the Video Dance Maker', *Dance Theatre Journal*, Summer 1986; with D. Watts, in
'An Impure Queer in a Dickhead World', *City Life*, April 1994; with Lynn Barber,
in 'Good Boy Now', *Independent on Sunday*, 7 June 1997; with Judith Mackrell in,
'Michael Clark in Focus', *Dance Theatre Journal*, 14(3), 1998; with Isabelle Graw in
'Tanzen Bis Zum Umfallen', *Texte Zur Kunst*, September 2000; with Greg Hilty
in, 'A Thousand Words: Michael Clark Talks About *Before and After: The Fall*',
Artforum International, October 2001; with Merce Cunningham in 'Dance: Pas de
Deux', *Tate: Arts and Culture*, November/December 2003; in 'Michael Clark',
DanceDanceDance, November 2005; with Alan Jackson, 'I Didn't Get Where I Am
Today Without . . .', *The Times*, 20 October 2007.

Articles: Alastair Macaulay, 'One at a Time', *Dance Theatre Journal*, Spring 1983;
Alastair Macaulay, 'Down at the Riverside', *Dancing Times*, October 1983; Chris
Savage-King, 'Maverick Makes Good', *Dance Theatre Journal*, Winter 1984; Sally
Watts, 'New British Dance', *Dancing Times*, May 1984; Nadine Meisner, 'Michael
Clark and Company', *Dance and Dancers*, September 1984; Chris Savage-King,
'Back to the Sixties with Michael Clark', *Dance Theatre Journal*, Winter 1985;
Judith Cruikshank, 'Michael Clark, Riverside Studios', *Dance and Dancers*, Novem-
ber 1985; Maureen Cleave, 'Leading Them a Dance', *Observer Magazine*, 18 May
1986; Alastair Macaulay, 'Michael Clark: The Angry Young Man with the Dispos-
able Hair', *Dance Magazine*, October 1986; Alastair Macaulay, 'Clarksville', *Dancing
Times*, November 1986; Catherine Debray, 'Michel ange et démon', *Danser*, Febru-
ary 1987; Alastair Macaulay, 'The Addict of Camp: Michael Clark, *Because We Must*',
Dancing Times, February 1988; Judith Mackrell, 'Post-modern Dance in Britain',
Dance Research, Spring 1991; Anita Finkel, 'Trying the Tempest, New *Dance Review*,
October/November 1991; Jann Parry, 'Mmm... Michael Clark', *Dance Now*, Sum-
mer 1992; David Hughes, 'Michael Clark's *Mmm...*', *Dance Theatre Journal*, Autumn
1992; Ann Nugent, 'Dream Ticket', *Dance Now*, Summer 1994; Clifford Bishop,
'Michael Clark', *Opera House*, 3 August 1994; Fiona Burnside, 'Michael Clark's
O', *Dance Theatre Journal*, Autumn 1994; Richard Glasstone, 'Michael Clark's Use

of Ballet Technique', *Dance Now*, Winter 1994; Jann Parry, 'Rites and Wrongs of an Outrageous Dancer', *Observer Review*, 15 May 1994; Richard Glasstone, 'Taramasalata and Pitta', *Dance Now*, Spring 1999; Jenny Gilbert, 'Dance Now: Flying High: Dance Umbrella 2001: The Michael Clark Company', *Dance Now*, Winter 2001–02; David Jays, 'Michael Clark and Trisha Brown', *Dancing Times*, November 2003; Luke Jennings, 'Silver Jubilee: Dance Umbrella at 25: Michael Clark', *Dance Now*, Winter 2003–04; Suzanne Cotter, 'Cross Over', *Afterall: A Journal of Art, Context & Enquiry*, 9, 2004; Catherine Wood, 'Let Me Entertain You', *Afterall: A Journal of Art, Context & Enquiry*, 9, 2004; Barbara Newman, 'Simply a Man: Michael Clark', *Dancing Times*, December 2005; Nicola Pearson, 'Always Welcome Back: The Enigmatic Michael Clark', *Dance Now*, Winter 2005/06; Ismene Brown, 'IgorFest', *Dance Now*, Winter 2006/07; Mike Dixon, 'Portrait: Michael Clark', *Ballettanz*, January 2008; Lizz Le Quesne, 'Dance Matters: Bad Boy Michael Clark Tours Again', *Dance Magazine*, June 2008, Mark Kappel, 'Michael Clark's Stravinsky Impressions', *Attitude – The Dancers' Magazine*, Summer 2008; Luke Jennings, 'Michael Clark Company', *The Observer*, 6 September 2009.

Books: Allen Robertson and Donald Hutera, *The Dance Handbook*, Harlow, Essex, 1988; Judith Mackrell, *Out of Line: The Story of British New Dance*, London, 1992; Sally Banes, *Writing Dancing in the Age of Postmodernism*, Hanover, New Hampshire, 1994; Jonathan Burrows, *Conversations with Choreographers*, London, 1998.

MERCE CUNNINGHAM

Editors' note: Merce Cunningham died in July 2009, during the final stages of preparation of this book. We have decided to include the entry on him here, despite the fact that the rest of the book covers only living choreographers – not least because of the huge importance of Cunningham's contribution to contemporary choreography.

Reminiscing at the time of his 75th birthday on a national general-interest programme shown on U.S. morning television, Merce Cunningham recalled that, according to his mother, he used to go dancing up the aisle in church as a child. With his sparse, crinkled grey hair framing his lined face like a platinum halo, the choreographer gave his anecdote with a simplicity and directness that were the hallmarks of his career.

Cunningham's smiling recall of his happy first dance steps bespoke the love he displayed over the years for both performing and creating dances. The year he turned 75 also marked the 50th anniversary of his career as a choreographer. He began his actual dance training at the age of 12 with Mrs J.W. Barrett, in what might be called all-round theatrical dancing. His entry into the then-budding world of modern dance came by way of the Cornish School in Seattle, Washington, an institute for the performing and plastic arts, where Cunningham had been studying to be an actor. There, dance teacher Bonnie Bird and composer John Cage – then a Cornish School faculty member and eventually Cunningham's lifelong partner in art and life – suggested that Cunningham study at the Bennington School of Dance, which was spending a summer at Mills College in California. Martha Graham was on its faculty and she subsequently encouraged Cunningham to move east, where he became a member of Graham's dance troupe.

Graham first cast Cunningham in the role of 'Acrobat' for *Every Soul is a Circus* (1939), next as the 'Christ Figure' in *El Penitente* (1940), and as 'March', the personification of Spring, in *Letter to the World* (1941) and 'Pegasus' in *Punch and Judy* (1941), as 'Yankee, an orator' in *Land Be Bright* (1942), as 'The Poetic Beloved' in *Deaths and Entrances* (1943) and finally as 'The Revivalist' in *Appalachian Spring* (1944). In looking back on his years with Graham, Cunningham repudiated some of her premises, taking issue with the idea 'that a particular movement meant something specific. I thought that was nonsense.' Still, when looking at Cunningham's far-reaching career, Graham's characterization of him in her dances provides a helpful guide to his various facets. The acrobatic, charismatic, aerial, American, poetic and intense lights in which Graham saw Cunningham continued to pertain to his own special qualities in his dancing and dances.

The start of Cunningham's career as choreographer can be traced back to 1944. The specific programme marking this beginning was a solo dance concert he performed on an evening shared with John Cage and his music. Characterizing the overall effect of both Cage's and Cunningham's work in this début concert as 'extreme elegance in isolation', the critic Edwin Denby noted that he had 'never seen a first recital that combined such taste, such technical finish, such originality of dance material, and so sure a manner of presentation'. However much these artistic partners and individual artists developed over the next 50-odd years (Cage died in 1992), the perceptions in Denby's initial reaction to their work remained consistently apt, particularly with regard to Cunningham.

From 1953 onwards, Cunningham had his own company of dancers on which to work. His variously constituted ensemble of male and female dancers grew more or less steadily in size over the years. In

1953, the troupe numbered five, including Cunningham; in 1994, there were 17, still including the choreographer. At his death at age 90 in 2009, the company numbered 14, equally split between men and women. Numerous alumni from the company have gone on to dancer-and-choreographer careers of their own, starting with Paul Taylor, who was part of the first five-person unit. Remy Charlip, Viola Farber, Margaret Jenkins, Douglas Dunn, Gus Solomons, Jr, Karole Armitage and Ulysses Dove – to name, but seven more of these – might be called (to borrow a term coined by Arlene Croce) 'Mercists'. But, however high the various members of Cunningham's 'flock' have soared, none has yet flown quite so high and majestically as the mentor himself, except possibly Taylor, who has flown in a non-Mercist direction very much his own.

As he began exploring ways of working dancers and dancing, Cunningham aimed for a modernism that was not anti-ballet (as was so much of modern dance at that point), but somehow beyond ballet. His desire was to combine what he saw as the pronounced use of legs in ballet technique with the strong emphasis on the upper body in modern dance methods. One of his technical advancements, related to ballet's five positions of the feet, he referred to as Five Positions of the Back: upright, curve, arch, twist and tilt.

For all those who have found the product of Cunningham's career richly poetic and deeply rewarding, there have been perhaps an equal number who have found it otherwise, to say the least. 'What would a Cunningham season be,' the Cunningham devotee's query goes, 'without a number of individuals fleeing the theatre, mid-programme or mid-dance, in semi-annoyed bewilderment?' Such may often be the knowing fan's lordly pleasure, but it does not seem to reflect Cunningham's view. 'No, no,' he once said when asked if he was interested in shocking people; rather, he elaborated, citing an aim of Cage's, 'I'm out to bring poetry into their lives'.

A good many viewers, trying to put their finger on what bothers people about Cunningham's dances, point accusingly at the unconventional sound element. Around the 1950s, this element became more and more unconventional, once the Cage (or school-of-Cage) scores Cunningham worked with stopped coming from piano or prepared-piano sources and started to come from every corner of 'left field' – that is, from nowhere predictable. Sometimes, electronic sound sources screeched or blared at high decibel levels, but it seems doubtful that the individuals put off by the works in which such sound effects occurred would find them much more agreeable had they some equally random, but more gently toned, sonic base.

Much has also been made, both for and against Cunningham, of his use of chance procedures. Like the stress on his dances' unconventional sound dimension, the focus on chance can also be overemphasized. Whatever part is played by this way of making decisions – that is, the use of forces outside the choreographer himself, such as tossed coins or a throw of the *I Ching*, to find a needed option – too much stress on it leads to thoughts of randomness, ambivalence and shapelessness. On the evidence of decades' worth of Cunningham's performing and choreography, three less Cunningham attributes are hard to imagine. As Denby noted instantly in 1944, taste, technical finish, originality and sureness of manner all intermingle undeniably in Cunningham's art.

Another of Cunningham's ways of working, while undoubtedly practised in the course of his dance making, can also be dwelt upon so narrowly as to miss the effect of the end result in the effort of recalling the process. This is the oft-noted independence of traditionally inter-dependent theatrical elements – music, décor and movement. Without doubt, this was Cunningham's way of working: neither the composer nor the designer created his part in close collaboration with the cho-reographer. But, this does not mean that a clash was desired or that Cunningham could not veto results that would obstruct the integrity of his dance. Just as he said he was not interested in shocking audiences, Cunningham said he was not actively being mysterious with his com-posers or designers: 'If they have questions, I try to answer them.' The list of visual artists who found Cunningham's way of working rewarding is long: among the most successful of these were Robert Rauschenberg, Jasper Johns, Charles Atlas, Mark Lancaster and Marsha Skinner.

Cunningham's consistency of working methods and his eager striv-ing for some unknown ('Every artist should ask,' he suggested in 1992, 'What is the point of doing what you already know?') have yielded a repertory of dances that reveals rewarding change amid singular artistic vision. In 1990, the dance-maker began devising ideas for dance move-ment on a computer, with a program called 'Life Forms', now known as 'Danceforms'. *Trackers* (1991) was partly the result of Cunningham's computer experimentation; its inclusion of unusually dense, complex grouping moves and of unfamiliar positions for the arms indicated how the choreographer was able to put computer 'choices' into the scheme of dance. After that time, all of Cunningham's dances were created, at least in part, in 'collaboration' with Danceforms.

Essentially, Cunningham's philosophy precluded any nostalgic looking back. Few of the dances we can read about in the substantial body of literature around Cunningham are available for us to see nowadays. Here and there, exceptions were made and dances have been revived. *Septet* (1953), for example, has been revived four times. The 2000s saw several major revivals: *Second Hand* (1970) in 2008; *Squaregame* (1976) in 2009 and *Ocean* (1994), a 90-minute dance performed in-the-round, was revived in full in 2005 and again, memorably, in 2008 in a granite quarry outside of St. Cloud, Minnesota. From the late 1970s, however, Cunningham was imaginatively involved with the making of moving picture dances (first on film, then mostly video tape). Therefore, Cunningham's canon has been given a 'retrospective' dimension by the presence of film and video dances, all directed in part by Cunningham himself.

Another practical and yet unconventional way in which Cunningham recalled his own rich past while showcasing the dancers of his current ensemble was to create what he called 'Events'. The first of these, *Museum Event No. 1*, was made in 1964 for a non-theatre space in a Vienna museum. After that, more than 800 'Events' were given. In them, Cunningham put together segments of older dances as a continuous programme of 'original' dancing, lasting approximately 90 minutes. For each presentation, given in a location that could not accommodate full-scale theatrical presentation, Cunningham used one-time-only music, lighting and costume design. A particularly grand example was the Beacon Events, a series of seven week-long, site-specific Events given from 2007 to 2009, each presented in a different gallery at the Dia Art Foundation galleries in Beacon, New York. It was through such performances that those who were nostalgic to remember Cunningham things past could find familiar, and often favourite, former dance moments.

Measures have been taken, especially in the wake of Cunningham's death, to preserve the past. The Merce Cunningham Dance Company (MCDC) has a very active and thorough archive department, which in 1995 was awarded a grant by the National Initiative to Preserve American Dance. Thanks to this, the Cunningham Archive has been able to collect and collate Cunningham's choreographic notes. The Company's archivist David Vaughan published *Merce Cunningham: Fifty Years* in 1999, and in 2000 Charles Atlas's documentary *Merce Cunningham: A Lifetime of Dance* was shown for the first time on Britain's BBC2. The Legacy Plan, created by Cunningham himself and put into place following his death, provides detailed and comprehensive arrangements for the company and the preservation of his vast body of work. One of its most startling features is its ultimate conclusion that, following an extended world tour, MCDC will cease to exist.[1]

The idea of a world without MCDC is, as of 2010, almost unfathomable. Age and illness did not prevent Cunningham from creating – indeed, up until the very end he said that 'he was still creating dances in his head' – and he made three works deserving of specific mention in the last decade of his life. *BIPED* (1999), which marked the first time Cunningham worked with motion-capture computer technology, could be considered his modern masterpiece, described by Alastair Macaulay as 'a brilliant success . . . projected on a gauze, in which he takes his work with the computer and incorporates it into the pieces. Virtual dancers appear alongside the flesh-and-blood performers.' *Xover* (2007) was another well-received dance, with the focal point being the extended duet at its centre. But *Xover* was also important because it again brought together Cunningham and his former collaborators, with music by Cage and décor based on a painting by Rauschenberg.

Finally, there is Cunningham's last work, *Nearly Ninety* (2009), the title referencing both its duration and his age, which had its premiere on his 90th birthday. It was praised, and the expectation of more from him was great. What else could he possibly have up his sleeve? In 2006, he had produced *eyeSpace*, using two scores, one to be played over loudspeakers and one to be heard by audience members on iPods, which they could control. In 2007, upon seeing *Xover*, one critic had commented on 'his revelation of possibilities'. With *Nearly Ninety*, Macaulay had noted that 'meanings pour from movement . . . Mr. Cunningham's dance imagination actually appears more fertile than ever before'. Just over three months later, Cunningham was dead.

Merce Cunningham's work made 'us better at watching', and doubtless also at listening and living. He was famous for his use of chance and for his experimentation with computer programs. But it should not be forgotten that his works remain, and in them is the proof: Cunningham's interest was, in the words of Anna Kisselgoff, 'first and foremost about movement'.

Robert Greskovic
(updated by Ellen Gaintner)

Note

1 Announcement in *The New York Times*, 26 January 2010, about the final tour of MCDC, which was to begin in Columbus, Ohio, and end in Manhattan on New Year's Eve 2011:

The Merce Cunningham Dance Company on Wednesday will announce its final tour, meant to give the world a last chance to view the works created by its founder, as performed by the men and women he trained. The modern-dance tour begins on Feb. 12 and wends its way through 35 cities before a final performance at the Park Avenue Armory. Cunningham, who died on July 26, had approved the tour as part of a plan to wind down the company's activities and preserve his legacy. The company will disband afterward. The tour will take it across the United States, to Montreal and then to France, England, Germany and Spain. Eighteen works will be performed, including seven pieces that have long been out of the repertory, the company said. The final New York performances will cost $10 a ticket, according to Cunningham's wishes.

Biographical details

Born Mercier Cunningham in Centralia, Washington, United States, 16 April 1919. **Died** in New York, 26 July 2009. Studied tap and ballroom dancing with Maude M. Barren; also attended George Washington University, Washington, DC; Cornish School (now Cornish Institute of Allied Arts), Seattle, Washington, 1937–39; Bennington College School of Dance summer session; Mills College, Oakland, California, 1939. **Career:** Danced with Martha Graham Dance Company, New York, 1939–45; first work as independent choreographer (with Jean Erdman and Nina Fonaroff), 1942, and fast solo concert with composer John Cage, 1944: frequently collaborated with Cage thereafter; toured Europe, with concerts in Paris, summer 1949; founder, Merce Cunningham Dance Company, at Black Mountain College, North Carolina, 1953, subsequently choreographing almost exclusively for the company, with regular composers Cage, David Tudor and with designers Robert Rauschenberg (resident designer, 1954–64), Jasper Johns (artistic adviser, 1967–80) and Mark Lancaster (artistic adviser from 1980), as well as other contemporary artists; collaborated on dance videos with Charles Atlas and Elliott Caplan; celebrated company's 50th anniversary in 2002–03 season. His work has been presented by numerous companies including New York City Ballet, American Ballet Theatre, Boston Ballet, White Oak Dance Project, Zurich Ballet and Rambert Dance Company. Major exhibitions on Cunningham and collaborators at Fundació Antoni Tàpies, Barcelona, 1999; Gallery of Fine Art, Edison College, 2002; the Museum of Contemporary Art, Miami, 2007 and the New York Public Library for the Performing Arts, New York City, 2007. **Awards and honours** include Guggenheim Fellowships, 1953 and 1959; Samuel H. Scripps/ American Dance Festival Award for Lifetime Achievement, 1982; Commandeur dans l'Ordre des Arts et des Lettres (France), 1982; Honorary Membership of American Academy and Institute of Arts and Letters, 1984; MacArthur Foundation Fellowship, 1985; Kennedy Center Honors, 1985; Olivier Award, 1985; Algur H. Meadows Award, Southern Methodist University, Dallas, Texas, 1987; Chevalier of the Légion d'honneur, France, 1989, elevated to Officier, 2004; National Medal of Arts (USA), 1990; Digital Dance Award, 1990; inducted to Hall of Fame at the National Museum of Dance, Saratoga Springs, New York, 1993; Golden Lion, Venice Biennale,1995; Nellie Cornish Arts Achievement Award, Cornish College of the Arts, 1996; Grand Prix of the Société des Auteurs et Compositeurs Dramatiques, France, 1997; Isadora Duncan Dance Award for Lifetime Achievement, 1999; Primo Internazionale 'Gion Tani', Rome, 1999; Nijinsky Special Prize,

Monaco, 2000; Dorothy and Lillian Gish Prize, 2000; named 'Living Legend' by Library of Congress, Washington, DC, 2000; Kitty Carlisle Hart Award for Outstanding Achievement in the Arts, 2002; Edward MacDowell Medal, 2003; Premium Imperiale, Tokyo, 2005.

Works

Seeds of Brightness (with Jean Erdman, 1942); *Credo in Us* (with Jean Erdman, 1942); *Ad Lib* (with Jean Erdman, 1942); *Renaissance Testimonials* (1942); *Totem Ancestor* (1942); *In the Name of Holocaust* (1943); *Shimmera* (1943); *The Wind Remains* (1943); *Triple-Paced* (1944); *Root of an Unfocus* (1944); *Tossed as it is Untroubled* (1944); *The Unavailable Memory Of* (1944); *Spontaneous Earth* (1944); *Four Walls* (1944); *Idyllic Song* (1944); *Mysterious Adventure* (1945); *Experiences* (1945); *The Encounter* (1946); *Invocation to Vahakn* (1946); *Fast Blues* (1946); *The Princess Zoodilda and her Entourage* (1946); *The Seasons* (1947); *The Open Road* (1947); *Dromenon* (1947); *Dream* (1948); *The Ruse of Medusa* (1948); *A Diversion* (1948); *Orestes* (1948); *Effusions avant l'heure* (later retitled *Games and Trio*; 1949); *Amores* (1949); *Duet* (1949); *Two Step* (1949); *Pool of Darkness* (1950); *Before Dawn* (1950); *Waltz* (1950); *Sixteen Dances for Soloist and Company of Three* (1951); *Variation* (1951); *Boy Who Wanted to Be a Bird* (1951); *Suite of Six Short Dances* (1952); *Excerpts from Symphonie pour un homme seul* (later retitled *Collage*; 1952); *Les Noces* (1952); *Theater Piece* (1952); *Suite by Chance* (1953); *Solo Suite in Space and Time* (1953); *Demonstration Piece* (1953); *Epilogue* (1953); *Banjo* (1953); *Dime a Dance* (1953); *Septet* (1953); *Untitled Solo* (1953); *Fragments* (1953); *Minutiae* (1954); *Springweather and People* (1955); *Lavish Escapade* (1956); *Galaxy* (1956); *Suite for Five in Space and Time* (later called *Suite for Five*; 1956); *Nocturnes* (1956); *Changeling* (1957); *Labyrinthian Dances* (1957); *Picnic Polka* (1957); *Collage III* (1958); *Antic Meet* (1958); *Summerspace* (1958); *Night Wandering* (1958); *From the Poems of the White Stone* (1959); *Gambit for Dancers and Orchestra* (1959); *Rune* (1959); *Theater Piece* (1960); *Crises* (1960); *Hands Birds* (1960); *Waka* (1960); *Music Walk with Dancers* (1960); Suite de Danses (for television, dir. Jean Mercure, 1961); *Aeon* (1961); *Field Dances* (1963); *Story* (1963); *Open Session* (1964); *Paired* (1964); *Winterbranch* (1964); *Cross Currents* (1964); *Variations V* (1965); *How to Pass, Kick, Fall and Run* (1965); *Place* (1966); *Scramble* (1967); *Rain Forest* (1968); *Walkaround Time* (1968); *Assemblage* (for television, dir. Richard Moore, 1968); *Canfield* (1969); *Tread* (1970); *Second Hand* (1970); *Signals* (1970); *Objects* (1970); *Loops* (1971); *Landrover* (1972); *TV Rerun* (1972); *Borst Park* (1972); *Un jour ou deux* (1973); *Exercise Piece* (1975); *Rebus* (1975); *Changing Steps* (1975); *Solo* (1975); *Sounddance* (1975); *Torse* (1976); *Squaregame* (1976); *Video Triangle* (for television, dir. Merrill Brockway, 1976); *Travelogue* (1977); *Inlets* (1977); *Fractions* (video, dir. Charles Atlas and Cunningham, 1977); *Exercise Piece I* (1978); *Exercise Piece II* (1978); *Exchange* (1978); *Tango* (1978); *Locale* (video, dir. Charles Atlas and Cunningham, 1979); *Roadrunners* (1979); *Exercise Piece III* (1980); *Duets* (1980); *Fielding Sixes* (1980); *Channels/Inserts* (video, dir. Charles Atlas and Cunningham, 1980); *10's With Shoes* (1981); *Gallopade* (1981); *Trails* (1982); *Quartet* (1982); *Coast Zone* (video, dir. Charles Atlas and Cunningham, 1983); *Roaratorio* (1983); *Inlets 2* (1983); *Pictures* (1984); *Doubles* (1984); *Phrases* (1984); *Deli Commedia* (video, directed by Elliott Caplan, 1985); *Native Green* (1985); *Arcade* (1985); *Grange Eve* (1986); *Points in Space* (video, dir. Elliott Caplan and Cunningham, 1986); *Fabrications* (1987); *Shards* (1987); *Carousal* (1987); *Eleven* (1988); *Five Stone* (1988); *Five*

Stone Wind (1988); *Cargo X* (1989); *Field and Figures* (1989); *August Place* (1989); *Inventions* (1989); *Polarity* (1990); *Neighbors* (1991); *Trackers* (1991); *Beach Birds* (1991); *Loosestrife* (1991); *Change of Address* (1992); *Enter* (1992); *Touchbase* (1992); *Doubletoss* (1993); *CRWDSPCR* (1993); *Breakers* (1994); *Ocean* (1994); *Ground Level Overlay* (1995); *Windows* (1995); *Tune In/Spin Out* (1996); *Rondo* (1996); *Scenario* (1997); *Pond Way* (1998); *BIPED* (1999); *Occasion Piece* (1999); *Interscape* (2000); *Way Station* (2001); *Loose Time* (2002); *Fluid Canvas* (2002); *Split Sides* (2003); *Views on Stage* (2004); *eyeSpace* (2006; new production, 2007); *Xover* (2007); *Nearly Ninety* (2009).

Further reading

Interviews with Arlene Croce, in *Current Biography Yearbook 1966*; with Peter Grossman, *Dance Scope*, 1970; with Elinor Rogosin, in her *The Dance Makers: Conversations with American Choreographers*, New York, 1980; with Jacqueline Lesschaeve, in *The Dancer and the Dance*, London and New York, 1985 (from the French edition of 1980); with R. Tracy in 'Bicycle in the Sky', *Ballet Review*, 20(3), 1992; with Christopher Cook, in 'Forms of Life', *Dance Now*, Summer 1997; with Donald Hutera, in *Dance Now*, Winter 2000/01; with Janet Lynn Roseman, in her *Dance Masters: Interviews with Legends of Dance*, New York, 2001.

Articles: Merce Cunningham, 'Space, Time and Dance', *trans/formation* (New York), 1952; Merce Cunningham, 'The Impermanent Art', *7 Arts* (Indian Hills, Colorado), 1955 (later in *Esthetics Contemporary*, edited by Richard Kostelanetz, Buffalo, New York, 1978); Michael Snell, 'Cunningham and the Critics', *Ballet Review*, 3(6), 1971; Jack Anderson, 'Dances about Everything and Dances about Some Things', *Ballet Review*, 5(6), 1975/76; Jill Silverman, 'Merce Cunningham on Broadway', *Performing Arts Journal*, Spring 1977; Holly Brubach, 'Cunningham Now', *Ballet Review*, 6(2), 1977/78; Stephanie Jordan, 'Freedom from the Music: Cunningham, Cage and Collaborations', *Contact*, Autumn 1979; David Vaughan, 'Merce Cunningham: Retrospect and Prospect', *Performing Arts Journal*, Winter 1979; Merce Cunningham, 'A Collaborative Process between Music and Dance', *TriQuarterly*, 54 (Evanston, Illinois), Spring 1982; Richard Kostelanetz, 'Avant-garde Establishment: Cunningham Revisited', *Dance Magazine*, July 1982; David Vaughan, 'Merce Cunningham: Origins and Influences', *Dance Theatre Journal*, Spring 1983; Robert Greskovic, 'Merce Cunningham as Sculptor', *Ballet Review*, Winter 1984; Marcia Siegel, 'Repertory in Spite of Itself', *Hudson Review*, Summer 1985; special Cunningham issue of *Dance Theatre Journal*, Summer 1985; 'The Forming of an Aesthetic: Merce Cunningham and John Cage' (discussion), *Ballet Review*, Fall 1985; David Vaughan, 'Cunningham, Cage, and James Joyce', *Dance Magazine*, October 1986; Alastair Macaulay, 'The Merce Experience', *The New Yorker*, 4 April 1988; 'Decision Making Dancers' (symposium), *Ballet Review*, Winter 1992; K. King, 'Space Dance and Galactic Matrix: An Appreciation of Merce Cunningham's Sounddance', *Chicago Review*, 37(4), 1992; Michelle Potter, 'A License to Do Anything: Robert Rauschenberg and the Merce Cunningham Dance Company', *Dance Chronicle*, 16(1), 1993; Bruce Fleming, 'Talking Merce' (conference report), *DanceView*, Spring 1994; Leslie Martin, 'Black Mountain College and Merce Cunningham in the Fifties: New Perspectives' (conference report), *Dance Research Journal*, Spring 1994; Nicole Dekle, 'Cunningham's World',

Ballet Review, Fall 1994; Lesley-Anne Sayers, 'Cunningham Revisited', *Dance Theatre Journal*, Autumn 1994; Alastair Macaulay, 'Merce Cunningham Dance Company', *Dancing Times*, December 1995; Roger Copeland, 'Fatal Abstraction, Merce Cunningham, Formalism and Identity Politics', *Dance Theatre Journal*, 14(1), 1998; Nancy Vreeland Dalva, '50 Years of Merce's Magic: The Cunningham Dance Company Has Gone Gold', *Dance Magazine*, July 2002; Joan Acocella, 'Double or Nothing', *The New Yorker*, 3 November 2003; Carolyn Brown, *et al.*, 'Four Key Discoveries: Merce Cunningham Dance Company at 50', *Theater* (Duke University), 34(2), Summer 2004; Gus Solomons, Jr, 'Move Your Feet! Merce Cunningham Technique', *Dance Magazine*, November 2007; Julie Bloom, 'An Old Mentor's New Medium', *The New York Times*, 20 January 2008; Alastair Macaulay, 'Merce Cunningham, Turning 90: Meanings Still Pour From Movement', *The New York Times*, 17 April 2009; Joan Acocella, 'Twos and Threes', *The New Yorker*, 4 May 2009; Alastair Macaulay, 'Merce Cunningham, Dance Visionary, Dies', *The New York Times*, 27 July 2009; Deborah Jowitt, 'Remembering Merce Cunningham', *The Village Voice*, 4 August 2009; Wendy Perron, 'Merce Cunningham', *Dance Magazine*, October 2009.

Books: Edwin Denby, *Looking at the Dance*, New York, 1949; Selma Jeanne Cohen (ed.), *Time to Walk in Space* (Dance Perspectives 34), New York, 1968; Merce Cunningham, *Changes: Notes on Choreography*, edited by Frances Starr, New York, 1968; Calvin Tompkins, *The Bride and the Bachelors: Five Masters of the Avant Garde*, New York, 1968; James Klosty (ed.), *Merce Cunningham*, New York, 1975; Moira Hodgson, *Quintet: Five American Dance Companies*, New York, 1976; Joseph H. Mazo, *Prime Movers: The Making of Modern Dance in America*, New York, 1977; Ann Livet (ed.), *Contemporary Dance*, New York, 1978; Marcia Siegel, *The Shapes of Change*, Boston, 1979; Cobbett Steinberg (ed.), *The Dance Anthology*, New York, 1980; Sali A. Kriegsman, *Modern Dance in America: The Bennington Years*, Boston, 1981; Arlene Croce, *Going to the Dance*, New York, 1982; Robert Coe, *Dance in America*, New York, 1985; Susan Leigh Foster, *Reading Dance: Bodies and Subjects in Contemporary Dance*, Berkeley, CA, 1986; Judy Adam (ed.), *Dancers on a Plane: Cage/Cunningham/Johns*, London, 1989; Richard Kostelanetz, (ed.), *Merce Cunningham: Dancing in Space and Time*, Pennington, New Jersey, 1992; John Cage, *John Cage: Writer*, edited by Richard Kostelanetz, New York, 1993; Janet Adshead-Lansdale (ed.), *Dance History: An Introduction*, London, 1994 (2nd edition); David Vaughan, *Merce Cunningham: Fifty Years*, ed. Melissa Harris, New York, 1997; Janet Lynn Rosmean, *Dance Masters*, London, 2001; Roger Copeland, *Merce Cunningham: The Modernizing of Modern Dance*, Boston, MA, 2004; Joyce Morgenroth (ed.), *Speaking of Dance: Twelve Contemporary Choreographers on their Craft*, New York, 2004; Merce Cunningham and David Vaughan, *Other Animals: Drawings and Journals*, New York, 2002.

SIOBHAN DAVIES

Siobhan Davies, one of Britain's leading modern dance choreographers, encapsulates in her work the contemporary dilemma between meaning and abstraction, showing her relation to the modernist tradition of strong dance values (the tradition of, for instance, Merce Cunningham and Richard Alston), while sharing in dance's more recent commitment to narrative.

In the 1980s, Davies seemed to be developing in two directions concurrently. There were works in which the pure dance values emerged strongly – like *New Galileo* (1984) for London Contemporary Dance Theatre (LCDT) and *Embarque* (1988) and *Sounding* (1989) for Rambert Dance Company – and pieces in which emotional states or progressions were more pronounced – like *Minor Characters* (1983), *Silent Partners* (1984) and *Wyoming* (1988), experiments using the intimacy of the small independent dance companies Second Stride and the Siobhan Davies Dance Company.

Yet, there was no firm borderline between these two types of her output, and in the 1990s, the boundaries became further blurred. While Davies refused to join the issue-based, politically overt tradition of the younger generation of choreographers, with its narrative-based structures, she also demonstrated the impossibility of abstraction in dance. She celebrates the fact that the most movement-led structuring devices produce resonances of meaning, and that even straightforward conventional dance moves contain feeling. Indeed, in *Wanting to Tell Stories* (1993), her starting point was to bring out the stories embedded within dance emotion itself, like the tenderness that a dancer might feel inherent in a particular dance gesture, or the joy or abandon within a dancerly jump.

Two years later, *Wild Translations* (1995) continued Davies's preoccupation with 'eloquence that parallels but is still different to that of language'. Here the expressive potential of gesture is suggestive of people in relationships rather than dictating particular events or experiences. Yet, Davies never surrenders the richness of the dance language that she has built up over the years, for the formal complexities and manipulation of movement material developed in her more abstract pieces can inform narrative and make subtle its personalities. Her conviction remains that 'dance can communicate on its own terms', and it is partly because of this commitment that her work has enjoyed a prominent position within the repertories of large established dance companies.

Davies, in any case, has always kept narrative or 'plot' extremely simple. The first of the 'narrative' works, *Then You Can Only Sing* (1978), set to the words and music of Judyth Knight, was a sequence of statements by five women, expressing aspects of individual personality and circumstance – loneliness, humour, uncertainty and confusion. It is significant that *Something to Tell* (1980) sprang from her response to the playwright Chekhov, developing out of what she perceived as his minimal plot development but extensive revelation of troubled personality. Later works developed the emotional base through gestural exploration, like *Silent Partners*, which tells of the history of a man and woman passing through a series of relationships until they meet one another in a duet of heightened passion and tenderness. But it is interesting that Davies puts forward a regular, symmetrical, formal proposition through which to develop the story, the man and woman taking 'learned' movement ideas from one encounter into the next.

Over the years, Davies has developed sophisticated techniques of cross-referencing and weaving together material. A contrapuntal complexity is evident in an especially compelling duet style, independent lines setting up their own countertensions and resolutions. There are imaginative territorial concepts within the stage space too, like the bodies resting motionless in *Make-Make* (1992), which affect the group island of action by their own stubborn lack of action. There is also the developing fluidity of her large structures – the irregular pacing and overlapping of solos, duets, ensembles – and of Davies's stage textures, involving brilliant regroupings and dissolves among clusters of dancers. These last aspects came to the fore most emphatically in big company pieces like *Embarque*, which, in its exuberant cavalcades of dancers in canon threading around each other in a path around the stage, achieved a powerful accumulation of energy.

The continuing tension between narrative and abstraction is clearly illuminated through Davies's developing vocabulary and syntax over the years. Like many other choreographers, her earliest task was to find an alternative to the Graham-based language in which she was trained. Many of the most interesting explorations she carried out using her own body. Later, she incorporated moves from technique class or from choreographers with whom she worked – for example, Robert Cohan and Richard Alston – even from ballet. But, by this time she had already established her own attitude to weight, allowing the body to yield to gravity as well as to resist it, and she had also located an unusual fluidity of motion (the turning point was 1977's *Sphinx*, in which she explored the qualities of animal movement). A new density of movement ideas developed, as she experimented with building a series of complex movement phrases as a starting point before structuring a piece through time.

In the 1980s, alongside her regular vocabulary, a new richness of gesture was introduced into her character pieces, freshly sparked off by working with Ian Spink, then her co-director of Second Stride; and there were also the 'speaking' full-body movements selected to indicate personality. By now, her work incorporated a rich dynamic and emotional range, from the gentleness and quiet (but often intense) passion of small gestures to the boldness and abandonment of whole-body motion.

The sensuality and speaking quality of Davies's style come across no more surely than in her work after her 1987 study trip to the United States: now she adopted working processes from the tradition of release and was able to work more democratically than before so that her dancers had a significant influence on the emerging vocabulary.

The new work used the principle that a private image behind the simplest movement makes it a sign, although that sign need not be developed further than a 'mood' ground. Here again is the tension between narrative and abstraction. In *Wyoming*, for instance, the dancers read the writing of Gretel Ehrlich, and there were images of a huge landscape, subtle textures of ground surface, weather conditions and the physical sensations produced by these external features. Although the inclusion of text suggests a more literal meaning, the dance concerns itself more with the play among areas of expansive space, and among intimate spaces in meetings between dancers.

Later dances continued to work from an image base, such as *Signature* (1990), where the dancers were invited to develop their own marks, and *The Glass Blew In* (1994), which developed from calligraphy, which the dancers studied as starting material. But she has continued to borrow vocabulary from external sources – the sign language of the deaf, for instance, for *Different Trains* (1990) and *Plants and Ghosts* (2002), and mimetic working hand movements for *Make-Make*. Indeed, hand gesture threads through many of her works, however subtle or fleeting.

A striking new sinuousness has characterized Davies's movement since 1988, showing a generous giving of weight as dancers fold over and around each other, with a melting of small joints into body and floor surfaces. Davies comes to rehearsal with physical ideas and structures in mind, like keys to unlock possibilities, but rarely with set material. Her approach is collaborative; her dancers regularly create their own material, dynamics and timing, and it seems that she now reaches movement images of extreme eloquence precisely because they are so deeply personal to the dancers.

At the beginning of her choreographic career, it seemed logical for Davies neither to work from music as a basis nor to integrate designs into her work. At first, she wanted her dance to establish its own rhythms and to explore rhythms based on breath- or body-timing rather than on musical phrasing or motor pulse. Once she felt secure in her own talents, she welcomed the challenge of other media. Early scores, therefore, provided primarily an atmospheric background and were created separately from the dance; several of them were tape scores. The collaborative process and musical style were typical of the rest of the LCDT repertoire in the mid-1970s. With *Then You Can Only Sing*, Davies explored, for the first time, fitting dance rhythms to sound, and since that piece she has used both commissioned and existing music, including several works by Britten.

From the mid-1980s, Davies has shown a major commitment to new music and sound scores, and she has used a series of scores by minimalist composers such as John Adams, Brian Eno and Steve Reich, although she has worked in closer collaboration with Kevin Volans, Gerald Barry, Gavin Bryars and Matteo Fargion for several recent commissions.

In the 1990s, Davies's modes of working varied, from deriving initial ideas from the music, to close give-and-take of ideas, to accommodating the score when most of the dance has been completed. She maintained certain stylistic preferences, still to allow dance to develop its own rhythm and phrasing, not to enter into a tight, regular relationship with the music, and not to use musical counts that work against the rhythms of body weight. Indeed, in parts of *White Bird Featherless* (1992), the dancers were invited to find their own points of contact with the music (an example of the creative freedoms given to her dancers). Occasionally, as seen in *Winnsboro Cotton Mill Blues* (1992) when the dancers reflected the mechanistic qualities of industrial looms, Davies has worked with, or in counterpoint to, rhythmic patterns.

Reflecting Davies's interest in continually challenging her response to sound and texture, *The Art of Touch* (1995) was set to harpsichord sonatas by Scarlatti juxtaposed with Fargion's *Sette Canzoni*. The speed and complexity of the harpsichord demanded an increased dexterity and wit from the dancers and set a feel for period, both modern and ancient, imbued with a sense of courtliness. Wild, furious and tightly structured at the start, *The Art of Touch* calmed to a more contemplative, meditative conclusion. The most recent chapter in Davies's career has seen her choreographing more experimentally with accompaniment, laying the foundations for a new way of working. For *Plants and Ghosts*, she commissioned a sound installation composition from Max Eastley, in which he drew from natural sounds and rhythms created by his own sculpture. In *Bird Song* (2004), Andy Pink provided a sound score that was a mix of fragmented sounds and music which surrounds the central section – the song of the Australian Pied Butcher bird – and from which the title is derived. The marriage between movement and sound is taken further still in Fargion's comic sound score for *Minutes*, performed as a witty counterpoint with dancer Catherine Bennett as part of *The Collection* (2009).

Davies's minimal design element in the 1970s distinguished her from most other LCDT choreographers. It was when she began to introduce narrative into her work that design became more prominent and the costumes less dancerly and more human. *Something to Tell* was an important early collaboration with the theatre designer Antony McDonald, who also contributed to later pieces, but Davies has worked most frequently with the photographer David Buckland and lighting designer Peter Mumford. A series of pieces in the 1980s used Buckland's blown-up photo images, which interrelated with the narrative content of the choreography, most provocatively in *Silent Partners*, where a landscape of presences functioned as a kind of history into which most of the dancers were finally subsumed.

Other Buckland and Mumford collaborations have offered a more abstract, geometrical concept, such as the set for *New Galileo*, which created a spatial and temporal framework for the choreography through a pair of ever-widening light beams, or the design for *Wanting to Tell Stories*, where two huge mesh screens turned and slid to reveal a range of different rooms and corridors. In *Trespass* (1996), Davies invited Buckland to design constructions as extensions to the dancers' bodies or to deliberately impose on and 'trespass' into the dancers' stage space. An even bolder design idea followed in the full-length work *Of Oil and Water* (2000), when a travelator was added as a new ingredient on stage. Real time could be momentarily abandoned as dancers were able to move back and forth across the stage as if in perpetual transit.

In the mid-1990s, Davies began to revisit selected earlier works, principally to explore ways in which setting material on different bodies, in different times, requires reworking to reproduce the original visual statement and effect. *White Man Sleeps* (1988), now regarded as a signature work, is perhaps the best known of these revivals, and it has continually evolved since its premiere. The 1997 restaging, set to the original instrumentation of Volans's music for harpsichords, viola da gamba and drums, revealed a subtle shift to a new percussive dynamic, though the expansive use of space and the fleet-footed, sinuous fluidity at the heart of the work remained. The most recent revival in 2005 is a reminder of Davies' continuing desire to investigate her own creative process.

The repertoire at the end of the 1990s was coloured by disquiet, a feeling of unrest, such as in *Bank* (1997), where movement was fragmented, angular, restless, yet pensive. This new dynamic went further in *Eighty Eight* (1998), where Davies found an urban, industrial quality in her response to the physicality of Conlon Nancarrow's score for pianola. In 1999, Davies created her first full-length work, *Wild Air*, a delicate and haunting essay in the opposing states of stillness and motion, absence and presence. Later that year, she ventured out of the theatre to make *13 Different Keys* (1999) at the Atlantis Gallery, London. This was followed by *A Stranger's Taste* (1999) for the Royal Ballet, the title reflecting well the challenge Davies found in translating her method to a very different context.

Plants and Ghosts (2002) marked a courageous step forward, not only in terms of presenting within a number of different sites and settings, each of which was allowed to infect the performance in particular ways, but also by bringing the audience into closer proximity with the dancers. Keen to break down the more usual polarized positions of audience and performer, *Plants and Ghosts* was about 'breaking moulds' and provided a new perspective on some familiar Davies devices, principally the layering of text, movement, gesture, sound and design, and the play with accumulative structures.

The theme of proximity continued in *Bird Song* (2004), which was initially performed in the round with the audience seated on four sides, thus bringing the focus inwards and reinforcing a sense of circularity. Audience members were able to see other audience members as much as dancers, providing new choices in what to view. The removal of the proscenium arch abandoned the 'them and us' relationship between performer and audience. One of the most striking aspects of *Bird Song* is the interweaving of meticulously composed movement with an emotionally charged sound score by Andy Pink and Adrian Plaut's lighting design, which together create diverse mood states.

In 2009, Davies ventured back into the art gallery to present *Minutes*, but this time to bring together dance artists, filmmakers and visual artists to explore the interface between contemporary art and dance. Set alongside art objects and installations, the piece allowed audiences wander in and around the dancers, in close proximity, contemplating the dance as they would a series of moving sculptures.

Now in her fourth decade of dance-making, Davies continues to develop her individual choreographic voice through rigorous exploration and investigation, focusing on movement itself and its ability to reveal the human condition. Initially regarded as a choreographer who made cool, intellectual and abstract work, Davies has found for some time that critics respond to the warmth, humanity and compassion that have always been at the core of her work. Still, Davies continues to focus predominantly on movement vocabulary and compositional structures rather than on overt narratives or explicit political themes. She believes that her work should enable a dancer to be 'revealed' in a movement style that is developed directly from personal history and idiosyncrasy.

Davies has shifted direction at various stages during her career, most obviously after 1981 when she developed a dual career between large and small independent companies, after 1987 in her pursuit of a more complex and tactile movement vocabulary, and since 2001 in her confident move away from traditional theatrical productions and to working with a broader range of artistic collaborators. Having reached a true distinctiveness of style, Davies has ensured her place as one of the Britain's most influential and enduring choreographers.

Stephanie Jordan and Sarah Whatley

Biographical details

Born Susan Davies in London, 18 September 1950. **Studied** at Hammersmith College of Art and Building, London, 1966–67 and with Robert Cohan, London School of Contemporary Dance, 1967–71. **Career:** Apprentice dancer at The Place (which became the London Contemporary Dance Theatre, LCDT), from 1969; danced with Ballet For All, London, 1971, and with LCDT, from 1971; also performed with Richard Alston's company, 1976–78; staged first choreography in 1970; associate choreographer for LCDT, 1974, becoming resident choreographer and member of company directorate (upon retirement as a dancer), 1983–87; founded own (part-time) company, Siobhan Davies and Dancers, 1980; joint director (with Ian Spink), Second Stride, 1981–86; founded Siobhan Davies Dance Company, 1988; company, renamed Siobhan Davies Dance, moved to new home, Siobhan Davies Studios, in 2006. Has also choreographed for Rambert Dance Company (associate choreographer, 1988–93), English National Ballet and the Royal Ballet; has worked as choreographer-in-residence and senior research fellow, Roehampton Institute, London (1995–97). **Awards and honours** include Greater London Arts Association Arts Award, 1980; Arts Award from the Fulbright

Commission, for travel and study in America, 1986–87; Digital Dance Awards, 1988, 1989, 1990, 1992; Olivier Awards, 1991, 1993, 1996; MBE, 1995; Prix d'Auteur, Bagnolet International Choreographic Competition, 1996; Prudential Award, 1996; *Evening Standard* Award, 1996; Honorary Fellowship of Trinity College of Music, 1996; South Bank Show Award, 2000; Creative Briton, 2000; CBE, 2002.

Works

Relay (1972); *Pilot* (1974); *The Calm* (1974); *Diary* (1975; with new music, 1976); *Step at a Time* (1976); *Nightwatch* (with Micha Bergese, Robert Cohan and Robert North, 1977); *Sphinx* (1977); *Then You Can Only Sing* (1978); *Celebration* (1979); *Ley Line* (1979); *Something to Tell* (1980); *Recall* (1980); *If My Complaints Could Passions Move* (1980); *Plain Song* (1981; television version, 1983); *Standing Waves* (1981); *Free Setting* (1981); *Mazurka Elegaica* (1982); *Rushes* (1982); *Carnival* (1982; television version, 1983; reworked as *Carnival of the Animals*, for Rambert Dance Company, 2009); *The Dancing Department* (1983); *Minor Characters* (1983); *New Galileo* (1984); *Silent Partners* (1984); *Bridge the Distance* (1985; television version, 1985); *The School for Lovers Danced* (1985); *The Run to Earth* (1986); *and do they do* (1986); *Red Steps* (1987); *Embarque* (1988); *White Man Sleeps* (1988; television version, 1989); *Wyoming* (1988; television version, 1989); *Sounding* (1989); *Cover Him with Grass* (1989); *Drawn Breath* (1989); *Signature* (1990); *Dancing Ledge* (1990); *Different Trains* (1990); *Arctic Heart* (1991); *Winnsboro Cotton Mill Blues* (1992); *White Bird Featherless* (1992; television version, 1995); *Make-Make* (1992); *Wanting to Tell Stories* (1993); *The Glass Blew In* (1994); *Between the National and the Bristol* (1994); *Wild Translations* (1995); *The Art of Touch* (1995); *Trespass* (1996); *Affections* (1996); *Bank* (1997); *Eighty Eight* (1998); *Wild Air* (1999); *13 Different Keys* (1999); *A Stranger's Taste* (1999); *Of Oil and Water* (2000); *Plants and Ghosts* (2002); *Bird Song* (2004); *Endangered Species* (2007, part of Cape Farewell exhibition, *The Art of Climate Change*); *In Plain Clothes* (2006); *Two Quartets* (2007); *Minutes* (part of *The Collection*, collaborative work at Ikon Eastside Gallery, 2009).

Further reading

Interviews with Chris de Marigny, *Dance Theatre Journal*, Winter 1985; in 'The Artist's View: Two Contrasting Interviews', *Dance Theatre Journal*, Autumn 1989; with Nadine Meisner, in 'Sound, Mood and Motion from the Floor', *Sunday Times* (Section 5), 8 September 1991; with Sanjoy Roy, in 'Making a Dance, *Dance Now*, Spring 1997; in Jo Butterworth and Gill Clarke (eds), *Dancemakers' Portfolio: Conversations with Choreographers*, Bretton Hall, 1998; with Richard Alston, in 'Artistic Directions', *Dance Theatre Journal*, 15(1), 1999.

Articles: Colin Nears, 'Bridging a Distance', *Dance Research*, Autumn 1987; Stephanie Jordan, 'Second Stride, The First Six Years', *Dance Theatre Journal*, Winter 1988; Stephanie Jordan, 'Siobhan Davies Company', *Dance Theatre Journal*, Spring 1989; Jann Parry, 'Watch Their Steps', *Observer Magazine*, 19 November 1989; Angela Kane, 'Siobhan Davies' (Dance Study Supplement 6), *Dancing Times*, March 1990; 'Choreographer on the Move', *Dance and Dancers*, October 1990; Allen Robertson,

'Letter from Europe', *Dance Ink*, December 1990; Helen Wallace, 'String Smiths', *Strad*, August 1991; Sophie Preston, 'Beyond Words', *Dance Now*, Winter 1992–93; Sanjoy Roy, 'From Studio to Stage', *Dance Now*, Winter 1995; Bill Bissell, 'Siobhan Davies in St Petersburg', *Dance Now*, Spring 1996; articles by John Drummond, Alan Franks, Richard Alston, Kevin Volans, David Buckland, in special Davies issue of *Dance Theatre Journal*, Spring 1996; articles by Christopher Cook, Sanjoy Roy, Sophia Preston, Stephanie Jordan, Nick Kimberley, in special Davies issue of *Dance Now*, Spring 1997; Sanjoy Roy, 'Creative Solutions . . . 25 Years of Siobhan Davies', *Animated*, Summer 1998; Sarah Whatley, 'Dance Study Aid; 'White Man Sleeps', Parts 1 and 2, *Dancing Times*, March and April 1999; Sarah Whatley, 'Siobhan Davies 50 this Year', *Dancing Times*, September 2000; Gill Clarke, 'Bank Account', *Dance Theatre Journal*, 17(4), 2001; Sanjoy Roy, 'Profile: Siobhan Davies', *Dance Theatre Journal*, 19(3), 2003; Sarah Whatley, 'Dance Identity, Authenticity and Issues of Interpretation with Specific Reference to the Choreography of Siobhan Davies', *Dance Research*, Winter 2005; Sarah Whatley, 'Archives of the Dance: Siobhan Davies Dance Online', *Dance Research*, Winter 2008.

Books: Joan W. White (ed.), *Twentieth-Century Dance in Britain. A History of Major Dance Companies in Britain*, London, 1985; Stephanie Jordan, *Striding Out: Aspects of Contemporary and New Dance in Britain*, London, 1992; Judith Mackrell, *Out of Line: The Story of British New Dance*, London, 1992; Jonathan Thrift (ed.), *Siobhan Davies in Residence: Summer Programme*, Roehampton Institute, London, 1996; Sanjoy Roy (ed.), *White Man Sleeps: Creative Insights*, London, 1999; Janet Adshead-Lansdale (ed.), *Dancing Texts: Intertextuality in Interpretation*, London, 1999; Bonnie Rowell, *Dance Umbrella: The First Twenty-One Years*, London, 2000; Rachel Duerden and Neil Fisher (eds), *Dancing off the Page: Integrating Performance, Choreography, Analysis and Notation/Documentation*, London, 2006.

JAVIER DE FRUTOS

'Maverick' is the term most often applied to Javier De Frutos by critics. In light of this, his approval of the disciplined training he received at London Contemporary Dance School in the mid-1980s is all the more interesting to note: 'it was very regimented then, thank god!'[1]

Discipline was also appreciated by De Frutos when performing with Laura Dean's company in New York: 'I was lucky to be there during her retrospective year'. Dean's work is known for its repetition of simple actions, geometric floor patterns and dervish-like spinning. De Frutos, who was fascinated by the structural 'unravelling logic' of Dean's dances, traces his own flexible use of space to her influence: constant spinning means 'you lose your sense of front and back'. His own choreographic style draws on an eclectic range of vocabulary, but he rejects notions of fusion because 'different styles can exist quite happily alongside each other; the aim is to get them to hang well together, like Laura did'.

De Frutos's first choreographic forays were solos, and music was the early catalyst for these. Although a novice, he chose complex scores, because they challenged him: 'the music dares you to do it, it provided my own laboratory to be experimental.' His ability to construct a new account from a familiar accompaniment drew public attention, as did his unusual response. For example, De Frutos used Stravinsky's *Rite of Spring* for *The Palace Does Not Forgive* (1994), but he also confounded stereotypes by presenting himself as the sacrificial virgin. This site-specific solo, commissioned by Chisenhale Dance Space, London, responded to the architecture of the K-Shed (Royal Victoria Docks) and it marked his début at Dance Umbrella.

Various trademarks were introduced in this solo that remain in evidence throughout his work. Repetition carried expressionistic interest. 'De Frutos ... travelled back and forth ... each return journey illustrating another facet of the peculiarly fey but brutish character which seemed to possess ... and govern his gestures'.[2] He acknowledged the dance heritage and made strong use of parody, teasing the audience 'with the imagery of a swan-armed Pavlova, a contracting Graham, and a Bausch minimalist'.[3] Nudity and the sense of irony with which this was undertaken were also significant. De Frutos lifted up the skirt of his gold lurex dress to flash at the spectators, 'carefully directing himself at each section of the audience, as if the gesture was intended to destroy the myth of dance's sacred cows'.[4]

To assume, however, that De Frutos uses nudity primarily for its shock value would be to misunderstand this. He explains that *The Palace Does Not Forgive* explores 'solitude, religion, sexuality, but it wasn't a representation of those things: I was using my body as a medium for getting them out'.[5] The fleshy, raw embodiment sharpened the issues of gender and victimhood raised by the historical connotations of the music, but personal issues also infused the solo. As a Catholic-raised homosexual, De Frutos states that he was 'still having to process "that guilt that marks you for life" ... [and he] became known as a man driven to expose everything on stage'.[6] What emerges as more broadly characteristic is his critique of hypocrisy and a brutal, revelatory honesty that might be likened to self-portraiture, such as that associated with painters like Egon Schiele.

Of significance is the use of music to trigger emotions in the exploratory phase of creating movement. De Frutos explains that 'theatre is memory, I am the source of that, I am the subject I know best but the end result must be to find the right vocabulary for the work'. This is further enhanced during performances by what De Frutos terms *method dancing,* which is a 'way to describe how immersed I get . . . on stage. It has to do with fully engaging myself with my personal experiences and finding ways to reproduce them onstage, not dissimilar to actors who practice the Method'.[7]

An unusual musicality ensures that De Frutos' work is not easily dismissed as gratuitous in its sustained exploration of nudity. In the solo *Transatlantic* (1996), for example, based on the eponymous stripper in *Gypsy,* De Frutos 'crawling across the floor, muscles quivering, to Everything's Coming Up Roses . . . somehow symbolised a deeper determination to survive . . . in a performance that cunningly mixed pathos with humour'.[8] Sly mischievousness is another characteristic, which invites audiences to see beyond shock tactics towards multi-layered meanings.

In addition to music, identity and sexuality continue to be the wellsprings of invention for De Frutos: 'I was playing with all the possibilities of being myself – extreme love, extreme fear, extreme campness, extreme childishness'.[9] This manifests itself in the need to press a theme to its limit, and *Grass* (1993) perhaps represents the epitome of this early period. The dancers in this trio, inspired by Puccini's *Madam Butterfly,* became mired in stage blood and a 'self-destructive eroticism . . . descended into an emotional hell of gruelling, flayed choreography'.[10] As De Frutos explains, method dancing ensured they performed 'to the maximum depth. The body takes the memory like a tattoo, then the head deals with it like a trigger to something else' – and because of this he felt that performing *Grass* was cathartic. Self-indulgence was avoided by having tight structures and careful research. Ideas from Greek tragedy provoked the gory staging, because 'they used blood on the walls too', although such full-on, Dionysian treatment can be difficult for audiences.

When De Frutos began creating for other companies, sexuality and identity remained uppermost as themes. *E Muoio Disperato* (1995), for Ricochet Dance Company, saw 'the cast, in short red velvet frocks, repeat the same series of kisses and embraces with different partners'.[11] An interest in exploring ballet themes and ballet music as a springboard for subversive reinterpretation also continued; for example, references to Fokine's *Dying Swan* of 1907 can be discerned in *The Hypochondriac Bird* (1998), a duet De Frutos created for his own company.

The emotional seam that De Frutos was mining took its toll. Temporarily exhausted, he immersed himself in the life and poetry of Tennessee Williams. During a two-year break, he followed some of the journeys described in Williams's diaries and 'the whole thing came alive'. Speaking to the older bartenders in New Orleans who knew Williams, for example, De Frutos felt that he was able 'to feel it closely in the body, reading with the body because I have a dancer's mind'.

On returning to the United Kingdom, where much of his career has been concentrated, De Frutos began a new phase as an itinerant choreographer. He found that having to make pieces quickly was 'a new discipline' to revel in. His work, now embraced by mainstream companies, became 'more elaborately danced, more overtly knowing in its referencing of academic steps'.[12] For example, *The Celebrated Soubrette* (2000), for Rambert Dance Company, was based on a play by Tennessee Williams about an ageing showgirl. Highly popular with audiences, this dance was remounted in 2004 for the Royal New Zealand Ballet: 'here ballet meets the bump-and-grind, in an homage to Vegas that captured the artificiality of strip and the bitchiness of backstage life . . . at the work's heart was a sad coarseness that the dancers captured pungently'.[13]

A chance meeting in 1945 between Tennessee Williams and George Balanchine in Mexico was the inspiration for De Frutos's *The Misty Frontier* (2001). This foray into ballet with dancers from the United Kingdom's Royal Ballet, as part of the Artist's Development Initiative at the Linbury Theatre, saw him (unusually now) performing a cameo role. His inclusion allowed a complex reading. He prowled around three couples, a 'black shadow, a presence subversively redolent of power teetering on the edge of vulnerability, of secret damage hidden beneath sexual flamboyance . . . [thus exposing] the complicated appeal of ballet . . . so pure and disciplined . . . so complicit with fetishism'.[14]

In 2003, De Frutos created another version of *Rite of Spring* for the Royal New Zealand Ballet. *Milagros* (2003) seemed to honour Tennessee Williams and Laura Dean. The whole cast wore long skirts: 'the women resemble yellowing Southern belles . . . the men look like whirling dervishes. They spin in a repressive carousel of coupledom, throwing each other to the floor when the rhythms speed up like a music box possessed by Satan'.[15] Sexuality and identity remained key themes, but a variety of working methods were now used. He teaches material having decided on this in advance, because 'it needs to be tight when working with new companies; then the challenge is working within this and elaborating with the dancers'. The layering of strong emotion and formal treatment was indicative of his current style: *Milagros*, nominated for an Olivier Award in 2005, presented 'a world warding off catastrophe . . . ugly standoffs and shivering revelations of desire hint at larger traumas . . . this ranks as one of the great *Rites*'.[16]

Elsa Canasta (2003), which won a Critics' Circle Dance Award, used a forgotten ballet score by Cole Porter and was De Frutos's second work for Rambert. 'Full of sly period references, echoing the violently erotic Apache dance of the music halls at one extreme and Balanchine's Apollo at the other',[17] *Elsa Canasta* illustrates that De Frutos continues to draw on dance heritage. Jean-Marc Puissant, a regular collaborator, designed a huge sweeping staircase. The dancers cascaded up and down this, driven by a 'repetitive energy that urges these bright young things towards destruction. They pause only for sex . . . [A]mid the crowd-pleasing wit and mischief lurks desolation'.[18]

With *Nopalitos* (2006), De Frutos began a two-year association with Phoenix Dance Theatre. Prior to creating this work, he stated, 'I might use Mexican music having travelled there and I'm falling in love with the idea of being Latin again which I wasn't before'. *Nopalitos* draws on his South American cultural roots and the Mexican Day of the Dead in a dance that mixes themes of seductive hedonism and riotous ceremonial. *Paseillo* (2007) and *Los Picadores* (2007), with titles drawn from bullfighting terms, continue these themes. *Los Picadores*, set to Stravinsky's *Les Noces*, illustrates that questions of sexuality and identity, and a willingness to expose these in extreme forms, remain of interest. Groups of dancers, smeared with stage blood, engaged in violent pugilistic ructions and erotic encounters which, at the same time, made reference to the stark realities in Nijinska's epic version of the ballet in 1923.

De Frutos stepped down as artistic director of Phoenix, 'by mutual consent so he can concentrate on new projects' according to the company's press release in September 2008. *Eternal Damnation to Sancho and Sanchez* (2009) demonstrates his continued commitment to exploring challenging themes. Made as part of 'In the Spirit of Diaghilev', a celebratory programme at London's Sadler's Wells Theatre, De Frutos's work drew on historical sources. Inspired by Cocteau's scenario and designs for the Ballet Russes, De Frutos presented a surreal, grotesquely proportioned Pope abusing an altar boy and a pregnant nun strangled with rosary beads. A mischievous sense of humour alleviated the violence when a neon sign, proclaiming Amuse Me, descended from above. Later, the BBC pulled *Eternal Damnation* from a television broadcast of the programme. Perhaps they wished to avoid showing it before the 9.30 p.m. watershed when children might be watching (although the content was always clear from the outset) or maybe the choreography seemed too strong a critique of the religious establishment at a time when the Catholic Church was embroiled in real-life child abuse scandals.

Strong convictions in respect of sexual politics are evident through all of De Frutos's work. Pressing a theme to its extreme sharpens his critique of hypocrisy and he does not shy away from engaging in subversive approaches. However, notoriety is not his aim: 'it's not . . . polemic, but you must put it out there. I hate work which has mere shock value or which entices or seduces me to agree with it, because it patronises the audience.'

Lorna Sanders
[This essay includes some material from
an article written for the Dancing Times, February 2006.]

Notes

1 Javier De Frutos in conversation with the author in summer 2005. All quotations unless otherwise stated are from this interview.
2 Sophie Constanti, 'Out of Chisenhale', *Dancing Times*, October 1994, p. 55.
3 Ann Nugent, 'Opening Out the Umbrella'. *Dance Now*, Winter 1994, p. 25.
4 Ibid. p.25.
5 Ibid.
6 Judith Mackrell, 'The Rite Stuff', *The Guardian*, 14 April 2004.
7 Javier De Frutos, online chat session, 23 November 2001: www.londondance.com.
8 Keith Watson, 'Solo Acts', *Dance Now*, Winter 1996/97, p. 33.
9 Mackrell (2004), op. cit.
10 Ibid.
11 Zoë Anderson, 'Dance on the Fringe', *Dancing Times*, October 1995, p. 21.
12 Mackrell (2004), op. cit.
13 Rachel Howard, 'Curious 'Rite' from New Zealand', *San Francisco Chronicle*, 6 June 2005.
14 Judith Mackrell, 'Misty Frontier', *The Guardian*, 4 December 2001.
15 Howard, op. cit.
16 Judith Mackrell, 'Royal New Zealand Ballet', *The Guardian*, 29 April 2004.
17 Judith Mackrell, 'Rambert', *The Guardian*, 27 November 2003.
18 Ibid.

Biographical details

Born in Caracas, Venezuela, 15 May 1963. **Studied** ballet and contemporary dance in Caracas, and later at London Contemporary Dance School and Merce

Cunningham School, New York; teachers included Barbara Mahler and Sara Rudner. **Career**: Performed with Laura Dean Dancers, 1988–92; appointed choreographer-in-residence at Movement Research, New York City, 1992; returned to the United Kingdom in 1994, founding Javier De Frutos Dance Company; artistic director, Phoenix Dance Theatre, 2006–08; appointed associate artist at Sadler's Wells Theatre, London, 2009; has also created works for CandoCo, Companhia Instravel, Gothenburg Ballet, Nuremberg Ballet, Rambert Dance Company, Ricochet Dance Company, Rotterdam Dance Group and Royal New Zealand Ballet. **Awards and honours** include Paul Hamlyn Award, 1995; Prix d'Auteur Bagnolet, 1996; South Bank Show Award, 1997; Arts Council of England Fellowship, 2000–02; *Time Out* Live Award, 2004; Critics Circle Award, 2005; Laurence Olivier Award, 2007.

Works

D (1990); *The Montana Affair* (1991); *J* (1991); *Trilogy + Country* (1991); *Consecration* (1991); *Almost Montana* (1993); *Meeting* (1993); *The Misty Frontier* (1993); *Hemisphere* (1993); *Jota Dolce* (1993); *Grass* (1993); *Weed* (1993); *The Golden Impossibility* (1993); *Simone and the Jacaranda Tree* (1994); *Dialogue Between* (1994); *Hemispheres* (1994); *Frasquita* (1994); *The Palace Does Not Forgive* (1994); *Gota a Gota* (1994); *Sweetie J* (1995); *E Muoio Disperato* (1995); *Mazatlan* (1995); *Meeting J* (1995); *Carnal Glory* (1996); *Out of J* (1996); *Transatlantic* (1996); *Affliction of Loneliness* (1996); *All Visitors Bring Happiness, Some by Coming Some by Going* (1997); *The Fortune Biscuit* (1998); *The Hypochondriac Bird* (1998); *The Long Road to Mazatlan* (film, 1999); *I Hastened Through My Death Scene to Catch Your Last Act* (2000); *The Celebrated Soubrette* (2000; restaged for Royal New Zealand Ballet, 2004); *Before My Heart Has Grown Dirty* (2000); *Sour Milk* (2000); *Montana's Winter* (2000); *But the Virgin was More Available* (2000); *Solitary Virgin* (2000); *Vagabondia* (film, 2000); *The Misty Frontier* (2001); *Milagros* (2003); *Wade in the Water* (2003); *Elsa Canasta* (2003); *The Saint of Lost Women* (2003); *J. Edna and Mother Tolson* (2004); *E Uno Y Medio* (2004); *Los Piadosos* (2005); *By the Heavenly Grass* (2005); *Nopalitos* (2006); *Banderillero* (2006); *Carousel* (musical, 2006); *Cabaret* (musical, 2006); *Los Picadores* (2007); *Paseillo* (2007); *Blue Roses* (2008); *Cattle Call* (2008); *Eternal Damnation to Sancho and Sanchez* (2009); *Death and the King's Horseman* (stage play, 2009); *Macbeth* (stage play, 2010).

Further reading

Interviews with Libby Snape in 'Javier de Frutos exposed', *Dance Theatre Journal*, 14(2), 1998; with Kevin Berry in 'Phoenix Dance Theatre', *Dancing Times*, October 2006.

Articles: Dawn Hathaway, 'Frames and Pictures', *Dance Now*, Autumn 1996; Michael Cominsky, 'Javier de Frutos, Purcell Room', *Dance Theatre Journal*, 13(3), 1997; Josephine Leask, 'In Bed with Violence', *Ballett International*, December 1998; Robert Penman, 'Dance on Television: A Bouquet from Javier', *Dancing Times*, March 1999; Josephine Leask, 'New Journey for Javier de Frutos', *Dance Theatre Journal*, 16(1), 2000; Lorna Sanders, 'Finding the Personal in the Mythic: Javier de Frutos', *Dancing Times*, February 2006; David Jays, 'Phoenix Dance Theatre at

Sadler's Wells', *Dancing Times*, July 2007; Jonathan Gray, 'Mixed Bill', *Dancing Times*, June 2008.

Book: Vida Midgelow, *Reworking the Ballet: Counter-Narratives and Alternative Bodies*, Abingdon, 2007.

ANNE TERESA DE KEERSMAEKER

Since the Belgian choreographer Anne Teresa De Keersmaeker began making dances, she has shown a prolific productivity for her well-praised work. De Keersmaeker has often revealed that music is her master, and over her long career she has developed various strategies in implementing music as well as choosing composers of significantly disparate genres. *Asch (I'm Tired)*, made in 1980, was her first piece, presented in Brussels. But, the spur for the beginning sections of her second and more important work, *Fase: Four Movements to Music of Steve Reich*, eventually completed in 1982, came in 1981 when she attended the Tisch School of the Arts in New York. De Keersmaeker met and worked with members of Reich's ensemble – Edmund Niemann and Nurit Tilles (piano) and Shem Guibbory (violin) – during her stay in the United States. Reich's score for *Fase* includes three duet sections for De Keersmaeker with Michèle Anne De Mey and a rare, passionate solo for the choreographer in the third section. *Fase* had its premiere in Brussels and was key to the choreographer's artistic evolution, with the music and movement minimalism providing a strong basis for future choreography. De Keersmaeker's keen rhythmic sense and intelligence in structuring complex movement patterns were realized in this compelling dance. The phrasing of Reich's pulsing music was not mirrored in her movement; rather it played against her own unique counterpoint configurations. The driving visual force and intense dramatic quality portrayed by these riveting women was a forecast of the tough expressionistic voice that was to emerge.

Fase was revived with the original cast at the Lincoln Center Festival in 1999. More than 15 years had brought maturity to the piece; not that De Mey or De Keersmaeker appeared less energetic, but the wisdom of their performance, enhanced by experience, gave this seminal work a piercing impetus. 'Piano Phase' is the first section and both women danced with fierce energy in white sleeveless dresses that hung just below the knees. Sparse vocabulary included complex pivoting patterns, in which the dancers, in a razor-shape simultaneous manner, changed their body facings towards or away from one another in a straight line, flinging their arms to shoulder height and adding more force to the turning action. In 'Come Out' they remained seated on stools in a block of light from two overhead lamps, dressed in grey trousers, pastel shirts and black high-heeled boots. Repetitive movements included violent backwards twisting of the upper body, lifting an elbow to place a hand behind an ear and pitching the torso forwards towards the knees as arms are pulled back. The angst in Reich's score was reflected in the dancers' faces and in their compulsively recurring gestures. This second section was a 14-minute scene of unresolved panic.

De Keersmaeker's solo in the third section, 'Violin Phase', displayed a seamless spectrum of expressions: mischievous, coy and enraged. Looking young and provocative in her white dress, she wrapped her arms around her body, thrust out her hip to the side, skipped and swung her legs high. At one point she lifted her skirt high above her waist as a child might. But, at the ending came a surprise. In a gamesome spirit, a major theme throughout *Fase*, the solo figure who had frolicked only minutes before suddenly ended in a taut painful posture, with eyes shut, before the lighted stage turned black.

Fase ends with 'Clapping Dance'. The duo wearing trousers lined up one behind the other at the upstage right corner. They performed light springing footwork, lifting off the floor to the tips of their shoes. The sound score was the clapping of human hands in an exciting musical round. In each previous section, the choreographer had used the stage space differently; here they travelled backwards to downstage right and returned to the starting point. The splendid performers were consistent in their intense concentration, but as in any serious gamelike play, *Fase* stopped when the time was up.

Rosas danst Rosas (1983), an intimate portrait of four women, remains a signature piece. It begins with clamouring industrial sounds and rhythmic clapping, followed by silence. The work, in five sections, starts in darkness, with the four women crouching and then coiling down flat to the floor. Quick urgent gestures alternate with long, sustained movements. The imagery suggests women who are weary and beaten down. The second section begins with careful placement of chairs and the putting on of shoes. (Chairs are frequently incorporated into De Keersmaeker's work; performers sit on them, lie on them, roll from one to another, fall off, roll and remount, stack them and carry them to new locations.) As in *Fase*, compulsively repeated gestures are a feature. They include a hand running through hair, the breast cupped with one palm, arms clenched tightly around the abdomen, both hands deep into the crotch, arms flung, clothing adjusted and the neck wrung to the furthest extent physically possible. These exaggerated naturalistic responses to life's frustrations are powerful images, which match the hard-driving percussive score. Solos are performed in the third section, accompanied by the sound of clarinets. The fourth section of turning and travelling through varying floor patterns is mesmerizing in its repetitive complexity.

De Keersmaeker's urgent and continuous patterning for this quartet is meticulously executed. As a needed relief, there are moments when the dancers seem to find a new energy, and take subtle delight in their virtuosity and in their sense of community. A dancer can move out from the group's synchronization, establish her own identity through idiosyncratic gestures, and then return to the ongoing movement phrase without losing the overall unity. Eventually, the driving music stops. The finale is short and, as in the beginning, it is in silence.

Elena's Aria (1984) was De Keersmaeker's third major work for her female ensemble, now numbering five. This piece featured the addition of classical music, including operatic arias, and cinematic images projected onto a screen. Still present were the repetitive movements and dramatic gestures of earlier work, but because of the abundance of new ingredients, the work was more obscure. There is an irony in De Keersmaeker's portrayal of women. While being shown as unhappy, lonely victims, her women also play *femmes fatales* in their short tight dresses, sexy stiletto heels and unabashed display of upper thighs. The women of Rosas are provocative and send out mixed messages.

Works that followed showed De Keersmaeker continually addressing gender issues in her own abstract communicative style. In *Verkommenes Ufer Medeamaterial Landschaft mit Argonauten* (1987), based on Heiner Müller's dramatic triptych on Medea, she used the 'Medea' characters to broaden her inspiration and expressiveness. This was a pivotal work in her use of manipulating a classic text.

She toured with 16 performers in *Ottone, Ottone* (1988), a work based on Claudio Monteverdi's opera *L'Incoronazione di Poppea*. The principal theme of *Poppea*, as the programme notes by Nikolaus Harnoncourt explained, is 'the destructive power – even in society – of Love . . . Monteverdi shows us what happens when Love has total power to rule'. The critic Alex Mallems (in *Ballet International*, February 1991), explained:

[De Keersmaeker] has chosen this work deliberately because of her affinity for both the music and the themes of the opera, but used the plot and characters rather flexibly – adding and changing character freely – slowed down music, improvised speeches in various languages and added quotations from other Rosas works.

Music of the Hungarian composer Györgi Ligeti was used for her work *Stella*, choreographed in 1990 for five women. Cultural references for this work are rich and include Kurosawa's film of *Rashomon* by Runosuke Akutagawa, *Stella* by Goethe, and the character of Stella from the play *A Streetcar Named Desire* by Tennessee Williams. Throughout her career De Keersmaeker has returned to themes of the mysteries of human behaviour, and perhaps here more poignantly reveals her ambivalence about the nature and role of the female gender. Her work in 1990 became more theatrical and her context more layered with literary and cultural references. During that same year she created *Achterland*, another piece where gender identity is a prime focus, for five women, three men and two musicians. But more interesting in this dance are the musical choices of two composers interacting and the choreographer's expanded development of her circular fall-and-rebound floor vocabulary. Doris Humphrey's classic work *Two Ecstatic Themes (Circular Descent and Pointed Ascent)*, is particularly brought to mind in this piece.

As is her practice, De Keersmaeker reconstitutes and embellishes her movement vocabulary and is not averse to recycling material or structures from previous pieces. She chose three of her favoured composers, including Thierry De Mey, for *Kynok* (1994). This was a work in three parts: *Rosa*, with music by Bartók, was reworked from the choreography in a short film by Peter Greenaway, 'Grosse Fuge'; the second part from *Erts* (1992), also reworked, had music by Beethoven and the last section entitled *Kynok* was newly choreographed. The word 'Kynok' is Russian for eye movements and is a term used by Russian *cinéma vérité* artists (to convey candid realism).

Woud (Forest, 1997) offered a large range of imagery inspired by love themes from the music of Berg, Schoenberg and Wagner. The two-and-a-half-hour work began with a lengthy film entitled *Tippeke*, choreographed and performed by De Keersmaeker. De Mey directed as well as composed the film's taped score. On a large screen, a solo figure (De Keersmaeker) wearing a dress and boots staggered through a stark forest while, periodically, a dancer attired in identical costume echoed the same movement on stage – a shadow image. In a desperate voice, De Keersmaeker repeated phrases concerning a boy named Tippeke. There were unexplained headlights, seen from the highway in the distance. Immediately following the end of the surreal film was the start of a live performance of Berg's haunting *Lyric Suite*. The music here, as in all De Keersmaeker's work, was essential to the structural frame and expressionistic themes that unfolded in layers. The male and female partnering and lifts were turbulent, intense and rich in movement material. *Woud* reintroduced the familiar spiral air turns into the floor and energetic rebounds, and the piece, exploring episodic love relationships, contained many thwarted climaxes.

The inspiration for *Rain* (2003), a 70-minute piece that saw her collaborating once again with Steve Reich, came from a novel of the same name by Kirsty Gunn, a story about a drowned child. This pure dance work made little reference to the story, but contained many strong emotionally driven passages. *Rain* opened with travelling steps and spatial patterns, which went from slow walks to runs and incorporated stillness, falls and directional changes. The most original choreography was seen in partnering for two or more dancers. Body contact in all configurations was both vivid and daring. The male–female coupling was passionate, as was much of the movement material. *Rain* was a well-matched journey for both dancers and musicians.

After an absence from performing, De Keersmaeker began dancing again in small group works. In 1999 she had created a dance-theatre piece based on the text of Heiner Müller called *Quartett*; she also choreographed and danced with Elizabeth Corbett for the production *with/for/by* in the same year, but a solo was not seen until she made *Once* in 2002. De Keersmaeker then, at 45, returned to New York City's Joyce Theater in 2005 with the American premiere of *Once*, set to the classic 1963 album *Joan Baez in Concert, Part 2*, and a bit of Bob Dylan, with projected scenes from D.W. Griffith's epic silent film *Birth of a Nation*. Baez's protest lyrics describe the disempowered and violated people of the world with some hope for the future with songs such as 'We Shall Overcome' and 'The Battle Hymn of the Republic'. De Keersmaeker demonstrated how she uses dance as a language that can illuminate and respond to the chaos and violence of the contemporary world.

The stage at the Joyce was completely exposed, with no attempt at theatrics except for subdued lighting, a chair and the Baez album jacket placed on the floor in front of a table holding a phonograph player. De Keersmaeker entered in a navy T-shirt worn over a dress with an uneven hem and long slits to allow the frequent high flinging of a leg or her long, deep lunges seen in profile. Her high heels were kicked off before walking downstage to quietly announce the name of her solo, '*Once*'. In silence, she retreated to a midpoint and began her revelatory 75-minute *tour de force*. In a parallel *demi plié* she glanced right and left, twisting and rising onto half toe to balance. Appearing to be testing her technical prowess, when ready, she moved on to a *grand plié* in a wide second position. Her mouth gestured as if attempting to speak. Several minutes into the piece, De Keersmaeker walked to the table and turned on the sound of the first of many memorable songs from the Baez recording which played without much interruption, except for the volume levels changing at the choreographer's whim. She responded to the words (projected on the rear wall) by her changes of mood and quality of movement, but she did not attempt to interpret their meaning in dance. Light skipping revealed an Isadora Duncan style of dance seen during the song 'Queen of Hearts'; her ability to create the various personae, from a girlish, gleeful youngster jumping and spinning with gusto to a downtrodden, aged woman collapsing in a crouch to the floor in grief, was remarkable. In the course of the work her costume was gradually removed, and the finishing moments, with projected battle scenes from Griffith's film on her almost nude body, were particularly poignant.

In recent years De Keersmaeker continues to be an active, creative presence. In 2008, the Brooklyn Academy of Music brought together Reich and De Keersmaeker in a special programme called *The Steve Reich Evening*, which included three works by the choreographer: 'Piano Phase', the first movement from the seminal *Fase: Four Movements*; two new (occasion) pieces, *Eight Lines* and *Four Organs*; and a rousing finale to the great score, *Drumming – Part One*. The choreography for *Eight Lines*, an octet for women, may have shown too much of the sameness as Reich's Balinese-inspired score, while *Four Organs*, for five men, made use of floor rolls, wild leaps and thrashing movement. But both new dances, which shared the twisting torso as a recurring motif, demonstrated De Keersmaeker's ingenious use of time and space. The exhilarating repeat of the duet from 'Piano Phase' served to prove that *Fase* is a work of enduring excellence.

A persistent dance maker, De Keersmaeker has a wide-ranging intellect and vision unique in European experimental dance. From her early support of Hugo De Greef (director of the Kaaitheater in Brussels) onwards, she continues to work with many of her close long-time collaborators.

Her passion for music brought an enormous range of scores to her *oeuvre*, from minimalism to her more recent interest in jazz and Indian raga. Never lacking in innovation, however, *Kassandra Speaking in Twelve Voices* (2004) was a text-driven piece with hardly any music. In Belgium and throughout Europe, Anne Teresa De Keersmaeker's presence and popularity are well established. She has a strong and fertile grounding in dance history and continues to gain global recognition as a gifted artist.

Sandra Genter

Biographical details

Born in Mechelen, Belgium, 11 June 1960. **Studied** classical ballet at the Lilian Lambert School and Maurice Béjart's Mudra School, Brussels, 1978–80; attended New York University's Dance Department, in the Tisch School of Arts, early 1980s. **Career:** Dancer in New York, early 1980s, also working with composer Steve Reich's group of musicians; returned to Belgium, 1982, then toured internationally with her work *Fase*; founder, Rosas dance company, 1983; artist-in-residence, with Rosas as resident company, at the Théâtre de la Monnaie, Brussels, from 1992; founder and director, PARTS (Performing Arts Research and Training Studios) dance course in Brussels, 1995, which replaced Mudra. Début as opera director, Théâtre de la Monnaie, 1998; has also choreographed for the Companhia Nacional de Bailado, Portugal. **Awards and honours** include New York Dance and Performance Award ('Bessie'), 1988, 1999; Grand Prix Video Danse, 1990; London Dance and Performance Award, 1991; Dance Screen Awards, 1992, 1994; Baroness for artistic merit, Belgium, 1996; Grand Prix International Video Danse, 1997; Officier dans l'Ordre des Arts et des Lettres, 2000, upgraded to Commandeur in 2008; Medal of the City of Paris, 2002; Medal of the Belgium Flemish Government, 2002.

Works

Asch (1980); *Fase: Four Movements* (1982); *Rosas danst Rosas* (1983; also film, dir. Thierry De Mey, 1997); *Elena's Aria* (1984); *Bartók/Aantekeningen* (1986); *Verkommenes Ufer Medeamaterial Landschaft mit Argonauten* (play by Heiner Müller, 1987); *Mikrokosmos* (1987); *Ottone, Ottone* (1988); *Hoppla!* (film, dir. Wolfgang Kolb, 1989); *Stella* (1990); *Achterland (Hinterland*, 1990); *Mozart/Concert Arias* (1992); *Erts* (1992); *Rosa* (film, dir. Peter Greenaway, 1992); *Kynok* (1994; includes reworkings of parts of *Erts* and *Rosa*); *Toccata* (1993); *Creation: Amor constante más allá de la muerte* (1994); *Erwartung: Verklärte Nacht* (1995); *Three Movements* (1996); *Woud (Forest*, 1997; includes film *Tippeke, Lyric Suite* and *Verklärte Nacht*); *Just Before* (1997); *Solo for Vincent* (1997); *Drumming* (1998); *The Lisbon Piece* (1998); *Quartett* (1999); *I Said I* (with her actor sister Jolentae, 1999); *with/for/by* (with Elizabeth Corbett, 1999); *In Real Time* (2000); *Rain* (2001); *Small Hands (Out of the Lie of No)* (2001); *Once* (2002); *(But if a Look Should) April Me* (2002); *Bitches Brew/Tacoma Narrows* (2003); *Desh* (2003, expanded, 2005); *Kassandra Speaking in Twelve Voices* (with her actor sister Jolente, 2004), *Raga for the Rainy Season/A Love Supreme* (2005); *D'un soir un jour* (2006); *Keeping Still* (with Ann Veronica Hanssen, 2007); *Eight Lines* (2008); *Four Organs* (2008); *Zeitung* (2008); *The Song* (2009); *3 Abschied* (with Jérôme Bel, 2010).

Further reading

Interviews with Marianne van Kerkhoven, in 'Time, Structure, Clarity', *Ballett International*, November 1987; with David Hughes, in 'Stop Making Sense', *Dance Theatre Journal*, Summer 1991; with Julia Pascal, in 'On Her Avantgarde', *Sunday Times*, 12 April 1992; with Roslyn Sulcas, in 'Space and Energy', *Dance and Dancers*, April 1992; with Marten Spangberg, in 'Organising Time and Space', *Ballett International*, June 1995.

Articles: Stephanie Jordan, 'Dance Umbrella Part 111', *Dancing Times*, January 1983; Marianne van Kerkhoven, 'The Dance of Anne Teresa De Keersmaeker', *Drama Review*, Fall 1984; Pascale Tison, 'Belgium: Between Tradition and Innovation', *Ballett International*, July/August 1986; Marianne van Kerkhoven, 'Rosas: Dance Theatre from Brussels', *Ballett International*, November 1987; Nadine Meisner, 'Anne Teresa De Keersmaeker', *Dance and Dancers*, February 1988; Alex Mallems, 'The Belgian Dance Explosion of the Eighties', *Ballett International*, February 1991; Virginia Brooks, 'Dance and Film: Changing Perspectives in a Changing World', *Ballett International*, February 1993; Leonore Welzein, 'What Men Are Moved By', *Ballet Tanz*, April 1994; Janet Adshead-Lansdale, 'Empowered Expression from Bausch and De Keersmaeker', *Dance Theatre Journal*, Winter 1995/96; Jochen Schmidt, 'Turning onto the High Road', *Ballet International*, March 1997; Nadine Meisner, 'Nadine Meisner Considers Continuity and Change in the Work of Anne Theresa de Keersmaeker', *Dance Theatre Journal*, Summer 1997; Rita Feliciano, 'Anne Teresa De Keersmaeker: A Love–Hate Affaire with Dance', *Dance Magazine*, March 1998; Helmut Pleobst, 'On Stage: Pentagrams to Spirals', *Ballett International*, October 1998; Nadine Meisner, 'Same Difference', *Dance Now*, Autumn 1999; Sandra Genter, 'Lincoln Center Festival 99', *Ballet Review*, Spring 2000; Thomas Hahn, 'Such Small Hands. . . ', *Ballett International*, October 2001; Ramsay Burt, 'Profile: Anne Teresa de Keersmaeker', *Dance Theatre Journal*, 19(4), 2003; Laura Shapiro, 'The Reich Stuff', *New York Magazine*, 1 December 2003; Sandra Genter, 'Next Wave Dance', *Ballet Review*, Winter 2004; Joan Acocella, 'Loners: What it Takes to Go Solo', *The New Yorker*, 12 December 2005; Deborah Jowitt, 'Steve Reich and Anne Teresa de Keersmaeker Get Phased', *The Village Voice*, 29 October 2008; Sandra Genter, 'The Next Wave 2008', *Ballet Review*, Summer 2009.

Books: Marianne Van Kerkhoven and Rudi Laermans, *Anne Teresa De Keersmaeker*, *Kritisch Theater Lexicon*, Brussels, 1998; E. Van Campanout *et al.* (eds), *Rosas/Anne Teresa de Keersmaeker: If and Only If Wonder*, Brussels, 2002.

PHILIPPE DECOUFLÉ

Philippe Decouflé defies classification. His video works include twenty-first century camera trickery, yet demonstrate a Dadaist sense of humour and penchant for the absurd that harks back to an earlier artistic sensibility, whereas his stage works are no less full of optical illusions, extraordinary surreal costumes and larger-than-life props. Absurd and poignant in equal measure, his dances are clever works of unbridled imagination bordering on the hallucinatory and offer affectionate glimpses of the past, from dance and art history, quoting from myriad different sources. They are also very funny.

His works are deceptive in more ways than one: they can fool people into thinking that they are nothing more than spectacle. His use of multi-media effects makes him easy to consign to the label of postmodern eclecticism without further debate. The style of presentation in a series of acts that are seemingly only loosely connected, similar in some ways to music hall turns, adds to the illusion. Yet, Decouflé poses serious questions about the nature of our interaction with art and his choreographies invariably centre on human issues, commenting on the absurdity and banality of existence. Furthermore, wherever his wild flights of imagination may take him, the dances demonstrate technical, artistic and structural control to an extreme: he refers to his 1986 piece, *Codex* for example as 'ensemble mathematics'.[1]

Born in Neuilly-sur-Seine in 1961, Decouflé studied at L'Ecole du Cirque from the age of 15 and at the Marceau Mime School, and from the age of 18 studied contemporary dance at the Centre National de Danse Contemporaine under Alwin Nikolaïs' direction. Decouflé has danced in the companies of Régine Chopinot and Karole Armitage and, alongside the influence of Nikolaïs, cites Nicholas Brothers' films and workshops with Merce Cunningham as formative experiences. This mixture of American modern and European New Dance influences is abundantly clear in his work, which typically includes elaborate Nikolaïs- or Bauhaus-inspired costumes and circus-inspired props, alongside text, mime, signing, film, theatrical effects and a disjointed Cunninghamesque movement style.

The numerous grand-scale projects with which he has been involved include multi-media shows, such as *Petites Pièces montées* (1993) and *Decodex* (1995), and stage spectacles, such as *Triton* (1990) and *Shazam!* (1998), all for his own Compagnie DCA. But, he has also been involved in projects as diverse as advertisements, numerous dance videos – the most acclaimed of which are *Codex* (1987) and *Le P'tit bal* (1994) – pop music videos; the 14th July Parade in 1989 in which the dancers wore clogs ('I like working with constraints'),[2] and the work that perhaps brought him to prominence, the opening and closing ceremonies of the XVI Winter Olympics at Albertville, in February 1992. Add to these diverse activities the orchestration of a vast parade in St Denis as part of the 2007 Rugby World Cup festivities, for which France played host, and the nomination to artistic directorship at the Crazy Horse cabaret in Paris in 2009, and we see a choreographer who is as unpredictable as he is open to new ideas and resistant to typecasting.

Decouflé founded DCA in 1983 and is typically enigmatic about the name, claiming at times that it could stand for Diversity, Cameraderie and Agility or elsewhere Decouflé's Company of Art: in short, the letters have tended to stand for something different with each new project. DCA was formed as a collective, with the dancers' individuality as important as their technical accomplishment, and members very often worked for free in the early years. The company was founded simply so that Decouflé would be eligible to enter the annual Bagnolet choreographic competition, which he won at the age of 21 for *Vague Café* (1983). Decouflé deliberately set out to make something very different to what had been seen there previously: 'I thought [Bagnolet] needed something short, something very dense which was physically very effective, very fast with four pieces of music, with four of us jumping in all directions ... a real burst of energy, and it worked'.[3] Compagnie DCA moved to La Chaufferie in 1993 at the invitation of the mayor of St Denis. Here, in a former thermo-electric station in a northern suburb of Paris, the company has offices and workshops plus a stage space complete with lighting rig and the potential to hang sets.

Decouflé's work first became available to UK audiences during the Festival of French New Wave, shown during the Dance Umbrella season in 1983. He is very much a product of the surge of freelance experimentation that took place during the 1980s in France, typified by a predilection for cinema. (The annual festival dedicated solely to video dance, which has been held every year since 1988 at the Centre Georges Pompidou, supports and partially explains this widespread enthusiasm.) Decouflé's interest in cinema, in its processes as well as in its history, together with multi-media eclecticism and a post-modern rediscovery of narrative, operates in contrast to the more formalist concerns of American post-modern dance. Decouflé is acutely aware of his French connections and often includes references to French cultural history, for example, the *guinguette* style songs in *Le P'tit bal* (1994) and *Abracadabra* (1998). However, unlike many of his contemporaries in France, Decouflé has chosen to work largely independently of the major grant system for dance and has resisted becoming a director of one of the generously supported Centres Chorégraphiques Nationales – in order, he says, to retain artistic freedom as well as freedom from the responsibilities that those appointments tend to bring.

Artistic openness in terms of inspiration, medium and collaboration seems to be the creative spur for Decouflé and he insists he is attracted to anything new. Nevertheless, Decouflé does have a tendency to rework and recycle ideas, sometimes developing a concept over a long period, perhaps spanning years. *Codex*, for example, was not only premiered as a stage work for DCA, then developed into an award-winning dance video in 1987, but also formed the basis for *Decodex*, created in July 1995 for the Festival Marseille Méditerranée. This whole stage spectacular was then reworked into a theatre production, which toured extensively throughout Europe over a period of almost two years. From this production evolved *Tricodex*, a part-dance, part-burlesque, part-circus work for Lyon Opera Ballet in 2004. All had their roots in the imaginary universe created by Italian artist and naturalist Luigi Serafini that inspired *Codex*, but *Tricodex* differed significantly in terms of its ballet company context, which gave an altogether different flavour to the work. From 2007 to 2010, the company toured extensively with three dances created prior to, or at the beginning of, this period: *Solo* from 2003; *Sombreros*, a new version of *Sombrero* (2006), and *Coeurs croisés* (2007), which explores striptease and eroticism.

Decouflé draws upon popular Western art forms and makes their disparate images coherent through the commitment of performance artists and the high energy of clubbers. But he delves beneath the surface of these elements through a fascination with language, communication and ambiguity: with how things mean in general. In *Le P'tit bal*, for example, two young people (Decouflé himself and Pascale Houbin) sit in a field full of long grass, behind a table from underneath which are produced a variety of different props. The dance includes visual and verbal puns; for example, the repeated refrain '*qui s'appelait . . .*' elicits first a telephone prop – '*qui s'appelait?*' – then a pint of milk – '*lait*'. Elements that constitute the video are inverted, so that while the two dancers sit (or occasionally stand), miming the words of the accompaniment but not otherwise leaving their places, everything else moves. The long grass that surrounds them is caught by a violent wind; a cow chews the cud; the light moves across the sky and the camera moves around the accordionist, even beneath and behind her. The production values and performance demonstrated high competence and professionalism, which contradicted the almost slapstick humour. The piece is haunting and affectionate, not least in its nostalgic reminiscence of post-war French culture.

In this dance, the features of post-modernism are fully displayed: eclecticism, irony, an obsession with semiotic analysis, the sentimentality of popular culture, plus of course the subversion of the medium. But, it also manifests an attitude to the post-modern condition, one that does not just reflect but also interrogates the disparateness of our lives in terms of the banality and profundity of our experiences, which occur in equal and equally unexpected measures. It is both reflexive and critical.

Codex demonstrates a similar humour involving the ambiguity of communication and the same commitment to the details of performance. The film includes what appear to be hieroglyphs introducing each section, together with dialogue in an unknown, probably non-existent, language and a song, again in an unrecognizable language but performed with intense emotional commitment. There are physical impediments to movement: dancers perform with fringed flippers on their feet in section one, for example. There is something about the dancers' various constraints that give them a quality of vulnerability and pathos. Their evident skills, when on display, serve to highlight this state of affairs further – as if we are glimpsing some very small but incredibly clever creatures who are struggling for survival against the laws of physics. At other times, we see strange creatures that are perfectly adapted to an alien environment. Whichever it is, it would seem that the decontextualization of the dancers is contrasted with their humanity, in a way that invokes empathy and affection. Decouflé's own movement style is unusually flexible, demonstrating his circus school training, at the same time as it is gauche and elegant in equal measures, and his face is as flexible as his body, evident in some clownish face-pulling at camera. This childish quality pervades all his dances and, juxtaposed with the sophisticated dance skills that are also evident, contributes strongly to their emotional effect.

Caramba, in 1986, was his first project with Christophe Salengro, an extraordinarily tall actor and comedian, and was a short film made on a shoestring budget with friends working for free. Other long-term collaborators who arrived at around this time are costume designer Philippe Guillotel, lighting designer Patrice Besombes and film artist and dancer Olivier Simola. Continuing the theme of 'different worlds and bizarre characters'[4] begun with *Caramba*, this team worked on *Codex*, which was very much a landmark piece for Decouflé. *Codex* the dance video, made the following year, allowed him to explore intensively the difference between stage and film, an interest that has persisted. Shortly afterwards, Decouflé and Guillotel were approached to work on the Winter Olympics ceremonies and this marked another turning point in Decouflé's career. The result had a huge impact and led to the company, as well as Decouflé himself, becoming extremely popular in France.

Decouflé's keynote style of mixing images, film and live dance began in *Shazam!* in 1998, the dance chosen by Decouflé to make his New York début during the France Moves festival in 2001. American critic Anna Kisselgoff acknowledged the formality and strength of the choreography and noted its perfect integration too with the other more spectacular elements, with dancers performing against live video, film and mirrors, without ever being swamped by them.[5] *Abracadabra*, Decouflé's 1998 dance film, continued with the same subject. An opening image of Salengro's head closes in on a yawn that reveals computer-generated creatures within the body. Shots of scientifically displayed skulls, brains and animal skeletons give way to acrobatic tumbling and various optical illusions, some computer generated and some physically generated. There are visual jokes, such as when the circus tumblers form ever more impossible feats of balance, but in amongst it all, a prolonged passage of virtuosic release-based dance forms an unexpected contrast that typifies Decouflé's tragicomic approach to his subject.

This contrast was also apparent in *Solo* in 2003. Subtitled *Le Doute m'habite* (The Doubt Within Me), with its obvious nod in the direction of Descartes, Decouflé appeared to be working on a more intimate scale – himself – but in reality was working alongside an impressive artistic and technical crew. *Solo* included the playful and intimate, with hand animals projected in silhouette contrasting with some superbly accomplished special effects: for example, a Busby Berkeley section that featured multiple reproductions of the soloist, slightly time delayed, which then morphed momentarily into an Esther Williams-style swimming sequence. Although the work was themed in terms of autobiography, including photographs of family and friends and a solo live performance of *Le P'tit bal*, it became clear that *Solo* was much more, and that despite the performer's self-deprecating comic persona, the real focus was on dance art and illusion. Decouflé's increasingly complex trickery and bizarre effects (at one point he tied up his accompanist with tape) served to draw attention to the live performance and its existence in real time and real space.

Decouflé seems to be fascinated by processes of all kinds (his own working, evolutionary change, bodily functions and personal development) and this fascination with how things work includes how dance communicates. His style involves theatrical illusion and self-deprecating mockery; however, on a more serious and profound level his dances address the problem of human ability and human frailty. Decouflé tells the story:

A childhood friend of mine had cancer and lost a leg. He was 18. In order to walk, he would bounce along on his remaining leg. I danced a duo with him. My desire to work with constraints comes from life, from chance.[6]

Decouflé's use of powerful and affecting movement vocabulary, set against the backdrop of spectacular theatrical effect, makes his droll take on the human condition all the more poignant.

Bonnie Rowell

Notes

1 Decouflé in François Roussillon (dir.), *The Planet Decouflé*, video, 1998.
2 Ibid.
3 Ibid.
4 Ibid.
5 Anna Kisselgoff, 'A Droll Illusionist Who Makes Old Tricks New', *The New York Times*, 27 April 2001.
6 Decouflé in Dominique Fretard, interview in *Le Monde*, 4 November 1993.

Biographical details

Born in Neuilly-sur-Seine, France, 22 October 1961. **Studied** at L'Ecole du Cirque, Marceau Mime School and Centre National de Danse Contemporaine. **Career**: Dancer in the companies of Régine Chopinot and Karole Armitage; founded own company, Compagnie DCA, 1983; also choreographer for the opening and closing ceremonies of the XVI Winter Olympics, Albertville, 1992, and opening ceremony of the Rugby World Cup, 2007. **Awards and honours** include First Prize for choreography, Concours de Bagnolet, 1983; Le Prix de la Qualité from Le Centre National du Cinéma, 1986; BRIT Award for Best Music Video, 1988; Silver Lion prize (for Polaroid advertisement), 1989; IMZ Dance Screen Award, 1994.

Works

La Voix des légumes (1982); *Vague Café* (1983); *Jump* (film, dir. Decouflé and Charles Atlas, 1984); *Tranche de Cake* (1984); *Le Trio épouvantable* (1984); *Caramba* (film, dir. Decouflé, 1986); *Codex* (1986; film version, 1987; reworked as *Decodex*,

1995 and *Tricodex*, 2004); *Tutti* (1987); *True Faith* (music video for New Order, 1987); *Technicolor* (1988); *You Drive Me Crazy* (music video for Fine Young Cannibals, 1988); *La Danse des sabots* (to commemorate the Bicentennial of the French Revolution, 1989); *Triton* (1990; reworked as *Triton et le petits Tritures*, 1998); *Petites Pièces montées* (1993); *Le P'tit bal* (film, 1994); *Dora, le chat qui a vécu un million de fois* (Musical, 1996); *Micheline* (1996), *Marguerite* (1997); *Shazam!* (1998); *Abracadabra* (film, dir. Decouflé, 1998); *Cyrk 13* (2001); *Iris* (2003; new version *1Iris*, 2004, *2Iris*, 2005); *Solo* (2003); *L'Autre défilé* (2006); *Sombrero* (2006; new version *Sombreros*, 2008/9); *Coeurs croisés* (2007); *Désirs* (Revue with Ali Mahdavi, Crazy Horse, Paris, 2009); *Face* (choreography for feature film, dir. Tsai Ming-Liang, 2009).

Further reading

Interviews in *Ballett International*, April 1994; with Thomas Hahn, in *Ballett International*, June 1999; with Anna Pakes, in 'Solo But Not Alone', *Dance Theatre Journal*, 20(4) 2005.

Articles: Bernadette Bonis, 'The Shaping of French Dance – A Phenomenon and Its History', *Ballett International*, August/September 1988; Stephanie Jordan, 'A Taste of Paris', *Dance and Dancers*, July 1989; Philippe Noisette, 'Decouflé's "Triton" Kaleidoscope of Phantasie', *Ballett International*, December 1990; Deidre Kelly, 'Review of Compagnie D.C.A. Théâtre de la Ville', *Dance Magazine*, April 1991; Martina Leeker, 'Ex Machina: Loosing the Body and Defying Death', *Ballett International*, June 1994; Jean-Marc Adolphe, 'Philippe Decouflé in Paris', *Ballett International*, April 1994; Roslyn Lucas, 'French Summer Festivals', *Dance Magazine*, November 1995; Keith Watson, 'Unnatural Histories', *Dance Now*, Winter 1996/97; Donald Hutera, 'Ringmaster Totally over the Big Top', *The Times*, 5 March 1997; Thomas Hahn, 'Decouflé Makes Ads Dance', *Ballett International*, March 1999; Anna Kisselgoff, 'A Droll Illusionist Who Makes Old Tricks New', *The New York Times*, 27 April 2001; Karyn Bauer, 'France Dances Through New York', *Dance Magazine*, April 2001; Doris Hering 'Dances with France', *Dance Magazine*, September 2001; Joan Acocella, 'Razzmatazz', *The New Yorker*, 10 May 2004; Ramsay Burt, 'Solo: Decouflé's Magic Isle', *Dance Magazine*, December 2004; Donald Hutera, 'Philippe Decouflé', *Dance Now*, 13(4) 2004; Sanjoy Roy, 'Dance Umbrella Curious Histories', *Dancing Times*, January 2005; Keith Watson, 'Lyon Opera Ballet Review', *Dance Now*, 14(4) 2005; Virginie Oks, 'Philippe Decouflé: The Unclassifiable Choreographer', *France-Diplomatie*, 23 March 2007; Liz Arratoon, 'Désirs', *The Stage*, 30 March 2010.

Book: Janet Adshead-Lansdale (ed.), *Dancing Texts: Intertextuality in Interpretation*, London, 1999.

MATS EK

Mats Ek is a prominent, and controversial, figure in contemporary European choreography. He has developed and established a personal choreographic style; yet his actual contribution to contemporary dance is contested, particularly when works such as the remade *Giselle* (1982) and *Swan Lake* (1987) – unanimously considered his most representative creations – are taken into account. Ek is the first European contemporary dance choreographer to have successfully revisited the masterworks of ballet history, by modifying radically the means of expression – namely the dance idiom – and updating the subject matter. His adaptations are often saluted as more accessible art forms than their antecedents in terms of style, vocabulary and content. On the other hand, some regard such translations of the nineteenth-century classics of ballet into contemporary dance as either desecration or lack of inventiveness.

In reworking ballet classics, Ek's creed is 'to render the characters alive, providing a clear description of their inner emotions and contrasts'.[1] The psychological characterization of the roles is thus enlarged; the characters' relationships and their emotional response to the development of the action are considered in greater depth. Although the transposition entails a careful process of revision and updating, the original essence and the original content of the work are neither betrayed nor altered; and as far as the music is concerned, the original score is also retained, although partly rearranged to suit the new dramatic structure. The outcome is a performance, prompted by an analytical reading of the old scenario, that aims to present the original message in an approachable way to contemporary audiences, addressing current issues. 'Clarity' is the choreographer's key word, as opposed to what he calls 'the ambiguity of the conventions and the clichés of classical ballet'.[2]

In Ek's case, however, 'clarity' should not be mistaken for simplicity. In both *Giselle* and *Swan Lake* there lies beneath an accessible, straightforward dramatic construction an intricate amalgam of social, political, cultural and literary references. This is a characteristic trait and a constant component of his choreographic productions. Political, social, racial and sexual concerns informed Ek's first three creations, *Kalfaktorn* (*The Batman*, based on Büchner's unfinished play *Woyzeck*), *St George and the Dragon* (both 1976) and *Soweto* (1977); psychological themes and gender issues played a part in both *The House of Bernarda* (based on Federico García Lorca's *The House of Bernarda Alba*, 1978) and *Antigone* (1979), long before *Giselle* and *Swan Lake*. Because of these themes, dance scholars and critics have often labelled Ek as a politically committed choreographer. The definition, however, is not entirely appropriate, for none of Ek's works can be regarded as a political manifesto. This is particularly evident in *Soweto*, inspired by the 1976 repression of a black students' revolt in Johannesburg. A little mechanical doll, representing white power, runs endlessly in a pre-designated pattern, shaking her head after witnessing the dramatic revolt, as conveyed by the dancers' stylized movements and gestures. The mechanical, repetitive movements of the doll symbolize the entrenched attitudes of the whites towards the blacks. Despite the immediacy of the theme and the metaphors, the work is imbued with a sense of detachment, as if the choreographer were merely an observer, lending a subtle, sombre irony to his vision.

Irony is a characteristic element of Ek's choreography, in which strong images and dramatic situations often contrast with brief, humorous episodes. Examples can be found in the first act of *Giselle*, wherein two male peasants dance a comic duet in front of Albrecht's fiancée, or in the many slapstick antics of the three jesters in *Swan Lake*. In the first example, the comic duet is placed within one of the most dramatic scenes before the conclusion of the act, heralded by the arrival of the aristocratic party. The dance, however, does not loosen the tension. On the contrary, it accentuates the theme of social conflict between one class and the other, as the dancers' humorous movements can be interpreted as mocking and irreverent gestures directed at the aristocrats.

Similarly, the three jesters in *Swan Lake* appear on stage whenever a dramatic situation reaches its climax, such as at the end of the lakeside scene. Their earthy antics can be seen as a reminder of reality, as opposed to Prince Siegfried's confused dream world, which reflects his uncertain sexuality. The juxtaposition heightens the sense of the principal character's introspective detachment, felt throughout the work. Human psychology, in all its varied facets, is one of Ek's more recurring preoccupations. In his works he has managed to encompass and explore virtually every possible form and variation of human relationship – man/woman, parent/child, rich/poor, white/black and society/outsider.

Ek's wider interests, for example his career as puppeteer, actor and director, have influenced the development of his choreography, especially in terms of subject matter. The significant role played by dramatic elements within the choreography can be detected in every one of his creations. Some of his works derive both their title and their subject matter explicitly from well-known masterworks of theatre history, such as Sophocles' *Antigone*, García Lorca's *The House of Bernarda Alba* and Büchner's *Woyzeck*, mentioned above. References to Shakespeare's

Hamlet are to be found in *Swan Lake*, where Siegfried is portrayed as the Danish prince and the Queen as Gertrude. Moreover, works such as *Gamla Barn* (*Old Children*, 1989), *Light Beings* (1991), respectively dedicated to his mother and to his father, or the video creation *Smoke* (1995) and its subsequent stage adaptation *Solo for Two* (1996), show clear echoes of the exploration of family issues and marital relationships that characterizes the *oeuvre* of Swedish director Ingmar Bergman, with whom Ek had worked as assistant director at the beginning of his theatre career – not to mention the fact that Anders Ek, Mats' father, had been one of Bergman's favourite actors.

Drama is also what Ek has returned to in more recent years. The provocative revisionist formulae that underscore his post-modern readings of ballet classics have found an equally successful application in Ek's stagings of Jean Racine's *Andromaque* (2002), Molière's *Don Juan* (1999) and William Shakespeare's *The Merchant of Venice* (2005). Traces of the thought-provoking approach to the choreographic rendition of García Lorca's *The House of Bernarda Alba* can easily be found in the much acclaimed and controversial staging of the Shakespeare play, in which the male role of Shylock is portrayed by an actress, Ek's sister Malin, in the same way as the character of Bernarda is portrayed by a man. Similarly, both *Andromaque* and, most notably, *Don Juan* stand out as a complex game of inter-textual solutions that echo the subplots and meta-narratives found in both *Swan Lake* and *Sleeping Beauty*. In each instance, the delivery of the text is constantly complemented and integrated by carefully planned and choreographed movements and pure dance images, which add extra layers of meaning to the acted lines.

Yet it would be erroneous to consider Ek as a theatre and dance maker who only works under the stimulus of a pre-existing narrative. Acclaimed dance works such as the amusingly provocative *She Was Black* (1995), the aforementioned *Smoke* and *Solo for Two*, as well as the more recent *Appartement* (1999) and *Fluke* (2002), do not revolve around given storylines, even though their content can hardly be deemed to be abstract, for the various situations that develop in front of the viewer always tell types of 'mini-stories', in line with Ek's own creed and thanks to a never-too-abstract choreographic idiom.

Ek's distinctive movement vocabulary derives mainly from the combination of his ballet training, his dancing experience with his mother, Birgit Cullberg, and his collaboration with the Nederlands Dans Theater. Although Ek may reject the conventional codes of ballet, his choreographic idiom clearly stems from principles of balletic technique.

Evidence can be found in the whole range of jumps and turns, in the footwork and in the constant use of basic positions (such as *plié à la seconde*), which recur in Ek's compositions. At the same time, these elements are treated from a contemporary perspective and interwoven with fundamentals of contemporary dance technique, such as freer pelvis movements and the use of the floor and of the body weight.

As mentioned, an important influence is that of his mother, Birgit Cullberg. In 1969, Ek contributed some group dances to Cullberg's *Romeo and Juliet*. That marked the beginning of a collaboration with the Cullberg Ballet, which was consolidated with his appointment as resident dancer and eventually co-director. A comparison between Cullberg's major works, such as *Miss Julie* (1950), and those by Ek reveals the extent to which her work influenced Ek's development. Although Cullberg's vocabulary is often strictly balletic, some features of her choreographic style recur as characteristic components in Ek's choreography. The attention to psychological characterization, the sensitive portrayal of human feeling, the juxtaposition of strong images and humorous episodes can be seen as typical attributes of both Cullberg's and Ek's creations.

Finally, his work as a choreographer for the Nederlands Dans Theater, which began in 1980, has contributed to the realization of Ek's choreographic style. Although Jiří Kylián's artistic formulae differ considerably from those of Mats Ek, there are some similarities between Kylián's works and those created by Ek after that date, particularly in terms of movement vocabulary. The fundamentals of what has generally become known as 'Northern European contemporary dance' have influenced, if not moulded, Ek's *œuvre*. The stylized but still dramatically expressive language of gesture, the use of the scenic space in terms of choreographic patterns, the particular sensitivity to the music and the fluidity of the movement with no apparent solution of continuity are elements of Ek's choreography that are not exclusive to his work but represent some of the common traits of that dance form. It is, however, the combination of these elements and their personal use within the choreographic texture that give a unique imprint to Ek's choreography. If Ek is considered part of the contemporary dance tradition, then his own individual dance style represents one of its most interesting expressions.

Giannandrea Poesio

Notes

1 Mats Ek in E. Vaccarino (ed.), 'Giselle di Mats Ek', *I grandi protagonisti della danza*, 13, Novara, 1993.
2 Ibid.

Biographical details

Born in Malmö, Sweden, 18 April, 1945 (son of choreographer Birgit Cullberg and actor Anders Ek). **Studied** dance with Donya Feuer on a summer course, 1962; undertook theatrical training at Marieborg Volks College; returned to dance training at Stockholm Ballet Academy, 1972. **Career**: Dance début at Riksteater, Stockholm, 1963; director at the Stockholm Puppet Theatre, 1966–73; also directed in the conventional theatre: worked at the Stockholm Stadsteater and the Dramaten (Royal Dramatic Theatre), collaborating with Ingmar Bergman and Alf Sjöberg; director at the Dramaten, 1968–72; dancer with his mother's Cullberg Ballet, 1973–74 and Düsseldorf Ballet, 1974–75, returning to Cullberg Ballet in 1975: began choreographing there, 1976, becoming joint artistic director with his mother, 1978; also dancer and choreographer, Nederlands Dans Theater, 1980–81; sole artistic director of the Cullberg Ballet (on Birgit Cullberg's retirement), 1985–93; freelance choreographer since 1993, including for television; recently writer and choreographer of theatre works for actors and dancers. Has also choreographed for the National Theatre in Oslo, Stuttgart Ballet, Hamburg Ballet, Paris Opera Ballet and for dancer Sylvie Guillem. **Awards** include Grand Prix de Video-Danse, 1988; two Emmy Awards since 1993; IMZ Dance Screen Award, 1996; Prix Italia, 1997.

Works

Kalfaktorn (1976); *St George and the Dragon* (1976); *Soweto* (1977); *The House of Bernarda Alba* (1978); *The Four Seasons* (1978); *Antigone* (1979); *Memories of Youth* (1980); *A God Disguised* (1980); *Cain and Abel* (1982); *Giselle* (1982; later staged for television); *Man and his Window* (1983); *Rite of Spring* (1984); *Grass* (1984); *På Norrbotten* (1985); *Eldstad* (1985); *Gräs* (1987); *Swan Lake* (1987); *Like Antigone* (1988); *Gamla Barn* (1989); *Over There* (1990); *Light Beings* (1991); *Journey* (1991); *Old and Door* (1991); *Carmen* (1992; staged for television, 1994); *Pointless Pastures* (1992); *Dans med nästen* (drama/dance work, 1993); *Wet Woman* (solo, 1993; video, 1995); *She Was Black* (1995); *Smoke* (video, 1995); *Sleeping Beauty* (1996); *Solo for Two* (stage version of *Smoke*, 1996); *A Sort of* (1997); *På Malta* (drama/dance work, based on Christopher Marlowe's play *The Jew of Malta*, 1996); *Johanna* (drama/dance work, 1998); *Don Juan* (drama/dance work, text by Molière, 1999); *Appartement* (1999; also for Paris Opera, 2000); *Andromaque* (drama/dance work, text by Racine, 2002); *Tulips* (2003); *Memory* (2005); *Fluke* (2002); *Aluminium* (2005); *The Merchant of Venice* (drama/dance work, text by Shakespeare, 2005); *Ställe* (2007); *The Other* (2009); *Casi-casa* (2009).

Further reading

Interviews with Ulrich Tegeder, in 'Mats Ek's *Giselle*: Create Characters, Special People', *Ballett International*, May 1983; with Rolf Garske, in 'Searching for a New

Complexity', *Ballett International*, March 1989; with Marinella Guatterini, in 'Ora pensa a *Carmen*', *Danza e danza*, February 1992; with Gunilla Jensen in *Dance Screen 99 Catalogue*, 7th International Festival for Dance in the Media, 1999; with Maggie Foyer, in 'Interview with Choreographer Mats Ek', *Dance Europe*, April/May 1999; with Hatmut Regitz, in 'Magazine: Mats Ek', *Ballett International*, January 2001.

Articles: Mark Kappel, 'Giselle in the Loony Bin', *Ballett International*, February 1983; Jochen Schmidt, 'Ballets d'action by Mats Ek, Heinz Spoerli and Uwe Scholz in Stuttgart, Basle and Zurich', *Ballett International*, March 1988; Mårten Spangberg, 'The Psychological Dimension of Classical Dance', *Ballett International*, March 1996; Horst Vollmer, 'Irreverently Classical', *Ballett International*, July 1996; Eva-Elisabeth Fischer, 'A Jewellery Box for Ballet's Gems', *Ballett International*, January 1997; Mårten Spangberg, 'Dancing on the Level?', *Ballett International*, January 1997; Gunilla Jensen, 'Mats Ek and the Cullberg Ballet', *Dancing Times*, August 1997; Emma Manning, 'A Speck of Ek', *Dance International*, Winter 1997/98; Mårten Spangberg, 'On Stage: A Family at the Stake', *Ballett International*, December 1998; Vida Midgelow, 'Reworking Texts – Inverting Bodies', *Dance Theatre Journal*, 15(2), 1999; Nadine Meisner, 'Edinburgh Festival '99: Surrealism and Sensuality', *The Independent*, 30 August 1999; Ann Nugent, 'Is Mats Ek a Great Choreographer?', *Dance Theatre Journal*, 17(3), 2001; Allan Ulrich, 'Cullberg Ballet on the Cusp', *Dance Magazine*, October 2002; Giannandrea Poesio, 'Mats Ek', *Dancing Times*, October 2003; Josephine Jewkes, 'Ställe', *Dancing Times*, October 2007.

Books: Andrée Grau and Stephanie Jordan (eds.), *Europe Dancing*, London, 2000; Stephanie Jordan (ed.), *Preservation Politics*, London, 2000; Ada D'Adamo, *Mats Ek*, Palermo, 2002; Bodil Persson, *Contemporary Dance in Sweden*, Stockholm, 2003; Vida Midgelow, *Reworking the Ballet*, Abingdon, 2007; Giannandrea Poesio, 'Elusive Narratives: Mats Ek', in Janet Lansdale (ed.), *Decentring Dancing Texts*, Basingstoke, 2008.

GARTH FAGAN

Throughout the 1970s, with quiet but absolute dedication, Garth Fagan nurtured one of the most exciting sensibilities in contemporary dance. The career of Jamaican-born Fagan followed a circuitous route: touring with Ivy Baxter's Jamaican National Dance Company while still in his teens; attending college in the United States, where he studied with the likes of José Limón, Martha Graham and Alvin Ailey; and involvement with a handful of Detroit companies as dancer, choreographer or artistic director. Soon after joining the faculty of the State University of New York, he began teaching dance in nearby Rochester to young adults more familiar with baseball pitches and inner-city streets than the stage. At about the same time, Arthur Mitchell was embarking on a similar adventure, shaping untrained urbanites into his Dance Theater of Harlem. Although Mitchell's goal had been to create classical ballet dancers who would excel particularly in the style of choreographer George Balanchine, Fagan had something else in mind. His fledgling dancers were trained in his own style, a synthesis of modern, jazz and African–Caribbean influences with just a tincture of balletic élan.

Fagan called his budding company 'The Bottom of the Bucket, But . . . Dance Theater', with a mixture of penurious apology and high hopes. By the mid-1980s the bottom had dropped out, so to speak, as Fagan's troupe, re-dubbed the Bucket Dance Theatre, was acclaimed one of the major dance discoveries of the decade. Now that they are secure in their status as a leading force in contemporary dance, the name is simply Garth Fagan Dance. Fagan is the company patriarch, working diligently to create intelligent artists capable of interpreting his choreography fully rather than dancers slavishly duplicating the master's steps. From the beginning, his dancers' education extended beyond the studio, with Fagan encouraging their exposure to other art forms and inviting group discussion on what they experienced.

As a dance maker, Fagan draws from a similarly broad background, blending the grounded, inner expressiveness and corporeal isolations of classic modern-dance pioneers like Graham, Limón and Doris Humphrey; the expansive theatrical buzz of Alvin Ailey's company; the abstract, yet dramatic, detachment of Merce Cunningham's work; the windmill arms, rubbery jumps and syncopated footwork of African dance; and the undulant rhythms propagated by Baxter and her fellow Caribbean dancer–teachers Pearl Primus and Lavinia Williams. This is not eclecticism for its own sake but an integral fusion of disparate African and European dance elements.

Fagan's ensemble bears the weight of this complex lineage with protean authority. The almost mystical air of concentration in which they dance is partly owed to Fagan's rehearsal studio set-up: he believes that mirrors promote narcissism; in their absence dancers perform more honestly, 'from the inside out'. His dancers possess a natural refinement and unadorned eloquent power; they are absorbed in the work, not in themselves. The men show vulnerability and the women resourcefulness, melting into virile grace in both sexes. They come across as real people capable of executing monumental actions, thanks to their strong backs, streamlined limbs, muscular amplitude and seemingly boneless flexibility.

Fagan's choreography allows them to shift expressively from lyrical serenity, to skittering mania and to joyful exuberance. His impish wit is evident in *Traipsing Through the May* (1987), an ensemble throwaway to Vivaldi. In total contrast is the long, dark solo, created for the company's superb 'benchmark' dancer Norwood Pennewell, that opens *Passion Distanced* (1987), a brooding, enigmatic sextet made the same year. The mood swings in Fagan's dances are aligned with the sharp changes in dynamics and shapes the dancers register. They are celebrated for their high, sometimes jagged, preparationless jumps followed by the softest of landings; for their smoothly held, crouching or asymmetrical balances and elegiac extensions; and for their prayerful stillness, disturbed by the most unexpected, unbridled bursts of energy. Fagan's ordering of these characteristic moves marks him out as a voluptuously original formalist.

The company's standard introductory piece is *Prelude* (1981), the subtitle of which, '*Discipline is Freedom*', serves as a collective philosophy. The piece is a perpetual flow of discontinuous movement, flecked with luxuriant oddities and propelled by Fagan's love of speed. It is his version of a company class-cum-showcase, climaxing with dancers fearlessly spilling, rocketing and spinning across the stage on diagonal paths. *Oatka Trail* (1979), an adagio male trio to Dvořák's moving *Cello Concerto*, is a fine example of Fagan's unpredictable musicality. Never content merely to ape rhythms, he eschews the obvious and the sentimental, preferring to get under the music's skin. The dance closes with the three men in alternately desperate opposition to, or physical harmony with, the music. *Easter Freeway Processional* (1983) weds exultant dramatic characterizations to the persistent rhythms of composer Philip Glass. *Never Top 40 (Juke Box)*, from 1985, is a kaleidoscopic suite of dances made in response to some of Fagan's favourite music (Puccini, Keith Jarrett and reggae). *Mask Mix Masque* (1986) is an intriguing and affectionate homage to pop singer Grace Jones.

The 1978 signature piece *From Before* trades in kineticized tribal ideas relevant to Fagan's background as a dark-skinned man influenced by white twentieth-century Westernism. Ten years later he made *Time After Before Place*, a piece taking those ideas to a sophisticated, primal and multi-cultural plane. A majority of Fagan's dancers are African-American, but to label the troupe 'black', he feels, is to limit its reach and narrow its possibilities. In 1995's *Earth Eagle First Circle*, Fagan celebrated the common ingredients of human cultures globally through an improbable, but exultant, fusion of the African-Latin rhythms of the late jazz pianist Don Pullen, the powerful chants, drumming and dances of native Americans, and his own varied choreography.

Griot New York (1991) is one of the best demonstrations of Fagan's belief that his work is about culture rather than folklore and ethnicity instead of race. In West African society, a *griot* is an oral historian and entertainer. Made in collaboration with jazz trumpeter-composer Wynton Marsalis and sculptor-turned-designer Martin Puryear, Fagan's *Griot* is a wise, roomy embrace of a city's heritage in all its uplifting, or ugly, glory. Exhilarating in its breadth and depth, and successfully revived in 2004, it is one of Fagan's crowning achievements.

Fagan has choreographed for theatre, most famously devising some earthy, vibrant and yet, by his standards, fairly rudimentary movement for the hit adaptation of Disney's animated feature *The Lion King* in 1997. Just over a decade earlier he had directed *Queenie Pie*, an unfinished street opera by Duke Ellington (to whom Fagan paid playful tribute in the 1983 duet *Postscript Posthumous: Ellington*).

Fagan has thrived since being embraced by Disney. As the fellowships, doctorates and awards have rolled in, he has added to his body of work. The pieces created for his company have drawn upon various cultural heritages, juxtaposed musical genres and even carried political implications in tones that have been either celebratory or tender. *Nkanyit* (a Kenyan term connoting respect for life, one's elders and each other), from 1997, was a depiction of the African-American experience that cinematically cross-cut between past and present. *Two Pieces of One: Green* (1998) fused contemporary jazz and sixteenth-century chants. Exploring different strains of Jamaican music, *Translation Transition* (2002) was described as 'a divine block party'. On a sober note, the central male duet in *Life: Dark/Light* (2005) was, in effect, an anti-war lament set to a score by jazz violinist – and Vietnam veteran – Billy Bang. *Senku* (2006), named after a Ghanian keyboard instrument, was a meditation on youth and maturity in Fagan's own hugely accomplished ensemble. Conceived as a series of inter-generational encounters, this dance melded African melodies and rhythms with Western classical structures. Interspersing effusive messages on his answering machine with solo piano pieces in *Phone Tag, Thanks & Things* (2008) yielded one of Fagan's rare missteps. He fared better in *Mudan 175/39* (2009), using six highly varied musical selections from a collective recording by Chinese-American composers as the soundtrack for an exquisite abstract ensemble dance that, with an almost magical calm, managed to dip into a deep well of human feeling.

One of Fagan's most extraordinary creations remains *Footprints Dressed in Red*, a large-cast piece *en pointe* made for the Dance Theatre of Harlem in 1986. A rigorous work of eccentric, searching intelligence, it challenged familiar classical syntax without violating it. The elimination of conventional transitions between steps, the brilliant contrasts and the novel use of space continue to justify the praise Fagan has received as an artist who 'reinvents the ordinary'.

Donald Hutera

Biographical details

Born in Kingston, Jamaica, 3 May 1940. **Studied** African–Caribbean dance with Pearl Primus and Lavinia Williams; attended Wayne State University, Detroit, majoring in psychology, graduated in 1968; took master classes from Merce Cunningham, José Limón, Lucas Hoeing, Sophie Maslow and Jean Erdman; studied in New York with Martha Graham, Mary Hinkson, Alvin Ailey and José Limón. Also received BA, Wayne State University, 1968. **Career**: Danced with Ivy Baxter and Rex Nettleford's Jamaican National Dance Company, touring Latin America, from 1957; studied and performed in Detroit, 1960–70, founding the East Side All-City Dance Company, and co-founding Detroit Contemporary Dance Company; principal soloist and choreographer for Dance Theater of Detroit, 1968; moved to New York; professor of dance at State University of New York at Brockport, from 1970 (awarded title of Distinguished Professor, 1986); founder, chief choreographer and artistic director, The Bottom of the Bucket, But. . . Dance Theatre, Rochester, New York, 1970 (becoming Bucket Dance Theatre in 1981, and Garth Fagan Dance from 1991). Has also choreographed for Dance Theatre of Harlem, Alvin Ailey American Dance Theater, José Limón Company, and Lyon Opera Ballet. **Awards and honours** include National Endowment for the Arts Choreography Fellowship, 1983; New York Dance and Performance Award ('Bessie') 1984 and 1990; Wayne State University Arts Achievement Award, 1985; New York State Governor's Arts Award, 1986; Guggenheim Fellowship, 1989; *Dance Magazine* Award, 1990; Fulbright 50th Anniversary Distinguished Fellowship, 1996; Tony Award, 1998; Jamaican Prime Minister's Award, 1998; Special Gold Musgrave Medal, Jamaica, 1998; Drama Desk Award (Outstanding Choreography), 1998; Outer Critics Circle Award, 1998; Astaire Award, 2000; inducted into American Academy of Achievement, 2001; Golden Plate Award, 2001; Samuel H. Scripps Award, 2001; Doris Duke Award, 2001; Laurence Olivier Award, 2001; Ovation Award, 2001; George Eastman Medal, University of Rochester 2003; Helpmann Award, 2004; Order of Distinction in the rank of Commander, Jamaica, 2001.

Works

Life Forms/Death Shapes (1967); *From Before* (1978); *Oatka Trail* (1979); *Of Night, Light and Melanin* (1981; video version, 1982); *Prelude: Discipline is Freedom* (1981; revised, 1983); *Touring Jubilee 1924 (Professional)* (1982); *Daylight Savings Time* (includes duet *Spring Yaounde*, 1982); *Easter Freeway Processional* (1983); *Postscript Posthumous: Ellington* (1983); *Never Top 40 (Juke Box)* (includes *Court Dance*

Contemporary, Dance Rainbow Revisited, Dance Psalmody 137, Dance Psalmody 69, Rainbow and Ballroom Romp, 1985); *Mask Mix Masque* (1986); *Footprints Dressed in Red* (1986); *Queenie Pie* (opera, 1986); *Traipsing Through the May* (1987); *Passion Distanced* (1987); *Scene Seen* (1988); *Time After Before Place* (1988); *Landscape for 10* (1988); *Telling a Story* (includes *Shorthand of Sensation, A Précis of Privilege*, 1989); *Until, By & If* (1990); *Griot New York* (includes *City Court Dance, Bayou Baroque, Spring Yaounde, Sand Painting, The Disenfranchised, Down Under, Waltz Détente, Oracabessa Sea, High Rise Riff*, 1991; revived, 2004); *Moth Dreams* (1992); *Jukebox for Alvin* (1993); *Postcards: Pressures and Possibilities* (1994); *Draft of Shadows* (1994); *Never No Lament* (1994); *Postcards: Pressures and Possibilities* (1994); *Earth Eagle First Circle* (1995); *Mix 25* (1996); *Nkanyit* (1997); *The Lion King* (stage version of Disney musical, 1997); *Two Pieces of One: Green* (1998); *Woza* (1999); *Trips and Trists* (2000); *Music of the Line/Words in the Shape* (2001); *Translation Transition* (2002); *Dancecollageforromie* (2003); *----ing* (2004); *Life: Dark/Light* (2005); *Senku* (2006); *Edge/Joy* (2007); *Phone Tag, Thanks & Things* (2008); *Mudan 175/39* (2009).

Further reading

Interviews with Francis Mason, in 'A Conversation with Garth Fagan', *Ballet Review*, Spring 1995; with Ian Bramley, in 'Animating Disney', *Dance Theatre Journal*, 15(3), 1999; with Donald Hutera, in 'Garth Fagan: Last Words', *Dance Europe*, December/January 1999/2000; in Renata Celichowska (ed.), *Seven Statements of Survival: Conversations with Dance Professionals*, New York, 2008.

Articles: Joan Acocella, 'The Bucket Dance Theatre, But No Longer at the Bottom', *Dance Magazine*, March 1986; Herbert Simpson, 'Quest for Perfection', *Ballet News*, March 1986; Kate Regan, 'Of the Bucket that Rose like a Rocket', *Connoisseur*, October 1987; Rex Nettleford, 'Afro-Caribbean Dance', *Dancing Times*, May 1990; David Vaughan, 'Two Leaders: Mark Morris & Garth Fagan', *Ballet Review*, Summer 1990; David Vaughan, 'Fagan Dance: Discipline is Freedom', *Dance Magazine*, November 1990; Tobi Tobias, 'Beauty and the Beast', *New York Magazine*, 6 January 1992; Helen Dudar, *'Griot New York* Sets the City's Rhythm to Dance', *Smithsonian*, September 1992; Susan Reiter, 'A Singular Vision', *Dance Australia*, February/March 1995; Valerie Gladstone, 'Broadway's Lion Tamer', *Dance Magazine*, June 1999; Joan Acocella, 'The Brains at the Top', *The New Yorker*, 27 December 1999; Roslyn Sulcas, '30 Years of Modern Dance', *Dance Magazine*, February 2001; Deborah Jowitt, 'It Takes Dedication', *The Village Voice*, 17 October 2006; Deborah Jowitt, 'Garth Fagan and Lar Lubovitch Celebrate Decades of Dancemaking', *The Village Voice*, 5 November 2008.

Books: Allen Robertson and Donald Hutera, *The Dance Handbook*, Harlow, Essex, 1988; Jamake Highwater, *Rituals of Experience*, New York, 1978, 3rd edition, 1992; Selma Jeanne Cohen (ed.), *Dance as a Theatre Art: Source Readings in Dance History from 1591 to the Present*, 2nd edition (new section by Katy Matheson), Princeton, NJ, 1992; Rose Eisenbaum (photographs and text) and Clive Barnes (foreword), *Masters of Movement: Portraits of America's Great Choreographers*, Washington, DC, 2004.

ELIOT FELD

Americans love to proclaim the next king even though the present one is alive and kicking. This over-eager, often foolish impulse had a reasonableness about it when applied to Eliot Feld. The occasion was the premiere of his first ballet, *Harbinger*, in May 1967, by American Ballet Theatre (ABT), the troupe Feld danced with at the time. Two months later came a second fine ballet, *At Midnight*, also presented by ABT. Feld was immediately and unanimously hailed as the genuine article, and for genuine reasons. Both ballets were absolutely fresh and original in style; yet they also fell within the historical continuum of ballet. They affirmed the cherished belief that an artist could recycle old ideas and make them new. Two other qualities in these ballets made Feld all the more impressive. They were very musical and very different in feeling from each other. *Harbinger*, set to a Prokofiev piano concerto, was youthful, frisky and optimistic. *At Midnight*, set to Mahler songs, was a darker piece, centred on an anguished Christ figure.

Within the next four years, Feld had more than a dozen ballets to his credit, most of them first rate. Although Feld's career started out as the quintessential overnight success story, he was to be no flash in the pan. He was downright prolific. Moreover, these early works enriched the diversity that his first two pieces had promised. *Intermezzo No. 1* (1969, set to Brahms) was rapturously lyrical, whereas pieces like *A Poem Forgotten* (1970) and *Theatre* (1971) had raw, expressionistic power. These latter two works incorporated strong narrative elements, whereas *Intermezzo No. 1*, *Early Songs* (1970) and many others followed a suite form of contrasting moods, conveyed primarily through movement and inspired by Feld's intelligent ear for music.

Feld's fecundity has never abandoned him. By the end of 2006, he had presented 133 works. The individualistic style that characterized his ballets 30 years earlier remains remarkably unchanged.

The unique 'look' of a Feld dancer derives from Antony Tudor. But whereas Tudor's style usually expressed a repressed state of mind, Feld's is able to sustain both happy and sad moods. What for Tudor was psychologically necessary is for Feld aesthetically pleasing.

The most characteristic aspect of this style is the *contraposto* line. Although a Feld dancer's body is not always as twisted as Hagar's in Tudor's *Pillar of Fire*, his or her head and shoulders are often posed in opposition to the trunk. In place of the traditional *effacé*, or open line of ballet, Feld favours the *croisé* line pushed into corkscrew complications. Like the Tudor torso, the Feld torso is held tightly. The body breaks at the joints; there is little bend. Feld's use of the pointe shoe is also influenced by Tudor. In more traditional ballet modes (namely by Petipa, Ashton and Balanchine), the action of the foot as it goes up and down is a focus of movement. A Feld woman sneaks up onto her toes; it's a rather shadowy business how and when she gets up there. Again, like Tudor, Feld likes to invent very convoluted and hence difficult ways of moving, yet he avoids virtuoso dancing. And when he does go in for show-off tactics, it is usually to satirize virtuosity, *à la* Tudor's *Gala Performance*.

Feld's love of *contraposto* lines, his ambivalence towards pointe work, and his hatred of audience-pleasing virtuosity are a few of the reasons why some observers wonder whether Feld can be viewed as a *bona fide* ballet choreographer. Another source of confusion is the fact that Feld never uses the traditional hierarchy of *corps de ballet* and soloists. All of his dances are conceived for an ensemble; accordingly stage centre is not necessarily the most important part of the stage. It is also true that, having studied modern dance as well as ballet, Feld has more authentic access to modern dance movement than most ballet choreographers, and it sometimes figures importantly in his ballets.

The difficulty some find in categorizing Feld's work is probably the best proof of his major achievement: Feld has indeed taken ballet in a new direction and in a profound way, not only by giving his dancers a contemporary physical profile but also by moving the very structure of a dance away from the nineteenth century and Balanchinian conventions. Radical in his avoidance of the chorus line and ballerina construct, he is nevertheless traditional in his use of music as prime motivation and in his adherence to theme and variations as the basic building blocks of his dances.

Feld's reliance on theme and variations has, in fact, grown over the years – unfortunately to detrimental effect, for what was originally a useful tool has now become an end in itself. Whereas his earlier works were concerned with evocations of atmosphere and feelings arising from music, his more recent body of work is about the number of ways a core movement can be manipulated. Feld's fascination with the mechanics of theme and variations was seen as early as 1974, in *The Real McCoy*, where the focus of this Gershwin dance was a chaise longue. In how many ways could it be made to glide? Feld counted them, all right. It was Feld's discovery of Steve Reich's modular music, however, that sealed the bond between Feld and the theme-and-variations device. Since that first Reich work in 1984, *The Grand Canon*, he has made 14 dances to Reich. In almost all his other works as well, be they set to Stephen Foster, Satie or Mozart, Feld's approach has been to squeeze as many variations as possible out of a basic theme.

An extraordinarily inventive manipulator, Feld has always found a few more variations than one would think possible – and than one would want. The passion with which he has pursued this game borders on the obsessional, which in turn makes the experience of watching a Feld ballet troubling to the mind as well as exhausting to the eye.

Quite aside from the issue of obsession, Feld's ballets are generally not the food for the conventional ballet audience. (Who knows whether he ever wanted them to be, although he did want to have artistic control over the mainstream ABT when he started choreographing for that troupe.) Feld's aversion to virtuosity and to choreography that brings individual personalities to the fore, and his preference for a more introverted, Tudoresque style over the more expansive, brilliant style embodied by Balanchine preclude his success within opera-house conditions.

Feld Ballets/NY has not toured as much as similar troupes and is virtually unknown abroad. It last visited Europe in 1986 and has never appeared in England. When it does tour it plays the college circuit rather than large theatres in big cities. And its repertoire is practically wholly by Feld, which often makes the company less appealing to audiences than the eclectic programming offered by other ballet groups.

Yet Feld is unique in the ballet world because he has survived and flourished on his own terms and without the institutional backing of an umbrella company. Instead, he has developed his own institutional protections. In 1982, he and his then executive director, Cora Cahan, raised funds to renovate a rundown movie theatre to form the superb Joyce Theater. Feld Ballets/NY was guaranteed seven weeks of theatre time in New York, an advantage few other troupes have. In 1986, Feld Ballets and ABT worked out a deal in which they were able to purchase the building in which they had been renting rehearsal space. Feld Ballets, as well as ABT, is thus in the enviable position of being landlords of prime real estate. Yet another coup has been the development of a ballet school, which opened in 1977. It is a tuition-free academy for students of New York's public school system, and has played an increasingly important role in Feld's endeavours. By the late 1980s, several members of Feld Ballets/NY were graduates of the school. In 1994, Kids Dance was launched, consisting of pre-professional students who performed in programmes designed for young audiences. In 1997, the name of the professional company was changed to Ballet Tech, with most of its roster drawn from the school. The ballets Feld made for Ballet Tech were less classically based than earlier works.

Ballet Tech's professional company disbanded in 2003 because of funding difficulties. Nevertheless, it has continued to support Feld's choreography in a more abbreviated scale. In 2004, Ballet Tech presented Mandance Project, featuring 12 new works performed by students. A similar season was presented in 2006, adding five more works to Feld's catalogue.

Without his own professional company, Feld took up a freelance life. To celebrate the centenary of New York's Juilliard School, which includes a theatre and dance department as well as its famed music conservatory, in 2005 Feld created an epic-sized piece called *Sir Isaac's Apples*, set to Reich's 80-minute *Drumming*. Mimi Lien's set, which filled the entire stage, consisted of a complex of ramps that were raked at a steep angle. Some 55 dancers moved up and down these in endless variations of speed and pattern. Of this piece, which Deborah Jowitt called 'stunning', Tobi Tobias wrote:

> Eliot Feld makes the laws of gravity visible – and thrilling. The initial configurations expand and escalate into new positions in the falling and rising, complex groupings, and varied speeds. The feat is Sisyphean; the calm, Olympian.[1]

In 2006, the New York City Ballet devoted an entire programme to Feld, the first time it had so honoured a choreographer other than Balanchine and Robbins. Of the six pieces on the bill, one was a premiere (*Etoile Polaire*, set to Philip Glass) and one a revival of Feld's *Intermezzo No. 1*, dating back to 1969. Set on a young apprentice dancer, *Etoile Polaire* left some critics nonplussed, but *New York Times* critic Jennifer Dunning hailed it as a 'tour de force', calling it 'typical of Mr Feld's most recent preoccupation with geometric line and form and repetition'.[2] As for the classic favourite, *Intermezzo No. 1*, Roslyn Sulcas expressed the view of many when she wrote, 'More than three decades later, it still offers a vision of ballet that is both slightly nostalgic and emotionally fresh'.[3]

In recent years, Feld's energies have been almost exclusively devoted to teaching and choreographing for student apprentices and children, which in many ways has given him the freedom to develop in new directions, producing dances that have been described as 'playful', 'witty' and 'smart'. In her enthusiastic review of Feld's 2008 piece for ballet pupils, *Dotty Polkas*, Jennifer Dunning wrote that Feld's dances for children 'tend to be a special pleasure because he often allows himself an expansiveness that he withholds from his adult performers'.[4] Although Feld has often frustrated critics and continued to defy classification with his choreographic pursuits, his energy, as witnessed by his prolific list of works, has not been in question. As Clive Barnes once explained, 'Feld was born as solo operator and a maverick'[5] and that continues to be true to this day.

Nancy Goldner
(Updated by the editors)

Notes

1 Tobi Tobias, 'Intelligent Design', *The Village Voice*, 11 October 2005.
2 Jennifer Dunning, *The New York Times*, 'For the City Ballet's Diamond Project, Choreographers Embrace their Inspiration', 1 May 2006.
3 Rosyln Sulcas, 'Visions Nostalgic and Utterly Fresh', *The New York Times*, 12 February 2007.
4 Jennifer Dunning, 'Challenging Dancers, Younger and Older', *The New York Times*, 11 April 2008.
5 Clive Barnes, 'Attitudes', *Dance Magazine*, September 2003.

Biographical details

Born in Brooklyn, New York, 5 July 1942. **Studied** at the High School of Performing Arts and the School of American Ballet; also trained with Richard Thomas, New York. **Career**: First professional stage appearances in off-Broadway productions, 1954, and then in Broadway musicals; also danced in Balanchine's *Nutcracker*, 1954; performed in modem dance companies under Pearl Lang, Sophie Maslow, Donald McKayle; danced with the American Ballet Theatre, 1963–68 and 1971–72, and choreographed his first work for the company in 1967; founder, director and choreographer, American Ballet Company, 1969–71; founder, Eliot Feld Ballet, 1974; remaining principal choreographer and artistic director: company renamed Feld Ballet, 1980; Feld Ballets/NY, 1990 and Ballet Tech – using only Feld-trained dancers – in 1997; established the New Ballet School to train children in 1977. Has also choreographed for Royal Winnipeg Ballet, London Festival Ballet, New York City Ballet, Royal Swedish Ballet and Royal Danish Ballet. **Awards** include *Dance Magazine* Award, 1990; Honorary Doctorate, Juilliard School, 1991.

Works*

Harbinger (1967); *At Midnight* (1967); *Meadowlark* (1968); *Intermezzo No. 1* (1969); *Cortège Burlesque* (1969); *Pagan Spring* (1969); *Early Songs* (1970); *A Poem Forgotten* (1970);

Cortège Parisien (1970); *The Consort* (1970); *Romance* (1971); *Theatre* (1971); *The Gods Amused* (1971); *A Soldier's Tale* (1971); *Eccentrique* (1971); *Winter's Court* (1972); *Jive* (1973); *Tzaddik* (1974); *Sephardic Song* (1974); *The Real McCoy* (1974); *Mazurka* (1975); *Excursions* (1975); *Impromptu* (1976); *Variations on 'America'* (1977); *A Footstep of Air* (1977); *Santa Fé Saga* (1977); *La Vida* (1978); *Danzón Cubano* (1978); *Half Time* (1978); *Papillon* (1979); *Circa* (1980); *Anatomic Balm* (1980); *Scenes for the Theater* (later retitled *Scenes*, 1980); *Song of Norway* (1981); *Play Bach* (1981); *Over the Pavement* (1982); *Straw Hearts* (1982); *Summer's Lease* (1983); *Three Dances* (1983); *The Jig is Up* (1984); *Adieu* (1984); *Moon Skate* (1984); *The Grand Canon* (1984); *Intermezzo No. 2* (1984); *Against the Sky* (1984); *Medium: Rare* (1985); *Aurora I* (1985); *Aurora II* (1985); *Echo* (1986); *Skara Brae* (1986); *Bent Planes* (1986); *Embraced Waltzes* (1987); *A Dance for Two* (1987); *Shadow's Breath* (1988); *The Unanswered Question* (1988); *Kore* (1988); *Petipa Notwithstanding* (1988); *Asia* (1988); *Love Song Waltzes* (1988); *Ah Scarlatti* (1989); *Mother Nature* (1989); *Contra Pose* (1990); *Charmed Lives* (1990); *Ion* (solo, 1991); *Fauna* (1990); *Common Ground* (1991); *Savage Glance* (1991); *Clave* (1991); *Evoe* (1991); *Endsong* (1991); *Wolfgang Strategies* (1992); *To the Naked Eye* (1992); *Hello Fancy* (1992); *Hadji* (1992); *Frets and Women* (1992); *The Relative Disposition of the Parts* (1993); *With Dew Upon Their Feet* (1993); *M. R. I* (1993); *Doo Dah Day* (1993); *Doghead and Godcatchers* (1994); *23 Skidoo* (1994); *Gnossiennes* (1994); *Ogive* (1994); *Ludwig Gambits* (1995); *Chi* (1995); *Tongue and Groove* (1995); *Meshungana Dance* (1996); *Paper Tiger* (1996); *Paen* (1996); *Shuffle* (1996); *Industry* (1996); *Yo Shakespeare* (1996); *Evening Chant* (1996); *Re:x* (1997); *Joggers* (1997); *Umbra Rumba* (1997); *Juke Box* (1997); *Yo Johann* (1997); *The Last Sonata* (1997); *On the Town* (Musical, 1997); *Simon Sez* (1998); *Cherokee Rose* (1999); *Mending* (1999); *Felix: The Ballet* (1999); *Apple Pie* (1999); *nodrog doggo* (2000); *Coup de Couperin* (2000); *Organon* (2001); *Pacific Dances* (2001); *Skandia* (2002); *Pianola: Raven* (2002); *Lincoln Portrait* (2002); *Behold the Man* (2002); *Pianola Indigo* (2002); *Mr XYZ* (2003); *French Overtures* (2003); *Yazoo* (2004); *Jawbone* (2004); *Proverb* (2004); *Gyorgy* (2004); *Hoodoo Zephyr* (2004); *Limbs* (2004); *Curious Air* (2004); *Rumors* (2004); *Backchat* (2004); *A Stair Dance* (2004); *This Dying is Killing Me* (2004); *Partootie* (2004); *Sir Isaac's Apples* (2005); *Étoile Polaire* (2006); *Ugha Bugha* (2006); *Sacred Steel* (2006); *Op. Boing* (2006); *Pursuing Odette* (2006); *Isis in Transit* (2008); *Undergo* (2008); *Dotty Polkas* (for children, 2008); *Radiance* (2009); *Dust* (2009); *The Spaghetti Ballet* (2009).

*Where published sources differ, the dates used here are those provided by Ballet Tech.

Further reading

Interviews with Charles E. France, 'A Conversation with Eliot Feld', *Ballet Review*, 3(6), 1971; in John Gruen's *The Private World of Ballet*, New York, 1975; in Elinor Ragosin's *The Dance Makers: Conversations with American Choreographers*, New York, 1980; with R.L. Cowser, in 'Eliot Feld Talks', *Dance Scope*, September 1980; with Joseph Mazo, in 'After 25 Years', *Elle*, March 1992; with Rena Subotnik, in 'Talent Developed: Conversations With Masters in the Arts Series', *Journal for the Education of the Gifted*, 25(3), 2002.

Articles: 'Eliot Feld', *Contemporary Biography Yearbook*, 1971; Doris Hering, 'Two Eliot Felds?', *Dance Magazine*, January 1971; Marcia Siegel, 'Feld Re-Fielded',

Dance Magazine, March 1974; Jack Anderson, 'Talking to Myself about Eliot Feld', *Dance Magazine*, February 1975 (reprinted in Anderson's *Choreography Observed*, Iowa City, 1987); Claudia Roth Pierpont, 'Contradictions in Eliot Feld', *Dance Life*, Summer 1976; Susan Reiter, 'His Own Man', *Ballet News*, June 1982; Patricia Barnes, 'Atmosphere, Jigs and Butterflies', *Dance and Dancers*, July 1984; Patricia Barnes, 'Dancing Together', *Dance and Dancers*, February 1988; Tobi Tobias, 'Plus ça Change...', *New York*, 19 June 1990; Clive Barnes, 'A Modern Classic: Eliot Feld', *Dance Magazine*, February 1992; Rick Whitaker, 'Buffy Miller: Three Feld solos', *Ballet Review*, Summer 1993; Ken Emerson, 'Feld's Foster', *Ballet Review*, Fall 1994; Jack Anderson, 'New York Newsletter', *Dancing Times*, June 1999; Clive Barnes, 'Field of Dreams', *Dance Magazine*, May 2001; Jack Anderson, 'Eliot Feld', *Dancing Times*, August 2002; Eliot Feld, 'Aphorisms, Piths, and Potshots', *Ballet Review*, Fall 2002; Jack Anderson, 'Baryshnikov and Eliot Feld', *Dancing Times*, May 2003; Clive Barnes, 'Attitudes', *Dance Magazine*, September 2003; Deborah Jowitt, 'Danger: Man at Work', *The Village Voice*, 19 October 2004; Joseph Carman, 'Deeply Feld', *Dance Magazine*, November 2004; Deborah Jowitt, 'Hang There', *The Village Voice*, 30 May 2006; Deborah Jowitt, 'Eliot Feld Mounts Two New Pieces and a Big Pot of Pasta', *The Village Voice*, 1 April 2009.

Books: John Gruen, *The Private World of Ballet*, New York, 1975; Moira Hodgson, *Quintet: Five American Dance Companies*, New York, 1976; Robert Coe, *Dance in America*, New York, 1985; Deborah Jowitt, *The Dance in Mind*, Boston, 1985; Marcia B. Seigel, *The Shapes of Change*, Berkeley, 1985; Nancy Reynolds and Malcolm McMormick, *No Fixed Points*, New Haven, CT, 2003; Rose Eichenbaum (photographs, text) and Clive Barnes (foreword), *Masters of Movement: Portraits of America's Great Choreographers*, Washington, DC, 2004.

WILLIAM FORSYTHE

From a high-school rock-'n'-roller in Manhasset on Long Island, New York, William Forsythe propelled himself along an upward path and continues as a radical, cutting edge, international choreographer of considerable reputation, especially among the *avant garde*. His passion as a dancer was established early in his teens and authenticated by winning high-school dance contests. The gyrating, disjointed, energetic movements he performed in the 1960s have filtered into his own unconventional and groundbreaking ballet lexicon.

Forsythe studied dance at Jacksonville University, Florida, trained in classical ballet and performed with Joffrey Ballet II in New York City. During the brief time with the Joffrey, he had opportunities as an understudy to perform with the senior company. The young dancer's charismatic nature surfaced rapidly; Robert Joffrey himself commented on how quickly Forsythe's ideas flowed. In 1973, Forsythe won director

John Cranko's approval and performed with the famed Stuttgart Ballet: his first piece, *Urlicht*, a duet to the music of Gustav Mahler, was made for that company in 1976. Soon his early choreographic success with the Stuttgart and Basel Ballet companies brought him recognition as an innovator in the dance world.

For 20 years (from 1984) Forsythe served as Ballett Frankfurt's artistic director and chief choreographer. His large company was based in a traditional German opera house, but there was nothing traditional about this controversial, risk-taking choreographer. Inheriting a city government-supported opera house enabled him to make grand-scale works with ambitious production possibilities. In his experimentation with classical ballet, *Swan Lake* was not on his agenda, and it is doubtful that it ever will be, at least in its traditional form. In a spring 1990 interview in *Ballet Review* Forsythe said, 'I have a good sense of the German culture, what might work for them.' He proved his point by developing a large, new and younger audience. Further, in 1999, under Forsythe's direction the company began performing at the Bockenheimer Depot (TAT), a more intimate performing space in Frankfurt-am-Main. However, a problematic relationship developed between the choreographer and Frankfurt's city government in 2002 over cuts in financial support, resulting in serious discontent on both sides. Unconventional ways of moving dancers' bodies, within a context of *non-sequitur* images that seldom result in a logical conclusion, can infuriate and confuse as well as excite audiences.

Ultimately, this determined the closure of Forsythe's relationship with Ballett Frankfurt and the establishment of his own company, which had its début in April 2005. The company planned to divide its time between two artistic homes, one in Dresden at the Festspielhaus Hellerau and one in Frankfurt at the Bockenheimer Depot.

Forsythe is a modern-day theatrical wizard, a man of many talents and a multitude of project ideas. In addition to choreographing for his own dancers, he has also made work and restaged his dances for a wide range of international companies. As in the *auteur* tradition of European filmmakers, Forsythe the scenographer controls all aspects of his works. These include lighting, set and costume designs; conceiving and writing texts often spoken in performances; creating the music (principally with Dutch composer Thom Willems) and/or sound effects; and often directing through microphones an entire work as it is happening. Idiosyncratic theatrical devices and eclectic activities have been employed, such as a fire curtain thudding to the floor – leaving the house in total darkness until it is lifted again to expose a complete change of stage activity. A curtain drop was repeated periodically throughout *Artifact* (1984), a piece seen at the Pepsico Summerfare Festival in Purchase, New York, in 1987. (*Artifact* was the first Frankfurt Ballet work performed in America and created strong but varied critical impressions.) For *New Sleep* (1987), made for the San Francisco Ballet, he created a unique lighting design, splitting the stage into quarters on diagonal lines, with the lighting downstage right/ upstage left very dark and that downstage left/upstage right very bright. The choreographer's lighting designs are a prime element in his *oeuvre*.

Full-length evening pieces such as *Artifact*, *France/Dance* (1983) and *Impressing the Czar* (1988), restaged in 2005 for the Royal Ballet of Flanders, have been likened to the creations of the American director Robert Wilson, who is also embraced enthusiastically by European cultural communities. However, there is a major difference between the two men. Forsythe's interest is in movement structures and in how his dancers produce the material in performance. The Forsythe dancers have necessary qualities beyond a strong ballet technique. In a 1989 interview with Burt Supree, Forsythe said:

> I've discovered there are two kinds of people who are dancing: there are dancers, and there are people who have learned to dance ... people who are just dancers [have] danced since they were this big [he gestures, child high], and they can dance, will always dance, and probably must dance.

These are the performers (like himself) that Forsythe wants because he needs people who can organize their bodies for whatever is necessary and commit themselves to the act of dancing.

Rudolf Laban, along with other philosophical and intellectual notables like Roland Barthes, Michel Foucault and Jacques Derrida, have been important to Forsythe. He became interested in Laban after studying and experiencing his spatial concepts in relationship to the body's movement possibilities. His dancers are not considered instruments to be moulded by his whim but an integral part of his creative process. For example, Forsythe said (in *Ballett International*, February 1994):

> I give the dancers my thoughts and not the results of them. I don't tell anyone what to do. I just tell them how they should do it. I've only created the conditions, but the movements are made manifest by the dancers themselves.

Dancers might be given a responsibility or task within a musical section to phrase the movement and be ready for the succeeding section. When setting his dances in the United States, Forsythe's approach to make movement was quite different for many classical ballet dancers. Both Leslie Carothers (Joffrey Ballet) in *Square Deal* (1983) and Lourdes Lopez (New York City Ballet) in *Behind the China Dogs* (1988) spoke of the creatively productive time they had with Forsythe. Improvisational work and personal problem-solving is not a customary practice with traditional ballet dancers and their choreographers.

In a 2009 interview with Rosyln Sulcas, Forsythe said:

> I think what I have introduced is the idea of intelligent sensation. I say to my dancers all the time, what you know is what you feel with your body. You don't need to think more, you need to feel, propriopreceptively, more.

He is very probably referring to kinesthetic perception/sense as described by Margaret H'Doubler in her book, *Dance: A Creative Art Experience* (1957).

The Forsythe Company takes a straightforward daily ballet class as a centring base. However, the choreographic work does not adhere to strict classical format. Forsythe pushes the ballet line far beyond the norm, especially for his women *en pointe* who jet out of verticality into wonderfully odd and impossible-looking silhouettes. Ballerinas are seen in daring off-centre lifts with legs rotated at 180 degrees, or being dragged across the stage *en pointe*. It is also not unusual for the arms to have a more inventive motion than the legs. To increase possibilities, the dancer's footwear varies from pointe shoes to work-boots, socks or anything that fits the bill. Performing movement at frantic speeds and showing a blatant strong physicality are elements that dominate Forsythe's work. Audiences who admire him are thrilled at the daring anti-establishment style of movement, whereas others are bothered by his bold departure from a 'pure' dance art.

Alie/nA(c)tion (1992) showed further development in his high-tech fragmented dance theatre. Described as one of his most difficult pieces to comprehend, its deconstructed title alone is cause for puzzlement. Here, he engages his audience in what is happening on the stage both in the construction and the deconstruction of the work process. During these events, his viewers are privy to benches being pushed around into place, seconds being counted for several minutes over a loudspeaker by a man with headphones, breathing sounds, gasps, squeals and sobs of performers equipped with personal microphones, the smell of smoke from a man's cigarette, the sound of rappers rapping and shouting obscenities, a man pretending to be a walrus and electric dancing that is exhilarating. Experiencing *Alie/nA(c)tion* was likened, by one young dancer, to an assault on one's entire physical being. Rolf Michaelis wrote in *Ballett International*, 'Even when Forsythe suspends the audience's comprehension – where else is the expressive range of contemporary dance being as vigorously extended as in Frankfurt?'

Conventional linear narrative is not part of Forsythe's repertory; a receptive audience has more than enough to feast their eyes on in his maze of activity. Yet Forsythe's work is not always hard edged and highly charged. His *Quintett* (1993) makes no use of high-tech feats, and has an atypical musical score, by Gavin Bryars (entitled *Jesus's Blood Never Failed Me Yet*). The song's words, continually repeated with subtle musical variations, are hauntingly beautiful. The choreography has been described as having a falling, swooping and skimming movement. A trapdoor with stairs leading below the stage, from which the dancers can move in and out of the audience's view, gives, along with the music, a dramatic context to explore.

Another key work of the 1990s was *Eidos: Telos* (from the Greek, meaning *Form: The End*), a highly charged three-part work with spoken text, lavish dancing by women in long bustled skirts and spectacular production values that left one with eyes and ears popping.

Although Forsythe's work has been seen in America, it was in Western Europe that it achieved early popularity and financial support. France, a great supporter of new dance, has commissioned his choreography and generously bestowed prestigious venues, such as the Théâtre Musical du Châtelet, for extended company residencies. Forsythe's fourth visit to the Montpellier Danse Festival in 2000, for instance, brought an array of four works divided in two sections; the first two were more classical in form, whereas the second two involved abandoning visible form and treating time differently. *Workwithinwork* (1998) presented 14 dancers performing an unorthodox treatment of the ballet lexicon minus text or any theatrical accessories. The music of Luciano Berio's *Duetti per violini* brought two musicians on stage interacting with the dancers, a familiar Forsythe device. That the women were as aggressive as the men in the duet was an enjoyable element. The subject of the work was episodic gatherings of dancing, sometimes alone but never isolated from the group.

Duo (1996), a 13-minute piece for two performers dressed in costumes by Forsythe (which exposed breasts and legs), was set to a piano score by Willems that was barely audible and contained stretches of silence. Dancers move in unison and separately, and perform risky surprise moves such as knee drops to the floor or legs sharply flinging into an unconventional back attitude. There are also still moments such as the dancers lying flat on their back. The work has been described as profoundly beautiful, and Forsythe's brilliant movement inventions are certainly striking. In *One Flat Thing, Reproduced* (2000), 14 dancers, without warning, violently pull 20 tables downstage in a matter of moments. Willem's score propels the piece, which is frenzied, urgent, machine-like in its activity, with dancers moving on top, beside and underneath the tables in solos, duets and trios.

In *The Room as it Was* (2002), eight dancers are challenged by Forsythe's ever-changing syntactical rules: at moments of contact the dancers have to connect visually to read and transpose each other's movements. Here also the women are *en pointe* and in contrast to being lifted aloft, they are often placed on the floor by their male partners, only to rise quickly and move on. These fast and complex episodes are interrupted by departure or arrival of one or more dancers walking in a natural gait to their next encounter. Slashing arms, spatial indirectness and lyrical duets keep the energy and involvement at a high pitch so that the ending, with its jolt of lights and blackout, is a surprise. Another 2002 work, entitled *(N.N.N.N.)*, is an engaging quartet for four men dressed in casual clothes, so unlike traditional ballet boys in their manner and style. Forsythe's dance is infused with a rich vocabulary and a sense of time that is constant in its bold language. Body strength is flaunted; there is no attention to the audience, no reason for the *non sequitur* action taking place, but these wild configurations of wrapping, slapping or simply connecting body parts, especially when all four men are entangled, are astonishing as well as amusing.

Never considered formulaic, Forsythe once again pushed the limits of performance with *Kammer/Kammer* (2000). This contemporary musical comedy is based on two texts, one by Anne Carson and one by Douglas A. Martin, and follows the fortunes of a college philosophy professor and a 'Garçon au Bonnet Bleu', both of whom are frustrated in love. In *Kammer/Kammer* we see provocative danced and spoken word-play, with performers spilling out their frustration in various rooms (*Kammers*) of an ingenious set with shifting walls designed by the choreographer. At the end of this highly visual and text-driven work, both characters strive, but fail, in their quest for something more than unrequited love.

Forsythe has attributed his creative inspiration to diverse branches of cultural, intellectual and political influences. *Three Atmospheric Studies* (2005), a theatre piece with a political voice that spoke of the current and continuing state of world affairs, clearly pointed at the ongoing war in Iraq. There is much dialogue, and the movement (such as young company members rushing, twisting and bumping into each other) is spare in comparison to the production elements. However, the work is passionate and remains relevant.

Decreation (2003), another Carson-inspired work, is a multi-media piece that awakens all the senses. The choreographic material is based on something Forsythe calls 'shearing'. The movement suggests that the performer is being pulled apart in the opposite direction from what would be normal. Clothes are pulled from the body and locomotion is irregular and off-balance. The loud sounds and emotionally driven movements evoke a madhouse.

Mastering a sophisticated computer system and other technological theatre tools of the twenty-first century has been an important learning requirement for Forsythe: he uses them to enhance the realm of possibilities and as a creative teaching tool. He has also contributed much of his time and talent to mentoring young dancers; and as a teacher he continues to work on educational projects such as introducing dance to children in Brazil.

In keeping with Barthes' philosophy of the goals of an artist, Forsythe is a man not preoccupied with the past, never dwelling on what has been accomplished but on what can be. He has said that dancing has nothing to do with closure or the exclusion of new possibilities. Site-specific work, installations and spoken text, as well as sections of pure dance, are among his current interests. *Human Writes* (2005), a joint project with Kendall Thomas, is an example of the artist's global concerns and has been described by Imanuel Schipper as a 'performance-installation that reflects the history of human rights and the continuing obstacles to their full implementation'. Forsythe has been commissioned to produce architectural and performance installations in cities including London, Paris and New York, often offering continuous admissions over a specified length of time without intermissions. *Human Writes* runs for three hours, and the video installations also typically run for long periods.

New ideas are a constant with William Forsythe. With unfailing energy and profound insight, the artist continues to make remarkable pieces that excite his vast audiences, providing them with eye-riveting work, challenges to the mind, stimuli to the senses and a desire to come back for more.

Sandra Genter

Biographical details

Born in New York, 30 December 1949. **Studied** initially for a degree in Humanities and Theatre in Florida; received first formal dance training with teachers Nolan Dingman and Christa Long; also studied with Jonathan Watts, Maggie Black, Finis Jhung at the Joffrey Ballet School, New York, from 1969. **Career**: Danced with Joffrey Ballet, 1971–73 and Stuttgart Ballet, 1973–80. First choreography for the Noverre Society Young Choreographers' Workshop, Stuttgart, 1976; resident choreographer for Stuttgart Ballet, 1976–80; freelance choreographer, staging ballets in Germany, Austria, Italy and the Netherlands, 1980–82; choreographer, Ballett Frankfurt, 1982, then its director and chief choreographer, 1984–2004; established The Forsythe Company, 2005. Has also choreographed for many other companies, including Basel Ballet, Munich Ballet, Nederlands Dans Theater, Deutsche Oper (Berlin), Royal Ballet (London), Joffrey Ballet, Paris Opera Ballet, Aterballetto, San Francisco Ballet, New York City Ballet and American Ballet Theater. **Awards and honours** include New York Dance and Performance Award ('Bessie'), 1988, 1999, 2004, 2007; Laurence Olivier Awards, 1992, 1999, 2009; Chevalier dans l'Ordre des Arts et des Lettres, 1992, 1999; Hessen Arts Prize (Germany), 1995; International Theatre Institute Award, 1996; Grand Prix Carina ARI, 1996; German Distinguished Service Cross, 1997; the Wexner Prize, 2002.

Works

Urlicht (1976); *Daphne* (1977); *Bach Violin Concerto in A-Minor* (1977); *Flore Subsimplici-Suit* (1977); *From the Most Distant* (1978); *Dream of Galilei* (1978); *Folia* (1978); *Orpheus* (with playwright Edward Bond, 1979); *Side 2 – Love Songs* (1979); *Time Cycle* (1979); *Joyleen Gets Up, Gets Down, Goes Out* (1980); *'Tis a Pity She's a Whore* (1980); *Famous Mothers Club* (solo, 1980); *Say Bye Bye* (1980); *Die Nacht aus Blei* (1981); *Whisper Moon* (1981); *Event 1, 2, 3* (1981); *Gänge 1 – Ein Stück über Ballett* (1982); *Gänge* (1983); *Mental Model* (1983); *Square Deal* (1983); *France/Dance* (1983); *Berg AB* (film, 1984); *Artifact* (includes *Artifact II*, 1984); *Steptext* (1984); *LDC* (1985); *Isabelle's Dance* (1986); *Skinny* (1986); *Die Befragung des Robert Scott* (1986); *Big White Baby Dog* (1986); *Baby Sam* (1986); *Pizza Girl* (1986); *New Sleep* (1987); *Same Old Story* (1987); *The Loss Of Small Detail* (1987; revised version, 1991); *Impressing the Czar* (includes *In The Middle, Somewhat Elevated*, 1988); *Behind the China Dogs* (1988); *The Vile Parody of Address* (1988); *Enemy in the Figure* (1989); *Slingerland I* (1989); *Limb's Theorem* (includes *Enemy in the Figure*, 1990); *Slingerland II and III* (1990); *Slingerland TV* (1990); *Marion/Marion* (1991); *The Second Detail* (1991); *The Loss of Small Detail* (1991); *Snap, Woven Effort* (1991); *Alie/nA(c)tion* (1992; revised version, 1993); *Quintett* (1993); *Herman Schmerman* (1992; revised version, 1993); *As a Garden in This*

Setting (1993); *Self Meant to Govern* (1994); *Pivot House* (1994); *Four Point Counter* (1995); *Firstext* (1995); *Invisible Film* (1995); *Of Any If And* (1995); *The The* (with Dana Caspersen, 1995); *Eidos: Telos* (1995); Solo (video; dir. Thomas Lovell, 1995); *Six Counter Points* (includes *The The, Duo, Trio, Four Point Counter, Approximate Sonata* and *The Vertiginous Thrill of Exactitude*, 1996); *Sleepers Guts* (1996); *Tight Roaring Circle* (with Dana Caspersen, 1997); *Hypothetical stream* (with *The Vile Parody of Address*, 1988, *Of Any If And*, 1995 and *Hypothetical Stream 11*, 1997); *Workwithinwork* (1998); *Small void* (1998); *Op. 31* (1998); *Endless House* (1999); *White Bouncy Castle* (1999); *From a Classical Position* (film, 1998/99); *One Flat Thing, Reproduced* (2000); *Kammer/Kammer* (2000), *Woolf Phrase* (2002); *The Room as it Was* (2002); *(N.N.N.N.)* (2002); *Scattered Crowd* (2002); *Decreation* (2003); *Wear* (2004); *Three Atmospheric Studies* (2005); *You Made Me a Monster* (2005); *Human Writes* (2005); *Heterotopia* (2006); *The Defenders* (2007); *Yes We Can't* (2008); *I Don't Believe in Outer Space* (2008); *Theatrical Arsenal 11* (2009). Also *Synchronous Objects* (interactive web project with Ohio State University, 2009) and *Transfigurations* (exhibition of Forsythe's installation work, Wexner Centre, Columbus, OH, United States, 2009).

Further reading

Interviews with Birgit Kirchner, in 'Good Theatre of a Different Kind', *Ballett International*, August 1984; with Elisa Vaccarino, in *Balletto oggi*, November 1989; with Senta Driver *et al.*, in 'A Conversation with William Forsythe', *Ballet Review*, Spring 1990; with Burt Supree, in *Proceedings of the Dance Critics Association Conference*, 1990; with Johannes Odenthal, in 'Conversation with William Forsythe', *Ballett International*, February 1994; with William Anthony, in 'William Forsythe Talks to William Anthony', *Dance Europe*, December/January 1996/97; with Gerald Siegmund, 'In the Mecca of Dance' *Ballett International*, April 1999; with Senta Driver (ed.) 'William Forsythe', *Choreography and Dance*, 5(3), 2000; with Roslyn Sulcas, 'Drawing Movements', *The New York Times*, 29 March 2009.

Articles: L. Shyer, 'Stuttgart Orpheus', *Theater*, Spring 1980; Mary Whitney, 'Prodigal Son', *Ballet News*, October 1983; Norbert Servos, 'The World Topsy-Turvey', *Ballett International*, August 1985; R. Langer and R. Sikes, 'New Directors, Part II: William Forsythe', *Dance Magazine*, January 1986; Norbert Servos, 'The Rigid Indifference of Things', *Ballett International*, July/August 1987; Otis Stuart, 'Forsythe's Follies', *Ballet Review*, Fall 1987; Arlene Croce, 'Wise Guys', *The New Yorker*, 31 July 1989; Eva Elisabeth Fischer, 'Aesthetic Norms and Today's Social Taboos: The Effect of Innovation and Creativity', *Ballett International*, January 1990; Nadine Meisner, 'Choreographer for Today', *Dance and Dancers*, April 1990; Eva van Schaik, 'What Will Come Next in the Forsythe Games?', *Ballett International*, October 1990; Senta Driver, 'Two or Three Things That Might Be Considered Primary', *Ballet Review*, Spring 1990; Roslyn Sulcas, 'William Forsythe: The Poetry of Disappearance and the Great Tradition', *Dance Theatre Journal*, Summer 1991; Stephanie Jordan, 'William Forsythe', *Dance Theatre Journal*, Autumn 1991; Nadine Meisner, 'Dangerous Dancing', *Dance and Dancers*, January/February 1992; Katherine Sorley Walker, 'Ashton and Forsythe', *Dance and Dancers*, April 1992; Claudia Jeschke, 'American Theatricality in Contemporary German Theater Dancing: John Neumeier and William Forsythe', *Society of Dance History Scholars Proceedings*, February 1992; Ann Nugent, 'Two Radicals in Europe', *Dance Now*, Winter 1992/93; Silvia Poletti,

'*Ali/en(A)ction*: Forsythe's Latest Comes to Italy', *Dance and Dancers*, March 1993; Edith Boxberger, 'Sucked into Hades: William Forsythe's new ballet *Quintet*', *Ballett International*, January 1994; Edith Boxberger, ' . . . want to be hypnotised . . . ', *Ballett International*, February 1994; D. Wilkins, 'Aesthetics and Cultural Criticism in William Forsythe's *Impressing the Czar*', *Ballet Review*, Spring 1994; Nadine Meisner, 'Dangerous Beauty', *Opera House*, January 1995; Judith Mackrell, 'Conflict, Confrontation and *Firstext*', *Dance Theatre Journal*, Summer 1995; Edith Boxberger, 'Breaking New Ground from Deconstruction: *Eidos: Telos*', *Ballett International*, March 1995; Edith Boxberger, 'Beyond the Images', *Ballett International*, March 1996; William Anthony, 'Forsythe in *Frankfurt*', *Dancing Times*, March 1996; Ann Nugent, 'Confounding Expectations', *Dance Theatre Journal*, Summer 1996; Roslyn Sulcas, 'Theorems and Counterpoints', *Dance Now*, Summer 1996; Helena Wulff, 'Composition and Crossover Collage, *Ballett International*, August 1995; Arnd Wesemann, 'Slumbering Forces', *Ballett International*, December 1996; Paige Perry, '*Sleepers Guts* in Frankfurt', *Dance Europe*, December/January 1996/97; Roslyn Sulcas, 'The Continuing Evolution of Mr Forsythe', *Dance Magazine*, January 1997; Gerald Siegmund, 'London Calling: William Forsythe's Castles of Air', *Ballett International*, June 1997; Ann Nugent, 'Eyeing Forsythe', *Dance Theatre Journal*, 14(3), 1998; Eva Elizabeth Fischer, 'On Stage: Forsythe's New Work', *Ballett International*, March 1998; G. Brandstetter, 'Defigurative Choreography', *The Drama Review*, Winter 1998; Arnd Weseman, 'On Stage. Whirlwinds', *Ballett International*, December 1998; William Forsythe, 'Improvisation Technologies: A Tool for the Analytical Dance Eye', *Dance Theatre Journal*, 15(3), 1999; Sandra Genter, 'Montpellier at Twenty', *Ballet Review*, Summer 2001; Ann Nugent, 'The Forsythe Saga', *Dance Now*, Spring 2001 and 'Who Dares Wins', *Dance Theatre Journal*, 16(4), 2001 and 'Profile: William Forsythe', *Dance Theatre Journal*, 19(2), 2003; Sandra Genter, 'Next Wave Dance', *Ballet Review*, Winter 2004; Senta Driver, 'Season XX', *Ballet Review*, Summer 2004; Sandra Genter, 'Montpellier at 25', *Ballet Review*, Spring 2006; Ann Nugent, 'William Forsythe, *Eidos: Telos*, and Intertextual Criticism,' *Dance Research Journal*, Summer 2007; Sandra Genter, 'New York', *Ballet Review*, Winter 2007/8; Sandra Genter, 'The Czar in Flanders', *Ballet Review*, Spring 2009.

Books: Janet Adshead-Lansdale (ed.), *Dancing Texts: Intertextuality and Interpretation*, London, 1999; Valerie Briginshaw, *Dance, Space and Subjectivity*, Basingstoke, 2001; Gerald Siegmund (ed.), *William Forsythe: Denken in Bewegung*, Berlin, 2004; Arnd Wesemann, *Forsythe – Bill's Universe*, Berlin, 2004; Agnès Noltenius, *Forsythe Detail* (Éditions Complexe/Arte Editions), a book of photographs by Noltenius and comments from Forsythe; Jo Butterworth and Liesbeth Wildschut (eds) *Contemporary Choreography: A Critical Reader*, London, 2009.

ITZIK GALILI

As a choreographer I am my own psychiatrist.[1]

Itzik Galili, the Israeli choreographer who has lived in the Netherlands since 1991, does not make a secret of the autobiographical elements he puts into his work. In interviews he is very open about his life, and watching his pieces one can follow his ups and downs. In the book *Open Circle: NND/Galili Dance*, which describes 10 years (1998–2007) of Galili's former company (based in the north of the Netherlands), he states: 'Theatre is also for me a therapeutic excursion or a voyage to discover experiences with myself and others'.[2] His work gives the audience a glimpse of his inner world, sometimes very overtly; for example, in *When You See God . . . Tell Him* (1993) and *Uhlai* (1995), performed by himself and his then wife Jennifer Hanna, it is clear that he is very much in love.

He does not give away all his secrets, however. What is in his 'black box', as he usually calls his inner world, is what he keeps for himself, but he transforms this into his dreams and fantasies. His difficult and violent youth in Tel Aviv inspired him to create the full evening's work *Below Paradise*, for Scapino Ballet Rotterdam in 1997. Although this piece is not as dark as one might expect, it is totally surrealistic, with white boxes like Dali's drawers: you open them and another amazing story starts, full of energy and the joy of living. What Galili wants to express is not only his personal experiences of life but also his position in the world: 'My work is a metaphor for my handling of the enormous pressure of what is happening around me'.[3] An example of this is an earlier dance for the Scapino Company created in 1994, *Ma's Bandage*, in which sexual violence and the maltreatment of women are the leading themes. Galili explores these themes with long texts chanted by the dancers and images projected onto their bare backs.

In 1991, love brought Galili from Tel Aviv to the Netherlands. He decided to stay because there was less stress and violence in his new home country. He needed a sheltered environment in which he wanted to discover and develop himself as a choreographer. The Groningen-based company, Reflex, offered him the opportunity to create *Trekidos* (1991). Then, with *The Butterfly Effect* (1991), he won the Public Prize at the International Competition for choreographers. These first choreographies were optimistic in mood, and at this time he also worked as a dancer, as well as a choreographer, on a programme with several Israeli Gulf War refugees who were in exile in the Netherlands. With them he created *Cage* (1991), which expressed the feelings – despair, fear, compassion – and tensions between people occasioned by the situation these dancers found themselves in.

Galili had started his dance career in Israel when he was in his twenties. A friend had taken him to a folk dance event, and the way Galili performed resulted in his being invited to take classes with the junior group of the internationally renowned Batsheva Dance Company. Once he had acquired a taste for dancing, he felt the urge to hurry and the drive to dance was to lead to the desire to create his own work. Eventually, he became a member of the Batsheva Dance Company itself, and by 1990 he had established his name as a choreographer with the award-winning *Old Cartoon* In the Netherlands, however, although he continued his relationship with the Batsheva Dance Company, he was also to work as a freelancer, invited by Dutch companies like Reflex, Scapino Ballet Rotterdam, the Nationale Ballet and Nederlands Dans Theater II, as well as by several other European companies. With Galili Dance he created his own productions and in 1997 he became artistic director of NND/Galili Dance, a new company based in Groningen.

Influenced by the Batsheva Dance choreographers Ohad Naharin and Daniël Ezralow, Galili's style became very energetic, sometimes even acrobatic, with horizontal jumps, bent knees and deep arches of the torso. But aggression, often seen in the work of Israeli choreographers, is not so much part of Galili's work. His movement phrases are often logical and fluent, even when body parts suddenly erupt in unexpected directions. The movement language is rich: turns and extensions, explosive kicks and swinging arms can be immediately followed by light-footed, humorous, tranquil or poetic motion.

His work, although it has received worldwide recognition, has not been without its detractors. However, Galili states that he feels the need to comment on what is fundamentally wrong in society. He is not primarily interested in realism, but rather it is abstraction that transforms his concerns.[4] Eva van Schaik writes:

> Not every choreography was received with equal enthusiasm and not every reviewer managed to appreciate his intellectual and often socially critical, if not politically oriented, intentions – on the one hand because this would presume his being morally in the right, and on the other because his dance vocabulary was seen as being too mysterious.[5]

Sometimes realism gains the upper hand. This is mostly the result of his use of texts that can be too explicit, like the repeatedly called out 'It was here, I know it was here! Where is it?' in *The Familiar Stranger* (1998). But more often than not, Galili is able to transform his experiences and his perceptions of the world around him into a performance that is universal and human, recognizable for individuals with their own perspectives on the themes he depicts. He combines fear and power, loneliness and comfort, aggression and tenderness, humour and seriousness, emotions and abstraction – not as contradictions, but as possibilities.

In the impressive *For Heaven's Sake* (2001), for example, one can recognize the Palestinian–Israeli conflict through the oriental sounds played by Arab-Israeli musicians and the furiously uttered monologue, which comes from a newspaper report of the 1982 attack on Chatila by Israel. The performance starts in the dark with slow slapping noises, and soon two men are seen, standing side by side beating themselves relentlessly. The speed increases; their skin becomes redder and redder. Are they offenders or victims? Eight minutes into the work and all of a sudden the stage is filled with people drumming. They galvanize the beat into an inflaming rhythm. Later, dancers enter the stage, a leg or arm fixed in a prosthesis or wearing a corset. With a leg dragging or stiff neck, they fall, push, turn and try to stay in pace with each other. As we watch them struggle, their effort becomes tangible. A fragile, intense duet closes the dance. In a ray of light, two dancers help each other very carefully and with much tenderness to make the next step on their path, leaving the audience with mixed feelings of despair and hope, aware of the violence that takes place not only in the Middle East but also everywhere in the world.

Characteristic of Galili is his dynamic group work. In his recent passionate *Sub* (2009), for example, individuals move in synchrony in constantly changing formations, escaping every now and then in solos, duets and trios, often integrated in a bigger whole. But the most touching works are his numerous duets, starting with his very first choreography, *Double Time* (1990), in which he shows the many possibilities of human relationships. With sometimes very subtle, meaningful gestures, he is able to communicate an emotion or a change in relationship between two people. They can express happiness as well as struggle – as in *When You See God . . . Tell Him* (1993) – or tenderness as well as cruelty – as in *Exile Within* (2006). In this later piece, several duets give expression to the longing for touch and tenderness. When a dancer tries to lay his head in another dancer's lap, and is pushed away again and again, or when two men touch each other very tenderly but break off when it becomes too close, the impact on the audience is palpable. In spite of the search for closeness, the dancers are alone even in the midst of a group.

Galili's strength lies in combining expressive movements with powerful images, often created by his own lighting designs. Spots and paths of light make darker areas of the stage resonate with a lurking and mysterious presence. In *Exile Within* the dancers are isolated in cones, pyramids, channels and squares of light; their movement is restricted by a square or circle of light projected on the floor, which varies in width. They have to stay within the bounds of this prison: it seems a metaphor for an inner struggle with their own history. One of the dancers speaks of what she is unable to erase: frictions, anger, disappointment, borders, narrow-mindedness, time, fear, safety, religion, regulations, fashion, infection and memories. At the end, the lyrics of a song are projected onto a screen – 'Nothing unusual, nothing strange' – and while the last performer is still moving, the stage technicians begin to dismantle the set. When one asks for the light to be dimmed, the dancer disappears. The reality of the language uttered by the technician merges with the magic of the words sung by Damian Rice.

When looking over Galili's body of work, one becomes aware of constant, intensive research into the interaction of movement with projected or spoken texts, uttered by the dancers themselves or by means of a voice-over. Sometimes the rhythm of the words is emphasized or words are translated into movements, often with hilarious result. Amusing anecdotes are told and manifestations of social commitment are expressed. Galili challenges his dancers to go beyond their borders by acting, using their voices, using their bodies as percussion instruments or by playing instruments they have never played before, like a piano in *Chronocratie* (1996).

Galili is not only interested in the physical possibilities of his dancers; he also wants to know what they think about their profession and lives. He works with individuals who can explore their own possibilities as dancers and as human beings. Furthermore, Galili also wants to nurture upcoming choreographic talent from within his company. In the programming of NND/Galili Dance he has often included work by his dancers, for example, Roni Haver, Guy Weizman, Stephen Shropshire and Sara Wiktorowicz.

Since January 2009, Itzik Galili has shared artistic leadership of the newly founded Dansgroep Amsterdam with Krisztina de Châtel, a Hungarian choreographer who also lives and works in the Netherlands. About his first full evening's programme, *The Casualties of Memories*, critic Sander Hiskemuller remarked in the journal *Trouw*:

Unprepared, we dive deeper into the world of Galili's mind ...The danger is to get lost in this expression of [his] mind-waves – the choreographer wants to achieve a lot – but he leads you out of the labyrinth purified.[6]

Weaving dreams and reality, past and present, Galili invites the audience to reflect about what remains hidden behind reality.

Liesbeth Wildschut

Notes

1 Annette Embrechts, 'Itzik Galili in het spoor van Dali', *Dans*, 3, 1997, p. 21.
2 Eva van Schaik, Alex de Vries *Open Circle: NND/Galili Dance*, Zwolle, 2007, p. 21.
3 Lucia van Heteren, 'Galili's nieuwe voorstelling kan niet om oorlog heen', *TheaterMaker*, December 2001–January 2002, pp. 20–21.
4 Lucia van Heteren, 'Galili's nieuwe voorstelling kan niet om oorlog heen', *TheaterMaker*, December 2001–January 2002, p. 21.
5 Van Schaik and de Vries, *Open Circle*, op. cit., p. 115.
6 Sander Hiskemuller, 'Itzik Galili', *Trouw*, 20 November 2009, p. 36. In English translation: http://ectopiadance.com/23/pressestimmen_406_en.htm

Biographical details

Born in Tel Aviv, Israel, 1961. **Studied** Israeli folk dance; and then ballet and contemporary dance with Nira Paz, his teacher in the junior group of the Batsheva Dance Company. **Career**: Performed with Bat-Dor Dance Company and then Batsheva Dance Company, Tel Aviv; moved to the Netherlands, 1991; founder and artistic director of NND/Galili Dance, 1997–2007; co-director of Dansgroep Amsterdam, from 2009; also director of International Competition for Choreographers, Groningen, 1997, 1998 and 1999. Has created works for Stuttgart Ballet, Ballets de Monte Carlo, Bayerisches Staatsoper Munich, Gulbenkian Ballet, Scapino Ballet, Nederlands Dans Theater II, Batsheva Dance Company, Les Grands Ballets Canadiens, Iceland Dance Company, Royal Finnish Ballet, Bale da Cidade de São Paulo, Royal Winnipeg Ballet, National Dance Company Wales, Norrdans, Rambert Dance Company, Koresh Dance Company, Cisne Negro Aspen Santa Fe, Geneva Ballet and National Ballet of the Netherlands. **Awards and honours** include Gvanim Choreographic Competition, 1990; Public Prize, International Choreographic Competition, Groningen,1992; Culture Award for Contribution to Dance in the Netherlands, 1994; VSCD Choreography Prize, 2002; Knighted, Royal Order of the House of Oranje Nassau, 2006.

Works

Double Time (1990); *Old Cartoon* (1990); *My Little Garden Party* (1991); *Black Donut* (1991); *Trekidos* (1991); *The Butterfly Effect* (1991); *Cage* (1991); *Gloves* (1992); *Facing* (1992); *For Tsouklamia, Just That* (1992); *Earth Apples* (1992); *Blind Kingdom*

(1992); *Cinderello* (1993); *Her Light Made of Sand* (1993); *Duet* (1993); *Perureim* (1993); *To Topography Too* (1993); *Dualis* (1989); *When You See God . . . Tell Him* (1993); *The Irony of Antimatter* (1994); *If* (1994); *Ma's Bandage* (1994); *Through Nana's Eyes* (1995); *Uhlai* (1995*)*; *Between L . . .* (1995); *Chronocratie* (1996); *Come Across* (dance film for Nederlands TV, 1996); *Below Paradise* (1997); *Fragile* (1997); *See under X* (1997; revised, 2003); *The Upper Room* (1997); *Blink* (1997); *Until. With/Out. Enough* (1997; revised, 2008); *The Familiar Stranger* (1998); *Is it Far to Go?* (1998); *Chameleon* (1998); *The Drunken Garden* (1999); *Beautiful You* (1999); *Blue Grass* (1999); *Enter* (2000); *Things I Told Nobody* (2000); *B-Side* (2000); *For Heaven's Sake* (2001); *There, There Is* (2002); *Drumming* (2001); *The Seventh Veil* (2002); *A Sense of Gravity* (BBC dance film, 2002); *Symbiosis* (2003); *Mona Lisa* (2003); *ME* (2004); *Peeled* (2004); *See Hear/Sea Here* (2004); *Hikarrizatto* (2004); *So Near, So Far* (2005); *A Linha Curva* (2005); *The Freckle Hunters* (2005); *Palm* (2005); *Shaker Loops* (2005); *U'd, Us and Hiccups* (2006); *If as If* (2006); *Exile Within* (2006); *Six* (2007); *Heads or Tails* (2007); *SoLow* (2007); *Kathy* (2007); *The Servant Voyager* (2007); *Heads or Tales-HoT* (2007); *Sub* (2009); *The Casualties of Memory* (2009); *Romance Inverse* (2010).

Further reading

Articles: John Percival, 'Reviews: *Kingdom, Cinderello*', *Dance and Dancers*, April 1993; Helma Klooss, 'Young Dutch Choreographers: The Crest of Holland's New Wave', *Dance Magazine*, October 1995; Fredrik Rutter, 'The Bergen International Festival', *Dance Europe*, August/September 1998; Michelle Man, 'Galili in Lisbon', *Dance Europe*, January 2001; Emma Manning, 'Going Places', *Dance Europe*, January 2002; Jeannette Anderson, 'So Near So Far Away', *Dancing Times*, August 2005.

Books: Eva van Schaik, Alex de Vries, *Open Circle*, NND/Galili Dance, Zwolle, 2007.

SHOBANA JEYASINGH

London-based Shobana Jeyasingh's artistic vision is shaped by a rich mix of international cultural forces. Generating debates about cultural identity, postcolonial power relationships and orientalist assumptions, her dances interrogate aesthetic issues of classicism, modernism and postmodernism as well as multiculturalism. Jeyasingh's choreography arises out of Bharatanatyam, a traditional dance form identified with the Indian nationalist movement prior to its independence from Britain in 1947. The dance's historical roots in Hindu religious practices and the Sanskrit treatise *Natyashastra* helped to construct a legacy untainted by colonial power, with many young women encouraged to study the dance as a link to the past. The power of heritage has often dominated critical writing about her choreography, as Sanjoy Roy notes, resulting in the use of 'crudely simplistic terms that do not do Jeyasingh's work justice ("East-West collaboration" or "Indian/contemporary dance fusion")'.[1] The focus on cultural questions negates the extent to which formal movement concerns are central to her artistry. Rather than the literary or religious references conveyed through the *natya* or dramatic components of Bharatanatyam, Jeyasingh uses its *nritta* elements, its formal structures, linear body designs and percussive footwork in which she finds objective principles of clarity, grace, vigour and precision comparable to ballet.[2] For Jeyasingh, 'rather than assisting the "plot", the dance *is* the plot where the characters are time, space and bodies'.[3] Deconstructing the complexities of her own sense of identity, Jeyasingh defies an East–West binary. In discussing the 'country' she is supposed to be representing, she challenges those who label it as 'Indian':

> . . . my heritage is a mix of David Bowie, Purcell, Shelley and Anna Pavlova, and it has been mixed as subtly as a samosa has mixed itself into the English cuisine in the last 10 years or so: impossible to separate . . . And in dance terms Rukmani Devi *and* Merce Cunningham are also part of my heritage.[4]

In 1997, Roy identified a back-to-basics phase which started Jeyasingh's choreographic career, placing Bharatanatyam's solo structure onto a group and breaking from its narrative conventions. Working closely with composer Michael Nyman, Jeyasingh created *Miniatures* (1988) for a television documentary, receiving a Digital Dance Award. *Configurations* (1988) evolved from *Miniatures* for her quartet of Bharatanatyam-trained female dancers: as Roy explains, 'its classical source is broken down into basic components – shape, direction and rhythm – and then reassembled, duplicated and refracted across space and among dancers to construct kaleidoscopic, crystalline geometries'.[5] *Correspondences* (1990), to Kevin Volans' commissioned score, was inspired by the immigrant experiences and early death of Indian mathematician S. Ramanujan (1887–1920) when he came to study at Cambridge University in England. Hunt writes that 'Jeyasingh convincingly equates the mathematical complexities of Bharatanatyam – its rhythms, precision and quickness, and the geometrical handling of the body and of space – with the mathematician's thought'.[6] Fragmentation of form and the abstraction of vernacular gesture produced an emphasis on formal qualities of movement, which has been a cornerstone of her aesthetic across the years. Her aesthetic is also shaped by input from prominent collaborators, as the sets, lighting, costumes and, increasingly, digital technology in her highly theatrical dances are as finely designed as the movement.

Further distance from a strict Bharatanatyam vocabulary was achieved by an increased fragmentation of traditional material through contemporary dance structures. *Late* (1991), to a score by Orlando Gough, integrates vernacular gestures such as 'a quick glance at a wrist watch, a fist impatiently striking the palm of the hand, an anxious glance over the shoulder'.[7] Other production aspects retained links to the dance style Jeyasingh was trained in, such as the musical mix evident in Christos Hatzis's minimalist score for *Byzantium* (1991). Created for an oboe soloist, Haztis combined south Indian rhythmic structures with Western forms, with Jeyasingh maintaining a close movement–music relationship.

In Roy's analysis, *Making of Maps* (1992) ushered in a choreographic phase that established a tension between classical clarity in 'the defined language of bharatanatyam and a more personal, exploratory way of moving'.[8] Inspired by the medieval Mappa Mundi that was orientated around Jerusalem, Jeyasingh's map marked out her personal journeys of identity through location and form. Bharatanatyam phrases were juxtaposed with contemporary dance floor work and physical contact not found in the classical form. Indian composer and singer R.A. Ramamani's score was layered with one by Arthur McDonald, comprised of city noises and other found sounds, along with violins and bells. *Making of Maps* signalled the institutionalization of Jeyasingh's choreography when it became a set work on the British secondary education 'A-Level' dance syllabus. Significantly, the education resource materials break down formal components of Bharatanatyam's classical structure, broadening awareness of the imported form while highlighting its trans-cultural potential as an abstract dance vocabulary.[9]

In *Romance . . . with Footnotes* (1993), sections of traditional south Indian *jathis* (mnemonic devices that correspond to the rhythmic footwork) composed by Karaikudi Krishnamurthy were layered with Glyn Perrin's score for three cellos and bass clarinet, with the musicians appearing onstage. Another contrast was referenced in the title – emotion (romance) and the intellect (footnotes as academic citations). In O'Shea's analysis, Jeyasingh alternates between the qualitative components of the dance tradition rather than shifting between abstract and thematic movement. The dancers use a different basic bodily stance and Bharatanatyam's codified hand gestures, or *mudras*, are used as 'spatial shapings which extend from gestures into full body movements that change levels and initiate contact between dancers'.[10]

Roy defines Jeyasingh's third phase as being marked by less emphasis on Bharatanatyam, although its lineage is still evident. In *Palimpsest* (1996), the vocabulary is wider and structurally layered, integrating martial arts (*chhau* and *kalari*) with Bharatanatyam and quotidian gestures. The Indian street game *Kabbadi* inspired *Raid* (1995), developing the theme of crossing various boundaries – between sides in the game and between sport and dance. But, in contrast to *Raid*, the *nritta* dance components in *Palimpsest* echo the layers of an overwritten manuscript the word defines. Inspired by the inversions of Shakespeare's *Hamlet* contained in Tom Stoppard's play *Rosencrantz and Guildenstern Are Dead*, Jeyasingh's dance phrases 'are rarely seen as blocks of movement; instead, they bubble up to the surface at different times, then sink to different depths, adjusting their specific gravities in the fluid matrix of the dance'.[11] Set to Graham Fitkin's score, the formality of classical phrases was interwoven with a freer movement style. When *Palimpsest* was restaged in 2000, Jeyasingh introduced male performers (such as Mavin Khoo), and male artists continue to feature in her work.

By the tenth anniversary of her company, Jeyasingh had accumulated an impressive list of tributes. Her dances embraced the relentless pace of contemporary urban life, developing a movement language that seemed to increase in intensity, complexity and energy. *Fine Frenzy* (1999), to Django Bates' jazz score, was inspired by Stoke Newington Church Street in North London. Described as 'a dazzling, jolting rollercoaster ride over the millennial edge' with 'fragmentary patterns and speedy directional shifts', the dance was seen by Donald Hutera as 'both a product of, and comment upon, our overloaded, explosive information age'.[12] In addition to referencing older dances, *Memory and Other Props* (1999, with music by Alistair McDonald) integrated video projections, which increasingly have featured in her more recent choreography.

Dance reviews are often peppered with terms such as fragmentation, layering and contrast, applied not only to the dance (classical and contemporary), but also to the music (recorded and live, Indian and western, electronic and conventional instruments), and to the use of live dancers and filmed projections. Site-specific works add additional layers for comparison, starting with *Défilé* (1989), performed on the Champs Elysées for La Marseillaise, the Paris celebration of the bicentennial of the French Revolution. In *Duets with Automobiles* (1993), choreographed for television, a fragmented Bharatanatyam movement vocabulary was set against views of contemporary London architectural landmarks.

Other dances integrate advanced technology to innovative levels, as in *[h]interland* (2002), which experimented with the disruption of perception via cyberspace. A live webcast of a dancer performing poolside at an elegant Bangalore hotel competed with Pete Gomes' looped film of the cacophony of a busy Indian street. Physical distances, disparate cultural ambiances and theatrical conventions were further subverted by having the audience placed onstage. Lucy Carter's dramatic lighting drew the eye to the balcony on top of the bar to watch solos and duets performed to Donnacha Dennehy's vocal score. Hale pondered whether the dance called for Jeyasingh to be categorized as a postmodernist, because of the range of subversions, unusual juxtapositions and innovative use of multimedia in the dance.[13]

As with many choreographers, there has been a wide range of critical responses to Jeyasingh's choreography. Praise for the choreographic structures, sets, lighting, costume designs and commissioned scores is occasionally tempered by criticism of a perceived absence of emotional resonance or an over-intellectualized approach. Densely packed, high intensity, rhythmically complex movements seemed to challenge some viewers and, in some early works, occasionally her dancers' capabilities. But criticisms of technical mastery became less common. Foyer wrote that *Surface Tension* (2000) revealed the dancers'

> ... explicit sense of both their own body shape and their part in the complex shape of the work. This, together with her minimal use of partner contact, gives Jeyasingh's form a unique poise and focus. At its best, it has a beautiful understated sensuality.[14]

Danced to Kevin Volans's prepared harpsichord music played live to a recorded electronic score, the piece also featured hanging paper cutouts by Madeline Morris washed by the rich hues of Lucy Carter's lighting.

The project-based character of her company enables Jeyasingh to work within a range of capacities, such as a NESTA Foundation grant that took her to Japan and China in 2005. Work with other companies spans styles, with Jeyasingh creating on groups who draw their movement foundation from Kathak, another South Asian classical dance form. She set *Curve Twist Gaze* (2002) and *Neon Dream* (2003) on the Sonia Sabri Dance Company and *Debris* (2004) on the Anurekha Ghosh Dance Company. An exchange of sorts occurred when Wayne McGregor set *Intertense* (1998) on Jeyasingh's company and she created *Polar Sequences* with his Random Dance Company in 2003. Sections of *Transtep* (2004) were choreographed by Lisa Torun, Filip Van Huffel and Rasphal Sing Bansal, with Jeyasingh's reworked section to music by Monteverdi touring as a separate dance the following year, in a rare instance of her choreographing to an existing score. Jeyasingh choreographed *2Step* for the celebrations of the Olympic Games handover in 2008, performed by 20 dancers on the steps of St Paul's Cathedral. Another site-specific commissioned work was part of Big Dance 2010, a national dance celebration set at London's historic Somerset House in conjunction with the English National Ballet.

Flicker (2005) was the result of collaboration with costume designer Ursula Bombshell and composer Michael Nyman. Jürgen Simpson manipulated segments of Nyman's music to create an electronic score overlaid by an electric guitar improvisation, and the result broke from the familiar Nyman style: 'its sound has been distilled into a more monochromatic world – an electronic heartbeat, the ice-cold spattering of glass'.[15] The title was a reference to the flicker of a computer screen, 'which we see as a malfunction, a disruption to the normal rhythms of perception', as explained in programme notes. Bharatanatyam's formal properties were visible, but inverted, fragmented and disrupted even further than before: 'Bodies wrench at, collide and melt against one another relentlessly, their movements broken down behind them into spidery veins of light that stutter into seismographic scratches'.[16] Guy Hoare lit linear pathways on the stage, occasionally constraining the action of four male and three female dancers. Projected motion-capture computer images, designed by Digit, responded to the rhythmically complex dance component, coming together only momentarily with the score.

The multi-faceted view of a bee's eye inspired *Exit No Exit* (2006), with two choreographic strands that interact with or overlay each other. Roy described them as being like two stories – one of a trapped lone woman interrupted by six dancers with freedom to enter and exit the stage. Core motifs of natural, organic movement were juxtaposed against angular and synthetic ones.[17] With her dancers credited in the programme as creative collaborators, 'Jeyasingh sets complex duets and group work against or inside rippling, stream-like film projections' (created by Nichola Bruce).[18] Judith Mackrell declared that *Exit No Exit* 'advances Jeyasingh right to the centre of her best form' in which a soloist 'periodically launches herself into spirited percussive solos', while 'around her, the rest of the cast ebb and flow in a series of sociable dance conversations' into a 'visceral, buoyant form of expression'.[19]

Contemporary identity issues re-emerged in later work, arising in part out of heightened tensions in the aftermath of terrorist attacks in London. *Faultline* (2007) was inspired by Gaultam Malhani's 2006 novel *Londonstani*, which explored the fraught existence and gang pressures of young British Asian men, confronted with generational, class and ethnic divides. Richly produced in all components, live vocals from Patricia Rozario overlaid with Pete Gomes' haunting film of the singer was projected onto panels, following from opening shots of young men in a street scene. Dance movement created a dramatic vision of a generation in a state of discord, slipping between aggression, confrontation and brief moments of tenderness. All darkly clad, four female dancers moved in and among the four men, occasionally slipping into recognizable Bharatanatyam phrases between expansive leaps, iconic sharp gestural phrases and acrobatic lifts. *Bruise Blood* (2009) originated in Steve Reich's manipulated recording of an African-American talking about a police beating in 1960s New York; and *Just Add Water?* (2009) explored ideas about citizenship and identity via memories of family meals from countries such as the United States, Malaysia, Spain and Laos, reworked into a text by Rani Moorthy.

Musing about the categories of East and West applied by authors writing about her work with non-Indian composers, Jeyasingh argues eloquently that much of the discourse results in a 'colonization through categorization'. She says:

> The fact that we share a common British culture is never highlighted. The assumption is that 'East', myself, must be a simple, unchanging essence which stands for tradition and the Past and 'West', the composer, represents change, modernity and dynamism.[20]

Evocative sources of inspiration, varied musical and movement styles continually defy stereotypes and embody concepts of dynamism and change linked to the West. Jeyasingh continues to push forward a cosmopolitan avant-garde dance that is anything but simple or unchanging. For Roy, 'looking over her work is like seeing a classical style become modern and then post-modern in the space of a decade'.[21] Although her style fuses a range of forms, it is increasingly seen as 'contemporary' in its own right, a label that appears more frequently without qualifiers such as 'multicultural' or 'hybrid'.

Stacey Prickett

Notes

1 Sanjoy Roy, 'Shobana Jeyasingh and Cultural Issues: Part I – Multiple Choices', *Dance Theatre Journal*, 13(4), 1990, pp. 4–7.
2 Shobana Jeyasingh, 'Getting off the Orient Express', *Dance Theatre Journal*, 8(1), 1990, pp. 36–37.
3 Shobana Jeyasingh, 'What is Dance?' *Dance Now*, Spring 1992, p. 22.
4 Shobana Jeyasingh, 'Imaginary Homelands: Creating a New Dance Language', in Alexandra Carter (ed.), *Routledge Dance Studies Reader*, London, 1998, p. 48.
5 Sanjoy Roy (1990), op. cit., p. 5.
6 Marilyn Hunt, 'Something in the Way Brits Move', *Ballet Review*, Fall 21(3), 1993, p. 7.
7 Sarah Rubidge, 'Shobana Jeyasingh and Chandralekha', *Dance Theatre Journal*, 9(3), 1992, p. 40.
8 Sanjoy Roy, op. cit., 1990, p. 6.
9 See *Making of Maps Resource Pack*, Shobana Jeyasingh Dance Company, 1993.
10 Janet O'Shea, 'Unbalancing the Authentic/Partnering Tradition: Shobana Jeyasingh's *Romance . . . with Footnotes*', *Society of Dance History Scholars Conference Proceedings*, 1998, p. 118.
11 Sanjoy Roy (1990), op. cit., p. 7.
12 Donald Hutera, 'Spring in the Step', *Dance Now*, Spring 1999, p. 12.
13 Catherine Hale, 'Peripheral Vision', *Dance Theatre Journal*, 19(1), 2003, p. 42.
14 Maggie Foyer, 'Shobana Jeyasingh', *Dance Europe*, June 2002, p. 58.
15 Judith Mackrell, 'Shobana Jeyasingh', guardian.co.uk, 25 March 2005.
16 Shiromi Pinto, 'Lightning Strikes in the Same Place', *Pulse*, Spring 2005, p. 10.
17 See Sanjoy Roy, *Exit No Exit: Education Resource Pack*, Shobana Jeyasingh Dance Company, 2006.
18 Donald Hutera, 'Shobana Jeyasingh', *The Times*, 13 March 2006.
19 Judith Mackrell, 'Shobana Jeyasingh Dance Company', guardian.co.uk, 9 March 2006.
20 Shobana Jeyasingh, 'Text Context Dance', in Alessandra Lopez and Royo Iyer (eds), *Choreography and Dance*, 4(2), 1997, pp. 31–32.
21 Sanjoy Roy, 'Step by Step Guide to Dance: Shobana Jeyasingh', guardian.co.uk, 21 October 2009.

Biographical details

Born in Chennai (formerly Madras), Tamil Nadu, India 26 March 1957. **Studied** Bharatanatyam with guru Valluvoor Samuraj Pillai; came to UK in 1981, receiving a BA in Shakespeare Studies and MA in Renaissance Studies, University of Sussex. **Career:** Toured internationally as solo performer; founded Shobana Jeyasingh Dance Company, London, 1988; Research Associate at ResCen, Centre for Research into Creation in the Performing Arts, Middlesex University, from 2006.

Awards and honours: Digital Dance Award, 1988; London Dance and Performance Award, 1988; Digital Dance Award, 1990; *Time Out* Award for Best Choreography, 1992, 1995; Arts Council Women in the Arts Award, the Prudential Premier Award for the Arts, 1993; MBE for services to Dance, 1995; NESTA Dream Time Fellowship, 2004; Asian Woman of Achievement Award, 2008.

Works

Miniatures (1988); *Configurations* (1988); *Janpath* (1988, National Youth Dance Company); *Défilé* (1989); *Correspondences* (1990); *Byzantium* (1991); *Late* (1991); *Making of Maps* (1992); *Duets with Automobiles* (1993); *Romance . . . with Footnotes* (1993); *Raid* (1995); *Palimpsest* (1996); *The Bird and the Wind* (1996); *Intimacies of a Third Order* (1998); *Fine Frenzy* (1999); *Memory and Other Props* (1999); *Surface Tension* (2000); *Phantasmaton* (2002); *[h]interland* (2002); *Curve Twist Gaze* (2002, Sonia Sabri Dance Company); *Triptych Self* (2003); *Neon Dream* (2003, Sonia Sabri Dance Company); *Polar Sequences* (2003, Random Dance Company); *Curve Chameleon* (2003); *Café Event* (2003); *Transtep* (2004 with choreography from Lisa Torun, Filip Van Huffel, Rasphal Singh Banjal); *Foliage Chorus* (2004); *Debris* (2004, Anurekha Ghosh Dance Company); *Flicker* (2005); *Transtep 2* (2005); *Pop Idol* (2005, Random Dance Company); *Skin Deep* (2005, Northern Contemporary Dance School); *Exit No Exit* (2006); *Counterfeit* (2006, Northern Contemporary Dance School); *city: zen* (2006, City Contemporary Dance Company, Hong Kong with co-choreographer Mui Cheuk-yin); *Taxon* (2007, Middlesex University); *Shibuya* (2007, London Studio Centre); *Faultline* (2007, DVD 2008); *2Step* (2008); *Breach* (2008, Ballet Black); *The Dancer's Cut* (2008–09); *Body Talk* (2008, 2009 for Chichester University); *Re:Mix* (2009, Laban students); *Just Add Water?* (2009); *Bruise Blood* (2009).

Further reading

Interview with Sanjoy Roy, in 'Elephants and Mayflies', *Animated*, Winter 1997; with Sanjoy Roy, in *The Dance Makers Portfolio: Conversations with Choreographers*, Butterworth, Jo *et al.* (eds), Wakefield, 1998; with Anne Sachs, in 'Sowing Seeds', *Dance Theatre Journal*, 17(2), 2001; with Gerald Dowler, in 'Out of the Suitcase . . .', *Dancing Times*, September 2008.

Articles: Shobana Jeyasingh, 'Getting off the Orient Express', *Dance Theatre Journal*, 8(1), 1990; Sarah Rubidge, 'Modern Movement . . . and Traditional Tales', *Dance Theatre Journal*, 10(3), 1993; Jann Parry, 'Jeyasingh: A Knight of Dance Journeys off into the Unknown', *Dance Magazine*, April 1997; Natasha Bakht, 'Shobana Jeyasingh and Cultural issues: Part 2, Rewriting the Culture', *Dance Theatre Journal*, 13(4), 1997; Shobana Jeyasingh, 'Text Context Dance', in *Choreography and Dance*, 4(2), 1997; Sanjoy Roy, 'Shobana Jeyasingh and Cultural Issues: Part I – Multiple Choices', *Dance Theatre Journal*, 13(4), 1997; Diana Evans, 'Subtle Movements and Small Details', *Dance Theatre Journal*, 16(1), 2000; Lorna Sanders, 'Shobana Jeyasingh', *Dancing Times*, September 2001; Maggie Foyer, 'Shobana Jeyasingh', *Dance Europe*, June 2002; Lorna Sanders, *Shobana Jeyasingh: A Choreographer Fact Card*, National Resource Centre for Dance, Guildford, 2004; Shobana Jeyasingh, 'Much More Talk, Talk, Talking, Than Dance', *Pulse*, Autumn 2005.

Books: Helen Thomas (ed.), *Dance and the City*, London, 1997; Alexandra Carter (ed.), *Routledge Dance Studies Reader*, London, 1998; Paul Allen, *Art, Not Chance: Nine Artists' Diaries*, London, 2001; Valerie Briginshaw, *Dance, Space, and Subjectivity*, Houndmills, 2001; Janet O'Shea, *At Home in the World*, Middletown, CT, 2007; Janet Lansdale (ed.), *Decentring Dancing Texts*, London, 2008.

BILL T. JONES

Bill T. Jones's significance as a choreographer is virtually inseparable from his eloquence as a performer. In both fields he exhibits a soul-searching, missionary zeal. He is a humanist with a multifarious political agenda, using dance to ask passionate questions about life.

It is impossible to consider Jones's output without taking into account the late Arnie Zane. Jones has described himself and Zane, partners in every sense of the word, as 'a continent of two'. Jones's career can be divided into roughly three phases: his early work with Zane; the pieces produced in the company, formed in 1982, that still bears both their names; and finally, all that Jones has done since 1988, when half of that continent submerged as a result of Zane's AIDS-related death.

A prime component of their creative relationship was the attraction of, and tension between, opposites. Zane was short and springy, with a speedy agility and pugilistic directness that bounced off the tall, muscular Jones's dark silkiness. They met at the State University of New York, Binghamton, in 1971. Jones, a college athlete who was the tenth of twelve children born to Baptist-Methodist migrant farm workers, was hoping to become a professional actor. Zane, of Italian-Catholic and Lithuanian-Jewish extraction, had a degree in art history with a particular focus on photography. Their initial kinetic common ground was contact improvisation, an intimate, free-form method of movement (traces are still detectable in Jones's work) that dovetailed arrestingly with their highly autobiographical onstage dialogues.

Jones was always a charismatic, even confrontational, talker with apparently little problem making public his private feelings. In the 1992 solo *Last Night on Earth*, Jones, clad only in white briefs, combined semi-spontaneous meditations on the history of his pin-up physique with gestures and poses abstracted into design. The result highlighted the fine line between self-aware honesty, a clarion issue for Jones, and attitudinizing self-indulgence, an accusation sometimes lobbed at him by critics.

In 1974, Jones and Zane co-founded American Dance Asylum in Binghamton, a forum for a series of experimental solos and duets. Zane was initially discomfited by the naked stream-of-consciousness story-telling and word-games that Jones pushed for. (In one of their early pieces he dealt with his fears by speaking in Dutch.) Jones eventually compromised, agreeing to a more scripted, less personal use of speech in their joint work. Between 1979 and 1980 they devised a trilogy (*Monkey Run Road, Blauvelt Mountain* and *Valley Cottage*) that put them on the international dance map. These were pieces marked by intel-lectual rigour and purposeful physical vitality, overlaid with their own mutual warmth and candour.

Given the interest generated by their work, the logical next step was to form a company of dancers. The new recruits were selected as much for individual personalities as for their technical strengths; differences and contrasts remain key company watchwords. Jones's and Zane's own differences, however stormy, served them well as co-artistic leaders. Zane was the organized thinker and director; Jones tended towards the intuitive, concentrating on developing shapes and phrases into a cohe-sive yet diverse movement vocabulary.

In 1983, Jones scored a hit with *Fever Swamp*, a crowd-pleasing, all-male sextet for the Alvin Ailey American Dance Theater. Ailey figures prominently among Jones's influences, along with Martha Graham, José Limón and the great wave of post-modernism that stretches from Merce Cunningham through the Judson Dance Theater, Grand Union and beyond. In addition, Jones, who sometimes refers to himself as a poet, admits an affinity with fragmentary forms of artistic expression such as modern music and structuralist filmmaking. *Fever Swamp* is one of his 'danciest' dances, proving that, as he put it, 'I don't have to wear my ideology on my sleeve.' When the dance was incorporated into his and Zane's troupe, the casting became gender-blind both by necessity (there were not six men in the company to do it) and philosophy (Jones and Zane believed in breaking down male/female dance stereotypes).

Together they received more attention with *Secret Pastures* (1985), an aggressively hip, wacky collaboration with graffiti artist Keith Haring, fashion designer Willi Smith and art-rock composer Peter Gordon and his Love of Life Orchestra. Add to this trendy line-up the gymnastic, jazzy and decidedly eclectic choreography, plus the semblance of a wildly allegorical, neo-Frankenstein plot, and you have a frank bid for commercial viability and accessibility. Jones danced the role of the Fabricated Man, the literal brainchild of Zane's Mad Scientist, fêted by society and, in turn, adopting its tenets of greed, lust and violence. The casting carried its own oblique commentary about a black man's role in a predominantly white creative milieu.

To some, the gutsy, uncompromising daring of the intense first phase of the Jones/Zane partnership seemed to have given way to a more streamlined urban chic. Their raw energy was refined to accommodate bigger stages, an increasingly global audience and a broadened comprehension of what their art could do. The company is still known for its risky, edgy, all-out style, but the theatricality now carries extra emotional charge. Zane's premature death, and Jones's own HIV-positive status, has lent urgency and depth to the latter's choreography. Rather than disband the company, Jones kept it going as a living memorial to Zane. He has injected his personal understanding of grief and survival into the spectrum of social and aesthetic concerns once shared with Zane.

The year following Zane's death, Jones produced three works, all of which dealt, directly or indirectly, with loss. White sheets and draperies set the tone in *Absence* (1989), a sombre piece about mourning and isolation, which uses statuesque silhouettes, waltzing, mime and crawling. *D-Man in the Waters* (1989), its polar opposite, is a sporty, joyous display of ensemble virtuosity, set to a Mendelssohn octet and dedicated to another company member who died of AIDS. The music of Kurt Weill and Bessie Smith permeates *Soon* (1988), five duets infused with romantic and sexual longing and separation that may be performed by one or two pairs of dancers of the same or opposite sex.

Mortality plays a part in Jones's later works. A death-like figure wearing a white hooded jacket stalks the emotional landscape of *Love Defined* (1992), commissioned by Lyon Opera Ballet. In this dance a balletic spin is given to expressive, syncopated street rhythms cued by the plaintive pop music of Daniel Johnston. *Achilles Loved Patroclus*, a 1993 *tour-de-force* solo for Arthur Aviles, a former company dancer with a compact power similar to Zane's, weds together notions of heroism, homoeroticism and death.

One of Jones's most accomplished pieces is the evening-length epic, *Last Supper at Uncle Tom's Cabin/The Promised Land* (1990). This controversial examination of racism, sexuality and faith was inspired by various sources: Leonardo Da Vinci's painting; Harriet Beecher Stowe's nineteenth-century novel about slavery during the American Civil War; African-American vaudeville, particularly 1920s Harlem, and a deck of soft-core porn cards. The artistic ingredients were equally varied: saxophonist/composer Julius Hemphill's dissonant yet elegiac score; text, including excerpts from playwright Leroi Jones's 1964 *Dutchman* and fragments of Martin Luther King's 'I have a dream' speech (1968), recited backwards; and movement ranging from ironic variations of popular steps to pungent modern dance. Combining the sweep of opera with the impact of political statement, the show presented images of power, struggle, sacrifice, humiliation and oppression. By the finale, however, the fury and desperation fuelling the whole piece were set aside, as a swarm of dancers of all shapes and sizes filed back and forth across the stage, united by their complete or (in some performances) partial nudity.

Jones has since choreographed and directed for opera and theatre. In the early 1990s, he launched the survival project, culminating in the full-length dance-theatre work *Still/Here* (1994). The subject was mortality. Content was culled from workshops held in 11 American cities with people coping with life-threatening illnesses. It is at once his most controversial and acclaimed work to date.

Still/Here, as its title indicates, is split into two parts. The first, more elegiac, half, relating to reactions to a diagnosis, uses the workshop members' own words, set to music by composer Kenneth Frazelle and sung by folk singer Odetta in a voice crackling with hard-won wisdom. The tone is internalized and spiritual, with the dancers clad in white, grey and pale blue outfits. The second section, more corporeal and affirmative, is about living with the prospect of death. The performers wear identical costumes, dyed red. Here the choreography is driven and dynamic, fuelled by the music of rock guitarist Vernon Reid. The vocabulary blends the odd balletic step with colloquial gestures and bold contemporary moves. Nothing the dancers do is conventionally literal, yet the shapes, forms and rhythms Jones uses convey tremendous feeling.

Jones has insisted that *Still/Here*, which features Gretchen Bender's extensive and haunting video footage of the workshop participants, was not about death but rather was intended as a tool for learning 'how we can become more alive'. In most quarters it was regarded as an unqualified artistic triumph. Arlene Croce, the dance critic for *The New Yorker* magazine, was the loudest voice of dissension. Her refusal even to see the production, on the grounds that as 'victim art' it begged her sympathy and therefore made itself impossible to be written about objectively, engendered both enormous debate within the arts world and additional publicity for the show itself.

Jones's subsequent dances have leaned towards the lyrical and abstract, although never at the expense of drama. For Lyon he made the evening-length *24 Images per Second* (1995), an impressionistic tribute to the 100th anniversary of the Lumière brothers' invention of cinema, and the smaller-scale *Green and Blue* (1997), a subtle and ghostly response to two lesser-known string works of Mozart. Poetry provided a life-affirming source for two 1996 pieces for Jones's own company. *Ballad*, a suite of ensemble and fleeting solo dances, is set to Dylan Thomas's readings of four of his own poems, while *Ursonate*, co-choreographed with dancer Darla Villani, draws on a 1928 sound-poem by Dada master Kurt Schwitters to impart an exciting sense of structured disconnection. The collage-like quality spilled over into the engaging, and deliberately disorientating, *Lisbon* (1997), virtually a choreographic retrospective marked by jarring changes of action, speed, light and music ranging from hard-driving rock to undulant Latin folk rhythms.

In 1997, Jones embarked on another evening-length work, *We Set Out Early . . . Visibility Was Poor*, which opts for a mysterious communal adventure in lieu of 'in-your-face' polemics. Hard to pin down, seamlessly constructed and loaded with vibrant movement, this cryptic, polished piece invited an intuitive response.

Jones has continued to think big, becoming overtly and urgently political in his choice of subject matter. In 2003, he adapted Flannery O'Connor's biting short story 'The Artificial Nigger' into *Reading, Mercy and the Artificial Nigger*. Two actors spoke the text while moving amongst the company dancers. *Mercy 10 × 8 on a Circle* was this bracing work's more abstract companion piece.

The themes of the full-length *Blind Date* (2005) included honour, valour and patriotism, particularly in America and in an atmosphere that Jones described as 'toxic certainty'. Rather than take the easy route by approaching such concepts with a didactically liberal mindset, he opted to wrestle with the moral questions that arose from them without sacrificing either choreographic ingenuity or theatrical flair. Over the years Jones's dancers have become, if anything, even more inclusive in their mix of races, genders, shapes and sizes. Here they were again cast as a microcosm of society negotiating its way through a set of shifting projection screens designed by Jones's partner and the company's resident designer, Bjorn Amelan.

The company's large-scale efforts are balanced by a variety of alternative artistic strategies. These include reshaping older pieces into new work, or stitching together combinations of work in a flexible fashion. Examples of the latter are *Another Evening: I Bow Down* (2006), a multi-media collage of new movement and excerpts from pre-existing repertoire, plus original music and text, and the modular *As I Was Saying . . .* (2005). The latter brings together 'With the Good Lord', a response to a recorded nightclub performance by the 1950s jazz artist Lord Buckley, regarded by many as a precursor of rap; *Chaconne*, a piece framed around spoken text and a Bach violin solo; and *22*, which updates Jones's 1983 talking solo *21* with digital technology. In this, as in the 1999 solo *The Breathing Show*, he performs with all the majesty and honesty that can be expected of such an uncompromising and sensitive provocateur.

Shaped specifically for the Venice Dance Biennal, *Another Evening: Venice* (2010) continues Jones's interest in referencing company repertory in tandem with newly created material. This is no mere exercise in artistic navel gazing. Jones' preoccupation with history is wide ranging and certainly not limited to his own creative past. *Serenade/The Proposition* (2008) considers the legacy of Abraham Lincoln, whereas the evening-length *Fondly Do We Hope . . . Fervently Do We Pray* (2009) focuses on key moments of the assassinated American president's life. As an offshoot of these works Jones's company offers *100 Migrations*, an ongoing project bringing together 100 diverse members of a local community who collectively explore the question, 'Had Lincoln lived, what would we be like today?'

The premise is typical of Jones's probing mind. Inspired by a short, absurdist play for two puppets, *A Quarreling Pair* (2007) examines the related notion of two people struggling to live together. Whatever the scale or subject matter, Jones tries to use his dances as a springboard from which we might begin to understand how people exist within themselves and alongside each other. This approach is equally relevant to the stage assignments he has undertaken away from his company. As a choreographer for hire, Jones was acclaimed for the 2006 Broadway musical adaptation of Frank Wedekind's seminal, pre-expressionist play about troubled German youth, *Spring Awakening* (2006). More recently he choreographed and directed *Fela!* (2009), another Broadway blockbuster, based on the life of the legendary Nigerian musician and political maverick Fela Kuti.

Donald Hutera

Biographical details

Born in Bunnell, Florida, United States, 15 February 1952. **Studied** African dance with Percival Borde, ballet with Ernest Paganano and Maggie Black, contact improvisation with Lois Welk, modern dance with Linda Grande and Humphrey Weidman, improvisation with Richard Bull and jazz ballet with Cova Pullman; attended State University of New York at Binghampton and State University College at Brockport, 1970–73. **Career**: Co-founder, with dancer-choreographer Arnie Zane, American Dance Asylum in Binghamton, New York, 1974–76; toured independently as dancer-choreographer; co-founder of Bill T. Jones/Arnie Zane Dancers, 1982; continuing as sole artistic director of Bill T. Jones/Arnie Zane Dance Company after Zane's death in 1988; resident choreographer (honorific title) for Lyon Opera Ballet, 1994–97. Has choreographed for Alvin Ailey American Dance Theater, Axis Dance Company, Boston Ballet, Diversions Dance Company; worked as choreographer and director for opera companies, including Houston Grand Opera, Glyndebourne Festival Opera, New York City Opera, Boston Lyric Opera. **Awards and honours**: Choreographic Fellowship, National Endowment for the Arts, 1980, 1981, 1982; New York Dance and Performance Award ('Bessie'), 1986 and 1989; Dorothy B. Chandler Performing Arts Award, 1991; *Dance Magazine* Award, 1993; MacArthur 'Genius' Award, 1994; named 'An Irreplaceable Dance Treasure' by Dance Heritage Coalition, 2000; Dorothy and Lillian Gish Prize, 2003; Wexner Prize, 2005; Samuel H. Scripps Award, 2005; Harlem Renaissance Award, 2005; Stage Directors and Choreographers Foundation CALLAWAY Award, 2006; Lucille Lortel Award, 2006; Tony Award for Best Choreography, 2007; Obie Award, 2007.

Works

Pas de Deux (with Zane, 1971); *Pas de Deux for Two* (with Zane, 1973); *A Dance with Durga Devi* (1974); *Negroes for Sale* (1974); *Entrances* (1974); *Track Dance* (1974); *Could Be Dance* (1974); *Across the Street There is a Highway* (1975); *Woman in Drought* (1975); *Impersonations* (1975); *Everybody Works/All Beasts Count* (1975); *For You* (1977); *Stomps* (1977); *Walk* (1977); *A Man* (1977); *Asymmetry: Every Which Way* (1977); *Da Sweet Streak to Love Land* (1977); *Floating the Tongue* (1978); *Naming Things is Only the Intention to Make Things* (1978); *Progresso* (1978); *By the Water* (1978); *Echo* (1979); *Addition* (1979); *Circle in Distance* (1979); *Monkey Run Road* (with Zane, 1979); *Blauvelt Mountain* (with Zane, 1979); *Dance in the Trees* (1980); *Open Places: A Dance in June* (1980); *Untitled Duet* (with Sarry Satenstrom, 1980); *Valley Cottage* (with Zane, 1980); *Balancing the World* (1980); *Sisyphus* (1980); *Social Intercourse: Pilgrim's Progress* (1980); *Break* (1980); *10: Prologue Performance* (1980); *Ah! Break It!* (1980); *Three Dances* (1982); *Shared Distance* (1982); *Duet x 2* (1982); *Continuous Replay* (with Zane, 1982); *Rotary Action* (with Zane, 1982); *Fever Swamp* (1983); *Naming Things* (with Phillip Mallory Jones and David Hammons, 1983); *Intuitive Momentum* (with Zane, 1983); *21* (1983; video version, dir. Tom Bowes, 1984); *Corporate Whimsy* (1983); *Casino* (1983); *Dances with Brahms* (1984); *Freedom of Information* (with Zane, 1985); *Secret Pastures* (with Zane, 1985); *1, 2, 3* (1985); *Holzer Duet . . . Truisms* (with Lawrence Goldhuber, 1985); *M.A.K.E.* (1985); *Pastiche* (1985); *Virgil Thompson Etudes* (1986); *Animal Trilogy* (with Zane; includes *How to Walk an Elephant, Water Buffalo: An Acquired Taste*, and *Sacred Cow: Lifting* a *Calf Every Day Until it Becomes an Ox*; 1986); *Where the Queen Stands Guard* (with Zane, 1987); *Red Room* (1987); *Chatter* (1988); *Soon* (1988); *History of Collage Revisited* (with Zane, 1988); *Don't Lose Your Eye* (1989); *Forsythia* (1989); *La Grande Fête* (1989); *It Takes Two* (1989); *Absence* (1989); *D-Man in the Waters* (1989); *Last Supper at Uncle Tom's Cabin/The Promised Land* (1990); *New Year* (opera, 1989); *Mother of Three Sons* ('dance/opera', 1990); *Havoc in Heaven* (1991); *Broken Wedding* (1992); *Die Öffnung* (1992); *Love Defined* (1992); *Our Respected Dead* (1992); *Aria* (1992); *Fête* (1992); *Last Night on Earth* (1992); *Lost in the Stars* (opera, 1992); *After Black Room* (choi. Zane, restaged by Jones, 1993); *Achilles Loved Patroclus* (1993); *War Between the States* (1993); *There were so many . . .* (1993); *And the Maiden* (1993); *Just You* (1993); *Still/Here* (1994); *I Want to Cross Over* (1994); *24 Images per Second* (1995); *Degga* (collaboration with Max Roach and Toni Morrison, 1995); *New Duet* (1995); *Bill and Laurie: About Five Rounds* (collaboration with Laurie Anderson, 1995); *Ursonate* (with Darla Villani, 1996), *Ballad* (1996); *Soon* (1996); *Blue Phrase* (1996); *Love Redefined* (revised version of *Love Defined*, 1996); *Some Songs* (1997); *Green and Blue* (1997); *Lisbon* (1997); *We Set Out Early . . . Visibility Was Poor* (1997); *Out of Some Place* (1999); *The Breathing Show* (1999); *Ghostcatching – A Virtual Dance Installation* (with Paul Keiser, Shelly Eshkar, Mark Downey, 1999); *You Walk* (2000); *Fantasy in C Major* (2000); *The Table Project* (2001); *Verbum* (2002); *WORLD WITHOUT/IN* (2002); *Black Suzanne* (2002); *WORLD II (18 Movements to Kurtag*; 2002); *There Were . . .* (2002); *Power/Full* (2002); *Another Evening* (2003); *Reading, Mercy and The Artificial Nigger* (2003); *Mercy 10 x 8 on a Circle* (2003); *and before . . .* (2003); *Blind Date* (2005); *As I Was Saying . . .* (2005); *Another Evening: I Bow Down* (2006); *Chapel/Chapter* (2006); *Spring Awakening* (musical adaptation of Frank Wedekind's play, 2006); *A Quarreling Pair* (2007); *Serenade/The Proposition* (2008); *Fondly Do We Hope . . . Fervently Do We Pray* (2009); *Fela!* (director and choreographer, 2009); *Another Evening: Venice* (2010).

Further reading

Interviews in Connie Kreemer (ed.), *Further Steps: Fifteen Choreographers on Modern Dance*, New York, 1987; with Maya Wallach, in 'A Conversation with Bill T. Jones', *Ballet Review*, Winter 1990/91; in 'Everything Feels a bit like Dancing', *Dance Theatre Journal*, 14(2), 1998; with Nicholas Rowe, in 'Bill T. Jones', *Dance Europe*, October/November 1998; with Debra Craine, in 'A Beautiful Body of Work', *The Times*, June 2004; in Joyce Morgenroth (ed.), *Speaking of Dance: Twelve Contemporary Choreographers on their Craft*, New York, 2004.

Articles: Julinda Lewis, 'Making Dances from the Soul: The Warm and Startling Images of Bill T. Jones', *Dance Magazine*, November 1981; Elizabeth Zimmer, 'Bill T. Jones and Arnie Zane: Solid Citizens of Post-Modernism', *Dance Magazine*, October 1984; B. Laine, 'Trendy Twosome', *Ballet News*, August 1985; Donald Hutera, 'Bill T. Jones Going Naked', *Dance Theatre Journal*, Autumn 1990; Maya Wallach, 'Bill T. Jones: In Search of the Promised Land', *Dance Magazine*, October 1991; R. Tracy, 'Bill T. Jones: Full Circle', *Dance Magazine*, October 1992; Henry Louis Gates, 'The Body Politic', *The New Yorker*, 28 November 1994; Arlene Croce, 'Discussing the Undiscussable', *The New Yorker*, 26 December 1994 and 2 January 1995 (double issue); Marcia B. Siegel, 'Virtual Criticism and the Dance of

Death', *Drama Review*, T150, Summer 1996; Raymond T. Ricketts, 'Working with Bill T. Jones', *Dance Now*, Autumn 1995; Donald Hutera, 'From *Enfant Terrible* to *Eminence Gris*', *Dance Now*, Summer 1998; Rose-Ann Clermont, 'Bill T. Jones Walks the Walk', *The Village Voice*, 11 July 2000; Deborah Jowitt, 'Rendezvous with Nimble Ghosts', *The Village Voice*, 16 September 2003; Elizabeth Zimmer, 'Bill', *Dance Magazine*, November 2003; Deborah Jowitt, 'Saith What Lord?', *The Village Voice*, 27 September 2005; Deborah Jowitt, 'Motion Sickness', *The Village Voice*, 5 December 2006; Sylviane Gold, 'Africa Rising', *Dance Magazine*, October 2008; Rebecca Milzoff, 'Nigerian Rhapsody', *New York Magazine*, 7 September 2008; Abigail Rasminsky, 'Tackling the Future: 'Bill T. Jones' Company at 25', *Dance Magazine*, February 2009; Deborah Jowitt, 'Bill T. Jones' Great Divide', *The Village Voice*, 17 November 2009; Joan Acocella, 'A Hero's Welcome', *The New Yorker*, 7 December 2009; Rita Felciano, 'Bill T. Jones/Arnie Zane Company', *Dance Magazine*, December 2009.

Books: Elizabeth Zimmer and Susan Quasha (eds), *Body Against Body*, New York, 1989; Bill T. Jones, *Last Night on Earth* (autobiography), New York, 1995; Merce Cunningham, Meredith Monk, Bill T. Jones, *Art Performs Life: Merce Cunningham, Meredith Monk, Bill T. Jones*, Minneapolis, 1998; Randy Martin, *Critical Moves*, Durham, NC, 1998; Jane Desmond (ed.), *Dancing Desires*, Madison, WI, 2001; Judith Chapman *et al.* (eds), *Dancelines: Writings by New Scholars*, Guildford, 2002.

AKRAM KHAN

Few newcomers equal Akram Khan in the intensity and speed of his impact on the international scene. Khan is a rare talent, a breathtaking soloist in the South Asian classical kathak dance form and a rising star as a contemporary choreographer and performer. One can rightfully use terms such as meteoric to describe his career, achieving early international acclaim and prestigious production funding with high-calibre collaborators. However, to label his style as a fusion of kathak and contemporary does not do it justice, and Khan is quick to point to other significant influences. A prodigious dancer from a young age, he was taught Bengali folk dances by his mother and was also immersed in music videos, particularly admiring Michael Jackson. London-born into a Bangladeshi family, Khan first came to contemporary dance at university. From these diverse strands, a unique movement language developed, already apparent in his initial foray into contemporary choreography in 1995. His mesmerising performance qualities in kathak spill over to his contemporary movement creations, even though he retains a strong commitment to the traditional form. The Akram Khan Company, founded in 2000 with producer Farooq Chaudry, has developed into a group of international performers who push stylistic boundaries.

As a child, Khan participated in various cultural events within his London diasporic community, studying kathak with Sri Pratap Pawar. Khan's choreography, shaped by Western and Eastern aesthetic visions, approaches contemporary and kathak collaborations through different processes.[1] His performance career started early, with him dancing in Pawar's works and in *The Adventures of Mowgli* (1983), an adaptation of Rudyard Kipling's *The Jungle Book* for the Academy of Indian Dance. At the other end of the spectrum, Khan's aesthetic is informed by the minimalist theatre approach of Peter Brook, with whom he worked on a production of the Hindu epic, *The Mahabharata*. Khan finds a purity in Brook's approach: 'his very honest and simple approach showed me that simplicity was much better than "too much"'.[2] He then started a dance degree at De Montfort University before moving to the Northern School of Contemporary Dance, achieving the highest degree scores in the institution's history.[3]

Khan's contemporary innovations are integrally linked to the dynamic and structural components of kathak. A strong dramatic component (*abhinaya*) is conveyed through gestural actions and facial expressions, bringing to life tales of Hindu gods. The abstract (*nritta*) elements can develop into highly complex and virtuosic movement, particularly in the percussive footwork accentuated by ankle bells and fast pirouettes (*chakkars*), both punctuated by sudden stops. Closely linked to the accompanying Hindustani music, dance phrases are structured in cycles, with rhythmic interplay between dancer and musician occurring within established rules. Mnemonic syllables (*bols*) emulate the *tabla* (drum) sounds and delineate variations in the cyclical rhythms. Khan's intense physicality is diverse, sharp yet fluid, displaying a virtuosic speed that can involve complex mathematics. His continued mastery of the traditional form is evident in spellbinding performances created by prominent kathak choreographers like Gauri Sharma Trapathi (*Polaroid Feet*, 2001; *Ronin*, 2003) and Kudmudini Lakhia (*Chakravyuh*, part of *Third Catalogue*, 2005).

Contemporary solos brought Khan into the limelight, with *Loose in Flight* (1995). The film version from 1999 reveals the extent to which multiple dance styles are seamlessly intertwined. To Angie Atmadjaja's score, the fluid grace of kathak's arm gestures and quick spins are combined with acrobatic vertical rolls and the release into gravity characteristic of many contemporary techniques. Dance critic Clement Crisp observed:

The curves and sinuosities of his style, gesture rippling and flickering, cobra-tongue fast, as his arms circled head and trunk, are eye-catching, eye-holding. He seems to pose in the centre of a magnetic storm of dance that he summons from the air.[4]

Fix (2000), his second solo, was inspired by whirling dervishes, different energy flows and spatial constraints, embodied in the blend of kathak, contemporary and breakdancing.[5] Lighting designer Michael Hulls and composer Nitin Sawhney, collaborators prominent in Khan's future creations, enhanced the work's theatricality. Former Royal Ballet dancer and contemporary choreographer Jonathan Burrows helped Khan explore new ways of working to expand and move beyond the form he was trained in – a lesson Khan learned during their collaborative duet, *Desert Steps* (mus. Kevin Volans, 1999).[6]

Rush (2000) was created as a quintet while at the X-Group choreographic project at the Performing Arts Research and Training Studios (PARTS), headed by Anne Teresa de Keersmaeker in Brussels. His inspiration came from the tension between the adrenaline thrills and silence of freefall experienced by parachutists, transformed into an abstract trio.[7] Khan's spatial and rhythmic manipulations were vividly apparent. A Hindustani nine-and-a-half beat rhythm underpins whirling arms that initiate quick turns with undulating arm ripples extending to the fingertips, propelling the dancers into dive rolls. Bursts of intensity end in poses, such as torsos bent parallel to the floor, arms out in 'V' shapes, or in a basic kathak stance in parallel with arms folded, chest-high, in a diamond formation. Black tunics and trousers contributed to an air of austerity that vanished as the intensity built. Solos then broke from unison phrases, danced to Andy Cowton's electronic score with metallic clangs and bells. *Related Rocks* (2001), created to Magnus Lindberg's electronic score with two live pianists, developed his style further. Khan 'kept his choreography on its own track, sometimes moving at a slower or faster pace than the music, sometimes fracturing into a dazzle of alternative rhythms'.[8]

Accounts of the early dances are filled with evocative movement metaphors, whereas Khan's full-length works tap richer symbolic depths. *Kaash* (2002), meaning 'if' in Hindi and 'if only' in Urdu, was inspired by physics and the cycles of destruction and renewal associated with the Hindu deity Shiva. The abstract treatment is explored in two high-velocity sections surrounding a meditative middle one. Nitin Sawhney's score builds to climactic volumes, as the windmill arm motions of five dancers' propel them out of lines only to be drawn back into place. In his response to *Kaash*, Alastair Macaulay compared Khan's accomplishments with Mark Morris, and his sophistication with Merce Cunningham, evoking the structural complexity of the string quartets of Mozart and Schubert, 'because of the way in which voices are combined, separated omitted, and reintroduced – often with dazzling command of space'.[9] In one quintet of dervish like spinning, 'you find that he's using that spinning to contract and expand the space'.[10] Aideen Malone's lighting of visual artist Anish Kapoor's black backdrop changed hues across the colour spectrum, transforming the materiality of the stage into a spatial void. Macaulay found beauty in moments of calm, explaining how the dancers

> ... show their authority by the simplest strokes: standing quite still facing that backdrop. Or, at the end of one terrific crescendo in the music, [Khan] enters alone, and exactly as it ends, just holds out one arm: holds it with limpid, unforced authority outward into space.[11]

In his second full-length work, *Ma* (2004), Khan expanded narrative strands further. Inspiration came from Arundhati Roy's essays about Indian farmers evicted from their land to make room for a dam. Themes linked to the translation of *ma* (Hindi for 'mother' and 'earth') provided poetic and physical imagery. Sufi vocals delivered by Pakistani singer Fazheem Mazhar, Riccardo Nova's score for cellist and a *mridangam* (a South Asian drum) percussionist, were interspersed with recorded passages by the Ictus Ensemble, and with text by Hanif Kureishi spoken by Khan. In pools of pale light, cast by lighting designer Mikki Kuntu, dancers occasionally paused and observed the action from behind bags suspended from the ceiling. Snippets of stories about love, childlessness and trees were told by two female dancers holding awkward yogic positions. The floor provided both a sounding board for percussive footwork and a launching pad for aerial work. *Ma* integrated a broader movement language – the stillness of strange body shapes alluding to an upside-down world set off by rapid flying rolls that skimmed across the floor. Khan's use of the lower body was more extensive as movement impulses travelled out into expansive leg gestures. Layers of physical and emotional interaction were summed up in Louis Armstrong's rendition of 'What a Wonderful World', ending the dance on a hopeful note.

Khan's performance role in *Ma* was minimal, the choreographer having accrued a strong company of stylistically diverse dancers, some of whom have now been with the company since its inception. Rules of classical dance are ingrained in Khan's body, in contrast to the relative freedoms he found in contemporary styles:

There is a right and a wrong, and the body is trained to identify where the parameters are. For me contemporary dance was about breaking the perception of where the parameters were about right and wrong. It was about breaking all the rules that were set in my body. It was liberating but it was a shock, and my body got confused, but the body has a way of finding balance again and finding sense in chaos, and that's what my body did.[12]

Other collaborations have brought together dancers trained in different genres. A question-and-answer session, for example, inspired the preliminary work on the trio *Red or White* (2003), commissioned for the George Piper Dancers (the company founded by former Royal Ballet dancers William Trevitt and Michael Nunn). Khan taught them the basics of kathak to identify a middle ground between their two styles.[13] Defying hierarchical categories of art, Khan then choreographed for pop star Kylie Minogue's 2006 *Showgirl* tour, while a collaboration with Lin Hwai-min's Cloud Gate Dance Theatre in Taiwan resulted in *Lost Shadows* (2007). Composer Nitin Sawhney and Khan's catalogue of work provided the material for *Confluences* (2009), comprising excerpts from their ten years of collaborations, while *Variations for Vibes, Strings & Pianos* (2006) celebrated the music of composer Steve Reich.

In 2005, Khan embarked on a trio of duets, beginning with *O°* (*Zero Degrees*) created with Belgium-based Sidi Larbi Cherkaoui. Similar identity issues inspired the work, as both are practising Muslims with dual ethnic and national influences (Khan is Bangladeshi–British and Cherkaoui is Moroccan-Flemish). Designer Antony Gormley's sculptures played a powerful role on stage and were made from castings of the choreographers' bodies. Devoid of expression, the lifeless dummies were an eerie presence; positioned as observers apart from the action, they later appeared to replace their live counterparts. When Cherkaoui aggressively manipulated Khan's sculpted twin, the physical reactions were channelled into Khan's body lying nearby. Gormley reshaped the stage into a white box, with musicians hidden behind a scrim and only fully revealed towards the dance's closing moments. Nitin Sawhney's score and Faheem Mazhar's vocals added a haunting resonance. The fragmented narrative alternated between humour and tragedy, self-assurance and insecurity, the dancers' impeccable timing bringing together their voices and intricate gestural choreography. Dramaturge Guy Cools's text was based on Khan's travels in India and Bangladesh, during which he encountered a range of experiences from a corrupt border guard to a dead man on a train with a grieving widow, while experiencing all along the longing for familiar comforts – basic amenities often taken so much for granted. The dance's starting point was discussions Khan had about

> ... the notion that you can never really achieve stillness. In life you are breathing, but in death your body continues to decompose. So what is the transitional point? When do you die? Nobody knows because once they go, they are on the other side. This is about that transition point, the point I call zero degrees.[14]

Distinctive physicalities and dance styles in his piece provided an innovative mix, as the dancers traded each other's steps whereas solo passages accentuated their differences. Cherkaoui's hyper-mobile, lanky limbs flicked into space or folded backwards to the floor in a contorted shoulder stand, while Khan's lightning quick kathak turns and flying dives traversed the stage, his compact body casting large shadows. Images of death, stillness, loss and belonging evoked through physical metaphors echoed those of the stories.

The trilogy of duets continued with *Sacred Monsters* (2006), created with former Royal Ballet prima ballerina Sylvie Guillem, in which the two mused physically and aloud about their relationships to their respective classical dance traditions. Hints of each were seen in solos, juxtaposed against duets that ranged from a humorous cartoonish fight to a magical transformation. In an otherworldly vision, Khan stood with Guillem's legs wrapped around his waist, their two torsos and four arms intertwining and pulling apart in mirror actions. *In-i* (2008), with actress Juliette Binoche, pushed each beyond their comfort zones as artists. The theme of love, supported by Cools's text and Philip Sheppard's score, ran the gamut of emotions (vulnerable tenderness to violent aggression) while Kapoor's monolithic red wall slowly inched forward, the claustrophobia of a relationship in the throes of break-up visually reflected in the decreasing stage space.

Cross-cultural journeys, real and metaphoric, inspired *Bahok* (2008), meaning 'carrier'. Set in an airport waiting room, the piece featured three dancers from the National Ballet of China who joined Khan's company in an exploration of the joys and insecurities of global travel. Alongside the thrill of adventure and the boredom of waiting, vignettes derived from the dancers' personal stories recalled the tensions of immigration interviews, language difficulties and loss of connection to home. Yet the warmth of fellow travellers also shone through evocative dance passages that celebrated the dancers' individual styles.

In *Gnosis*, advertised for 2009 but delayed by injury until 2010, Khan returned to the Hindu epic *Mahabharata* and contemporary dance, with choreographic input from kathak exponent Gauri Sharma Trapathi. Partnered by Japanese taiko drummer, singer and dancer Yoshie Sunahata, Khan told a story of faith, love and loss that was fulfilled through inventive movement, music and vocals. Khan explained that 'classical to me is clarity, where the boundaries are clear and visible. Contemporary is chaotic'.[15] Yet his contemporary dances are increasingly infused with a clarity that transcends the boundaries between the two. Central to his artistic vision is a rich theatricality with influences drawn from other arts, most of which are vivid production components (music, lighting, design and, increasingly, text). But Khan also speaks of being inspired by the entangled and non-linear narrative styles of some cinema directors, thus expanding on the traditions of storytelling that underpin his kathak roots.[16] It is not just the stories he tells, but the way he tells them that enthrals global audiences.

Stacey Prickett

Notes

1 Preeti Vasudevan (with Akram Khan), 'Clarity within Chaos', *Dance Theatre Journal*, 18(1), 17, 2002, p. 18.
2 Quoted by Margaret Willis, 'Dancer Profile: Akram Khan', *Dancing Times*, March 2001, p. 588.
3 Emily Eakin, 'The Agile Ambassador at Large', *New York Times*, Magazine section, 12 October 2003.
4 Clement Crisp, 'Artist who Dazzling Explores Boundaries', *Financial Times*, 29 October 2002, p. 17.
5 Lorna Sanders, *Akram Khan's Rush: Creative Insights*, Alton, 2004.
6 Lorna Sanders, 'Choreographers Today: Akram Khan', *Dancing Times*, May 2003, p. 19. In some references, including early Akram Khan Company material, the title of the dance is listed as *Duet*.
7 Ibid. Sanders notes that initial publicity material mistakenly identified Khan's inspiration as 'paragliders' rather than 'parachutists'.

8 Judith Mackrell, 'Related Rocks', *The Guardian*, 11 December 2001.
9 Alastair Macaulay, 'A Fusion of Youth and Maturity', *Financial Times*, 17 May 2002, p. 18.
10 Ibid.
11 Ibid.
12 Akram Khan, interviewed by Samantha Ellis in 'Dance Was about Breaking All the Rules that Were Set in My Body', *The Guardian*, 22 April 2004.
13 Sanders (2003), op. cit., p. 23.
14 Akram Khan, quoted by Rosie Millard, in 'Spiritual Mould', *The Times*, 25 June 2005, p. 9.
15 Akram Khan, quoted by Preeti Vasudevan in 'Clarity within Chaos', *Dance Theatre Journal*, 18(1), 2002, p. 18.
16 See Akram Khan interviewed by Sanjoy Roy, in 'Akram Khan & Nitin Sawhney, the Mould-Breakers', *Pulse*, No. 106, Autumn 2009, p. 8.

Biographical details

Born in London, 29 July 1974. **Studied** Bengali folk dancing as a child with his mother and kathak with Sri Pratap Pawar, becoming his disciple; also studied at Kathak Kendra in New Delhi as well as diverse contemporary and ballet styles at De Montfort University, 1994–96, and Northern School of Contemporary Dance, 1996–97. **Career:** Performed as a teenager in Sir Peter Hall's production of the *Mahabharata*, which toured internationally, 1987–89, and in the televised version, 1988; also appeared in *Hamlet* (dir. Hall, 2001) with the Royal Shakespeare Company; official début in classical performance (*Ragmanch Pravesh*) in 1992, continuing as solo dance performer in the 1990s; founded Akram Khan Company in 2000; choreographer-in-residence, 2001–03, and associate artist, 2003–05, South Bank Centre, London; associate artist at Sadler's Wells Theatre, London, from 2009. Has also choreographed for George Piper Dances, Cloud Gate Dance Theatre, National Ballet of China and Kylie Minogue. **Awards and honours** include Jerwood Foundation Choreographic Award, 2000; Time Out Live Award, 2000; Dance Critics' Circle Awards, 2000, 2002; International Movimentos Dance Prize, 2004; Critics Circle National Dance Award, 2005; South Bank Show Award, 2005; Outstanding Artist (Modern), National Dance Awards, 2005; two Helpmann Awards, 2007; International Theatre Institute Award, 2007; *Dance Magazine* Award, 2008; MBE for services to UK dance community, 2005

Works

Loose in Flight (1995; film version for Channel 4 TV, 1999; UK tour 2000)*; *No Male Egos* (with Mavin Khoo, 1999); *Desert Steps* (with Jonathan Burrows, 1999); *Fix* (2000); *Rush* (2000); *Related Rocks* (2001); *Polaroid Feet* (2001); *Kaash* (2002); *Ronin* (2003); *Red or White* (2003); *A God of Small Tales* (2004); *ma* (2004); *Zero Degrees* (initially *O°*; 2005); *Third Catalogue* (programme title, 2005); *Sacred Monsters* (additional choreography by Lin Hwai Min, 2006); *Variations for Vibes, Strings & Pianos* (2006); *Lost Shadows* (2007); *Bahok* (2008); *In-i* (2008); *Confluences* (retrospective programme with Nitin Sawhney, 2009); *Gnosis* (additional choreography by Gauri Sharma Trapathi, 2010); *Vertical Road* (2010).

*Akram Khan Company website cites only 2000.

Further reading

Interviews with Margaret Willis, in 'Dancer Profile: Akram Khan', *Dancing Times*, March 2001; with Donald Hutera, in 'The Big Rendezvous', *Dance Europe*, March 2001; with Preeti Vasudevan, in 'Clarity within Chaos', *Dance Theatre Journal*, 18(1), 2002; with Sanjoy Roy, in 'Akram Khan & Nitin Sawhney, the Mould Breakers', *Pulse*, No. 106, Autumn 2009; with Alison Kirkman, in 'Space Outside', *Dancing Times*, November 2009.

Articles: Klaus Witzeling, 'On Stage: Concentration on the Body', *Ballett International*, May 2001; Reginald Massey, 'Dance Scene International: Kathak Conquers London', *Dancing Times*, June 2001; Anonymous, 'Akram Rocks On', *Pulse*, I, Spring 2002; Lorna Sanders, 'Choreographers Today: Akram Khan', *Dancing Times*, May 2003; Joan Acocella, 'Hard and Fast: What an Indian Tradition Can Do For Modern Dance', *The New Yorker*, 23 October 2006; David Jays, '*Bahok*', *Dancing Times*, July 2008; Zoë Anderson and Reginald Massey, 'Svapnagata Festival', *Dancing Times*, January 2010.

Books: Lorna Sanders, *Akram Khan's Rush: Creative Insights*, Alton, 2004; Lorna Sanders, 'Akram Khan's *ma* (2004): An Essay in Hybridisation and Productive Ambiguity', in Janet Lansdale (ed.), *Decentring Dancing Texts*, Basingstoke, 2008.

JAMES KUDELKA

Creating dance for me is a way of being less afraid of life.

(James Kudelka, 1995[1])

A child prodigy is a rare thing among choreographers, but Kudelka produced his first piece at the age of 14, and by 21 he had created the deeply disturbing, utterly adult ballet, *A Party* (1976). This prompted Toronto dance critic Penelope Doob to ask in 1977, 'How many choreographers, especially at twenty-one, can make convincingly realistic ballets about grown-ups? ... [H]e just might turn out to be the special choreographer we have been waiting for.'[2] He was. According to Karen Kain, Kudelka's successor as Artistic Director of the National Ballet of Canada, he has become 'the foremost choreographer in this country',[3] internationally recognized, both for his art and for his compelling new vision of 'what a classical ballet repertory should look like in the 21st century.'[4]

A Party already exhibited in embryo the essential Kudelkian characteristics: 'physical drive' (to quote first-cast dancer, Frank Augustyn), sculptural form, precarious weight-sharing between partners, psychological depth and a troubling theme. (In the 'date rape' *pas de deux*, for instance, Nadia Potts had to support herself arched backwards on one arm, while clinging to her 'rapist' (Augustyn) with the other: the effect was both sculpturally striking and all too sadly appropriate to the nature of date rape itself.[5]) As David Earle has said of Kudelka's work generally, 'freeze-frame any part of his dances, and you'll have a gorgeous three-dimensional sculpture'[6] – and this is true even in this early piece.

Kudelka's time in Toronto's National Ballet, from 1972, was memorable for his innovative interpretations of hitherto unnoticed characters and his skill at mime. His intense stage presence also won him more important roles. But, it was claustrophobic and emotionally damaging: the company was under the directorship of Alexander Grant, whose fixation on the Ashton repertoire Kudelka found stifling; he increasingly sought relief in Graham classes at Toronto Dance Theatre. The chance to work with Les Grands Ballets Canadiens in Montreal (1984–91) was revivifying, and it was there that he produced his first works of international acclaim, like *In Paradisum* (1983). The then artistic co-director Daniel Jackson says, 'We not only gave him *carte blanche* to experiment, we made him a principal dancer so he would be challenged both ways . . . My head still floats with the images of his invention'.[7]

His success as both choreographer and artistic director surely springs, in part, from his self-confessed concern to 'care about every dancer'.[8] Kudelka's choreography, however, is notoriously difficult (he prefers his dancers to be *thinking* constantly). Ballet mistress Anita Paciotti of San Francisco Ballet has said:

> It was clear . . . that he had been influenced by modern dance, because he challenges the classical notion of dance as balanced and vertical. James isn't interested in watching something comfortable . . . he loves using off-balance, with dancers sharing weight, which is precarious in *pointe* shoes.[9]

She also described Kudelka's choreography as 'the most dangerous' she had ever worked with, 'but also the most exciting'. Kudelka speaks of his penchant for off-balance *pas de deux* work as 'sculptural opportunity', a way of exploring risk because 'having a partner allows you to be off-balance'. His daring technical experimentation translates into immediate emotional impact on stage, as in, for instance, the slow, tense off-balance turn *en pointe* in the *pas de deux* from *The Actress* (1994): at this moment the relationship, hitherto enigmatic, between the actress and a former acquaintance takes on a startlingly menacing quality effected by the physics of uneasy dependence.

Kudelka's major works, apart from *A Party*, are *Washington Square* (1977), *In Paradisum* (1983), *Fifteen Heterosexual Duets* (1991), *The Miraculous Mandarin* (1993), *The Actress* (1994), *The Four Seasons* (1997), *Some Women and Men* (1998) and his utterly reinvented *Cinderella* (2004), repatriating Prokoviev's score into the elegant *art nouveau* world of the 1920s. One is struck, looking over this list, by several things: first, only two of these works (*In Paradisum* and *Fifteen Heterosexual Duets*) are offpointe. Second, many of them are narrative ballets and many deal with serious social or psychological issues. These points are not unrelated: Kudelka himself notes the scarcity in North America of contemporary choreographers working in the classical idiom. He attributes this to the 'all-encompassing . . . [and] unhelpful' influence of Balanchine's detached aestheticism.[10] A choreographer more unlike Balanchine would be hard to imagine. Although he has worked in the United States and Europe, Kudelka's is a distinctively Canadian voice.

But, what exactly does Kudelka do? And what is Canadian about his voice? Themes like insignificance, victimization and emotional repression have been identified in Canadian literary criticism and they also proliferate in Kudelka's ballets; programme notes to *The Miraculous Mandarin*, for instance, describe this narrative ballet as dramatizing 'the salvation and ultimate empowerment of the youngest son', and much (perhaps too much) has been made of the autobiographical implications of that theme for its choreographer.[11] But the theme can work on a national level too, as the painful rescue and emergence from cultural colonialism (European and American) that has taken place precisely in Kudelka's generation. Broader Canadian themes arise as well, such as passion for the natural world and awe at its untamed power, a particular emphasis evident in Kudelka's reworking of *Swan Lake* (1999). The ballet's traditional opposition between the sophistication of the court and the lake as the evil, wild domain of Baron von Rothbart, becomes in Kudelka's retelling an idyllic natural setting, while the court becomes, in his own words, 'a decaying bastion of martial values, repressive and authoritarian'.

As for what Kudelka represents in his own original works, critics have complained that he has no consistent style. He has no visible lineage (although he has been compared to Massine, whose works he does not know).[12] Graham technique, however, supplemented by David Earl's gift for mime, has been the most visible influence on the contemporary side of this otherwise innately classical (though never conservative) choreographer. Perhaps a closer look at the offpointe work for which he has become famous will illustrate the unique character of his work better than labels and generalizations.

In Paradisum is quintessential Kudelka, the natural flexibility and range of modern dance here supported, not emasculated, by the classical precision. As such, it is worth detailed investigation. The piece is a complex blend of his rare intellectual and interdisciplinary range, with raw emotional and absolutely autobiographical conflict. It combines driving and turbulent movement with emphatic gesture, memorable tableaux and (surprising) moments of ethereal serenity. The sharp changes in mood throughout *In Paradisum* are partly a response to composer Michael Baker's deceptively neutral minimalistic music, periodically disturbed by bursts of quick chromatic half-scales, urgently repeated upwards and downwards, giving the piece its alternating frantic and controlled sensibilities. Its use of the modern idiom is so pure and effortless, it could have been choreographed by Graham herself, although its appearance is more like the work of contemporary choreographers such as Jiří Kylián or even Nacho Duato.

The costumes are Grahamesque, with their simple, tailored lines and flowing skirts; designer Denis Joffre has deftly captured something of the universality Kudelka strives for in the movement, the slightly Grecian full-length tunics evoking a classical and timeless dignity and stoicism. Yet there is also a strong sense of Christian tradition – both angelic and monastic – in the overall effect. A more universal quality is what Kudelka was striving for: in response to terminal illness, he says, 'we have to look inside ourselves to see how vast the damage is – one life is many lives.' This is the essence of *In Paradisum's* message and rarely do choreographers speak so articulately on their own works.

In Paradisum has the Kudelka trademark of fast-paced, intricate movement patterns and an emotional power. Yet in spite of the emotional resonance for its choreographer, the work finds control through its use of pure technique, which in turn transforms, even masks, the emotionalism for the dancers. The piece progresses through Elizabeth Kuebler-Ross's five stages of dying: it opens with Denial and Isolation when, in Kudelka's words, the 'whole family or community boils up' in shock and resistance to the news of a death; and it then proceeds recognizably, though never slavishly, through Anger, Bargaining, Depression and Acceptance. Kudelka's gifts as a mime artist emerge in several *leitmotif* gestures: the centuries-old one for grief, for instance, of holding one's head in one's hands is stylized by Kudelka, so that the fingers are fanned out to convey starkness and the hands do not quite touch the head – a brilliant suggestion of abstraction and distraction blended in one gesture.

The most important *leitmotif*, often photographed, is the opening tableau of the work, in which the dying man reaches upwards (fingers fanned open), while his companion, one arm wrapped lovingly around him, nevertheless turns away, his head buried in grief, while the community swirls about them. This same tableau ends the piece, this time with the addition of the third principal, the angelic guide, who kneels beside the dying man with both the arms wrapped around him. The guide figure comes onstage only towards the end of the piece. He has a unique mimic gesture – an arm fully extended to the side with hand sharply angled upwards from the wrist, performing a series of rigid fluttering motions, as if of a single wing. Is Kudelka's angel so powerful as to need only one wing – or is he slightly crippled? Interpretation is open to each viewer.

Kudelka's most famous *en-pointe* work, *The Four Seasons* (1997), similarly hovers between transcendence and passion and also explores forebodings of death, even during the vivacious 'Spring' and 'Summer' episodes. Set to Vivaldi's famous score, it was created on the National's towering dramatic talent, principal dancer Rex Harrington (playing 'A Man'), whom Kudelka partnered successively with four women. Although the piece is unapologetically classical, with breathtakingly difficult pointe work, all four duets have a Grahamesque penchant for falling and rising turns in contraction.

The Four Seasons is about everyman's life journey and every dancer's, a factor underscored by the inventive 2001 film version, which opens with real-life footage of backstage warm-up scenes and closes with the dancers melting off stage and into real conversations (one is reminded of Bergman's *Magic Flute*, with its backstage-life vignettes). The piece lends itself to life allegory, as does the tableau (the group clustered pietà-like around the Man at his death is like a family). This is not the dysfunctional family of *Miraculous Mandarin*, or the androgynous groupings of *In Paradisum*, but a mourning family, joined by the Man's lovers (Spring, Summer and Autumn), all gathered to bid farewell. The piece is strong in choreographic virtuosity: despite the 'furious intoxication of the steps' and the 'split-leg poses as the women wrap around [Harrington's] body or drop into fantastic fish-dives,' the choreography is 'never merely gymnastic: in its musicality and finesse, the movement is always pure dance'.[13]

The Four Seasons is also trademark Kudelka in its use of same-sex pairings, played off against heterosexual pairings in unexpected ways. In Autumn, for instance, men lift men alongside men lifting women, reminiscent not only of *In Paradisum*, but also of pieces like *Some Women and Men*, created for the San Francisco Ballet in 1998. In *Four Seasons*, the pairings and their movements are propelled by the Baroque score; in *Some Women and Men* by the jazzy Poulenc score. Kudelka creates intimacy out of any kind of music, and the intimacy is as often non-sexual as not. His choreography explores relationships and themes of all sorts, from the social oppression of evangelicalism in *The Contract* (2002) to the carnage caused by weaponry in *Swan Lake* (1999), to the emotional thunder storms of summer in *Four Seasons*.

Kudelka's success as a choreographer is related to his success as an artistic director: in both capacities he thinks like a dancer. 'I hate the idea of becoming one of *them* – the Artistic Staff,' he said in 1995.[14] But by 1996, the luxury of rebellion was vanishing, as he progressed from artist-in-residence to artistic director of the National Ballet of Canada at bewildering speed. Half-nostalgic for the days when a corps of six (*The Actress*) was his largest staging headache, he was now worrying about how to put 120 people on stage in a new *Nutcracker* (1995).[15] He took on the job when finances were so scarce that, by 2001, his 50-dancer troupe could hardly stage one of the longer works in the repertoire for the 50th anniversary season. But, he never compromised on artistic seriousness just because the company was forced to down-size (or as he preferred to call it, 'distil'). Even in the big box-office successes (like his revisionary *Swan Lake*, 1999, *The Firebird*, 2000 or *Cinderella*, 2004) mounted to help keep the company afloat, his artistry never bowed to commercial pressure. He learned to ask questions like, 'If it's a tutu ballet, what should a tutu look like now, and how should you dance in it?'

His idea of what a 'tutu ballet' should look like in the twenty-first century is glimpsed in the eco-politics of his *Swan Lake* but is most successfully captured in *Cinderella* (2004). With Chaucerian originality, Kudelka retells a familiar story to speak with wit and poignancy to the social issues of his own generation. In his hands, for instance, the wicked stepmother becomes an alcoholic, 'lurching through the action like a superannuated silent film star'; the setting becomes the *art nouveau* world of the 1920s, suiting the modernisms of Prokoviev's score perfectly. Cinderella, at the ball, looks like no other Cinderella has ever looked, fashionably swathed flapper-style in a straight, floor-length silken, fur-collared coat, supported *en-pointe* by four adoring gentlemen in tails. The allusion to the Rose Adagio is unmistakable, but there are no fairytale tutus here. The opulent *art nouveau* world is just remote enough to conjure magical elegance for the present generation, just close enough to lend an historical authenticity Disney cannot (Kudelka is very aware that he is competing with Disney in mounting family-entertainment blockbusters).[16] As in his even more iconoclastic *Firebird* (2000), with its fierce Inca-style costuming, moving staircases and spectacular scenery, Kudelka is able to compete even with Harry Potter, all the while, however, making sophisticated allusions to dance history for the adults in the audience. *Firebird*, for example, as Crabb noted at its premiere, alludes to the 'flattened, frieze-like character of Nijinsky's *Afternoon of a Faun*' and it reworks Prince Ivan's role to meet the expectations for male roles in contemporary ballet.[17]

Freed of the pressures of company directorship, Kudelka now works with a range of companies, including San Francisco Ballet and American Ballet Theatre. Far from the tyranny of fund-raisers and boards of directors, many of his ballets, including *Cruel World* (2009), can be seen by everyone on YouTube, along with commentary by the dancers on whom they were created. Watching the emotional climax of *Cruel World*, with Julie Kent leaning dangerously *en-pointe* at a 45-degree angle, one knows that some things never change in Kudelka's choreography, even if the medium of delivery is now one's home computer.

Whatever fear of life (or death) Kudelka is exorcising through his choreography, the single most important emotion in all his work is courage. As he has himself said, 'safe is not one of the words you use to describe a dancer or choreographer because you are always at risk', and *In Paradisum* and *The Four Seasons*, perhaps, best exemplify the combination of sacrifice, pain and courage that represent at once the cost and the beauty of Kudelka's creativity.

Kathryn Kerby-Fulton

Notes

1 Quoted from the interview in *Originals in Art*, executive producer Mozes Znaimer (Sleeping Giant Productions, in association with Bravo Television, copyright 1995).
2 In 'Spotlight on James Kudelka', *Dance Magazine*, March 1977, pp. 72–3.
3 Karen Kain, with Stephen Godfrey and Penelope Reed Doob, *Movement Never Lies: An Autobiography*, Toronto, 1994, p. 19.
4 Michael Crabb, 'Notebook', *Dance International*, Summer 2005, p. 67.
5 See the photo of this moment in *Kain and Augustyn: A Photographic Study* by Christopher Darling, Toronto, 1977, pp. 118, and 114 for Augustyn's comment.

6 Quoted by Paula Citron in 'James Kudelka: Out of the Depths', *Dance Magazine*, February 1994, p. 96.
7 Quoted by Paula Citron in 'James Kudelka: Out of the Depths', *Dance Magazine*, February 1994, p. 96.
8 Penelope Doob, 'Balancing Virtue and Necessity: The Dual Roles of James Kudelka, *Performance*, February 12–16 (1997), pp.11–17.
9 Cited in Citron, op. cit., p. 97.
10 From *Originals in Art*, op. cit.
11 See, for instance, Leland Windreich, 'Full Circle: Love, Sex and Death in James Kudelka's *The Miraculous Mandarin*', *Dance International*, Fall 1993, pp. 10–15, which is typical of Kudelka criticism in stressing the autobiographical.
12 Ibid., p. 14.
13 Kaija Pepper, 'Vancouver Update,' *Dance International*, Winter 2003, pp. 44–5.
14 *Originals in Art*, op. cit.
15 Penelope Doob, 'Balancing Virtue and Necessity: The Dual Roles of James Kudelka', *Performance*, 12–16 February 1997, pp. 11–17.
16 Michael Crabb, 'Calgary/Toronto Update', *Dance International*, Fall 2004, pp. 45–6.
17 Michael Crabb, 'Toronto Update', *Dance International*, Winter 2001, pp. 47–8.

Biographical details

Born in Newmarket, Ontario, Canada, 10 September 1955. **Studied** as a child at the National Ballet School (director Alexander Grant), Toronto, 1965–72; also studied Martha Graham technique at the Toronto Dance Theatre, under David Earle. **Career**: Danced with the National Ballet of Canada, Toronto, from 1972, becoming soloist in 1976 and principal dancer from 1981 to 1986; early choreography was for the National Ballet of Canada workshops, 1973–80; then company choreographer in Toronto, 1980–82; principal dancer and (from 1984) resident choreographer, Les Grands Ballets Canadiens, Montreal, 1984–91; artist-in-residence, from 1992, then artistic director (succeeding Reid Anderson), National Ballet of Canada, 1996–2005. Has also choreographed for Joffrey Ballet, San Francisco Ballet, Montréal Danse, Toronto Dance Theatre, Margie Gillis, Les Ballets Jazz de Montréal, American Ballet Theatre, Birmingham Royal Ballet, Hubbard Street Dance (Chicago), Peggy Baker and the Joyce Triller Company. **Awards and honours** include Jean Chalmers Award (National Ballet of Canada), 1975; Isadora Duncan Award, San Francisco, 1988; Dora Mavor Moore Awards, 1992, 1996; Officer of the Order of Canada, 2005.

Works

Sonata (Moods of Intimacy) (1973); *Apples* (1974); *Sonata* (1974); *A Party* (1976); *Washington Square* (1977; revised version, 1979); *Bach Pas de Deux* (1979); *Windsor Pas de Deux* (1979); *The Rape of Lucrece* (1980); *Playhouse* (1980); *All Night Wonder* (1981); *Passage* (1981); *Intimate Letter* (1981); *Genesis* (1982); *Dido and Aeneas* (with David Earle and others; 1982); *Hedda* (1983); *In Paradisum* (1983); *Court of Miracles* (with David Earle, Christopher House and others; 1983); *Alliances* (1984); *unfinished business* (1984); *Dracula* (1985); *Death of an Old Queen* (1985); *Diversion* (1985); *The Heart of the Matter* (1986); *Vers la glace* (with Margie and Christopher

Gillis; 1986); *Collisions* (1986); *Soudain l'hiver dernier* (1987); *Dreams of Harmony* (1987); *Le Sacre du Printemps* (1987); *'the wakey nights'* (solo; 1987); *Concerto Grosso* (1988); *In Camera* (1988); *La Salle des pas perdus* (1988); *Signatures* (1988); *Love, Dracula* (1989); *The Comfort Zone* (1989); *Ouverture Russe* (1989); *There, Below* (1989); *Divertissement Schumann* (1989); *Schéhérazade* (with David Earle; 1989); *Romance* (1990); *CV.* (1990); *Pastorale* (1990); *Romeo and Juliet before Parting* (1990; also video, 1990); *Violin Concerto* (Misfits) (1990); *This Isn't the End* (1991); *The Kiss of Death* (1991); *Musings* (Fare Well) (1991); *Mirror* (1991); *Mixed Program* (1991); *Fifteen Heterosexual Duets* (1991); *Désir* (1991); *The First Dance* (duet; 1992); *The End* (1992); *Making Ballet* (1993); *New York* (duet; 1993); *Ghosts* (1993); *The Miraculous Mandarin* (1993); *Vittoria Pas de Deux* (1993); *Vestiges, ou, Les Ratées du coeur or Six Tableaux for the Sexually Challenged* (1993); *Spring Awakening* (1994); *Heroes* (1994); *Cruel World* (1994); *The Actress* (1994); *Gluck Pas de Deux* (1994); *The Nutcracker* (1995); *Missing* (1995); *States of Grace* (1995); *Terra Firma* (1995); *Solo for Rex* (1995); *Daisy's Dead* (1996); *A Piece for Walter* (1996); *Le Baiser de la fée* (1996); *I'm a Stranger Here Myself* (for television, 1996); *The Four Seasons* (1997); *Musings* (1997); *Some Women and Men* (1998); *Swan Lake* (1999); *A Disembodied Voice* (1999); *The Book of Alleged Dances* (1999); *The Firebird* (2000); *Sin and Tonic* (2002); *The Contract* (2002); *Gazebo Dances* (2003); *Cinderella* (2004); *Charcony* (2004); *An Italian Straw Hat* (2005); *It is as it Was* (with counter tenor Daniel Taylor, 2006); *See #1* (2007); *Little Dancer* (2008); *Hush* (2008); *The Ruins Proclaim the Building Was Beautiful* (2008); *The Goldberg Variations – Side 2: Adam & Eve & Steve* (2009); *Cruel World Pas de Deux* (2009).

Further reading

Interview with Penelope Doob, in 'Spotlight on James Kudelka', *Dance Magazine*, March 1977; with Peter Darbyshire, in 'I'm a Caustic, Difficult Person and I Made Myself Unemployable', *The Globe*, 21 July 2008; with Marene Gustin, 'Life After the National', *Dance International*, Summer 2008.

Articles: Ellen Shearer, 'James Kudelka', *Dance in Canada*, Summer 1979; Paula Citron, 'James Kudelka – Profile of an Enigma', *Dance in Canada*, Spring 1984; Linda Howe-Beck, 'Kudelka Charts the Land of Heart's Desire', *Dance Magazine*, May 1991; Leland Windreich, 'Full Circle: Love, Sex and Death in James Kudelka's *The Miraculous Mandarin*', *Dance International*, Fall 1993; Paula Citron, 'James Kudelka: Out of the Depths', *Dance Magazine*, February 1994; 'James Kudelka', in *Current Biography Yearbook, 1995*; Debra Craine, 'Kudelka's Nutcracker', *Dance Now*, Spring 1996; Cormac Rigby, 'Sugar and Ice', *Dance Now*, Winter 1996/97; Penelope Doob, 'Balancing Virtue and Necessity: The Dual Roles of James Kudelka', *Performance* (O'Keefe Center for the Performing Arts, Toronto), February 12–16 1997; James Neufield, 'New Swan Lakes 1', *Dance Now*, Summer 1999; Michael Crabb, 'National Ballet of Canada's Swan Lake and San Francisco Ballet's Giselle', *Dancing Times*, July 1999; Michael Crabb, 'Toronto Update, *Dance International*, Winter 2001; Michael Crabb, 'The National Ballet of Canada's *The Contract*', *Dancing Times*, June 2002; Kaija Pepper, 'Vancouver Update', *Dance International*, Winter 2003; Michael Crabb, 'The National Ballet of Canada', *Dancing Times*, September 2004; Michael Crabb, 'Canadian Artistic Director Steps Down', *Dancing Times*, July 2005; Michael Crabb, 'Notebook', *Dance International*, Summer, 2005; Tobi Tobias,

'American Ballet Theatre Performs "Cinderella" at the Met', *The New York Times*, 28 May 2006; Marene Gustin, 'James Kudelka: Life after the National', *Dance International*, Summer 2008; Fiona Morrow, 'A Second Act for James Kudelka', *The Saturday Globe and Mail*, 20 February 2009.

Books: Karen Kain, with Stephen Godfrey and Penelope Reed Doob, *Movement Never Lies: An Autobiography*, Toronto, 1994; James Neufeld, *Power to Rise: The Story of the National Ballet of Canada*, Toronto, 1996; Iro Valaskakis Tembeck (ed.), *Canadian Dancing Bodies Then and Now*, Toronto, 2002; Jennifer Fisher, *Nutcracker Nation*, New Haven, CT, 2003.

JIŘÍ KYLIÁN

It has become the custom to think of great choreographers as those who are particularly innovative with the language of movement, who have provided what can be called a new language for dance. Jiří Kylián, then, is perhaps something of a throwback to an earlier age, one that is less thirsty for the 'new' than now; for if Kylián has a claim to greatness, it is not so much as a starkly original formal innovator but as a master craftsman contributing to the overall evolution of his art. Whatever his comparative standing, Kylián has undeniably strengthened the art of dance by building on its foundations, and will therefore hand on not just the products of an individual creative talent but an enriched heritage.

Kylián certainly has something in common with all the most significant creators – that his formative years took place at a special time and in a special place. The place was Stuttgart and the time became known as the 'Ballet Boom'. Kylián joined the Stuttgart Ballet in 1968 in the middle years of John Cranko's remarkable directorship, when choreographers Cranko, Maurice Béjart and Hans van Manen were providing a lively new approach to ballet characterized by athletic, theatrical movement.

Kylián began choreographing prolifically from 1970, occasionally working for Nederlands Dans Theater (NDT), a company that had come to the forefront of the contemporary-dance revolution in Europe during the 1960s. Founded in 1959, NDT was the first European ballet company to institute a regular modern-dance class and thus was a pioneer in the combination of classical and modern-dance traditions within one company. In its early days, its prime mover was Hans van Manen, whose choreography for the company drew on a wide range of composers including Stravinsky, Satie, Stockhausen and Cage. After van Manen resigned as artistic director in 1970, the company entered a period of decline and it was Kylián who brought it back to international prominence during the 1970s and 1980s.

Kylián brought to NDT the ethos of Stuttgart, an approach to ballet that was firmly based on the classical technique and neoclassical in style. In addition, however, Kylián's work teems with references to folk dance, which can add another textual level to the dance, like an old dialect breaking through the sophisticated, highly evolved and constraining balletic language he has adopted and made his own. His vocabulary is convoluted and dense; the vision from which he forms his steps and gestures is driven by expressionism but schooled in neoclassicism and informed by a profound musicality.

Ballet's straight, sharp leg extensions coupled with the contracted body of the Graham technique has made the female body a particularly potent expressive tool for embodying dualism and conflict. This has been powerfully exploited by Kylián. Like many choreographers working in ballet since the 1960s, Kylián uses the balletically trained body at its extremes. Yet his motivation does not appear theatrical, virtuosic or purely abstract; it comes from within, from an emotion or idea which resonates outwards. Kylián is a master of tension, providing potent, dramatic ballet, inventive and profound. He has proved himself prolific and diverse, not only as one of the most consistently stimulating but also as one of the most accessible of contemporary choreographers.

Kylián's normal *métier* is the non-narrative, dramatic ballet, though he has made ventures into other terrains such as narrative in *L'Histoire du soldat* (1986) and explorations of aboriginal rituals in *Nomaden* (*Nomads*; 1981), *Stamping Ground* (1983) and *Dreamtime* (1983). Just as you fix him in one rich interior, Kylián will undoubtedly show you another. In general, however, it could be said that his vocabulary is informed by a basically modernist consciousness; certainly his vivid descriptive talent deals well with a range of human emotions and with a complexity that is unusual in ballet.

As If Never Been (1992), for example, explores a sense of nihilism and despair. Two dancers are locked together in an internal drama on the basis of dependency and exploitation. Against a background of silent, abstractly gestural commentators, who provide something of a Greek chorus, a hellish duet of mounting tension takes place – a kind of expressionistic *paso doble*. The woman is manipulated by her partner into various contorted shapes and exaggerated extensions, or thrown into passages of forced abandon, her legs flying around his head like windmills. The shapes they make together are typical of Kylián's style and evocative power, such as when she wraps around his body and with her bony arms and legs gives him skeletal wings, or when he walks her up the proscenium arch and over onto her back to pose in the air like an upturned cockroach.

Kylián can deal equally well with classical sublimity. If Tudor's *Dark Elegies* is ballet's *Paradise Lost*, then Kylián's *Sinfonietta* (1978) is surely its *Paradise Regained*. This is Kylián at his most optimistic and life affirming. To the uplifting opening of Janácek's score, Kylián sets six men in tights and billowing shirts against a painted landscape. With simple leaps, runs and turns they announce and celebrate the musical theme. When only two are left on stage, they are joined by two women who, rushing across the stage, are stopped by the men and pose for a moment in a detached halted run. Although the couples are inter-changeable partners, often passed from one to the other (in Kylián's work there is very little sense of the dancers as individuals), the work is essentially romantic, sensual and supremely lyrical. Undercurrents of folk rhythms run through the music and when they break out in the choreography they momentarily add another dimension, taking away any sense of pre-Fall innocence from these otherwise joyous creatures. Overall the mood is wonderfully serene. One of the loveliest moments is when four dancers lie down centre-stage, one behind the other; in unison they raise their arms in a slow, broad sweep that brings to mind the tail of a whale waving in the air before plunging into the deep.

Kylián's dancers can be classically sublime, as in *Sinfonietta*, and then again they can sculpt themselves into space in a way that has conflict and angst screaming out of every contortion; Kylián can uplift your spirit one minute and set your teeth on edge the next. In watching his ballets one enters a strongly defined world in which the dancers are not characters as such but they certainly embody ideas. What makes his work particularly accessible is that it is dramatically expressive, lyrical, virtuosic and profoundly musical. He is renowned particularly for his use of late-Romantic composers, but has in fact worked with quite a wide variety of scores and soundscapes.

For example, *Falling Angels* (1989), set to Part One of Steve Reich's *Drumming* (1971), consists of one basic rhythmic pattern which is var-ied only in terms of phrase position, pitch and timbre. It is simple but labyrinthine and so dominating in its power and density, so over-whelming an aural experience, that one might think it would leave no room for choreography. Kylián shows us otherwise. *Drumming* is compelling because it is such a wildly inventive exploration of a single isolated and confined idea. The tension inherent in this combination of contradictory qualities is similarly exploited by Kylián; the tightly controlled choreography uses mesmeric choral movement and repeated phrases but with an exhilarating sense of wildly creative energy.

Falling Angels begins with a group of dancers walking slowly towards the audience out of the darkness; they are all women. They contort on the beat and retreat a couple of steps, all in unison. They look like a cross between the figures on an Egyptian frieze, in terms of their angular two-dimensional shapes, and something more Germanic with their red lipstick, fixed focus, strong projection and black swimsuits – a Pina Bausch-style line-up with a touch of cabaret. They flash an angular figure of eight with a dreamlike flow of crisscrossing arms and legs. Hands slap, caress, cover, flick, move body parts, splay. Flat-footed jumps with bent knees recall Nijinsky's faun. In spirit it is primitive, ritualistic; they look rather like insects totally in command of their prey. Dancers break free, duets break out, but the group always reclaims them. Contrasting moments of dramatic stillness create a surreal sense of space, even in the midst of this frenzied drumming. They are pious one minute, military another, but can then subvert it all with a fey lean to the side, hands draping diagonally across their bodies or by flirtatiously pulling their swimsuits away from their flesh as if to taunt the audience.

In a very different style we can find a similar musicality and mastery of choral movement in Kylián's earlier work, *Symphony of Psalms* (1978), set to the driving rhythms of Stravinsky's score. The music is concerned with praising God; however, Kylián's choreography, sublime as it is, is rather more earthily sensual, set against a sumptuous background of oriental carpets. Again he does far more than visualize the music; his dialogue with it brings out the music's subtleties but then insists on its own contrasting statements. Perhaps most breathtaking of all in this work is Kylián's use of deep space. Space is always emotionally resonant with Kylián; dancers reach out to it rather than simply stretch into it, but here the pleasure is also intellectual, a visual feast of layered movement. The eye moves out from the lucidity of the individual dancers' bodies to the larger scale of the mass and back again. Curves counter angles in the body, mesmerizing flow counters stark shape (it is difficult to believe that so many parts can move in so many different directions), creating a complex message of joy and sorrow, sensual pleasure and anxiety even within one movement. Kylián calls for a dramatic power in his dancers that they can switch on and off whenever the piece warrants it; they must be detached but involved, expressive but not 'acting' – everything is in the movement and apparently every muscle can be choreographed.

There is in Kylián's work a celebration of the creative spirit that spills over into a joyous playfulness. His ability to be witty is well represented by two works set to Mozart, *Six Dances* (1986) and *Petite Mort* (1991). These works are an amusing romp through the music of the great composer but are intended as more than merry dances of bawds and cuckolds. For all their foppish wigs, headless crinolines on wheels, sword play and bubbles, there is a level of social comment without which they would not be Kylián but some other choreographer.

Kylián's moral consciousness and intelligence are easily located within his work; he is accessible without being populist and there is a depth to his ballets that makes them very rewarding to watch. His dancers are not presented as extraordinary performers to be admired for their physical virtuosity but as expressive figures in a landscape or situation that has dramatic and social resonance. Judith Lynne Hanna notes that *Symphony in D* (1976) reverses the partnering conventions of classical ballet and challenges the *status quo*.[1] Kylián's social and political consciousness, however, runs deeper than simple reversals of the norm. *Fallen Angels*, for example, has been read as a profound examination of the struggling female psyche.[2] There are a number of ways in which Kylián could be said to have questioned, and gently shifted, the norms of Western theatre dance. For example, the superficiality of an art-form shackled to youth and good looks for its splendours is something that he has directly addressed. Recognizing the power of the older, experienced dancer and the profound eloquence that can be the product of a career spent working with a wide range of choreographers, Kylián established NDT3 in 1991, giving a new lease of life to dancers whose careers would normally have come to an end around the age of 40. This was an important step in developing a deeper, more sophisticated appreciation of dancers.[3]

In terms of his choreography, Kylián's morality, spirituality and bouts of existentialism can seem rather old-fashioned today, though his work is none the weaker for that. The sensuality and sexuality of his works can also appear a little outdated when compared to many contemporary choreographers. Yet there are passages of his work where its tremendous physicality moves towards the starker terrain of a more brutal and violent eroticism, which has been explored more fully by choreographers such as Lloyd Newson and Michael Clark. Examples are the male duet from *La Cathédrale engloutie* (1975) or passages of *Torso* (1975). But it is doubtful that Kylián could explore images of today's brutalized consciousness without intellectually commenting on it and setting it in some form of moral and social framework. This is perhaps central to what makes him a great choreographer, as opposed to merely a strong contemporary voice.

Kylián's work often presents us with a potent dialogue between classical (and perhaps also Christian) ideals and the contorted angularity of modernism. He can choreograph the divine light and equally well explore our fractured twentieth-century consciousness full of angst and godless doubt. Although not directly religious, his works often embrace the kind of duality that is a part of Christian consciousness: a sense of the double possibility of elation and despair, agony and ecstasy, heaven and hell, the sacred and profane, order and meaninglessness. As bodies sink down to earth, eyes often search upwards. There are shapes that seem shot through with Christian imagery (e.g. there is a photograph of dancer Bryony Brind hanging down from outstretched arms in a crucifixion-like pose from the Royal Ballet's 1975 production of his *Return to the Strange Land*). Above all else Kylián is a great humanist; he is not concerned with abstraction; and he sites his ideas firmly within the human sphere. He presents human struggles, passions and prayers, elation and despair; he is a choreographer of potent dualisms lucidly expressed through a mixture of classical sublimity and contemporary expressionism. Although the medium in which Kylián works – a combination of classical and modern dance languages – is familiar rather than formally innovative, it is difficult to think of a more *eloquent* living choreographer.

Lesley-Anne Sayers

Notes

1 Judith Lynne Hanna, *Dance, Sex and Gender: Signs of Identity, Dominance, Defiance, and Desire*, University of Chicago Press, 1988, p. 213.
2 See Ann Nugent: 'Two Radicals in Europe', *Dance Now*, 1(4), Winter 1992/93.
3 NDT3 existed until 2006.

Biographical details

Born in Prague, Czechoslovakia (now Czech Republic), 21 March 1947. **Studied** at the National Ballet School, Prague Conservatory, from 1962, and at the Royal

Ballet School in London from 1967. **Career**: Danced with Stuttgart Ballet, Germany, becoming soloist, 1968–75; choreographed first work for Stuttgart Ballet in 1970; co-artistic director at Nederlands Dans Theater (NDT), 1975, becoming artistic director in 1977; established NDT3 in 1991 for dancers over the age of 40; retired as director in 1999, working as resident choreographer until end of 2009. Has choreographed mostly for NDT, but many of his works have been reproduced by other companies, notably in the United States and Germany, and in the UK by Scottish Ballet, Ballet Rambert and the Royal Ballet. **Awards and honours** include Carina Ari Medal, Sweden; Society of West End Theatre Award, London; Netherlands Choreography Prize; Hans Christian Andersen Ballet Award, Denmark; Grand Prix International Video-Danse, France; Sonia Gaskell Prize, Netherlands; *Dance Magazine* Award, 1994; Dutch Orde van Oranje Nassau, 1995; Benois de le Danse, 1998; Laurence Olivier Award, 2000; Grand Prix, Montreal International Festival of Film, 2007; Golden Lion, Venice, 2008; Medal for Art and Science of Her Majesty Queen Beatrix, 2008; Zwaan (Swan) Award, Dutch VSCD, 2009.

Works

Paradox (1970); *Kommen und Gehen* (1970); *Incantations* (1971); *Der Einzelganger* (1972); *Der stumme Orpheus* (1972); *Viewers* (1973); *Blue Skin* (1974); *Der Morgen danach* (1974); *Rückkehr ins fremde Land* (*Return to the Strange Land*, 1974; extended version, 1975); *Stoolgame* (*The Odd One*; 1974); *La Cathédrale engloutie* (1975); *Verklärte Nacht* (*Transfigured Night*; 1975); *Torso* (1975); *Nuages* (1976); *Elegia* (1976); *Symphony in D* (two-part version; 1976); *November Steps* (1977); *Ariadne* (1977); *Symphony in D* (three-part version, 1977); *Kinderspielen* (*Children's Games*, 1978); *Sinfonietta* (1978); *Intimate Pages* (1978); *Rainbow Snake* (1978); *Symphony of Psalms* (1978); *Glagolitic Mass* (1978); *Dream Dances* (1978); *Field Mass* (1980); *Overgrown Path* (1980); *Forgotten Land* (1981); *Nomaden* (*Nomads*; 1981); *Symphony in D* (1981); *Svadebka* (*Les Noces*; 1982); *Lieder eines fahrenden Gesellen* (1982); *Stamping Ground* (1983); *Dreamtime* (1983); *Curses and Blessings* (with Christopher Bruce, 1983); *Wiegelied* (1983); *Valencia* (1984); *L'Enfant et les sortilèges* (1984); *Heart's Labyrinth I* (1984); *Heart's Labyrinth II* (1985); *Piccolo Mondo* (1985); *Silent Cries* (1986), *L'Histoire du Soldat* (1986); *Six Dances/Sechs Tanze* (1986); *Heart's Labyrinth* (1987); *Frankenstein!* (1987); *Sint Joris rijdt uit* (1987); *Evenings Songs* (1987); *Kaguyahime* (1988); *No More Play* (1988); *Tantz-Schul* (1989); *Falling Angels* (1989); *Sweet Dreams* (1990); *Sarabande* (1990); *Petite Mort* (1991); *Obscure Temptations* (1991); *Stepping Stones* (1991); *Un ballo* (1991); *As If Never Been* (1992); *No Sleep Till Dawn of Day* (1992); *Whereabouts Unknown* (1994); *Double You* (1994); *Tiger Lily* (1995); *Quando Corpus* (1995); *Arcimboldo* (1995); *Bella Figura* (1995); *Anna and Ostriches* (1996); *Trompe l'oeil* (1996); *Compass* (1996); *If Only . . .* (1996); *Wings of Wax* (1997); *A Way A Lone* (1998); *One of a Kind* (1998); *Indigo Rose* (1998); *Half Past* (1999); *Doux Mensonges* (1999); *Click-Pause-Silence* (2000); *Birth-day* (2001); *27'52"* (2001); *Black Bird* (2006); *Claude Pascal* (2002); *When Time Takes Time* (2002); *Last Touch First* (2002); *Far Too Close* (2003); *Sleepless* (2004); *Il Faut qu'une porte* (2004); *Toss of a Dice* (2005); *Tar and Feathers* (2005); *Car Men* (film, dir. Boris Pavel Conen, 2006); *Vanishing Twin* (2008); *Gods and Dogs* (2008); *Zugvögel* (*Migration Birds*; 2009); *Mémoires d'oubliettes* (2009).

Further reading

Interviews with Sue Merrett, in 'Spotlight on Jiří Kylián', *Dancing Times*, May 1991; with Peta Koch, in 'Jiří Kylián: Outlining Dance', *Dance Australia*, December 1993; with Benjamin Harkarvy, *Dance Magazine*, November 1994; with Arnd Wesemann, 'Back to the Aborigines', *Ballett International*, July 1998; with Eva-Elisabeth Fischer (in German), *Ballettanz*, June 2009.

Articles: Norma McLain Stoop, 'Jiří Kylián of the Netherlands Dance Theatre', *Dance Magazine*, October 1979; Patricia Barnes, 'New Faces: Jiří Kylián', *Dance News*, December 1979; Norma McLain Stoop, 'Midsummer Nights' Dreams', *Dance Magazine*, July 1982; James Monaghan, 'Amsterdam and Kylián', *Dancing Times*, May 1984; Rolf Garske, 'In Love with Music and Movement', *Ballett International*, March 1987; Louisa Moffett, 'Kylián Changes Keys', *Dance Magazine*, May 1987; Horst Koegler, 'Pledged to the Spirit of Our Times: Nederlands Dans Theater, 1959–89', *Ballett International*, May 1989; Rolf Garske, 'At the Crossroads: NDT – 1989', *Ballett International*, May 1989; Janet Sinclair, 'Choreographer's Luck', *Dance and Dancers*, June/July 1991; Jiří Kylián, 'What is Dance?', *Dance Now*, Winter 1992/93; Lesley-Anne Sayers, 'Dreams and Discontent: The Choreography of Jiří Kylián', *Dance Theatre Journal*, 10(2), 1992; Ann Nugent, 'Two Radicals in Europe', *Dance Now*, Winter 1992/93; Helmut Scheier, 'Choreographing in Symbols', *Ballett International*, October 1994; Ann Nugent, 'Ripe Tomatoes, Sweet Grapes – and Arcimboldo', *Dance Theatre Journal*, Summer 1995; Janet Sinclair and Leo Kersley, 'Celebration in The Hague', *Dancing Times*, June 1995; Eva van Schaik, 'Master of Ceremonies, Seeker of Truths', *Ballett International*, June 1995; Jochen Schmidt, 'He Wanted His Little Joke', *Ballett International*, July 1996; Janet Sinclair, 'Cabrioles and Choreographers', *Dance Now*, Autumn 1996; William Anthony, 'NDT3', *Dancing Times*, August 1997; Horst Koegler, 'On the Dance Floor of Democracy', *Ballett International*, June 1998; Jiří Kylián, 'An Australian Diary', *Ballett International*, July 1998; John Percival, 'Jiří Kylián at NDT', *Dance Now*, Summer 1999; Deborah Jowitt, 'Worlds Apart', *The Village Voice*, 9 March 2004; Alison Kirkman, 'NDTII in *Celebrating Kylián* and Het Nationale Ballet in *Partners*', *Dancing Times*, January 2006; Katja Werner, 'Jiří Kylián', *Ballettanz*, June 2009.

Books: Arlene Croce, *Going to the Dance*, New York, 1982; Jack Anderson, *Choreography Observed*, Iowa City, 1987; Gerard Mannoni, *Kylián* (in French), Arles, 1989; Isabelle Lanz, *A Garden of Dance: A Monograph on the Work of Jiří Kylián* (in Dutch and English), Amsterdam, 1995; Annette Embrechts, Maja Landeweer et al., *Dancing Dutch: Contemporary Dance in the Netherlands*, Amsterdam, 2000; Arlene Croce, *Writing in the Dark: Dancing in The New Yorker*, New York, 2000; Elisa Guzzo Vaccarine, *Jiří Kylián*, Palermo, 2001; Jaap Hulsmann, Marain Sarstadt et al., *Nederlands Dans Theater Yearbook, 2002–2003*, The Hague, 2003.

LIN HWAI-MIN

Founder, artistic director and main choreographer of Cloud Gate Dance Theatre of Taiwan, Lin Hwai-min is an internationally renowned choreographer, whose innovative dance works have received critical acclaim both at home and abroad. Lin Hwai-min's artistic achievement lies in his ability to integrate Eastern and Western culture in a serenely elegant and seamless style. Despite the heavily coded ethnic characteristics, his choreography rises above geographical and political boundaries, creating an intercultural dance phenomenon that enchants viewers with its aesthetic qualities.

Born in 1947 to an educated family in Chiayi, Taiwan, Lin Hwai-min was the son of a senior member of the Nationalist (KMT or Kuomintang) government. Originally trained as a journalist, Lin is also a published novelist, holding a Master of Fine Arts degree from the Writers' Workshop at the University of Iowa. Lin used the proceeds from his early published works to fund his interest in dance, initially receiving training in ballet and modern dance, but then going on to study Peking Opera movement, Graham and Cunningham techniques, and the classical court dances of Japan and Korea.

Lin founded Cloud Gate in 1973, with the intention of performing works 'composed by Chinese, choreographed by Chinese, danced by Chinese for Chinese audiences'. The company was named after a Chinese ritual dance dating from the era of the legendary Huang Ti (Yellow Emperor c. 2697–2589 BCE). Cloud Gate was the first professional dance company to be established in Taiwan and was to become inextricably linked with Lin Hwai-min's artistic development.

Most of Lin's dances are full-length, large-scale works that were premiered by Cloud Gate Dance Theatre in Taiwan. Many have subsequently been restaged for the national and international stage and are widely considered to be his landmark works.

Despite Cloud Gate's monopoly on Lin's output, a good number of his works have thus also found their way into the repertoires of other dance companies. Among these are the Zurich Ballet, which restaged *Smoke* in 2004, the Dutch company Introdans which restaged *White* in 2005, and Sylvie Guillem, who, in London in 2006, premiered *Sally*, a new solo created for the ballerina as part of Akram Khan's *Sacred Monsters* production. In 2002, Lin's landmark work *Legacy* was restaged by a collective of international companies and individuals for the World Dance Alliance Festival in Düsseldorf, Germany. Lin has also directed two opera productions, *Rashomon* (1996) and *Tosca* (2002).

Under Lin's influence, Cloud Gate has developed a unique Taiwanese contemporary style that fuses elements of Chinese, Western, Taiwanese and other Asian cultures. The evolution of Cloud Gate's repertoire, although contributed to from time to time by other choreographers, has been primarily influenced by Lin's personal ethos. This is characterized by two main elements: first, the need to develop a new form of contemporary dance, which reflects Taiwan's unique cultural environment (itself consisting of indigenous, Japanese, mainland Chinese, Western and other Asian influences), and second, the integration and exploration of Taiwanese sociocultural and political phenomena. The result is a body of work that serves to reflect Taiwan's sociopolitical condition and to address important questions of cultural and national identity.

This dual nature of Lin Hwai-min's creative output has spurred discussion and at times controversy about the various issues relating to the connection of dance, art and politics, and the questions of Taiwanese identity, nationalism and tradition. Consequently, part of the legacy of Lin's work will always be related to his unique ability to embody and reflect important aspects of the Taiwanese political, cultural and social environment. The combination of journalistic observation, poetic expression and choreographic melancholy inherent in his work not only draws comprehensive and sometimes exhaustive coverage from journalists and critics alike but also attracts considerable research interest from the wider dance and academic community.

Nevertheless, politics and society aside, Lin's work functions most importantly at an aesthetic level. His work appeals to wider audiences through its sheer beauty, choreographic structure and the profound elegance of a movement vocabulary developed through the powerful use of symbolism and theatrical elements. On a national level, his work takes on even more striking poignancy with its wide use of Taiwanese and Sino-cultural themes, symbolism and metaphor. This multi-dimensional characteristic allows critics to move from a regional to a more universal interpretation. Commenting on *Nine Songs* at the 1995 New York premiere, Anna Kisselgoff stated, 'What seems like an allegory about the seasons and human existence is turned finally into a protest piece . . . Lin refers to these gods of shamanistic times with a similar approach, moving from the universal to the specific.'[1] When writing on the 2003 New York premiere of *Moon Water*, Kisselgoff pointed out, '*Moon Water* is not about meditation but is a meditation in itself. Lin has accomplished what creative artists rarely succeed in doing today: challenging the audience with a work unlike any other.'[2]

Although dance movement has been a major focus of Lin's work, as his career expands, he no longer limits himself to the simple task of making dance steps. Costume, props, lighting, décor and multi-media projection are just as important as movement in the overall make-up of his work. Ballet, Graham technique and Peking opera movements are combined with the use of an umbrella, for example, to perform a psychological interpretation of a Chinese legend in *The Tale of the White Serpent* (1975). Or, to the sound of pounding drums, a huge white cloth is manipulated by dancers to symbolize a sail, a stormy sea and the crossing of the Straits of Formosa in *Legacy* (1978). White canes are used by a group of celebrants to reiterate the trance rhythm of the shaman woman in *Nine Songs* (1993). Chinese characters are projected onto dancers' bodies, creating a picture of shifting calligraphy in *Cursive* (2001). In *Dreamscape* (1985), flying Buddhist celestials and ancient Chinese personalities share the stage with modern businessmen, bandaged casualties and a motorcycle stunt man. The dance ends with a man in Western outfit standing facing a giant red Chinese gate as if confronting his destiny. The result of all this is a repertoire that is neither Chinese nor Western, neither traditional nor modern. It is a Taiwanese product, reflecting modern Taiwanese culture through the transformative power of dance. The development of Lin's work can be seen as a constant re-processing of materials, a re-interpretation and re-transformation of stylistic elements from his seminal works – a mode of working that has preoccupied Lin for the best part of his career.

Nationalism was an important motive in Lin Hwai-min's creation of Cloud Gate. He once said in an interview:

> When I first arrived I was full of enthusiasm, hoping to integrate Chinese tradition with new techniques from the West . . . the nation needed a dance company . . . it seemed that no one was willing to do it. So I did.[3]

It was a nationalist passion, evoked by diplomatic defeats in the international arena – for instance the Tiao-yu-tai Incident (1971–72), Taiwan's withdrawal from the United Nations (1971), and the consequent loss of many allies – that stimulated the creation of Cloud Gate. The company's mandate, as Lin articulated, was 'maybe it was a different form of "Tiao-yu-tai" protest'.[4]

The evolution of Cloud Gate's repertoire follows Lin Hwai-min's search for a cultural identity in a diasporic society. He began his search with a re-evaluation of the Chinese culture in Taiwan, then the re-evaluation of Taiwanese culture. As he stated,

I do love the Yellow River; I do love the Yangtze. When I grew up, I realized that this kind of love is dangerous. It is autistic and unreal, unless I know the Tanshui River [Taiwan] and love the Choshui River [Taiwan].[5]

After clarifying his cultural identity, Lin attempted to develop vocabularies 'matching the pulse of the time'. Realizing that both modern ballet and traditional opera movements were 'out of touch with Taiwanese reality', and what Cloud Gate had achieved was a 'transitional phenomenon', Lin turned to the Taiwanese vernacular arts.[6] Taiwanese dance rituals, vernacular literature (Xiang Tu Wen Xue), legends and songs thus contribute to his dance creations. In his words, 'those materials are more effective than Peking Opera, they still have live roots'.[7] The creation of *Legacy* (1978) and Cloud Gate dances with Taiwanese themes such as *The Day When She Sees the Ocean* (1977), *Liao Tien Ting* (1979), *Rite of Spring* (1984) and *My Nostalgia, My Songs* (1986) was Lin's reaction to the surge of Taiwanese ideology.

Responding to growing international touring demands and the changing social, cultural and political environment in Taiwan, Lin Hwai-min gradually played down the link between his dance works and contemporary sociopolitical issues. His attention shifted from social criticism to aesthetic meditation. His creative impulse has evolved from the multicultural to what might be called the intercultural, dealing with the realms of both reality and symbolism, which challenge audiences' preconceptions of dance, exoticism and theatricality. In *Songs of the Wanderers* (1994), for instance, a monk's silent prayer was transformed into Georgian folk songs, and a pilgrim journey of peace and humanity was set against a constant changing landscape of golden rice grains. In *Bamboo Dream* (2001), a bamboo forest that earlier reverberated with Arvo Pärt's music was to be physically dismantled by the dancers and stage crews, mocking the artificial nature of theatricality. Finally, in the *Cursive* Trilogy (2001–05), Chinese characters were deconstructed, reassembled and transformed by choreography of kinetics and visual images. Old figures were given a new look, unreadable words acquired new meaning, empty space filled with tension and attraction. Lin's choreography leads the viewer to a unique forum where Orient merges with Occident, tradition is juxtaposed with modern, and individual decision confronts group destiny.

Most of Lin's dances are not recorded, and many of them are lost or have hardly been performed since their premieres. Nevertheless, some dances have been kept in the current repertoire and have been reproduced in recent years. Since 1991, Cloud Gate has been working with film directors on restaging Lin's dances for film and digital media. As a result, more than 17 of his dances are published as dance videos or DVDs. In 2003 *Legacy* was preserved in the form of Labanotation.

Yu-Ling Chao

Notes

1 Anna Kisselgoff, 'Birth and Purification via Lotuses and Water', *The New York Times*, 20 October 1995.
2 Anna Kisselgoff, 'The Syncretism of Tai Chi and Bach', *The New York Times*, 20 November 2003.
3 Paul Shackman, 'The Dance Writer', in Lin Hwai-min *et al.*: *Brief Encounters*, Taipei, 1989.
4 Lin Hwai-min *et al.*, 'Fragmentary Works' in *Brief Encounters*, Taipei, 1989.
5 Lin Hwai-min, 'My Nostalgia, My Songs', in CGDF House Programme, live performance of Cloud Gate Winter Season, Taipei, December 1986.
6 CGDF, House Programme, live performance of Cloud Gate Autumn Season, Taipei, September 1977.
7 Chen-I, 'That Fierce Power of Judgment', in CGDF House Programme, live performance of Cloud Gate Spring Season, Taipei, May 1978.

Biographical details

Born in Chiayi County, Taiwan, 19 February 1947. **Studied** opera movement in Taiwan, modern dance at the Martha Graham and Merce Cunningham studios, New York and classical court dance in Japan and Korea; also received a BA in journalism, National Chengchi University, Taiwan, 1968, and an MFA, Writer's Workshop, University of Iowa, 1972. **Career**. Founder and Artistic Director of Cloud Gate Dance Theatre of Taiwan, from 1973, establishing Cloud Gate Dance School in 1998 and Cloud Gate II, the junior company, in 1999; founding chairman of the Department of Dance, Taiwan's National University of the Arts, 1983–88, and founding Dean of their graduate dance programme, 1993–94; also artistic director of 'Novel Hall New Dance Series', introducing international artists to Taiwan, from 2000; has directed opera, including *Rashomon* (Graz, 1996) and *Tosca* (Taipei, 2002). Author of *The Cicadas*, Taipei, 1969, and *Metamorphic Rainbow*, Taipei, 1968. **Awards and honours** include Fulbright Fellowship, 1989; National Award for Arts, Taiwan, 1980; *Dance Europe* Choreographer of the 20th Century, 2000; Best Choreographer at Lyon Biennial Festival, 2000; Citation of Honour, World Dance Alliance, 2004; Taishin Arts Awards, 2004, 2006; Joyce Award, New York, 2005; John D. Rockefeller Award, 2006; Distinguished Artist Award, International Society of Performing Arts, 2006; Lifetime Achievement Award, International Movimentos Prize, 2009.

Works

The Butterfly Dream (1971); Landscapes (1971); Autumn Thoughts (1973); Summer Night (1973); After the Rice-Reaping (1973); Blind (1973); Wu Lung Yuan (1973); Mien (1973); Yuin Hsin (1973); Han Shih (1974); Revenge of a Lonely Ghost (1974); No Cha (1974); The Tale of the White Serpent (1975); Phenomenon (1975); Hair Tree (1975); One More Clear Night (1975); The Little Drummer (1976); Wu Shung Kills the Tiger (1976); A Slap on the Face (1976); Forward Look (1976); Vivaldi Concerto (1976); Wu Fong (1976); Peacocks Fly South-Eastern Bound (1977); Kua Fu Pursues the Sun (1977); Red Strings (1977); The Day When She Sees the Ocean (1977); Legacy (1978); Liao Tien Ting (1979); Nu Wa (1979); Milky Way (1979); Spring Breeze (1980); Street Game (1980); Duet (1981); Spring Ripple (1981); Nirvana (1982); Shen Ming (1982); Prelude (solo concert, 1982); Souvenir Shot (solo concert, 1982); Smoke (solo concert, 1982); Times 3 (solo concert, 1982); I Am a Macho (solo concert, 1982); To Wei Chin-shen (solo concert, 1982); The Dream of the Red Chamber (1983); Concerto for Bamboo Flute (1984); Adagietto (1984); Rite of Spring (1984); Taipei, 1984 (1984); Fantasy on Aspirin (1984); Notebook (1984); Dreamscape (1985); Peacock Variations (1986); My Nostalgia, My Songs (1986); Four Seasons (1987); Spring (1987); Requiem (1989); The Fortune-Number Card and Change of Costumes (1991); Song of Plowing (1991); As The River Flows On (1991); Shooting the Sun (1992); Nine Songs (1993); Rice Grains (1994); Songs of the Wanderers (1994); Symphony of the Sorrowful Songs (1995); Portrait of the Families (1997); Moon Water (1998); Burning of the Juniper Branches (1999); Green (2000); Bamboo Dream (2001); Cursive (2001); Smoke (2002; restaged by Zurich Ballet, 2004); Cursive II (2003); The Road to the Mountain (2004); Wild Cursive (2005); White (2006); Wind Shadow (2006); Sally (solo for Sylvie Guillem, in Sacred Monsters, chor. with Akram Khan, 2006); Whisper of Flowers (2008); Listening to the River (2010).

Further reading

Interview with Nicholas Rowe, in 'Interview with the Choreographer Lin Hwai-min', Dance Europe, June/July 1999; with Arnd Wesemann in 'A Sign From Buddha', Ballett International, June 1999; with Zachary Whittenburg, in 'Beyond Words', Time Out Chicago, 21–27 January 2010.

Articles: Jochen Schmidt, 'On the Threshold', Ballett International, February 1986; Daryl Reis, 'Cloud Gate's Director sees Hong Kong as Lynchpin of Change', Dance Magazine, October 1986; Daryl Ries, 'Building Contemporary Dance Expression in Asia', Ballett International, March 1988; Andre Lepecki, 'Postcolonialism, Interculturalism', Ballet International, January 1996; Jochen Schmidt, 'A Shining Example for Asia', Ballett International, January 1998; David Mead, 'The Dance of Ink on White Paper', Dancing Times, June 2007; Zoë Anderson, 'Moon Water', Dancing Times, July 2008; Jonathan Gray, 'Wind Shadow', Dancing Times, November 2009.

Books: Chen Ya-ping and Chao Chi-fang (eds), Dance Studies and Taiwan: the Prospect of a New Generation, Taipei, 2001; Chen Ya-ping, 'In Search of Asian Modernity: Cloud Gate Dance Theatre's Body Aesthetics in the Era of Globalization', in Jo Butterworth and Liesbeth Wildschut (eds), Contemporary Choreography: A Critical Reader, London and New York, 2009.

LAR LUBOVITCH

Lar Lubovitch's dances evoke descriptions such as exuberant, energetic, sweeping, luscious and impassioned. A prodigious choreographer, Lubovitch's new commissions and restaged older dances abound in the repertories of internationally renowned ballet and modern dance companies. From the New York City Ballet to the Paris Opera Ballet, Alvin Ailey American Dance Theater to Israel's Bat-Dor Dance Company, San Francisco Ballet to Hubbard Street Dance Chicago and his own Lar Lubovitch Dance Company, his appeal transcends boundaries of style and nation. Despite dissenting opinions from some critics, audiences respond vociferously to his mainstream and entertaining dances, which, although often devoid of narrative, are emotionally charged.

Pursuit of his talents as a visual artist led Lubovitch to major in art at Iowa State University, where he encountered the José Limón Dance Company. Seeing a professional dance performance for the first time awakened a long-held ambition to dance. He abandoned his brushes for the dance studio, eventually taking up a full scholarship at the Juilliard School, where some of Lubovitch's teachers ranked among the *Who's Who* of twentieth-century dance: Anna Sokolow, Louis Horst, Lucas Hoving and Antony Tudor among them. A painterly and sculptural vision continues to inform his creations, reflected in Lubovitch's interviews, which are peppered with visual art terminology.

Lubovitch choreographed his first full work and started his own company in 1968, in the midst of a performance career encompassing both modern dance and ballet. (Members of his company, then and now, reflect the diversity of Lubovitch's own training. He has worked with dancers known for their strength and versatility, of both ballet and modern dance techniques; notable dancers over the years include Rob Besserer and Mark Morris.) In 2008, the Lar Lubovitch Dance Company celebrated its 40th anniversary. The company had survived financial fluctuations, a brief year-long hiatus in 1974 and a break in touring from 1995 to 2007, although the commitment to new creations and staging older works did not wane during the time off the road.

Distinct choreographic phases are evident over Lubovitch's career. *The Time Before the Time After (After the Time Before)* (1971) was a duet about a tortured relationship in which the lovers constantly hurt each other yet are unable to walk away. *Scherzo for Messah Jack* (1973), an evocation of the Deep South of the United States, combined figurative and abstract movement. Other dances, *Whirligogs* (1969), *Some of the reactions of some of the people some of the time upon hearing reports of the coming of the Messiah* (1970) and *Joy of Man's Desiring* (1972), link movement and music to create 'a teeming meeting of the psychological and the physical' resulting in 'high-voltage aesthetic results'.[1] In contrast, Marcia B. Siegel characterized the early works as rhythmic with 'huge simultaneous body changes', without 'lightness or upward swing to this choreography, no sense of flying out into space'.[2]

Photographs of the signature work *Cavalcade* (1980) epitomize a second choreographic phase that began in the late 1970s. With limbs stretched taut in explosive leaps, beautiful bodies caught mid-air in stylized all-in-one leotards, the message is the movement. Rhythmically driven by the scores of the minimalist Steve Reich in *Marimba: A Trance Dance* (1976) and *Cavalcade* and of Philip Glass in *North Star* (1978), dancers responded directly to the music, passing bodily undulations on to each other, 'ricocheting a movement phrase through a line of dancers'.[3] Trance-like flowing and circular qualities dominated some dance sections, while in others a controlled energy built up until the dancers burst out in leaps across the stage. Harnessing what he termed 'energy reverberations' in *Cavalcade*, Lubovitch draws on the individual strengths of his dancers, shaping them into a fast-paced virtuosic 'parade of dancers'.[4] Yet the mass, the contemporary *corps* of eight, retain their individuality when dancers step out to perform solos and duets.

Lubovitch described the middle years of working as taking 'the theoretical approach rather than the exclusively physical approach' to create movement.[5] In contrast to his popular success, critical responses were not unanimously favourable, as some found his choreography repetitive and derivative. Arlene Croce focused on the impact of the minimalist scores on the choreography, writing that the dance 'never transcends procedural mechanics, and it always seems to begin and end in the same spot without having gone anywhere in between'.[6]

Brahms Symphony marked a transformative period in 1985, as Lubovitch turned back to early composers for inspiration, searching for a 'primal spirit of movement'.[7] In dances 'so warm, and sensuous and pretty', Jennifer Dunning wrote that 'he seems to have created a new category – dance to bask in', in which intricate patterns, tilting torsos and lifts of surging motion compel the dancers.[8] A revitalized confidence was noted by Jack Anderson in a paring down and use of fewer steps.[9] Significantly, Lubovitch explained that his return to the intuitive and the physical occurred when he became reintegrated into the choreographic process by moving his own body.

Lubovitch distinguishes between the creation of movement and dance technique itself. Although his works are technically demanding, 'movement is what dance is about' and he focuses on transitions rather than static poses.[10] Traditionally, he sets the choreographic structure to the music first, prior to working with visual shapes, although venturing away from the familiar on occasion. 'I search for the relationship between my shape and the music . . . Then the combination of the shape, emotional suggestions and musical correlation is the finished phrase'.[11] He explains that choreographing a dance is like solving a problem that is approachable through various methods.

The movement questions Lubovitch sets himself lead to unexpected results with varying degrees of success. In *Of My Soul* (1987), he drew on the text of J.S. Bach's *Cantata No. 78*, with American sign-language for the deaf integrated into the choreography. Here, the character of The Sermon admonishes The Fallen (a role taken by either a female or male dancer) set against a chorus, combining signing gestures with dancerly movement. For *Fandango* (1989), danced to Ravel's *Bolero*, Lubovitch eschewed the critical musical relationship during its creation and generated movement from the dancers by using verbal descriptions of drawn abstract shapes.

Beau Danube (1981), a humorous piece set to Johann Strauss's music; *Rhapsody in Blue* (1988), commissioned by the New York City Ballet, *American Gesture* (1992) for the Pacific Northwest Ballet, set to Charles Ives; and *Do You Be* (2004) danced to Meredith Monk scores represent the eclectic range of composers Lubovitch uses. In '. . . *smile with my heart*' (2002), danced to Marvin Laird's original score *Fantasie on Themes by Richard Rodgers*, Lubovitch draws together the popular with modern dance technique. Increasingly, jazz stimulates new choreography, as seen in *Love Stories* (2005) for Hubbard Street Dance Chicago, set to songs by Kurt Elling and *Elemental Brubeck* (2005), to accompaniment by Dave Brubeck, commissioned by the San Francisco Ballet. Lubovitch spoke of his teenage years listening to jazz in Chicago, feeling at home with a musical form that 'assaults my solar plexus and causes a response in the rest of my body'. For *Coltrane's Favorite Things* (2010), the musical impulse came from John Coltrane's improvisations on Richard Rodgers' famous tune from *The Sound of Music*. Performed in front of a reproduction of Jackson Pollock's *Autumn Rhythm (Number 30)*, Lubovitch characterized this dance as responding to Coltrane's 'sheets of sound' and Pollock's 'field of action' with his own 'ribbons of movement'.[12]

Undaunted by the complex beauty of the symphonies and concertos of master composers, Brahms, Mozart and Stravinsky among them, the physical responses to musical impulses create 'kinetic feasts for the eye',[13] which highlight musical passages in unexpected ways instead of through musical equivalents.[14] France's Centre National de Danse Contemporaine commissioned a signature Lubovitch dance, inspired by Mozart's *Concerto for Clarinet and Orchestra* (K. 622). The first and third movements of *Concerto Six Twenty-Two* (1986) celebrate a sense of community, which frames a male duet in the adagio movement. Often performed independently, the duet was created in response to the AIDS crisis, but is 'more about love than lovers'.[15] Lubovitch focused on the dignity of male friendship rather than the agony of death and loss. One partner's physical support translates into a caring relationship between men, yet it speaks beyond a friendship of two. *Concerto Six Twenty-Two* was set on the José Limón Dance Company in 2004, bringing the Limón connection full circle. Although Deborah Jowitt saw stylistic similarities to Limón, Lubovitch created distinctive characteristics, where 'rapture lifts the dancers' bodies, they breathe into their curving, arching patterns'.[16]

Another choreographic phase is marked by the full-length ballet *Othello* (1997), created in collaboration with composer Elliot Goldenthal and designer George Tsypin. In addition to being nominated for a Grammy award, the ballet was also set on the Joffrey Ballet in 2009 and remains in the American Ballet Theatre and San Francisco Ballet repertoires. Noted for breaking from a traditional ballet narrative format, his 'psychological storytelling'[17] was accompanied by his signature style in 'a surge of movement that sweeps its dancers along into lifts or waves of eddies on the stage'.[18] Although fragments of stories can be identified, other story-telling dances eschew a strict narrative. Initially performed in churches and a former synagogue, *Pentimento* (2004) saw Lubovitch looking to his painterly, choreographic, personal past and towards an aesthetic shaped, in part, by the urban landscapes of Chicago and New York City. In *Men's Stories* (2000), set to Scott Marshall's score based on Beethoven piano concertos, he focused on what the nine male dancers' bodies reveal when they dance rather than on 'what they're dancing'.[19] Male camaraderie is also celebrated in the trio *Little Rhapsodies* (2007). The male duet *Dogs of War* (2010), to Prokofiev's 'War Sonatas', embodies a confrontation between soldiers and inevitable death and anguish, supported by Paul Vershbow's photographic projections documenting the horrors of battle.

During the break from touring, which ended in 2007, Lubovitch devoted his energies to the creation of new work rather than the maintenance of existing repertoire. His company's 40th anniversary celebration performances at New York's City Center Theatre set classics such as *North Star* alongside newer creations, reinforcing perceptions of his mastery of movement. In *Dvořák Serenade* (2007), duets flowed out of an undulating corps, while in *Jangle: Four Hungarian Dances* (2008) the rich rhythms of Bartók's folk-inspired rhapsodies were emphasized by grounded movement and group formations. His dancers' enjoyment of performance is often palpable as they find an organic fluidity in choreography, which feels 'right' on their bodies.[20]

Success on Broadway has also marked Lubovitch's career as choreographer for Sondheim and Lapine's *Into the Woods* (1987), a musical based on fairytale characters; a London production of *Oklahoma!* (1994); in new dances for Rodgers and Hammerstein's *The King and I* (1996); and Cole Porter's *High Society* (1998). And despite the 1993 critical failure of the Broadway musical adaptation of the movie *The Red Shoes* (1993), American Ballet Theatre bought the performance rights to Lubovitch's choreography. Collaborations with Olympic ice skaters John Curry and Peggy Fleming in *Tilt-a-Whirl* (1979), followed by *The Sleeping Beauty* for Robin Cousins and Rosalyn Summers (1987), have extended Lubovitch's expertise beyond the proscenium frame. His ice dance choreography for French Olympic stars Isabelle and Paul Duchesnay in 1994, to Holst's *The Planets* (1994), was broadcast on American television and nominated for multiple awards, including Emmy and Grammy awards. Other ice dances for Paul Wylie (*Adagio* and *Touch Me*), Roca and Sur (*I'll Be Seeing You*) and for the Ice Theatre of New York (*Gershwin Variations*) were also created in 1996.

In Robert Altman's film *The Company* (2003), Lubovitch appeared as an actor and his duet *My Funny Valentine* (2001) was nominated for an International Emmy award. Appealing to a diverse audience base, Lubovitch strives to broaden physical access to contemporary dance through projects such as Lar's Dance your Dreams (for New York City's schools), just one component of a multifaceted outreach programme. He also established the non-profit Chicago Dancing Company organ-ization to help support the annual Chicago Dancing Festival, which has grown to five days of free performances since it began in 2007.

Lubovitch's choreography continues to divide opinion among critics and, at times, opposing perspectives are found in the same review. Laura Shapiro feels he is 'disinclined to make waves . . . It's as if he's tapped into some innate comfort zone and discovered exactly what people want bodies to look like when they're moving to music, and which emotions will be most pleasant to experience'.[21] For Lubovitch's audi-ences, the smooth ride he offers is an exuberant one. His choreography celebrates life and its range of emotional states, while emphasizing the music/movement relationship. As Lubovitch explains, 'All of my dances are about dancing. Dancing is really a superior metaphor for humanity and emotions'.[22]

Stacey Prickett

Notes

1 John Gruen (ed.), *People Who Dance: 22 Dancers Tell Their Own Stories*, Princ-eton, NJ, 1988, p. 80.
2 Marcia B. Siegel, *At the Vanishing Point: A Critic Looks at Dance*, New York, 1972, p. 126.
3 Sally R. Sommers, 'Review', *Dance Magazine*, June 1981, p. 46.
4 Eleanor Rachel Luger, 'Lar Lubovitch: In Command of Method and Mad-ness', *Dance Magazine*, March 1981, p. 68.
5 John Gruen, 'Confrontation with Dance: Lyricism and Craft, Lar Lubovitch', *Dance Magazine*, February 1990, p. 48.
6 Croce, Arlene, *Going to the Dance*, New York, 1982, p. 364.
7 Quoted in Gary Parks, 'New Lease on Lar', *Dance Magazine*, November 1986, p. 55.
8 Jennifer Dunning, 'Dance: Premiere by Lar Lubovitch', *The New York Times*, 9 May 1985.
9 See Jack Anderson, 'Lubovitch and Brahms: Exuberant Partnership', *The New York Times*, 22 March 1988, C20.
10 Lubovitch, quoted in Parks, op. cit., p. 54.
11 Lubovitch in Gruen (1988), op. cit., p. 87.
12 Lubovitch in Gia Kourlas, 'Choreography Inspired by Coltrane', *The New York Times*, 21 February 2010, p. AR15.
13 Anne Tobias, 'Lar Lubovitch Dance Company', *Dance Magazine*, September 1992, p. 71.
14 Anna Kisselgoff, 'Lubovitch the Earth-Shaker Takes a Breather', *The New York Times*, 17 March 1988, III, p. 23.
15 Anna Kisselgoff, 'The Wider Dimension of Lubovitch's Male Duet', *The New York Times*, 13 May 1993, p. C15.

16 Deborah Jowitt, 'Lar Lubovitch Celebrates Decades of Dance Making', *The Village Voice*, 6 November 2008, n.p.

17 Jennifer Dunning, 'A Drama Built More on Character than Dancing', *The New York Times*, 12 June 1998, n.p.

18 Anna Kisselgoff, 'A Downtown Experiment Has an Uptown Premiere', *The New York Times*, 26 May 1997, n.p.

19 Jennifer Dunning, 'Where Men Reveal Their Stories and Souls', *The New York Times*, 27 November 2000, n.p.

20 Joseph Carman, 'Unwavering', *Dance Magazine*, September 2008.

21 Laura Shapiro, 'Comfort Food', *New York Magazine*, 31 May, 2004.

22 William Harris, 'For Lubovitch, Dance is a Verbal Art', *The New York Times*, 25 February 1990, II, p. 1.

Biographical details

Born in Chicago, United States, 9 April 1943. **Studied** art at Chicago's Art Institute and Iowa State University; studied dance at Connecticut College, New London, with José Limón and Alvin Ailey, at New York's Juilliard School of Performing Arts from 1964, and with Anna Sokolow, Martha Graham, Louis Horst, Lucas Hoving, Antony Tudor and Leon Danielian; also attended classes at the Joffrey Ballet School and the Martha Graham School. **Career**: Danced with several ballet, modern and jazz companies, including Pearl Lang Company, 1964; Manhattan Festival Ballet (soloist) and Harkness Ballet (soloist), 1967–69. First choreography for opera productions, 1965; formed own group the Lar Lubovitch Dance Company in 1968, disbanded 1974 and reformed in 1975; has been guest choreographer for various companies, including Pennsylvania Ballet, Bat-Dor Dance Company (Israel), Gulbenkian Ballet, Dutch National Ballet, Paris Opera Ballet, Ballet Rambert, Baryshnikov's White Oak Dance Project, Pacific Northwest Ballet, New York City Ballet, Alvin Ailey Dance Theater and American Ballet Theatre. Has also choreographed a number of works for ice dancers and for Broadway and West End musicals. **Awards and honours** include International Emmy Award (for film of *Fandango*), 1992; National Education Film and Video Festival Golden Apple, 1993; Astaire Award (Theater Development Fund), 1993–94; US International Film and Video Festival Gold Camera Award, 1995; Worldfest Gold Award (Houston, Texas), 1995; Gemini Award (Canada, for ice-dance film *The Planets*), 1996; Elan Award (Dance Spirit Magazine and Capezio) 2004; Chicagoan of the Year, 2008; Ice Theater of New York Choreography Award, 2009.

Works*

Don Giovanni (opera, 1965); *The Marriage of Figaro* (opera, 1965); *Carmen* (opera, 1965); *Blue* (1968); *Freddie's Bag* (1968); *The Journey Back* (1968); *Greeting Sampler* (1969); *Transcendant Passage* (1969); *Unremembered Time – Forgotten Place* (1969); *Incident at Lee* (1969); *Whirligogs* (1969); *Variations and Fugue on the Theme of a Dream* (1970); *Ecstasy* (1970); *In a Clearing* (1970); *Sam Nearlydeadman* (1970); *Some of the reactions of some of the people some of the time upon hearing reports of the coming of the Messiah* (1970); *Air* (1970); *Social* (1971); *Clear Lake* (1971); *The Time Before the Time After (After the Time Before)* (1971); *Joy* (1972); *Considering the Lilies (Joy of*

Man's Desiring) (1972); *Sans titre* (1972); *Scherzo for Messah Jack* (1973); *Chariot Light Night* (television version, 1973; stage version, 1974); *Three Essays* (1974); *Zig Zag* (1974); *Eight Easy Pieces* (1974); *Avalanche* (1974); *Girl on Fire* (1975); *Rapid Transit* (1975); *Session* (1975: new version titled *Cité Veron*, 1977); *Marimba: A Trance Dance* (1976); *Les Noces* (1976: re-imagined in 2000 and titled *The Wedding*); *Exultate, Jubilate* (1977); *Scriabin Dances* (1977); *Cité Veron* (1977); *North Star* (1978); *Valley* (1978); *Tilt-a-Whirl* (ice dance, 1979); *Up Jump* (1979); *Mistral* (for television, 1979); *Cavalcade* (1980); *American Gesture* (1981; expanded version, 1992); *Beau Danube* (1981); *Big Shoulders* (1983; revised version 1985); *Tabernacle* (1983); *Adagio and Rondo for Glass Harmonica* (1984); *Court of Ice* (ice dance; 1984); *Brahms Symphony* (1985; revised version, as *A Brahms Symphony*, 1995); *Concerto Six Twenty-Two* (1986); *Blood* (1986); *Of My Soul* (1987); *The Sleeping Beauty* (ice dance, 1987); *Into the Woods* (musical, 1987); *Musette* (1988); *Rhapsody in Blue* (1988); *Fandango* (1989); *From Paris to Jupiter* (1990; later retitled *Just Before Jupiter*); *Quartet for Oboe and Strings* (1990); *Hautbois* (1990); *Sinfonia Concertante* (1991); *Waiting for Sunrise* (1991); *Dance of the Seven Veils* (play *Salomé* by Oscar Wilde, 1992); *American Gesture* (1992); *The Red Shoes* (adaptation of film musical by Jule Styne, 1993); *So in Love* (1994); *The Planets* (ice dance, 1994, broadcast by A&E in 1995); *Oklahoma!* (musical, 1994); *The King and I* (musical, 1996); *Touch Me* (ice dance, 1996); *Adagio* (ice dance, 1996); *I'll Be Seeing You* (ice dance, 1996); *Gershwin Variations* (ice dance, 1996); *Othello* (1997); *High Society* (1998); *Yiddish Songs of Love And Wonder* (1998); *Thus is All* (1998); *The Hunchback of Notre Dame* (1999); *Meadow* (1999); *All Ye Need to Know* (1999); *Men's Stories* (2000); *The Wedding* (new version of *Les Noces*, 2001); *My Funny Valentine* (2001); *'...smile with my heart'* (2002); *Artemis* (2003); *Pentimento* (2004); *Do You Be* (2004); *Nature Boy* (originally *Love Stories*, 2005); *Elemental Brubeck* (2005); *Recordare* (2005); *Little Rhapsodies* (solo version, 2006); *Cryptoglyph* (2007); *Little Rhapsodies* (expanded version, 2007); *Dvořák Serenade* (2007); *Angel's Feet* (2007); *Jangle: Four Hungarian Dances* (2008); *Coltrane's Favorite Things* (2010); *Vita Nova* (duet from *Meadow*, 2010); *Dogs of War* (2010).

* Where discrepancies in published dates exist, those listed here conform to the company website.

Further reading

Interviews in 'Lar Lubovitch: American Dancer and Choreographer', *Dance and Dancers*, October 1972; with Gary Parks, 'New Lease on Lar: Passion's Progress', *Dance Magazine*, November 1986; with John Gruen, in 'Confrontation with Dance: Lar Lubovitch', *Dance Magazine*, February 1990; with Gia Kourlas, in 'Top 40', *Time Out New York*, Issue 683, Oct 30–Nov 5 2008.

Articles: Doris Hering, 'Choreography by Lar Lubovitch', *Dance Magazine*, February 1970; Norma McLain Stoop, 'A Human Being Who Dances: Lar Lubovitch', *Dance Magazine*, April 1972; Horst Koegler, 'The Lisbon Story – Part One', *Dance and Dancers*, August 1972; John Gruen, 'Lar Lubovitch: Choreographer in Search of Meaning', *Dance Magazine*, February 1977; Eleanor Rachel Luger, 'Lar Lubovitch: In Command of Method and Madness', *Dance Magazine*, March 1981; Allen Robertson, 'Right on Target', *Ballet News*, February 1984; Alastair Macaulay, 'Umbrellissima', *Dancing Times*, December 1984; Clive Barnes, 'Outsiders Moving In', *Dance and*

Dancers, February 1987; Kevin Boyd Grubb, 'Broadway and Beyond', *Dance Magazine*, April 1988; Maya Wallach, 'Lubovitch Strikes Out', *Attitude*, Winter 1989/90; Tobi Tobias, 'Rites of Passage', *New York Magazine*, 7 January, 1991; 'Lar Lubovitch', in *Current Biography Yearbook 1992*; Sheryl Flatow, 'Page Two: The Red Shoes Dance on Broadway', *Dance Magazine*, November 1993; George Dorris, The Red Shoes Onstage', *Dancing Times*, February 1994; Gus Solomons, 'Reviews', *Dance Magazine*, February 1995; John Gruen, 'Dance Returns to Broadway', *Dance Magazine*, April 1996; Robert Johnson, 'A New 'Othello' by Lar Lubovitch', *Ballett International/Tanz Actuell*, January 1997; Hilary Ostlere, 'Dancetheater: Swing High, Swing Low', *Dance Magazine*, July 1998; Arnd Wesemann, 'The Phantoms of the Musicals', *Ballett International/Tanz Aktuell*, July 1999; Gus Solomons, 'View: A Guy thing', *Dance Magazine*, March 2001; Laura Shapiro, 'Comfort Food', *New York Magazine*, 31 May, 2004; Susan Yung, 'Lar Lubovitch Dance Company', *Dance Magazine*, July 2004; Joseph Carman, 'Unwavering', *Dance Magazine*, September 2008; Deborah Jowitt, 'Garth Fagan and Lar Lubovitch Celebrate Decades of Dancing', *The Village Voice*, 5 November, 2008; Gia Kourlas, 'Choreography Inspired by Coltrane', *New York Times*, 21 February, 2010; Deborah Jowitt, 'Lar Lubovitch Raises a Jazz Soufflé', *The Village Voice*, 23 February, 2010.

Books: Max Niehaus, *Ballett Faszination*, Munich, 1972; John Gruen, *The Private World of Ballet*, New York, 1975; Don McDonagh, *The Complete Guide to Modern Dance*, Garden City, New York, 1976; Cynthia Lyle (ed.), *Dancers on Dancing*, New York and London, 1977; Arlene Croce, *Going to the Dance*, New York, 1982; John Gruen (ed.), *People Who Dance: 22 Dancers Tell Their Own Stories*, Princeton, NJ, 1988; Rose Eichenbaum (photographs and text) and Clive Barnes (foreword), *Masters of Movement: Portraits of America's Great Choreographers*, Washington, DC, 2004.

VINCENT MANTSOE

Vincent Sekwati Koko Mantsoe's recognition as a choreographer demonstrates that to be successfully integrated into the performance arena as a contemporary artist, one does not have to disavow one's cultural heritage. Quite the contrary.

Growing up in Diepkloof, one of the South African townships outside Johannesburg known as Soweto, Mantsoe developed his musical understanding of movement and its transformational potential in his early years. When still a boy, he would assist in the dancing and drumming that his grandmother, his mother and two of his aunts performed in their capacity as *sangomas* (the Zulu term for traditional healers). The *sangoma* ceremonies involve the shifting of body and mind into a state of trance, from where the ancestral spirits may be consulted for guidance in curing physical and psychological disorders. Growing up in Soweto in the late 1970s and 1980s also meant going to school at a time when the education of black children was a low priority for the apartheid government. As a result Mantsoe spent a substantial part of his teenage years practising the 1980s styles of township street dancing, which combined popular African dance forms with influences from American pop culture picked up from videos, such as Michael Jackson's.

In the township youth group known as The Joy Dancers, with whom Mantsoe performed, Gregory Maqoma (who has since earned acclaim as a contemporary choreographer in his own right) was also a member. In 1990, both Mantsoe and Maqoma were accepted into the newly established trainee programme of Moving Into Dance Mophatong (MIDM), one of the first integrated dance companies in South Africa. Instead of being a 'punk with a perm', Mantsoe, an ambitious student, immersed himself in the discipline of formal dance training, while discovering his creative powers in solving choreographic tasks.[1] Having had little academic training, he battled with assignments in subjects such as the history and anthropology of dance.

Still under the mentorship of MIDM founder and artistic director Sylvia Glasser, his education was nurtured through exposure to the world outside South Africa. Among the formative contexts that influenced Mantsoe's artistic approach and provided him with movement inspiration were residencies with NAISDA (The National Aboriginal Islander Skills Development Association) in Australia in the early 1990s. Here, he was introduced to movement philosophies embodied in traditional dance forms from Australia and Asia, such as Balinese dance. Another important learning process was as a dancer in Glasser's choreographies, most notably in *Tranceformations* (1991), based on the trance dance of the San people of the Kalahari Desert as depicted in their rock art. As explained by Mantsoe, whose own ancestral heritage combines influences from Zulu, Pedi, Xhosa, Venda and Shangaan dance, the preoccupation with the spiritual life of the San taught him the importance of being humble when engaging with dance forms not his own.[2] Describing the work on Glasser's choreography as a turning point, Mantsoe recalls it as the moment when he realized how he could make choreographic use of the ancestral knowledge embedded in the dance he had known since childhood.

Afrofusion, an approach to dancing taught at MIDM, was introduced in the late 1970s as a combination of dance forms. Starting with African dance and music styles and rituals, and blending them with the techniques and aesthetics that Sylvia Glasser had studied in Europe and the

United States, Afrofusion was a point of departure for Mantsoe's own choreographic work. He has developed an approach drawing on his own movement inspirations, placing emphasis on the spiritual qualities that may be accessed at a deep level of the body tissue. In the process, the dancer acquires not only strength and energy as a performer but also a deeply humane gentleness in expression. Concerned first and foremost with an embodied ethics of dance, his approach replaces what he considers the misleading binaries of contemporary/traditional or Western/African dance with a profound sensitivity to the power of movement itself. The process is described in the choreographer's own words as a re-education about the spirit of the dance and a rebalancing of the past with the present, through which the interconnectedness of humanity and nature is revealed. In a unique manner, a preoccupation with identity, shared with many artists in post-apartheid South Africa, is implicit in his works rather than explicit.

The concepts of transformation and fusion carry additional meaning on a political level in the South African context of the 1990s. Mantsoe's emergence as a choreographer may thus be seen as closely linked to the ending of the era of apartheid. *African Soul* (1991), his first solo created while he was still a student at MIDM, won him the Stepping Stones Award in the FNB Dance Umbrella in Johannesburg. As a festival and a competition, the FNB Dance Umbrella had been established a few years earlier with a commitment to nurture the growth of contemporary choreography and dance from the wealth of creative talent previously working in isolation. When Mantsoe was chosen the following year, together with Boyzie Cekwana, as recipient of the FNB Dance Umbrella's Young Choreographer's Grant, it was among 90 choreographic entries. The figure gives an idea of the explosion of contemporary dance in South Africa, which fostered a number of contemporary choreographers who today enjoy international recognition, such as Robin Orlyn, Boyzie Cekwana, Gregory Maqoma and Elio.

The next seminal event in Mantsoe's career took place in 1992, at the time when negotiations between the apartheid government and the African National Congress (ANC) were showing promise, and the Ministry of Foreign Affairs, eager for a positive response from the international community, gave MIDM their first governmental grant. This allowed them to represent South Africa at the world exhibition EXPO in Spain. The programme featured a work by Sylvia Glasser, together with a duet version of Mantsoe's *African Soul*. International response was overwhelming. During the following years, Mantsoe was celebrated in festivals in Australia, Japan, Africa, Europe and North America. Although these opportunities provided him with the all-important space and support to allow for his artistic growth, in return he earned MIDM fame on stages around the world.

Among the many distinctions awarded in recognition of Mantsoe's choreographic talent in these years, the most important was the first prize granted to *Gula Matari* (1993) at the First Contemporary African Dance Competition in Luanda, Angola, in 1995. Once more the choreography, set on MIDM dancers, had initially been a solo. Like *Gula*, which for many years held signature status in his solo repertory, the group piece shows the dancers' transformation into bird-like beings. On the tour of sub-Saharan Africa that followed in the wake of the Angolan award, MIDM performed in the capitals of Kenya, Ghana, Togo, Ivory Coast, Gabon, Congo-Brazzaville and Angola. The programme, which presented the award-winning choreography together with Mantsoe's newly commissioned *Speaking with Tongues* (1994) and *Ngoma* (1994), as well as works by Sylvia Glasser and other members of MIDM, was held together by a ritualistic and spiritual thread. Yet it was undeniably contemporary. This puzzled some, provoked others and resonated with many in the audiences across Africa.[3]

A similar, but overall positive, response was granted for Mantsoe's work in Europe, where *Gula Matari* earned him an award in the French Rencontres Chorégraphiques Internationales de Seine-St. Denis in 1996. Two years later, the turn came to *Hanano Blessing of the Earth* (1995) in the Rencontres in Bagnolet. The successful exposure in France was followed by an enthusiastically received appearance in the 1999 London Dance Umbrella, where Mantsoe was the first choreographer from the African continent to perform. His solo programme included *Gula*, *Mpheyane* (*Deceit*, 1997), about a man in search of his ancestral heritage and *Phokwane* (1998), a tribute to his parents in gratitude for their spiritual support. An interest in his work was generated, which culminated in a solo tour of the United Kingdom in the spring of 2006. A similar track was drawn in North America, where his introduction as a soloist at the Jacob's Pillow festival with *Motswa Hole* (*Person from Far Away*, 2001) in 2003 was followed by repeated and extensive touring in both the United States and Canada with more recent works such as *Bupiro-Mukiti* (*Dance of Life*, 2002), *NDAA* (*Greetings*, 2003) and *NTU* (*Nothing*, 2005).

As the choreographic commissions increased through the 1990s, so did international demands on Mantsoe's solo performances and workshops.

With less time spent in South Africa, the ties between Mantsoe and MIDM gradually loosened. Holding the position of Associate Artistic Director from 1997 to 2001, he continued in the capacity of artistic consultant of MIDM before separating himself from the company to pursue his international career from a base in France. In South Africa, Mantsoe's inspiration to younger generations of dancers and choreographers has continued through his appearances at the FNB Vita Dance Umbrella in Johannesburg, which has remained his preferred venue when it comes to premiering new works.

Returning to Johannesburg on a regular basis is, moreover, imperative, because it provides Mantsoe with the opportunity to reconnect through ritual acts with his ancestors, who continue to inform the investigations of individual freedom and collective norms on which his artistic practice relies. Repeatedly in programme notes, in documentary films about his work, in commentaries as well as in numerous interviews, Mantsoe makes continued references to his ancestral beliefs and the voices to which he opens himself when dancing. His creative preoccupation revolves around the existential challenge of building bridges between the past, the present and the future. Creating a universe through the dance, he invites the audience to join him on his sometimes humorous, more often painful, and always extremely physical journey.

While Mantsoe is primarily known for his enticing solos, the most recent of which is *Ebhofolo* (*This Madness*, 2007), he has also choreographed a substantial number of group works. Many of them have been set on dancers who share neither his dance background nor his spiritual approach to movement and, therefore, have to work hard in order to access the same depths in the movements. The first company to take on this challenge was Dance Theatre of Harlem with *Sasanka* (1997); others include the Ballet Theatre Afrikan in South Africa with *Thari* (1998), Inbal Dance Company in Israel with an unnamed piece in 1998, COBA (Collective of Black Artists) in Canada with *Bodika* (*Sessions*, 2005); Skånes Dansteater in Sweden with *Majara* (*The Carrier*, 2002) and Ace Dance and Music in the United Kingdom with *Letlalo* (*Skin*, 2007).

The artist's quest in creating group works seems increasingly preoccupied with finding ways to enhance the dancers' confidence in their own physical resources in order that they may experience the fluidity of both movements and the mind that his choreography calls for. In the process, Mantsoe encourages a very deliberate connecting of the breath with movement, while allowing the articulations of the arms, torso and hips to support the inner release of energy. Much of the work relies on the *koba* position (flexion of knees and hips), which enables the dancers to connect with the ground and to control speed as well as the direction of the movements. Coming from his mother tongue Southern Sotho, the term *koba* also describes the position he remembers his grandmother in, as she would sweep the yard for hours without getting tired.

As a mature artist, Mantsoe founded his own dance company, Association Noa/Compagnie Vincent Mantsoe, which is registered in France. With a multi-ethnic cast of five dancers, his first creation for the company was a reworked *Men-Jaro* in 2006, a piece originally created for MIDM in 1996. Premiered in Johannesburg, the work was performed to newly written music by award-winning South African composer Anthony Caplan, played live on stage with four musicians on traditional instruments, which have (or have had) a functional use in ritual practices.[4] Subsequent works include *Mobu* (2007), a trio in which the dancers explore a range of sensory qualities associated with sand, and *SAN* (2009), a piece inspired by the journeys and spirits of the San aboriginal inhabitants of the Southern African Plains.

Although elements of trance have been present as an energetic and dramatic device in almost all of his performances, only recently have critics paid attention to this dimension of his work. In carrying trance with him from the context of his upbringing in Soweto to theatre spaces around the world, Mantsoe's choreographic works point to the potential of theatricalized dance to bridge the sacred and the vernacular. With Mantsoe, the shift is not one that suggests the loss or release of its footing in the sacred, from which it departs; rather, it is the kind of shift that finds confidence, even joy, in a new way of distributing the balance between the two. In so doing, his work interweaves a multitude of performative practices drawn from the choreographer's personal politics of survival as an artist while speaking in a confident voice about the powers of dance.

Karen Vedel

Notes

1 Vincent Mantsoe as quoted in interview by South African dance critic Adrienne Sichel in *The Star Tonight*, 14 February 2006.
2 Discussed by Sylvia Glasser in 'Transcultural Transformations', *Visual Anthropology* 8(2), 1996, pp. 287–309.
3 The reception of MIDM's African tour is discussed by David April in *20 Years of Moving Into Dance Mophatong*, compiled and edited by Jill Waterman and Sylvia Glasser, Johannesburg, 1998.

4 Anthony Caplan is a graduate of the Department of Music at Rhodes University in Grahamstown, where he was a student of ethnomusicologist Andrew Tracey at the International Library of African Music (ILAM). He has also contributed to Laurie Levine's *The Drum Cafe's Traditional Music of South Africa*, Johannesburg, 2005.

Biographical details

Born in Soweto (Johannesburg), South Africa, 26 April 1971. **Studied** dance, including 'Afrofusion' with Sylvia Glasser, contemporary dance with Bev Elgie and Jazz with Nadine Benger at Moving Into Dance Mophatong (MIDM), Johannesburg, from 1990; also studied at Melbourne University, Australia, 1993; has studied a variety of techniques including Graham, Limón, release, ballet, Alexander, Balinese, Australian aboriginal, Classical Indian and Cambodian forms. **Career:** Resident choreographer and associate director of MIDM, 1997–2001; moved to France and founded his own company, Association Noa/Cie Vincent Mantsoe in 2005; also appointed visiting dance artist, Duke University, North Carolina, 2009. Has also created works for Ballet Theatre Afrikan, South Africa; Dance Theatre of Harlem; Collective of Black Artists in Toronto; Skånes Dansteater, Sweden, and Ace Dance and Music, UK. **Awards and honours** include IGI Dance Umbrella, 1992, and variety of awards at FNB Vita Johannesburg Dance Umbrella 1993, 1994, 1995, 2000, 2001, 2006; Standard Bank Young Artist of the Year, 1995; First Prize, Contemporary African Dance Competition, Angola, 1995; Rencontres Chorégraphiques Internationales, 1996 and 1998; Prix du Peuple, International Festival of New Dance, Montreal, 1999; Black Theatre Alliance Award, Chicago, 2007.

Works

African Soul (1991; duet version in 1992); *Gula Matari* (expanded from *Gula Bird*, a solo, 1993); *Ngoma* (1994); *Speaking with Tongues* (1994); *Hanano Blessing of the Earth* (1995); *Men-Jaro* (1996; reworked, 2006); *Mpheyane* (*Deceit*, 1997); *Sasanka* (1997); *Thari* (1998); *Phokwane* (1998); *Naka* (1999); *Falla* (1999); *Traduction simultanée* (2000); *Barena* (*Chiefs*, 2000); *Motswa Hole* (*Person From Far Away*, 2001); *Bupiro-Mukiti* (*Dance of Life*, 2002); *Majara* (*The Carrier*, 2002), *NDAA* (*Awakening of the Self* – also translated as *Greetings*, 2003); *Bodika* (*Sessions*, 2005); *NTU* (*Nothing*, 2005); *Letlalo* (*Skin*, 2007); *Ebhofolo* (*This Madness*, 2007); *Mobu* (2007); *SAN* (2009); *Lefa* (2009).

Further reading

Interviews with Thea Nerissa Barnes, on-line interview, www.ballet-dance.com, February 2004.

Articles: Sylvia Glasser, 'Is Dance Political Movement?', *Journal for the Anthropological Study of Human Movement*, 6(3), 1991; Sylvia Glasser, 'Transcultural Transformations', *Visual Anthropology*, 8(2), 1996; Valerie Gladstone, 'Dance Theatre of Harlem: Crashing Through', *Dance Magazine*, March 1997; Caitlin Simms, 'International

View', *Dance Magazine*, October 1997; Jann Parry, 'If the Spirit Moves You . . .', *The Observer*, 2 November 2003; Funmi Adewole, *Heritage: Crossing Academia and Physicality*, Seventh NOFOD Conference, Reykjavik, April 2004; Miranda Young-Jahangeer (ed.), *African Contemporary Dance? Questioning Issues of a Performance Aesthetic For a Developing and Independent Continent*, Seventh Jomba Contemporary Dance Conference, University of KwaZulu-Natal, August 2004; Deborah Jowitt, 'Call to Earth', *The Village Voice*, 27 February 2007; Karen Vedel, 'World Dance, Trance Dance: A Contextualized Look at Vincent Mantsoe's Solo in *Men-Jaro*', *Nordic Theatre Studies*, 19: *Currents and Trends in Contemporary Scholarship*, 2007; Rosalyn Sulcas, 'Beyond the Body, Making Spirit Move', *New York Times*, 22 February 2007; Sanjoy Roy, 'Vincent Mantsoe', *The Guardian*, 14 October 2009.

Books: Germaine Acogny, *Danse Africaine / Afrikanischer Tanz / African Dance*, Frankfurt, 1980; Jill Waterman and Sylvia Glasser (eds), *20 Years of Moving Into Dance Mophatong*, Johannesburg, 1998; Salia Sanou, *Afrique: Danse contemporaine*, Paris, 2008; Karen Vedel, 'The Use of Trance in Vincent Mantsoe's *Men-Jaro*', in Bent Holm, Bent Flemming Nielsen and Karen Vedel (eds), *Religion, Ritual, Theatre*, Frankfurt, 2008.

MAGUY MARIN

Although it is generally acknowledged that *Tanztheater* is a genre exclusive to German culture, its equivalent in English, the term 'dance-theatre', is conventionally used to designate contemporary productions that do not rely on the language of dance as the sole means of expression. If considered from this standpoint, the works of Maguy Marin are fitting examples of 'dance-theatre', for the dance medium is often circumscribed by the concomitance of other elements, including aural, vocal and visual ones. It is not incidental, therefore, that some dance historians and reviewers have labelled Marin's choreography the 'French answer to *Tanztheater*'. At the same time, her formulae differ considerably from those of, for example, Pina Bausch and Susanne Linke, whose works refer more or less explicitly to the canons of German Expressionism and indeed do not stem from any specific artistic or cultural movement.

An overview of Marin's works reveals that, through the years, she has constantly changed her artistic principles, approaching the art of dance from different angles and experimenting with different forms of expression. In her early works, such as *La Jeune Fille et la mort* (*Death and the Maiden*, 1979) and *Cante* (1980), the movement vocabulary, stemming from the combination of classical dance with contemporary techniques and her choice of subject matter, reflected her experience as a member of both Mudra and Béjart's Ballet du XXème Siècle. After 1981, a deeper investigation of theatre led Marin to the creation of some of her most distinctive dances, such as *May B.* (1981), *Babel Babel* (1982) and *Hymen* (1984). It is possible that these works were conceived under the influence of *Tanztheater*, which significantly affected European choreography in the early 1980s. Yet, it should be remembered that the combination of theatre elements with dance was also one of the characteristic traits of Béjart's spectacular performances. Finally, the rediscovery of ballet, which had constituted an integral part of Marin's dance training, has been the impetus behind more recent works, such as *Cendrillon* (*Cinderella*, 1985), *Groosland* (1989) and *Coppélia* (1993).

Despite such a varied *oeuvre*, it is still possible to identify some recurring elements in Marin's choreography. Perhaps the most characteristic aspect is her ability to create metaphorical and allegorical images. The symbolism that permeates Marin's works is neither obscure nor self-indulgent but reflects the choreographer's wide range of thematic concerns. In *La Jeune Fille et la mort*, considered Marin's first major creation, Schubert's quartet provided the inspiration for a dance that focused on the difficulty of existing and of communicating. Similarly, in *May B.*, unanimously regarded as the work that confirmed her pre-eminence within European contemporary choreography, Marin alluded to Samuel Beckett, particularly to some of his most significant plays, to explore and to portray the 'tortuous paths of human relationships'.[1]

One year after the creation of *May B.*, the biblical myth of Babel prompted *Babel Babel*, which dealt with the contrast between the simple language of an idealized, original world – to which societies will eventually revert – and the restrictive, often absurd conventions of the various idioms created by man through different eras of civilization. *Hymen*, perhaps the least narrative and most allegorical of Marin's creations, was a celebration of mystical love through a sequence of contrasting images derived from well-known, recognizable sources, such as the paintings of Velásquez and the films of Fellini. In *Cendrillon*, the familiar fairytale of Cinderella became the pretext for a psychological investigation of a child's world, addressing issues such as children's innate cruelty and children's vision of love and parenthood. More recently, with *Coppélia*, Marin explored the constraints and oddities of male erotic ideals, as analysed from a witty feminist perspective.

Marin's symbols and metaphorical images rely on a complex combination of different means of expression. At the beginning of *Babel Babel*, for example, the dancers appeared in the nude (thus conveying that idealized, pure, original world) and performed, to music by Mahler, steps and sequences derived from the combination of contemporary dance and ballet. Then, in a rapid crescendo of images, various stages of human history were shown: a rural community moving to the rhythmic sounds of rustic tools; a fashionable beach with bodybuilders posing; a rock group singing tunes from the 1960s and the advent of the punk movement. After a cathartic explosion, the action reverted to the opening sequence, as a message of hope. The members of the company, including the choreographer (who appeared as one of the rock singers, thus referring ironically to her previous artistic experiences) expressed themselves through a variety of means, exploiting all their possibilities as actors, singers, mimes and musicians.

The use of masks, and of body-masks in particular, characterized *Cendrillon*; according to the choreographer, their purpose was to 'transcend the limits of traditional pantomime'.[2] The set resembled a doll's house, divided into several compartments corresponding to the locations of the action. Prokofiev's ballet score was interpolated both with recordings of electronic sounds, to accompany the movements of the fairy godmother, portrayed as a science fiction character, and with sounds of children's voices, underlining some of the most dramatic moments, such as the ballroom scene where the party-goers ended up fighting over lollipops.

In *Coppélia*, the action took place both on stage and on a screen. *Coppélia*, the doll, was portrayed as a celluloid sex-symbol, starring in movies that Frantz and Coppelius enjoyed watching in private. Her image was suddenly multiplied into 12 identical starlets, who came out of the screen to haunt the two men, as the Wilis do in the Romantic ballet *Giselle*.

Coppélia can be regarded as the last of Marin's narrative works to date. The encounter with composer and music theorist Denis Mariotte in 1987 started a gradual but steady shift of Marin's creative interests towards less strictly narrative solutions. The early successful outcomes of the collaboration with Mariotte – *Cortex* (1991), *Waterzooi* (1993), *Ram Dam* (1995), *Pour ainsi dire* (1999), *Quoi qu'il en soit* (1999) – exemplify this change in performance making. Although Marin's distinctively postmodernist approach to theatre narratives remains a constant recurring feature, in each of these creations there is no identifiable storyline. The text is thus more of a combination of mini-stories, or events, which contribute, each in its own way, to the creation of a final message – namely the topic of each work.

Such changes seem to have been somewhat prompted by the beginning of a new chapter in the history of Marin's own company. In 1990, the choreographer and her dancers consolidated their longstanding collaboration with the Maison de Culture in Créteil by creating a Centre Chorégraphique National (National Centre of Choreography, known as CCN). After eight years, the CCN moved to Rillieux-la-Pape, from which the company began an intense work of cultural expansion, opening satellite choreographic centres in the nearby cities.

The work undertaken in different centres to generate more awareness of the CCN heightened Marin's personal awareness of social problems, which soon became the main themes of her new creations, such as *Pointes de fuite* (*Points of Escape*, 2001) and *Les Applaudissements ne se mangent pas* (*One Cannot Eat Applause*, 2002) which ponders on the social and political tension in Latin America. Political critique and satire are also the main traits of the internationally acclaimed *Umwelt* (*Environment*, 2004) in which the performers appear in a seemingly endless sequence of snapshots encased in mirror cubicles, from which they keep throwing all sorts of items onto the stage, towards the public. By the time the performance reaches its climax, the stage is littered with a pile of garbage, including a foetus.

Because of the presence of diverse theatre idioms in all her works, dance critics have often considered Marin more as a 'director' than a choreographer. But that definition is inappropriate, for the language of dance remains the distinctive common denominator of all her works, whereas other means of expression are used only occasionally, depending on their compatibility either with particular subjects or with particular moments in the action. It is not difficult to identify the principles of Marin's dance style, much as the movement vocabulary may vary in relation to dramatic, musical and cultural context. What the choreographer refers to as 'my language'[3] is a personal adaptation of the dance style absorbed from Mudra, Carolyn Carlson (with whom she worked briefly) and Béjart's company, a style that was itself derived from a concoction of combining contemporary technique and modern ballet. In Marin's works, the dance movement is always smooth and fluid, interwoven with contrasting angular motions and an often predominant language of gesture.

Indeed, gesture is a significant element in Marin's choreography. If her dance vocabulary is the constant, then different types of gesture represent the variants that distinguish, both technically and stylistically, each work. In *May B.*, for example, the fast, neurotic movements echoed Beckett's writing, whereas in *Cendrillon* gestures provided a stylized portrayal of children's physical behaviour. These gestures, however, never become trite pantomime. Indeed it is the perfect balance between diverse elements that is the successful formula of Marin's creations and reveals her in-depth knowledge of theatre arts.

Giannandrea Poesio

Notes

1 Jean Claude Diénis, 'Maguy Marin, Femme on the rock', *Danser*, November 1985.
2 Maguy Marin, as quoted in Diénis, op. cit.
3 Ibid.

Biographical details

Born in Toulouse, France, 2 June 1951. **Studied** classical ballet at the Toulouse Conservatoire from 1959, with Nina Vyroubova in Paris, and at Maurice Béjart's newly created Mudra school in Brussels, 1970–73. **Career**: Danced with Strasbourg Opéra Ballet, *c.* 1969; joined the Chandra group (directed by Micha van Hoecke), which split away from the Mudra school in 1974; joined Béjart's Ballet du XXème Siècle in 1972 as dancer: first choreography for the company, 1976; together with Daniel Ambash formed her own company, Le Ballet Théâtre de l'Arche, 1978, based in Créteil from 1981, renamed Compagnie Maguy Marin, 1984, becoming a Centre Chorégraphique National in 1990, and relocated to Rillieux-la-Pape, 1998. Has also choreographed for the Groupe de Recherche Chorégraphique de l'Opéra de Paris (GRCOP), Paris Opera Ballet, Lyon Opera Ballet, Dutch National Ballet and Nederlands Dans Theater. **Awards and honours** include First Prize, Nyon Choreography Competition, 1977; First Prize, Bagnolet Festival International Choreography Competition, 1978; Grand Prix National de Chorégraphie, 1983; Chevalier dans l'Ordre des Arts et des Lettres, 1988; Samuel H. Scripps Award, 2003.

Works

Yu-ku-ri (1976); *Evocation* (1977); *Nieblas de Nino* (1978); *L'Adieu* (with Daniel Ambash, 1978); *Dernier Geste* (1978); *Puzzle* (1978); *Zoo* (1979); *La Jeune Fille et la mort* (1979); *Contrastes* (1979); *Cante* (1980); *Réveillon Eve* (1980); *May B.* (1981); *Babel Babel* (1982); *Jaleo* (1983); *Hymen* (1984); *Cendrillon* (1985); *Calambre* (1985); *Eden* (1986); *Leçons de ténèbres* (1987); *Otello* (opera by Verdi, 1987); . . . *Des Petits Bourgeois Les sept pechés Capitaux* (1987); Coups d'états (1988); *Groosland* (1989); *Eh, qu'est-ce-que ça m'fait à moi!?* (1989); *Cortex* (1991); *Ay Dios* (1992); *Made in France* (1992); *Coppélia* (1993; also film version); *Waterzooi* (1993); *Ram Dam* (1995); *Soliloquy* (1995); *Aujourd'hui peut-être* (1996); *Pour ainsi dire* (1999); *Vaille que vaille*

(1999); *Quoi qu'il en soit* (1999); *Grosse Fugue* (2001); *Points de fuite* (2001); *Les Applaudissements ne se mangent pas* (2002); *Ça, quand même* (2004); *Umwelt* (2004); *Ha!Ha!* (2006); *Cap au pire* (2006); *Turba* (2007); *Description d'un combat* (2009).

Further reading

Interview with Martine Plenells, in 'Moi, je fais du spectacle', *Danser*, March 1991; with Pascaline Dussurget, in 'Maguy Marin: retour à l'opéra', *Saisons de la Danse*, April 1993; with Mary Körner, in 'Maguy Marin', *Dance Europe*, July 2001.

Articles: Raphael de Gubernatis, 'Maguy Marin', *Danser*, April 1983; Allen Robertson, 'Danse Nouvelle: The New Wave of French Modern Dance', *Ballet News*, July 1983; Norbert Servos, 'Vintage Avant-garde', *Ballett International*, January 1985; Jean Claude Diénis, 'Maguy Marin, Femme on the Rock', *Danser*, November 1985; Malve Gradinger, 'Surface Values: French Dance Theatre', *Ballett International*, February 1986; Bruce Merrill, 'France's Marin', *Dance Magazine*, March 1986; Malve Gradinger, 'Punk Counterworlds', *Ballett International*, April 1986; Claudia Roth Pierpont, 'Nouvelles *Cendrillons*', *Ballet Review*, Summer 1987; Malve Gradinger, 'Lyon (France): Revue-type Dance of Death', *Ballett International*, February 1988; Bernadette Bonis, 'French Choreographers Creating New Worlds', *Ballett International*, November 1989; Jean-Marc Adolphe, 'The Source and the Destination: Concepts of Memory, Movement, and Perception in French Dance', *Ballett International*, January 1991; André Philippe Hersin, 'Avant-premières: Marin/Hoffmann/Eifman', *Les Saisons de la Danse*, February 1991; Bruce Merrill, 'Baby Doll', *Dance Magazine*, September 1993; Camille Hardy, 'Compagnie Maguy Marin', *Dance Magazine*, December 1995; Susanna Sloat, 'May B: Compagnie Maguy Marin', *Attitude*, Spring 1996; Isabelle Ginot, 'Back to a Clarity of Forms', *Ballett International*, March 1997; Rose Anne Thom, 'Compagnie Maguy Marin', *Dance Magazine*, January 1999; Wiebke Hüster-Meyer, 'Meditating while Vacuuming', *Ballett International*, May 1999; Thomas Hahn, 'Maguy Marin', *Ballett International*, May 2001; Jean Pierre Pastori, 'Maguy Marin: Avant Propos', *Tanz und Gymnastik*, 58(4), 2002; Deborah Jowitt, 'Hell and Heaven', *The Village Voice*, 6 April 2004; Laura Shapiro, 'In Brief: Applaudissements', *New York Magazine*, 26 April 2004; Deborah Jowitt, 'Compagnie Maguy Marin: Moving Days', *The Village Voice*, 2 July 2008; Deborah Jowitt, 'Lyon Opera Ballet's Postmodern Whirlwind', *The Village Voice*, 16 March 2010.

Books: Allen Robertson and Donald Hutera, *The Dance Handbook*, Harlow, Essex, 1988; Janet Adshead-Landsdale, *Dancing Texts: Intertextuality in Interpretation*, London, 1999.

SUSAN MARSHALL

To choreographer Susan Marshall, dance is about people, not performers. Marshall designs movement choices that encourage audiences to see modern dance as the reality of men and women. She explores interior states to convey a sense of the struggle involved in intimate relationships. Marshall constructs time, movement and focus to reveal human intent.

Marshall's 'intelligently calibrated constructions reveal nuances of human emotions, complexities of intimate relationships, absurdities and hidden hostilities that form part of even the tenderest friendship'.[1] One dance implies that success is unattainable and life is an endless, arduous struggle yet the drive for excellence can be a virtue; another suggests that people striving for success are genuinely supportive of each other.[2] They provide commentaries on American life 'with its headlong drive for individual distinction and achievement'.[3] They are icons of our ravenous need to be loved and our undeniable fear of loneliness. We see lovers who can neither quite live together, nor bear to be separate. We experience friends giving the impression that they are trying to ignore, yet also impress, each other. We witness duets rooted to the spot, suspended in the air, defying gravity or sinking under the weight of weakness. Her characters express helplessness through arm movements that embrace, fondle and support while gripping, manipulating and repelling space or each other. Discrete gestures register alternatively as lethal blows or tender caresses.

Subtexts of relationships and their subtleties are natural subject matter for Marshall; they were learned at home. As a youngster she grew up with parents who were active in the Civil Rights Movement. Her father was a behavioural scientist and scholar and her mother was best known as a leading feminist writer. The nature of discussions at the family dinner table shaped Marshall's working aesthetic early in life, an aesthetic she sought to pursue with equal intensity as a dancer and choreographer.

In preparation, Marshall studied dance at the Juilliard School of Music in New York City. After two years she decided to explore the craft of choreography on her own. In the early 1980s, Susan Marshall & Company was formed, and with it she gained recognition and acceptance. Marshall's first evening-length work, *Interior With Seven Figures*, was premiered in 1988 at the Brooklyn Academy of Music. As austere black figures enter a harshly lit stage, they inhabit a frigid landscape that consists of a massive empty metal frame hanging at the back and a matching square of mauve laid on the floor; and the seven dancers behave like participants in a series of arduous matches whose goals are ambiguous. As critic Deborah Jowitt explained it,

[What] powers these encounters . . . is the dash to seize, the grab of manipulative hands, the slap of body against body against the floor . . . . The most potent imagery seems subtly derived from drowning, rescuing, and . . . from those frightening early swimming lessons that plague many adult nightmares.[4]

Marshall's dances reaffirm 'the dualities and complexities of a troubled and often unsympathetic society' by combining social comment with psychological insight.[5] Her works emerged in an era characterized by a social shift from a concern solely with oneness to pluralism.

As a choreographer, Marshall's working methods reflect the influence and lineage of the choreographers of the 1960s and 1970s, including Trisha Brown, Yvonne Rainer, David Gordon, Steve Paxton and Meredith Monk. Stripped-down structures and pedestrian vocabulary are put to a purpose that is unique among contemporaries. In her early dance works, Marshall contrived an action and response technique. Each character might become outlined as one dancer reacted to another character's movements. This collaborative volleying with the dancers became a method to create movement as well as providing a narrative function.

Marshall is not a mercurial worker but draws on her dancers' reactions and inputs, systematically videotaping each rehearsal, then studying the tapes between rehearsals. She extracts or condenses a recorded movement motif and develops it further in rehearsal. 'There's a lot of give and take with the dancers in the creation of the work and they give a great deal of material and feedback,' Marshall says, continuing:

I outline the structure and tell them what I think the work is about . . . . [They] bring to the process their personal lives and stories as well . . . . There is another layer which is our lives together as a company – this feeds into the work as well . . . . The dance [becomes] steeped with all these different layers of individual experiences and contributions and . . . it ends up being very tangible to an audience.[6]

Marshall's dances elevate non-traditional movement and everyday action into theatrically expressive gestures while retaining a formalistic sense of architecture and emotional edge. For instance, *Contenders* (1990) is a metaphor for life's challenges. The dancers appear as 'generic jocks . . . sprinters, long-distance runners, wrestlers, swimmers, acrobats . . . relentless strivers' attempting to surpass their own capabilities.[7] The dancers, dressed in workout apparel, line up over and over again, moving forward through a series of sport manoeuvres in competitive postures. They strut, vogue and roughneck. Their manic behaviour makes strong social statements compelling us to view them as attention seekers. Yet, *Contenders* is also about heroic efforts, about not giving up – 'going for it, making it, pushing beyond all reasonable limits of strength, speed, endurance and courage'.[8]

Just when you think you have finally grasped the meaning of Marshall's dances, she will present something unexpected compared to her previous creations; for example, she might add a scripted text and actors in collaboration with the dancers to present a *film noir*-style detective story like *One and Only You* (2001), which alternates between the real world of an author and the imaginary world of his creation.

> I'm taken by all kinds of simple everyday movements, say the way someone might leave or enter a room . . . [or] two people walking toward each other in a corridor . . . all movement is there for me to use as material, just as with a writer all language is there for them to use as their medium . . . . [Choreographers] often use embraces, kisses, touches, things of this nature as punctuation – as meaningful signifiers . . . . I might use an embrace, over and over and over again with subtle variations as you see it repeated. The embrace becomes recognizable again as something other than a cliché – a gesture with depth and possibilities . . . . [A] familiar gesture takes on more shades of meaning than if it were used as a theatrical punctuation.[9]

Often the same characters, or character types, continue through different dances. Within a single choreography, role reversal and mutual dependency may occur. Examples of this technique may be seen in *Ward* (1983), *Standing Duet* (1992), *Untitled (Detail)* (1992) and *Interior with Seven Figures* (1988).

Marshall works pragmatically and thematically with a vocabulary of limited movement. She thinks not only of defining parameters for the art of dance (what is dance, who does it, where and how?) but also concentrates rigorously on individuals reacting. She wants to know the why and wherefore of her dancers as characters move about. Marshall describes the approach as one of wanting the 'audience thinking about the dancers as characters, thinking, "what's happening here?"'[10]

In her creations, a recognized 'Marshall' language of movement speaks out. It is accompanied by the intentionally limited vocabulary that she creates for each new dance. Often a movement motif will thread itself through many pieces. For instance, the ending segment of *Trio in Four Parts* (1983) becomes the thematic motif of *Arms* (1984), a signature work of Susan Marshall & Company. Marshall's repeated use of arm gestures takes on different dramatic intentions when placed in different theatrical contexts. Repetitious arm movement motifs occur in works such as *Trio in Four Parts, Arms, Interior with Seven Figures, Contenders* and *The Most Dangerous Room in the House* (1998). The gesturing arms symbolically reinvent new and complex dramatic moments of the human spirit. A raised arm motif in *Interiors with Seven Figures* may signify messages of 'I'm okay, everything is fine,' while in *The Most Dangerous Room in the House* that same hand lift may suggest a 'stop right there' signal that also doubles persuasively as a greeting. They reveal Marshall's exquisitely crafted use of multilayered, multidimensional images of emotional states and universal themes. Her attention to carefully chosen gestural detail of arms and torsos allows us to 'read' the emotion in her work.

Fields of View (1994) and *Spectators at an Event* (1994) are different meditations on death and loss. *Fields of View* was Marshall's new foray into work that focused more on the relationship between movement, design and music rather than highlighting narrative. The swirls and moves are continuously set to Philip Glass's *Fourth String Quartet*. Some of the most visually arresting moments appear as the dancers walk backwards while snow falls on stage, blowing gently across the performance space. Marshall points out that:

> At the center of [the] work was the tangled relationship between experience and time . . . our interior lives move fluidly through time uninterrupted by barriers . . . [even] as we live in the present, we revisit and rethink the past. We dream and rearrange the future. This dance unfurled like a scroll containing many smaller dances that recurred, advanced, receded and coexisted.[11]

In creating other choreography in the mid-1990s, such as *Spectators at an Event*, Marshall presented complex occurrences that could be frozen into a moment or that float in our minds as a solitary memory. *Spectators* drew its inspiration from the 1940s journalistic photographer, WeeGee (Arthur Fellig), and the crime scenes he portrayed. WeeGee was a theme-and-variation photographer who depicted a wide range of strong emotions by showing close-up shots of spectators. 'Marshall's interest was in WeeGee's stark realism that captured the reactions of individuals and groups at the exact moment of witnessing images of murder, disorder and other dramatic events in New York City during the thirties and forties'.[12]

Drawing on WeeGee's voyeuristic photographs, Marshall structured *Spectators* with multiple layers of images of people watching each other. For example, using video and video cameras to acquire this effect, one member of the cast aims a camera at the audience, which creates images of the audience watching themselves on a screen on stage, or the camera videos a dancer whose image hangs above him. Her initial images were 'about those who are left behind. How their lives go on and how some people's lives don't go on'.[13] Marshall was interested in the idea of reaction, instead of action. She created abstract groups of anxious, disbelieving spectators who crowded around a constantly replaced victim, until just the empty space itself conjured dread.

Articles of Faith (1990) is a dance-theatre piece that was commissioned for the World Financial Center at the Winter Gardens in New York. Structural and gestural repetition and emotional aggression are once again present throughout this dance. Multiple images of falling press a dramatic point about aggressive behaviour and how a community reacts, or does not react, to the plight of one of its own. For example, one dancer strikes another but a different performer on stage cries out. Pain and loss emerge as constant themes.

Inspired by Jean Cocteau's 1929 novel *Les Enfants Terribles*, a surreal, menacing story about the complex psychological tragedy of two siblings, Marshall, in collaboration with composer Philip Glass, choreographed and directed a dance-opera called *Les Enfants Terribles: Children of the Game* (1996). The production, a hybrid of singers, dancers, musicians and projected text, created a rich amalgam of aural and visual components expressing Cocteau's belief in the transformative powers of the imagination.

Marshall's 1998 collaborative dance project with composer David Lang, *The Most Dangerous Room in the House*, is a full evening's performance in three acts, which uses text and movement. This piece, inspired by Marshall's anticipation of motherhood, explores the unsettling fear of events and forces that are beyond our control. The text becomes a word game and a window into Marshall's choreography, 'capturing the eternally contradictory nature of our desire'.[14] Marshall also strings suggestive memories from the past in diverse movement combinations to produce subtle shades of meaning. *One and Only You* (2001) marries a comic literary aesthetic with dance theatre, throwing us into an unpredictable world of urgent dramatic power with a scenario that revolves around a lost manuscript.

According to dance critic Tobi Tobias, 'poetic richness coupled with economic poverty ... is the state of dance in America at the beginning of the 21st century' and *Cloudless* (2005), which involved working 'smaller, tighter, faster', is a statement of these financial constraints.[15] These imposed limitations became the form and structure of *Cloudless*, which also contained her familiar mixture of structural formality, emotional heat and everyday behaviour. Marshall created a series of solo, duet and group vignettes with a performance duration running from four-and-a-half minutes to no more than eleven minutes.

Through these mini-solos, duets and vignettes, fleeting bodies are seen everywhere: dancing alone in a corner, piercing the performance space from the wings only to be shoved off stage over and over again by another dancer who will not relinquish his spot; bodies climbing ladders, turning pages in a book, casting bits of paper into a fan that suspends them forever in space; prone bodies mirroring bodies lying on furniture. At times there are no real bodies on the stage at all, only virtual bodies on moving monitors. Our mind becomes flooded with Marshall's imagistic magic.

Unlike Marshall's early dance works, a larger display of stage sets is incorporated into *Cloudless*; some remain static and bound to the space, whereas others appear and disappear before we become attached to them. The use of props like ladders, furniture, fans, TV sets, books or tiny pieces of white paper that are blown skyward or across the stage like falling snow have been added to enhance or confound Marshall's powerful movement imagery. The space continually shifts, re-defining itself with familiar everyday objects, as dancers like voyeurs enter, linger quietly, frantically pass through or momentarily disappear only to reappear again and again. Life is messy, life is short, life goes on.

As we have learned from early on in Marshall's career, collaboration is important in all aspects of her creations.

> All the actual movement in my work is generated by the dancers ... I start by setting them in motion with instructions about space, timing and the nature of the activity. I give them physical goals – the more abstract, the better. The dramatic or psychological subtexts

evolve as the dance develops, through our group discussions about where the work wants to go. I like to create through the back door ... because that's where the discoveries – and surprises – are.[16]

Throughout her choreography, Marshall has created art that focuses on the intrinsic defining condition of dance: the human body in motion, forever recognizing and expressing itself. Her imagery is derived from everyday action and events, yet repeating and restating themes visually and viscerally. Her dance works are microcosms of life's intrinsic struggle with emotional and situational conflict. They tell the audience how humans accept, yet are afraid to acknowledge, their own vulnerability.

Throughout Marshall's career, both tiny, terse creations for a nearly bare stage and big works with lavish production values have conveyed the same message: We are of two minds about what we do. Defining, then articulating, our own state of mind is tough enough, but understanding that of others is well nigh impossible. Inevitably ... Marshall's work tends to be dark ... 'if you're working with complexity and you're working with the body, some of those overtones and undertones are going to be dark. I like to think ... that they're always counterbalanced by upward movement – and tenderness'.[17]

We strive to be self-sufficient, yet crave companionship. We discover the intoxicating ecstasy of love, yet harbour hostility toward others and ourselves. This is Susan Marshall.

Jennifer Predock-Linnell

Notes

1 Tobi Tobias, *New York Magazine*, 4 January 1988.
2 Jack Anderson, 'For Susan Marshall, Eloquence is Movement', *The New York Times*, 22 August 1993.
3 A. Kreigsman, 'The Drive of "Contenders"', *Washington Post*, 2 February 1991.
4 Deborah Jowitt, 'Love as a Knockout', *The Village Voice*, 27 December 1988.
5 Bill Deresiewicz, 'Susan Marshall's Small Pleasures', *Dance View*, Summer 1993.
6 Susan Marshall in *An Interview with Susan Marshall*, published by the Kreisberg Group, 1 June, 1994.
7 Tobi Tobias, 'Down for the Count: Dance', *New York Magazine*, 17 December 1990.
8 Kreigsman, op. cit.
9 Marshall, op. cit.
10 M. J. Cowell, *Dance about People*, programme notes, Washington, DC, 1990.
11 Marshall, op. cit.
12 Ibid.

13 Ibid.
14 Tobi Tobias, 'House Rules', *New York Magazine*, 24 August 1998.
15 Tobi Tobias, 'Dancing as Fast, and as Tightly, as She Can', *The New York Times*, 31 July 2005.
16 Ibid.
17 Ibid.

Biographical details

Born in Pensacola, Florida, 17 October 1958. **Studied** at the Dance Department of the Juilliard School of Music (having first trained as a gymnast), New York, 1976–78. **Career**: Began choreographing in 1982, founding her own small performing group, Susan Marshall & Company, with residency at The Yard, from 1982. Has also choreographed works for New York company CoDanceCo, Boston Ballet, Dallas Ballet, Groupe de Recherche Chorégraphique de l'Opéra de Paris (GRCOP), Frankfurt Ballet, Montréal Danse and Lyon Opera Ballet and has staged dances for Los Angeles Opera and New York City Opera. **Awards and honours** include New York Dance and Performance Award ('Bessie'), 1985, 1997, 2005, 2006; fellowships from New York Foundation for the Arts, 1985 and National Endowment for the Arts, 1986–91; American Choreographer Award, 1988; Brandeis University Creative Arts Citation, 1988; Guggenheim Fellowship, 1990; *Dance Magazine* Awards, 1994, 1995, 2000; MacArthur Genius Award, 2000.

Works*

Fault Line (1982); *Trio in Four Parts* (1983); *Ward* (1983); *Arms* (1984; television version, 1989); *Routine and Variations* (1984); *Opening Gambits* (1985); *Common Run* (1985); *Kin* (1986); *Arena* (1986); *Gifts* (1986); *The Refrain* (1986); *Overture* (1987); *Kiss* (1987); *The Aerialist* (1987); *Companion Pieces* (1987); *Interior with Seven Figures* (1988); *Figures in Opposition* (1989); *In Medias Res* (1989); *Articles of Faith* (1990); *Contenders* (1990; film version, dir. Mark Obernhaus, 1991; revised version, 1992), dances in *Les Troyens* (opera by Berlioz, 1991); *Untitled (Detail)* (1992); *Standing Duet* (1992); *Solo* (1993); *Walter's Finest Hours* (1993); *Entr'Acte I* (1993); *Entr'Acte II* (1993), dances in *Midsummer Marriage* (opera by Tippett, 1993); *Central Figure* (1994); *Ne me quitte pas* (1994); *Avatar* (1994); *Private Worlds in Public View* (1994); *Fields of View* (1994); *Spectators at an Event* (1994); *Lines from Memory* (1995); *Portrait of Jack* (1996); *Portrait of Drew* (1996); *Les Enfants Terribles* (1996); *The Most Dangerous Room in the House* (1998); *The Descent Beckons* (1999); *One and Only You* (2001); *Sleeping Beauty* (2003); *Other Stories* (2003); *Cloudless* (2006); *Sawdust Palace* (2007); *Frame Dances* (2008); *Adamantine* (2009).

*Where discrepancies exist in published sources, dates cited above are those listed on the Susan Marshall company website.

Further reading

Interviews *An Interview with Susan Marshall*, The Kreisberg Group, Ltd., 1 June 1994.

Articles: Elizabeth Zimmer, 'Susan Marshall & Company', *Dance Magazine*, April 1985; Sally Sommer, 'Susan Marshall & Company', *Dance Magazine*, May 1986; Otis Stuart, 'Susan Marshall and Company at BAM: Marshalling the Next Wave', *Dance Magazine*, December 1988; Jennifer Dunning, 'Rituals of Complex Relations', *New York Times*, 8 December 1988; C. Hardy, 'Susan Marshall and Company', *Dance Magazine*, March 1989; Robert Sandla, 'Freedom of Expression', *Dance Magazine*, February 1990; Anna Kisselgoff, 'Aggression in an Atrium', *New York Times*, 8 March 1990; Joan Acocella, 'Desire under The Palms', *Dance*, 21 March 1990; Sally Sommer, 'Susan Marshall & Company', *Dance Magazine*, August 1990; Tobi Tobias, 'Down for the Count', *New York Magazine*, 17 December 1990; Jack Anderson, 'Choreography in the Pursuit of Happiness', *New York Times*, 6 January 1991; David Hughes, 'The Poetics of Exhaustion', *Dance Theatre Journal*, Spring 1991; Judith Mackrell, 'Post-Modern Dance in Britain: An Historical Essay', *Dance Research*, Spring 1991; Sally Banes, 'American Postmodern Choreography', *Choreography and Dance*, 1(2), 1992; Anna Kisselgoff, 'An Explorer Traverses Some Emotional Terrain', *New York Times*, 21 December 1992; Bill Deresiewicz, 'Susan Marshall's Small Pleasures', *Dance View*, Summer 1993; Jack Anderson, '*For Susan Marshall, Eloquence is Movement*', *New York Times*, 22 August 1993; Lisa Traiger, 'Gender Bending', *Dance View*, Autumn 1992; Doris Hering, 'Susan Marshall and Company', *Dance Magazine*, March 1993; Ann Tobias, 'Susan Marshall: A Place Beyond', *Dance Ink*, Summer 1994; Andre Lepeckie, 'How Radical is Contemporary Dance?', *Ballett International*, February 1995; Anne Tobias, 'Reviews: Susan Marshall Company', *Dance Magazine*, March 1995; Lilo Weber, 'Frames of Reference', Cocteau's Myth of Childhood', *Ballett International*, July 1996; Jack Anderson, 'New York Newsletter', *Dancing Times*, January 1997; Molly McQuade, 'Reviews: New York City, Susan Marshall and Company', *Dance Magazine*, March 1999; Susan Sloat, 'The Most Dangerous Room in the House', *Attitude*, Brooklyn, 14(1), Spring 1999; Karen Dacko, 'Marshall Mystery Moves Between Two Worlds', *Dance Magazine*, January 2002; Deborah Jowitt, 'Saying it Again. And Again', *The Village Voice*, 28 October 2003; Tobi Tobias, 'Dancing as Fast, and as Tightly, as She Can', *New York Times*, 31 July 2005; Deborah Jowitt, 'One Act at a Time', *The Village Voice*, 21 February 2006; Joan Acocella, 'From a Marriage', *The New Yorker*, 29 January 2007; Deborah Jowitt, 'Madcap Cabaret', *The Village Voice*, 10 July 2007; Deborah Jowitt, 'Susan Marshall and Sally Silvers Entrance the Eye', *The Village Voice*, 25 March 2009.

WAYNE McGREGOR

> Throughout all my work I have been reaching the conclusion that the most sophisticated technology is the body. In the last few years, the focus has not been on external equipment but rather on how to use scientific knowledge to access the technology of the body.[1]

Wayne McGregor's own words operate as a powerful corrective to those who view his choreographic practices as driven primarily by an overarching desire to engage dance with the latest innovations in new technology. McGregor's reputation as the most prolific UK-based choreographer to operate at the interface between dance and technology is intrinsic to his status as 'probably the most significant' British-born choreographer at work today.[2] Yet, to read his choreography in terms of this dimension alone is not only to overlook the more recent turn his work has taken in favour of the dialogue between dance and science, in particular cognitive psychology and neuroscience, but also risks trivializing the very considerable role technology has played in McGregor's work.

No mere prop, adjunct or structuring device, technology has powered, in the most fundamental terms, the overriding commitment to probing, exploring, questioning and, ultimately, affirming the human body, which emerges as the constant, defining feature across his career. As McGregor puts it:

> When I choreograph I generate a vocabulary for movement that in some way challenges, exploits, explores and rediscovers the potential of the human body. With the dancers we generate a physical alphabet that's different from one piece to the next. Then I create the composition.[3]

Of his training at Bretton Hall, McGregor remembers, 'I did a kind of community dance degree in many ways . . . what that really taught me is that all I do as a choreographer is work with individuals, each with a different physicality.' From this early awareness of bodily difference springs an abiding interest in what McGregor terms 'dysfunctional physicality'.[4] Nowhere is this more evident than in *AtaXia* (2004), an exploration of the effect of a neurological disorder that causes loss of muscular co-ordination, in some cases destroying speech and mobility, which McGregor created for Random Dance. 'We have such a normalized view of the body, and it's very restricting. Some of the questions for me are about when the behaviour of the body is different; that's actually very dynamic and interesting,' explains McGregor.[5] The culmination of the six months he spent as a fellow at Cambridge University, working with neuroscientists and experimental psychologists, *AtaXia* was also created in dialogue with Sarah Seddon Jenner, who has the condition.

Sanjoy Roy described how, for this piece, McGregor created conditions in which his dancers could experience for themselves the effects of perturbations, the medical term given to interventions that disrupt normal relationships between the brain and the rest of the body. Wearing prisms to distort their sense of spatial geography, or purposefully given one set of instructions to interfere with another, the dancers felt their perceptions deliberately manipulated in ways that enabled them to confront at firsthand what it is to inhabit a body dealing with tasks it is unable to perform. Michael Gordon's musical score extended this approximation of experiencing ataxia to the audience. 'The experience of watching *AtaXia* has been likened "to an overload of sensory information that you can't keep up with"',[6] and the music mimics the sensation of being overwhelmed with a surfeit of information felt by those with the condition. *AtaXia* marked a critical shift in McGregor's own evolving understanding of the body. No longer conceiving of the dysfunctional body as a body in trauma, he came to view it instead 'as a body with an extended behaviour'.[7]

Receiving early support from John Ashford, in 1992 McGregor was appointed choreographer-in-residence at The Place, the first holder of the post not to have trained at London Contemporary Dance School. He founded Wayne McGregor/Random Dance that same year and *Xeno 123* followed in 1993. Initially, McGregor made short pieces on himself and his dancers and for commissions from regional and national dance agencies. Community dance projects, their frequent simultaneous operation over multiple sites relayed telematically, endure as a key part of his choreographic output.

McGregor's early choreography was imbued with his idiosyncratic dance style, rooted in his own body, its unusually long, loose limbs especially, which facilitated a fluid way of moving at intense speed. The resultant work was dense and highly textured. Dancers, sometimes struggling, juggled the extreme juxtaposition of fractured, rapier sharp angularity with a 'seemingly boneless' but rapid-fire transmission of movement that appeared to pulse about their hyper-extended bodies.[8] *Labrax*, his first full-length piece, was presented at The Place in 1994. *Cyborg* (1995), created for Dance Umbrella, explored kinetic architecture in Tokyo.

It was a digital trilogy in the late 1990s that secured McGregor's reputation for pioneering a highly inventive relationship between dance and new technology, in turn facilitating a more secure funding platform for Random. *Sulphur 16* (1998) forged a dialogue between live dancers and virtual figures, while *Aeon* (2000) engaged its dancers with digitally created landscapes. *The Millennarium* (1997) paired ideas of mind/body disconnection (anticipating *AtaXia*, except that the focus here was on the exterior manifestation, rather than internal triggers of dislocation) with a digital aesthetic that subverted conventional expectations of three-dimensional space. A digitally animated architecture of huge voids opened up behind dancers in ways that conjured space as a degenerating electronic image.

Technology was reconfigured, in the works that followed, as something the dancers were pitched against. It was grafted directly onto the body as animatronic prostheses worn by the dancers in *Nemesis* (2002) and crafted as a giant kinetic limb suspended overhead in *detritus* (2001). Created to mark Random's tenth anniversary and the first work following its appointment as company-in-residence at Sadler's Wells, *Nemesis* pushed the dancers to experience space differently, as they renegotiated familiar terrain in the struggle to accomplish movement that accommodated their artificially extended arms. In keeping with McGregor's conception of dancers as 'in some way displacing space', bodies in *detritus* fought the giant limb for ever-depleting space.[9]

McGregor has been compared to William Forsythe in the extremity of his choreographic vocabulary. Although both choreographers share a fascination with the intensely heightened sense of proprioception that ballet facilitates for the dancer, McGregor's interest in ballet is not deconstructionist in the Forsythian sense of entering into a radical critique of the Cartesian rationalist philosophy especially enshrined in the ballet body. For McGregor, ballet's appeal lies rather in its particularized attainment of another type of extremely altered body. Ballet's 'extremity of line, the conformity, the detail, the precision, [and] the difficulty of clean technique [are] all amazing places from which to excavate, push, contradict, relearn,' he observes. 'Ballet vocabulary to me is a mine of potential, a breathtaking idea[s] bank!'[10] It is perhaps not surprising that pointe work holds special appeal for McGregor. In a sense another kind of prosthetic, as the pointe shoe propels the body into new relationships to and through space.[11]

Works such as *PreSentient* (2002) for Rambert and *Duo:Logue in Three Parts* (2001), a collaboration between Random Dance and the Royal Ballet, repositioned contemporary dance and ballet in a new dialogue that sought to delve beyond facile ideas of pastiche or fusion. For Michelle Potter, the dancing bodies mobilized by *Dyad 1929* (2009), choreographed as part of the Australian Ballet's Ballets Russes project, 'become an experimental field'.[12] *Outlier* (2010), created as part of New York City Ballet's 'Architecture of Dance' festival, and McGregor's first commission for an American company, registered as 'a new anti-illusion form of ballet theater' for Alastair Macaulay, who cites 'the force with which Mr McGregor contrasts individual body parts' as particularly 'anti-classical'.[13] And McGregor's interest in ballet is reciprocated. No doubt triggered in part by the desire to see how McGregor's lack of interest in creating a collective look might emancipate ballet from its tendency towards uniformity, world-ranking ballet companies, including those at the Mariinsky and the Paris Opéra, have acquired or commissioned work from him. *Chroma* was created for the Royal Ballet in 2006. Driven by 'the desire to offer the brain an opportunity to see movement freshly', it led to McGregor's appointment as their choreographer-in-residence, the first since Kenneth MacMillan held the position.[14]

If McGregor's regard for ballet runs counter to widely held assumptions about contemporary choreography, his work seems similarly resistant to those prevalent post-humanist readings that view new technology as heralding the body's impending obsolescence. Whereas performance artist Stelarc's robot 'third arm' prosthesis reduces his body 'to little more than an empty shell: a human cadaver to be jerked like a puppet in some macabre computer game', for McGregor, technology is ultimately an affirming tool through which to extend, experiment with, but it can never replace the body.[15] The exploration, in works such as *Skindex* (2006) for Nederlands Dans Theater, of 'how technology has become an extension of our skin',[16] may spring from Marshall McLuhan's conception of communication technologies 'as prosthetic devices that extend the body',[17] but for McGregor, technology's effect is not to render the body redundant. Its very liveliness remains his touchstone. The way in which a version of *Nemesis* (reworked for the Adelaide Festival and Commonwealth Games Cultural Festival in Melbourne in 2006) moves, as McGregor describes, 'from live bodies, to "extended" bodies with live animatronics, to the solo dancer with the virtual dancers, and finally back to the unmediated live body', makes this very clear.[18]

Given cognitive psychology's 'epistemological basis' in information theory, its conception of 'the mind as an information-processing system, as software that runs on the hardware of the brain', McGregor's recent shift in focus away from digital technologies in favour of the intersection of dance, neuroscience, experimental psychology and information technologies marks a logical progression.[19] Beyond *AtaXia*, other outcomes of the Cambridge-based Choreography and Cognition project McGregor devised with Scott deLahunta include a study undertaken with Random dancers of the gulf between dance phrases 'articulated through verbal explanation' and those 'grasped at a more intuitive level by other cognitive or sensorial means'.[20] And *Entity*, for Random Dance in 2008, explored McGregor's 'preoccupation with the idea of "an artificially intelligent choreographic entity" – a piece of software which can "think" for itself and help generate movement'.[21]

McGregor's characteristic willingness to question his own assumptions is evident in his working practices in the Cambridge project and elsewhere. Reflecting on the role that work on paper plays within his dance-making process, McGregor described the page 'as a tool to dialogue with' not in a traditional documentary sense but 'as an active, living, ideas score'. 'The "product" may be without words,' he observes but 'the process of creativity is heavily reliant on them'.[22] Words are often the points of origin for McGregor's choreographies. 'The idea for *The Millennarium* came from a cross between millennium and aquarium, a bastardized fusion of a word ... this was the starting point,' recalls McGregor.[23] And *Qualia*, created for the Royal Ballet in 2003, derives its title from 'a term used in brain science to refer to a kind of perception', 'a raw, primary, sensory experience'.[24]

This same open-mindedness, directed towards the co-option of new technologies and the bodily extremity thus enabled, is ultimately humanist in its affirmation of the body. Altered states and an abiding sense of humanism characterize McGregor's choreography. 'Could I generate a hybrid form of naturalistic, i.e. *humanistic*, almost gestural movement, and very digital movement?' McGregor asked himself in creating *Millennarium*.[25] And he views his career in similar terms, as one of 'experiment with new technologies, experiment with the live body, so never really to replace the live body but really to experiment [with] and extend it'.[26] 'Technology has become the body's new membrane of existence' yet 'human to human contact is irreplaceable – and it will stay like that, I think forever,' McGregor maintains.[27]

This conception of the relationship of science and technology with the body reverberates in the formation of individual works. *Entity*, for instance, 'is not about science,' says McGregor.

> The process behind it may dictate the nature of the piece, but it's not . . . a dance about Einstein where I'm trying to convert his ideas into movement and communicate that to an audience. I've always been just as interested in making people think as I am in

making them feel, and one of the things this scientific process allows me to do is make the audience look differently at dance.

This 'fascination' impacts on the kind of dancers McGregor seeks out as collaborators. 'Obviously they have to have the technical ability to do the work,' he says, 'but just as importantly, they have to have an open curiosity, be able to converse with the neuroscientists and generate movement themselves based on tasks I set them'.[28]

Looking to the future, these processes – or, to use McGregor's term, these 'operations'-driven choreographic dialogues with science – coupled with a commitment to community dance are set to endure as cornerstones of McGregor's creative output. The Big Dance 2012 sees him working with 12,000 young people. And of neuroscience, McGregor says:

> . . . it's going to be a constant fascination for me. Because brain science is still in its infancy, and the more information they find out, the more things will open up to us in terms of the creative process, the possibilities are endless.[29]

Helena Hammond

Notes

1 Sophie Travers, 'Dancing, Prosthetically: Interview with Wayne McGregor', *Realtime Arts*, Issue 71, 2006.
2 Luke Jennings, 'One Step Beyond', *The Observer*, 13 April 2008.
3 McGregor in Catherine Hale, 'The Science of Making Dances', *Dance Gazette*, Issue 2, 2004, pp. 16–19.
4 This and previous quotation of McGregor from *Dysfunctional Physicality: A Portrait of Wayne McGregor*, documentary broadcast as BBC Knowledge Dance Night, February 2001.
5 McGregor in Janice Steinberg, 'Troupe Explores the Body, Mind Connection', *The San Diego Union-Tribune*, 20 October 2006.
6 Sanjoy Roy, 'Random Dance Company's *AtaXia*', *Contemporary*, Issue 65, 2004, pp. 34–37.
7 McGregor in Emma Crighton-Miller, 'Physical Thinking', Royal Opera House World Stage Supplement, *The Guardian*, Autumn 2006, p. 4.
8 Judith Mackrell, *AtaXia* programme notes, 2004.
9 McGregor in *Dysfunctional Physicality*, op. cit.
10 McGregor in 'Wayne McGregor on Ballet into the Twenty-First Century', interview with Brendan McCarthy, accessed 04.05.2007, www.ballet.co.uk/magazines/yr_02/dec02/interview_wayne_mcgregor.htm
11 Simon Shepherd views the modifying function of the pointe shoe similarly in 'Lolo's Breasts, Cyborgism, and a Wooden Christ', pp. 170–189 in *Cultural*

Bodies: Ethnography and Theory, ed. Helen Thomas and Jamilah Ahmed, Oxford, 2004, p. 181.

12 Michelle Potter, '*Concord*: The Australian Ballet', 23 August 2009.

13 Alastair Macaulay, 'Different Approaches and Grand Designs in a City Ballet Premiere', *New York Times*, 16 May, 2010.

14 McGregor in Emma Crighton-Miller, op. cit., p. 4.

15 Steve Dixon, 'Metal Performance: Humanizing Robots, Returning to Nature, and Camping About', *The Drama Review* 48(4) (T184), Winter 2004, pp. 15–45, p. 30.

16 Ali Mahbouba, '*Shoot the Moon, Skindex, Claude Pascal*', *Dance Europe*, June 2006, p. 45.

17 Lev Manovich, 'Visual Technologies as Cognitive Prostheses' in *The Prosthetic Impulse: From a Posthuman to a Biocultural Future*, edited by Marquard Smith and Joanne Morra, Cambridge, MA, 2006, p. 204.

18 Travers, op. cit.

19 Manovich, op. cit., p. 211.

20 Scott deLahunta and Phil Barnard, 'What's in a Phrase?' in J. Birringer and J. Fenger (eds) *Tanz im Kopf: Jahrbuch 15 der Gesellschaft für Tanzforschung*, Williamshaven: Florian Noetzel-Verlag, Autumn 2005, pp. 253–66, p. 258.

21 Jennings, op. cit.

22 Scott deLahunta, Wayne McGregor and Alan Blackwell, 'Transactables', *Performance Research*, 9(2), pp. 67–72, p. 68.

23 'Wayne McGregor in Conversation with Jo Butterworth', in Jo Butterworth and Gill Clarke (eds), *Dance Makers Portfolio: Conversations with Choreographers*, Bretton Hall, 1998, pp. 103–114, p. 103.

24 Crighton-Miller, op. cit., p.4.

25 McGregor in Butterworth and Clarke, op. cit., p. 104.

26 McGregor in *Dysfunctional Physicality*, op. cit.

27 McGregor in Sandra Heerma van Voss, 'Wayne McGregor: Head, Shoulders, Knees and Toes', *Nederlands Dans Theater Yearbook 2005–2006*, n.p.

28 All quotations in this paragraph are from Kelly Apter, 'Interview: Wayne McGregor – Scientist and Choreographer', *The Scotsman*, 14 May 2010.

29 McGregor in Apter, op. cit.

Biographical details

Born in Stockport, Cheshire, 12 March 1970. **Studied** at Bretton Hall College, gaining a degree in dance; and later at the José Limón School, New York. **Career**: Founded his own company, Wayne McGregor/Random Dance, while choreographer-in-residence at The Place, London, 1992, with Random Dance becoming resident company at Sadler's Wells Theatre, London, in 2002; AHRB/ACE Research Fellow in Cognition and Choreography, School of Experimental Psychology, University of Cambridge, 2003–04; resident choreographer at the Royal Ballet from 2006; appointed as UK government's first Youth Dance Champion in 2008; curator of *Deloitte Ignite* festival, London, 2009. Has also choreographed for San Francisco Ballet, Stuttgart Ballet, NDT1, English National Ballet, Adam Cooper Dance Company, Olympic Ballet, La Scala, Paris Opera Ballet, Gothenburg Ballet, Shobana Jeyasingh Dance Company, Ricochet Dance Company, Australian Ballet and New York City Ballet. **Awards and honours** include Arts

Foundation Fellowship, 1998; *Time Out* Awards, 2001, 2003; IMZ Dance Screen Award, 2002; Laurence Olivier Awards, 2004, 2007; Innovator-in-Residence, University of California San Diego's Sixth College, 2007; *South Bank Show* Awards, 2007, 2009; International Theatre Institute Award, 2009; Prix Benois de Danse, 2009; *Ballett Tanz* Choreographer of the Year, 2009; Movimentos Award, 2009; Critics Circle Awards, 2006, 2007, 2010.

Works*

Xeno (1992); *Xeno 123* (1993); *9.7 Recurring 2% Black* (1994); *Artificial Intelligence* (1994); *Labrax* (1994); *Sever* (solo, 1994, as duet 1995); *AnArkos* (1995); *CeBit Dances* (1995); *For Bruising Archangel* (1995); *Jacob's Membrane* (1995); *Dragonfly* (1995, 2004); *Cyborg* (1995); *A Little Night Music* (theatre, 1995); *Slam* (1996); *Cybergeneration* (1996); *Vulture (Reverse Effect)* (1996); *Sheer* (1996); *Urban Savage* (1996); *8 Legs of the Devil* (1996); *Bent* (film, 1996); *Encoder* (1996); *Bach Suite* (1996); *Neurotransmission* (1997); *Skinned Prey* (1997); *x2* (1997); *Chameleon* (1997); *Black on White* (1997); *S.I.N.* (1997); *The Millennarium* (1997); *53 Bites* (1997); *Dance of the Broadband* (1997); *Pointe* (1997); *Trial by Jury* (1998); *Angel* (1998); *Medusa* (1998); *Intertense* (1998); *Interplay* (1998); *Sulphur 16* (1998); *Zero Hertz* (1999); *Equation* (1999); *net/Work Narrative(s)* (2000); *The Field* (2000); *Telenoia* (2000); *Fleur de Peux* (2000); *Aeon* (2000); *Trilogy Installation* (live web cast of *The Millennarium*, *Sulphur 16*, *Aeon*, 2000); *Symbiont(s)* (2000); *Velociraptor* (2001); *brainstate* (2001); *detritus* (2001); *Codex* (2001); *Duo:Logue in Three Parts* (2001); *Castlescape* (2001); *HIVE* (2001); *digit01* (2001); *11 Digital Mantras* (2001); *Horizone* (film, 2001); *Castlescape* (2001); *Nemesis* (2002); *Phase Space* (2002); *BodyScript* (2002); *Game of Halves* (2002); *L.O.V.E.* (2002); *PreSentient* (2002); *chrysalis* (film, 2002); *Alpha* (2003); *2 Human* (2003); *Nautilus* (2003); *Bio-logical* (2003); *Binocular* (2003); *Xenathra* (2003); *Polar Sequences 3* (2003); *Series* (2004); *AtaXia* (2004); *Trance* (2004); *Qualia* (2003); *Dance USA* (film, 2004); *Dice Life* (film, 2004); *Cloaca* (theatre, 2004); *Aladdin* (theatre, 2004); *Woman in White* (theatre, 2004); *Eden/Eden* (2005); *Engram* (2005); *The Midsummer Marriage* (opera, 2005); *You Can Never Tell* (2005); *Tremor* (film, 2005); *Eden/Eden* (2005); *Amu* (2005, also as *Amu@Durham*, 2006); *Ossein* (2006); *Skindex* (2006); *Dido and Aeneas* (opera, 2006); *Much Ado About Nothing* (theatre, 2006); *Chroma* (2006); *Harry Potter and the Goblet of Fire* (feature film, dir. Mike Newell, 2006); *Erazor* (2006); *Genus* (2007); *[memeri]* (2007); *Chroma* (2007); *Kirikou et Karaba* (2007); *Nimbus* (2007); *Proprius* (2008); *Infra* (2008); *Entity* (2008); *Renature* (2008); *Dyad 1909 (In the Spirit of Diaghilev)* (2009); *Dyad 1929* (2009); *Limen* (2009); *Outlier* (2010).

*Dates as cited by Random Dance, except where earlier premiere has been clarified.

Further reading

Interviews with Jean Cameron, in 'Random's Numbers', *Animated*, Winter 1996; in 'In the Flesh: Wayne McGregor in Conversation, *Dance Theatre Journal*, 15(3), 1999; with Sophie Hansen, in 'An Artist's Development Initiative Collaboration', *Dancing Times*, April 2001; with Zoë Anderson, in 'Wayne McGregor: Something in the Way He Moves', *The Independent*, 18 December 2006; with Mike Dixon, in

'Interview with Wayne McGregor', *Dance Europe*, January 2007; with Zoë Anderson, 'McGregor's Covent Garden', *Dancing Times*, March 2007.

Articles: Josephine Leask, 'On Stage: Fire and Brimstone', *Ballett International*, April 1999; Sophie Hansen, 'Wayne McGregor: Twenty-First Century Choreographer', *Dancing Times*, June 2001; Emilyn Claid, 'Seduced by Odette', *Dance Theatre Journal*, 17(3), 2001; Deborah Bull, 'Time Zone Unknown', *Dance Now*, Autumn 2001; Debra Craine, 'A Strange and Super Trouper', *The Times*, 18 February 2002; Steve Dixon, 'Absent Fiends: Internet Theatre, Posthuman Bodies and the Interactive Void', *Performance Arts International*, 'Presence' special online issue, 2003; Scott deLahunta *et al.*, 'Densities of Agreement', *Dance Theatre Journal*, Autumn 2005; Rosaleen McCarthy *et al.*, 'Bodies Meet Minds: Choreography and Cognition', *Leonardo*, 39(5), October 2006; David Jays, 'Entity', *Dancing Times*, May 2008; Zoë Anderson, 'Wayne McGregor's Deloitte Ignite', *Dancing Times*, November 2008; Roslyn Sulcas, 'Tiny Human Dramas in a Digital World', *The New York Times*, 28 November 2008; Sophie Travers, 'Concord', *Dancing Times*, October 2009; Euan Ferguson, 'Wayne's World', *The Observer*, 11 October 2009.

Books: Jo Butterworth and Gill Clarke (eds), *Dancemakers' Portfolio: Conversations with Choreographers*, Wakefield, Yorkshire, 1998; Gavin Carver and Colin Beardon, *New Visions in Performance: The Impact of Digital Technologies*, Amsterdam, 2004; Steve Dixon and Barry Smith, *Digital Performance: A History of New Media in Theatre, Dance, Performance Art and Installation*, Cambridge, MA, 2007; Jo Butterworth and Liesbeth Wildschut, *Contemporary Choreography: A Critical Reader*, Abingdon, Oxfordshire, 2009.

BEBE MILLER

Bebe Miller, one of the best, most unpretentious exponents of downtown New York dance, works in the post-modern idiom with confidence. Her work, steeped in urban sensibility, frequently employs everyday movement, but it is always grounded in Miller's impressive understanding of her craft. Her choreography, which could be called semi-narrative, is never merely abstract for its own sake. She devises movement that is deeply rooted in recognizably human dynamics. For her there is a direct, visceral link between mind and motion. The result is the creation of warm, urgent, kinetic drama.

Miller does not make an issue of being an African-American woman. She is far more keen to make dances than to make either feminist or ethnic manifestos. Born in Brooklyn, she began taking dance workshops as a child on Manhattan's Lower East Side. Her tutors included Murray Louis and Alwin Nikolais. Composition and improvisation were the strong suits of her training, factors still evident in Miller's work today: her dancers' seemingly off-the-cuff, stream-of-consciousness spontaneity is usually supported by a strong structure. She majored in art at Indiana's Earlham College, before securing a dance fellowship at Ohio State University College, where she encountered Nina Wiener, a dancer-choreographer in the Twyla Tharp mould (Wiener was a member of Tharp's company in the early 1970s). Miller signed on with Wiener's troupe for six years. By the time she left, she had begun to make dances of her own. She toured with Dana Reitz, another Tharp alumna and a maverick minimalist, before starting her own company in 1984.

As a performer, Miller is compelling, compact and essentially without any apparent ego. She not only favours fast, clear moves but is also capable of idiosyncratic delicacy: witness her signature solo, *Spending Time Doing Things* (1985). This pensive, private, highly gestural piece begins and ends in silence. Miller's beautifully modulated phrasing seems to summon up the music, Duke Ellington's *In My Solitude*. When the music, as it were, vanishes, Miller is alone again, with her body and her thoughts.

If *Spending Time* is an ingenious dance equivalent of a soliloquy, *Two* (1986) is an anguished dialogue. In this small masterpiece, a collaboration with Ralph Lemon, Miller explores the terrible weight of wanting, but being unable to connect with, another person. The man and woman in this haunting dance wage a gripping, compulsively watchable war of see-sawing need and rejection. Their emotional agitation is at once explicit and fraught with ambiguity. In Miller's best works, the atmosphere may be charged with feeling, yet some mystery is preserved. This makes viewing her dances a discovery of, rather than a lesson in, human behaviour.

Miller is a dancer's dancer-choreographer, who extracts a high degree of input from dancers, whether part of her company or when working on commissioned pieces. Miller treats them as individuals whose duty is to make her movement their own. Consequently, they tend to exhibit an unforced alertness, as they must, given the precisely inflected, unexpected shifts of weight, tone, energy and nuance she demands. Miller's dancers boldly glide on complexity. They thrash, pause, wander, and whip themselves about, swooping, hopping, crashing to the floor and rising again in vertical jumps. There are quiet moments, too, of tenderness and trust. To negotiate all this lush, galvanizing turbulence requires considerable control while pulling out all the stops.

Miller's ensemble pieces run the gamut from infernally dark to red-hot, to irrepressibly playful. She drew on her experiences as a waitress to make *Working Order*, a 1986 study in blue-collar despair and survival. *The Hendrix Project* is her exuberant, exhaustive 1991 response to guitarist Jimi Hendrix's music. (Miller's aural selections lean towards jazz, rock or electronics.) The group moves are sleek, ample, loopy and filigreed. Like many choreographers who dance, from Merce Cunningham to Trisha Brown, Miller planted into the piece a central solo for herself, full of airborne splits, slicing arm thrusts and circular rhythms. Then there is the strung-out but amiable belligerence of *Trapped in Queens* (1984), the high, partying rhythms of *Gypsy Pie* (1985), the rollicking fluidity of *Cantos Gordos* (1995) and a big, liquid finger-paint of a dance called *Thick Sleep* (1988).

These fun (and much more) works may all ultimately be of less interest than the 1987–88 trilogy of *Hell Dances*, in which Miller marks out every available inch of space in the prison of interpersonal intimacy. *This Room Has No Windows and I Can't Find You Anywhere* (1987) is an entangled tango of ruthless relationships, with the dancers cruising each other, offering occasional support minus affection. The double duet *Habit of Attraction* (1987) amplifies *Two*, counterpointing the struggles of couples for whom conflict is a bond. *Simple Tales* (1988) brings the power-playing elements of eroticism and aggression from the other two dances to a head.

Miller's dances sometimes meander and doodle, as if the intentions behind them are temporarily lost. The 1994 female quartet *Tiny Sisters*, her response to the poignant real-life story of the 'silent twins', a pair of West Indian siblings living in Wales who developed their own secret language, is more tantalizing fragment than finished work. Miller took greater risks with *Nothing Can Happen Only Once* (1993), her most overtly theatrical, and frustratingly unfulfilled, experiment to date. This 70-minute piece used text, and fairly elaborates settings and effects, as much as movement to examine the arbitrary nature of memory. As an attempt to put the thought process on stage it failed but honourably so. Embedded in the half-baked ideas and the characteristically alternating floppy/sharp choreography was at least one gorgeous duet.

Miller was the first American choreographer to work in post-apartheid South Africa. She drew upon this experience for the 1996 *Yard Dance*, a piece incorporating her readings of passages from the journal she kept during her month-long residency there. Her dancers' joyous stomps are inspired by the percussive boot dances of street children she observed in Soweto and Johannesburg.

In the mid-1990s, Miller began to move in the direction of collaborative and larger-scale theatrical undertakings encompassing choreography, writing, film, video and digital media. Working with a composer and videographer, *Drummin': The Rhythms of Miami* (1997) was a multimedia, interdisciplinary performance revolving around ethnic drumming traditions in communities throughout greater Miami. This, in turn, led to *Rhythm Studies* (1999), a solo that demonstrated anew her startling mix of boldness and vulnerability as a performer. In between came *Going to the Wall* (1998). Featuring eight dancers and Miller's own voice-over text, this was a highly physical examination of race, culture and identity, conveyed in part through an inquiry into our assumptions about the people we see onstage. This piece was planned as a touring performance with residency activities involving both local artists and the community at large. Miller is just the person to spearhead this blending of the socio-political and the creative.

The award-winning quartet *Verge* (2001) continued a collaboration with the playwright and dramaturg Talvin Wilks that began with *Wall*. Here bursts of his fragmented text, repeated questions and comments were used to establish an ambiguous context for human behaviour in a dissociated world. *Landing/Place* (2005) expanded those ideas via interactive video and digital animation in an examination of how ideas of 'place' are often at the heart of social interaction. It, too, received plaudits and awards. Influenced by a trip Miller took to Eritrea, this quintet addressed the instability arising from the necessity to decode our own and other cultures. It may sound high-concept but, typical of her, the work was grounded in a rough-and-tumble yet fluid movement vocabulary. As with all of her pieces, it posed far more questions than it answered.

In 2000, Miller was appointed as a full professor at Ohio State University; since then she has collaborated with the dance department there on digital documentation of her output. Her company, meanwhile, has ceased to operate as a traditional touring troupe. Rather, it has been restructured as a 'virtual company' whose members live in various US locations. Miller's dance projects are now developed over a period of years via longer-term residencies. One of these, called *Necessary Beauty* (2008), is built out of component parts that can be presented singly, as a recurring event or in a series adding to an hour-long performance. Featuring the same creative team as *Landing/Place*, this highly adaptable work continues Miller's probing investigations into dance, theatre and digital technology. It demonstrates anew her ongoing interest in using dance to artfully address matters that range from the intimate to the cosmic.

Donald Hutera

Biographical details

Born Deryl Adele Miller, in New York City, 20 September 1950. **Studied** with Murray Louis at Henry Street Settlement, New York, 1954–62; attended Earlham College, Richmond, Indiana, 1967–71, receiving BA degree; trained at the Louis Nikolais Dance Theater Lab, 1972–73, and at Ohio State University, 1973–75, receiving MA in dance. **Career**: Danced with Nina Wiener Company, 1976–82 and with Dana Reitz Company, touring, 1983; first choreographic work, 1978, and regular choreographer from 1981; formed own group, the Bebe Miller Company, in 1984. Also, choreographed for Concert Dance Company, Zenon Dance Company, Creach/Koester Company, Alvin Ailey Repertory Ensemble, Boston Ballet, Phoenix Dance Company (UK), Dayton Contemporary Dance Company, Pennsylvania Dance Company, Oregon Ballet Theater, PACT Dance Theatre (Johannesburg) and others. Has served as board-member of Dance Theater Workshop, Gotham Dance, Wiener Center for the Arts International Advisory Council, Bates Dance Festival, and Colloquium, Contemporary Dance Exchange. **Awards** include Creative Artists' Public Service Fellowship, 1984; New York Foundation for the Arts Fellowships, 1984 and 1991; National Endowment for the Arts Fellowship, 1985–88; New York Dance and Performance Award ('Bessie'), 1986, 1987, 2001 and 2005; Guggenheim Fellowship, 1988; American Choreographer Award, 1988; Earlham College Outstanding Alumni Award, 1988; Dewar's Emerging Artist Award, 1990; honoured as Distinguished Professor, Ohio State University, 2009.

Works*

Tune (1978); *Square Business* (1981); *Task/Force* (1981), *Jammin'* (1981); *Task/Force* (1981); *Vespers* (1982); *Story Beach* (1982); *Gotham* (1983); *Guardian Angels* (1983); *Trapped in Queens* (1984); *Reet City* (1984); *Spending Time Doing Things* (1985); *Gypsy Pie* (1985); *No Evidence* (1985), *Walt's* (1986); A *Haven for Restless Angels of Mercy* (1986); *Working Order* (1986); *Two* (in collaboration with Ralph Lemon, 1986); *The Habit of Attraction* (1987); *This Room Has No Windows and I Can't Find You Anywhere* (1987); *Butte* (1988); *Simple Tales* (1988); *Hell Dances* (trilogy comprising *The Habit of Attraction, This Room . . .* and *Simple Tales*, 1988); *Cracklin' Blue* (1988); *Thick Sleep* (1988); *Heart, Heart* (1988); *Vital Boulevard of Love* (1988); *Allies* (1989); *Rain* (1989); *The Hidden Boy: Incidents from a Stressed Memory* (in collaboration with Jay Bolotin, 1990); *The Hendrix Project* (1991); *Sanctuary* (1991); *Paisley Sky* (1992); *Spartan Reels* (1992); *Nothing Can Happen Only Once* (1993); *Things I Have Not Forgotten* (1994); *Daughter* (1994); *Tiny Sisters* (1994); *Heaven + Earth* (1994); *A Certain Depth of Heart, Also Love* (1994); *Arena* (1994); *Cantos Gordos* (1995); *Tiny Sisters in the Enormous Land* (1995); *Blessed* (1996); *Yard Dance* (1996); *Voyages plein d'espoir* (1997); *Roses from a Righteous Garden* (1997); *Drummin': The Rhythms of Miami* (1997); *Field* (1997); *Going to the Wall* (1998); *Rhythm Studies* (1999); *Three* (film, dir. Isaac Julien, 1999); *Eritrea* (1999); *My Science* (2000); *Prey* (2000); *Verge* (2001); *Aerodigm* (2002); *Landing/Place* (2005); *View: with an eye towards romance* (2005); *Necessary Beauty* (2008).

*Published sources vary; works cited here are in accordance with Bebe Miller Company website.

Further reading

Interview with Tom Pepys in 'Curtain Up', *Dance and Dancers*, September/October 1992; in Heidi Henderson (ed.), *Growing Place: Interviews with Artists, 25 Years at the Bates Dance Festival*, Lewiston, Maine, 2007.

Articles: E. Zimmer, 'Bebe Miller Comes Home', *Dance Magazine*, December 1989; Jann Parry, 'Bebe Miller and Company', *Dance Theatre Journal*, Autumn 1989; Jann Parry, 'Now for Something Completely Different', *Observer*, 8 November 1992; Chris Callis, 'Full Force', *The New Yorker*, 29 April 1996; Christy Adair, 'Two into the Making of Three', *Dance Theatre Journal*, February 1999; Joseph Carman, 'Bebe Miller Company', *Dance Magazine*, August 1999; Paula Citron, 'Lights, Camera, Dance!', *Dance International*, Spring 2000; Deborah Jowitt, 'Going On', *The Village Voice*, 11 October 2005; Deborah Jowitt, 'Veteran Choreographers Bebe Miller and Risa Jaroslow', *The Village Voice*, 19 November 2008; Kevin Giordano, 'Bebe Miller: Going to the Wall', *Dance Magazine*, May 2009.

Books: Allen Robertson and Donald Hutera, *The Dance Handbook*, Harlow, Essex, 1988; *Current Biography Yearbook*, New York, 1999.

MEREDITH MONK

> I definitely feel that I am a humanist. I really am involved with trying to figure and deal with how we, as people, are going to survive in this environment on a large scale. I want every element of the human being to be utilized – the spiritual, the instinctive, the emotional, the intellectual, and I feel that if a piece doesn't have all of these things, at least for me, it's not complete.
>
> (*Thrust*, March 1970, p. 2)

When the Houston Grand Opera presented the premiere of Meredith Monk's opera *Atlas* in 1991, many of the varied aspects of her career were brought together: here was a large-scale work of musical theatre for which Monk had prepared the scenario, organized the text, composed the music and movement and overseen the production, in addition to singing the leading role. Indeed, the only major aspect of her work that was not prominently represented was filmmaking.

The story of the explorer Alexandra Daniels (loosely based on the explorer Alexandra David-Néel) presents a voyage of self-exploration that takes us into spiritual realms only hinted at in earlier works, but reflecting Monk's long interest in the writings of Gurdjieff and Eastern mysticism. Combining scenic spectacle (including music and dance to shape the dramatic situations) with great simplicity in a journey towards inner truth, *Atlas* recalls elements from such earlier works as *Vessel* (1971), *Education of the Girlchild* (1972–73), *Quarry* (1976) and *The Games* (1983), all of them products of collaborations with close associates whose contributions inextricably became part of the works' richness.

Above all, Monk is a musician and a choreographer, a maker of movement. 'I think of myself as a composer: of music, of movement, and of images,' Monk has said. 'There are actually three branches of my work: the music concerts, the large multi-media performance pieces, and the films. The concerns of one overlap into another.' Most of her work grows from her efforts as composer, choreographer and performer, whether alone or with members of the collective known as The House. Although each work bears her unmistakable imprint, she has consistently worked with collaborators who share her vision while bringing highly individual qualities to the work. Monk's associates are as physically disparate (conventional notions of beauty seldom being relevant) as they are multitalented. Over the years, members of The House come to seem like parts of one's family – perhaps like distant relatives seen on special occasions – and as familiar faces disappear new ones gradually join the group. As music has become increasingly central to her work, singing has become one of the expected skills of a Monk performer, in the wide-ranging vibrato-less style she developed. Yet each must have the physical control of the actor-dancer. In this way a social and spiritual ideal of the 1960s – the idea of the collective – becomes merged with Monk's musical/dramatic vision. (In 1972, after a Liverpool performance, she told *The Guardian* about The House: 'We don't want our life and work to be separate. We want our work to be an expression of our lives, which are striving to be good.')

Gesture in Monk's work may derive from familiar movements, but it is selected, slowed, abstracted, sometimes framed, so that the characters seem archetypes: a sick child, an old woman, a group of women sitting at a table, perhaps pouring coffee. The movements of the Inuit couple which Monk and Robert Een enact (and sing) in *Facing North* (1990) are circumscribed by their bulky garments, but their solemn gaiety shows that they are at one with their demanding world. 'Narrators' sometimes appear framing works (often wordlessly), like the two who hop through *Education of the Girlchild*.

Blending music and dance came naturally to Monk, whose early training combined both. Her mother was a singer, her maternal grandparents musicians and great-grandfather a cantor who sang for the Tsar. In addition to music, Monk studied Dalcroze Eurhythmics, ballet and later modern dance. At Sarah Lawrence College, she fortunately found the right mentor in Bessie Shoenberg, who encouraged her students to become the very best of whatever they were. Therefore, when coming on to the New York dance/music/art scene in the early 1960s, Monk moved easily into the performing and creative world that was beginning to show work at the Judson Church and other spaces, those alternatives to the established theatres and studios, where more traditional modern dance was seen. Along with newcomers like Phoebe Neville and Kenneth King, and the slightly older Yvonne Rainer and Trisha Brown, Monk performed in 'happenings' and avant-garde events that broke the formal constraints of dance as practised by Martha Graham, José Limón and even Merce Cunningham. On the West Coast Anna Halprin was another influence, especially through her task-oriented, site-specific works, which often incorporated performers without prior dance training.

Monk was soon recognized as a choreographer with a highly individual way of combining theatrical elements, usually in a non-proscenium space, while controlling and distancing powerful emotional overtones. Thus, *Duet with Cat's Scream and Locomotive* (1966) was a nonerotic *pas de deux* that stressed physicality through large close-ups of mouths rocking around the area and a taped score associating the locomotive with him, the cat with her. The long solo *16 Millimeter Earrings* (1966) introduced singing (her first original score) and film, with images of her face projected onto a paper globe covering her head. The piece moved from a film of a burning doll to the projection of flames on Monk's nude body as she crumpled into a trunk, in an image combining martyrdom and desire.

In these early works one can see the basis of Monk's fascination with the narrow line between the real and artificial, and her involvement with space that makes the later works designed for conventional theatres so striking. *Blueprint* (1967) moved among usually private and public spaces within the large Judson Church complex, where one saw things close-up, then framed at a distance through a doorway or window. At one point, Monk, in traditional costume, danced *The Dying Swan* (not badly), shaking real feathers from a pillow. *Juice* (1969) began in Frank Lloyd Wright's Guggenheim Museum, with its great spiral ramp, and concentrated first on the viewers at the bottom looking up into the light, and then on the viewers on the ramp looking down. Later the audience shifted to a small theatre, and the third night ended in Monk's studio, where no performers were present, only photographs of what had been seen. *Vessel* (1971) derived from the idea of Joan of Arc, moving from the confines of Monk's studio, where everyday activities took place in slowed time, to a theatre where 'medieval' figures clambered around an obviously artificial cloth mountain, to a vast parking lot where armies seemed to sweep across the space, figures appeared on the steps of a distant church, motorcycles churned around the area and finally Joan was immolated in the light of a welder's torch. These spectacles brought together a dazzling array of elements from life, theatre, dance, music and village pageants but were always controlled by a sensibility that gave them shape, depth and focus.

Education of the Girlchild, Paris/Chacon (1972/1974) and *Quarry* began the body of musical/dramatic works that have formed the core of a repertory that leads towards *Atlas*. *Girlchild* began as a remarkable solo in which a crone-like figure, cackling with glee at having thus far evaded death, begins a journey down a white cloth path that reverses time, ending as a numinously innocent child. The first part, added later, includes a favourite Monk image: women of various ages and shapes sitting at a table engaged in ordinary activities, 'the tribe of companions'. Each is distinct, yet part of a defined group. Monk's feminism, like her mysticism, is simple and practical, never doctrinaire.

Paris/Chacon (made with a frequent collaborator, Ping Chong) contrasted a Parisian couple enjoying a stroll (why Monk wore both a dress and a moustache, typically, was never explained) with a community of dancers actually larger than tiny Chacon, New Mexico. In *Quarry*, however, the dreams of a sick child reveal modern horrors: 'The sick child, in a sense, is a metaphor for the diseased world,' Monk says. The ordinary events of life are transformed by gesticulating dictators into an endless emigration (covering centuries), leading towards inevitable death, while a crowd carrying artificial clouds returns with airplanes, instruments of death. Through music, spectacle and the carefully recalled details of daily life, she has dug deeply in the uneasy foundations of modern life. On a smaller scale, *Recent Ruins* (1979) suggests similar concerns as we become archaeologists patiently reconstructing our lives. *Specimen Days: A Civil War Opera* (1981) put this in a specifically American context, presenting a museum of scenes from Walt Whitman's time, representing the quintessentially American struggle for freedom, political and spiritual. *The Games* (again with Ping Chong) takes us into a future world in which simple pleasures of life are only memories to be recreated ritually. The concerns of the moral and physical world are evident in Monk's work, although she is seldom tendentious.

Since forming a vocal ensemble in 1978, Monk's music has become richer in its textures, more contrapuntal in the clarity of its interweaving lines, often suggesting medieval music without literally imitating it. (She especially admires the twelfth-century French composer Pérotin Le Grand.) Her own voice is a pure soprano with a remarkable three-octave range and no vibrato, a cool pure sound that would be ideal for 'early music', yet can cackle, keen or croon as easily as soar. (An evening of art songs at the Whitney Museum in 1974 called *Raw Recital* was as remarkable for its musical variety and vocal purity as for the way she and her pianist circled the space on a small platform.) Not one to compromise artistically, Monk is now able to support some of her large-scale ventures by solo recitals, although these can be carefully planned theatrically, like the 1994 programme *Volcano Songs*, where visual images proved as memorable as the music.

Although Monk has often been ranked with Steve Reich and Philip Glass as a minimalist, her use of *ostinato* is not to create clock-like structures but to provide a foundation for the vocal lines that develop above and beyond its harmonic implications. A synthesizer often provides that basic continuity, blending with the voices while asserting its own independence. Like the music, the vocal techniques draw on many sources, from medieval organum and hocketing through African music to Mongolian hoomi (to produce very high fundamentals and overtones). Supporting instruments range from the Jew's harp and glass harmonica (*Our Lady of Late*, 1973) to the shawm, sheng recorder and didgeridoo played by Wayne Hankin, who conducted *Atlas*.

Her film *Ellis Island*, made for *Recent Ruins*, juxtaposed past and present with images of immigrants coming through the dusty, decaying halls of the great building where so many, like Monk's ancestors, first set foot in America. In *Turtle Dreams* (1983), the turtle crawls across maps, a creature from the past totally out of scale, finally filling the empty streets of a deserted city, an image of desolation. *Book of Days*, her 1989 feature-length film, expands this intertwining of present and past when a fourteenth-century Jewish girl has visions of the future, such as the silver bird she draws that we recognize as an airplane. Her grandfather interprets her visions through the past – the Bible – and only a madwoman with compassion for suffering (played by Monk) understands her clairvoyance. The past is shown in black and white. Only when modern workmen rediscover her village, which was overtaken by plague, do we have colour, the sense of our own lives.

Returning to where we began, *Atlas* reveals many stages of Monk's archetypal journey, after the girl who is its central character is prepared for exploration by the Spirit Guides. Her companions chosen, their way takes them through idyllic farm communities to the Forest, then to the seductive, terrifying hell of the Ice Demons and on to the Desert, until all but one can ascend to a timeless, radiant place of spiritual knowledge. At the end we return to that familiar, but now extraordinary image, a woman quietly pouring and drinking a cup of coffee. The true journey is not without but within. To convey such a vision in musical and dramatic terms is Monk's achievement.

While Monk has recently devoted much of her attention to her music (including *Possible Sky* for orchestra, commissioned by Michael Tilson Thomas, and *Stringsongs* by the Kronos Quartet), her later theatre work has continued to develop themes of transience and transcendence, surely reflecting her Buddhist faith. Thus, in *The Politics of Quiet* (1996), amid images of disconnection and decay, everyday objects like a telephone and a roller skate are dipped in hot wax, becoming exhibits from a distant past before moving towards the stars, then back to the hectic present. In *Magic Frequencies* (1998), an astronomer and a television anchorwoman observe a couple munching corn on the cob and a man quietly dying, our everyday world also observed through the cracks of time by extraterrestrials.

The larger scale *Mercy* (2001) was developed with the installation artist Ann Hamilton, who like Monk has been awarded a MacArthur 'genius' grant. It moved from the small live images of Monk's vocal cords and Hamilton drawing a line to a doctor diagnosing a patient before an enormous blow-up of her face and a crowd of seeming refugees. As in all of her works, these disparate images are bonded by Monk's spellbinding music and together remind us of the brevity, terror and triumph of human life – themes reflected in *Impermanence* (2006), again dealing with loss and acceptance, of being and becoming, within the framework of eternity. *Songs of Ascension* (2008), in which the six instrumental musicians are required to move almost as much as her singer-dancers, develops these themes while adding a new gentleness as the work closes in silence.

George Dorris

Biographical details

Born in New York City, 20 November 1942. **Studied** Dalcroze movement, ballet and music from childhood; technique and composition at Sarah Lawrence College, Bronxville, New York, receiving BA degree in 1964; studied dance in New York with Mia Slavenska, Merce Cunningham, Martha Graham and at Ruth Mata/ Eugene Hari studio and the Joffrey School. **Career**: Performance début in 1963, and subsequent career has been as choreographer, composer, singer, performer, film director and recording artist, frequently combining several of these capacities in individual projects. Performed briefly with Judson Dance Theater, New York, 1960s; founded own interdisciplinary arts group, The House, 1968, remaining as artistic director and chief choreographer and composer. Has directed several video and film projects (including some versions of stage works), and recorded several albums of her music. **Awards and honours** include Guggenheim Fellowship, 1972 and 1986; Obie Award, 1972, 1976 and 1985; Venice Biennale First Prize, 1975; New York Dance Festival Merit Award, 1980; *Ciné* Golden Eagle Award, 1981; New York Dance and Performance Award ('Bessie'), 1985 and 2005; Creative Omega Award, 1987; Rockefeller Foundation Distinguished Choreographer Award, 1987; Honorary Doctorate, Bard College (Annandale-on-Hudson, New York), 1988; *Dance Magazine* Award, 1992; John D. and Catherine T. MacArthur Fellowship, 1995; Samuel H. Scripps American Dance Festival Award, 1996; Sarah Lawrence College Distinguished Alumnae Award, 1996; New York Foundation for the Arts Fellowship, 1996; Fellow, American Academy of Arts and Sciences, 2006; Demetrio Stratos International Award for musical experimentation, 2007; Premio Arlecchino d'Oro, Mantova Festival, 2008; honorary doctorates from Bard College, New York, 1988, University of the Arts (Philadelphia), 1989, The Juilliard School, 1998, San Francisco Art Institute, 1999, and Boston Conservatory, 2001.

Works

Me (1963); *Timertop* (1964); *Untitled* (1964); *Diploid* (1964); *Arm's Length* (1964); *Cowell Suite* (1964); *Break* (1964); *Cartoon* (1965); *The Beach* (1965; revised version, 1969); *Relache* (with Dick Higgins, 1965); *Blackboard* (1965); *Radar* (1965); *Portable* (1966); *Duet with Cat's Scream and Locomotive* (1966); *16 Millimeter Earrings* (1966; film version, 1966); *Blueprint (1)* (1967); *Overload (Blueprint 2)* (1967); *Blueprint (3)* (1968); *Blueprint (4)* (1968); *Blueprint (5)* (1968); *Co-op* (1968); *Title: Title and Untidal: Movement Period* (1969); *Tour: Dedicated to Dinosaurs* (1969); *Tour 2: Barbershop* (1969); *Juice: A Theater Cantata* (1969); *Tour 4: Lounge* (1969); *Tour 5: Glass* (1970); *Tour 6: Organ* (1970); *Tour 7: Factory* (1970); *Needle-Brain Lloyd and the Systems Kid: A Live Movie* (1970); *Tour 8: Castle* (1971); *Vessel. An Opera Epic* (1971); *Education of the Girlchild* (solo, 1972); *Paris* (with Ping Chong, 1972); *Our Lady of Late* (mus. Monk, 1973); *Education of the Girlchild: An Opera* (complete version, 1973); *Chacon* (with Ping Chong, 1974); *Roots* (with Donald Ashwander, 1974); *Anthology and Small Scroll* (1975); *Quarry* (opera by Monk, 1976); *Venice/ Milan* (with Ping Chong, 1976); *Tablet: House of Stills* (1977); *The Plateau Series* (1978); *Recent Ruins: An Opera* (includes *Ellis Island*, 1979); *Specimen Days: A Civil War Opera* (1981); *Turtle Dreams: Cabaret* (film, 1983); *The Games* (with Ping Chong, 1983); *The Ringing Place* (1987); *Book of Days* (1985; television version, 1988, film version, 1989); *Acts from Under and Above* (with Lanny Harrison, 1986);

Facing North (with Robert Een, 1990); *Atlas: An Opera in Three Parts* (1991); *Three Heavens and Hells* (1992); *Street Corner Pierrot* and *Evanescence* (in *Particular People* by Donald Ashwander, 1993); *American Archaeology #1: Roosevelt Island* (1994); *Volcano Songs* (1994); *A Celebration Service* (1996); *The Politics of Quiet* (1996); *Magic Frequencies* (1998); *Mercy* (2001); *Impermanence* (2006); *Voices of Ascension* (2008).

Further reading

Interviews with Brooks McNamara, in *'Vessel*: The Scenography of Meredith Monk', *Drama Review*, March 1972; with Carole Koenig, in 'Meredith Monk: Performer-Creator', *Drama Review*, September 1976; with Connie Kreemer, in her *Further Steps: Fifteen Choreographers on Modern Dance*, New York, 1987; with Nicholas Zurbrugg, *Dance Theatre Journal*, Winter 1992/93.

Articles: Constance H. Posner, 'Making it New: Meredith Monk and Kenneth King', *Ballet Review*, 1(6), 1967; Rob Baker, 'Landscapes and Telescopes: A Personal Response to the Choreography of Meredith Monk', *Dance Magazine*, April 1976; Sally Banes, 'Meredith Monk and the Making of *Chacon*', *Dance Chronicle*, 1(1), 1977; Sally Banes, 'The Art of Meredith Monk', *Performing Arts Journal*, Spring/Summer 1978; Kenneth Bernard, 'Some Observations on Meredith Monk's *Recent Ruins*', *Yale/Theater*, Spring 1980; Bonnie Marranca, 'Meredith Monk's *Recent Ruins*: Essaying Images', *Performing Arts Journal*, 4(3), 1980; Marianne Goldberg, 'Transformative Aspects of Meredith Monk's *Education of the Girlchild*', *Women and Performance*, Spring/Summer 1983; Allen Robertson, 'Renaissance Ms', *Ballet News*, October 1984; Susan Foster, 'The Signifying Body: Reaction and Resistance in Postmodern Dance', *Theatre Journal*, March 1985; Meredith Monk, 'Some Thoughts about Art', *Dance Magazine*, September 1990; Rob Baker, 'Material Worlds', *Parabola*, Fall 1991; David Finkelstein, 'The Films of Meredith Monk', *Ballet Review*, Summer 1991; Bonnie Marranca, 'Meredith Monk's *Atlas of Sound*: New Opera and the American Performance Tradition', *Performing Arts Journal*, January 1992; Meredith Monk, 'Ages of the Avant-Garde', *Performing Arts Journal*, 16(1), 1994; Nancy Vreeland Dalva, 'Meredith Monk', *Dance Magazine*, December 1994; Gia Kourlas, 'Meredith Monk: A Verb, Not a Noun', *Dance Magazine*, April 1998; Logan Hill, 'The Accidental Icon', *New York* magazine, 24 July 2000; Gus Solomons, 'Meredith Monk: A Voice in Motion', *Dance Magazine*, July 2001; Kyle Gann, 'The Moving Pencil Writes', *The Village Voice*, 31 October 2006; Deborah Jowitt, 'Meredith Monk Makes the Guggenheim Dance and Sing', *The Village Voice*, 4 March 2009; Alex Ross, 'Primal Song', *The New Yorker*, 9 November 2009.

Books: Don McDonagh, *The Rise and Fall and Rise of Modern Dance*, New York, 1970; Marcia Siegel, *At the Vanishing Point*, New York, 1972; Marcia Siegel, *Watching the Dance Go By*, Boston, 1977; Sally Banes, *Terpsichore in Sneakers: Postmodern Dance*, Boston, 1980; Selma Jeanne Cohen (ed.), *Dance as a Theatre Art: Source Readings in Dance History from 1591 to the Present*, 2nd edition (new section by Katy Matheson), Princeton, NJ, 1992; Deborah Jowitt, *Meredith Monk*, New York, 1997; Nick Kaye, *Site-Specific Art*, London, 2000; Susan Key and Larry Rothe (eds), *American Mavericks*, Los Angeles, 2001; Rose Eichenbaum (photographs and text) and Clive Barnes (foreword), *Masters of Movement: Portraits of America's Great Choreographers*, Washington, DC, 2004; Bonnie Marranca, *Performance Histories*, New York, 2008.

MARK MORRIS

Mark Morris's historical importance, at least in the early part of his career, was that his work united what were, before him, two divergent trends. One was traditional modern dance, with its weightiness, its musicality and its liberal humanism. The other was the postmodern sensibility – with its insistent irony, its self-conscious historicism and its political emphasis – that dominated American art, including dance, in the 1980s. When Morris began showing his work to New York audiences, these two trends were following widely separate paths. In traditional modern dance, there seemed to be no young talent; in what the young were doing, there seemed to be no dance but rather a sort of political theatre. Morris's work bridged the divide. It was up-to-date, full of 'styles' and mordancy and taboo-breaching (particularly gender-violation: unisex dances, women lifting men etc.). Yet it was dance, modern dance: plastic, musical and fundamentally earnest. And the combination seemed completely natural.

In view of Morris's education, it *was* natural. Born in Seattle, Washington, in 1956, he grew up as the third and last child of an ordinary middle-class family. (His father taught at the high school down the block; his mother stayed home with the children.) At the age of eight, he received the *coup de foudre* at a performance of José Greco's flamenco troupe, and he soon began lessons in Spanish dance. Thereafter – and this is the crucial point about his dance background – most of his training was in folk dance. He also began ballet training at the age of 10, but his primary dance education was in flamenco (which he also studied in Madrid in 1974) and Balkan dance, which he learned when, at the age of 13, he joined the Koleda Folk Ensemble, a Seattle troupe devoted to Balkan forms. In artistic terms, the latter experience was the main event of his youth. For three years, the Koleda Folk Ensemble was socially and artistically the centre of his life. From that troupe he learned how he wanted a dance ensemble to look – like regular people, full of human variety – and how he wanted the dancing body to look – sturdy, solid, with the weight held low and the feet flat on the ground. From the post-1960s spirit with which the members of Koleda imbued their dances, he learned the utopianism that was to mark his later work. Finally, Balkan dance and also flamenco – both highly sophisticated musically – taught him to see dance as grounded in music. (He pursued music independently as well. His father showed him how to read music as a child, and he taught himself to play the piano.)

Morris had almost no training in modern dance, with the result that he was never affected by its generational disputes, never saw himself as needing to throw off the past – as well he might have done, for he had grown up into a bad-boy type: long haired, loud-mouthed, provocative and forthrightly homosexual. Yet, from ethnic dance he was learning all the values that would eventually enable him to become an unself-conscious practitioner of modern dance, and to place his new-style sensibility in the service of that old form.

Morris began choreographing at the age of 14 and went on making dances for school plays, recitals and the like throughout his adolescence. In 1976, when he was 19, he moved to New York, where for the next seven years he danced with various troupes. In 1980, he founded his own company, the Mark Morris Dance Group, and his fame, together with his skill and productivity, grew yearly. By 1986, the year he turned 30, he was being reviewed by national magazines, two major ballet companies had premiered dances by him, and he had been the subject of an hour-long Public Broadcasting Service television special. He was the foremost young choreographer in the United States.

In 1988, Morris moved his troupe to Brussels, to replace Maurice Béjart's Ballet of the 20th Century as the resident dance company of Belgium's national opera house, the Théâtre Royal de la Monnaie. The troupe spent three turbulent years in Brussels, receiving, for the most part, harsh reviews from a press unaccustomed to American modern dance (Morris's third Brussels season was greeted by the front-page headline 'Mark Morris, go home!' in the city's leading paper, *Le Soir*.). Meanwhile, the company was undergoing painful internal changes. Essentially, the troupe's first generation was yielding to its second. Veteran dancers quit; new dancers arrived; the company became larger, younger, more technically skilled. Through all these disruptions, Morris went on working steadily. During the Belgian years, he created – for his company and others (including Mikhail Baryshnikov's modern dance troupe, White Oak Dance Project, which he helped to found) – 11 dances, including two acknowledged masterpieces, *L'Allegro, il Penseroso ed il Moderato* (1988), to Handel's oratorio, and *Dido and Aeneas* (1989), a danced version of Purcell's opera. In recognition of this show of strength and courage, he was awarded a MacArthur Fellowship in 1991. Shortly afterwards, the company returned to New York, becoming the fourth-largest modern dance troupe in the United States and probably the most discussed.

One of the first impressions to strike most spectators at a Mark Morris event is the seeming naturalness of his dances. This quality is not as insistent today as it was in his early dances. Still, it is there. His dancers look like people one might meet on the street: tall and small, black and white. They move with weight and effort, they squat and strain and they hurl themselves into the air. This gives them a note of vulnerability, of candour, and also an extreme physical immediacy, compounded by the fact that the dances are often performed to live vocal music (about half of Morris's works have been set to song), so that the music too reverberates with the force of the body. This is profoundly visceral choreography. Yet, unlike other naturalistic styles, Morris's makes no claim to be life rather than art. His work is artifice: largely abstract and a structure of open symbols. Though the dancers may drag themselves across the floor by their arms – which they do in Morris's popular *Gloria* (1981, revised in 1984) – they do so in a line of seven, in canon, in imitation of the structure of the music. Naturalism, for Morris, is an artistic strategy.

The basis of Morris's choreography is music. From adolescence he has been a passionate and erudite music lover. He has set works to the music of more than 60 different composers, together with many popular songs. He favours Baroque music, by reason of its structural clarity, emotional directness and danceability. (He has set four dances to J.S. Bach; his two most ambitious pieces, *L'Allegro* and *Dido and Aeneas*, were to Handel and Purcell, respectively.) And since his youth, he has shown a fondness for choreographing to the West Coast experimental composers Harry Partch, Henry Cowell and Lou Harrison. Still, his taste is very eclectic. Whatever the music, he does not so much choose it; it chooses him. It is because that piece of music has given him choreographic ideas that he decides to set a dance to it, and the dance that he makes reflects the musical structure. (He ordinarily choreographs with the score in hand.) Musical ensembles become dance ensembles; musical solos become dance solos. Rhythm, harmony, counterpoint, dynamics and key structures all become part of the dance. In consequence, some reviewers have chided Morris for 'music-visualizing', though the relationship between the musical structure and the dance structure in his work is usually quite elastic. Music may be his muse, but it is not the direct source of his choreography. The source is the imaginative process – a compound of thought and emotion, experienced as movement images – set off in his mind by the music. This process is something that an external pattern can only influence, never dictate. The pattern is necessary to him, however. Morris almost never commissions music. The music must be pre-existent; he has to hear it in order to want to make a dance to it.

A number of Morris's finest works are narrative. *One Charming Night* (1985) tells of a vampire seduction; *Bedtime* (1992) of the theft of a child by a goblin. *Dido and Aeneas* and *The Hard Nut* (1991), Morris's *Nutcracker*, tell the usual tales. Others of his dances, if they do not have stories, have clear subjects, in keeping, often, with their vocal text: love (*New Love Song Waltzes*, 1982; *I Don't Want to Love*, 1996), death (*The Vacant Chair*, 1984), fear (*Behemoth*, 1990; *The Office*, 1994), dreaming (*Bedtime*), religious feeling (*Gloria; O Rangasayee*, 1984; *Stabat Mater*, 1986; *Strict Songs*, 1987; *Beautiful Day*, 1992; *Jesu, Meine Freude*, 1993). Another persistent theme is community, group love. (Morris, almost alone among choreographers, is not especially interested in romantic love. He has created a few beautiful love duets – notably in *A Garden*, 2001 – but he prefers solos, small groups and ensembles.) Though he uses 'subject matter', he develops it not in a literary way – a linear way – but in a musical way, through the repetition and development of movement themes. The movements may begin as story, but they end as dance.

Morris's works tend to have double emotions. They present two opposing sides of an experience simultaneously: sorrow and dryness (*Love Song Waltzes*), reverie and absurdity (*Ten Suggestions*, 1981), exultation and anguish (*Stabat Mater*) and brassiness and horror (*Lucky Charms*, 1994). As an overarching opposition, they tend to use beautiful old music – which puts the audience into a worshipful mood – in combination with blunt, vernacular movement that disrupts that mood. This persistent doubleness has caused Morris, at times, to be mistaken as simply an ironist. He is in fact quite earnest, but he is also witty and unsentimental, and there is a long streak of darkness in his vision of life. Many of his dances have great pathos, but it is won from difficulty, from a criticism of pathos.

Morris is remarkably prolific. Since 1980, when he founded his company, he has created close to 130 works – about five per year. This includes 14 classical ballets for the Joffrey Ballet, Boston Ballet, American Ballet Theatre, Paris Opera Ballet, Les Grands Ballets Canadiens and, most frequently, the San Francisco Ballet. He has directed six opera productions. (In *Die Fledermaus*, Seattle, 1998, and *The Marriage of Figaro*, Brussels, 1991, his work was limited to directing, though there was a small amount of dancing. In *Orfeo ed Euridice*, Iowa City, 1996, and *Platée*, Edinburgh, 1997, there was copious dancing, but the singers too were onstage. *Dido and Aeneas*, Brussels, 1989, and *Four Saints in Three Acts*, London, 2000, were through-danced, with the singers offstage.) He has also created dances for operas, directed by others, notably Peter Sellars' *Nixon in China* (1987) and *The Death of Klinghoffer* (1991). His rifle-toting ballerinas in *Nixon* were much admired.

Morris's style has changed over the years. In 1985–86, when he began his immersion in Baroque music, he became more interested in tight, complex dance structures – 'perfect systems', as he calls them – both as a reflection of that music and, it seems, as an organizer and container for themes of grief. Also, in 1986, he broke his foot and had to stop dancing for five months. Up to that time, Morris had always been the star dancer of his company, but the injury forced him to watch his work from the sidelines, and he began to design his dances more in accordance to how it would be to look at them rather than how it would feel to dance them. And, it seems, he began more purposefully to design choreography for specific dancers rather than for a notional general dancer based on himself. From that time on, he took himself out of certain pieces, though he went on creating superb roles for himself. In *Dido and Aeneas*, he played both Dido and the Sorceress – the greatest role of his career. Now in his fifties, he dances occasionally, in specialized parts.

Another turning point in Morris's working life was the period in Brussels. With the resources of the national opera house at his disposal, he was able to double the size of the company, and, for the first time, to command set and costume shops, orchestras and choruses. His work expanded in every way, not only in size (*L'Allegro* has a cast of 24, *The Hard Nut*, 33) but also in clarity and boldness. In certain works of this period – *L'Allegro, Dido* and *Behemoth* – there are neither soft parts, nor fat; it is impossible to imagine this thing being said with greater imaginative force. At the same time, his style changed, as a result of several circumstances. He had many new dancers, and he had to train them. Furthermore, he now had a studio of his own (actually, several studios) so that he could train them. He began teaching a company class every morning, and it was a ballet class, for another influence of this period was ballet: he became more interested in it. At the same time, he was caught up in a burst of creativity, with ideas newly clear to him, new things to say. Under all these pressures, his dances took on a new look. They shaded from the 'vernacular' style to something more formal, more designed and legible, with the body more 'worked', the steps more complicated, the rhythms more difficult and exact. This change had been building for years, but in Brussels it became most noticeable, partly because one saw it on new dancers, who had not been trained in the older, shaggier style. Since the Brussels interlude, his work has not altered as much. The middle-period style has simply become more stable. With important exceptions, his work is increasingly abstract. Stories and emotions are there, but they must be inferred. Style apart, one notable development of the 1990s was Morris's exploration of new media: dance on video (*Falling Down Stairs* and *Dido and Aeneas*, both 1995 for Rhombus Media); opera (*Orfeo, Four Saints, Platée*); musical theatre (*The Capeman*, 1998).

One thing has never changed in Morris's work, and that is its amalgamative nature. He himself is a combination of oddly assorted parts. In the words of David White, founding director of Dance Theater Workshop, where much of his early work was produced, 'Mark is a sort of car crash of personalities. There's this working-class guy and there's this music scholar guy, and there's this folk-dance guy and this gay guy, and they've all washed up into the same body.'[1] His work, likewise, is a great gathering-in. While Spanish and Balkan dance, together with ballet, have been his major influences, he has also been deeply affected by Asian dance, European court dance and indeed major figures of American modern dance: Isadora Duncan, Ruth St Denis, Martha Graham, Merce Cunningham, Paul Taylor, Laura Dean, Lucinda Childs and Trisha Brown. Though music is the law of his mind, he is also passionately involved with stories that work by an opposite logic. While his is a very modern mind – sophisticated, ironical and self-critical – he is also attached to old values and old music: Bach, Handel and the things they felt were important. While he may be in one mood about something, he can see the other mood too. This is not to say that Morris 'can't be pigeonholed'. He can be. He has a specific style and specific concerns. But his habit has always been to join opposing things. This makes his work more difficult and more durable. It also produces a largeness of vision that has endeared him to the public.

Joan Acocella

Note

1 Quoted in Joan Acocella, *Mark Morris*, New York, 1993.

Biographical details

Born in Seattle, Washington, United States, 29 August 1956. **Studied** flamenco dance from age nine, with Verla Flowers and ballet with Perry Brunson in

Seattle. **Career**: Danced with semi-professional Balkan dance troupe, the Koleda Folk Ensemble, from ages 13 to 16; later danced with numerous companies, including those of Eliot Feld, Lar Lubovitch, Hannah Kahn and Laura Dean; began choreographing as a young student; founded Mark Morris Dance Group in 1980, bringing group to Europe to become the resident company of the Théâtre Royal de la Monnaie, Brussels, 1988–91; co-founded, with Mikhail Baryshnikov, White Oak Dance Project, in 1990. Has choreographed for numerous other companies, including Joffrey Ballet, Boston Ballet, American Ballet Theatre, Les Grands Ballets Canadiens, San Francisco Ballet and Paris Opera Ballet; has also directed opera. **Awards and honours** include New York Dance and Performance Award ('Bessie'), 1984, 1990 and 2007; Guggenheim Fellowship, 1986; MacArthur Foundation Fellowship, 1991; *Dance Magazine* Award, 1991; Olivier Award, 1998 and 2002; *Evening Standard* Award, 1997; New York State Governor's Award, 2001; *Time Out* Live Award, 2002; Critic's Circle National Dance Awards (UK), 2002; Doris Duke Award, 2002; Fellow, American Academy of Arts and Sciences, 2005; New York Mayor's Award for Arts and Culture, 2006; WQXR Gramophone Special Recognition Award, 2006; Samuel H. Scripps Award, 2007; Independent Award, Brown University Club of New York, 2007; Member, American Philosophical Society, 2008.

Works

Barstow (1973); *Zenska* (1975); *Brummagem* (1978); *Rattlesnake Song* (1980); *Castor and Pollux* (1980); *Dad's Charts* (1980); *Ten Suggestions* (1981); *Etudes Modernes* (1981); *I Love You Dearly* (1981); *Gloria* (1981); *Rattlesnake Song* (1981); *Canonic 3/4 Studies* (1982); *Jr. High* (1982); *New Love Song Waltzes* (1982); *Not Goodbye* (1982); *Songs That Tell a Story* (1982); *Bijoux* (1983); *Ponchielliana* (1983); *Caryatids* (1983); *Celestial Greetings* (1983); *The Death of Socrates* (1983); *Deck of Cards* (1983); *Dogtown* (1983); *Minuet and Allegro in G* (1983); *The 'Tamil Film Songs in Stereo' Pas de Deux* (1983); *Come on Home* (1984); *Forty Arms, Twenty Necks, One Wreathing* (1984); *Love, You Have Won* (1984); *My Party* (1984); *Championship Wrestling after Roland Barthes* (1984); *O Rangasayee* (1984); *Prelude and Prelude* (1984); *She Came from There* (1984); *The Vacant Chair* (1984); *Vestige* (1984); *Frisson* (1985); *Handel Choruses* (1985); *Jealousy* (1985); *Lovey* (1985); *Marble Halls* (1985); *One Charming Night* (1985); *Retreat from Madrid* (1985); *Aida* (1986); *Ballabili* (1986); *Esteemed Guests* (1986); *Mort Subite* (1986); *Mythologies* (1986); *Pièces en Concert* (1986); dances in *Salomé* (opera by Richard Strauss, 1986); *Shepherd on the Rock* (1986); *Stabat Mater* (1986); dances in *Nixon in China* (opera by John Adams, 1987); *Scarlatti Solos* (1987); *Sonata for Clarinet and Piano* (1987); *Strict Songs* (1987); La *Folia* (1987); *Drink to Me Only with Thine Eyes* (1988); dances in *Die Fledermaus* (opera by Richard Strauss, 1988); *Fugue and Fantasy* (1988); *L'Allegro, il Penseroso ed il Moderato* (1988); dances in *Le Nozze de Figaro* (opera by Mozart, 1988); *Offertorium* (1988); dances in *Orphée et Euridice* (opera by Gluck, 1988); *Dido and Aeneas* (1989; television version, 1995); *Love Song Waltzes* (1989); *Wonderland* (1989); *Behemoth* (1990); *Ein Herz* (1990); *Going Away Party* (1990); *Motorcade* (1990); *Pas de Poisson* (1990); dances in *The Death of Klinghoffer* (opera by John Adams, 1991); *The Hard Nut* (1991); *A Lake* (1991); *The Marriage of Figaro* (also dir., 1991); *Paukenschlag* (1992); *Beautiful Day* (1992); *Polka* (1992); *Three Preludes* (1992); *Bedtime* (1992); *Excursion to Grenada: A Calypso Ballet* (1992); *Grand Duo* (includes *Polka*, 1993); *Home* (1993); *Mosaic and United* (1993); *Jesu, Meine Freude* (1993); *A Spell*

(1993); *Falling Down Stairs* (film, 1995; stage version, 1997); *The Office* (1994); *Lucky Charms* (1994); *Rondo* (1994); *Maelstrom* (1995); *Quincunx* (1995); *Somebody's Coming to See Me Tonight* (1995); *Pacific* (1995); *World Power* (1995); *Three Russian Preludes* (1995); *Orfeo ed Euridice* (1996); *I Don't Want to Love* (1996); *Rhymes with Silver* (1997); *Anger Dance* (1997); *Waltz in C* (1997); *Platée* (opera by Rameau, 1997); *The Capeman* (musical by Paul Simon, 1998); *Medium* (1998); *Greek to Me* (1998); *Dancing Honeymoon* (1998); *The Argument* (1999); *Dixit Dominus* (1999); *Sandpaper Ballet* (1999); *Flight* (1999); *Zwei Harveytanze* (1999); *Peccadillos* (2000); *Four Saints in Three Acts* (opera by Virgil Thomson, 2000); *Sang-Froid* (2000); *From Old Seville* (2001); *A Garden* (2001); *Gong* (2001); *V* (2001); *Later* (2002); *Foursome* (2002); *Kolam* (2002); *Resurrection* (2002); *Something Lies Beyond the Scene* (2002); *Non Troppo* (2003); *Serenade* (2003); Act III ballet in *Idomeneo* (opera by Mozart, 2003); *All Fours* (2003); *Sylvia* (2004); *Violet Cavern* (2004); *Rock of Ages* (2004); *Cargo* (2005); *Candleflowerdance* (2005); *Up and Down* (2006); *King Arthur* (2006); *Mozart Dances* (2006); *Italian Concerto* (2007); *Orfeo ed Euridice* (opera by Gluck, 2007); *Looky* (2007); *Joyride* (2008); *Excursions* (2008); *Romeo and Juliet, On Motifs of Shakespeare* (2008); *L'isola disabitata* (2009); *Empire Garden* (2009); *Visitation* (2009); *Cease Your Funning* (2009); *Socrates* (2010).

Further reading

Interviews with David Vaughan, in 'A Conversation with Mark Morris', *Ballet Review*, Summer 1986; with Roslyn Sulcas; in 'Man on the Move', *Dance and Dancers*, January/February 1992; with Maura Keefe and Marc Woodworth, in 'An Interview with Mark Morris', *Salmagundi*, Fall/Winter 1994/95; with Donald Hutera, in 'The Big Rendezvous', *Dance Europe*, August 2000; with Beth Genné, in 'A New Home for Mark Morris', *Dancing Times*, October 2001; in Janet Lynn Roseman, *Dance Masters: Interviews with Legends of Dance*, London and New York, 2001; in Joyce Morgenroth (ed.), *Speaking of Dance: Twelve Contemporary Choreographers on Their Craft*, Abingdon and New York, 2004; with Meryl Cates, in 'Mark Morris Dance Group Returns to the UK', *Dancing Times*, April 2010.

Articles: Tobi Tobias, 'Mark Morris: Manchild in the Promised Land', *Dance Magazine*, December 1984; Laurie Lassiter, 'Mark Morris Dance Group', *Drama Review*, Summer 1985; John Gruen, 'Mark Morris: He's Here', *Dance Magazine*, September 1986; Clive Barnes, 'Mad about the Boy', *Dance and Dancers*, January 1987; Alastair Macaulay, 'Vivamus atque Amemus', *The New Yorker*, 20 June 1988; Lynn Garafola, 'Mark Morris and the Feminine Mystique', *Ballet Review*, Fall 1988; Don Daniels, 'Alone Together', *Ballet Review*, Winter 1988; Arlene Croce, 'Mark Morris Goes Abroad', *The New Yorker*, 16 January 1989; Christine Temin, 'The Triumph of Mark Morris', *Boston Globe Magazine*, 19 February 1989; Arlene Croce, 'Wise Guys', *The New Yorker*, 31 July 1989; Joan Acocella, 'L'Allegro, il Penseroso ed il Moderato', *Ballet Review*, Summer 1989; Christine Temin, 'Mark Morris: Brussels and Boston', *Ballet Review*, Fall 1989; William James Lawson, 'In the Monnaie', *Ballet Review*, Summer 1989; Sophie Constanti, 'Mark Morris, Béjart Pulp, and Belgian Bores', *Dance Theatre Journal*, February 1990; David Vaughan, 'Two Leaders: Mark Morris and Garth Fagan', *Ballet Review*, Summer 1990; David Vaughan, 'Mark Morris Here and There', *Ballet Review*, Winter 1990/91; David Vaughan, 'Mark Morris: Here and There – II', *Ballet Review*, Spring 1991; Marcia Siegel, 'Decomposing

Sugar Plums & Robot Mice', *Ballet Review*, Spring 1991; John Percival, 'The Mark Morris Dance Group', *Dance and Dancers*, November 1992; Arlene Croce, 'An American Ritual', *The New Yorker*, 28 December 1992 and 4 January 1993 (double issue); Joan Acocella, 'Mark Morris: The Body and What it Means', *Dance Now*, Summer 1994; Alastair Macaulay, 'The Last Great American Choreographer', *Dance Theatre Journal*, Summer 1995; John Gruen, 'Mark Morris: Breaking New Ground', *Dance Magazine*, July 1995; Roger Copeland, 'Mark Morris, Postmodernism, and History Recycled', *Dance Theatre Journal*, Summer 1997; Graeme Kay, 'Lost for Words', *Dance Theatre Journal*, Summer 1997; Roger Copeland, 'Mark Morris, Postmodernism and History Recycled', *Dance Theatre Journal*, 13(4), 1997; Susan Reiter, 'The Very Individual Mark Morris', *Dance Australia*, April/May 2000; Allan Ulrich, 'Mark Morris: 20 Years of Serious Fun', *Dance Magazine*, April 2001; Debra Craine, 'The Ruling Class: Twenty Years of Mark Morris', *Dance Now*, Winter 2001/2; Zoë Anderson, 'Mark Morris Dance Group', *Dancing Times*, February 2002; Henrietta Bannerman, 'Profile: Mark Morris', *Dance Theatre Journal*, 18(4), 2002; Mark Morris, 'Creating Sylvia: Eros triumphs over Diana', *Dance Magazine*, May 2004; Joan Acocella, 'Sylvia Grows Up', *The New Yorker*, 24 May 2004; Zoë Anderson, 'Mark Morris Anniversary', *Dancing Times*, May 2006; Deborah Jowitt, 'Mark Morris Matches Wit with Beethoven and Ives', *The Village Voice*, 25 August 2009; Deborah Jowitt, 'Message from Mark Morris: Look, But Don't Forget to Listen', *The Village Voice*, 2 March 2010.

Books: Arlene Croce, *Sight Lines*, New York, 1987; Tom Brazil, *Dances by Mark Morris* (photographs), New York, 1992; Selma Jeanne Cohen (ed.), *Dance as a Theatre Art: Source Readings in Dance History from 1591 to the Present*, 2nd edition (new section by Katy Matheson), Princeton, New Jersey, 1992; Joan Acocella, *Mark Morris* (biography), New York, 1993; Janet Adshead-Lansdale (ed.), *Dancing Texts: Intertextuality in Interpretation*, London: 1999; Jeffrey Escoffier and Matthew Lore (eds), *Mark Morris' 'L'Allegro, il Penseroso ed il Moderato': A Celebration*, New York, 2001; Rose Eichenbaum (photographs and text) and Clive Barnes (foreword), *Masters of Movement: Portraits of America's Great Choreographers*, Washington, DC, 2004; Vida Midgelow, *Reworking the Ballet: Counter-Narratives and Alternative Bodies*, London and New York, 2007.

GRAEME MURPHY

In many ways, Graeme Murphy – choreographer, dancer, artistic director – can be regarded as the personification of Australian contemporary dance. Australian-born, he has a commitment to Australian dance and dancers, which has been unrelenting, as has his commitment to other Australian artists – choreographers, composers, musicians, painters and designers among them. Through the auspices of the Sydney Dance Company (SDC), Murphy has also been instrumental in bringing Australian dance to the wider international stage. Thus, few would challenge the claim that not only dance but also the performing arts as a whole in Australia owe a great deal to this highly innovative, often iconoclastic, but quintessentially Australian, artist.

If one were to pinpoint the characteristics of Murphy's dance, then 'eclectic' and 'theatrical' are perhaps the two most definitive terms: whether in the choice of artistic medium or in the choice of theme, movement style and music, Murphy ranges over a wide field, drawing on whatever he considers appropriate to realize his creative vision. That vision is firmly anchored in the belief that dance should be theatre that excites, stimulates and provokes: thus, riding on the edge, taking risks and 'ruffling feathers' has always been at the heart of the Murphy canon.

Murphy's movement style is a case in point. Classical ballet lies at its core.[1] At the same time, however, he freely calls on any number of other movement sources (both dance and non-dance) if it suits his purpose to do so. The result is a rich tapestry of movement that goes beyond any readily definable stylistic category. *Daphnis and Chloë* (1980), for example, shifts freely across time periods and movement styles, distorting them while still working recognizably within them. Greek shepherds and shepherdesses dance an elegantly stylized folk dance; the tough punk-rocker Bryaxis and his sewer rats rummage around with somersaults and hand-stands, while Cupid careers about on a skateboard and Daphnis and Dorcan compete for the lovely Chloë's favour with a duel of the ballroom-disco competition kind.

Another dimension of Murphy's eclecticism is the frequent interplay between fact and fantasy, past and present, age and youth. Although *Poppy* (1978), *After Venice* (1984) and *Beauty and the Beast* (1993), among others, show this thematic mix, it is arguably in the highly original version of Tchaikovsky's *Nutcracker* (created for the Australian Ballet in 1992, and in collaboration with designer Kristian Fredrikson) that these dynamic shifts reach their peak. Here, the essence of the original ballet is woven in and around a contemporary storyline that has a distinctively Australian orientation but draws on Russian dance and political history at the same time. Clara (the work's subtitle is in fact *The Story of Clara*) is portrayed as an elderly Russian *émigrée* looking back over her life as a famous ballerina, who made her début with the Imperial Ballet as the *Nutcracker's* Sugar Plum Fairy. After fleeing the 1917 Revolution, she joins Diaghilev's Ballets Russes, arriving in Australia in 1940 with the De Basil company. Her career ends with the newly fledged Borovansky Ballet (the precursor to the Australian Ballet).

Murphy's eclectic approach, together with his commitment to highly theatrical collaborative ventures with other leading artists (composers, set and lighting designers, choreographers and musicians), and his commitment to breaking boundaries and challenging conventional norms, suggests more than a hint of the Diaghilevian about the man and his work. Thus it is, perhaps, not at all surprising to find that a significant number of works in his extensive repertory relate in some way or another to Diaghilev or the Ballets Russes.

The full-length *Poppy*, for example, takes the life and art of Jean Cocteau as its theme. Part biography and part journey in the fantasy world of Cocteau's opium-charged imagination, this critically acclaimed work includes not only a larger-than-life Diaghilev but also refers choreographically to some of the Ballets Russes masterpieces (*Le Spectre de la rose* and *Le Sacre du printemps* among them). *Shéhérazade* (1979), *Daphnis and Chloë* (1980) and *Late Afternoon of a Faun* (1987) further reinforce the Diaghilev connection, as of course does *Nutcracker*.

As the above works also suggest, the reinterpretation of classics (whether dance, literary text or film) is another feature of Murphy's work. The high-tech *Beauty and the Beast* similarly identifies the choreographer's interest in taking a classic and interpreting it in a way that is both entertaining and thought-provoking. Elements from the familiar Gothic tale and others from Cocteau's film version are reworked into a contemporary moral fable that includes not only the Gothic Beast but also his robotic Corporate Beast and drug-ravaged Rock Beast counterparts. Although serious messages are embedded in the work, they are offset by an irreverent and somewhat camp sense of humour – yet another Murphy trademark.

Central to Murphy's choreography is the belief that dance should surprise rather than lead an audience comfortably along a predictable path: Diaghilev's aphoristic 'astonish me!' could well be taken as one of Murphy's fundamental artistic credos. As many of his works reveal, he is an inveterate risk-taker who is prepared to challenge conventional practices in, and perceptions about, dance. To take his *Nutcracker – The story of Clara* again: the work departs radically from the original, but rather than being yet another reinterpretation of the rather improbable story, it is an entirely logical reflection and commentary both on the work itself and on the origins of Australian ballet, emphasizing its Russian roots. His internationally acclaimed *Swan Lake* (2002) is likewise a re-interpretation of a great Petipa/Tchaikovsky classic: set in Geneva in the 1930s, the work takes the essential elements of love, deception and betrayal, and reshapes them into something contemporary both in content and relevance.

The principle of surprise also underpins the music Murphy uses. Hence, new contemporary music dominates the repertory, with commissioned scores from leading Australian composers (Carl Vine and Graeme Koehne in particular) playing a major role. The diversity that marks Murphy's choreographic *modus operandi* similarly underlies his choice of music: the rock music of Iva Davies/Bob Kretschmer in *Boxes* (1985), the percussion scores used for *Synergy with Synergy* (1992), and the music of Iannis Xenakis (*Kraanerg*, 1988) or Karol Szymanowski (*King Roger*, 1990) give some indication of its extent.

Yet another aspect of Murphy's challenge to conventional norms and expectations is the fact that he does not shy away from nudity and sexuality in his works. Although bare flesh undeniably abounds, it rarely gives the sense of being there solely for gratuitous display. Murphy simply revels in the body and its physicality, and as he points out, he has 'never looked at dance removed from sensuality and sexuality'.[2] The nudity ranges from the humorous (Cupid displays a cheeky pair of bare buttocks in *Daphnis and Chloë*), through the provocatively sensual (in the 1994 television work, *Sensing*), to the more overtly sexual (e.g. in *Beauty and the Beast*).

Any commentary on Graeme Murphy would be incomplete without mention of the close relationship between him and his life partner (and acknowledged muse) Janet Vernon, as well as between him and the SDC itself.[3] The relationship with the latter is essentially symbiotic, and one that has been of enormous mutual benefit, not only to those directly concerned but also to Australian dance itself.

Although Murphy and the SDC are regarded by many as one and the same, he has never insisted on exclusive artistic ownership over 'his' company.[4] Instead, he has ensured that its dancers have been consistently exposed to the influences of other choreographers and other companies. Louis Falco's feisty *Black and Blue* (1982),[5] Barry Moreland's *Daisy Bates* (1982) and *Mansions* (1982), Ohad Naharin's *Arbos* (1989) and Douglas Wright's *Gloria* (1991), for example, were either set on, or created for, the company. Importantly, Murphy also encouraged dancers from within the company to test their choreographic wings: Paul Mercurio,[6] Kim Walker,[7] Stephen Page[8] and Gideon Obarzanek[9] are among those who took up the challenge.

Co-company enterprises have also been an important part of the SDC agenda. *Boxes*, for example, saw the collaboration between the company and the rock band Icehouse, whereas the exciting *Synergy with Synergy* saw Australia's leading percussion ensemble Synergy as an integral part of the performance.[10] Perhaps, one of the most ambitious, both artistically and logistically, of these collaborative ventures came about in 1988 with Australia's bicentenary celebrations: Murphy created the full-length *VAST* using 70 dancers from four widely dispersed companies – the SDC, the Australian Dance Theatre, the Western Australia Ballet and the Queensland Ballet.[11] More recently, *Hua Mulan* (which opened the 2005 Shanghai International Arts Festival) was another huge co-production, which brought together dancers from SDC, 60 performers from the Shanghai Song and Dance Ensemble and the Synergy ensemble.

In May 2006, Murphy, along with Vernon as SDC's Associate Director, celebrated 30 years at the company's helm, marking the occasion with *The Director's Cut*, a special triple bill fusing past, present and future. In an interview at the time, Murphy made the comment:

> It's nice to be at a point where we can say, my God we're tough, we've survived, and it's 30 years down the track. We still feel as if we're on this mad, bad, dangerous ride. And it is wonderful.[12]

But the mad, bad ride came to a sudden and unexpected end ('astonish me' at its most dramatic perhaps) when Murphy and Vernon announced their resignation less than a month later (July), citing lack of support from both the government (in the form of funding) and the public and crystallized this in their provocative, but unanswerable, question – 'How can the arts flourish in a society where war and sport take centre stage?' But, far from retiring from the dance scene, Murphy (and Vernon) continue to do what, in their own words, they have always done: 'follow passion, encourage talent, be creatively opportunistic, and continue to believe in Australian artists and their importance globally.'[13]

Murphy now spends his time freelancing, with his most recent work being the creation of *Water* (Shanghai Ballet, 2009), *Firebird* (The Australian Ballet, 2009), choreographing for film director Bruce Beresford's acclaimed movie *Mao's Last Dancer* (2009) and reworking *The Silver Rose* (first created for the Bavarian State Ballet in 2005) for its Australian Ballet premiere in 2010.

Anita Donaldson

Notes

1 Thus, giving rise to the description – at times used somewhat pejoratively – of the SDC style as 'neo-classic'.
2 Quoted from the video documentary *Astonish Me!*
3 As Murphy's words in *Astonish Me!* suggest,Vernon has played a pivotal role in his artistic life:

> When JanetVernon first pointed her immaculate foot on stage, that was like a key opening a door that could not be closed for the next fifty minutes . . . or perhaps forever. In my mind, that door having been opened really has changed me.

4 Murphy took charge of SDC in 1976, named until then as The Dance Company (NSW).
5 It was created for Falco's NewYork company in 1982 but set on SDC in 1984.
6 Paul Mercurio achieved international fame after he starred in Baz Lurhmann's hit movie *Strictly Ballroom*.
7 After leaving SDC, Kim Walker became Artistic Director of The Flying Fruit Fly Circus, Australia's premier youth circus, and was appointed Director of the NAISDA College of Dance in 2007.
8 Stephen Page is Artistic Director of the indigenous Aboriginal company Bangarra Dance Theatre.
9 Founder and Artistic Director of Chunky Move, Gideon Obarzanek has also created work for a range of international companies including Nederlands Dans Theater 1 and 2.
10 The dancers, musicians and the percussion instruments themselves become an interactive sound and movement ensemble.
11 Given the 'tyranny of distance' that is a hallmark of Australian life, the logistics of getting these four companies together in the first instance, and then touring them around the country, was no small achievement. The work was 'vast' in more than name alone.
12 www.smh.com.au/news/arts/graeme-murphys-dangerous-liason
13 www.graememurphy.com/News.html

Biographical details

Born in Melbourne, Australia, 2 November 1950. **Studied** with Kenneth Gillespie in Launceston, Tasmania, from 1961; and at the Australian Ballet School 1966–68. **Career**: Joined Australian Ballet as dancer, 1969, touring the United States in 1970; first choreography in 1971; spent six months with the Sadler's Wells Theatre Ballet in London and on tour, 1972; danced with the Grenoble-based Ballets Félix Blaska, touring Europe, 1972–74; returned to Australia via Southeast Asian tour with Ballet Caravan, 1974–75; freelance choreographer in Australia, working for Tasmanian Ballet, Queensland Ballet and Australian Ballet School; rejoined Australian Ballet, as dancer and resident choreographer, 1976, and toured the United States and the United Kingdom; Artistic Director and Chief Choreographer, Sydney Dance Company (Dance Company New South Wales until 1979) 1976–2007. Has choreographed for the Nederlands Dans Theater, the Australian Ballet Theatre, the Australian Opera Theatre, West Australian Ballet, Opera Australian, Mikhail Baryshnikov's

White Oak Dance Project, Shanghai Ballet and the ice dancers Torvill and Dean; has also directed opera productions. **Awards and honours** include *Canberra Times Dance Competition Award*, 1976; Order of Australia medal, 1982; named Australian of the Year, 1987; Sydney Opera House Honours for Services to Dance, 1993; *The Age* Performing Arts Award, 1995; Dancers Hall of Fame, 1997; Helpmann Award for Best Choreography, 2000; Australian Dance Awards Best Choreography, 2001; James Cassius Award for Lifetime Achievement, 2002; Australian Government Centenary Medal, 2003; Australian Dance Awards Best Achievement in Choreography, 2003; Cultural Leader of the Year: Dame Elisabeth Murdoch Cultural Leadership Award, 2004; Australian Dance Awards Best Achievement in Choreography, 2005; Australian Dance Awards Lifetime Achievement Award, 2006; Gold Camera Award, 2007; Award for Contribution to Cultural Exchange by the Ministry of Culture, People's Republic of China, 2008; Green Room Award, 2009.

Works*

Ecco (1971); *Off* (1974); *Sequenza V11* (1975); *Three Conversations* (includes *Third Conversation*, 1975); *Glimpses* (1976); *Up* (1976); *Papillion* (1975); *Pandora's box* (1975); *Volumina* (1977); *Tip* (1977); *Fire Earth Air Water* (1977); *Poppy* (1978); *Tekton* (1978); *Rumours I* (1978); *Shéhérazade* (1979); *Rumours II and III* (1979); *Signatures* (1979); *Scintillation* (1977); *Viridian* (1980); *Beyond Twelve* (1980); *Daphnis and Chloë* (1980); *An Evening* (1981); *Hate* (1982); *Homelands* (1982); *Wilderness* (1982); *Limited Edition* (1982); *The Selfish Giant* (1983); *Some Rooms* (1983); *Flash Backs* (1983); *Meander* (1984); *Old Friends, New Friends* (1984); *After Venice* (1984); *Deadly Sins* (1984); *Death in Venice* (opera, 1984); *Song of India* (ice dance, 1984); *Boxes* (1985); *Sirens* (1986); *Nearly Beloved* (1986); *Shimmering* (1985); *Metamorphosis* (opera, 1985); *Shining* (1986); *Fire and Ice* (ice dances, 1986); *Late Afternoon of a Faun* (1987); *Afterworlds* (1987); *An Evening Part 111* (1987); *Song of the Night* (1987); *Gallery* (1987); Torvill and Dean world tour (1987); *VAST* (1988); *Kraanerg* (1988); *Soft Bruising* (1990); *In the Company of Women* (with Paul Mercurio, 1991); *King Roger* (1990); *Bard Bits* (1991); *Nutcracker – The Story of Clara* (1992); *Piano Sonata* (1992); *Synergy with Synergy* (1992); *Salomé* (opera, 1993); *Beauty and the Beast* (1993); *The Protecting Veil* (1993); *Sensing* (for television, 1994); *Les Troyens* (opera, 1994); *Fornicon* (1995); *Berlin* (1995); *Embodied* (1996); *Free Radicals* (1996); *Salome* (1998); *Party* (1998); *Samson et Dalila* (opera, 1998); *Air and Other Invisible Forces* (1999); *urtdot* (1999); *Body of Work* (2000); *Mythologia* (2000); *Ellipse* (2002); *Tivoli* (2001); *Swan Lake* (2002); *Shades of Gray* (2004); *Hua Mulan* (2005); *Grand* (2005); *The Silver Rose* (2005); *The Director's Cut* (2006); *Ever After Ever* (2007); *Water* (2009); *Aïda* (opera, 2008); *Ainadamar* (opera, 2008); *Firebird* (2009); *Mao's Last Dancer* (film, dir. Bruce Beresford, 2009); *The Silver Rose* (new version, 2010).

*Published sources sometimes differ; all dates listed here have been verified by the Graeme Murphy company.

Further reading

Interviews with Hazel Berg in 'Growing in Australian Soil', ed. Michelle Potter, *Brolga: An Australian Journal about Dance*, December 1994; with Karen Van Ulzen in 'Murphy's Word', *Dance Australia*, April/May 2000.

Articles: Peter Rosenwald, 'The Other Australian Company', *Dance News*, December 1977; John Cargher, 'The Spice of Life: The Sydney Dance Company', *Ballet News*, May 1981; Jill Sykes, 'The Sydney Dance Company', *Dance Magazine*, May 1981; Jill Sykes, 'Vigour and Variety', *Dance and Dancers*, June 1982; John Byrne, 'Hurried Creation', *Dance Australia*, September/November 1984; Patricia Laughlin, 'A Murphy Showcase', *Dance Australia*, December/January 1987/88; Andrea Borsay, 'Graeme Murphy: *Kraanerg* and the Rest', *Dance Australia*, December/January 1988/89; Andrea Borsay, 'Ideas Without Words', *Dance Australia*, February/March 1990; Karen Van Ulzen, 'Murphy's Back on Deck', *Dance Australia*, April/May 1990; Andrea Borsay, 'Another Murphy Success', *Dance Australia*, June/July 1990; Karen Van Ulzen, 'Tasteless and Silly', *Dance Australia*, October/November 1990; Karen Van Ulzen, 'The Past Revisited', *Dance Australia*, June/July 1991; Karen Van Ulzen, 'A Return to Integrity', *Dance Australia*, August/September 1991; Patricia Laughlin, 'Reviews International: Sydney Dance Company', *Dance Magazine*, May 1994; Kathryn Sorely Walker, 'The Australian Ballet', *Dancing Times*, August 1995; Michelle Potter, 'Reviews: Powerful Theatre', *Dance Australia*, February/March 1996; Leland Windreich, 'Melbourne', *Ballet Review*, Spring 1996; Karen Van Ulzen, 'Dance Greats: The Choreographer: The Making of Murphy', *Dance Australia*, April/May 1996; Karen Van Ulzen, 'Is the Crisis Over?', *Dance Australia*, October/November 1997; Roslyn Sulcas, 'Reviews: New York City', *Dance Magazine*, March 1998; Nicholas Rowe, 'Sydney Dance Company, *Dance Europe*, December/January 2000; Michelle Potter, 'Reviews: Air and Other Invisible Sources', *Dance Australia*, December/January 2000; Patricia Laughlin, 'Reviews: the Australian Ballet', *Dance Australia*, April/May 2000; Patricia Laughlin, 'Dance Down Under', *Dance International*, Fall 2000; Lee Christofis, 'Odette's Evolving Nightmare', *Brolga*, June 2003; Graeme Murphy, 'Side-Stepping the World', *Dance Australia*, April/May 2004; Jack Anderson, 'The Sydney Ellipse', *Dancing Times*, May 2004; Hilary Crampton, 'Grand', *The Age*, 11 July 2005; Jill Sykes, 'Graeme Murphy and the SDC', *Brolga*, June 2007.

Books: Michelle Potter, *A Passion for Dance*, Canberra, 1997; Anonymous, *Sydney Dance Company: Graeme Murphy's Body of Work – A Retrospective*, playbill, 2000.

OHAD NAHARIN

Ohad Naharin has brought contemporary spirit and high artistic standards to the dance world in Israel since 1990, when he was appointed artistic director of the Israeli Batsheva Dance Company. His professional career was launched at the age of 22, when he joined Batsheva in 1974 as an apprentice. In that same year, Martha Graham, who founded Batsheva with the Baroness Batsheva de Rothschild (in 1964) and served as its first artistic advisor (1963–75), came to Tel Aviv to create *Jacob's Dream* (1974) for them. Graham noticed the talented young dancer and created the character of Esau for him in this biblically themed dance.

At the invitation of Graham, Naharin went to New York to join her company as well as to study. A year later, he left for the School of American Ballet, and in 1977 he moved to the Juilliard School and he also studied with Maggie Black and David Howard. The following year, he joined the Béjart Ballet of the 20th Century in Brussels as a dancer for a year. Although he has learned from all these experiences, Naharin says that artistically he was influenced by Merce Cunningham, William Forsythe and Pina Bausch. Naharin's emphasis on movement points to the work of the first two choreographers, since the subject matter of their dances is the dance. The theatricality, the physically and emotionally aggressive and charged episodes, all link his work with Bausch's.

The core of Naharin's distinctive dance language is the human body and the physical experience, conveyed by rough and sensual movement that arouses primordial and animal-like sensations. His movement language is characterized by a supple spine and limbs along with broad and deep movement. Another prominent and recurring element is the use of instantaneous changes from rapid movement to stillness, which allows time for minuscule details, impulses that originate from deep within the torso, to emerge. It is a different virtuosity with a sense of distortion. At the same time, the movement in his dances is succinct, and like poetry the tension is related both to pain and pleasure.

Despite his late professional start, Naharin has become a widely known choreographer, one who has revolutionized the international dance scene. In 1980, he started to create dances for his New York-based Ohad Naharin Dance Company, and toured the United States as a dancer with the company. At the same time, he started to create dances for various dance companies as a freelance choreographer, and he has been producing almost one dance a year for Batsheva. In 1987, Jiří Kylián, then artistic director of Nederlands Dans Theater (NDT), was impressed by Naharin's innovative creativity and invited him to create for the company. Since then, Naharin has created works for many other companies around the world.

In Naharin's first works for Batsheva, his preference for harsh, rock music culture, risky movement and pushing the limits, while yet inspiring devotion from his dancers, was already clear. Naharin's innovative style brought the company again to the forefront of new dance internationally. For example, *Kyr* (1990; meaning 'wall' in Hebrew) and *Anaphasa* (1993), a performance made for the opening ceremony of the Israeli Festival, drew the attention of a wide audience beyond the limited framework of dance lovers.

In *Kyr* (1990), Naharin drew on local and personal material to make references to the army, the family and the Israeli pioneering spirit, while using an energetic and non-polished movement language. Live music on stage by the Tractor's Revenge, an Israeli rock group, added to the dance's intensity and was considered innovative and bold. In this work, Naharin used a traditional, conventional and worn-out format, and presented it in a new context. The text, 'Echad Mi Yodea' (Who Knows One?), a traditional Passover song, was performed by dancers seated on chairs in a half-circle, performing cumulative movements of a ritual nature, yet with individual personal characteristics. At the end of each cycle, the last one in the row fell down and then revived when the song resumed. This dance constituted a breakthrough: the dancers, in outbursts of movement and voice from a confined framework, showed neither the ability nor the wish to break free. They did not present a story or an overall theme, but through powerful gesture and movement managed to convey the pain, pleasure and consolation of the individual.

In 1998, a performance of *Kyr* turned into the 'Gatkes incident' ('Gatkes' is Yiddish slang for long winter underwear). Batsheva was supposed to perform *Anaphasa* (1993), which included part of *Kyr*, at a festive performance for Israel's 50th anniversary of Independence Day. However, the process of undressing down to underwear and throwing clothes to the centre of the stage, in the context of a traditional religious text being performed aloud, provoked a political storm. Pressure was put on Naharin by the prime minister's office and by the president as well to have the dancers wear an alternative outfit – 'Gatkes'. However, Naharin and his dancers insisted on their right to remain true to the piece and refused to perform. Later on, this incident turned into a symbol of Naharin's artistic independence and integrity.

Tension – created by integrating tenderness with savagery, vulnerability with bursts of violence, for example – is a prominent theatrical motif in Naharin's dance style. Such contrasts enable a sense of division, an awareness of the gulf between extremes, to operate on the spectator. In *Z/na* (1995), Naharin interjects brief moments of sensual lovemaking between sharp and wild movement sections. In *Naharin's Virus* (2001), based on Peter Handke's play *Offending the Audience* (1966), no attempt is made to seduce the audience with the theatrical glamour and movement virtuosity that he creates within the void of negating theatrical conventions. He presents human and vulnerable dancers who make the spectators respond to the artistic sincerity of his piece. In *Three* (2005), a trilogy engaging in the issues of body and passion,

Naharin juxtaposes dance sections in which the dancers move skilfully, with restrained strength, with sections in which dancers immediately afterwards perform movements suggestive of passion, exaggeration, outbursts of force and momentary pleasure. In this, the expressive movement of the subjective body, exposed and vulnerable, confronts the 'coolness' of the dance structure.

Another extreme gap is created when Naharin juxtaposes the movement of single individuals with that of homogeneous groups. In *Mabul* (1992), for example, this theme is clear. The dance makes reference to the sin and punishment of the biblical story (*Mabul* is the Hebrew word for 'flood'). An individual's pain and madness bursts out against a restrained Baroque style – in movement, singing and costumes – represented by the group. A heart-rending cry from a trembling female dancer's body is immediately absorbed into the group's movement, and a short solo expressing pain and dread in movement is assimilated into the theatrical whole. In addition, in this dance one can see the beginning of Naharin's estrangement from direct engagement in the Israeli reality, a characteristic that appears later in his other works. In *Naharin's Virus* (2001), Naharin sets up what are apparently autobiographical and revealing words spoken by the dancers from within the group's restrained movement; this radical juxtaposition shakes the audience, engulfed in the auditorium darkness.

Another subject Naharin engages in is the experience of spectating. In *Naharin's Virus*, he undermines the feeling of distance and non-involvement in the occurrences on stage when a hidden dancer, in a monotonous voice (Handke's text), hurls a flow of insults at the audience, and the dancers emphasize the feeling of strain through an abundance of movements. In *Zachacha* (1998), Naharin challenges the subject by means of humour. Several audience members are enticed on stage for what turns out to be an amusing sequence. One couple (a dancer and a spectator) dance intimately, unaware that they are left alone on stage. When the dancer drops onto the floor, the stunned spectator becomes the subject of the audience's laughter. *Mamootot* (2003; the title refers to the pre-historic mammoth) is a landmark in Naharin's work, since in it he breaks radically the physical and psychological distance between the audience and the performers. In the dance, created after the death of his wife Mari Kajiwara, Naharin invites the spectators to experience intimacy with the Batsheva dancers in an unexpected way – from within the dance. The audience, surrounding the performance space on all sides, turn into an integral part of the performance. The traditional social alienation between the spectators and the performers breaks when the latter relate to the spectators during the dance, seat themselves next to them and at the end of the performance even shake their hands. By doing this, Naharin not only demands total involvement from spectators as performers but also rejects the act of voyeurism that is part of the viewing experience.

While working with Batsheva, Naharin has developed artistic associations with prominent Israeli designers, including lighting designer Avi Yonah Boeno (Bambi) and costume designer Rakefet Levy. Naharin often collaborates in the musical compositions for his work (he was musically trained before he started to dance), using widely divergent musical sources, from Arvo Pärt and John Zorn to Johann Strauss. Many of his works include live accompaniment performed on stage with such musicians as The Tractor's Revenge, Avi Belleli and Dan Makov or Ivry Lider.

Naharin collaborated with Dutch musicians Peter Zegveld and Thijs van der Poll on *Sabotage Baby* (1997), which is an extended version of *Diapason* (1997); in both pieces, Zegveld and Poll play on 19 music machines, which they have created from parts of various musical instruments and which look like big toys. In the newer work, the movement and the music receive equal dramatic weight. Naharin creates a world of illusion and fantasy: Zegveld and Poll play on the music machines; there is a dance on crutches; dancers wear spectacular costumes, and animation films designed by Zegveld are screened. Naharin is also involved with the music of some of his dances, such as *In Common* (1981), *Kyr* (1990), *Mabul* (1992), *Opening Ceremony* (1993) and *Anaphasa* (1993), writing a part of it himself. In *Max* (2007), Naharin not only composed the music, using Maxim Warrat as his pseudonym, but also his chanting in gibberish fuelled the repetition and accumulation of the movement phrases.

The most recent significant project Naharin has embarked on is something he terms Gaga (the name comes from baby gibberish), a training method he developed during his ongoing work with Batsheva's dancers. Because he selects dancers not according to conventional or uniform physical beauty but for their personal uniqueness, this improvisation-based method enables him to foster, enhance and present their captivating qualities, which stir audiences worldwide. The learning of Gaga, which serves today as the official training of Batsheva, relies, in general, on exercises in which the teacher gives instructions based on images and tasks, guiding the student to choose the movements he/she will perform.

It allows significant discoveries and breaks conventional boundaries between the dancers and the creator. Gaga, according to Naharin, enhances the alertness of the senses and the use of imagination. Contrary to conventional dancing lessons, which emphasize development of muscular memory by means of daily repetitions of given movements, Gaga releases the individual from physical fixations. In addition, this language enables the sensation of pleasure to be related to physical effort, not only for dancers but also for any person wishing to improve his physicality.

Currently, Naharin creates mostly for Batsheva since the intensive work, the familiarity with his unique movement language and the dialogue with the dancers is a highly significant element in the process of making dances.

Henia Rottenberg

Biographical details

Born in Kibbutz Mizra, Israel, 22 June 1952. **Studied** at the Graham school and the School of American Ballet, 1975, and at the Juilliard School, New York, 1976. **Career**: Danced with the Martha Graham Dance Company for a season; danced with Béjart's Ballet of the 20th Century in Brussels, 1978; worked with Bat-Dor (Israel) briefly, and then choreographed for his own small troupe in New York, Ohad Naharin Dance Company, 1980–90; also worked as a freelance choreographer in Israel and abroad; choreographer for Nederlands Dans Theater, 1987; Artistic Director of the Batsheva Dance Company, 1990–2003 and House Choreographer from 2005; also founded the Batsheva Ensemble, 1991. Has choreographed for Frankfurt Ballet, Opéra National de Paris, Grand Théâtre de Genève, Sydney Dance Company, Lyon Opera Ballet, Les Grand Ballets Canadiens, Rambert Dance Company, Compañia Nacional de Danza, Cullberg Ballet, Finnish National Ballet, Ballet Gulbenkian, Balet da Cidade de Saõ Paulo, Bavarian State Ballet, Pittsburgh Ballet Theatre and Hubbard Street Dance Chicago. **Awards and honours** include Chevalier dans l'Ordre des Arts et des Lettres (France), 1998; Ministry of Education and Culture Award (Israel), 2001; New York Dance and Performance Award ('Bessie'), 2002 and 2004; honorary member of the Sam Spiegel Film and Television (Jerusalem), 2003; honorary doctorate, Weizmann Institute of Science, 2004; Israel Prize for Dance, 2005; honorary doctorate, Hebrew University of Jerusalem, 2008; Samuel H. Scripps American Dance Festival Award for lifetime achievement in dance, 2009; Art, Science and Culture Prize (Israel), 2009 and *Dance Magazine* Award, 2009.

Works*

Haru No Umi (1980); *Pas de Pepsi* (1981); *Interim* (1981); *In Common* (1981); *Inostress* (1983); *Black Milk* (1985); *Sixty a Minute* (1985); *Tabula Rasa* (1986); *Chameleon Dances* (1987); *Queens of Golub* (1989); *Passomezzo* (1989); *Sinking of the Titanic* (1989); *Arbos* (1989); *King of Wara* (1989); *Kyr* (1990); *Axioma 7* (1991);

Mabul (1992); Off White (1992); *Perpetuum* (1992); *Opening Ceremony* (1993); *Anaphasa* (1993); *Dancing Party* (1994); *Kaamos* (1994; revived 2009); *Z/Na* (1995); *Yag* (1996); *Two Short Stories* (1997); Diapason (1997); *Sabotage Baby* (1997); *Zach-acha* (1998); *Quotations 1–9* (1999); *Moshe* (1999); *Minus 16* (1999); *Deca Dance* (2000), *Naharin's Virus* (2001); *Plasticine* (2001); *Mamootot* (2003); *Camooyot* (based on *Mamootot* and *Moshe*, 2003); *Playback* (2004); *Three* (2005); *Telophaza* (2006); *George and Zalman* (2006); *Furo* (2006); *Max* (2007); *Order* (2007); *B/olero* (2008); *Hora* (2009).

*Published sources vary; works and dates cited here were provided by the Batsheva Dance Company.

Further reading

Interviews with Gaby Aldor in 'Ohad Naharin talks to Gaby Aldor', *Israel Dance*, October 1994; with Emma Manning, *Dance Australia*, February/March 1996; with Norbert Servos, 'A Place of Storms which Speaks of Calm', *Bullett International*, October 1996; with Wendy Peron, 'Truth in Movement', *Dance Magazine*, October 2006.

Articles: Nadine Meisner, 'NDT3: Dance Theater, Den Hag', *Dance and Dancers*, January 1993; Giora Manor, 'A Kibbutz Childhood', *Ballet International*, April 1994; Giora Manor, 'Batsheva the Flagship of Modern Dance in Israel', *Israel Dance*, October 1994; Alexandra Tomalomis, 'Batsheva Dance', *Dance Magazine*, June 1998; Gaby Aldor, '"Invisible Unless in Final Pain": About Ohad Naharin', *Dance Today*, March 2001; Gaby Aldor, 'Virus', *Dance Today*, June 2001 (in Hebrew); Tobi Tobias, 'Heir Craft', *New York Magazine*, 27 May 2002; Gaby Aldor, 'The Borders of Contemporary Israeli Dance', *Dance Research Journal*, Summer 2003; Deborah Jowitt, 'Life Squad', *The Village Voice*, 22 November 2005; Henia Rottenberg, 'The Present Body and the Body's Presence: *Three* By Ohad Naharin', *Dance Today*, December 2005 (in Hebrew); Deborah Jowitt, 'Divide and Re-form', *The Village Voice*, 18 July 2006; Joan Acocella, 'World Stage', *The New Yorker*, 21 August 2006; Deborah Jowitt, 'Violent Repetition', *The Village Voice*, 12 June 2007; Gia Kourlas, 'Conjuring up a World Where Images Abound', *The New York Times*, 5 March 2009; Deborah Jowitt, 'Ohad Naharin Brings the Gaga to BAM in *Max*', *The Village Voice*, 11 March 2009.

LLOYD NEWSON

As a choreographer who has made a dramatic impact on the contemporary dance scene in Britain and Europe by challenging it and defining a new language, Lloyd Newson, with his company DV8 Physical Theatre, has pushed dance-theatre into areas previously unexplored by dance. He has also been influential in the rise of issue-based work across the arts. Having originally trained and practised as a psychologist in Melbourne before becoming a dancer, Newson has created works like a psychologist's playground, exposing human emotions and feelings, and investigating questions of sex, identity and relationships. Together with his insight into human behaviour, Newson's skill at evoking images, structuring movement and creating theatre makes for gripping, disturbing and thought-provoking performances. The raw 'in-your-face' portrayal of extreme human behaviour, particularly among homosexual men, is intended to question assumptions that society makes and to communicate with, rather than to shock, audiences, while the honesty and vulnerability with which the dancers perform reveals a deep self-questioning on the part of both themselves and Newson.

Newson began his career dancing with the New Zealand Ballet. After spending one year at London Contemporary Dance School on a scholarship, he went on to work with the repertory company Extemporary Dance Theatre, as both a dancer and choreographer, from 1981. His frustration with the general direction of contemporary dance and the lack of meaning for the sake of technique prompted him in 1986 to form his own company, DV8 (which refers to the 'deviant' homosexual identity Newson declares in his work), along with the independent dancers Nigel Charnock, Michelle Richecoeur and Liz Rankin. Newson's first hit was *My Sex, Our Dance* (1986), a charged duet for himself and Charnock in which the physical risks evoked the emotional risks of two men in love, struggling with their sexuality, and with masculinity and the restrictions it imposes. Newson's choice to call his performance style 'physical theatre' indicated a departure from the accepted contemporary dance styles in that it did not rely on a traditional dance vocabulary, but demanded athletic physicality and stamina from his dancers, as well as the ability to improvise. The use of weight exchange, lifts and holds in Newson's work is rooted in contact improvisation but is usually performed with a faster, more violent dynamic, and is mixed with pedestrian movement and body language, while the repetitions and heightened stylization can be traced back through to Pina Bausch's expressionistic dance theatre. Hurling the body onto another at speed, climbing up a body, falling or being thrown, often repeated until a state of real exhaustion and desperation is reached to evoke the nihilistic aspect of relationships in an unsympathetic society, recall the movement and themes often apparent in a Bausch performance. Another similarity with Bausch is the importance of the individuality of each performer and the way that this is projected onto the audience.

Newson works closely and collaboratively with his performers, sharing the artistic process, channelling ideas and improvising to uncover material that is always drawn from the performers' characters or their personal experiences. Each performance is so physically and mentally demanding for the dancers, who have to maintain authenticity and honesty throughout, that the works only have a limited performance life. Newson does not believe in churning things out on demand, stating, 'I only create when I have something to say ...The work is always about issues; things that concern or affect my life at this given time' (*Dance Now*, Summer 1993), and dancers are chosen according to their appropriateness to the given subject matter for each new project.

From the stark, non-narrative, almost workshop-like qualities of the earlier works – such as *My Sex, Our Dance* and *Deep End* (1987), a gruelling quartet which explored female–male partnerships, and *My Body, Your Body* (1987), which exposed traps and rituals in such relationships with its cast of eight men and eight women playing out sexual stereotypes in tortured movements – Newson's subsequent work has incorporated the raw energy and themes while layering them with more theatrical devices, such as text, sets, sound scores and even linear narratives, as in *Strange Fish* (1992). In *Dead Dreams of Monochrome Men* (1988), based on the life of the London serial killer Dennis Nilsen, traces of a 'pick-up' nightclub environment and a flat where the killer took his victims were suggested by minimal set designs; and action poses, surreal images and body language carried a deeper probing of homoeroticism with its dark, sadomasochistic message powerfully evoked by the four male performers. *Never Again* (1989), which was filmed in a derelict warehouse, developed the nightmarish surrealism hinted at in *Dead Dreams*, showing a room filled with naked bodies hanging upside down and a public lavatory in which frozen poses of bizarre people standing in the cubicles included two ballet dancers wearing tutus. Shots of the performers running down endless corridors and entering dark empty rooms suggested the psychological fear of not belonging anywhere and of being ostracized by society.

Strange Fish marked another departure, as it merged dance with a more sophisticated use of theatre and conceptual art. Newson also here avoided exploiting physical risk as he had done so much in previous work and instead focused more on subtleties and teasing out not only the pain of not belonging or of being alone but also the humour of people playing the fool to attract attention. Elaborate images of religion were offered, including a dominating crucifix, with a naked female Christ, and a singer who sang in Latin and was part of the cast. A subterranean water tank suggested the subconscious or death, while a cascade of rocks evoked chaos and confusion. *MSM* (1993) was a piece of text-based theatre for seven actor-dancers based on 'cottaging', the activity of men picking up other men for sex in public lavatories. The text was extracted from interviews with 50 homosexual and bisexual men, and was accompanied by a sound score by Jocelyn Pooks (with whom Newson has collaborated on several works) and by a revolving set of washbasins, cubicles and stalls. Receiving rave reviews from theatre critics, it expanded Newson's reputation as a choreographer into that of a theatre director.

Enter Achilles (1995) took straight male bonding as its theme and was a physical manifestation of the 'new lad' imagery that was being promoted in the media at the time. This work was both nationally and internationally an enormous success and was made into a film. It was a striking piece of popular culture, which exposed the crisis of masculinity through movement, sound and design. *Bound to Please* (1997) also focused on popular media themes and was partly inspired by Elizabeth Wurtsel's pop psychology book, *Prozac Nation*. Newson was interested in how our Western consumer culture rejects bodies that are not economically or sociably viable, such as the old, the fat and the disabled. Newson's point – that the dance world is particularly to blame for this – was conveyed through a send-up of the dance profession. *Bound to Please* was full of technical dance steps, a parody of how beauty-obsessed dancers behave. 'Beautiful' dance images were constantly juxtaposed with seamier events – the realities, according to Newson, of a dysfunctional society. The climax of this work was a steamy naked duet between an elderly woman and a young man, which boldly questioned society's attitude to the older woman, especially in a sexual context. With this work, Newson had tackled yet another taboo.

Indeed, Newson's works have been more preoccupied with exploring the truths and falsehoods about how we as individuals 'manage' to live, love and work in an aggressively competitive Western society. *The Happiest Day of my Life* (1999) explored themes of rejection and failure within a highly pressurized society, where relationships seemed doomed before they had even begun. With an elaborate set that converted the stage into a huge swimming pool, into which the desperate characters plunged as if to drown their sorrows, Newson's fascination with water as metaphor for the subconscious was made more boldly than ever.

The productions of DV8 this century have built on themes of image, success, failure and low self-esteem. Newson has questioned the lengths we go to in our pursuit of perfection, as well as a media-imposed value system that privileges the superficial and trivial above all else. While tackling a different set of psychological issues that have arisen in our 'celebrity' culture, Newson has also forged more ambitious collaborations with set designers and musicians, and with the backing of international co-producers who have been attracted to DV8's spiralling fame the productions have become much bigger. In order to maintain the rigorous artistic integrity and quality for each new project, Newson takes the necessary time, sometimes a couple of years, to research and develop as well as to find the necessary funding for this much larger scale of production.

Can we afford this/the Cost of Living, which was commissioned by the Sydney Olympics Arts Festivals 2000, had a huge cast of multi-talented performers who showed off their impressive skills but at the end, as described by Judith Mackrell (*The Guardian*, 21 September 2000), finished by standing in a line and 'offer[ing] up their eccentricities and pain, like victims of some gruesomely inverted beauty competition'. Newson has used the theatrical device of line-up confessional in recent productions, which turns faultless performers 'inside out' to reveal scarred and tormented souls; the work of Pina Bausch springs to mind once again.

In the unprecedented event of a choreographer being asked to make a work for the Tate Modern, *Living Costs*, a site-specific performance piece, was made in 2003 as part of the Tate and Egg Live series. This was initially a daunting prospect and Newson described it in terms of having to conquer an animal. Featuring clowns, showgirls, trapeze and hoop artists, an obese man, an octogenarian, and actors as well as dancers, Newson used all the levels of the massive gallery. The audience were taken on a guided tour by former DV8 performer, Wendy Houstoun, to witness the 'exhibits' on each floor. Covering the terrain from freakish acts to commercially viable entertainment, to the elite 'purity' of contemporary dance and ballet, Newson seem to be questioning the elitism not only within the art world but also, more importantly, within our culture.

A multi-award winning film was also adapted from the show and dealt with similar themes. It was produced by DV8 Films for Channel Four Television and while it continued DV8's long relationship with film, it also marked Newson's début as a film director.

Newson's obsession with image and illusion was behind his next work, *Just for Show* (2005), where in the words of one of the performers, 'faking it was all about making it'. For this work, Newson gathered together a cast of 'beautiful' people, most of whom looked like models and were virtuosic in dance, yoga and whatever movement form they were required to perform. They were equally accomplished delivering the witty, sharp verbal exchanges and monologues of the narrative, highlighting the fact that Newson looks for performers who are highly eclectic as well as being unique individuals and outstanding performers. As DV8 is project based, Newson, while usually keeping a core from previous works, employs new performers for each production and usually holds auditions internationally.

Newson also delved into the world of new technologies in *Just for Show* as he used virtual projection and film to interrogate how 'illusion' plays such an important part in our dreary monotonous lives. The projection turned the stage into a field of pink roses swaying gently in the summer's breeze, which covered up the dull, stark bedsits of reality. Once again, the physically perfect performers, who seemed on the surface to have it all, hung up their dirty washing at the end of the show: the man with AIDS, the slightly fat dancer, the anorexic, the fake, the woman addicted to abusive relationships.

In 2009, Newson returned to the theme of homosexuality in *To Be Straight with You*, but this time in the format of largely text-based, documentary-style theatre. Using dance, text, documentary, animation and film, Newson explored issues relating to the tolerance and intolerance of homosexuality as well as religion, with his multi-ethnic cast of performers. The work drew on hundreds of hours of audio interviews held with people who had been affected by these issues in a variety of countries. Slickly designed with a seamless cycle of fact-based footage bombarding the audience in the form of text, dialogue, movement, photographs and film, the production featured performers who imparted the brutal information efficiently and dispassionately in the manner of news readers, but the overall effect was undisputedly lyrical.

Now, attracting hugely diverse audiences and basking in its reputation as one of the most effective and provocative dance companies in the world, what is the reason for DV8's success? While fabulous performers, great collaborators, supportive funders are all reasons, one of the most important factors must be that Newson is still committed to challenging himself, his performers and his audience – and finally, our preconceptions about dance, and about what dance can and should address.

Josephine Leask

Biographical details

Born in Albury, New South Wales (date not publicly known). **Studied** dance when at college; gained degree in psychology, University of Melbourne (before 1979); attended London Contemporary Dance School (scholarship), 1980–81. **Career**: Dancer with New Zealand Ballet, 1979; came to the United Kingdom, 1980; after LCDS, company member and occasional choreographer, Extemporary Dance Theatre, 1980–85; has also danced with Karole Armitage, Michael Clark, David Gordan, Daniel Larrieu and Dan Waggoner. Freelance music-video choreographer by mid-1980s; co-founder, dancer and principal choreographer, DV8 Physical Theatre, from 1986, with Nigel Charnock, Michelle Richecoeur and Liz Rankin; DV8 Films founded in 1991. Has also choreographed for opera and directed for film. **Awards and honours** include *Manchester Evening News* Theatre Award, 1987; Digital Dance Awards, 1987, 1988, 1990; London Dance and Performance Awards for Choreography, 1988, 1990, 1991; *Time Out* Award, 1989; *Evening Standard* Ballet Award, 1989; IMZ Dance Screen Awards, 1990, 1993, 1996, 2005; Golden Pegasus Award (Australia), 1990; Prudential Awards, 1991, 1992; SADAC Award (France), 1992; Festival International du film sur l'art Award, 1992; Grand Prix International Video-Danse (Pierre Cardin Award), 1993; TZ Rose (Germany), 1993; Prix Italia, 1994, 1996; Festival of Dance Visions Award, 1994; International Emmy for Performing Arts, 1997; Montreal Festival for Films on Art, Jury Prize, 1998, 2005; VideoDance (Athens), audience award, 2004; Moving Pictures Festival, NOW Audience Choice Award, 2004; Belgrade International Festival, Jury's Special Prize and Audience Award, 2005; Dance on Camera festival, New York, Jury Prize, 2005; *Time Out* Live Award, outstanding achievement in dance, 2005; Dance Camera West Award, Los Angeles, 2007; Grand Prix de Danse, Paris, 2009.

Works

Breaking Images (1982); *Beauty, Art and the Kitchen Sink* (1984); *Bein' a Part, Lonely Art* (1985); *My Sex, Our Dance* (duet, 1986); *eLeMeN t(h)ree Sex* (1987); *Deep End* (1987); *My Body, Your Body* (1987), *Dead Dreams of Monochrome Men* (1988; film version, dir. David Hinton, 1989); *Never Again* (for television, 1989); *'if only...'* (1990); *Strange Fish* (1992; television version, 1992, dir. David Hinton, revival and rework, 2010/11); *MSM* (1993); *Anodanie* (opera by Mozart, 1993); *Enter Achilles* (1995; television version, dir. Clara van Gool, 1995); *Bound to Please* (1997); *The Happiest Day of my Life* (1999); *Can we afford this/the cost of living* (2000); *Living Costs* (2003); *The Cost of Living* (2003; film version, dir. Lloyd Newson, 2004); *Just for Show* (2005); *To Be Straight with You* (2009).

Further reading

Interviews with Andy Solway, in 'Lloyd Newson Interview', *New Dance*, Autumn 1985; with Nadine Meisner, in 'Strange Fish', *Dance and Dancers*, Summer 1992; with Louise Levene, 'Fish out of Water', *The Independent*, 11 July 1992; with Ellen Cranith, 'Quest for an Unholy Grail', *Sunday Times*, 26 July 1992; in Jo Butterworth and Gill Clarke (eds), *Dancemakers' Portfolio: Conversations with Choreographers*, Bretton Hall, 1998; with Libby Snape, 'Lloyd on Love', *Dance Theatre Journal*, 15(2), 1999; Louise Levene, 'First-person-singular Sensation', *Sunday Telegraph*,

1 May 2005; with Gia Kourlas, in 'Not-so-straight Talk', in *Time Out New York*, 2–7 October 2008.

Articles: Sophie Constanti, 'Spring Loaded: The Opening Shots', *Dancing Times*, March 1988; Sophie Constanti, 'Giving Birth to Dead Dreams', *Dance Theatre Journal*, Spring 1989; Christopher Winter, 'Love and Language, or Only Connect the Prose and the Passion', *Dance Theatre Journal*, Spring 1989; 'DV8 Physical Theatre in Rouen', *Dance Theatre Journal*, Summer 1990; Nadine Meisner, 'You Must Go On', *Dance and Dancers*, October 1990; Sophie Constanti, 'Dance Scene: DV8', *Dancing Times*, October 1990; Allen Robertson, 'Letter from Europe', *Dance Ink*, December 1990; Alex Mallems, 'DV8 Refusing to Compromise', *Parachute* (Montreal), July–September 1993; Lloyd Newson, 'Lloyd Newson on... Dance', *Dance Now*, Summer 1993; Ian Somerville, 'Black and White Dance on Brown Tape', *Dance Now*, Autumn 1994; Josephine Leask, 'The Silence of the Man: An Essay on Lloyd Newson's Physical Theatre', *Ballett International*, August/September 1995; Paul Jackson, 'Becoming Lloyd', *Dance Now*, Autumn 1995; Allen Robertson, 'DV8 x 2', *Dance Now*, Winter 1995; Keith Watson, 'Enter Achilles', *Dance Theatre Journal*, Winter 1995/96; Lloyd Newson, 'Talkback', *Dance Europe*, February/March 1996; Rupert Christiansen, 'Weakness in the Heel', *Dance Theatre Journal*, Summer 1996; Josephine Leask, 'Not the Body Beautiful', *The Independent on Sunday*, 27 July 1997; Beth Cinamon, 'Newson and Bacon', *Dance Now*, Autumn 1997; Stacey Prickett, 'Profile: Lloyd Newson', *Dance Theatre Journal*, 19(1), Winter 2003; David Jays, 'DV8 in Just for the Show', *Dancing Times*, January 2006; Lyn Gardner, 'To Be Straight with You', *The Guardian*, 15 April 2008, Donald Hutera, '"Straight" Talk', *Dance Magazine*, October 2008.

Books: Allen Robertson and Donald Hutera, *The Dance Handbook*, Harlow, Essex, 1988; Stephanie Jordan and Dave Allen (eds), *Parallel Lines: Media Representations of Dance*, London, 1993; Janet Lansdale, *Ancestral and Authorial Voices in Lloyd Newson and DV8's 'Strange Fish'*, Cambridge, 2004; Janet Lansdale, *The Struggle with the Angel: A Poetics of Lloyd Newson's Strange Fish*, London, 2007.

HENRI OGUIKE

2009 was a watershed year for Henri Oguike. He created *Tread Softly*, his first commission for Rambert Dance Company, and celebrated his company's tenth anniversary in retrospective mode with a tour of past works, including *Front Line* (2002), *White Space* (2001), *Falling* (2008) and *Finale* (2003). It also saw him in a contemplative mood, undertaking an extended period of research and development. Taking stock of his career and having time for reflection provided not only a sense of freedom to refresh his choreographic interests but also provoked some challenging thoughts. He says, 'I found myself standing at a cross roads, poised with one foot lifted, undecided as yet where the weight will fall.'

This is both an exciting and a disturbing place to be. It arises out of Oguike's need to 'keep the boundaries flexible enough, to open myself further'.[1]

Oguike is considered unusual in the United Kingdom for his ongoing exploration of the relationship between music and dance. Not many choreographers of his generation share this interest. Critics who review his work value traditional outcomes, in that they prefer choreography that integrates with the music. Oguike certainly does this at times. For example, in *Tread Softly* (2009) a syncopated, flat-footed, percussive gallop focuses sharpened attention onto the accompanying rhythms of Schubert's *Death and the Maiden*. But, the cacophonous force of this movement also provides a striking contrast with the composer's melancholy strains. Oguike's approach tends not to be a conventional one, as this example indicates.

Oguike does not treat music as an unproblematic familiar partner, expected only to provide an underpinning structure for the dance or to suggest an overt theme that explains the movement in some way. He is clear that 'music provides a foundation for asking questions, to frame something else which lies out there waiting to be discovered'. This 'something else' is usually intangible, redolent with emotion and always thought provoking. Music is a stimulus and not merely accompaniment.

From taiko drums to Scarlatti, Bartók to Piazolla, Oguike's choice of music is unusually wide-ranging. At one level, like his early mentor Richard Alston in whose dance company he performed, he mines the accompaniment to provide structural and thematic emphasis. Commonly referred to in the media as Oguike's signature work, *Front Line* (2002) falls into three clear sections based on three movements from Shostakovich's Ninth String Quartet. Oguike draws on the music's irregular phrasing and emotionally charged mood to create a tense atmosphere in the dance. It evokes the turbulence of the Stalinist era in Russia, the period through which Shostakovich lived; the psychological horrors born of political oppression; and the need for human warmth and trust. But, straightforward music visualization is avoided: dance and accompaniment are not mirror images. To the brief intervals of silence *between* the pizzicato notes of Shostakovich's fourth movement, a male dancer propels gestures that seek urgent, abrupt, sound-producing contact against his partner's body. Sharp dynamic qualities are shared across action and music but without correspondence in timing. The duet resonates with the desperation of alienation.

Although occasionally movement and accompaniment mirror each other closely, as in *Green in Blue* (2007) where a sinuous use of the spine and swivelling hips directly reflect the jazzy syncopations of Iain Bellamy's saxophone score, Oguike often uses rhythm to drive material which runs counter to the style of the music. This is not an approach he shares with Alston. Oguike is able, through this, to produce dramatic images that tread a fine line between abstraction and implied narrative, as examples demonstrate. In *Dido and Aeneas* (2003) a spiky, broken-limbed, insect-like descent to the floor is juxtaposed with Purcell's measured, harmonious tones but somehow finds an unexpected rhythmic echo. Structural contrast is highlighted and the agony of Dido's death is evoked. In *Little Red* (2007), thrown-away, quirky gestures are pitched against Vivaldi's Baroque precision. This suggests the collision of contradictory sets of manners and asserts a modern sexiness in the female dancers. In *All Around* (2008) a pair of dancers bowls across the stage, their bodies closely entangled, to ritualistic Native American chanting. The duet appears supportive, playful or trapped. Disjuncture between the style of movement and the aural environment forces recognition, the body can be read in various ways to elicit a range of possibilities.

Further to this, Oguike sometimes constructs hints of folk dance in his use of footwork. Simple steps, small jumps and percussive rhythmic pattering feet suggest a sense of community. There is no attempt at authenticity or to place the action in a specific location, even when these aspects might be indicated by the style of the accompaniment. In *Finale* (2003) for example, the dancers cascade up and down the stage evoking a carnival mood with their syncopated stepping patterns. Accompanied by René Aubrey's cheerful music and the sunny irides-cent glow of Guy Hoare's lighting, swishing hips and skimming, grounded travelling suggest earthy qualities. The dance phrases are also structured as a complex canon that echoes the music. By this, attention is drawn to individual movement and kaleidoscopic shifts in the group-ings. It is not a mere manifestation of the stabilities of peasant life.

Lighting design is also a feature that Oguike is interested in. A con-tinued collaboration with Hoare began in 2000 when the latter relit some previously created pieces, but their first work together was *Shot Flow* (2001). Hoare devised a lighting plan that did not alter at set points but which could change at every performance in response to the dance. Parts of the bodies were captured in the light, adding to the spatial restriction evoked in the dance.

Shot Flow was unusual for another reason too. It was the first work in which Oguike explored his Points Network System (PNS). An adjunct to Oguike's questioning of music is his pursuit of improvisation as a process for generating movement. He developed PNS as a method for this. It begun life as a notion that points in space might be mapped onto a geometric image, such as a square for example, which could help with designing pattern in the body. By asking his dancers to connect point to point by direct or indirect routes or find movement within or outside of the preconceived shape, Oguike set up a system that allowed collaborative experimentation within a structured approach. *Shot Flow* produced a duet of fragmentary gestures in a spatially compressed area, an aspect further enhanced by Hoare's lighting design. A shifting combative relationship was evoked by the dancers.

PNS provided an abstract system for organising and exploring the spatial aspect of movement, as rhythm provided an abstract way to respond to musical structure. Emotion is an allusive aspect arising from the outcome. During 2009, Oguike reflected on these aspects. He now suggests that time and space 'remain something to be re-identified' and that development of PNS could help to guide the way in which he asks future questions. He expresses the need to move beyond linear processes in the creative act. Rather than singular points in space, he is constructing the system as an imagined network of relationships where oppositions and contradictions can have a place. It will consist of 'a healthy collection of potent components where the points of reference lead you to another unseen, unknown point'. Again, Oguike points to an interest in making discoveries, and the 'something else' referred to earlier might be opened up by new processes of working.

The choreographic characteristics of Henri Oguike might be summarized thus: use of lighting as a collaborative aspect; a rhythmical emphasis in feet and legs; a Cunningham–Alston influenced, complex use of the torso; abstract treatments, based upon questions elicited by the music, with elusive and more directly emotional narrative elements; and a strong interest in the use of the ensemble with canon, unison, contrast and complementing choreographic relationships to the fore, sometimes with a soloist or small group set against the larger group. *Front Line* (2002), his signature work, is a clear illustration of these aspects, as is *Tread Softly* (2009). If PNS develops in the way that he envisages, however, it is likely to have a considerable impact on Oguike's thinking in the future. By late 2009, he was expressing how he felt himself to be at a crossroads. 2010 and beyond may well point to the new direction that Oguike has found.

Lorna Sanders

Note

1   This and subsequent quotations of Henri Oguike are from a personal interview with the author, October 2009.

Biographical details

Born in West Glamorgan, Wales, 26 September 1970. **Studied** at London Contemporary Dance School, 1991–93, becoming a member of '4D', their graduate performance group, in 1994, for whom he made *Doors and Sundials*. **Career**: A founder member of Richard Alston Dance Company, 1994–98; founded the Henri Oguike Dance Company in 1999; artistic director of National Youth Dance Wales, 2004–07. Has also choreographed for Bare Bones Dance Company, Companhia Portuguesa de Bailado Contemporaneo (Lisbon), Phoenix Dance Theatre, Rambert Dance Company and Ballet Black; and has created works for numerous youth dance companies as well, including Intoto Dance, Swindon Youth Dance Company, Transitions, and the National Youth Dance Company. **Awards** include Robin Howard Foundation Awards, 1997 and 1999; Jerwood Award, 1997; *Time Out* Live Award, 2001.

Works

Amongst Shadows (1994); *Spool of Threads* (1994); *The Brutality of Fact* (1998); *Prime Origin* (1998; revised version, 1999); *Ile aye* (1998; revised version, 1999); *A moment of give* (1999); *Seen of Angels* (2000; revised version, 2005); *Play to Win* (2000; co-produced with Yellow Earth Theatre); *Travel Matrix* (2000); *Apollo New Apollo* (2001); *Shot Flow* (2001); *Of Death and Stillness* (2001; revised version, renamed *Front Line*, 2002); *White Space* (2001; revised version, 2004); *Melancholy Thoughts* (2001); *Casual Grace* (2001); *F.P.S. (Frames Per Second*, 2002; revised version, 2003); *Violet* (2002); *In broken tendrils* (2002); *Finale* (2003); *Dido and Aeneas* (2003); *Duet* (2003); *Signal* (2004); *F.P.S (Frames Per Second) Part 2* (2004); *Tiger Dancing* (2005); *Tippett's Concerto for Double String Orchestra* (2005); *Second Signal* (2005); *Expression Lines* (2006); *How I Look* (2006), *Green in Blue* (2007); *Little Red* (2007); *Touching All* (2008); *All Around* (2008); *Falling* (2008; film for Channel 4, dir. *Dan Faberoff*); *Tread Softly* (2009); *Da Gamba* (2010).

For youth dance companies: *Doors and Sundials* (1994); *Pulse* (1996); *Sketches to Portraits* (1996); *Train (Ride to the Abyss*; 1998); *Language* (2000); *La, La, La...* (2001); *Butterfly Grid* (2002); *Broken Strings* (2002); *Brightside* (2002); *Splinter* (2003); *With My Sighs* (2003); *Spatial Signatures* (2004); *Parade* (2004); *Working Lights* (2005); *Small Theatres* (2006); *Quackers* (2006); *Just For Me* (2007); *Ex 1 To ...* (2007); *Start To Fall* (2007); *Finding Red* (2007); *Thought Like Raindrop* (2007); *Fish Tale* (2008).

Further reading

Articles: David Jays, 'Resolution', *Dancing Times*, April 1996; Donald Hutera, 'British Dance Edition', *Dance Now*, Spring 2002; Lorna Sanders, 'Choreographers Today: Henri Oguike', *Dancing Times*, March 2003; Zoë Anderson, 'Phoenix Dance Theatre 04', *Dancing Times*, May 2004; David Jays, 'Henri Oguike Dance Company', *Dancing Times*, June 2004; Mary Clarke, 'Henri Oguike', *Dancing Times*, April 2005; Clement Crisp, 'Henri Oguike at the QEH', *Dancing Times*, May 2007; Ian Palmer, 'Mixed Bill', *Dancing Times*, April 2009; Jonathan Gray, 'Mixed Bill', *Dancing Times*, December 2009.

Book: Lorna Sanders, *Henri Oguike's Front Line: Creative Insights*, Alton, 2004.

STEVE PAXTON

To watch Steve Paxton dance is to witness an insatiable curiosity about the movement potential of the human body. As the lights come up and the music begins, Paxton nonchalantly plunges into a series of skips, spins, twists and tilts, taking his body (and his audience) on an adventure across the last five decades of American contemporary dance. The corporeal is clearly his medium, the raw material that he forms and reforms depends on his particular focus. His recent physical obsession has been the spiralling and unspiralling of the spine and the various ways the arms and legs can complete or disrupt that core movement direction.[1] Although his work may be motivated primarily by an investigation of muscle and bone, Paxton's dancing is never simply a matter of physical actions. For Paxton, the physical is never a simple matter. It is, rather, 'a complexity of social, physical, geometric, glandular, political, intimate and personal information which is not easily renderable.'[2] Despite his protestations to the contrary, Paxton, in fact, has spent a lifetime attempting to render just that.

In a 1993 solo work, Paxton weaves his way back and forth across the performing space to the quick, classically complex beats of *Some English Suites* (J.S. Bach, played by Glenn Gould), pirouetting at one moment and then crawling across the floor at the next. Clearly enjoying himself, he seems to be revelling in the legacy of his long dancing career, which bridges the historical shift from modern to post-modern dance. His early training in the dance styles of Martha Graham and then Merce Cunningham has infused his body with a proud, almost classical deportment that the relaxed pedestrian demeanour he has cultivated since the 1970s cannot completely dislodge. In his dancing, there are breathtaking moments of a crystal-clear motion – such as a spin that turns fiercely, yet elegantly, to stop on a dime – which exude the quiet groundedness of a Zen master. Yet these moments may immediately give way to clowning with a highly exaggerated and slightly awkward drop to the floor, executed with a slight smile that seems to acknowledge the restrictions of his ageing body and, at the same time, to remind the audience not to take him or themselves too seriously.

Although he has been a major catalyst for many of the significant innovations in American dance over the past four decades, Steve Paxton is less well known to the general public than are some of his contemporaries. Rather than building a company to showcase his own choreography, Paxton has chosen to focus his intellectual and physical energies on improvisational dance. Because he is committed to the flexible, open, often anti-hierarchical structure of much contemporary improvisation, Paxton has eluded a more public recognition for the less marketable, but nonetheless influential, work of teaching and performing improvisation. Among contemporary dancers, he is best known as the man who pioneered the earliest form of contact improvisation. Yet his influence spans beyond the genre of contact improvisation to include almost all dancers studying a form of contemporary dance technique.

Arriving as a young dancer in New York City at the end of the 1950s, Paxton quickly became a key figure in the development of postmodern dance. He danced with Merce Cunningham's company and participated in Robert Dunn's legendary composition course, which was taught at the Cunningham studio and included a number of important dancers, choreographers, artists and composers. This class and Paxton's friendships with the likes of Yvonne Rainer and Robert Rauschenberg paved the way for the extraordinary collaborations of the Judson Dance Theater. By all accounts, Paxton played a seminal role in forming the Judson aesthetic.

Judson Dance Theater was formed in 1962, and although it officially lasted only two years, it set the stage for the evolution of American postmodern dance. Throughout all the wacky experimentations with a variety of compositional forms and contents (including storytelling and musical theatre, as well as minimalist assemblage), much of the work that came out of Judson Dance Theater's collaborations with dancers, artists and musicians highlighted the performer's body emphasizing the raw materiality and potent concreteness of that dancing body. This desire to unmask the dancing body as a pedestrian body as well as a culturally determined body plugged the Judson experiments directly into the 1960s' burgeoning ethos of radicalism and freedom.

If we look at several of Paxton's dances from that time, we can see a number of typical Judson stylistic innovations at work. Similar to his peers, Paxton became increasingly interested in working with movement repetition, uninflected dynamics, the use of props and alternative performance sites (including a wood in *Afternoon*, 1963), as well as working with pedestrian and found movement. For instance, *Proxy* (1961) was a dance piece based on a visual score made up of sports photographs and other printed images. Paxton asked the dancers to copy the poses as directly as possible, making their own choices about how to achieve the necessary transitions from one pose to another. *Proxy* also included staged actions culled from everyday living such as eating, drinking and walking.[3]

In her extensive research on Judson Dance Theater, Sally Banes identifies the preoccupation with walking as a significant break from the traditional modern-dance aesthetic. Walking refuted the elitism of dance training and suggested that a dancer could be an ordinary person who was interested in looking at and experiencing some of the simplest kinds of everyday actions as dance movements. Similarly, this belief opened the door for 'average' bodies to participate in the new crop of Judson dances. Paxton was particularly attracted to this new openness to what could constitute dance movement and to who could be identified as a dancer. As Banes comments in her discussion on the development of Paxton's work, walking was crucial:

> It opened up a range of nondance movement, a variety of nonhierarchical structures, a performance presence that could be simultaneously relaxed and authoritative. It became the currency of Paxton's populist stance. Walking is something that everyone does, even dancers when they are not 'on.' Walking is a sympathetic link between performers and spectators, a shared experience that allows for personal idiosyncrasies and individual styles. There is no single correct way of walking.[4]

Paxton made quite a few dances in the late 1960s that incorporated large groups of people walking. *Satisfying Lover* (1967) and *State* (1968) both used 30 or more performers who walked and stood at different intervals according to a predetermined score.[5] Jill Johnston's description of *Satisfying Lover* in her 14 April 1968 *Village Voice* column gives us a good sense of its countercultural priorities:

> The fat, the skinny, the medium, the slouched and slumped, the straight and tall, the bowlegged and knock-kneed, the awkward, the elegant, the coarse, the delicate, the pregnant, the virginal, the you name it, by implication every postural possibility in the postural spectrum, that's you and me in all our ordinary everyday who cares splendor.[6]

It was this sort of egalitarian ideology, combined with a growing curiosity about the possible physics of human bodies, that brought Paxton to the form of duet partnering called contact improvisation.

Contact improvisation began as a communal experiment. During the summer of 1972, Paxton was joined by a group of dancers, mostly students, from Oberlin, Bennington and Rochester – places where he had taught workshops the previous winter and spring. Working and living together in a loft space in New York City, the group spent two weeks investigating different states of dancing, including standing still (and feeling the small adjustments that one's body makes to keep standing – what Paxton calls the 'small dance'), falling, and hurling one's body at another person. The development in that time was the seeds of a dance form based on the exchange of touch, energy, weight and momentum between two (or more) people. Influenced by Asian martial arts, such as Tai Chi and Aikido, as well as the release work being taught by Mary Fulkerson, contact improvisation literally embodied many of the cultural values being championed in the early 1970s.[7]

It is telling that when Paxton and some of the group that worked together that summer later went on an *ad hoc* tour of the West Coast, they entitled their performances *You come, we'll show you what we do*. As it developed under Paxton's guidance, contact improvisation became a relatively unpretentious, democratic dance form. Dance events called 'jams' integrated people from all walks of life and of all different dance abilities. The casual, spontaneous nature of the dancing allowed many people (especially men) who could not (or would not) think of themselves as dancers to participate in this movement form. Contact improvisation also incorporated into its movement training many of the Eastern philosophical principles that Paxton was absorbing at the time. Contact dancers try to cultivate a full yet easy awareness in their minds and a readiness in their bodies to prepare them for the unexpected. This ability to observe and react, rather than to manipulate and direct the dancing, is one of the core principles in contact improvisation.

Although Paxton is considered the founder of contact improvisation and although he still teaches workshops in the form throughout the world, contact improvisation has grown beyond his influence into a complex, multi-dimensional dance genre, complete with its own journal (*Contact Quarterly*) and multinational network. One of the most recent developments in this hybrid genre is the inclusion of dancers with different disabilities. In his work with Anne Kilcoyne at Touchdown Dance in England and his presence at the yearly DanceAbility workshops in Eugene, Oregon, Paxton has played a key role in furthering this work.[8]

Given Paxton's devotion to improvisation, and his belief that dancing should be an experience available to everyone, it is not surprising that he should enjoy the challenges of teaching and dancing with people whose movement styles are determined by physical disabilities.[9] Yet it is important to note that Paxton is not limiting his involvement with this work to that of altruism. The experience of dancing with a blind person or a dancer with cerebral palsy informs his own physicality in myriad ways, becoming a part of the movement material that he relies on for his solo improvisational performances. Knowing about his movement history makes watching Paxton's solo performances especially delightful, as one can pick out the physical movements and theatrical images that seem to point to key moments in his long and multifaceted dancing career.

Ann Cooper Albright

Notes

1 See his recent DVD-ROM 'Material for the Spine' produced by Contredanse, 2008, available from *Contact Quarterly* website.
2 Steve Paxton, 'Drafting Interior Techniques', *Contact Quarterly*, Spring/Winter 1993.
3 Sally Banes, *Terpsichore in Sneakers*, Boston, 1980.
4 Ibid.
5 After the chapter on Steve Paxton in *Terpsichore in Sneakers*, there is a published score of this dance.
6 Reprinted in Jill Johnston, *Marmalade Me*, New York, 1971.
7 For a detailed discussion of the development of contact improvisation see Cynthia Novack, *Sharing the Dance: Contact Improvisation and American Culture*, Madison, WI, and London, 1990.

8 For more information see the 'Dancing with Different Populations' issue of *Contact Quarterly*, Winter 1992.
9 Steve Paxton, '3 Days', printed in *Contact Quarterly*, Winter 1992.

Biographical details

Born in Phoenix, Arizona, United States, 21 January 1939. **Studied** at the American Dance Festival, Connecticut College, New London, 1958–59, and with Merce Cunningham, from 1958; also studied with José Limón, 1959, and composition with Robert Dunn, 1961–62. **Career:** Danced with José Limón Company in 1959; member of the Merce Cunningham Dance Company, 1961–64; also danced with Trisha Brown, Lucinda Childs, Yvonne Rainer, Robert Rauschenberg, Robert Whitman and Simone Forti; founding member of Judson Dance Theater, 1962; founding member of the Grand Union, 1970–76; member of the improvisational ensemble Free Lance Dance, 1977–79; numerous improvisational performances and solos around the world include with Crash Landing (Vienna), with Kathy Duck (Leuven, and Amsterdam), with the Lisbon Group, with Pastforward, and with White Oak Dance Project (world tour). Has also worked extensively in Europe and North America as a teacher of his contact improvisation methods since 1972, particularly in Amsterdam, Bennington College (Vermont, 1973–76), Darlington College of Arts (Devon, England, 1978–1980), and in courses at Oberlin College (Ohio), Rochester (New York), and Eugene (Oregon), as well as at the American Dance Festival (Durham, North Carolina), Touchdown Dance (1987–93), Dance-Ability (Eugene, Oregon; annually) and Diverse Dance (Vachon Island, Seattle; annually). Has also been a contributing editor of *Contact Quarterly*.

Works

Proxy (1961); *Transit* (1962); *Music for Word Words* (1963); *English* (1963); *Afternoon* (1963); *Left Hand* (1963); *Flat* (1964); *Rialto* (1964); *Jag Ville Görna Telefonera* (1964); *title lost Tokyo* (1964); *Section of a New Unfinished Work* (1965); *Augmented* (1966); *The Deposits* (1966); *Physical Things* (1966); *AA* (1966); *Earth Interiors* (1966); *Somebody Else* (1967); *Love Songs* (1967); *Satisfying Lover* (1967); *The Sizes* (1967); *Walking There* (1967; later retitled as *Audience Performance #1*); *The Atlantic* (with spoken text, 1968); *Lecture on a Performance* (1968); *Audience Performance #2* (with texts read by the audience, 1968); *Salt Lake City Deaths* (1968); *State* (1968); *Beautiful Lecture* (1968); *Intravenous Lecture on Sponsors and Producers* (1969); *Lie Down* (1969); *Smiling* (1969); *Collaboration with Winter Soldier* (and film *Winter Soldier*, 1971); *Benn Mutual* (with Nita Little; 1972); *Air* (1973); *With David Moss* (1974 and later versions); *You Come, We'll Show You What We Do* (1975); *Backwater: Twosome* (1977 and later versions); *Part* (with Lisa Nelson, 1978); *Ave Nue* (1981); *Audible Scenery* (1986); *Suspect Terrain* (with Laurie Booth, Dana Reitz and Polly Motley, 1989); *Flipside* (1993); *Some English Suites* (1993); *Long and Dream* (with Trisha Brown, 1994); *O X 2* (lecture on space, 2000); *Night Stand* (with Lisa Nelson, 2004).

Further reading

Interviews in Jane McDermott, 'An Interview with Steve Paxton', *New Dance*, Autumn 1977; in 'Trance Script: Judson Project Interview with Steve Paxton',

Contact Quarterly, Winter 1989; with Helmut Ploebst, 'Improvisation', *Ballett International*, May 1999; in 'Steve Paxton's Talk at CI36', Contact Improvisation's 36th Birthday Celebration, 13 June 2008, reprinted in *Contact Quarterly*, 34(1), Winter/Spring 2009.

Articles: Steve Paxton, 'The Grand Union', *Drama Review*, September 1972; Rob Baker, 'Grand Union: Taking a Chance on Dance', *Dance Magazine*, October 1973; Elizabeth Kendall, 'The Grand Union: Our Gang', *Ballet Review*, 5(4), 1975/76; Eleanor Rachel Luger, 'A Contact Improvisation Primer', *Dance Scope*, Fall/Winter 1977/78; Sally Banes, 'Steve Paxton: Physical Things', *Dance Scope*, Winter/Spring 1979/80; Yvonne Rainer, 'Backwater: Twosome, Paxton and Moss', *Dance Scope*, Winter/Spring 1979/80; Allen Robertson, 'Newer Than New: The PostModern Choreographers', *Ballet News*, October 1981; 'Performing Improvising Performing Improvising', *Contact Quarterly*, Spring/Summer 1981; Barry Laine, 'In Search of Judson', *Dance Magazine*, September 1982; Marcia B. Siegel, 'The Death of Some Alternatives', *Ballet Review*, Fall 1982; Sarah Rubidge, 'Steve Paxton', *Dance Theatre Journal*, Winter 1986; Barbara Newman, 'Steve Paxton', *Dancing Times*, November 1986; Robert Ellis Dunn, 'Judson Days', *Contact Quarterly*, Winter 1989; 'Dancing with Different Populations', *Contact Quarterly*, Winter 1992; Josephine Leask, 'Festival: The Year of the Solo', *Ballett International*, January 1996; Mary Prestidge, 'Beyond the Fringe', *Animated*, September 1997; Steve Paxton, 'Surfing with Steve Paxton' (e-mail dialogue), *Dance Theatre Journal*, 14/1, 1998; Elizabeth Zimmer, 'Contact Improvisation Comes of Age', *Dance Magazine*, June 2004; Joan Acocella, 'Think Pieces: Return of the Judsonites', *The New Yorker*, 24 May 2010.

Books: Don McDonagh, *The Rise and Fall of Modern Dance*, New York, 1970; Jill Johnston, *Marmalade Me*, New York, 1971; Don McDonagh, *The Complete Guide to Modern Dance*, Garden City, New York, 1977; Peter Wynne (ed.), *Judson Dance: An Annotated Bibliography of the Judson Dance Theater and of Five Major Choreographers*, Englewood Cliffs, NJ, 1978; Sally Banes, *Terpsichore in Sneakers: Post-Modern Dance*, Boston, 1980; Sally Banes, *Democracy's Body: Judson Dance Theater 1962–1964*, Ann Arbor, MI, 1983 (reprinted Durham, NC, 1993); Deborah Jowitt, *The Dance in Mind*, Boston, 1985; Cynthia Novack, *Sharing the Dance: Contact Improvisation and American Culture*, Madison, WI, 1990; Margaret Hupp Ramsay, *The Grand Union: 1970–1976*, New York, 1991; Selma Jeanne Cohen (ed.), *Dance as a Theatre Art: Source Readings in Dance History from 1591 to the Present*, 2nd edition (new section by Katy Matheson), Princeton, NJ, 1992; Ann Cooper Albright and David Gere, *Taken by Surprise: Improvisation in Dance and Mind*, Middletown, CT, 2003.

PILOBOLUS

Pilobolus, sometimes called Pilobolus Dance Theater and once upon a time known as Vermont Natural Theater, has been as pervasive an influence on American dance theatre in the latter part of the twentieth century as was Denishawn during the earlier part. In impact, this small ensemble – more or less consistently limited to a core company of four men and two women – recalls the popularity held by the St Denis and Shawn enterprise during the 1920s. In kind, the mixed bills put on by Pilobolus are more artfully outrageous, somewhere between naughty and nice, where the Denishawners were lofty and decoratively exotic. However, both aesthetics can be said to focus on the sensual projection resulting from the direct display of the dancer's body.

Indeed, with almost 40 years to its credit, Pilobolus has proven itself to have even greater staying power than Denishawn. Since its very modest beginnings in 1971, when the burgeoning group was little more than one three-man work entitled *Pilobolus*, this innovative and hard-to-categorize entity has remained popular with its public and influential over its fellow practitioners in dance theatre. The influence of Pilobolus on various kinds of choreography in the 1980s and 1990s is not hard to recognize: intriguingly massed clusters of bodies and gymnastically levered processes of partnering or grouping. A few other distinguishing Pilobolus characteristics, such as artful nudity and a taste for surreal twists of visual logic, also tend to be emulated, although to a lesser extent.

The most common misinformation regarding the troupe is that its founders were gymnasts. In fact, the original trio grew out of Alison Chase's dance composition class at New England's Dartmouth College, then an all-male institution where dance was not a major subject and where the future Pilobolus founders were athletic collegians, not college athletes. Moses Pendleton was an English literature major and a cross-country skier; Jonathan Wolken was a philosophy and science major who fenced, did folk dancing and played the banjo; and Steve Johnson was a pre-medical student who pole-vaulted. (Lee Harris and Robert Barnett joined up when Johnson left to continue his medical studies. The former, who also left shortly afterwards, was a computer science major; the latter, who stayed on and served as an artistic director once he stopped performing, was an art major.)

The individuals who brought Pilobolus to its first flowering made up the group's first sextet unit. Half were founding (or nearly founding) members: Pendleton, Wolken and Barnett. The other half were Michael Tracy, who replaced Harris; Chase, who joined her former students as an equal; and Martha Clarke, a Juilliard Dance School graduate and former performer with the Anna Sokolow Dance Company, who had been working with Chase on experimental choreography. Chase and Clarke were the first female Pilobolus members. These six, who were in place by 1974 for the reworking of *Ciona* (a 1973 sextet and the first Pilobolus piece integrating women into its work), formed the company that put the Pilobolus aesthetic indelibly in the minds of the 'dance-eager audiences of the United States' so-called 'dance boom'. In one sense, both the audience for Pilobolus and the troupe itself developed along similarly fresh and unpredictable lines. In the 1960s, with its freewheeling, flower-power, youth cult aspects, dance and dancers caught media attention as the 'hot' art form. The growing audience for dance and the dance-like theatre of Pilobolus were encumbered by few preconceptions regarding dance's historical traditions or expectations.

Central to the post-1960s pedigree of Pilobolus was its very way of working. Instead of following the pervasive single-choreographer scheme that had dominated American modern-dance companies since the birth of the art form in the earlier part of the century, Pilobolus chose a communal angle. Every performer was directly involved in the creation of choreography. Any work they appeared in, they had in some way helped to develop.

The fashion for communal living situations during this age was mirrored in the artistic process promoted by Pilobolus: collective improvisation, followed by periods of streamlining and revision by the 'choreographers', who could perhaps more accurately be called the 'orchestrators'. Longstanding Pilobolus repertory staples such as the sextets *Monkshood's Farewell* (1974) and *Untitled* (1975), *Pseudopodia* (a 1973 solo) and *Shizen* (a 1978 duet) all date from this period. By 1978, Clarke had left to do her own work – which, sometimes classified as 'theatre of images', she continues to do. (She was replaced by Elisa Monte, who is now a choreographer and director of her own echt-Pilobolus troupe). By 1992, Pendleton was no longer an artistic director although his work, notably the lush, sensual and playful *Debut C* (a 1988 sextet), continued to be a staple of the Pilobolus repertory. This well-known and, arguably, most talented member from the founding trinity was by this time concentrating on directing and creating works for Momix, the Pilobolus offshoot Pendleton founded in 1979. By 2002, Pilobolus was starting to move away from its standard way of working, with more pieces being created by the artistic directors individually (Chase and Tracy) or collaboratively (Barnett and Wolken). In 2005, Chase, whose class had been the catalyst for this eventually highly successful enterprise, left the company due to artistic differences with the new executive director, Itamar Kubovy, and board of directors. Chase herself had once likened the Pilobolus experience to 'six radios, all on different stations at the same time'. Although many stayed on and thrived amid the commotion of large collaborative efforts, it has become increasingly clear that the one big family-of-artists way of working is not an easy thing to keep in order.

One of the most enthusiastic and powerful champions of Pilobolus has been Charles Reinhart, director since 1969 of the American Dance Festival (ADF), an institution devoted to the development and promotion of modern dance. An outgrowth of the Bennington College festivals that supported early modern-dance artists such as Martha Graham and Doris Humphrey, ADF frequently commissioned Pilobolus work, starting in 1973. A 1998 work, *The Hand That Mocked, the Heart That Fed*, for example, was co-commissioned by ADF and the Kennedy Center for the Performing Arts as part of the Doris Duke Millennium Awards. In 2000, Pilobolus received its own 'millennium award' when ADF honoured it with the Samuel H. Scripps American Dance Festival Award for lifetime achievement in choreography.

Despite its self-sufficient, collaborative style of creation, Pilobolus does bring in guest choreographers. The first, and perhaps still the most notable, of these instances was in 1999, when Pilobolus joined with Maurice Sendak to create *A Selection*. This work, deemed 'admirably ambitious' by Jack Anderson, tells a story of a small group of travelling players stranded on a train platform in Central Europe during the Nazi era. After three years, in 2002, a documentary film called *Last Dance* was made about the collaboration and production of this work, one of the more aggressively emotional dances presented by Pilobolus. Since then, Pilobolus has launched the International Collaborators Project, inviting outside artists to work with the group.

Both those admiring and those leery of Pilobolus have tussled with the question of dance. Reinhart recalled the controversy surrounding the group and remembered its work being described as 'interesting, but not dance'. Dance critic Arlene Croce, a champion of classicism, especially Balanchine's, noted in her first major review of the troupe in 1976, '"Dance" is not what I would say Pilobolus does, and it is not what I would want it to do. Its art, which is based on gymnastics, is already complete.' She further observed that 'Gymnastics present the body in complicated feats of coordination without reference to what dancers call dynamics.' This lack of 'dynamics' proved to be a more serious problem for other critics, often those grounded in Rudolf Laban's effort/shape theory of dancing. In 1977, the dancer/choreographer/writer Deborah Jowitt countered Croce, reporting on the 'seductive designs' of Pilobolus that tended to 'bewitch' audiences. She noted there were quite a few at the ADF (in the case of this report), who're appalled by the heartless beauty of the company's jointly made dances'.

Pilobolus did not dance, *per se*, partly because the group came into being out of a non-dance environment. A hybrid at best, the Pilobolus product remained a kind of visual poetry shaped from movement theatrics, although not necessarily danced moves. Leveraged, counter-balanced weight, acrobatic emphases, anthropomorphic shape modulations and often surreal, pictorial groupings all inter-related to give life and force to Pilobolus creations. The group's somewhat frequent use of unashamed nudity or semi-nudity consistently reinforced art critic Kenneth Clark-like theories that distinguished the 'nude' from the 'naked'. Anna Kisselgoff, chief dance critic of *The New York Times*, identified the nudity of Pilobolus as consistently being 'on the skinny-dipping level: fun and intended to make a splash with the audience'. She elaborated her observation by adding that the company's dancers 'have always had a healthy uninhibitedness'. However, such perceptions are not shared far and wide; the troupe has encountered producers around the United States who ask the performers to exclude nude-dancer works from their local repertory, or to add 'figleaf' costuming to soften the 'shock'.

By the late 1980s, when the first generation had all graduated to positions of artistic authority, the troupe was made up of individuals with more traditional dance backgrounds. Although the repertory in this period included some Pilobolus 'classics', it continued to include new works made by the 'artistic directors' in collaboration with the newer Pilobolus members. By the 1990s, Pilobolus had introduced an education division that taught the 'Pilobolus Method' in workshops, residencies and summer programmes. In 1991, The Pilobolus Institute was born to send Pilobolus into smaller spaces and schools, giving audiences who may never have had the chance to see the troupe the opportunity to see them perform. By 1997, Pilobolus Creative Services was established to handle commercial work, with offers rolling in from companies that ranged from MAC cosmetics to Hyundai. Pilobolus received its biggest commercial assignment in 2007 when the troupe depicted – symbolically, in its most acrobatic style – the films nominated for the Best Picture Oscar. Two years later it was nominated for an Emmy Award for its performance during a Saturday Night Football game. Pilobolus had arrived on primetime.

The mass national viewing in 2007 (some 40 million people tuned into the Oscar telecast) was followed in 2008 by new and exciting international appearances for Pilobolus. Its tour of the Holy Land was photographed by Robert Whitman and exhibited in New York. The photographs show members of the group creating shapes throughout the landscape, some beautiful, some witty, juxtaposing a contemporary acrobatic sensibility with an ancient setting. Pilobolus was then distinguished by the US Department of State, which co-sponsored its tour of Armenia, making it the first American modern dance company to perform there. And then, in 2009, Pilobolus performed for Queen Elizabeth II at the Royal Variety Performances in Blackpool, England. The company's schedule in 2010 revealed non-stop touring for the first half of the year. Pilobolus, it seems, has fashioned itself into perpetual motion.

Robert Greskovic
(updated by Ellen Gaintner)

Biographical details

Foundation and history: Dance company, based in Washington Depot, Connecticut, founded by dancer–choreographers Moses Pendleton, Jonathan Wolken and Steve Johnson (all students of dance composition teacher Alison Chase) at Dartmouth College, Hanover, New Hampshire, in 1971; joined by Lee Harris and Robert Barnett (on departure of Johnson, 1971); made New York début in December 1971; joined by Michael Tracy (on departure of Hams, 1974), and by Alison Chase (1973) and Martha Clarke (1973–78, and then guest performances); has retained original name and stylistic identity throughout various subsequent changes of personnel, including Pendleton's departure (1979) to form Momix. In 1997, the artistic directors of Pilobolus were Barnett, Chase, Tracy and Wolken; in 2010, they were Barnett, Tracy and Wolken. Pilobolus has also choreographed for Hartford Ballet, the Juilliard School and the National Theater for the Deaf. **Awards and honours** include Berlin Critics' Prize; Brandeis Award; New England Theatre Conference Prize; Primetime Emmy Award, 1997; Samuel H. Scripps American Dance Festival Award, 2000; Dartmouth College fellowships for Barnett, Tracy and Wolken, 2007.

Works

(Choreographers in parentheses)

Geode (Barnett, 1971); *Pilobolus* (Johnson, Pendleton, Wolken, 1971); *Walklyndon* (Barnett, Harris, Pendleton, Wolken, 1971); *Anaendrom* (Barnett, Harris, Pendleton, Wolken, 1972); *Ocellus* (Barnett, Harns, Pendleton, Wolken, 1972); *Spyrogyra* (Barnett, Harris, Pendleton, Wolken, 1972); *Aubade* (Barnett, Clarke, 1973); *Cameo* (Chase, Clark, 1973); *Ciona* (Barnett, Chase, Clarke, Pendleton, Tracy, Wolken, 1973); *Pseudopodia* (solo; Wolken, 1973); *Terra Cotta* (Barnett, Clarke, 1974); *Monkshood's Farewell* (Barnett, Chase, Clarke, Pendleton, Tracy, Wolken, 1974); *Alraune* (Chase, Pendleton, 1975); *Untitled* (Barnett, Chase, Clarke, Pendleton, Tracy, Wolken, 1975); *Pagliaccio* (solo; Clarke, 1975); *Vagabond* (solo; Clarke, 1975); *Lost in Fauna* (solo; Chase, Pendleton, 1976); *Bone* (solo; Barnett, 1977); *The Garden Gate* (solo; Clarke, 1977); *The Eve of Samhain* (Barnett, Chase, Pendleton, Tracy, Wolken, 1977); *Renelagh on the Randan* (solo; Wolken, 1977); *Molly's Not Dead* (Barnett, Chase, Pendleton, Tracy, Wolken, 1978); *Moonblind* (solo; Chase, 1978); *Shizen* (Chase, Pendleton,

1978); *The Detail of Phoebe Strickland* (Kammy Brooks, Chase, Pendleton, 1979); *Tendril* (Tracy, 1979); *The Empty Suitor* (Jamey Hampton, Tracy, Wolken, 1980); *A Miniature* (Chase, 1980); *Momix* (Pendleton, 1980); *Day Two* (Pendleton); *Tarleton's Resurrection* (Barnett, Félix Blaska, 1981); *Elegy for the Moment* (Chase, 1982); *What Grows in Huygen's Window* (Wolken, 1982); *Stabat Mater* (Pendleton, 1982); *Mirage* (Tracy, 1983); *Hot Pursuit* (Wolken, 1984); *Return to Maria La Baja* (Barnett, Chase, 1984); *Carmina Burana, Side II* (Pendleton, Tracy, 1985); *Televisitation* (Barnett, Chase, 1985); *Land's Edge* (Barnett, Chase, Wolken, 1986); *I'm Left, You're Right, She's Gone* (Barnett, Chase, Tracy, Wolken, 1987); *The Golden Bowl* (Barnett, Chase, 1987); *Debut C* (Pendleton, 1988); *The Particle Zoo* (Barnett, Tracy, Wolken, 1989); *Coming of Age in the Milky Way* (Barnett, Tracy, Wolken, 1989); *Axons* (Chase, 1990); *Cedar Island* (Chase, 1990); *Clandestiny* (Tracy, 1990); *Ophelia* (Barnett, 1990); *Sweet Purgatory* (Barnett, Chase, Tracy, Wolken, 1991); *Duet* (Barnett, Chase, Tracy, 1992); Solus (Wolken, 1992); *Slippery Hearts* (Barnett, Félix Blaska, 1992); *Bedtime Stories* (Wolken, 1993); *A Portrait* (Chase, 1993); *Rejoyce* (Barnett, Tracy, Wolken, 1993); *Animundi* (Chase, Tracy, 1994); *Collideoscope* (Chase, Tracy, 1994); *Quatrejeux* (Barnett, Wolken, 1994); *Vestidigitations* (Barnett, Wolken, 1994); *The Doubling Cube* (Barnett, Chase, Tracy, Wolken, 1995); *Pyramid of the Moon* (Chase, Tracy, 1995); *Masters of Ceremony* (Barnett, Chase, Wolken, 1995); *Aeros* (Barnett, Chase, Tracy, Wolken, 1996); *Elysian Fields* (Chase, Tracy, 1997); *Peer Gynt* (play by Henrik Ibsen; with the National Theater for the Deaf, 1997); *Gnomen* (Barnett, Wolken, 1997); *Solo* (Chase, 1997); *Apoplexy* (Barnett, Tracy, Wolken, 1998); *Orangotango* (Chase, 1998); *The Hand that Mocked, the Heart that Fed* (Barnett, Tracy, Wolken, 1998); *A Selection* (Barnett, Sendak, Tracy, Wolken, Yorinks, 1999); *Femme Noire* (Chase, 1999); *Uno Dos Tray* (Chase, 1999); *Sweet Dreams* (Tracy, 2000); *Tantra Aranea* (Barnett, Wolken, 2000); *Tsu Ku Tsu* (Chase, with master Taiko drummer Leonard Eto, 2000); *Davenen* (Barnett, Wolken, 2001); *Monkey and the White Bone Demon* (Chase, 2001); *Symbiosis* (Tracy, 2001); *Ben's Admonition* (2002); *The Brass Ring* (Tracy, 2002); *The Four Humours* (Barnett, Tracy, 2002); *My Brother's Keeper* (Tracy, 2003); *Star-Cross'd* (Chase, 2003); *Wedlock* (Wolken, 2003); *Megawat* (Wolken, 2004); *Night of the Dark Moon / Orpheo and Euridice* (Chase, 2004); *Warm Heart* (Tracy, 2004); *Aquatica* (Tracy, 2005); *BUGonia* (Chase, 2005); *Megawatt Full Strength* (Wolken, 2005); *Momento Mori* (Wolken, 2006); *Prism* (Tracy, 2006); *B'yzrk* (Wolken, 2007); *Persistence of Memory* (Tracy, 2007); *Rushes* (Pinto, Pollak, Barnett, 2007); *Darkness and Light* (Barnett, Wolken, with puppeteer Basil Twist, 2008); *Lanterna Magica* (Tracy, 2008); *Razor: Mirror* (Wolken, 2008); *2b* (Pinto, Avshalom, Del Rosario, Herro, Kuribayashi, Sheaff, 2009); *Redline* (Wolken, Del Rosario, Herro, Huang, Kuribayashi, Mendez, Sheaff, Whitney, 2009); *Shadowland* (Banks, Barnett, Jaworski, Kent, Kubovy, Tracy, 2009).

Further reading

Interview with Elvi Moore, in 'Talking with Pilobolus', in *The Vision of Modern Dance*, edited by Jean Morrison Brown, Princeton, New Jersey, 1979, London, 1980.

Articles: Iris Fanger, 'Pilobolus', *Dance Magazine*, July 1974; J. Bulaitis, 'Pilobolus', *Dancing Times*, May 1978; John Gruen, 'Dance Vision', *Dance Magazine*, July 1985; Patricia Barnes, 'Welcome Variety', *Dance and Dancers*, February 1986; Susan Reiter, 'Dance Watch', *Ballet News*, February 1986; Clive Barnes, 'Turning to the Light', *Dance and Dancers*, March/April 1987; Alastair Macaulay, 'Fantasia', *Dancing Times*, June 1987; John Percival, 'Summer Assortment', *Dance and Dancers*, August 1987; Larry Stevens, 'A Fabulous Company with a Fabulous Name', *Dance Pages*, Summer 1993; Terry Teachout, 'And They Dance Their Terrible Dance', *The New York Times*, 20 June 1999; Jack Anderson, 'Dark Theme Ushers in Pilobolus', *The New York Times*, 7 July 1999; Christopher Reardon, 'Keeping Pilobolus Safe for Democracy', *The New York Times*, 11 July 2004; Catherine Kerr, 'Pilobolus', *Ballet Review*, Spring 2005; Ann Murphy, 'Pilobolus Dance Theater', *Dance Magazine*, May 2005; Andrea K. Hammer, 'Pilobolus: The Shape of Things to Come', *Dance International*, Fall 2007; Amanda Smith, 'Pilobolus and the Middle School: Utopianism Meets Reality', *Dance Magazine*, June 2007; Susan Yung, 'Pilobolus "Rushes"', *Dance Magazine*, November 2007; Sarah Kaufman, 'With a Light Touch, Pilobolus Casts a Long Shadow', *The Washington Post*, 5 October 2009.

Books: Arlene Croce, *Afterimages*, New York, 1977; Tim Matron, *Pilobolus*, New York, 1978; Arlene Croce, *Going to the Dance*, New York, 1982; Deborah Jowitt, *The Dance in Mind*, Boston, 1985; Arlene Croce, *Sight Lines*, New York, 1987; Deborah Jowitt, *Time and the Dancing Image*, New York, 1988; Allen Robertson and Donald Hutera, *The Dance Handbook*, Harlow, Essex, 1988.

ANGELIN PRELJOCAJ

Internationally, Angelin Preljocaj is probably the best-known French contemporary-dance choreographer of the generation that came to prominence during the 1980s. His company frequently performs in the world's major theatres and festivals, and he has created works for major ballet companies including New York City Ballet, Opéra de Paris and Berlin Staatsoper. Indeed, he seems to be equally appreciated by both contemporary-dance and ballet audiences. Born in France of Albanian immigrant parents, he learned classical ballet from an early age, going on to study both European and American modern-dance techniques. As he himself admits, the twin poles of his creative process are German expressionism and US abstraction.[1] His works are often set to European classical music or to scores by contemporary composers. He seems to have a particular affinity for the music of Prokofiev and Stravinsky, which has inspired him to choreograph some dynamic, intense works. While Preljocaj is an intellectual, his work is never cerebral; rather, it invariably direct and strips away formal conventions to focus on basic human needs and drives. It often combines abstract passages of characteristically angular and asymmetrical choreography with fragmented dramaturgical structures that hint at narrative without telling stories. Although not minimalist, his work sometimes takes on a ritualistic quality, or proceeds with an irresistible, almost machine-like inevitability that gives it a disturbing or menacing edge.

Preljocaj's parents were political refugees who, following threats, had escaped from Albania by walking over the mountains into neighbouring Montenegro. He was born shortly after they settled in France, and he grew up feeling Albanian at home while speaking French at school and with his friends. Having studied ballet from an early age, he turned to contemporary dance taught by Karin Waeher, who had herself been a pupil of the great German choreographer Mary Wigman. After studying in New York at the Cunningham studio, he worked for the Centre National de Danse Contemporaine in Angers, directed at the time by ex-Cunningham dancer Viola Faber.

Of all the American companies who, during the 1960s and 1970s, had acted as catalysts for the revival of European modern dance, the Cunningham company had the greatest impact. Europeans recognized in Cunningham's work a continuation of the European avant-garde tradition of Dada. They also found in his hybrid fusion of ballet and modern-dance movement a way of adapting and developing the modernist tradition of post-war European ballet choreography. In the late 1940s and early 1950s, ballet seemed more in tune with Europe's new internationalist aspirations than the modern dance, which had been so intimately associated with German nationalism. Cunningham's influence on the 'new wave' of French contemporary dance in the 1980s can be found in the cool, crisp clarity with which choreographers such as Preljocaj developed their own somewhat idiosyncratic, fragmented styles.

After dancing with Faber, Preljocaj spent three years as a member of Dominique Bagouet's company. At this time, the French Ministry of Culture was setting up 'national' dance centres and companies throughout the French regions. Bagouet was based in Montpellier. He was probably the most innovative and influential pioneer of the French new wave, Preljocaj working with him at a key early stage in its development. When Preljocaj left Montpellier to start making his own work, some of Bagouet's fans saw this as a betrayal.

Preljocaj first attracted wider attention in 1984 when his piece *Marché noir* won first prize at the international choreographic competition at Bagnolet. In 1985, his newly founded company (in December 1984) was established in Champigny-sur-Marne with regular funding from the Ministry of Culture, and that year he created *Larmes blanches*.

This title is ambiguous, meaning 'white tears' (*larmes*) while sounding like 'white weapon' (*l'arme*), and this uncertainty was also present in the choreography, which seemed poignantly idiosyncratic but was at the same time aggressively impersonal. Made for two men and women, and including same-sex duets, it was set to Baroque music played on a harpsichord whose quasi-mechanical ticking combined with the choreography's complex, geometrical precision to give the piece a modernist quality. The movement material itself consisted of tiny obsessive gestures, unexpected sideways hops, and sudden collapses, often performed in nervous but uncanny unison.

In contrast with the fastidious surface of *Larmes blanches*, Preljocaj choreographed *Noces*, his 1989 version of *Les Noces*, a fast moving, menacing ritual to Stravinsky's jarring, discordant choral music. This had initially been choreographed in 1923 by Bronislava Nijinska for the Ballets Russes. Preljocaj retained the piece's premise that marriage for a young Russian peasant bride was a terrifying prospect, but abandoned the ballet's libretto to make an abstract ensemble piece for five couples who sit on, jump over, or upend five benches, and play violently with five life-size rag dolls that are dressed like brides. As Anna Kisselgoff observed, 'There is nothing exploratory or learned about the relationships on view; the couples throw themselves into each others' arms or laps with a regularity that implies pre-ordained roles – male–female confrontations ruled by instinct'.[2] *Noces* drew the attention of the film director Roman Polanski, whose discussions with Preljocaj formed the basis for a 1992 book of interviews.[3]

The younger generation of more conceptually orientated French choreographers in the 1990s criticized Preljocaj's generation for pretending they were starting from scratch in developing new movement vocabularies, like those found in works like *Larmes blanches* and *Noces*, when these were actually derived from established historical traditions. This is, however, to misunderstand the way the French new wave in the 1980s and early 1990s experienced their new-found choreographic freedom as an alarming loss of what had until then seemed certainties. The resulting aesthetic of boundarylessness was particularly resonant at a time when many Europeans were suffering the unsettling and disorienting effects of globalization and the collapse of Soviet communism. In 1993, Preljocaj himself described choreography as a way of accessing the unknown:

> Only the language of the body can bring out the difficult transmission of the unspeakable. What seems so magnificent to me

about the craft of choreography is its potential for grasping the unspeakable and unnameable, and expressing meanings in its name.[4]

The 1980s saw several modern reworkings of well-known ballets, including Mats Ek's *Giselle* (1982) and *Swan Lake* (1987) for the Cullberg Ballet and Maguy Marin's surreal *Cendrillon* (*Cinderella*, 1985) for Lyons Ballet who commissioned Preljocaj, in 1990, to make a new version of *Roméo et Juliette*. Setting this in a dystopian future, Preljocaj chose to collaborate with cult fantasy and sci-fi illustrator Enki Bilal. Their Capulets became a rich elite, living in a futuristic gated community patrolled by helmeted, leather-clad security men with guard dogs. Tybalt and his crew let off steam on excursions to beat up local vagrants – the Montagues. Thus, although the Capulets wore tight black clothes and moved in a brutal, angular way that recalled Nazi goose-stepping, the Montagues wore soft, loose grey shirts and tattered trousers, and moved with the provocative insouciance of the three sailors in Jerome Robbins's *Fancy Free* (1944). The encounters between the two gangs had the same menace as those between Sharks and Jets in Robbins's choreography for the musical *West Side Story* (1957). Preljocaj counted on audience familiarity with Shakespeare's play, with Prokofiev's score and with previous versions of the ballet including the one danced famously by Nureyev and Fonteyn. However, this also gave him opportunities to trouble their sense of the familiar by introducing disorientating elements and abstracting or ritualizing scenes. The role of the Nurse thus became two sinister female minders whose dancing had an almost robotic, or clone-like, mirrored symmetry. The climax of the bedroom scene saw four duplicate couples emerge in the background moving in perfect synchronization with Roméo and Juliette's passionate embraces.

Following the success of *Roméo et Juliette*, Preljocaj was commissioned in 1993 to create an evening of work as a tribute to the Ballets Russes, for which he revived *Noces* and created characteristically idiosyncratic versions of *Le Spectre de la rose* (1993) and *Parade* (1993). In 1994, the Paris Opéra commissioned *Le Parc*, around the idea of eighteenth-century aristocratic libertinage danced to music by Mozart, and Preljocaj returned to explore again the same theme for the company in 1998 with *Casanova*. He has choreographed two more reworkings of Ballets Russes ballets, both with Stravinsky scores: *L'Oiseau de feu* (1995) for Munich Ballet and, in 2001, *Le Sacre du printemps* for dancers in the Berlin Staatsoper, supplemented with his own dancers for performances conducted by Daniel Barenboim. The final sacrifice of the Chosen One in Preljocaj's *Le Sacre* was more or less initiated with a rape scene as she struggled to get away but was assaulted by the rest of the cast, both male and female. As she tried to resist, they held her down and, tearing off her clothes, left her completely naked and ashamed. Such explicit scenes of sexual predation and violence proved controversial after the work's premiere.

Preljocaj has created several works that celebrate the male dancing body. In 1988, with the gay novelist and filmmaker Cyril Collard, he created the short dance film *Les Raboteurs* (the floor planers), inspired by a French impressionist painting by Gustave Caillebotte of workmen planning floorboards with their shirts off on a hot day. Caillebotte had not romanticized the back-breaking nature of the work, and nor did Preljocaj's choreography, which emphasized the contrast between its intense physicality and the mundane nature of the event, with Preljocaj himself dancing as one of the three workmen. The film also invented a bourgeois couple who sipped wine while voyeuristically watching them working. Preljocaj returned to the spectacle of intensely physical, half-clad male bodies in his 2001 work *MC 14/22*. The title refers to the story of the Last Supper: St Mark's Gospel (Chapter 14, Verse 22) reads, 'Take, eat; this is my body which is given for you.' The piece began with the cast of semi-naked male dancers ritualistically washing one another and ended with choreographed sequences of defiant heroics set to the sounds of bombs and helicopters. Preljocaj seems to allow for the fact that the male dancing body is attractive both for female and gay male spectators, the bourgeois voyeurs in *Les Raboteurs* being matched by a disembodied female voice in *MC 14/22* that whispers mystically about male erections.

In 1994, Ballet Preljocaj was invited to settle in Toulon. Shortly after the move, however, a prominent member of the far-right, anti-immigration Front National was elected as Mayor of Toulon. Ballet Preljocaj's plans to undertake outreach projects with underprivileged North African immigrants in some of the city's suburbs caused the Mayor to cut their funding and mount a vicious campaign against the company, predictably suggesting that Preljocaj should go back to Albania. The Ministry of Culture intervened and, in 1996, Ballet Preljocaj relocated to Aix-en-Provence.

In 1998, Preljocaj was made a Chevalier of the Légion d'Honneur. The rebellious outsider of the 1980s had become an establishment figure. Asked in 2003 to name his favourite choreographer, he replied that there were two, both called Jerome: Robbins and Bel, the latter having danced for Preljocaj in the late 1980s.[5] This wry comment hints at the way that Preljocaj's work had developed from the edgy, impersonal radicalism of works such as *Larmes blanches* into the more explicitly humanist intentions of works such as *MC 14/22* and *Near Life Experience* (2003), a work inspired by the breathlessness Preljocaj had experienced on holiday that year while climbing Mount Kilimanjaro without the aid of oxygen. The same year he also created a filmed version of his 1997 ballet *The Annunciation*. He remains extremely productive, almost addicted to the process of choreography, sometimes making as many as three new works a year. For each one, he prepares by reading, writing and analysing movement ideas, but this, he says, evaporates and is forgotten as soon as he reaches the rehearsal studio: 'When I have before me my dancers, then I am inspired by what vibrates in their bodies, which is biological and organic. The dance pours out of this forgetting'.[6]

Ramsay Burt

Notes

1 Bettina Wagner-Bergelt, 'The Classical Choreographer Between Abstraction and Expressionism', *Ballett International*, April 1996.
2 Anna Kisselgoff, 'A French Company's Version of *Noces*', *The New York Times*, 22 June 1991.
3 Jean Bollack, Ismail Kadaré and Brigitte Paulino-Neto (eds), *Angelin Preljocaj, Roman Polanski*, Paris, 1992.
4 In Aline Apostolska, 'Angelin Preljocaj: Capricorne', *Saisons de la Danse*, March 1993.
5 Dominique Frétard, 'Danse: l'escalade vertigineuse d'Angelin Preljocaj', *Le Monde*, 26 June 2003.
6 Ibid.

Biographical details

Born in Sucy-en-Brie, France, 9 January 1957. **Studied** classical ballet and then modern dance with Karin Waehner at the Schola Cantorum, and at the Cunningham Studios in New York, 1980; also studied Noh in Japan, 1987. **Career:** Joined Quentin Rouiller Company in Caen, then worked at Centre National de Danse Chorégraphique at Angers, 1981–82; dancer for Dominique Bagouet, 1982; choreographer, making his first work, *Aventures colonialis* (in collaboration with Michel Kélménis) in 1984; established his own company in Champigny-sur-Marne, in 1984, becoming the Centre Chorégraphique National de Champigny-sur-Marne and du Val-de-Marne, 1989; the company now known as Ballet Preljocaj-Centre Chorégraphique National de la Région Provence based in Aix-en-Provence from 1996, moving into new, purpose-built premises, Pavillon Noir, 2006. Has also created works for Lyon Opera Ballet, Ballet de l'Opéra de Paris, Munich Ballet and New York City Ballet, with his work also staged by companies around the world, including Helsinki Ballet, Gulbenkian Ballet, Finnish National Ballet, Ballet of La Scala, Nederlands Dans Theater, São Paulo Balé de Cidade, and Staatsoper, Berlin. **Awards and honours** include First Prize at Concours de Bagnolet, 1984; Grand Prix, 1992; Benois de la Danse, Moscow, 1995; New York Dance and Performance Award ('Bessie'), 1997; Chevalier of the Légion d'Honneur, 1998; Grand Prix International de Vidéodanse, 1999; Order of Merit, 2006; Cristal Globe, 2009.

Works

Marché noir (1984); *Larmes blanches* (1985); *Peurs bleues* (1985); *A Nos Héros* (1986); *Hallali Romée* (1987); *Le Petit Napperon bouge* (1987); *Liqueurs de chair* (1988); *Les Raboteurs* (film, 1988); *Un Trait d'union* (1989); *Noces* (1989); *Amer America* (1990); *Roméo et Juliette* (1990; restaged 1996); *La Peau du Monde* (1992); *Hommage aux Ballets Russes: Parade* and *Le Spectre de la rose* (1993); *Le Parc* (1994); *Petit Essai sur le temps qui passe* (1995); *L'Anoure* (1995); *Annonciation* (1995); *L'Oiseau de feu* (1995); *Paysage après la bataille* (1997); *La Stravaganza* (1997); *Casanova* (1998); *Centaures* (1998); *Personne n'épouse les méduses* (1999); *Portraits in corpore* (2000); *Le Sacre du printemps* (2001); *MC 14/22 (ceci est mon corpore;* 2001); *Helikopter* (2001); *Near Life Experience* (2003); *Le Songe de Médée* (2004); *'N'* (2004); *Empty Moves (part I)* (2004); *Les 4 Saisons . . .* (2005); *Fire Sketch* (2006); *Empty Moves (parts I & II)* (2007); *Eldorado (Sonntags Abschied)* (2007); *Blanche Neige* (2008); *Le Funambule* (2009), *Siddharta* (2010).

Further reading

Articles: Laurence Louppe, 'Angelin Preljocaj, '*Larmes blanches*, côté coeur', *Pour la Danse*, January 1986; Dominique Passet, 'Preljocaj roule pour vous', *Danser*, October 1986; Anna Kisselgoff, 'A French Company's Version of *Noces*', *The New York Times*, 22 June 1991; Jean-Michel Plouchard, 'Entretien avec Angelin Preljocaj', *Les Saisons de la Danse*, December 1991; Aline Apostolska, 'Angelin Preljocaj: Capricorne', *Saisons de la danse*, March 1993; Gus Solomons, 'Review of Choreography Performed by the Lyon Opera Ballet', *Dance Magazine*, December 1994; Bettina Wagner-Bergelt, 'The Classical Choreographer Between Abstraction and Expressionism', *Ballett International*, April 1996; Jean Claude Diénis, 'Angelin Preljocaj: un contemporain en terre classique', *Danser*, July/August 1997; Thomas Hahn, 'You See, Willi!: Preljocaj's *Casanova* in Paris', *Ballett International*, May 1998; Alice Naude, 'Ballet Preljocaj' *Dance Magazine*, January 1999; Suki John, 'From Louis XIV to Le Hip-Hop: French Choreographers Transform American Moves', *The Village Voice*, 17 April 2001; Thomas Hahn, 'On Stage: Angelin Preljocaj, *Flight 14/22 Delayed*', *Ballett International*, May 2001; Anne Gilpin, 'Ballet Preljocaj: *Helikopter* and *Rite of Spring*', *Dance Europe*, June 2002; Jenny Gilbert, 'Blissed Out!', *The Independent on Sunday*, 9 May 2004; Allan Ulrich, 'Preljocaj Meets Grendel', *Dance Magazine*, July 2006; Deborah Jowitt, 'Bridal Party', *The Village Voice*, 28 November 2006; Victoria Looseleaf, 'Ballet Preljocaj', *Dance Magazine*, July 2009; Luke Jennings, '*Siddharta*', *The Observer*, 21 March 2010.

Books: Jean Bollack, Ismail Kadaré, and Brigitte Paulino-Neto (eds), *Angelin Preljocaj, Roman Polanski,* Paris, 1992; Isabelle Ginot (ed.), *Danse et utopie: Mobile 1,* Paris, 1999; B. Raffali, *Preljocaj ou la tentation de l'épique,* Paris, 2001; Guy Delahaye and Agnès Freschel, *Angelin Preljocaj,* Arles, 2003.

GARRY STEWART

For a late starter in dance, Garry Stewart has developed an arresting choreographic style to which critics give such labels as 'explosive', 'wracked', 'visceral', 'daring', 'dangerous' and 'ballistic'. Stewart himself told the *London Times* critic Debra Craine that his choreography is 'an incredibly dextrous physical form, which is equivalent to sport' and that his work was 'about the execution of extreme virtuosity and taking the body into an entirely new realm'.[1] His performers train in Korean martial arts, gymnastics, *capoeira,* break-dancing and other forms as well as classical ballet. They hurl themselves into the air, spin with vertiginous speed, leap over, under and around each other, crash to the floor, and yet are capable of quiet tenderness and delicacy when needed.

The youngest of four children in a poor rural family, the Australian Stewart was born near Gunnedah in northern New South Wales. His parents divorced when he was seven. When he was a teenager he moved with his mother to Sydney, where he completed his secondary schooling and was 'bowled over' on first experiencing classical music; he began playing trumpet in a school orchestra. What he calls a 'tumultuous' family background gave him an early feeling for social justice and political awareness. Seeing education as a way out of domestic confinement, he completed his schooling, worked for a time in a bank and with blind and deaf people, and then began a university course in social work; he became something of an activist and helped to find the university's Gay Society.

But then he saw the Sydney Dance Company in *Poppy,* Graeme Murphy's interpretation of Jean Cocteau's life. It was Stewart's first sight of theatrical dance, and he was 'blown away'. He thought the dancers 'like gods'. Giving up the university, he saw as much dance as he could and worked at anything to make enough money to keep going. On the brink of turning 20 years old, he began classes with Margaret Chapple at the Bodenwieser studio, then Sydney's leading modern dance centre, but realizing classical training was necessary he began learning, and (to his surprise) was accepted into the Australian Ballet School in Melbourne when almost 22. Although more than merely coping with the classical classes of Kelvin Coe and Gary Norman, he was more at ease with Gayrie MacSween's Graham technique and other modern teaching, and suggested that there should be a season of student choreography. In retrospect, he thought his own contribution, *Conversation with an Ironing Board* (1985 – there was no ironing board in it) 'a dreadful little piece . . . a bit DaDa-ist', but it was his first serious attempt at choreography.[2]

Before completing the three-year course, he was accepted into the Australian Dance Theatre, making his professional début in *A Descent into the Maëlstrom*, commissioned for the 1986 Adelaide Festival of Arts from choreographer Molissa Fenley and composer Philip Glass, both Americans. This intensely rhythmic fast-moving work was based on a story by Edgar Allan Poe in which a Norwegian fisherman emerges from a cataclysmic whirlpool alive but transformed into an old man. If Fenley's rapid, athletic style drew him, it had little influence on a short workshop piece, *Zen Do Something*, later in the year, or *Childscape*, which he made for Expressions, the Queensland company he joined in 1987. After a brief stint appearing in contemporary works with the Queensland Ballet, he returned to Sydney in 1988, discovering a strong connection with acting as a member of Kai Tai Chan's One Extra Company. Kai Tai's works, more dance theatre than dance itself, were usually based on social issues, an added attraction for Stewart, who danced Iago in a version of *Othello* where Shakespeare's Moorish general became an Australian Aboriginal businessman caught between two cultural worlds. More acting experience came with *Harold in Italy*, a collaboration between One Extra and Sydney Dance Company, but after 18 months with One Extra Stewart made his first overseas trip, to Spain, where working with Carmen Senra and her small experimental group in Madrid led to a feeling that it was not acting or even dancing but choreography that would be his future path.

Back in Sydney, he made a few short works before snapping an anterior cruciate ligament in 1991. During the following enforced year off, he began a University of Technology course in film and video, made his first dance film and choreographed two short works. He continued to study, discovering the post-modern philosophers, especially Michel Foucault, and in 1995 produced *The Velocity of Sex*, a robust, even violent, expression of sexualized dance in which he first used the particular kind of fast movement that became his stylistic hallmark. Creating this work made him realize how psychologically satisfying it was to see his own choreography delivered with great speed and power. Later that year, he pushed the technique further in *Spectre in the Covert Memory* for the début season of his friend Gideon Obarzanek's company Chunky Move. For one reviewer, the dancers 'appeared galvanized by electric shocks'.[3]

In late 1997, a three-month Australia Council grant took him to study release technique with Susan Klein in New York. He returned to create for the Victorian College of the Arts the first, small, version of *Birdbrain* (1998), a deconstruction of *Swan Lake*, which evolved through several transformations to become his first international success. By now realizing he needed his own group to develop his particular style of movement, he formed Thwack! for which in 1999 he made *Plastic Space*, a commentary on our fascination with Outer Space, combining his fast-moving, athletic choreography with film and video images.

But bigger things were in store. Later in the same year, Stewart was appointed as an Artistic Director of Australian Dance Theatre. Based in Adelaide, ADT, as it is affectionately known, was founded in 1965 by Elizabeth Dalman and Leslie White and is Australia's oldest modern dance company. Subsequent directors have included Jonathan Taylor, Leigh Warren and Meryl Tankard, each with a distinctive style. More than any of his predecessors, Stewart has pushed boundaries, explored the use of technology with dance and created an individual mode of movement. His first work after appointment could hardly have been more spectacular: for *Housedance*, he slung six dancers and a violinist on ropes to perform his acrobatic choreography on the outside of the main sail of the Sydney Opera House roof. Made for the International Millennium Broadcast on New Year's Eve 1999, it was seen by an estimated two billion people.

His evolutionary working method is exemplified by *Birdbrain*, which began as a piece for students, underwent development at the Australian Choreographic Centre in Canberra, had its professional premiere at the 2000 Adelaide Festival, and has since toured widely. Stewart mostly dispenses with the narrative of Petipa's ballet, but dresses his dancers in T-shirts with characters' names – 'Sieg' and 'Fried', 'Hero', 'Lover', for example; with scenery – 'Woods', 'Lake'; and with phrases – 'Peasant Joy', 'Royal Disdain' and even 'More Pointless Revelling'. Helpful hints to the story flash on a screen from time to time, and on one occasion a soloist combines rapid breakdance and classical mime to summarize the plot. The cygnets begin decorously enough but rapidly become four wrestlers flinging themselves at, through and around each other while remaining were firmly attached. The 32 fouettés are stolidly performed by four dancers as the numbers count down on the screen behind them, while there are several Odettes, Odiles and other characters, Von Rothbart is played by a contortionist, half-seen behind a scrim at the back of the stage.

A video of famous Odettes gives historical context (at times mockingly), and last of all a film loop shows a ballerina taking her bow as dancers carry the limp bodies of their lovers slowly across the misty stage – a sober conclusion until five appear with light boxes spelling out 'Begin', returning us to the start of the work, and asserting the continuance of the ballet itself. For all its daring gymnastic exuberance, variety of movement and humour, *Birdbrain* takes an affectionate, not a contemptuous or harshly satirical, view of *Swan Lake*. *The Guardian's* Judith Mackrell remarked that part of the work's 'considerable comedy derives from [Stewart's] knowing and often loving manipulation of the original choreography', and when John Percival wrote in *The Independent* that '*Birdbrain* is fun, but not only fun' he was in full agreement with *The New York Times's* Jack Anderson's view that 'It was also fun to think about'.[4]

A restless thinker, Stewart pushes ideas just as he pushes his dancers' bodies, and he sees his choreographies as being in dialogue with one another. After the post-modern ironies of *Birdbrain*, for example, came the somewhat whimsical *Monstrosity* (2001), with the dancers first as dotty sheep and cows, then as hyperactive gymnasts, barrelling through the air, leaping and twisting at great speed, and later as red-spotted monsters. Then came *The Age of Unbeauty* (2002), a commentary on cruelty, violence and the negation of truth and beauty in today's world, originally inspired by revulsion at Australia's treatment of certain asylum seekers. Against a wall of parquet flooring, a series of episodes depict torture, corpses piled on a cart, bandaged bodies being manipulated, riot and street chaos and other aspects of inhumanity. A few sequences nevertheless offer caring and nurture. In a hopeful conclusion, the frenetic, tormented movements of the dancers become calmer, more elegant, giving a sense of release and connection between people. Videos, still projections and the sound design of Luke Smiles were integral to the production, which had great success, although some found it needed more emotional and intellectual engagement with its audience.[5]

Always a photography enthusiast, Stewart found an immediate chemistry when he met dance photographer Lois Greenfield in New

York. The result was *Held* (2004), in which Greenfield spends about two-thirds of the hour-long work on stage, freezing the spectacular movements of the whirling, leaping dancers in 1/2000th of second shots that are projected on two huge screens a fraction of time later behind the still-moving performers. Further playing games with visual perception, Stewart also uses shadow, darkness (the dancers lit by strobe lighting), different coloured backgrounds and videos when Greenfield is off stage, and varies the choreography with a couple of slow solos in contrast to the high-velocity twists, jumps and mid-air rolls that comprise most of the movement. *Held* won awards for Stewart and members of his company.

Collaboration with Melbourne filmmaker Gina Czarnecki (with whom he had made the award-winning film *Nascent* in 2005), Canadian robotics designer Louis-Philippe Demers and Melbourne composer Darrin Verhagen led to *Devolution* (2006), based on the metaphor of ecosystems and placing humans and machines in conflict and confluence with one another. The dancers, uncharacteristically floor-bound and dressed in scaly insect-like costumes, not only shared the stage with various robots (from the small and crablike to the huge and clomping) but also eventually appeared to grow metal, glass and plastic prosthetic limbs – the most extraordinary a long, unpredictably lashing whip sprouting from a dancer's back. Although critical reception was somewhat cool as to the success of contextualizing humans in a futuristic mechanical world, *Devolution* pleased audiences greatly and won significant awards.

Stewart's long concern with social issues, particularly justice, was given 'shatteringly good' expression in *Honour Bound* (2006), inspired by the five-year incarceration without trial of Australian David Hicks in the American prison for suspected terrorists at Guantanamo Bay.[6] Stewart's choreography, which was conceived and directed by Nigel Jamieson, put the six performers in a giant wire cage and 'into dizzying spins . . . heart-stopping drops . . . disorienting situations in which we seem[ed] to be observing them from above. Savage emotions of despair [were] counteracted by the poignancy of glimpses of compassion'.[7] Stewart links this with *The Age of Unbeauty* (2002), in which he said, 'Dramaturgically I was investigating the history of torture and incarceration and oppression'.[8] His next work, *G*, a reworking of *Giselle*, had a studio showing in 2008 and premiered in August 2009. For this, the basics of *Giselle*'s story and words relating to her emotional state were spelled out on a large LED display hung against the black backcloth. Chronological development was replaced by a constant current of action across the stage, the barefooted dancers at first walking with slow, classical steps, disappearing left, reappearing right, in a continuous flow, until Luke Smiles' electronic score ramped up the beat. The dancers now moved rapidly, criss-crossing feet in tiny steps until one suddenly bent low, distorting and twisting her body, her face tortured. From then on, the choreography raced and slowed with relentless energy, expressive particularly of anguish, hysteria and fear ('I am so frightened' flashing on the display). Extracting and amplifying such elements from *Giselle* and eschewing the humour of *Birdbrain* made *G* a comment on the anxieties of modern life as much as a deconstruction of a great classical ballet. While touring internationally with *G*, Stewart developed *Be Your Self* for the 2010 Adelaide Festival, an examination of the stability of the concept of self – through dance, video graphics, spoken text and architectural design. In 2009, he also choreographed a community dance, *The Sydney*, performed by 300,000 for the opening night of that year's Sydney Festival; *The Centre and Its Opposite* for Birmingham Royal Ballet; and *Un-Black* for Ballet de l'Opéra National du Rhin in Mulhouse.

Garry Stewart is nothing if not adventurous.

Alan Brissenden

Notes

1 *The Australian,* 11 February 2005.
2 Interview with the author, 1 February 2007.
3 Patricia Laughlin, *Dance Magazine,* January 1996.
4 Judith Mackrell, *The Guardian,* 9 May 2003; John Percival, *The Independent,* 12 May 2003; Jack Anderson, *The New York Times,* 6 January 2002.
5 See Alan Brissenden, *The Australian,* 1 March 2002; Debra Craine, *The Times,* 8 March 2005.
6 Jill Sykes, *The Sydney Morning Herald,* 8 August 2006.
7 Ibid.
8 Jacqueline Pascoe, 'A Cry for Justice', *Dance Australia,* No. 146, 2006.

Biographical details

Born near Gunnedah, New South Wales, Australia, 19 May 1962. **Studied** at the Bodenwieser Studio and Tanya Pearson Classical Academy, Sydney, 1982–84, and Australian Ballet School, Melbourne, 1984–86; also studied video at the University of New South Wales and Media and Communications at the University of Technology, Sydney. **Career**: Performed in drag shows 1982–84, making his professional début with Australian Dance Theatre in 1986; also dancer with Expressions Dance Company, 1987, Queensland Ballet, and One Extra Company, 1988. First choreography as a student, 1985, going on to create works for One Extra, Darc Swan, Chunky Move, Sydney Dance Company and several tertiary dance courses, 1991–98; founded his own company *Thwack!*, 1998; artistic director, Australian Dance Theatre, from 1999, taking the company on 16 international tours by 2010. **Awards and honours** include Robert Helpmann Scholarship, 1998; Australia Council for the Arts Fellowship, 1999; Australian Choreographic Centre Fellowship 1998, 1999, Australian Dance Awards, 2002, 2004, 2005, 2006, 2008; Adelaide Critics' Circle Awards, 2002; Helpmann Awards 2004, 2006; IMZ Dance Screen Award 2005; Reeldance Award 2006; Ruby Award (*Devolution*), 2006.

Works

Conversation with an Ironing Board (1985); *Zen Do Some Nothing* (1986); *Childscape* (1987); *N.Y.* (1988); *The Year My Leg Broke* (1991); *The Sex, Flesh/Love, Lust Axis* (1992); *Arlene Harper* (1992); *The Kweer and the Unfamilia* (1993); *This* (1993); *The Velocity of Sex* (1995); *Bonded* (1995); *Spectre in the Covert Memory* (1995); *West Side Story* (1996); *THWACK!* (1996); *Danger is Imminent* (1997); *Two Step Crush* (film, 1997); *Birdbrain* (evolving versions, 1998, 2000, 2001); *Fugly* (1998); *Smiles Miles* (film, 1998); *Amnesia* (1999); *Space* (1999); *Plastic Space* (1999); *Currently under Investigation* (1999); *Housedance* (1999); *Monstrosity* (2001); *The Age of Unbeauty* (2002); *Nothing* (2003); *Held* (2004); *Nascent* (film, dir. Gina Czarnecki, 2005); *Present Tense* (2005); *Devolution* (with Louis-Philippe Demers and Gina Czarnecki, 2006); *Honour Bound* (with Nigel Jamieson, 2006); *Infinity* (2008); *G* (2008–09); *The Sydney* (Sydney Festival, 2009); *The Centre and Its Opposite* (2009); *Un-Black* (2009); *Be Your Self* (2010).

Further reading

Interviews with Lee Tran Lam, in 'Nothing if Not Inspired', *Limelight*, July 2003; with four other choreographers in 'Not Strictly Dancing', *State of the Arts*, March/April 2005; with Mark Baechtel, in 'The Body Heroic', *Anchorage Daily News*, 7 April 2005; with Karen van Ulzen, in 'Limelight', *Dance Australia*, No. 140, October/November 2005; with Erin Brannigan, in 'Dance Evolution in the Land of Robotics', *RealTime*, February/March 2006.

Articles: Catherine Taylor, 'No Holds Barred', *Weekend Australian Review*, 7–8 August 1999; Jack Anderson, 'Taking Liberties with Ballet's Archetypes', *The New York Times*, 6 January 2002; John Percival, 'Birdbrain', *The Independent*, 12 May 2003; Ashley Hay, 'Frieze Frame', *The Bulletin*, 10 August 2004; Zoë Anderson, 'Birdbrain', *The Independent*, 8 March 2005; Patrick McDonald, 'Danger! Machines in Motion', *Advertiser Review*, 18 February 2006; Jacqueline Pascoe, 'A Cry for Justice', *Dance Australia*, 146 October/November 2006; Michael Bollen, 'Maybe We're Not Human: Translating Actions and Affects Between Humans and Machines in Australian Dance Theatre's Devolution', *Brolga*, 31, 2009.

ELIZABETH STREB

Elizabeth Streb's choreography does not look much like other contemporary dance. Although compellingly physical, it is not at all 'dancerly'; its technical vocabulary – created anew, depending on the task the dancers are to perform – seems to have more in common with that of the circus aerialist or the Hollywood stunt artist than with conventional modern dance. Her company, Streb/Ringside, incorporates gymnasts, climbers, divers and other elite athletes alongside traditionally trained performers.

Nevertheless, Streb's work is firmly rooted in the ideology of American post-modern dance. Her pieces owe much of their conceptual basis to Merce Cunningham's ideas about choreography, but they give that tradition a unique interpretation. Like Cunningham, with whom she studied for several years and whom she revered, Streb pursues movement that is insistently present in time and in particular places. Like Cunningham, she is interested in expanding possible perceptions of space and time. Although Cunningham used chance structures, indeterminacy and computer simulation to reconfigure the predictable line and habitual kinaesthetics of a formal style of movement, Streb choreographs the performance of tasks in restricted risky settings to generate high-intensity movement that keeps her dancers constantly off balance and hyper-aware – illuminating the natural laws with which the dancer is always engaging.

She refers to her style of dare-devil movement as 'honest', by which she means that it cannot be marked or faked and must be performed with full commitment; otherwise the dancer could get hurt. In Streb's earliest dances, her engagement with natural forces seemed literal and unadorned. She manipulated poles or rings, tossing them in the air, catching them, sliding them around her body and jumping over them. The issue was not simply discovering all the things that could be done with a particular piece of equipment, but it was also about sensing the effects of gravity on the object, learning how to engage with momentum and, in constructing a dance, figuring out how lift, weight and momentum define the choices with respect of the sequencing of tasks. Over the years, Streb commissioned increasingly elaborate sets from articulated harnesses to a giant 'hamster wheel' designed by Michael Casseli. As Streb herself described it in a press release for *Space Object* in 1983, 'With these objects, I confront space to create movement that becomes functional and integral to that object.'

In her early signature piece *Little Ease* (1985), Streb performed in a box a little bigger than a coffin, turned on its side, thus dramatically framing her inability to initiate any movement from an upright position. This very calculated and constrained use of space framed and condensed the energy of her effort so that what was dramatized was the supremacy of natural laws as well as the heroic effort of the dancer.

In 1985, Streb began choreographing dances, or what she calls 'Action Events', for increasingly large groups of dancers, multiplying the energy and momentum of her dances as well as the risk of collisions and their need for attentiveness, collaboration and precision. She ventured into sophisticated theatrical décor such as projections of digital video and closed-circuit cameras to establish different points of view on the action. 'Dancing in the air,' Streb has said, 'is like being in the center of space. I want to be in places seemingly too unnameable to mention . . . on every point between two points, onward and into infinity' (Streb, talking during rehearsals in New York, July–August 1993). In one of Streb's many aerial dances, *Lookup* (1993), four dancers wearing omni-directional harnesses walked, spun, dived and swooped against a 40-foot high wall (which was also a floor) as they were slowly lowered down the wall. At any given moment in the dance, the performers might be head down, face down, back down or side down, as they did everything from forward somersaults to *chainé* turns. In the different environments in which this dance was shown, Streb tried to let the audience experience maximum disorientation by being as close as possible, even directly beneath, the dancers.

Like many post-Cunningham choreographers, Streb honours the injunction that a movement takes as much (and only as much) effort and time as the movement itself dictates: a rejection of either expressive or musical phrasing. In its functionalism and emphasis on pure movement, Streb's work resonates with allusions to first-generation post-modern choreography of the 1960s and 1970s. Some of her pieces seem like direct descendants of early post-modern dances: *Lookup*, for example, seems to be an elaboration of Trisha Brown's walking-on-the-wall dances; and Streb's preoccupation with risk and planned chaos seems to hark back to Brown's and Yvonne Rainer's dances in which, for example, participants took turns falling and catching one another.[1]

But Streb goes further: the apparatus she uses, and the momentum required for much of her choreography, tend to mobilize the whole body as a unit and necessitate timings that are often at the edge of human comfort and control. In *Up* (1995), the dancers rebound, often at high speed, off an Olympic-quality trampoline whose extremely live surface can be touched by only one dancer in any given instant, lest the dancers ricochet in unexpected and dangerous directions. In *Gauntlet* (2004), groups of dancers navigate and lie flat beneath swinging cinder blocks suspended on wires as the audience witnesses a series of near-misses.

Streb prides herself on her technical awareness of physical encounters, occasionally projecting mathematical formulae and diagrams behind the word to indicate the mechanisms of bodies in motion, and she designed an idiosyncratic course of study for herself at New York University's Draper Programme to earn a graduate degree in Time and Space. Streb's dances deliberately 'push' both dancers' and audiences' perceptions of time by taking the body outside the kinaesthetic parameters that conventionally determine timing, making palpable the warping of conventions of time and space that come with a brutally immediate movement. At the same time, performing (and watching) Streb's work not only sharpens one's sense of timing; it also increases the actual speed at which one can perceive movement, allowing one to see images that seem to defy natural laws.

In recent years, Streb has amplified the surfaces and floor of her performance spaces so that each rebound and fall is intensely jarring. It almost seems as though Streb is using sound as a Brechtian alienation effect, disrupting the audience's easy pleasure in the dances' athleticism and shocking viewers into seeing movement in a fresh way. Streb has also carried cognitive dissonance into some dances made specifically for video in collaboration with the videographers Michael Schwartz and Mary Lucier, especially Schwartz's and Streb's *Airdance* (1987). In 2003, Streb established the Streb Lab for Action Mechanics (SLAM) in Williamsburg, Brooklyn, which offers the company a 'laboratory' for experimentation as well as open-to-the-public rehearsals and a full schedule of community classes and workshops for adults and children.

In 1997, Elizabeth Streb was awarded a MacArthur Foundation 'Genius' award, and in addition to a full touring schedule has worked increasingly towards more commercial projects, including an off-Broadway season. Although primarily appearing in performance venues on tour, Streb is committed to presenting accessible work in public spaces such as parks and beaches. For example, the company has appeared during a baseball game at the Minnesota Metrodome, in the streets of Montreal with Cirque de Soleil, in the cultural programming at the 2010 Winter Olympics in Vancouver and in 'the hugely public medium of television'.

This theatricality expands Streb's restless concern with exploring and communicating the intensity and immediacy of movement. As she put it in a 1990 *Dance Magazine* interview, 'I've tried to examine a "real move" for a long time now. Not to fabricate movement but to get at the inside gut of it . . . this wild, untamed animal.'

Judy Burns
(revised and updated by Debra Cash)

Note

1 See Marianne Goldberg, *Reconstructing Trisha Brown: Dances and Performance Pieces* 1960–75, PhD dissertation, New York University, 1990.

Biographical details

Born in Rochester, New York, United States, 23 February 1950. **Studied** at the State University of New York, Brockport, 1968–72, obtaining a BS (*cum laude*) in Modern Dance: taught by Susannah Payton, Daniel Nagrin, Irma Plyshenko and Mary Edwards; she also received tuition under Diana Byer, Janet Panetta, Viola Farber, Merce Cunningham, Jocelyn Lorenz and June Finch. **Career:** Dancer with Margaret Jenkins, San Francisco, 1972–74; based in New York from 1974; founder, dancer and choreographer, Streb/Ringside company, 1985; established SLAM (Streb Lab for Action Mechanics) in 2003. **Awards and honours** include Creative Artists Public Service Program Award, 1981; National Endowment for the Arts Choreography Award, 1984, and Fellowships, 1985–88, 1989–92, 1992–94, 1994–96; Foundation for Contemporary Performance Arts Fellowships, 1985, 1988; Art Matters Fellowship, 1985, 1987, 1992; New York Foundation for the Arts Fellowship, 1987, 1990, 1994; Corporation for Art and Television Award, 1987; New York Dance and Performance Award ('Bessie'), 1988, 1998; Guggenheim Fellowship, 1989; Brandeis University Creative Arts Award, 1991; MacArthur Foundation 'Genius' Award, 1997; appointed to the Mayor's Cultural Affairs Advisory Commission, 2008.

Works

Springboard (1979); *Pole Vaults* (1980); *Fall Line* (1981); *Fall Line Inside Out* (video; dir. Michael Schwanz, 1982); *Ringside* (1982); *Space Object* (1983); *P.S.I.* (1983); *Whiplash 1* (1983); *Add* (1983); *Runway* (1983); *Marathon Dance* (1983); *Blackboard* (1983); *Blackboard 1* (1984); *Target* (1983)*; *Whiplash 4* (1985); *Blackboard 4* (1985); *Little Ease* (1985); *Roller Board* (1985); *Free Flight* (1985); *Amphibian* (video;

dir. Mary Lucier, 1985); *Airlines* (1986)*; *Midair* (1987); *Freeflight* (1987); *Airwaves* (1987); *Pole Vaults* (1987); *Airdance* (video; dir Michael Schwanz, 1987); *Soaring* (1987 and 1990); *If I Could Fly I Would Fly* (video; dir. Mary Lucier, 1987); *Massfloat* (1988); *Mass Dance* (1989); *Spacehold* (1989); *Log* (1990)*; *Rebound* (1990); *Mass* (video; dir. Mary Lucier, 1990); *Impact* (1991); *Groundlevel* (1992)*; *Dive* (1991); *Wall Drive* (1991); *Link* (1992); *Surface* (1993); *Lookup* (1993); *Bounce* (1994); *Line* (1995)*; *Up* (1995); *Rise* (1995); *Breakthru* (1995); *Echo* (1995); *Q/Action* (1995); *Pop Action* (1996); *Paint Action* (1997); *Across* (1997); *Fly* (1997); *Punch the Jump* (1999); *Swing* (2000); *Writhe* (2000); *Squirm* (2000); *Jump* (2000); *Gravity* (2000); *Air Impact* (2000); *Edge* (2000); *Dive Through Hoops* (2000); Action Heroes (2001); *SlipandSlide* (2002); *Heavy Metal* (2002); *Bilevel* (2002); *Against the Wall* (2002); *Tied* (2002); *Rise and Fall* (2002); *Slap Stick/Buster* (2002); *AirSwim* (2002); *Wall Fall* (2002); *Up and Down* (2002); *Air* (2003); *Splash* (2003); *Wild Blue Yonder* (2003); *Stay* (2004); *Gauntlet* (2004); *Falling Everywhere* (2005); *Orbit* (2005); *Crash* (2005); *Moon* (2006); *Tip* (2006); *Ricochet* (2006); *Ripple* (2006); *Revolution* (2006); *Group Gravity* (2006); *Streb vs Gravity* (2006); *Invisible Forces* (2009); *Brave* (2009); *Raw* (2010).

*Published sources vary; dates cited here are in accordance with Elizabeth Streb's website.

Further reading

Interviews with Michael Sapir, *Dance Theatre Journal*, Autumn 1994; with Nancy Vreeland Dalva, in 'Elizabeth of Anchorage', *Dance ink*, New York, Winter 1993/94, with Joseph Carman in 'Death-Defying Dance', *The Advocate*, 28 May 2002, with Michelle Vellucci, in 'Elizabeth Streb', *Dance Teacher*, February 2010.

Articles: Iris Fanger, 'Elizabeth Streb: Action and Reaction', *Dance Magazine*, March 1990; Judy Burns, 'Wild Bodies, Wilder Minds: Streb, Ringside and Spectacle', *Women and Performance*, 7(1), 1994; Robert Greskovic, 'Elizabeth Streb Ringside', *Dance Magazine*, October 1994; Romi Goldwasser, 'Streb's 'Pop-action' to Kennedy Center', *Dance Magazine*, February 1997; Susanne Sloat, 'Streb', *Attitude*, Spring/Summer 1998; Alice Naude, 'Reviews: New York City', *Dance Magazine*, April 1998; Susan Reiter, 'In Step: Action Packed', *Dance Australia*, October/November 1998; Diedre Sklar, 'Artists' Forum: Matthew Bourne, Rennie Harns, Elizabeth Streb', *Ballet Review*, Spring 1999; Sanjoy Roy, 'Up, Down, Turn Around', *Dance Now*, Summer 1999; Rose Eichenbaum, 'Faces in Dance: Elizabeth Streb – Lady of Action', *Dance Magazine*, November 1999; Mary Jo Thompson, 'The Sound of Dance', *Dance International*, Fall 2000; Gigi Beradi, 'Hero Worship', *Dance Magazine*, March 2001; Nancy Dalva, 'Wham Bam Streb', *Dance Magazine*, June 2003; George Jackson, 'Streb', *Dance Magazine*, December 2003; Deborah Jowitt, 'Quantum Leaps', *The Village Voice*, 4 July 2006 and 'On the Fly', *The Village Voice*, 11 July 2006; Robyn Sulcas, 'Gravity May Eventually Triumph, but Not Without a Fight', *The New York Times*, 4 December 2007; Deborah Jowitt, 'Elizabeth Streb Spins Her Whizzing Gizmo', *The Village Voice*, 13 May 2009.

Books: Rose Eichenbaum (photographs and text) and Clive Barnes (foreword), *Masters of Movement: Portraits of America's Great Choreographers*, Washington, DC, 2004; Joyce Morgenroth (ed.), *Speaking of Dance: Twelve Contemporary Choreographers on Their Craft*, New York, 2004; Elizabeth Streb, *How to Become an Extreme Action Hero*, New York, 2010.

PAUL TAYLOR

Paul Taylor has described himself as an 'American mongrel'. It is an apt assessment, given the range of ideas and influences that permeate his choreography, and it is also indicative of his resistance to being pigeon-holed. Critics have referred to the 'dark' and 'light' sides of Taylor's choreography, his dance vocabulary is an ingenious mix of pedestrian movements alongside the most rhythmic and sweeping of steps (some-times within the same work), his musical choices are wide-ranging and his collaborations with visual artists have been equally eclectic.

Taylor's early career provides several clues to the rich diversity that characterizes his choreography. He created his first work, *Hobo Ballet* (1952), while still a student at Syracuse University, where he divided his time between courses in painting and the demands of a swimming scholarship. During the 1950s, he worked with a variety of teachers and choreographers and he came into contact with many of New York's most avant-garde artists. Taylor's first work for the experimental New York group Dance Associates, *Jack and the Beanstalk* (1954), was designed by Robert Rauschenberg. They collaborated on ten subse-quent productions, including *Three Epitaphs* (1956)[1] and *Seven New Dances* (1957). It was through Rauschenberg that Taylor met Gene Moore, the designer of later works such as *Images* (1977), *Airs* (1978), *Arden Court* (1981) and *Musical Offering* (1986).

During this period, Taylor's choreographic musings seemed at odds with his parallel development as a performer. As a member of the Martha Graham Dance Company in the late 1950s, he was dancing in increasingly prominent roles. A pinnacle of success was his starring role in George Balanchine's choreography for *Episodes* in 1959, which helped to establish Taylor as one of New York's leading dancers. However, Taylor's choreography received less support at first, mainly because some critics regarded it as an apparent rejection of the dra-matic, all-dancing, 'grand' modern tradition.

Much has been written about the iconoclastic nature of Taylor's early choreography, and particularly of *Seven New Dances*, a concert that critics claimed had notoriously little dancing in it. Ironically, it was Louis Horst's non-review of the concert (a blank column with only the place and date printed), rather than the seemingly non-dance content of the programme itself that caused the greater furore; and, indirectly, it also brought Taylor his first taste of fame.[2]

Taylor had, in fact, spent several months evolving the programme through a series of choreographic discoveries; his intention had been to find an 'alphabet' from which he could form steps, phrases and, ultimately, dances. It was a turning point in his career. As he confirms, 'after that my dances began to move, a lot of movement, very wild, flung, I call it "scribbly"'. These 'scribbles' evolved into large, legible phrases in which each movement was defined spatially, but with such fluency that body shapes registered without ever being fixed in a position. Certain contours and steps soon became Taylor's hallmarks. Recurrent features are the spiralling, open-chested torso; extended 'V' or curved 'C' shaped arms; and skimming *sissonnes* and successive jumps in first position (both performed with the legs in parallel and rarely fully stretched).

Seven New Dances also taught Taylor much about stillness. In many of his works, he illuminates the dance 'moment' and its dramatic intent through such theatrical means as posture and timing. (The 1982 collage, *Lost, Found and Lost*, actually draws on many of the poses and postural changes in *Seven New Dances*.)

Taylor's theatrical manipulation of dance time is matched by an instinctive (and sometimes irreverent) response to music. When he first choreographed to Baroque music – *Junction* (1961), to Bach; and *Aureole* (1962), to Handel – many of his avant-garde colleagues felt that he had abandoned experiment in favour of more mainstream and popular aims. But in creating *Junction*, Taylor's intention was 'to find what musicality meant'. By matching the mellow rhythms of Bach's cello music to the quirky, grounded movements of his choreography, he began to forge complex, contrapuntal dance–music relationships. Importantly, *Junction* initiated a familiarity with, and mastery of, music by Bach – an interest that led, ultimately, to *Musical Offering* and to Leopold Stokowski's orchestral transcriptions of Bach for *Promethean Fire* (2002). Taylor developed his musical sensibility with speed and competence, evident in the lyricism and detail of *Aureole* and, by 1966, in his sophisticated handling of Beethoven's last quartets for the hour-long work *Orbs*.

It was the success of *Aureole* that persuaded Taylor to commit himself full-time to his own choreography and company. The international appeal of this work and its complementary role in his rapidly evolving repertory meant that the Paul Taylor Dance Company became one of the world's busiest touring groups. Even today, *Aureole* remains one of his most popular works, both within his company repertory and when staged by other ballet and modern-dance companies.

Another pivotal work was *Esplanade* (1975), not only because of its exuberant physicality but also because it confirmed that Taylor's company could be successful after he retired from performing. By this time, he had evolved a repertory where the central male presence of Taylor himself had dominated the work. From 1975 onwards, Taylor became one step removed from the realization of his ideas and, working in this way, he became open to new possibilities, both in his own selection and structuring of material and in the particular talents of individual dancers.

During the next decade, Taylor assembled a company of outstanding performers while, simultaneously, creating a series of great works. *Runes* (1975), created only months after *Esplanade*, celebrates Taylor's interest in symbolic gesture, ritual practices and transformation. Its subtitle, 'Secret Writings for Use in Casting a Spell', hints at the exhaustive attempts made by Taylor and his dancers to find appropriate material for the series of danced incantations that feature in the work. As with *Musical Offering*, it is the originality and unprecedented stylization, particularly for the two female soloists, that makes *Runes* distinctive.

Originality of a different kind prompted *Le Sacre du printemps (The Rehearsal)* in 1980. The title alludes to the context within which Taylor set his version of Stravinsky's well-known scenario. Instead of the primitivism of most previous productions, his *Sacre* is set in the post-modern present, with its downtown locations (a dance studio and gangland Chinatown) and its pastiche of 1920s movie stereotypes. Taylor mixes his narratives: the daily rituals of a dance company are enacted while a detective story about a kidnapped baby unfolds. (Taylor has described it as 'a sort of Runyonesque gumshoe story'.) Curiously, despite this duality *Sacre* is Taylor's most linear storyline. With the death of the baby and the mother's frenzied solo, the detective story reaches a clear dénouement and, as if to reaffirm the Taylor company's perpetual round of rehearsal performance, *Sacre* ends where all its dances begin – back in the studio.

Le Sacre du printemps (The Rehearsal) was Taylor's last collaboration with the designer John Rawlings, who died that same year. Rawlings first worked with Taylor on *Piece Period* in 1962 and, subsequently, created designs for several key works, including the Americana epic *From Sea to Shining Sea* (1965) and *Esplanade*. Taylor later claimed that Rawlings was 'one of the few people I've ever really collaborated with', and this is borne out by accounts of Rawlings's ongoing discussions with Taylor and his involvement during rehearsals. At the opposite extreme is Taylor's association with Alex Katz, whose designs have sometimes been produced before Taylor begins a work. These 'obstacle courses' as Taylor refers to them, such as the stand-up metal dogs in *Diggity* (1978) and the mirrored prisms in the apocalyptic *Last Look* (1985), thus became an organizing principle of the choreography.

Another designer, 'George Tacet', was featured in programmes from the 1960s to the late 1970s. Tacet is, in fact, Taylor himself and although financial constraints may have been the main reason for in-house designs at times, they prompted important works such as *Aureole, American Genesis* (1973) and *Runes*.

The intermittent use of the design contributions of Katz, Rawlings and Gene Moore is typical of Taylor's tendency to work with a small, select group of designers while staggering the sequence of their involvement. (Other designers include Rouben Ter-Arutunian, Alec Sutherland and William Ivey Long.) An exception to this pattern is Taylor's association with Santo Loquasto who, from *Speaking in Tongues* (1988) onwards, has designed the vast majority of Taylor's work. Since the mid-1960s, Jennifer Tipton has lit almost all his dances including *Polaris* (1976), in which the work's environment changes, based on two different styles of lighting.

Another long-term associate is Donald York, who has composed music for several works, including *Diggity, Last Look* (1985) and the evening-length *Of Bright and Blue Birds and the Gala Sun* (1990). Especially crucial has been York's contribution as a music director and conductor of Taylor's company. Since first working with them in 1976, a time when Taylor's creativity was reaching new heights, York has guided the musical choices. Taylor's use of 'difficult' scores, such as those by Scriabin (*Nightshade*, 1979), Radzynski (*Profiles*, 1979), Milhaud (*House of Cards*, 1981), Varèse (... *Byzantium*, 1984) and Ligeti (*Counterswarm*, 1988), increased noticeably under York's presence.

Most telling of all, in terms of Taylor's musical development, is his glorious command of Bach's *Musical Offering*. Significantly, the score was a product of years of musical experimentation and development by the composer; similarly, Taylor's *Musical Offering* is a consummate synthesis of several previously explored elements in his choreography. Some critics consider it Taylor's greatest rite, and once again a subtitle, 'A Requiem for Gentle Primitives' (added after the work's premiere), helps to contextualize the subject matter and movement style. A single female protagonist, the chief celebrant, begins and ends the dance. She introduces all the main themes of the work and, as the fugal and canonic accumulations of Bach's music become more densely textured, other dancers become part of the requiem. Although Taylor cannot read music notation, the parallels between the choreography and score of *Musical Offering*, particularly in terms of their structural and sectioning correspondences, are unequivocal.

Some time after the premiere of *Musical Offering*, Taylor revealed why he had interpreted the score, one of Bach's last compositions, as a requiem; 'I see this old man saying goodbye', he said, and to a degree, this farewell can be seen as autobiographical. Taylor has created, on average, two works each year since 1986, and as he entered his eighth decade he continued to create, so *Musical Offering* was certainly not his 'last' work. However, it represented the end of one phase of his career and a farewell to many influential colleagues.

More than 30 years on from *Esplanade*, Taylor has presided over new generations of dancers and seen his works staged by numerous companies worldwide. Age distinctions are now more pronounced in his dances, and historicity, especially related to Taylor's own past, has emerged as a subject matter. In *Kith and Kin* (1987), contrasting pieces for three generations of a familial group are the focus; in *Speaking in Tongues* (1988), generational stereotypes of a small-town community are the social fabric around which Taylor weaves his themes of wrong-doing and redemption; in *Company B* (1991), the war-time milieu of Taylor's youth is recalled in the ten dances set to songs by the Andrews Sisters; in *Oh, You Kid!* (1999), the sunshine of Taylor's nostalgic ragtime is clouded over by the jarring presence of a quintet in Ku Klux Klan hoods; and in *Black Tuesday* (2001), first performed by American Ballet Theatre, jitterbugging optimism brushes against the harsh realities of the Great Depression. *Promethean Fire* (2002), with its pile of bodies and lucid inter-weavings among the full-company ensemble, was rapturously received as a response to the terrorist attack on New York's World Trade Center (although Taylor noted that rehearsals for the work had already begun when the towers fell).

Taylor's work is represented in a number of media including nine different programmes made for American public television. *Dancemaker* (1998), the Academy-award nominated documentary by Matthew Diamond, captured the creation of *Piazzolla Caldera* (1997), an idiosyncratic meditation on basic human yearnings conjured by the soul of the tango. Repertory footage was also included in the film: *Esplanade* seen from the wings; and archival footage of *Aureole*, with Taylor's magisterial solo intercut with clips of a compelling younger dancer, Patrick

Corbin. In 2003, Diamond again documented Taylor's work with a public television taping of *Black Tuesday* and *Promethean Fire*. To celebrate the milestone of the company's 50th anniversary season in 2004/05, Paul Taylor Dance Company made an unprecedented tour of all 50 of the United States. Forever the 'mongrel', Taylor's legacy is a wealth of more than 125 dances that remain excitingly unpredictable.

Angela Kane
(revised and updated by Debra Cash)

Notes

1 Taylor's first version of the work was in 1956. It was briefly performed later the same year as *Four Epitaphs*, but was revised and staged as *Three Epitaphs* in 1960. In 1991, Taylor created new choreography and costumes for *Fact and Fancy* (1991), a work that begins with a complete performance of *Three Epitaphs* in Rauschenberg's original costumes.

2 Horst in 'Reviews of the Month', *Dance Observer*, 24(9), November 1957.

Biographical details

Born in Allegheny County, Pennsylvania, United States, 29 July 1930. **Studied** fine arts at Syracuse University, New York, 1950–53; studied modern dance with Martha Graham, Doris Humphrey, José Limón and Merce Cunningham; also ballet with Antony Tudor and Margaret Craske. **Career:** Danced with various modern companies, including those of Merce Cunningham in 1953–54, Pearl Lang in 1955, and Martha Graham in 1955–62. Made first choreography in 1952; founded Paul Taylor Dance Company in 1954 and retired from performing in 1974. Works widely as a guest choreographer; more than 75 companies have performed his work. **Awards and honours** include Théâtre des Nations Dance Festival Best Choreographer Award (Paris), 1962; Premio de la Critica (Chile), 1965; Capezio Dance Award, 1967; Chevalier dans l'Ordre des Arts et des Lettres, 1969 (upgraded to Officier, 1984, and Commandeur, 1990); *Dance Magazine* Award, 1980; MacArthur Foundation 'Genius' Award, 1985; Emmy Award, 1991; Kennedy Center Award, Washington, DC, 1992; US National Medal of Arts, 1993; Algur H. Meadows Award for Excellence in the Arts (United States), 1995; Doris Duke Awards, 1998, 2002, 2007; Légion d'Honneur, 2000; Critics' Circle National Dance Award, 2003; 10th Annual American Choreography Award, 2003; Association of Performing Arts Presenters (APAP) Award of Merit, 2005; Americans for the Arts Lifetime Achievement Award, 2005.

Works

Hobo Ballet (1952); *Jack and the Beanstalk* (1954); *Circus Polka* (revised as *Little Circus*, 1955); *The Least Flycatcher* (1956); *Three Epitaphs* (1956; briefly performed as *Four Epitaphs* later that year); *Untitled Duet* (1956); *Tropes* (1956); *Obertura Republicana* (with Remy Charlip, Marian Sarach, David Vaughan and James Waring, 1956); *The*

Tower (1957); *Seven New Dances: Epic, Events I, Resemblance, Panorama, Duet, Events II, Opportunity* (1957); *Rebus* (1958); *May Apple* (1958); *Images and Reflections* (1958, duet version in 1960); *Option* (1960); *Meridian* (1960); *Tablet* (1960); *Three Epitaphs* (revised version, 1960); *The White Salamander* (1960); *Fibers* (1961); *Insects and Heroes* (1961); *Junction* (1961); *Tracer* (1962); *Aureole* (1962); *Piece Period* (1962); *Fibers* (duet version, 1963); *Poetry in Motion* (1963); *La Negra* (1963); *Scudorama* (1963); *Party Mix* (1963); *The Red Room* (1964); *Duet* (1964); *Nine Dances with Music by Corelli* (1965); *Post Meridian* (revised version of *The Red Room*; 1965); *From Sea to Shining Sea* (1965); *Orbs* (1966); *Agathe's Tale* (1967); *Lento* (1967); *Public Domain* (1968); *Private Domain* (1969); *Duets* (1969); *Churchyard* (1969); *Foreign Exchange* (1970); *Big Bertha* (1970); *Book of Beasts* (1971); *Fêtes* (1971); *Guests of May* (1972); So *Long Eden* (1972); *West of Eden* (1973); *American Genesis: Before Eden, So Long Eden, West of Eden, Noah's Minstrels* (1973); *Sports and Follies* (1974); *Untitled Quartet* (a reworking of *Fibers*; 1974); *Esplanade* (1975); *Runes* (1975); *Cloven Kingdom* (1976); *Polaris* (1976); *Images* (1977); *Dust* (1977); *Aphrodisiamania* (1977); *Airs* (1978); *Diggity* (1978); *Nightshade* (1979); *Profiles* (1979); *Le Sacre du Printemps (The Rehearsal)* (1980); *Arden Court* (1981); *House of Cards* (1981); *Lost, Found and Lost* (1982); *Mercuric Tidings* (1982); *Musette* (1983); *Sunset* (1983); *Snow White* (1983); *Equinox* (1983); . . . *Byzantium* (1984); *Last Look* (1985); *Roses* (1985); *Musical Offering* (1986); *Ab Ovo Usque ad Mala (From Soup to Nuts)* (1986); *Kith and Kin* (1987); *Syzygy* (1987; revised 1989); *Brandenburgs* (1988); *Counterswarm* (1988); *Danbury Mix* (1988); *Speaking in Tongues* (1988); *Minikin Fair* (1989); *The Sorcerer's Sofa* (1989); *Of Bright and Blue Birds and the Gala Sun* (1990); *Fact and Fancy* (1991); *Company B* (1991); *Oz* (for White Oak Dance Project, 1991; for Taylor Company in 1992); *A Field of Grass* (1993); *Spindrift* (1993); *Moonbine* (1994); *Funny Papers* (with other company members, 1994); *Offenbach Overtures* (1995); *Prime Numbers* (1997); *Eventide* (1997); *Piazzolla Caldera* (1997); *The Word* (1998); *Fiddlers Green* (1998); *Oh, You Kid!* (1999); *Cascade* (1999); *Arabesque* (1999); *Dandelion Wine* (2000); *Fiends Angelical* (2000); *Black Tuesday* (2001); *Antique Valentine* (2001); *Promethean Fire* (2002); *Dream Girls* (2002); *In the Beginning* (2003); *Dante Variations* (2004); *Klezmerbluegrass* (2004); *Le Grand Puppetier* (2004); *Banquet of Vultures* (2005); *Spring Rounds* (2005); *Troilus and Cressida (reduced)* (2006); *Lines of Loss* (2007); *De Sueños* (2007); *De Sueños que se Repitem* (2007); *Beloved Renegade* (2008); *Changes* (2008); *Brief Encounters* (2009); *Also Playing* (2009).

Further reading

Interviews in 'Down with Choreography', *Modern Dance*, Middletown, CT, 1965; with Cynthia Lyle, in *Dancers on Dancing*, New York, 1977; with Lillie F. Rosen, in 'Talking with Paul Taylor', *Dance Scope*, Winter 1979; with Jack Anderson, in 'Choreographic Fox: Paul Taylor', *Dance Magazine*, April 1980; with Tobi Tobias, in 'In Conversation with Paul Taylor and George Tacit', *Dance Magazine*, April 1985; with Jeffrey Brown, *PBS News Hour*, 19 June 2007 (available at www.pbs.org).

Articles: Selma Jeanne Cohen, 'Avant-Garde Choreography', *Dance Magazine*, 3 parts: June, July, and August 1962; Don McDonagh, 'Paul Taylor in Orbit', *Dance Scope*, Fall 1966; Clive Barnes, 'Paul Taylor', *Ballet Review*, 2(1), 1967; L.E. Stern, 'Paul Taylor, Gentle Giant of Modern Dance', *Dance Magazine*, February 1976; Jack Anderson, 'Paul Taylor: Surface and Substance', *Ballet Review*, 6(1), 1977/78; Elizabeth Kendall, 'American Mongrel', *Ballet News*, April 1980; Ron Daniels, 'Paul

Taylor and the Post-Moderns', *Ballet Review*, Summer 1981; C. Adams, 'The Paul Taylor Mystique', *Dance Theatre Journal*, 1(1), 1983; Joel Lobenthal, 'Christopher Gillis: Dancing for Paul Taylor', *Ballet Review*, Spring 1985; Mania Siegel, 'Thirty Years in Eden's Dustbin', *Hudson Review*, Autumn 1985; Carolyn Adams, 'Lifeline to Taylor', *Ballet Review*, Winter 1986; Ina Sorens, 'Taylor Reconstructs Balanchine', *Ballet Review*, Summer 1986; Susan Reiter, 'Baroque and Beyond with Paul Taylor', *Ballet Review*, Fall 1986; Alastair Macaulay, 'The Paul Taylor Dance Company', *Dance Theatre Journal*, Summer 1987; Daniel Jacobson, 'Private Domains in Public Spaces', *Ballet Review*, Spring 1989; Laura Jacobs, 'Light and Dark', *Ballet Review*, Fall 1990; Nancy Dalva, 'Paul Taylor: A Very Appealing Genius', *Dance Magazine*, October 1991; Joseph Mazo, 'Paul's Women: Motivator, Matriarch, Muse', *Dance Magazine*, October 1991; Christopher Bowen, 'Paul Taylor Dance Company at the Edinburgh Festival', *Dance Theatre Journal*, Winter 1995/96; Paul Taylor and Angela Kane, 'A Catalogue of Works Choreographed by Paul Taylor', *Dance Research*, Winter 1996; Craig Dodd, 'Paul Taylor at Sadler's Wells', *Dancing Times*, January 2001; Allen Robertson, 'The Paul Taylor Dance Company', *Dance Now*, Summer 2003; Angela Kane, 'Through a Glass Darkly: The Many Sides of Paul Taylor's Choreography', *Dance Research*, Winter 2003; Harris Green, 'Paul Taylor's Golden Age', *Dance Magazine*, March 2004; Angela Kane, 'Paul Taylor Dance Company at 50 – parts 1 and 11: Past, and Present Triumphs', *Dancing Times*, May and June 2004; Paul Taylor *et al.*, 'Taylor Made', *Dance Magazine*, March 2005; Jack Anderson, 'Paul Taylor's Anniversary Season', *Dancing Times*, May 2005; Jack Anderson, 'Paul Taylor Premieres', *Dancing Times*, May 2006; Jack Anderson, 'Paul Taylor Dance Company in New York', *Dancing Times*, May 2007; Jack Anderson, 'Mixed Bills', *Dancing Times*, May 2008 and May 2009.

Books: Selma Jeanne Cohen, *Modern Dance: Seven Statements of Belief*, Middletown, CT, 1967; Don McDonagh, *The Rise and Fall of Modern Dance*, New York, 1970; A.V. Coton, *Writings on Dance*, London, 1975: Moira Hodgson, *Quintet: Five American Dance Companies*, New York, 1976; Arlene Croce, *After Images*, New York, 1977; Cynthia Lyle, *Dancers on Dancing*, New York, 1977; Joseph H. Mazo, *Prime Movers: The Makers of Modern Dance in America*, New York, 1977; Marcia Siegel, *The Shapes of Change: Images of American Dance*, Boston, 1979; Arlene Croce, *Going to the Dance*, New York, 1982; Arlene Croce, *Sightlines*, New York, 1984; Robert Coe, *Dance in America*, New York, 1985; Edwin Denby, *Dance Writings*, ed. Robert Cornfield and William Mackay, New York, 1986; Paul Taylor, *Private Domain* (autobiography), New York, 1987; Jack Anderson, *Choreography Observed*, Iowa City, 1987; Nancy Reynolds and Susan Reimer-Torn, *Dance Classics*, Chicago, 1991; Stephanie Jordan *et al.*, *Preservation Politics: Dance Revived, Reconstructed, Remade*, London, 2000; Arlene Croce, *Writing in the Dark, Dancing in The New Yorker*, New York, 2000; Beth Soll, *Will Modern Dance Survive?*, New York, 2002; Paul Taylor Dance Company, *Paul Taylor Dance Company: The First Fifty Years*, New York, 2004; Suzanne Carbonneau, authorized biography (forthcoming).

TWYLA THARP

Twyla Tharp began her career in 1965, at the age of nearly 23, with *Tank Dive*, a work in three movements that was choreographed for herself and four non-dancers. It was performed partly to the accompaniment of Petula Clark's recording of 'Downtown', in Room 1604 – a small, Bauhaus-style auditorium – of Hunter College in New York City. *Tank Dive* lasted for seven minutes. Tharp began the first section wearing high-heeled bedroom slippers. She then changed into wooden shoes with rigid, flipper-like extensions in front. These confined her to one spot, but allowed her to move her upper body freely. Soon, she discarded the shoes, performing the rest of the work barefoot. At the end, she threw herself to the floor, face downwards, and then made her exit. She took no bows, declining to acknowledge the presence of the small group of people who had been watching her, though the fact that the performance was given in public, and that she had mailed out notices for it, implied her desire to make contact with an audience.

Although Tharp had also invited the press, there were no reviews. This critical silence disconcerted her. From the start, she was filled with ambition, a drive to succeed beyond the ordinary. Success took eight years to arrive, and once it came there was no stopping her – for a while, at any rate. By the end of 1973, she was big news, not simply in the newspapers, but also in weeklies, monthlies and glossy magazines. The watershed in her career was *Deuce Coupe* (1973), which leading dance director Robert Joffrey commissioned for his New York ballet company. Set to a montage of recordings by The Beach Boys, the piece brought together, for the first time in a major dance piece, the techniques and attitudes of both classical ballet and post-modernism, the latter enriched by movements taken from teenage dancing: limply held hands, raised shoulders, undulating hips, snapping fingers and eyes lowered in an ecstatic-seeming withdrawal from reality. The juxtaposition of styles – the work was performed simultaneously by the Joffrey Company and by Tharp's own dancers – was not only enjoyable to watch but was also resonant with meaning, a metaphor for the coexistence of tradition and youth. Although essentially conceptual – and though, as Tharp's autobiography has since revealed, its audience-pleasing effects were all carefully calculated – the piece was also emotionally reverberant. The references to love in The Beach Boy's songs were bodied forth with warmth and conviction.

Deuce Coupe, first presented at New York's City Center Theater, was an instant hit, bringing Tharp for the first time to the attention of the public at large. Over the years, the Joffrey Ballet had cultivated with great success an audience responsive more to the thrills of cultural modishness than to the niceties of classical ballet. To these Joffrey fans, *Deuce*

Coupe made an instant appeal, if only on account of its novelty. In 1973, ballet companies had hardly yet begun to use pre-recorded pop music. Nor, apart from Balanchine, had they started to mix high art and low; and they had only rarely invited non-ballet dancers to join them onstage, though again, Balanchine had anticipated Tharp in this respect. Intriguing though these features were, it soon became clear that what lifted the ballet out of the ordinary and made it worth seeing more than once was the visceral excitement it communicated, the energy and passionate commitment to dance that Tharp drew from her cast. However, titillating the ballet's references to contemporary social attitudes were its ultimate worth lay in its dynamism, inventiveness and grace.

The courage shown by Robert Joffrey in asking a choreographer without any experience of working with classically trained performers to make a piece for his company paid off handsomely, both at the box office and in terms of prestige. Joffrey was praised for having sponsored a significant development in American dance: because of him, at the beginning of the 1970s a choreographer had succeeded in expressing the attitudes of the younger generation in a work that linked the iconoclasm of the previous, revolutionary decade with a centuries old, traditional art. Although Tharp was praised for having made a major populist statement, some people remained seemingly unaware that *Deuce Coupe* was also fastidiously constructed and, despite its flippant and trendy tone (augmented by the presence on stage of a bunch of kids who, during the performance, created graffiti with spray cans at the back of the stage), was a serious work of art.

Success brought not only the fame Tharp had yearned for but also a certain amount of carping for the first time: *Deuce Coupe* offended those guardians of aesthetic purity who felt that the use of elements from rock-and-roll constituted a threat to the artistic integrity of ballet, apparently unaware that ballet over the centuries had been enriched by absorbing elements from social dancing and popular theatre. However, criticism of this kind tended to disappear after Tharp's 1976 creation of *Push Comes to Shove* for American Ballet Theatre (ABT). By the mid-1970s, the juxtaposition of pop dancing and ballet no longer produced much of a shock. However, there was now criticism from the standard bearers of avant-garde dance. Because *Push Comes to Shove* was an even greater hit than *Deuce Coupe* – indeed it proved to be the most successful American dance work since Jerome Robbins's *Fancy Free* of 1944 – many felt that Tharp had sold out, that her extraordinary ability to reach big, popular audiences had necessarily entailed the loss of artistic integrity. For these critics, the accessibility of *Push Comes to Shove*, which made use of the same blend of styles as in *Deuce Coupe*, but with a new, comic component derived from Old-Time vaudeville, was proof of Tharp's self-betrayal. For everyone else, *Push Comes to Shove* was a revelation, a brilliant comic gloss on classical ballet that demonstrated the latter's infinite adaptiveness.

Push Comes to Shove, set to Haydn's *Symphony No. 82*, and preceded by a rag by Joseph Lamb, also provided Mikhail Baryshnikov, the ballet's star and the most gifted male dancer of his day, with the finest new role he had found since his defection from the Soviet Union – indeed, with what remains the only starring role of real artistic distinction to have been made for him by a Western choreographer. Tharp had long since demonstrated that she could enhance and refine the natural qualities of dancers as different as the tall Rose Marie Wright and the dark, intensely lyrical Sara Rudner, two of the pillars of her company. She proceeded to extend the range of Baryshnikov.

In *Push Comes to Shove*, she created a new personality for him: a blend of the sly, the unpredictable, the wryly self-mocking, the witty and the prodigiously virtuosic – though in *Push Comes to Shove* he displayed his virtuosity so insouciantly that his brilliance seemed almost inadvertent. Technically, Tharp's demands on Baryshnikov were nearly superhuman. From him, she wanted speed, not merely in performing specific movements, but in making transitions from one to the other. She also wanted him to dance in a manner that minimized the decorum inherent in the *danse d'école*. Thus, he had to perform multiple *pirouettes* with great velocity, but at the same time keep his body off-centre. In addition, she offered him the chance to reveal a hitherto unsuspected stage persona that of the cool cat/wise guy/prankster/lady-killer. With this ballet, Baryshnikov received, so to speak, his naturalization papers as an American dancer.

Tharp's progression from *Tank Dive* to *Push Comes to Shove*, from avant-garde iconoclasm to mainstream populism, took her just over a decade. On the way, she created a variety of avant-garde, often non-theatrical works, some austere in mood and dauntingly rigorous in structure. In *The Fugue* (1970), three dancers performed 20 variations on a 20-count theme. At the climax of *The One Hundreds* (1970), a hundred people (for the most part non-dancers) executed a hundred different eleven-second movement phrases. Other works from this period were frankly rebarbative: in the final section of *Re-Moves* (1966), the dancers performed inside a large plywood box and were thus invisible to the audience. Some works were geographically diffuse, such as *Sunrise, Midday March, Evening Raga* (1971), which took place in different locations of New York, beginning before dawn in Fort Tryon Park and ending at dusk in City Hall.

During these years, Tharp and her dancers took no curtain calls. At the end of each piece, they simply left the stage or performing space. Until almost the end of 1971, the company was entirely female. Tharp's decision to take in Kenneth Rinker opened up new creative possibilities for her, at once technical and expressive. In 1971, moreover, she created her first piece to music: *Eight Jelly Rolls*. (The Petula Clark record she had used in *Tank Dive* was an incidental feature of the piece.) Before then, she and her dancers had performed, if not to silence, then without music – the sound of footfalls in *The Fugue* was a constituent expressive element of the piece, and one she made more important in due course by amplifying the stage on which *The Fugue* was danced.

From *Eight Jelly Rolls* on, music, to which Tharp is remarkably responsive, became central to her work, supplying the dances in which she used it with rhythmic impetus, structural guidelines and an overall mood. In *Eight Jelly Rolls*, first seen at Oberlin College, Ohio, and then revised for the New York Shakespeare Dance Festival in Central Park, she used jazz recordings from the 1920s by Jelly Roll Morton and his Red Hot Peppers. The first performance of the revised version elicited so enthusiastic a response that Tharp decided her dancers would henceforth acknowledge the audience's applause. Two months after this, she created *The Bix Pieces* (1971), set to recordings by jazzman Bix Beiderbecke, and, a year later, *The Raggedy Dances* to music by Scott Joplin. These works, all clearly designed to appeal to the taste of general audiences, confirmed the change in her outlook. No longer did she feel that she had to be so aggressively earnest and uncompromisingly ascetic to win respect. These three works foreshadowed the more complex *Deuce Coupe*.

After *Push Comes to Shove*, Tharp found herself sought out as a choreographer. As a result she began to ask for substantial financial recompense; today, she is in all likelihood among the best-paid choreographers of her time. She also received invitations to collaborate on movies, a medium to which she felt a strong attraction – as indeed, she did to any performing art that would extend her expertise as a performer and a creator. In 1982, she appeared in New York in an experimental play, *Bone Songs* opposite to its author, André Gregory, but she proved to have no skills as an actress. Unfortunately, none of the films on which she worked (*Hair, Ragtime, Amadeus* and *White Nights*, with Baryshnikov and the great tap dancer Gregory Hines), offered her opportunities worthy of her gifts. In *Hair*, she made an appearance as a dancer. For *Amadeus*, she not only provided the choreography but also staged and directed the operatic scenes. Both *Amadeus* and *Ragtime* required period dances, the former from the eighteenth century and the latter from the early twentieth century. Although *Ragtime* did not do her career much good, it taught her a great deal about ballroom dancing, knowledge she put to use two years later in *Nine Sinatra Songs* (1982), one of her finest achievements.

Tharp's eagerness to work in films – like her forays into ice skating, theatre and television – is evidence of a deep-seated urge to diversify, and thus more certainly to conquer. In 1984, she teamed up with Jerome Robbins to create a work for New York City Ballet, *Brahms/Handel*. In 1985, she directed as well as choreographed a stage version of the classic Gene Kelly musical, *Singin' in the Rain*, an ambitious venture but a failure artistically and a flop commercially.

Some of Tharp's ambitiousness can no doubt be traced to the choreographer's relationship with her powerful mother, who saw to it that her eldest child took lessons in ballet, flamenco, acrobatics, tap, violin, viola and baton twirling, as well as various languages. The memory of her childhood, revealed in Tharp's 1992 autobiography *Push Comes to Shove* to have been very unhappy, has clearly haunted her for many years. In 1980, she created a quasi-autobiographical full-length work, *When We Were Very Young*, which incorporated a framing text by the playwright Thomas Babe. It is characteristic of the desperate need she has to master her past that she should have accepted a script as sophomoric as Babe's.

Although it dispensed with words, *The Catherine Wheel*, which followed a year later, was another confused act of psychic exorcism, a convoluted and cloudy family psychodrama to music commissioned from the talented David Byrne. What saved *The Catherine Wheel*, which, like *When We Were Very Young*, was aimed at general audiences and performed in a regular Broadway house, was its final abstract sequence that Tharp called *The Golden Section*. This, unlike everything that had preceded it, was daring, thrilling and clear, a succession of brilliant, demanding and non-stop dances that showed very clearly where Tharp's talent lay. *The Golden Section*, in excerpted form, is now performed alone as a show-stopper by companies as diverse as Miami City Ballet and Alvin Ailey American Dance Theater.

Most of her failures since *When We Were Very Young* have either implied or presented a narrative, such as *Short Stories* (1980), *Bad Smells* (1982), *Bum's Rush* (1989) and *Everlast* (1989). Her greatest success, artistic and commercial alike, since *Push Comes to Shove* has been *Nine Sinatra Songs*, and it expresses its insights about men and women through a love of dance rarely visible in the works with stories or literary themes. Both *Bum's Rush* and *Everlast* were given their premieres by ABT, where she made a variety of interesting works in non-narrative modes and where she created a joyous piece for the young virtuoso Julio Bocca, called *Brief Fling* (1990), the only new ballet of his career to make him look like a star.

Since that time, Tharp has begun to choreograph again for the troupe. In May 1995, she was accorded the honour of providing all the works that made up the programme of ABT's annual fund-raising gala at the Metropolitan Opera House. The evening was a disappointment. All three premieres lacked coherence and, more surprisingly, originality. The vapid *Americans We* invoked memories of other choreographers' work, principally that of Tudor and Robbins – the first Tharp ballet ever to do so. *Jump Start*, danced to live contemporary jazz, was a new and exhausted version of her early youth-dance ballets. *How Near Heaven*, to music by Britten, was simply unfocused. However, her 1998 *Known by Heart*, to music by Mozart, Donald Knaack and Steve Reich, was declared 'the best thing ABT has commissioned in years' by Joan Acocella in *The New Yorker*. And dating from before her departure, the powerful and aggressive *In the Upper Room* (1986), which always wins an ovation, is part of ABT's basic repertoire. Her relationship with ABT, then, is not entirely a series of expensive disappointments.

Tharp has not had a permanent company in some time. Both Tharp! (1995 to 1998) and Twyla Tharp Dance (2000) were short-lived. Instead, she choreographs, as she always has, for other companies. For example, she has worked repeatedly with the Joffrey since *Deuce Coupe*; the classic *As Time Goes By*, made for them in 1973, is superb. She worked with the Martha Graham dancers in 1993 (*Demeter and Persephone*), with London's Royal Ballet for the first time in 1996 (*Mr Worldly Wise*), and successfully returned to New York City Ballet, where she had collaborated with Robbins, for *The Beethoven Seventh* (2000).

But recently Tharp's most high-profile works have been for Broadway: *Movin' Out* (2003), a major hit to the music of Billy Joel that won her the Tony Award for Best Choreography, and *The Times They*

Are a-Changin' (2006), a major flop to the music of Bob Dylan. After creating works in 2008 for three major American ballet companies (ABT, Miami City Ballet and Pacific Northwest Ballet), she went on in 2009 to create another show, this time using music of Frank Sinatra, which had brought her luck in the past. *Come Fly with Me* had its premiere in Atlanta and seemed to be a return to form, described by one critic as 'exhilarating'. By the start of 2010, the musical, re-titled *Come Fly Away*, was bound for Broadway.

Tharp remains an active and sought-after choreographer. Her work, which she began licensing in 2003, is in demand internationally. The Tharp archive contains teaching and performing tapes of 132 dances, which, together with former Tharp dancers, are sent to companies who receive a piece so that the work may be preserved with her vision intact. And what is that vision? Simply, dance. As she once put it, 'I think movement is movement.'

Dale Harris
(updated by Ellen Gaintner)

Biographical details

Born in Portland, Indiana, United States, 1 July 1941. **Studied** at Pomona College, California, transferred to Barnard College, New York, obtained a BA degree (majoring in art history) in 1963; while at college, studied ballet with Igor Schwezoff, American Ballet Theatre School and with Richard Thomas and Margaret Craske in New York; studied modern dance with Martha Graham, Merce Cunningham and Alwin Nikolais and jazz with Eugene 'Luigi' Lewis and Matt Mattox. **Career**: Made début as a dancer with Paul Taylor Dance Company, 1963; founder, dancer and choreographer of own company, 1965, which became the Twyla Tharp Dance Foundation in 1973; artistic associate, American Ballet Theatre (ABT), 1988–90; re-formed own company as the 12-member Tharp!, 1995–98 and Tharp Dance, 2000. Has choreographed for Joffrey Ballet, American Ballet Theatre, John Curry (Olympic ice skater), Paris Opera Ballet, the Martha Graham Company, the Royal Ballet, London, New York City Ballet, The Boston Ballet, Pacific Northwest Ballet and Miami City Ballet, as well as for feature films, including *Hair* (dir. Forman, 1979), *Ragtime* (dir. Forman, 1981) and *White Nights* (dir. Hackford, 1985) and television, including *Baryshnikov Dances Tharp* (PBS 'Dance in America' series, 1984). Has also published several books. **Awards and honours** include Brandeis University Citation, 1972; *Dance Magazine* Award, 1981; Mayor's Award of Honor, New York, 1984; Emmy Award 1985; Golden Plate Awards, 1987 and 1993; Samuel H. Scripps Award, 1990; Laurence Olivier Award, 1991; MacArthur Fellowship, 1992; Tony Award, 2003; Astaire Award, 2003; National Medal of the Arts, 2004; Critics Circle Dance Award (UK), 2006; Jerome Robbins Award, 2008; Kennedy Center Honor, 2008.

Works

Tank Dive (1965); *Stage Show* (1965); *Stride* (1965); *Cede Blue Lake* (1965); *Unprocessed* (1965); *Re-Moves* (1966); *Yancey Dance* (1966); *One Two Three* (1967); *Jam* (1967); *Disperse* (1967); *Three Page Sonata for Four* (1967); *Forevermore* (1967); *Generation* (1968); *One Way* (1968); *Excess, Idle, Surplus* (1968); *After 'Suite'* (1969); *Group Activities* (1969); *Medley* (1969); *Dancing in the Streets of London and Paris, Continued in Stockholm and Sometimes Madrid* (1969); *Pymffyppmfynm Ypf* (1970); *Sowing of Seeds* (1970); *The Fugue* (1970); *Rose's Cross Country* (1970); *The One Hundreds* (1970); *The History of Up and Down, I and II* (1971); *Eight Jelly Rolls* (1971); *The Willie Smith Series* (video, 1971); *Mozart Sonata, K.545* (1971); *Sunrise, Midday March, Evening Raga* (1971); *Torelli* (1971); *The Bix Pieces* (1971); *The Raggedy Dances* (1972); *Deuce Coupe* (1973); *As Time Goes By* (1973); *In the Beginnings* (1974); *All About Eggs* (1974); *The Bach Duet* (1974); *Deuce Coupe II* (revised version of *Deuce Coupe*, 1975); *Sue's Leg* (1975); *The Double Cross* (1975); *Ocean's Motion* (1975); *Push Comes to Shove* (1976); *Remembering the Thirties* (for television, 1976); *Give and Take* (1976); *Once More, Frank* (1976); *Country Dances* (1976); *Happily Ever After* (1976); *After All* (1976); *Mud* (1977); *Simon Medley* (1977); *Cacklin' Hen* (1977); *1903* (1979); *Chapters & Verses* (1979); *Baker's Dozen* (1979); *Hair* (film, dir. Milos Forman, 1979); *Three Fanfares* (for closing of the Winter Olympic Games, 1980); *Brahms' Paganini* (1980); *When We Were Very Young* (1980); *Dance is a Man's Sport Too* (for television, 1980); *Assorted Quartets* (1980); *Short Stories* (1980); *Third Suite* (1980); dances in *Ragtime* (film, dir. Milos Forman, 1980); *Uncle Edgar Dyed His Hair Red* (1981); *The Catherine Wheel* (1981); *Nine Sinatra Songs* (1982); *Bad Smells* (1982); *Once Upon a Time* (later re-titled *The Little Ballet*, 1983); *Bach Partita* (1983); *Fait Accompli* (1983); *Telemann* (1983); *Amadeus* (film, dir. Milos Forman, 1984); *Brahms/Handel* (with Jerome Robbins, 1984); *Sorrow Floats* (1985); *Sinatra Suite* (1985); *Singin' in the Rain* (musical by Comden and Green, 1985); *White Nights* (film, dir. Taylor Hackford, 1985); *In the Upper Room* (1986); *Ballare* (1986); *Quartet* (1989); *Bum's Rush* (1989); *Rules of the Game* (1989); *Everlast* (1989); *Brief Fling* (1990); *Grand Pas: Rhythm of the Saints* (1991); *The Men's Piece* (1991); *Octet* (1991); *Sextet* (1992); *Cutting Up* (1992); *Bare Bones* (1993); *Let's Forget Domani* (1993); *Brahms' Paganini (Book Two)* (1993); *Demeter and Persephone* (1993); *Waterbaby Bagatelles* (1994); *Red, White & Blues* (1994); *Noir* (1994); *Americans We* (1995); *How Near Heaven* (1995); *Jump Start* (1995); *Mr Worldly Wise* (1996); *The Elements* (1996); *Heroes* (1996); *66* (1996); *Sweet Fields* (1996); *The Story Teller* (1997); *Roy's Joys* (1997); *Moondog* (1998); *Sam and Mary* (1998); *Yemaya* (1998); *Known by Heart* (1998); *Diabelli* (1998); *Hammerklavier* (1999); *The Beethoven Seventh* (2000); *Variations on a Theme by Haydn* (2000); *Mozart Clarinet Quintet K.581* (2000); *Surfer at the River Styx* (2000); *Known by Heart Duet* (2001); *Westerly Round* (2001); *Hammerklavier II* (2001); *Movin' Out* (2003); *Even the King* (2003); *The Times They Are a-Changin'* (2006); *Armenia* (2008); *Nightspot* (2008); *Rabbit and Rogue* (2008); *Brahms Opus 111* (2008); *Afternoon Ball* (2008); *Come Fly with Me* (2009).

Further reading

Interviews in 'Space, Jazz, Pop . . . ', *Dance and Dancers*, May 1974; with Suzanne Well, in *Contemporary Dance*, New York, 1978; with Elinor Rogosin, in *The Dance Makers: Conversations with American Choreographers*, New York, 1980; with Deborah Jowitt, in 'The Choreographer and the World', *Ballett International*, June/July 1984; with Emma Manning, in 'Twyla Tharp', *Dance Europe*, October/November 1997;

with Laura Shapiro, in 'She's Got Way', *New York* magazine, 28 October 2002; with David Shank, 'A Conversation with Twyla Tharp', *Atlantic*, 26 February 2010.

Articles: Deborah Jowitt, 'Twyla Tharp's New Kick', *New York Times Magazine*, 4 January 1976; Allen Robertson, 'Tharp Comes to Shove', *Ballet News* March 1980; Michael Robertson, 'Fifteen Years: Twyla Tharp and the Logical Outcome of Abundance', *Dance Magazine*, March 1980; Marcia Siegel, 'Success Without Labels', *Hudson Review*, Spring 1983; Marcia Siegel, 'Couples', *Hudson Review*, Summer 1984; Alastair Macaulay, 'Twyla Tharp Dance', *Dancing Times*, August 1984; David Vaughan, 'Twyla Tharp: Launching a New Classicism', *Dance Magazine*, May 1984; Matthew Gurewitsch, 'Kinetic Force', *Ballet News*, October 1984; Steven Albert, 'Utopia Lost – and Found?', *Ballet Review*, Spring 1986; Clive Barnes, 'Twyla Tharp and the Modern Classicism', *Dance and Dancers*, September 1987; Clive Barnes, 'Daring, Newness and Occasion', *Dance and Dancers*, September 1989; Marcia Siegel, 'Strangers in the Palace', *Hudson Review*, Autumn 1989; Joan Acocella, 'Balancing Act', *Dance Magazine*, October 1990; Barbara Zuck, 'Tharp Moves', *Dance Magazine*, January 1992; Joan Acocella, 'Twyla Tharp: Divided Loyalties', *Art in America*, May 1992; Marcia Siegel, 'Both Doors Open', *Hudson Review*, Summer 1992; Clive Barnes, 'Attitudes: Cunningham and Tharp – Originals', *Dance Magazine*, March 1993; Marcia Siegel, 'Twyla's Tour', *Ballet Review*, Spring 1993; Ann Nugent, 'Till and Twyla: A Myth and a Legend', *Dance Now*, Spring 1994; Mary Clarke, '*Mr Worldly Wise*', *Dancing Times*, January 1996; Susan Manning, 'Cultural Theft – or Love?', *Dance Theatre Journal*, 13(4) 1997; Nadine Meisner, 'Conquering Hero?', *Dance Theatre Journal*, 14(1), 1998; Deborah Jowitt, 'Flying Blind into Brooklyn' (feature), *The Village Voice*, 13 February 2001; Alex Witchell, 'To Dance Beneath the Diamond Skies', *The New York Times Magazine*, 22 October 2006; Deborah Jowitt, 'Tightrope Walk', *The Village Voice*, 31 October 2006; Joan Acocella, 'Guy Stuff', *The New Yorker*, 30 June 2008; Wendy Perron, 'Twyla Tharp's *Come Fly with Me*', *Dance Magazine*, December 2009; Joan Acocella, 'High Hopes', *The New Yorker*, 5 April 2010.

Books: Moira Hodgson, *Quintet Five American Dance Companies*, New York, 1976; Don McDonagh, *Complete Guide to Modern Dance*, New York, 1976; Arlene Croce, *Afterimages*, New York, 1977; Cynthia Lyle (ed.), *Dancers on Dancing*, New York, 1977; Joseph H. Mazo, *Prime Movers: The Makers of Modern Dance in America*, New York, 1977; Anne Livet (ed.), *Contemporary Dance*, New York, 1978; Marcia Siegel, *The Shapes of Change*, Boston, 1979; Arlene Croce, *Going to the Dance*, New York, 1982; Robert Coe, *Dance in America*, New York, 1985; Deborah Jowitt, *The Dance in Mind*, New York, 1985; Arlene Croce, *Sight Lines*, New York, 1987; Twyla Tharp, *Push Comes to Shove* (autobiography), New York, 1992; Twyla Tharp, *The Creative Habit: Learn it and Use it For Life*, New York, 2003; Marcia B. Siegel, *Howling Near Heaven: Twyla Tharp and the Reinvention of Modern Dance*, New York, 2006; Twyla Tharp, *The Collaborative Habit: Life Lessons for Working Together*, New York, 2009.

WIM VANDEKEYBUS

It is tempting, when contemplating an artist's *oeuvre*, to consider his work as a causal outcome of earlier life. Such an approach could be easily applied to the work of Wim Vandekeybus. The son of a veterinarian, Vandekeybus may well have brought his childhood experience to bear on his adult work, which would explain his use of animals as a recurring motif in his work, as well as the distinct viscerality that he has brought to the stage since the start of his choreographic career. As a young man, Vandekeybus began his studies in psychology, and one might also see the influence of psychology borne out in the complex mythology of the psyche that runs through many of his pieces, rich with a demanding symbolism free of conventional narrative. Then, there was what one could regard as his apprenticeship with Jan Fabre and the intense physicality shaped in the Flemish choreographer's theatre. All these elements clearly have played a role in the forming Vandekeybus's public world.

Yet we must go beyond simple biographical explanations to consider the resonant complexities of Vandekeybus's vision. A challenge to the viewer was announced both in the title and content of what was essentially his début as choreographer (following earlier workshop pieces), *What the Body Does Not Remember* (1987), a work that provoked audiences with its rhythmic force and perplexed viewers with its own theatre of esoteric ritual, which eschewed easy 'get-outs' to decode what was on view. Although it was well received in Europe, it took the American reception of *What the Body Does Not Remember* for the dance world to sit up and take notice, in particular in Anna Kisselgoff's review in *The New York Times*: 'Tough, brutal, playful, ironic and terrific. Adjectives seem unduly passive to describe *What the Body Does Not Remember*'.[1]

So what earned this response, culminating with a 'Bessie' Award for 'a brutal confrontation of dance and music'? Here was a production with a new kind of vocabulary, rich with risk of all kinds, from the invasive tensions of the women being frisked by the men to the borderline violent physicality of the leaps and rolling falls repeatedly braved by the dancers of Ultimata Vez (which translates as 'Last Time'), Vandekeybus's multinational company. It was a style that seemed to become an almost instantaneously pervasive influence as the 1980s turned to the 1990s, as reflected in the coinage 'Eurocrash', with all the scepticism of the sensation it implied – and with some justice as regards those who were inspired only at the most superficial level by the opportunities offered by Vandekeybus. As Keith Watson puts it, 'Just as Kurt Cobain's Nirvana had to suffer the indignities of identikit grunge, so Vandekeybus inspired a lamebrain bunch who thought

Eurocrash was all about trashing your bones on the floor'.[2] For Vandekeybus, the surface is emphatically only the end point. 'We mustn't forget that dance emerged as a kind of communication, as a kind of ritual, an expression of something,' he has said.[3] What does his work communicate? Perhaps here biography can point the way, as shown in Vandekeybus's boyhood memories of accompanying his father on his rural rounds as a vet: 'We would be confronted with an atmosphere of catastrophe. My father would have to put things right, and quickly ... Sometimes death was the only salvation he could offer. Quickly and efficiently, without pathos'.[4] That confrontation with chaos, the existential implications of the physical, the exploration of these things, free of sentiment: such is the viewer's experience of Vandekeybus's work.

Such exploration continued in *Les Porteuses de mauvaises nouvelles* (1989), for which Vandekeybus received a second 'Bessie'. In this piece, the performers were pushed to their limits, but there was a purpose beyond grandstand showmanship, as the extremity of the games of trust and falling, and the near-lethal props – including a flaming cord – accumulated to create an environment of danger and abandonment, the absolute antithesis of the technical convention that threatens to render dance moribund. The sheer brute force of the earlier work was still on display, but now there appeared moments of beguiling invention: the emergence of a shirt (to be worn by a dancer) from a melting block of ice embodied the multiple tensions and wilful contradictions that structure Vandekeybus's world.

These tensions cut across a range of ideas: gender, music and dance, myth and the contemporary, and expectation and reality. Conflict is at the heart of Vandekeybus's work: 'For me it is important that we work with physical and mental aggression. To make the public question the authenticity of things. Right from the beginning, one of my mottos has been: Back to reality'.[5]

Given that viewers of *Les Porteuses de mauvaises nouvelles* found themselves seemingly assailed by a dart thrown by one of the performers, it was perhaps for the best that the maturing choreographer found a gentler way to the real using the experience of specific individuals. A chance meeting between Vandekeybus and the retired German variety artist Carlo Verano (also known as Carlo Wegener) gave rise to *Immer das Selbe gelogen* (1991). To the now-characteristic speed and rolling falls, Vandekeybus added a mixture of text, snippets of narrative, film, individual performance and an omelette cooked onstage. Vandekeybus purposefully abandoned control to this eclectic mix of elements while somehow reining them into resonant effect with his vision and sense of timing. The affecting juxtaposition between the images of the 89-year-old Verano and the surrounding action introduced a dimension of unaffected humanity that has come to play an increasingly greater role in his work.

'If dance is just about movement, it says nothing to me,' Vandekeybus has commented. 'I want to create some space again for the bizarre, the unpredictable that eludes any kind of control'.[6] To that end he has chosen performers who are more collaborators than mere ciphers for his choreographic scheme, who offer experience beyond technique and training; in the stage/film melds, *Her Body Doesn't Fit Her Soul* (1993) and *Mountains Made of Barking* (1994), Vandekeybus worked with the blind Moroccan dancer Saïd Gharbi.

As the unexpected almost becomes the norm in a sensation-hungry age, so perhaps it was inevitable that Vandekeybus's edgy impact was to be blunted, at least in terms of critical reception. By the mid-1990s the shock of the new had been dissipated by audience familiarity with Eurocrash and its dilution into the work of other European choreographers. Purists began to carp at the increasing layering of mythic imagery and the burgeoning theatrical accoutrements that threatened to overwhelm the choreography. It was easy to get lost in the externals of a stage full of musicians in the chaotic *Bereft of a Blissful Union* (1996). For one critic, the complex symbolism of superstition in *7 for a Secret never to be told* (1997) and the forceful bodily contortions that took place on this elaborate canvas were all for nought: 'Aesthetically ... nothing stirred'.[7]

Such reactions are determined by the viewer's expectations of a certain dance aesthetic, but Vandekeybus has always conceived of his work within a wider context:

> I don't come from dance, more from theatre or film, and I make performances ... we are always concerned with not just what we are doing, but why we are doing it. What is the theatrical foundation? What story can we transpose to another medium? Do we need text? Do we need something else?[8]

Thus, Vandekeybus has increasingly used film not only as an element within stage pieces – witness the surrealist short *The Last Words* (1999) bisecting the abstract exploration of masculinity that was *In Spite of Wishing and Wanting* (1999) – but as a discrete medium in its own right. Prompted by the death of his father, the film '*Inasmuch as life is borrowed*. . . . .' (2000) and its imagistic contemplation of mortality and existence is charged with far more spiritual resonance that many other contemporaneous dance works. The stage and video versions of *Blush* (2002) offered two very different surveys of human behaviour united by an edgily animalistic tension between modern living and mythic ritual. It is not surprising that Vandekeybus embarked on the project of creating his first feature film, *Galloping Mind*, a natural development for a career of gargantuan artistic appetite.

Yet Vandekeybus is still a vital figure in stage-based contemporary dance, not only for his legacy but also for the work he continues to produce. Who else could have had the theatrical imagination to devise *Scratching the Inner Fields* (2001)? This visceral work tossed its all-female cast around a stage of earth decorated with stretched membranes to create a living tableau of primal force. For performers and audiences alike, Vandekeybus is emphatically not there to make life easy; we would be bereft without the challenge he offers.

Ben Felsenburg

Notes

1 Anna Kisselgoff, 'Dance: A New Work by Wim Vandekeybus,' *The New York Times*, 22 November 1987.
2 Keith Watson, 'Aim for the Head. Go for the Gut', *Dance Now*, Summer 1996.
3 Robert Ayers, '*Scratching the Inner Fields*: Listening to Wim Vandekeybus', *Dance Theatre Journal*, 18(1), 2002.
4 Claire Diez, 'Danser ce qui s'échappe de la conscience', *La Libre Belgique*, 20 December 1996.
5 Wim Vandekeybus, 'Ik zou alles willen stilleggen en dan tot ontploffing brengen', *De Schouwburgkrant*, Royal Flemish Theatre, 3 November 1993.
6 Watson, op. cit.
7 Arnd Wesemann, 'One For Sorrow? Wim Vandekeybus' New Work', *Ballett International*, November 1997.
8 Ayers, op. cit.

Biographical details

Born in Herenthout, Belgium, 30 June 1963. **Studied** psychology in Leuven (but did not complete studies); took part in workshops with theatre director and playwright Paul Peyskens; also studied classical dance, modern dance and tango. **Career**: Danced with Jan Fabre for 2 years from 1985; worked on first production with own company, Ultima Vez, 1986; artist-in-residence at KVS (Royal Flemish Theatre), 1993–99; Ultima Vez guest Dance Company at Teatro Comunale di

Ferrara, Italy, 2000–02. **Awards and honours** include New York Dance and Performance Award ('Bessie'), 1988 and 1990; IMZ Dance on Screen Award, 1991; Special Prize from the Jury, Brussels International Film Festival, 1993; Prize for Creativity, National Film Board of Canada/International Festival Films on Art, 2003; SACD Oeuvre-Prize Herman Closson, 2003; Best Feature Film, Festival du Film d'Aubagne, 2005.

Works

What the Body Does Not Remember (1987; revived 1995); *Les Porteuses de mauvaises nouvelles* (1989); *The Weight of a Hand* (1990); *Roseland* (video, 1990); *Immer das Selbe gelogen* (1991; film version *Le Mentira*, 1992); *Her Body Doesn't Fit Her Soul* (1993); *Elba and Federico* (film, 1993); *Mountains Made of Barking* (1994; film version, 1994); *Alle Grössen decken sich zu* (1995); *Bereft of a Blissful Union* (1996; film version, 1996); *Duet* (film, 1996); *Exhaustion from Dreamt Love* (for Batsheva Dance Company, 1996); *7 for a Secret never to be told* (1997); *Body, body on the wall . . .* (with Jan Fabre 1997; film version, 1997); *The Day of Heaven and Hell* (1998); *In Spite of Wishing and Wanting* (1999); *The Last Words* (film, 1999); '*Inasmuch as life is borrowed . . .*' (2000; film version, 2000); *Scratching the Inner Fields* (2001); *Silver* (film, 2001)*; *it* (for Sidi Larbi Cherkaoui, *Le Vif du sujet* Festival, 2002; full evening version, 2003); *Blush* (2002; film version 2005); *Sonic Boom* (2003); *Puur* (2005); *Spiegel* (2006); *Quiebro* (for Companhia Nacional de Danza, 2006); *MENSKE* (2007); *Here After* (2007, a film version of *Puur*); *Lichtnacht* (2008); *Black Biist* (2009); *nieuwZwart* (2009).

*As on company website; sometimes listed elsewhere as 2002.

Further reading

Interview: Robert Ayers, '*Scratching the Inner Fields*: Listening to Wim Vandekeybus', *Dance Theatre Journal*, 18(1), 2002.

Articles: Katie Verstockt, 'Belgian Impressions', *Ballett International*, June/July 1988; Katie Verstockt, 'Belgian Prospects: The Explosion Has Not Yet Come to Pass', *Ballett International*, November 1989; Fiona Burnside, 'Games Belgians Play and the Way Germans Feel', *Dance Theatre Journal*, Late Summer 1990; Alex Mallems, 'The Belgian Dance Explosion of the Eighties', *Ballett International*, February 1991; Sabrina Weldman, 'Belgian Dance: Fertile Ground', *Ballett International*, July/August 1991; Keith Watson, 'Aim for the Head, Go for the Gut', *Dance Now*, Summer 1996; Mary Brennan, 'Eurocrash: The Bane of Physical Theatre?', *Dance Theatre Journal*, Spring 1997; Elisa Vaccarino, 'The New Wim Vandekeybus', *Ballett International*, May 1999; Erin Branningan, 'Instinctive Man', *Dance Australia*, Oct/Nov 1999; Arnd Wesemann, 'On Stage: One Jumps the Net', *Ballett International*, June 2000; Tobi Tobias, 'Avant-Guarded', *New York* magazine, 14 August 2000; Gus Solomons, 'With a Wim There's a Way', *Dance Magazine*, October 2000; Peter Boenisch, 'In Spite of Wishing and Waiting', *Ballettanz*, August/September 2002; Jason Beechey, 'Wim Vandekeybus', *Dance Europe*, November 2002; Arnd Wesemann, 'Sonic Boom', *Ballettanz*, July 2003; Jennifer Dunning, 'Creating a World Onstage with Film', *The New York Times*, 19 November 2004; Judith Mackrell, 'Ultima Vez',

The Guardian, 12 February 2007; Jenny Gilbert, 'Dance: *Spiegel*', *The Independent*, 18 February 2007.

Books: Erwin Jans, *Wim Vandekeybus*, Brussels, 1997; Johannes Birringer, *Media and Performance: Along the Border*, Baltimore, 1998; Luk van den Dries *et al.*, *Body Check; Relocating the Body in Contemporary Performing Art*, Amsterdam, 2002.

DOUG VARONE

In the world of dance, Doug Varone is a rare truthteller. Another choreographer might ask his dancers to convey emotion or make eye contact; Varone asks his dancers simply to interact, without pretence. Although Varone's dances capture and distil aspects of the human experience, their true power lies in the fact that real human experiences take place on stage. Yet it would be simplistic and erroneous to suggest a lack of orchestration on the choreographer's behalf. The effect of Varone's most successful work is akin to the experience of watching a drama so skilfully directed and honestly acted that its fiction is forgotten in a temporary yet complete suspension of disbelief.

Attempts to fit Varone into a school or movement meet with challenges. He is influenced by Broadway musicals and José Limón, and inspired by Merce Cunningham and William Forsythe. His works can be comic, romantic, ruminative and violent. Neither abstract nor narrative, his dances range from the explosively physical to the subtle, slow and gestural. He is at once in love with movement and enamoured of stillness, blending dancerly technical prowess and casual, pedestrian elements. He has created traditional stage dances, site-specific and multimedia works, and dance for film and television, theatre and opera. What holds his work together is not so much an immediately recognizable aesthetic as a kind of humanist ethos. In Varone's dances, movement always stems from an emotional impulse. It is never abstract; there is always meaning, no matter how open to interpretation that meaning may be. Human experience is primary and that experience goes on in real time before an audience. His dancers are collaborators in that process, and they tend to be loyal, long-time company members who value the agency they are given as co-creators of the work.

At the same time that it achieves an organic, instinctive quality, Varone's work is sophisticated, layered and carefully crafted. His musicality is reminiscent of Mark Morris, in that movement arises from a response to the score, though for Varone that response is more emotional than literal. In certain group passages, the effect is one of controlled chaos: the music seems to sweep the dancers into seemingly disorderly formations, comparable with the wind swirling dry leaves, while underlying the apparent wildness is a finely wrought structure – a phenomenon Varone himself has described as 'a design in space that defies organization, yet is so utterly choreographed that it appears the reverse'.

Varone does not oversimplify his work and makes no concessions to popularity, which places him some distance outside the realm of 'accessible' contemporary dance. Yet, in his deeply musical approach, his strong dramatic instinct and his rigorous attention to emotional honesty, Varone has become a favourite of dance audiences and critics alike.

Varone grew up tap dancing and performing in musical theatre – his idols were Gene Kelly and Fred Astaire – and his boyhood dream was to dance on Broadway. After attending college and completing a degree in dance, he transferred his allegiances to contemporary dance, dancing for a year with the José Limón Dance Company before joining the Lar Lubovitch Dance Company, where he stayed for eight years. He began creating work for his own company, Doug Varone and Dancers, in 1986, and soon works like *Nocturne* were displaying his own distinctive movement aesthetic: a curious blend of the various influences of his training, infused with an inherent delight in dancing. From musical theatre, he borrowed the kind of physical exuberance that translates all the way to the back of the house, and also the habit of falling in and out of pedestrian movement and casual, tossed-away gestures. Conservatory training gave him technical precision, while Limón technique appeared in flowing, spiralling motion.

The result was an idiosyncratic, hybrid style in which passages of subtle gesture were punctuated by an almost crazed dynamism, and fluidity of the spine and arms contrasted with sharp, linear use of the lower body. Splayed fingers and toes, successional turns that whipped the body in a circle leading from the toe to the top of the head, fast shuffles executed in deep *pliés* or in *relevés* – these signature movements would form the core of the company's vocabulary: a vernacular from which they would at times depart dramatically, but would always make reference. It was a quirky language full of amplified gesture, impulsive jerks and spasms, marionette-like stiltedness and moments of unbridled, joyful abandon.

Bel Canto (1998), an irresistibly comedic look at the nature of love and relationships set to excerpts from the Bellini opera *Norma*, exhibits some of the more emphatic, frenetic aspects of this style, including bird-like pecking movements of the head and shoulders, flapping arms and fastidious, rapid footwork. Of a different mood but equally characteristic of Varone's movement aesthetic is *Rise* (1993), which Varone considered the critical turning point in his career. Against the swelling backdrop of John Adams's *Fearful Symmetries*, dancers congregate and disperse, their energy building to climax, then retreating, like ocean waves. *Rise* exemplifies the controlled chaos and architectural vision of bodies in space that have become especially significant in his more recent work in theatre and opera.

Many of Varone's works are characterized by the use of gesture in direct response to a musical score. *The Bench Quartet*, part of the larger work *Cantata 78/Every Waking Hour*, which the company performed in 1986 at their first concert at the New York experimental arts centre PS 122, marks the beginning of Varone's fascination with following a musical structure (in this case, a Bach libretto), with an invented gestural language. Arm and hand gesticulations, subtle adjustments of the head and shoulders, even dances confined to the face (as in *The Bottomland*, 2002) form a kind of sign language that expresses non-linguistic experiences. This practice of imposing limitations on physical movement to tap new realms of creativity is exemplified in *Boats Leaving* (2006), which relies heavily on gesture, poses and stillness, rather than the dynamic physicality that constitutes many of Varone's dances.

The direction of a given work is determined as much by the contributions of individual dancers as by the choreographer's vision. The diversity of Varone's company is often remarked on; although the company usually consists of no more than nine dancers, they range widely in age, size, body type, ethnicity and technical background. What they have in common is not so much physical appearance or even movement styles, but qualities like maturity, intelligence, intuition and self-awareness. 'When I locate dancers that understand the art of "being" rather than performing,' Varone has said, 'I am drawn to them immensely.' Because the dancers are given a great deal of autonomy and creative liberty, the work reflects their natural impulses – it lacks pretence. Varone's dancers tend to remain with the company for long periods of time, and the depth of communication and understanding between them speaks far more powerfully than if they were chosen because of superficial similarities.

Varone achieves accessibility not by compromising the complexity of his vision, but by holding his work and his dancers to rigorous standards of honesty. Paradoxically, it is in avoiding the relative homogeneity that characterizes many dance companies, and encouraging his dancers to 'be real' on stage rather than to attempt absolute unison or technical perfection, that Varone attains a new level of accessibility. Dance critic Tobi Tobias, writing for the *Bloomberg News*, noted that Varone's dancers look 'like real people who happen to dance'.

In keeping with this interest in presenting dances without pretence, the company is known for engaging the audience in meaningful ways. *Momentary Order* (1992), created over an extended period of social and historical research into the Franco-American community of Lewiston, Maine, and *Neither* (2000), performed in the cramped quarters of an abandoned Manhattan tenement building, explored the relationship between performer and audience, and aimed to open a dialogue and exchange of ideas. In the former case, company members lived in residence in Lewiston over a period of weeks, sharing meals and discussions with members of the community to gain a deeper understanding of their culture. In the latter case, audiences were limited in size to 20, and the claustrophobic rooms confronted viewers with the unusual position of watching the dance from within the performance space. Through such projects, and through a strong programme of education and community outreach, the company has shed light on the dance-making process, and engaged new audiences in contemporary dance.

Varone did not gain significant recognition for his choreography for almost a decade. Part of the reason may be that he did not follow fashion or fad, a fact that gave his work a timeless quality but also made it difficult to categorize. He never fitted comfortably into the catalogue of dualities that tend to distinguish New York choreographers: uptown/downtown, abstract/narrative, dancerly/pedestrian, lighthearted/serious. Whitney Vaughan of *The Village Voice* reflected that this 'aesthetic homelessness' actually translated into 'artistic maturity'.

That aesthetic homelessness could also be described as a taste for ambiguity. Dance writer Suzanne Carbonneau once described Varone as revelling 'in the indefinable, in the indescribable, in the enigmatic . . . fascinated by the power of movement to embody ambiguities and mysteries, to sustain emotional complexity'. Powerful juxtaposition is a Varone hallmark. Intense physicality and subtle gesture; haunting scenes filled with longing and side-splittingly comic episodes; spare, simple constructions and dense, ornate passages – all coexist within single works. The 2004 masterpiece *Castles* shows Varone at his most chameleon-like – dealing in duets and group sections that are thrillingly explosive one moment, tender and intimate the next, and always on the edge of conflict, a response to the complex layers of Sergei Prokofiev's *Waltz Suite.*

In the mid-1990s, the company emerged from relative obscurity into central focus. Yet critics continue to comment on Varone's changeable choreographic nature, sometimes lamenting his lack of a singular identity, sometimes praising his versatility. Still others claim to experience a sense of repetition — a sameness that pervades his work despite thematic variation.

His versatility, though, is unarguable. Particularly in the twenty-first century, Varone has turned increasingly towards theatrical work, creating movement that conveys some kind of narrative, whether literal or implied. Varone is by nature a master of evocation. Even earlier, non-linear dramas like *Home* (1988), which focuses on domestic tension, and *Possession* (1994), based on the novel by A.S. Byatt, demonstrate Varone's talent for building dramatic atmosphere and his fascination with dialogue and relationship expressed through dance. The year 2001 marked another turning point: Varone directed his first opera, *Orpheus and Eurydice*, an experience he referred to as requiring a scope of vision larger than anything he had ever contemplated in the dance world. Later operas *The Barber of Seville* (2004), *The Elephant Man* (2006) and *Faust* (2009) further expanded his directorial capacity. The heightened theatricality of opera seems to have spilled over into *Alchemy* (2008), a pure dance work set to Steve Reich's *Daniel Variations.* Like Reich's score, *Alchemy* took as its subject the kidnapping and murder of Jewish-American journalist Daniel Pearl by Islamist extremists in Pakistan. Critics noted the work not so much for its formal characteristics as for its 'profound humanity'.

In 2005, Varone underwent surgery for a hip replacement, which forced him to remove himself physically from the choreographic process and to articulate his ideas verbally instead. The work that evolved during this period, including *Boats Leaving* (2006), relied more heavily than usual on the dancers' interpretative skills, and resulted in less step-oriented, more dramaturgically driven work. Even the most formal, abstract Varone works are never fully abstract — always there is an emotional undercurrent. Masterpieces such as *Rise* and *Castles* triumph because they are at once movement paintings that bring their scores to life and deeply dramatic works that illuminate the very essence of the human experience, just as the music of John Adams and Sergei Prokofiev draw out all that is rich yet conflicted, chaotic yet beautiful, explosive yet subtle, in the experience of living.

In the sense that he returns to an emotionalism largely rejected by the previous generation of choreographers,Varone belongs to the post-postmodernist era. He embraces complexity, ambiguity and enigma, evading predictability and avoiding the obvious, and at the same time his work points again and again to our shared humanity. Never reductive or didactic,Varone's work insists on our need for one another and our common vulnerability. If he were to belong to a choreographic subgroup, he might share the 'humanistic, truth-seeking, theatrically oriented' category with Joe Goode, another dance artist drawn to mature performers with unusually direct stage presence and a willingness to explore the fringes of dance and theatre. Perhaps more significantly, Varone's approach to dance-making has influenced a new generation of dance artists, whose taste for emotionally honest work and exploration of 'the art of being' they owe in part to him, often, perhaps, without even realizing it.

Elizabeth Schwyzer

Biographical details

Born in Syosset, New York, 5 November 1956. **Studied** dance at Purchase College, State University of New York (SUNY), gaining BFA in 1978. **Career**: Danced with José Limón Dance Company, 1978–79 and Lar Lubovitch Dance Company, 1979–86; founded Doug Varone and Dancers, 1986 (work supported by the National Endowment for the Arts from 1988); has created work for José Limón Dance Company, Dancemakers (Canada), Bern Ballet, Batsheva Dance Company, An Creative (Japan), Hubbard Street Dance Chicago, Colorado Ballet, Ailey II, Rambert Dance Company and other companies. Has also choreographed for opera, including New York's Metropolitan Opera, Washington Opera, New York City Opera; for theatre, including for Broadway, Baltimore's Centre Stage, Yale Repertory Theatre, Walnut Street Theatre, Princeton's McArthur Theater; film, including the Patrick Swayze film *One Last Dance*; television and fashion shows. **Awards and honours** include Guggenheim Fellowship, 1996; two New York Dance and Performance Awards ('Bessies'), 1998 and 2007 (for Sustained Achievement in Choreography); OBIE Award for *Orpheus and Euridice*, 2006; Presidential Distinguished Alumni Award, Purchase College, SUNY, 2007.

Works

Cantata 78/Every Waking Hour (1986); *The Bench Quartet* (section of *Cantata 78*, 1986); *Four Variations on a Theme* (1987); *Feet of Clay* (1987); *Barcarolle* (1987); *Nocturne* (1987); *Voix Bulgare* (1987); *Straits* (1988); *Home* (1988); *In Middle Ground* (1988); *Ever Faithful* (1989); *Taken Pieces* (1989); *Augury* (1989); *Care/Volpe Sisters* (1989); *Force Majeure* (1990); *Two Mozart Arias* (1990); *Confidence* (1990); *Dilluvium* (1990); *Oscillating Thirds* (1990); *Kiss My Eyes Goodnight* (1990); *Liszt Sonnets*

(1990); *Stranded Landfish* (1991); *Beauty* (1992); *Momentary Order* (1992); *Motet* (1992); *Brash Grid* (1992); *Rise* (1993); *On the Field of Destiny* (1993); *Aperture* (1994); *Peak Sacred* (1994); *Possession* (1994); *Smashed Landscapes* (1994); *Strict Love* (1994); *After You've Gone/Mr. Al* (1995); *In Thine Eyes* (1996); *Let's Dance* (1996); *Proverb/Valley* (1997); *Democracy* (1997); *The Triumph of Love* (Broadway musical; 1997); *Need* (1998); *Knave* (1998); *Bel Canto* (1998); *Mercury* (1998); *Assembling a Common Language* (1998); *Eclipse* (1999); *String Quartet #2* (1999); *Agora* (1999); *Sleeping with Giants* (1999); *And Their Words to the End of the World* (1999); *The Plain Sense of Things* (1999); *Breaker* (2000); *Polonaise #4* (2000); *Neither* (2000); *As Natural as Breathing* (2000); *Tomorrow* (2000); *The Drawing Lesson* (2001); *Ballet Mécanique* (2001); *Short Story* (2001); *Approaching Something Higher* (2001); *Orfée et Euridice* (opera, 2001); *The Bottomland, Part I* (2002); *The Bottomland, Part II* (2002); *The Beating of Wings* (2002); *Distance* (2003); *Of the Earth Far Below* (2003); *La Sacre du printemps* (2003); *Heaven* (2003); *Beats and Stomps* (2003); *The Thing of the World* (2004); *Castles* (2004); *Deconstructing English* (2004); *Desert Tango* (2004); *The Barber of Seville* (opera, 2004); *Orpheus and Euridice* (opera, 2005); *The Invisible Man* (choreographer and director, play, 2005); *The Elephant Man* (opera, 2006); *Boats Leaving* (2006); *Lux* (2006); *The Constant Shift of Pulse* (2006); *Victorious* (2007); *Beyond the Break* (2007); *Dense Terrain* (2007); *Alchemy* (2008); *Scribblings* (2008); *Faust* (opera, 2009).

Further reading

Interview in Heidi Henderson, *Growing Place: Interviews with Artists, 25 Years at the Bates Dance Festival*, Lewiston, Maine, 2007.

Articles: Paul Jackson, 'Umbrella Music', *Dance Now*, Winter 1996, David Jays, 'Dance Umbrella', *Dancing Times*, December 1996; Valerie Gladstone, 'Musical Comedies: Postmodern Dance's Season on Broadway', *Dance Magazine*, December 1997; Rose Anne Thom, 'Reviews: New York City, Limón Dance Company', *Dance Magazine*, February 1998; Tobi Tobias, 'Uncommon Sense', *New York Magazine*, 25 October 1999; Gia Kourlas, 'A Knave of Hearts', *Time Out New York*, 2 January 2000; Kate Mattingly, 'Doug Varone's Decade of Dance', *Dance Magazine*, January 2000; Jennifer Dunning, 'Works with a New Ring in the Wake of Sept. 11', *The New York Times*, 9 December 2001; Jack Anderson, 'Doug Varone', *Dancing Times*, February 2002; Roslyn Sulcas, 'Varone Takes High Ground', *Dance Magazine*, April 2002; Cheryl Tobey, 'Doug Varone and Ballet Mécanique', *PAJ: A Journal of Performance and Art*, September 2002; Joan Acocella, 'Let Yourself Go', *The New Yorker*, 27 October 2003; Karen Campbell, 'Daring Dances on a Human Scale', *Boston Globe*, 5 March 2004; Deborah Jowitt, 'Take Me with You', *The Village Voice*, 28 November 2006; Deborah Jowitt, 'Victory!', *The Village Voice*, 10 July 2007; Elena Hecht, 'Dance out of Darkness', *Dance Magazine*, October 2008; Deborah Jowitt, 'Doug Varone and Jodi Melnick Swim Deep Rivers', *The Village Voice*, 25 February 2009.

Books: Suzanne Carbonneau, *A Momentary Order: An Arts-Community Partnership*, Lewiston, ME, 1994; Rose Eichenbaum, *Masters of Movement: Portraits of America's Great Choreographers*, Washington, DC, 2004.

JAWOLE WILLA JO ZOLLAR

It was not until her college years that Jawole Willa Jo Zollar knew that dance would be her profession. At the University of Missouri–Kansas City she was exposed for the first time to formal modern dance and ballet, after a childhood of joyous, though demanding, classes in Afro-Cuban dance taken in a community centre in her home town of Kansas City. In those classes, she learned about rhythm, style and communicating with an audience. At college, she committed to be a dance major but happened to be, she discovered, a very imperfect one.

'Everybody was so neurotic about their bodies,' Zollar told Ellen Ashdown in a 2002 interview (published in the Florida State University journal *Research in Review*). 'I suddenly became aware of this whole idea that my body wasn't right. But the African idea is that you celebrate yourself through movement. If you had hips, that was a good thing because you had more to move.'

Both the earlier and subsequent dance influences are fused in her work, with an emphasis on modern dance. Of greater importance are the themes that work addresses. Many of the dances that Zollar has created since 1984, when she founded the modern-dance company Urban Bush Women, have focused on social and cultural issues and their impact on women, though in a way more exuberant than doctrinaire. She selected her company name after hearing an ensemble of Chicago musicians called the Urban Bush Men. 'I knew I wanted a concept name,' she told Ashdown, 'not "The Jawole Zollar Company".'

The name, chosen with the musicians' permission, also made her think of 'the sense of "bush" as incredibly dense, tangled growth; deep forest,' she said in the Ashdown interview. 'Growing up in the inner city, I was also in a dense, thickly populated place, rough. But people tried to make gardens of it. When they did, it became something else entirely.' Her own form of 'gardening', the process of making work, was like 'diving for pearls' deep into the thick of life, Zollar said, without becoming stuck there.

From the start, she saw a major goal of the ensemble, for most of its existence an all-black, all-female company, as exploring the use of cultural expression as a catalyst for social change, focusing on 'the transformation of struggle and suffering into the bittersweet joy of survival'.

Zollar, who has often talked of her fondness for teaching, spends considerable time with her company making dance with local people in far-flung neighbourhoods. 'Community outreach' has been a popular activity of socially-minded – and cash-strapped – American dance companies from the 1970s onwards. But these residencies did more than acquaint locals with the art of dance. Instead, Zollar and her company gave the 'lions' a chance to tell their stories in their own voices. For, as a favourite African proverb puts it, 'Given a hunter and a lion, the history each tells will be very different. The hunter's is familiar. The lion's still needs to be told.' And it was, in workshop productions like the 2001 *Dixwell*, in which residents of a minority community near New Haven, Connecticut, joined with the dancers to explore issues such as Caribbean migration to the neighbourhood, the imprisonment there of rebellious Africans from the *Amistad* slave ship, and the destruction of grassroots local landmarks through urban renewal. The performers included a local jazz band, a singing policewoman and a 100-member drill team.

In a similar vein, Zollar and her company established a Summer Dance Intensive in 1997 at Florida State University, where she received her MFA in dance. For the annual workshops, Zollar drew men and women, many of them were non-dancers and all drawn from applicants throughout the United States and from abroad, into heady sessions in which art was eventually created by everyone in the group to address contemporary social issues head-on, incorporating the skills and experiences of the participants. In 2004, the programme moved to Brooklyn, New York, where Urban Bush Women has its headquarters. There, two years later, the programme produced a provocative and immensely poignant re-envisioning of the Hurricane Katrina disaster.

Zollar had attacked the problem of homelessness in her powerful 1988 work *Shelter*, revived for the Alvin Ailey American Dance Theatre in 1992, though with more nuance than most artistic treatises on the subject. It alluded not only to governmental disregard of the poor but also to the notion that many who pass by are a paycheck away from such a life. Zollar's approach is more to embrace the stereotype, however, and find the richness and persistent life within it. Her sly, exuberant *Batty Moves*, choreographed in 1995, rejoiced in black women's big bottoms, 'batty' being Jamaican slang for that part of the anatomy. *Girlfriends* (1986) and *Lipstick . . . A Doo-Wop Dilemma* (1988) evoked young black women's giddy bonding and despair.

HairStories, created in 2001, incorporated video interviews that mostly dealt, comically and caustically, with black women's attempts to combat the problems and social disgrace of 'nappy' hair. In one video, Zollar washed her thick curly hair and then struggled to comb through it. The title for another dance, her 1986 *Anarchy, Wild Women and Dinah*, says it all. Life as a black woman, the piece suggests in one long, raucous burst of song and movement, is anarchic and wild for all that it is infused with tenderness.

Praise House, co-choreographed in 1990 with Pat Hall-Smith, is a linear narrative, unusual for Zollar. A layered, complex piece with the style and look of visionary outsider or folk art of the American South, *Praise House* tells the story of three generations of women living together and of the gradual pulling away of a grandmother and young girl into the world of spiritualism as the girl's mother watches help-lessly, rooted in everyday reality.

Like much of Zollar's work, the piece incorporated spoken words, written by the Appalachian playwright and sculptor Angelyn DeBord. The set, by Leni Schwendinger, was unusually sprawling and detailed and made use of ordinary objects such as tablecloths for angels' wings and a cheese-grater and wooden spoon as angelic musical instruments. These last were actually used on stage to help perform a musical score by Carl Riley, which evoked the religious shouts and hymns of Southern church services.

Praise House suggested a total immersion in a culture quite unlike the urban arts environments in which Zollar has worked during much of her career. A similar immersion was suggested by her jewel-like, intensely evocative *Walking with Pearl: Africa Diaries* (2004) and *Walking with Pearl: Southern Diaries* (2005). The dances were drawn from the writing of Pearl Primus, the influential modern-dance pioneer of the 1940s, who died in 1994. Her work, which Zollar had studied and written about as a college student, was drawn from the traditional dances and cultures of Africa, the Caribbean and black American slaves, all of which Primus, who had a doctorate in anthropology, saw in part from the perspective of a social scientist. (Interestingly, Zollar, as a small child in Kansas City, took classes with Joseph Stevenson, who had per-formed early on in the company of Katherine Dunham, the other great choreographer-anthropologist of American modern dance.)

Zollar had studied Primus and her work in depth after being asked to stage Primus's dance *Bushache*. Researchers at the American Dance Festival in Durham, North Carolina, introduced Zollar to Primus's journals on Africa and the American South. Reading them, Zollar became aware, as she told *The New York Times* in 2005, that 'I don't think I'm finished with Pearl, and I don't think she's finished with me.' She had realized, she said, that whatever she made of the diaries would not be 'about me telling her life. It's about me connecting my artistic heart to her artistic heart, through her writing.'

'What I really appreciate about Pearl Primus is that she became a dancer against all odds,' Zollar continued in the *Times* interview:

> She was this thick, dark-skinned black woman who had started training in dance late. She had been an athlete, so she had this incredibly powerful jump. She had a vision of dance that was bigger than the concert stage and that was about a kind of personalization of experience and letting it come out in a very rough-hewn manner, which I absolutely identify with.

The 'diary' dances that Zollar went on to choreograph captured ordinary individual lives in villages in Africa and the American South as well as the loneliness and openness to beauty felt by Primus as she journeyed through and observed those places so foreign, yet so familiar, to her.

Although Zollar has never made much of an issue of it, her career has largely been centered on the work of women in dance. She moved to New York City in 1980 to study with Dianne McIntyre, a quietly influential performer, choreographer, and teacher who maintained a Harlem dance studio that was a mecca for black dancers, musicians and artists. There McIntyre passed on her ideas about dance improvisation, drawn from her intensive collaborations with jazz musicians. (Improvisation has remained a choreographic tool for Zollar and her dancers.) McIntyre also encouraged her students to persist in expressing their own personal truths, and to perform every dance, as she would call out in the studio, 'as if your lives depend on it'.

The black choreographers and ensembles that emerged in modern dance and ballet, first in the 1920s and then, more strongly and cohesively, from the 1950s onwards, were for the most part male or male-directed. But Zollar came of age in a time that produced highly individual black women choreographers whose gender went unremarked upon, among them not only McIntyre but also Blondell Cummings, an evoker of simple, age-old stories in dance and Bebe Miller, a more mainstream modern-dance formalist. And the dances in Zollar's first full New York programme of choreography, performed in a loft studio theatre in 1984 by her newly founded Urban Bush Women, were inspired in part by Jamaica Kincaid's *At the Bottom of the River* as well as her studies with the stark Korean minimalist Kei Takei, also a woman.

One shimmering piece, *River Songs* (1984), was filled with skinny little girls at play, a mother tenderly combing and oiling her daughter's hair, and two exorcized women. Zollar has occasionally included male dancers in her company and she has long collaborated with male musicians, as she did in this first concert. But the heart of her work has been the sense it creates of community, a quality attributable in large part to the unaffected performing of her dancers and to a choreographic style and philosophical perspective whose directness, simplicity, and strong emotions give Zollar's work an appeal that transcends race, class and gender.

Jennifer Dunning

Biographical details

Born in Kansas City, Missouri, 21 December 1950. **Studied** as a child with Joseph Stevenson, a student of Katherine Dunham; received a BA in Dance, University of Missouri-Kansas City, 1975, and an MFA in Dance, Florida State University, Tallahassee, 1979; also studied with Dianne McIntyre at Sounds in Motion, New York, 1980–83. **Career**: Founded Urban Bush Women, acting as artistic director and choreographer from 1984; has also choreographed for Alvin Ailey American Dance Theater, Ballet Arizona, Philadanco, Dayton Contemporary Dance Company, Union Dance Company, UK, and others. Has held numerous teaching positions, including Worlds of Thought Resident Scholar, Mankato State University 1993–94, Regents Lecturer, UCLA, 1995–96, Visiting Artist, Ohio State University, 1996, and the Abramowitz Memorial Lecturer at Massachusetts Institute of Technology, 1998. **Awards and honours** include Fellowship, New York Foundation for the Arts, 1984; Fellowship, National Endowment for the Arts (Choreography), 1988–90; New York Dance and Performance Award ('Bessie'), 1992 and 2006; Outstanding Alumni Achievement Award, University of Missouri-Kansas City, 1993; Capezio Award, 1994; Alumna of the Year, Florida State University, 1997; Dr Martin Luther King Jr. Distinguished Service Award, Florida State University, 1999; Master Artist, Atlantic Center for the Arts, New Smyrna Beach, Florida, 2001; History Maker, National Heritage Project, Chicago, 2006; Doris Duke Award, 2008; Wynn Fellow, 2008.

Works

River Songs (1984); *Xpujla* (1984); *LifeDance . . . The Fool's Journey* (1984); *Working for Free* (1985); *Anarchy, Wild Women and Dinah* (1986); *Madness* (1986); *Girlfriends* (1986); *LifeDance I . . . The Magician* (1986); *Bitter Tongue* (1987); *LifeDance II . . . The Papess* (1987); *Song of Lawino* (1988); *Heat* (1988); *Lipstick* (adaptation from *Heat*, 1988); *Shelter* (adaptation from *Heat*, 1988); *Lipstick . . . A Doo-Wop Dilemma* (1988); *I Don't Know, But I Been Told, If You Keep on Dancin' You Never Grow Old* (1989); *Praise House* (1990); *LifeDance III . . . The Empress* (1992); *The LifeDances* (incorporating all *LifeDance* pieces, 1993); *Nyabinghi Dreamtime* (1994); *Vocal Attack* (1994); *Batty Moves* (1995); *BONES AND ASH: A Gilda Story* (1995); *Transitions* (1996); *Self Portrait* (1997); *Hands Singing Song* (1998); *Soul Deep* (2000); *Dixwell . . . When the Lions Tell History – A Community Collaboration* (2001); *HairStories* (2001);

Shadow's Child (2002); *Are We Democracy? . . . Susan B. Anthony* (2004); *Walking with Pearl: Africa Diaries* (2004); *Walking with Pearl: The Southern Diaries* (2005); *Flashback/Flash Forward . . . Cool Baby, Cool* (2006); *Bring 'Em Home* (2009); *The Walkin', Talkin', Signifying Blues Hips, Lowdown Throwdown* (2009); *Zollar: Uncensored* (2010).

Further reading

Interview with Tessa Triumph, in 'Jowale Willa Jo Zollar Interviewed', *New Dance*, July/September 1987; with Ellen Ashdown, in 'The Journey of Jawole', *Research in Review* (Florida State University), Summer 2002.

Articles: Veta Goler, 'Life Dances: Jawole Willa Jo Zollar's Choreographic Construction of Black Womanhood', *Choreography and Dance*, 5(1), 1988; Jowale Willa Jo Zollar, 'A Constant State of Premiere', *Dance*, Fall 1993; Joan Acocella, 'The Brains at the Top', *The New Yorker*, 27 December 1993–3 January 2000 (double issue); Ananya Chatterjea, 'Jawole Willa Jo Zollar's Womb Wars: Embodying Her Critical Response to Abortion Politics', *Dance Research Journal*, Summer 2001; Ananya Chatterjea, 'Reading "Difference": The Interventionary Performance of Jawole Willa Jo Zollar's *Batty Moves*', *Discourses in Dance*, 2(1), 2003; Brenda Dixon Gottschild, 'Urban Bush Women: Telling It with Sass and Style', *Dance Magazine*, May 2003; Jennifer Dunning, 'Urban Bush Women: Rough, and Proud of It', *The New York Times*, 19 June 2005; Deborah Jowitt, 'The Hip Crowd', *The Village Voice*, 15 May 2007; Paul Taylor, 'Urban Bush Women Mixed Bill', *Dancing Times*, January 2008; Deborah Jowitt, 'Dark Magic', *The Village Voice*, 2 February 2010.

Books: Edward Thorpe, *Black Dance*, Woodstock, 1989; Mark O'Brien and Craig Little (eds), *Reimaging America: The Art of Social Change*, Philadelphia, Pennsylvania, 1990; David Gere, Lewis Segal, *et al.* (eds), *Looking Out: Perspectives on Dance and Criticism in a Multicultural World*, New York, 1995; Sharon Friedler and Susan Glazer, *Dancing Female: Lives and Issues of Women in Contemporary Dance*, Amsterdam, 1997; Thomas F. DeFrantz (ed.), *Dancing Many Drums: Excavations in African American Dance*, Madison, WI, 2002; Ananya Chatterjea, *Butting Out: Reading Resistive Choreographies Through Works by Jawole Willa Jo Zollar and Chandralekha*, Middletown, CT, 2004.